THE CAMBRIDGE ILLUSTRATED HISTORY OF

British Theatre

SIMON TRUSSLER

CAMBRIDGE
UNIVERSITY PRESS

PUBLISHED BY THE PRESS SYNDICATE OF THE UNIVERSITY OF CAMBRIDGE
The Pitt Building, Trumpington Street, Cambridge, United Kingdom

CAMBRIDGE UNIVERSITY PRESS
The Edinburgh Building, Cambridge CB2 2RU, UK   www.cup.cam.ac.uk
40 West 20th Street, New York, NY 10011-4211, USA   www.cup.org
10 Stamford Road, Oakleigh, Melbourne 3166, Australia
Ruiz de Alarcón 13, 28014 Madrid, Spain

First published 1994
First paperback edition 2000

Project management, picture editing and design by Stuart McCready, Oxford OX2 7SE

Picture research by Callie Kendall

Additional design by P.D. Terre-Brei

Artwork by G.A. Moores

Typeset by Country Setting, Kingsdown, Kent CT14 8ES

Printed in the United Kingdom at the University Press, Cambridge

A catalogue record for this book is available from the British Library

Library of Congress Cataloguing in Publication data

The Cambridge Illustrated History of British Theatre / Simon Trussler
p.   cm.
Includes bibliographical references and index
ISBN 0 521 41913 1
1. Theatre–Great Britain–History. 1. Title
PN2581.T78 1994
792' .0941–dc20
94-25635
CIP

ISBN 0 521 41913 1 hardback
ISBN 0 521 79430 7 paperback

Overleaf: Emma Fielding, Clive Wood,
and Billie Brown in *Twelfth Night*,
Royal Shakespeare Company, 1994

Page 1: From the title page of *The Wits,
or, Sport upon Sport, Select Pieces of
Drollery, Digested into Scenes by way of
Dialogue*, London 1662

THE CAMBRIDGE ILLUSTRATED HISTORY OF
British Theatre

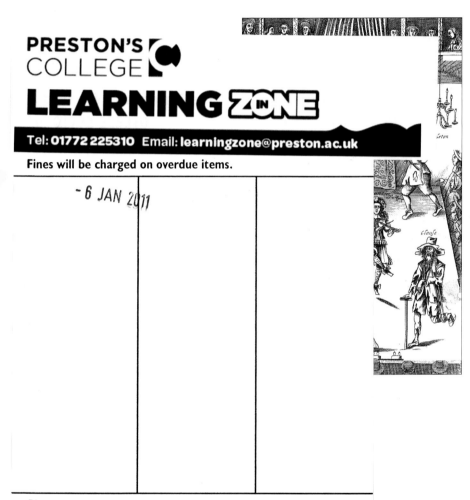

Contents

Introduction

This is a difficult moment in history at which to be writing a history – especially a history of theatre. Not only are the ideologies which pervade all histories now subject to rigorous examination (and properly so), but the very possibility of writing history is being challenged from a variety of deconstructive and post-modernist viewpoints. The theatre historian, in particular, has a hard enough task reading the traces of ephemeral events and elusive personalities without being told that he (for it is a he) is being 'reductive' or that his work 'lacks theoretical rigour'. It is not in ignorance of such dangers that I have none the less written what may be perceived as a fairly 'conventional', chronologically driven history: rather, it is in recognition that history, much like the theatre, is *shaped* by conventions, understood as the shorthand which is shared between authors (or performers) and their readers (or their audiences). So long as the conventions are understood, if not necessarily shared, I hope that the endeavour will be perceived as worthwhile.

I do believe that this book fills a gap. There have been very few recent histories of British theatre – as distinct, that is, from a fair number which have taken on the world, and as even more distinct from those which have dealt more or less exclusively with the written word. But the play in print is (or should be), like the musical score, a form of notation for the play in performance – as it is also, like a playbill or a press-cutting, one of the few vestigial traces of its survival. What the script records is only one element (and by no means an invariable one) in the complex process of creating the 'finished' – and eternally unfinished – theatrical event.

A history of theatre needs, then, to be not only a history of plays, but of players and of playing places; of the ways the players have been instructed in their roles by authors, stage managers, or directors; of how the playing places have been organized, decorated, and illuminated; and of the ways audiences have been accommodated, which will influence whether they feel intimately involved with what they 'receive' or are reduced to a state of passive observation. It is also important to know something about the social composition of those audiences – whether they were drawn from all sections of the population or from a social elite, whether different kinds of theatres were catering to different classes – as also to understand how critical preconceptions, and wider social and political developments, have shaped prejudices and expectations, and affected the kinds of performance it is possible or permissible to see.

The further back we delve, the scantier the evidence. We have often to deal in realms of probability and conjecture – most of all, when we attempt to reconstruct what a particular theatrical performance or a particular actor's style was *like*. A novel or a poem – literature which survives as words on a page – provides a 'text' which may be 'read' whether the death of the author be proclaimed by the Bills of Mortality or by Roland Barthes. Paintings and sculptures persist as their artists shaped them, however divorced from their original settings. Great works of music can be played on instruments supposedly identical with those on which they were first performed. And film, of course, builds permanence into its very rhetoric of composition, seeking to perfect a definitive version for posterity's completion. But even the now widespread use of video does little more than mummify the theatrical event it seeks to conserve. For the living theatre creates a *different* event every night: and, in doing so, it is dependent upon an interrelationship with its audience which no mechanical medium can ever reproduce. If we had videos of Burbage, Betterton, Garrick, or even Irving in performance we would find them at worst entirely alien to our ways of thought, speech, and behaviour – at best, historical curiosities, observing conventions that we no longer understood or could hope fully to recapture.

And this, of course, is before we begin to take into account all the other kinds of performance which the persisting double meaning of 'play' suggests. For we are concerned here not only with those formally constructed theatre pieces which, for a few hours set-aside every afternoon or evening, wholly or partially occupy what we recognize as the stage of a theatre. 'Play' is any pretence which entertains, and as soon as the entertainment by its nature extends beyond the participants to invite an audience, as soon as its 'actors' make of it a continuing or even intermittent occupation, it merits our attention here. This is why, in my early chapters, I argue that the work of itinerant mime players, of singers of epic lays, or performers from the multi-faceted tradition of minstrelsy are as much a part of our history – arguably, in the consciousness of their intentions, more so – than the Christian priests tentatively putting their ceremonies into that quasi-dramatic form so long regarded by scholars as the 'rebirth' of a drama that had, in truth, never died.

Thankfully, all this is now the very grist of theatre scholarship. But theatre scholarship is a young discipline in Britain: it is less than fifty years since the first Department of Drama was established in a British university (Bristol), and since the still-surviving and honourable tradition of 'amateur' scholarship (its amateurishness extending only to a lack of monetary reward) found its voice in the creation of the journal *Theatre Notebook* by the Society for Theatre Research. This book could not have been written without the flourishing of research thus happily enabled: but (Allardyce Nicoll's pioneering work notwithstanding) scholars have generally been too busy bringing out the finer details of a previously blurred picture to have stood back to examine the broader canvas. So what follows does not aspire to be a work of original scholarship: rather, I have aimed to offer a conspective overview of the research and discoveries of others – as partially but none the less gratefully acknowledged in the Bibliography.

However, I have intended and do believe that the resulting synthesis, evolved from conflicting viewpoints and interpretations, is original, and that some of the connections I have made – not least, perhaps, with the life being lived beyond the traditionally rather confined boundaries of the theatre as such – should help to place theatrical activity in closer conjunction with its times. Necessarily, personal choice is involved simply in the selection of material, and here I have wished to strike a corrective balance between, on the one hand, the activities of the 'official' theatre and the production of conventional plays, and, on the other, the kinds of popular, 'unofficial', and often oppositional performance which in the past have been marginalized, condemned, or simply ignored. Hence my stress, for example, on the importance of the jig in the Elizabethan theatre, on the theatres of the fairs in the eighteenth century, or on the role of the Workers' Theatre Movement in the inter-war years of our own. Hence, conversely, the absence of the usual chapter devoted exclusively to Shakespeare – whom, like Garrick and Irving, I have tried to place rather in context than on a pedestal.

It is not possible fully to avoid the dangers of 'periodization', but by dividing this work into a large number of chapters, most of which cover no more than a few decades at a time, I have tried to avoid a surfeit of generalizations. Thus, any references here to 'eighteenth-century' or 'nineteenth-century theatre' may be taken to *intend* a longer view, not to have been imposed by that unwieldy and unhelpful conflation of times and manners which (for example) has in the past stretched the 'Restoration' from an event of 1660 (or at most a mood sustained for a limited portion of the reign of Charles II) into a label for theatre practice loosely allowed to slip into the early years of Queen Anne.

Certain restrictions have been imposed by necessity rather than choice. From the late sixteenth century, London became and remained the centre of theatrical activity in the kingdom: and the kind of plays written for its audiences were those which the theatre in the regions imported, as the circuits established themselves in the eighteenth century and 'provincial tours' supplanted these in the nineteenth. And while popular performing traditions were more broadly based, they remain elusive. In that sense this history may be found at times as parochial as it is also, by definition – at least from the aftermath of the Norman Conquest until late in the present century – ethnocentric.

Feminist scholarship is rightly recovering the history of women in theatre, and I have stressed the female leadership of many early mime troupes, the continuing involvement of women in itinerant performance, and the significance of the plays of Hrotsvitha – the first playwright of the post-classical period for whom we have a name. But most folk performance and all church-sanctioned dramatic activity was exclusively male, and the cruel fact is that even in the one branch of the profession, acting, in which after 1660 women found their place, all too often it was only to be maligned as little better than whores. And the rediscovery of Aphra Behn cannot disguise the fact that such 'disreputable' associations for long made the novel the genre of choice for women writers. One of the few optimistic notes struck in my final chapter thus concerns the belated equalizing not only of opportunity but of actual participation by women in all branches of a previously patriarchal profession.

This prejudice was the theatre's, not my own: but this is not to claim that in other respects I have written an unprejudiced history. *All* histories are prejudiced, however hard they claim to strive for objectivity. For if the new historicism has taught us anything, it is that the moment *from* which we write shapes our view of the moment *of* which we write no less inescapably than our accumulated cultural baggage of personal opinion and experience. 'Objective' historians once set up arbitrary (and so subjective) criteria by which they decided that medieval theatre 'originated' in the introduction of the Quem Quaeritis trope, a 'fact' which would render my first chapter redundant. 'Objective' historians decided that the demonstrations so frequent in the late eighteenth and early nineteenth century theatre were the work of a disruptive element, to be conveniently segregated as 'the mob': my own 'subjective' view, inevitably influenced by my class origins, is that the ordinary people who comprised 'the mob' (usually far less violent than the forces of 'law and order' which suppressed them) were demonstrating for rights I now enjoy, but take for granted at my peril.

This is, then, a radical history which, while it recognizes the role of the ever-shifting West End (not to mention the South Bank) in shaping the official theatre, tries also to reconstruct and reclaim the unofficial theatre which no less influenced the lives of those it touched. As a radical, I 'place' myself as both a product and a continuing supporter of the post-war political consensus which – through the good education, housing, and health care it provided – gave me 'chances in life' which my own younger children would lack, had not those same chances allowed me the resources to assist them. Parents of today who have to start from the under-privileged base of my own will find such chances harder if not impossible to secure.

This book would not exist without the help, forbearance (and Macintosh knowhow) of my wife, Laverne Anderson, the stimulus of our children, Jonathan and Meryl, and the encouragement and support of my older children, Anna and Nicholas. Colleagues at Goldsmiths' College, especially Nesta Jones and Bill Naismith, have been invaluably supportive, and I am also grateful to the Warden and Council of the College for the grant of a term's sabbatical leave at a time when a 'clear run' at the book was most needed. I am indebted to William Tydeman for his helpful comments on my treatment of the medieval period, as to Peter Holland for his careful eye over the whole project. At Cambridge University Press, the peripatetic nature of modern publishing has given this book three editorial godparents – Ann Stonehouse, who conceived and commissioned it; Peter Richards, whose unstinting support saw most of it into final draft; and Kendall Clarke, whose light touch was appreciated at a time when less tactful editors might have required its recasting in their own image. Sarah Stanton also offered constant background support. My thanks, too, to Callie Kendall for picture research, and to Stuart McCready for not only recognizing that the new technology permits authors a large collaborative share in the production process, but for allowing and encouraging me to claim it.

Simon Trussler

THE CAMBRIDGE ILLUSTRATED HISTORY OF
British Theatre

CHAPTER 1

Roman Britain and the Early Middle Ages

The first performer in Britain known by name was a woman. On a shard of Italian redware pottery found at Leicester, dated somewhere between the first and fourth centuries AD, the name Verecunda, described as a 'ludia', or player, is scratched alongside that of Lucius the gladiator – an appropriate pairing, for itinerant actors and gladiators no doubt rubbed shoulders in the theatres of England under the Roman occupation as they did elsewhere in the far-flung Empire.

Traces of large theatres in the Roman style, some dating from the first century AD, have been found in six English cities of the time, including Canterbury, Colchester, and St Albans, while sites of a dozen amphitheatres, probably used for theatrical among other purposes, have also been identified. And eight theatrical masks, both tragic and comic, have come to light, often in yet different locations – the property, perhaps, of strolling players, who did not necessarily require a purpose-built theatre. The sum of the archeological evidence suggests a broadly-based tradition

Mosaic believed to depict a scene from a play by the Greek dramatist Menander. The masks, musical skills, and deportment here depicted – not to mention the attendant midget – might equally have characterized a troupe of itinerant mimes. Signed by Dioskorides of Samos, and finely preserved amidst the volcanic ash at Pompeii, the mosaic dates from *c.* 100 BC

of performance in Roman Britain, stretching from Yorkshire down to Kent and from Caerleon in South Wales across to Essex.

Despite such physical traces of theatrical activity, we know almost nothing about what forms it might have taken. Conjecturally – which could well be our watch-word for this chapter – we must assume that British players followed, at an appropriate provincial distance, the fashions set in imperial Rome. And there, even before the building of the earliest British theatres, the comic dramas of Plautus and Terence (recognizable to us as part of a tradition which survives in the plots of situation comedy) were being supplanted by the silent art of the *pantomimus*, and by the rougher and readier 'mimes'. The *pantomimus* was a masked, solo player of dance-dramas performed in dumb-show, who himself acted all the roles to spoken and musical accompaniment. The performer's themes were usually taken from myth – which, for all his pretensions to high art, also provided plenty of opportunities for sexual display.

THE SURVIVAL OF THE MIMES

With no such pretensions, so too did the Roman 'mimes' – a term which, confusingly for us, denotes not only these short spoken playlets but the itinerant actors, or *mimi*, who performed them. (The name derives from the *mimetic* or imitative quality which Aristotle perceived as being at the heart of the dramatic instinct.) Played both in public and in the many private or household theatres of Ancient Rome, the mimes at the height of their popularity are said to have required companies numbering up to sixty. On the evidence of the handful that remain extant, all in fragmentary form, they were short and sometimes scurrilous pieces, catching up men and gods alike in mixtures of farce, satire, and burlesque, and of song, dance, and acrobatic skills.

Earthy, even bawdy, the mimes may have been, but scarcely objectionable – still less contributory to the decline and fall of the Roman Empire, as you might think from some descriptions. Indeed, the Roman mimes form part of a tradition of popular theatre which can be traced back even further than the golden age of the Athenian drama, to the Dorian farces of the sixth century BC. They were praised by so astute a writer as Seneca (who evidently did not expect his own, closet tragedies to find favour in performance), and at least tolerated by Juvenal, as if a lesser evil than the 'bread and circuses' he was otherwise the first to deride. In the view of the theatre historian Allardyce Nicoll, the typical mime was probably similar in style to an eighteenth-century ballad opera – while a later critic likened it to 'a kind of revue or variety'. Since it functioned also as what we might today call a 'star vehicle', not least in its evident subordination of plot to personality, I suspect that we might equally well compare its crossbred style to that of a television variety sketch or Christmas celebrity special.

One suspects that the abuse so casually heaped upon these mimes derived as often from disapproval of such formal irregularity as from outrage at supposed moral impropriety. It is probably true enough that in the first century AD the

Ivory miniature of a tragic theatre mask, possibly forming the side of a lady's workbox, found at Caerleon, site of a Romano-British settlement near Newport in Gwent, where the grassed-over remains of an amphitheatre are also well preserved

Emperor Domitian ordered that the role of a bandit in the *Laureolus*, by the popular mime-writer Catullus, should be taken over by a condemned criminal in the final scene, so that a real execution could be carried out. And it is notorious that in the third century the adolescent Emperor Elagabalus wanted to see simulated adulteries replaced by the real thing. Yet, as so often in history, it may be that such excesses are remembered and recorded, while the less scandalous and run-of-the-mill goes unremarked.

In any case, it is doubtful whether such imperial indulgences within the confines of metropolitan Rome would have been imitated in a far province such as Britain. It is more helpful to imagine the likes of our unknown Verecunda as the *archimima*, or leading female performer, in one of the mimes discovered in a papyrus at Oxyrhincus in Egypt, and apparently dating from the second century AD. This is usually known after its leading character as *The Faithless Wife* – who, having failed to seduce a slave who prefers the charms of a fellow-servant, orders the couple to be put to death. She persuades a more susceptible slave first of her own attractions, then of the need to kill her husband – whose supposed corpse turns out to have been merely drugged. Justice is done, and slave gets slave-girl. The prose dialogue, mainly for the wife, is probably only an outline around which the mime players, or *mimi*, would have improvised – no doubt carefully playing up to their actress-manager, who would have assembled her company's repertoire with an eye for just such juicy roles.

When Christianity began to emerge as a force within the Empire, the *mimi* mocked its more risible practices – such as baptism by immersion, which must have offered good potential for theatrical water-play. But it was unwise of the *mimi* to make enemies of a sect which was becoming not only more powerful but increasingly ascetic in its doctrines: and, following the conversion of the Roman Empire to Christianity under the Emperor Constantine, the members of their companies were duly excommunicated. It is said that the Emperor Justinian closed the theatres during his brief recapture of Rome, before it finally fell to the barbarians in 568 – although, ironically, he also took as empress the Byzantine mime-actress Theodora, once notorious for shedding her clothes before enraptured audiences.

Although the last of the legions had withdrawn from Britain early in the fifth century, the influence of the Romans was by no means forgotten, and the more ambitious local chieftains liked to regard themselves as their natural successors. The briefly powerful King Edwin of Northumberland even built himself a theatre modelled on Roman lines, as recent excavations at one of his chief residences at Yeavering have revealed. It is impossible now to say whether the place was used merely for councils and social gatherings, or for something akin to theatrical entertainment – not that the two were by any means mutually exclusive. What is important is the sense of cultural continuity sought by Edwin – and the related possibility that there remained strolling players, travelling singly or in groups, carrying on the traditions of the *mimi*, whose performances needed nothing more elaborate than the cleared space and the receptive audience which have always been the fundamental requirements of theatre. In the seventh century, Isidore of Seville (writing, confessedly, about Spain), significantly referred to theatre *buildings* in the past tense, but to the *mimi* always in the present.

In the scholarly debate over whether or not the *mimi* survived, however exiguously, through the so-called Dark Ages in Britain, most such evidence, though not as scarce as is sometimes claimed, is similarly indirect. The Council of Rome in 679 required English clerics to ban 'both jesters and players' from their premises, while Alcuin, an English diplomat of the eighth century, made many references to *mimi*, typically advising that it is 'better to please God than the actors', and 'better to have a care for the poor than for the mimes'. An ordinance of 789 prescribed beating or banishment for *histriones* who donned clerical garb (presumably in order to mimic its wearers), and among the laws of Charlemagne in the early ninth century was a similar decree, with death now the alternative to exile for any actor who 'puts on a garment belonging to a priestly rank'. Over a century later, in a speech of

Aerial view of the remains of the Roman theatre at Verulamium (St Albans). First constructed around the middle of the first century AD, in its present form it probably dates from around 300, by which time the originally round orchestra had been blunted by the jutting stage here visible – the discovery on the site of an iron counter-weight suggesting that the stage may even have been fronted by a curtain

969, King Edgar of Kent was complaining that 'a house of clergy is known . . . as a meeting place for actors . . . where mimes sing and dance'. What all these references have in common is that they take the activities of the *mimi* or *histriones* or *ludi* or whatever (and these distinctions of vocabulary may be important, as we shall see) very much for granted – but only worthy of notice when the dignity of the church is threatened.

We actually have a name and a verse epitaph, here translated from the Latin by the scholar Richard Axton, for a protean continental mime, probably of the eighth or ninth century, who went by the name of Vitalis, and who could clearly combine the talents of *pantomimus* and mime actor:

> I used to mimic the face, manner, and words of those talking,
> So that you would think many people spoke from one mouth.
> The subject, presented with a twin image of himself before his eyes,
> Would tremble to see a more real self existing in my faces.
> Oh, how often a lady saw herself in my performance,
> And blushed for shame, horribly embarrassed.
> Thus, as many human forms as were seen in my body
> Were snatched away with me by the dismal day of death.

THE NARRATIVE PERFORMANCES OF THE GLEEMEN

While the stress here is mainly on Vitalis's genius for imitating physical appearances and mannerisms, other solo performers there undoubtedly were whose chief skill lay in telling a story. These were the *scops*, or gleemen, who performed 'partly as a narrator, and partly by assuming characters other than their own' – the description is Aristotle's, in the *Poetics*. There, back in the fourth century BC, Aristotle was setting out to define the qualities of the *epic* mode – distinguishing it both from the *dramatic*, in which actors consistently assume the identity of their characters, and from the *lyric*, in which the performer speaks consistently in his own voice. But what is important from our point of view is that Aristotle was making these distinctions not between forms of *literature* but between kinds of *performance* – for most of what we think of as 'poetry' remained a performing medium throughout the Middle Ages. So alongside the mimes, of whose continuing existence we know very little, we need to consider the relatively large body of extant verse which was written for performance both in the epic (or narrative) and the lyric mode.

Scholars are generally agreed that the earliest poem extant in the Old English language, 'Widsith', dates from the late sixth century, though it only reached the shape in which we have it after many succeeding years of recitation in the great halls of early medieval England. But what must be of special interest for us about 'Widsith' is that it is also *about* a performer – the 'Far Traveller' of its title, who reflects on his life as a wandering *scop*, and even gives us what reads like a catalogue of the Germanic heroes about whom he can sing. In other Old English poems, too,

Opposite: The biblical King David, accompanied on his lyre by medieval minstrels – and (top left) by a juggler with balls and knives. This illustration is from the eleventh-century Tiberius Psalter

Tertullian, one of the greatest early Christian apologists. In his *De Spectaculis* of *c.* 200, he admonished the faithful against their continuing attendance at theatrical arenas. In God's sight, he warned, 'everything fabricated is corrupt' – and pagan spectacles were part of a demonic plot to subvert mankind

the narrators speak of themselves and their fortunes – Deor, in the lament so-named (which probably dates from the eighth century, but is perhaps earlier), bemoaning the loss of his 'good office' as gleeman, a rival 'skilled in song' having displaced him in the favour of his 'gracious lord'.

Like Widsith, Deor also offers a sort of 'trailer' of the tales he can recount. Tantalizingly, none of these have survived: but they presumably took the form of short 'lays', which could perhaps have been reworked into more expansive format as an epic cycle – for it was surely one of the skills required of the *scop* that he should have been able to fit his material to the nature and duration of a gathering. Of such larger epics, only *Beowulf* – as some scholars suggest, itself a blending-together of shorter pieces – remains extant in Old English; but it casts no such light on the life of its performers as do 'Widsith' and 'Deor' – although, sure enough, gleemen are said to 'sing loudly in Heriot', the great hall of Hrothgar, who himself takes his turn at the harp. But in form *Beowulf* is entirely suited to the circumstances of its performance, for recitation during grand occasions of feasting by a *scop* such as Widsith or Deor.

As compared with the *mimi* who survived the departure of the Romans, and presumably had to scratch their livings as best they could among all sorts and conditions of men, the *scops* thus sang before the nobler and more powerful members of society. They enjoyed a dignified status, and could hope to amass considerable wealth – although Deor, as the poem's narrator tells us, has been deprived of his lands as well as his job, suggesting not only the high favour to which a *scop* might rise, but also (a favourite theme) the precariousness of such good fortune.

The epic performing modes of the *scops* were, presumably, those with which the ruling classes of the early medieval world found themselves most comfortable – for both performers and audiences were drawn from the waves of Teutonic invaders, whose sensibilities were steeped in the heroic myths and legends of the Germanic tribes. Yet the *scops* recited not only before aristocratic but also clerical audiences: and, because these were literate, their work stood some chance of being written down and so of surviving – albeit in manuscripts which, often dating from centuries after a poem's likely origins, had soaked up centuries of oral accretion.

The overtones of jesting and mockery in the etymology of the word may even indicate that the *scop* – who was, after all, a professional entertainer – might have included occasional or comic pieces in his repertoire, too topical to have reached such written form. Yet the variety even of the surviving Old English monologues is considerable. They range in length from the elegaic brevity of 'Widsith' or 'Deor' to the broad epic sweep of *Beowulf*, and in mood from the personal and reflective, or 'lyric', to the narrative and discursive, for the historic or legendary themes appropriate to the epics – which themselves drew not only on the heroic deeds of Germanic legend but also on stories from the Bible.

For us, the biblical narratives are particularly interesting, in part for their 'visualization' of their scriptural originals, and in part for their choice and treatment of their material: thus, 'Exodus' is no mere vernacular paraphrase, but an adventure story focusing upon the predicament of the Israelites as they find themselves trapped between their Egyptian pursuers and the sea, and then watch as the waves which have parted to allow them safe passage close inexorably over their enemies.

No word distinguished the role of the *scop* or gleeman as creator of his songs from his role as performer of them – mainly, no doubt, because the two functions were so closely identified as to make such a distinction meaningless. Also, however, there was simply less sense in the Middle Ages than in our own of a work of art as an assertion of personal 'authorship': rather, the feeling was that it celebrated the values of its community. However, the great eighth-century English historian, the Venerable Bede, does give us a name for the author of the 'Exodus' and other poems – Caedmon, a humble cowherd employed by the Abbess Hild of Whitby. Visited by an angel as he slept, Caedmon, according to Bede, was inspired with the gift of improvising divine songs, which he performed for the company assembled in the abbey.

THE INFLUENCE OF CHRISTIANIZATION

This legend usefully bears out that there were two kinds of audience for such recitations: on the one hand the assemblies of aristocrats and warriors, who no doubt preferred something on the lines of *Beowulf*, and, on the other, the gatherings in monasteries and abbeys before which Caedmon first improvised his 'Exodus'. And this, in turn, reminds us of the ambiguous attitude of the Christian Church towards the arts of performance. The *mimi* had been excommunicated and the theatres apparently closed, yet in the celebration of the Mass the Church had itself created a compelling spectacle which, as we shall see, it was later to make more purposefully 'dramatic'. Churchmen were forbidden to entertain strolling players, or to be entertained by them, yet such a *scop* as Caedmon was held capable of divine inspiration, and expected to reshape the most sacred material in his songs. Beyond the Roman experience and the Platonic precedents usually cited, what were the causes for the continuing (although increasingly ambivalent) opposition of the Church to the theatre?

Tertullian, building on Old Testament injunctions against 'dressing up' and transvestism, first formulated Christian objections to the Roman theatre in his *De Spectaculis* of *c.* 200. Claiming that, in God's sight, 'everything fabricated is corrupt', he condemned the actor's falsification of his identity (with the *pantomimus*, also of his sex) as a mortal sin: for not only did an actor imitating a villain take on the evil he portrayed, but one pretending to be a good person committed sacrilege by daring to mimic virtue. Seemingly, then, to pretend to commit a murder on stage, or even to watch the enactment of that pretence, was an endorsement of evil – although to read of it in scripture, or even to see it in a painting, was to commit no such sin.

Two centuries later, St Augustine, whose writings are saturated with references to the theatre, wasn't even sure about the painting: but he had himself loved the theatre in his youth, and was not the first or last to acknowledge that 'we too are acting in life this mime of ours'. Not only is Augustine much more self-aware than Tertullian, but his arguments reveal a deeper understanding alike of history and of the theatrical process: yet he comes, in the end, to no less condemnatory conclusions.

It was the second St Augustine who, through the conversion of Kent at the end of the sixth century, began the process whereby Christianity finally took on its Roman form throughout the seven kingdoms of Anglo-Saxon England. And this second Augustine pursued the missionary policy advocated by the first – aiming not so much to eradicate all traces of paganism as to overlay them, as it were, with Christianity. So 'heathen temples' were transformed into churches, or new churches built on sites once sacred to pagan gods – just as Christian festivals were already being fixed to coincide with and hopefully supplant periods of pagan celebration.

Given that 'conversion' was usually a matter of a local chieftain imposing his will from above, and that it was accomplished partly by means of this calculated confusion between the sites and calendars of the old religion and the new, it is not surprising that ordinary people should have seen nothing wrong in preserving traditional, often quasi-dramatic forms of celebration – notably those age-old calendar celebrations which probably made sense to their participants less in terms of theology, old or new, than of their experience of living.

From our point of view, to search for physical traces of the origins of such types of folk performance would be futile: most of the 'plays' were probably ambulatory (as they remain today), so their 'theatres' were the whole of a village, and if a focal point were needed it could only be the church, itself sharing the site of some more ancient place of worship. (Today – a sign of the adaptability of these plays – the local pub usually offers a final, festive welcome.) And, just as medieval man had no need to seek a special place for such celebrations, nor did he need to invent an occasion – which the overlapping calendars of old and new religions provided.

Here we need to take account of the distinctive way in which medieval man perceived the passage of time. The Christian understanding of 'sacred history', as stretching from Creation to Day of Judgement (in some ways a virtually accomplished process, awaiting imminent fulfilment) anticipated our modern sense of time as a 'linear' process, driving inexorably forwards. But secular assumptions and modes of living in the Middle Ages were rather shaped by the cycle of the seasons – by a feeling for time as *recurrence*, a sort of stepping-stone from year to year. And to this sense Christianity paid due obeisance, through its calendar of feasts and 'holy days' which paralleled the recurring pattern of the seasons.

Unlike, say, his long-distant descendants in a nineteenth-century factory or sweatshop, medieval man was thus allowed the opportunity to celebrate the rhythms of his year by this sequence of 'holy days' – only a few of which (most notably Christmas) survive among the largely secularized 'holidays' of today. King Alfred's laws of 876 thus stipulated holidays amounting to well over a month in each year, and, as we shall see, this 'official' free time tended to increase as the

centuries passed: but in a period when the expectation of no more than subsistence-living made 'work for work's sake' a pointless exercise, in actuality people probably enjoyed their leisure more often, whenever there was no necessary work to do.

The feast of Christmas, celebrated midway between the Germanic season of Yule and the Roman Saturnalia and Kalends, and intended to absorb the pagan energies of both, thus provides its twelve days or more of celebration at a time of no urgent agricultural activity. And the mummers – the folk performers whose descendants still claim this season as their own – were probably setting out on their rounds long before the Church first Christianized the festival, and subsequently seized the occasion for its own dramatic purposes. Overleaf we explore the significance of this and other aspects of the tensions between pagan calendar customs and the attempted Christianization of such popular celebrations.

It is not needful to try to tie up the three strands of theatrical activity we have begun to unravel – the activities of professionals intent on earning a living, the potentially dramatic rituals of the Church, and the popular performances of the people – within some neat, bow-ribboned theory of 'the origins of British drama'. For the drama, as we have seen in this chapter, had no need to originate: it never went away. We pause, therefore, at the point when many theatre histories begin, or begin again: at that moment, late in the first millennium, when the Church recognized that it too might make fuller use of the dramatic impulse, now being satisfied in semi-pagan ceremonies and by those elusive companies of strolling players, in order to celebrate its own beliefs through dramatic performance, as it had long been doing through epic.

And if we need more evidence that the Church had no need to 'discover' theatre when, around the middle of the tenth century, it came to introduce a dramatic note into its liturgy, we need look no further abroad than a German nunnery. For just as the first known performer in England was a woman, so too was the first named playwright of medieval Europe.

'Wild men' and 'wild women' such as these (from Walter de Milemete's *De Nobilitatibus*) cleared the way for folk performances and pageants later in the medieval period. By then they were perhaps professional entertainers, but their green-clad 'grotesque bodies' have an earlier ancestry, deriving from the uneasy relationship between the medieval peasant and his often hostile environment

Roman theatre had largely been an urban affair, and had probably passed by the scattered inhabitants of the countryside. But following the withdrawal of the legions early in the fifth century AD, most towns that had been large enough to support theatres were destroyed or largely deserted – as were those long, straight Roman roads which linked them. The remaining, predominantly rural settlements were separated by great distances, dense forests – and habits of mind which saw no need for travel beyond boundaries which were at least familiar, if not at all secure.

Within such small agrarian communities, early medieval man did not, as is sometimes romantically assumed, feel at one with the natural forces which shaped his life, but was rather involved in a constant struggle to keep them at bay, with difficulty taming those few he could make productive of his meagre subsistence. Much more than the urbanized Roman citizen, let alone modern man, he led his life in what the Russian historian A. J. Gurevich has called 'an undifferentiated relationship between people, both individuals and groups, and the earth'.

There is in medieval art a recurrent, emblematic rendering of this 'undifferentiated relationship', variously portraying man as half-animal or half-tree, or even as a humanoid mountain or bunch of vegetables. The 'grotesque body' is how the influential Russian cultural critic Mikhail Bakhtin described such attempts by visual artists to convey a sense of man as both emerging from yet trapped within his natural surroundings. And folk performance, too, was (and remains) crowded with 'grotesque bodies', which had probably been integral to its celebrations from the very beginnings. They had even, long since, found their way into the more 'literary' drama, in the goat-like dancers of the 'satyr plays' of Ancient Greece.

The relationship and the dividing-line between such 'performance' and what we may loosely call 'ritual' – whether communal and predictably recurrent, or marking out 'rites of passage' in individual lives – has been the subject of endless debate. Anthropologists, for example, once tended to distinguish, rather arbitrarily, three types of seasonal folk play as representing 'arrested' stages in the development of what was originally 'pure' ritual towards performance. The 'sword play', which typically culminates in a 'lock' of swords being placed round the neck of a fool who is later brought back to life by a doctor, was thus regarded as closest to its totemistic origins; the 'wooing ceremony' as more developed in its mythic interpretation of the theme of fertility and of the triumph of youth over age; and the 'hero combat', with its fight to the death and subsequent resurrection, as the most dramatically sophisticated, on account of its individualized characters and clearer narrative line.

Other scholars suggest that the plays have survived according to the capacities of generations of performers to effect the transition (made necessary by Christianization) from pagan

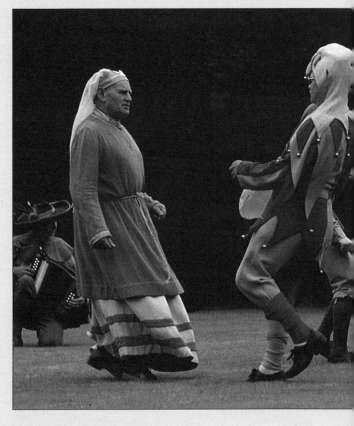

ritual, first into folk entertainment and then into play – the final stage of this process, it is argued, having occurred between the thirteenth and fifteenth centuries. Others again, pointing to no less distinct groups of 'Robin Hood plays', 'Old Horse plays', and 'Old Tup plays', dispute such schematic arrangements, and today stress tends to be laid on the communal and recreative nature of most 'folk' activities – not to mention their economic potential, since many performances end in appeals for money, or at least in the expectation of refreshment. This may suggest either a formalized acknowledgement of social obligations – or simply an opportunistic deployment of the time-honoured techniques of the mimi.

Though early texts were not, of course, written down – indeed, the earliest extant text of an English mumming play dates only from the eighteenth century – it is, however, clear that analogues for most types of folk drama are to be found throughout Europe and even beyond, suggesting that elements of such performance may be older even than the pagan religions which Christianity supplanted, and return us close to the primeval origins of the religious as of the dramatic impulse, in fertility ritual, sympathetic magic, and human sacrifice.

To this day, sanitized versions of these ancient ceremonies, most with 'grotesque bodies' in their casts, take place throughout the length and breadth of Britain, according to their time-honoured calendar – from the Haxey Hood Game in early January

Six horn dancers, a man-woman 'Maid Marion', a primitive hobby horse, and a jester are the chief 'characters' in the Abbots Bromley Horn Dance, whose participants traverse some twenty miles as they call at farms and stately homes. As 'recently' as three centuries ago this, like the mummers' play, was a Christmastide celebration, but it is now danced in early September. No play is enacted, suggesting that the origins of the dance lie deep in a past when such ritual performance was scarcely distinguishable from the sympathetic magic in which it probably originated

and the sword dances of Plough Monday, to the prancing Hobby Horses and the Furry Dance at Helston in the spring, and the Padstow 'Oss on May Day; from the parade of the Burry Man at South Queensferry in August to the Horn Dance at Abbots Bromley in September; and from all those corn dollies of Harvest Home to the mumming plays which predominate from All Hallows-cum-Samhain to Christmas-cum-Yule.

If we now find such an unlikely figure as the Turkish Knight (or Turkey Snipe), who presumably first appeared during the Crusades, cheerfully co-existing with Napoleon or the Black Prince, and Father Christmas keeping no less incongruous company with Old King Cole or St George, this may be because so many of the 'scripts' or scenarios of these plays were 'frozen' during the late-eighteenth or nineteenth centuries, when some well-intentioned antiquary wrote down what had previously been passed on and developed by oral tradition. However, it may alternatively be because a 'new' tradition was created much more recently – for while many surviving 'folk' dramas are connected with communities which retain a sense of contact with their rural past, others are to be found in younger, industrial environments, perhaps in response to the pressures felt by the urbanized poor during the most oppressive years of the industrial revolution.

Certainly, such traditional plays were accessible enough at the time, in the cheaply-printed pamphlets, or chapbooks, which constituted the poor man's literature. It's worth comparing here the difficulties experienced by some early folklorists in prising the words of certain folk songs from their singers – not always because these would have raised a blush from the maiden ladies or earnest curates concerned, but because they formed part of a 'secret literature' through which the ordinary man cocked a snook at authority. Indeed, Robin Hood plays – a few of which, adapted from ballads, were even published in the sixteenth century – celebrate the outlaw as a hero persecuted by the establishment. And it seems quite likely that the survival or revival of folk performance in some areas is due in part to its ability over the years to speak for the social and political oppression of the people, as well as of their religious or 'ritual' needs.

To suggest that 'folk' plays might no less have served as a 'secret literature' for the poor even in early medieval England would be … well, mere conjecture – but conjecture was, after all, to be our watchword, so far as the elusive nature of the evidence for this period is concerned. Certainly, we may now feel that the strand of anarchy in much 'unofficial' drama is not so much dramaturgically clumsy as creatively carnivalesque. No less certainly, the Church was finding such popular festivities as worthy of its prohibitions as the secular performances of the mimi – although, as we shall see, it was soon to find a way of integrating dramatic elements into its own 'seasonal celebrations'.

CHAPTER 2

The High Middle Ages

This imaginary scene of Hrotsvitha kneeling to present a book of her plays to the Emperor Otto is attributed to the great German engraver, Albrecht Dürer, and served as frontispiece to the edition of her works printed by Conrad Celtes in 1501. She thus came early into print, along with the great classical writers of Ancient Greece and Rome – her own supposed model, Terence, among them

It used to be argued that the half-dozen or so dramatic pieces written around the middle of the tenth century by Hrotsvitha, an obscure German nun cloistered within the confines of an abbey, could not have been intended for performance. They were, it was assumed, mere literary exercises, written in an attempt to clean up and Christianize the plays of the Roman comic dramatist Terence, on which they were confessedly modelled.

There are many misconceptions in this view – not least, that the abbey where Hrotsvitha lived and worked was remote from the world. As the scholar Peter Dronke describes it, the abbey of Gandersheim in Lower Saxony was nothing less than 'a small, proudly independent principality ruled by women', and its members, apart from the servants, were all of noble birth. Gandersheim was an imperial foundation, whose abbess was a member of the reigning family of the Emperor Otto: it boasted its own court, militia, ambassadors, and even a royal mint. Hrotsvitha in all probability never took vows, and as a canoness would have been able to remain in close contact with the cosmopolitan imperial court.

Dronke also points out that a contemporary life of the Emperor's brother, Bruno, Archbishop of Cologne, remarks both upon his 'relations with Gandersheim' and his taste for the 'scurrilia et mimica' – obscene jests and mimetic antics – that 'in comedies and tragedies are presented by various personages'. We cannot be certain what 'presented' implies here, along the spectrum between a mere reading-aloud and a fully 'acted' performance, nor can we know whether the 'various personages' were other courtly amateurs, resident entertainers, or visiting troupes of *mimi*. No less is it guesswork whether Hrotsvitha's own plays were among those 'presented': but there seems no reason of proximity, opportunity, or dramatic viability why they should not have been.

HROTSVITHA AND THE 'TERENCE STAGES'

Hrotsvitha's plays, so far from purifying the Terentian mode of anything offensive to Christian morality, are full of potential for those 'scurrilia et mimica' on which Bruno's biographer comments. It is true that chastity is always triumphant, but it is under constant, often titillating siege. There is, for example, a scene in the play named after the three virtuous sisters who are its heroines, *Agape, Chionia, and Hirena*, in which the villainous Roman governor Dulcitius makes love to bits and pieces of kitchenware under the delusion that they are the Christian maidens – who are meanwhile mocking his antics through cracks in the wall. The governor, blackfaced from his encounters, is then mistaken for the Devil by the waiting guards, who flee from him in terror. Such a scene is not only frankly bawdy, but as much in the tradition of the *mimi* as of Terence – and, full of action and reaction as it is, it would not seem to have been worth the writing were it not also meant to have been performed.

Copies of the works of Terence were fairly widely available in monastic libraries (including those at Canterbury, Durham, and St Albans in England). And Hrotsvitha's plays do appear to adapt well to the Terentian staging convention which was to become common throughout the Middle Ages, whereby a scene might either occur in a definite location – a 'house', 'mansion', or *locus* – or occupy instead a generalized, neutral foreground known simply as the *platea* or 'place'. However, it is actually a medieval *misconception* concerning the practice of Ancient Roman theatre which may provide a clue to the way Hrotsvitha intended her own dialogue to be handled. For it was presumed – the belief perhaps even deriving from the working methods of the *scops* – that a narrator would have recited all the roles, while the action was mimed by players. The plays of Hrotsvitha can readily be visualized with this kind of staging in mind – the Emperor Bruno's brother perhaps serving as 'Terentian' narrator, while he relished the 'obscene jests and mimetic antics' for which his biographer claims he had a taste.

But why should we concern ourselves here whether plays were being written, read, or staged in the court of the Holy Roman Empire? It was to this court that Alcuin, who issued some of the cautions against the *mimi* which we noticed in the previous chapter, had come as ambassador from England in the time of its founding Emperor, Charlemagne. Now, the Emperor Otto was striving to preserve his great ancestor's ideal of a Christian Europe built on the foundations of Roman civilization. Hrotsvitha's plays, which contributed towards the richness of the so-called Ottonian Renaissance, embodied this Carolingian ideal – not least in their use of the Latin language, which was both a vehicle and a symbol of cultural continuity. But, for us, the crucial importance of Hrotsvitha is not so much that she wrote in

The Roman playwright, as understood in the Middle Ages. The 'narrator' (Calliopus) reads from a sort of puppeteer's booth, while performers (described as *joculatores*) play in an open arena (the *theatrum*) before a throng of spectators. Some illustrations of these so-called 'Terence stages' are wildly impractical: yet the method they assume would have resolved the problem of illiterate players unable to read or learn lines in Latin. While these hired *mimi* were displaying their gestic miming and improvisation, a clerical narrator would be quarantined from undesirable proximity

Latin (though her work *would* thus have been accessible to English as it was to German clerics), or even that her plays reveal a sophisticated awareness of the nature, techniques, and potential of theatrical performance, and a strong feeling for comic business and timing. Rather, it is because she combined *all* these attributes at a time when, according to many scholars, other clerics were, quite unconsciously, engaged in 're-inventing' drama – and were doing so in a primitive and embryonic fashion, apparently ignorant not only of the itinerant mimes but of that respectable pagan Terence and his Christian imitator besides.

THE LITURGICAL DRAMA

Among the relatively recent historians of medieval theatre who spoke for a belief which stretched back to E. K. Chambers at the beginning of the twentieth century, the respected scholar Hardin Craig was unequivocal:

> It happens that at a definite time and place there came together in an exercise of representative art the three factors that are the constituents of drama, namely, impersonation, action, and dialogue. The ecclesiastical persons responsible for this combination of elements were at first and for a long time entirely ignorant of what they had done, and it was perhaps two hundred years before anybody realized that drama had again been invented, that the achievement attributed to the sixth-century BC Greek, Thespis, had been independently repeated.

Before we can dispute, as we must, the common fallacy encapsulated here, we need to examine just what Professor Craig believed to have been 'invented', and at what 'definite time and place'. And before we can do this, we need to understand a little more about the ways in which the Christian Church had been edging its way towards enabling 'ecclesiastical persons' thus to combine 'impersonation, action, and dialogue' in a manner not only acceptable to the Church, but capable of being integrated into its most sacred ceremonies.

An ecclesiastical 'theatre' was already there. Indeed, in its simple, rectangular shape, the Saxon and early Norman church bears a curious resemblance to the form of the English playhouse of the later seventeenth century – the oblong nave equivalent to the ground-level of the auditorium, or pit; the intermediate chancel akin to the 'apron stage', or forward-thrusting acting area; and the 'set-piece' of the altar framed by a sanctuary arch comparable to the proscenium beyond which the Restoration theatre displayed its 'scenes'. I am not, of course, suggesting any direct descent or even influence, only remarking on the shared suitability of these architectural forms for their very different dramatic purposes.

When the Church wished to sanctify such a building for the faith, or to dedicate to Christ a temple previously used for pagan worship, it carried out a rite of consecration which to us seems poised between folk ceremony and drama. In the version employed at Metz in the ninth century, the Bishop, having completed a circuit of the building, would approach the door, knock thrice with his mitre, and (in Latin, of course) command it to open in the words of the Twenty-Fourth Psalm: 'Lift up your heads, O ye gates, and be ye lift up ye everlasting doors, and the King of Glory shall come in.' A priest already concealed inside the building then responded, 'Who is this King of Glory?'. Thereupon the circuit, command, and question would be twice repeated, until, in answer to the third putting of the question, the Bishop and his train would finally reply: 'Even the Lord of Hosts, he is the King of Glory.' The door would then be flung open, and the hidden priest rush out as if he were the spirit of evil fleeing the holy place.

This ceremony was clearly 'invented' and 'acted', involving as it did both dialogue and impersonation. And as much could even be claimed of the Mass itself, with its processional movement, elaborate spectacle, and sharing-out of the spoken liturgy between celebrant, priests, and participants – all leading to the climactic

The early Norman church of St Mary's, at Kilpeck in Herefordshire, looking from the nave through the inter-mediate chancel towards the altar, framed by the sanctuary arch. The intrinsic theatricality of this simple arrangement was well adapted to the ceremonies of the early Church as they assumed an increasingly 'dramatic' form

'representational' or symbolic act of communion. Moreover, as in classical drama, there is a crucial choral involvement, and a prominent function for music and stylized movement.

To regard this as constituting a 'dramatic' occasion is not retrospective special pleading. As early as 821, Bishop Amalarius of Metz had set out in the *Liber Officialis* an allegorical view of the Mass in terms which seem to recognize no distinction between ritual and drama, while by the early twelfth century Honorius of Autun was explicitly comparing the officiating priest to a *tragicus*, or tragic actor, who (in the translation of the medieval scholar David Bevington) 'represents to the

Dramatic 'tropes' for Eastertide and Christmas

On high occasions, the mass would include embellishments known as tropes. Some were dramatic. For example, around 975 a version of the Quem Quaeritis trope (named from its opening question, 'Whom do you seek?') appeared in the Regularis Concordia. The outcome of the long deliberations on monastic life of a council set up at Winchester by King Edgar, the Regularis was an 'agreed code of practice', as the title roughly translates, formulated by Bishop Ethelwold. The Winchester Quem Quaeritis is fleshed out with quite detailed 'stage directions' which suggest that it had already been fully integrated into the service (the Regularis Concordia codifying, as it were, an established custom for the benefit of those as yet unpractised in its conduct).

Christmas was the other main occasion on which liturgical 'dramas' were 'performed' – invariably, like the rest of the service, in Latin. Although there are far fewer extant examples of a Christmas trope than of the Easter version, these include not only the Officium Pastorum of Christmas Day itself, involving the shepherds' visit to the manger, but the Ordo Prophetarum of Advent, with its procession of prophets foretelling the coming of the saviour, and the

Officium Stellae of the Epiphany, celebrating the star-led visit of the Magi to the baby Jesus. There also exists a trope for Ascensiontide (forty days after Easter) which probably originates from Canterbury – one of the very few to have survived from an English source, perhaps owing to the wholesale plunderings of monastic libraries at the time of the Reformation.

Liturgical dramas continued to be written throughout Europe into the twelfth and thirteenth centuries. Although their actors were invariably drawn from the monastic brethren, and their dialogue was normally sung, those that have come down to us do vary considerably in complexity – from simple antiphons, comprising a few responses with accompanying 'actions', to more substantial, almost cosmic dramas, which would have required an elementary form of 'simultaneous staging'.

The visit of the three Maries – clearly in priestly garb – to the sepulchre on Easter morning. A stone bas-relief of the early twelfth century representing a dramatic trope.

Christian people in the theatre of the church, by his gestures, the struggle of Christ, and impresses upon them the victory of his redemption'.

In the liturgical calendar which regulated the Church's forms of worship as it celebrated the Christian year, the focal points were, of course, Christmas and Easter – the first celebrating the birth, the second the death and glorious resurrection of Christ. We have already noticed how the date of Christmas had been fixed to coincide with the midwinter festivities of the pagan and Roman calendars – while Easter, no less significantly, is not a fixed but a moveable feast, its date being calculated in relation to that of the first full moon after the vernal equinox. The Christian Easter – even its name deriving from that of Eostre, the pagan earth goddess of the Saxons – thus took its place in a pattern of celebrations of fertility and new life which, from time immemorial, had expressed man's sense of renewal in the coming of Spring.

Already there existed within the Church forms of dramatic ceremony for Eastertide. One such began on Good Friday, when the cross was taken down from the place it usually occupied high above the nave, by means of the stairs used solely to gain access to the 'rood loft' (these stairs, apparently leading from nowhere to nowhere, may still be seen in surviving Saxon churches). The cross was reverently wrapped in a 'shroud', and laid beside the altar or in a specially constructed 'sepulchre'. Here, priests stood guard as over the body of their crucified Lord until Easter morning, when the cross, with pomp and rejoicing, was restored to its elevated position, to celebrate Christ's miraculous resurrection.

There also already existed within the liturgy of the Church decorative but as yet undramatic textual interpolations known as 'tropes'. These had previously taken a musical form – at its simplest, an elaboration of the choral exclamation 'Alleluia!'. Then, by the early tenth century, tropes in dialogue form began to be introduced on the Continent as a coda to the Easter ceremony just described. Usually known as the *Quem Quaeritis*, from the question ('Whom do you seek?') with which it begins, this trope took the form of a dialogue between the women who find Christ's empty tomb and the angel who offers them comfort and hope.

As dramatized 'troping' became more common and more complex, the ampler, cruciform shape of the Romanesque church probably served to encourage the extension of the 'stage area' from the chancel into the nave and even the transepts – from which the three Magi thus emerge in the Rouen play of the Epiphany. Having first (quite unliturgically) encountered Herod and later (quite unscripturally) the three shepherds, the Magi follow the guiding star towards the altar crib – while in another continental example they first 'visit' the pulpit, representing Jerusalem, before making their way to the altar with gifts for the infant Christ in Bethlehem.

However, while there were certainly both simple and more ambitious liturgical dramas, the old habit among scholars of shuffling these into a sort of evolutionary sequence, in which primitive forms give way before more sophisticated versions, is now known to be misleading. The detailed researches of Oscar Hardison demonstrated in 1965 that however scrupulous earlier scholars had been in assembling

The stairs to the rood loft in the nave wall of St Peter's Church at Iver, Buckinghamshire, from which the cross would have been taken down on Good Friday, to be shrouded in its sepulchre until its restoration on Easter Day

their evidence, their chronology had been adapted to suggest a 'development' that simply had not taken place. Thus, Hardison revealed not only that some 'primitive' tropes emerged later than supposedly more 'complex' ones, but also that the former existed alongside the latter, instead of being displaced by them as the evolutionists assumed. 'Sophistication', seemingly, related to ceremonial function (and perhaps to geography) rather than to a growing awareness of dramatic potential.

It was, however, in the combination of 'impersonation, action, and dialogue' of this liturgical drama that Hardin Craig (himself the last heavyweight 'Darwinian') discerned that 'exercise of representative art' through which drama was again 'invented'. But quite apart from the heresy that, once invented, it had then to be 'perfected' until it turned into Shakespeare, and even leaving aside all the earlier manifestations of theatricality we have discussed, to talk of the participating priests as 'imitating' their 'characters' and 'conversing' in a form of dramatic 'dialogue' is not so much mistaken as beside the point.

Thus, while efforts at costuming and disguise, and even 'stage directions' for movement and gesture, may suggest 'imitation', Craig's belief that this was with the aim of creating dramatic illusion was, quite simply, anachronistic: for the medieval mind was no more concerned with illusion than with niceties of Aristotelian taxonomy. Rather, these clerics were striving to create a microcosmic version of an enduring macrocosmic reality – expressing their sense of the continuities and correspondences between their own here-and-now and a somehow co-existing elsewhere of the past. Their drama was on a scale both cosmic and eternal.

We may, then, perhaps best understand the practice of troping as part of that cultural moment, distinctive to the High Middle Ages, of which the Church was the focus and Christianity the subject. It is not that this 'embryonic' form of drama 'developed' in the later medieval period, but that the infiltration of more secular concerns at every level of life manifested itself in new kinds of dramatic activity: and some of these were sanctioned by the Church as it began to recognize that Christ's humanity could communicate itself to the laiety more readily than his divinity. Among the plays which remain extant, most are thus overtly religious in subject – though some display not only independence of clerical origins but even that more critical attitude towards the Church which begins to characterize the medieval sensibility from the fourteenth century onwards.

As the theatre historian Glynne Wickham has put it in his masterly study of *Early English Stages*, there were essentially two *separate* kinds of medieval religious drama, which were 'of single Christian origin but of independent motivation: the drama of the Real Presence within the liturgy and the imitative drama of Christ's humanity in the world outside'. This second kind of drama will be among our concerns in the next chapter. Suffice it here to note that not only was it indeed more 'imitative', and no longer integrated into forms of Church worship or confined to Church premises, but it was also largely written and performed in the vernacular – features we should, then, bear in mind in seeking its possible antecedents.

Opposite: conjectural reconstruction by Richard Leacroft, based on Southwell Minster, of a setting within the church for a fully developed form of 'mansion' staging, based here on a twelfth-century French liturgical drama of the Resurrection

Interestingly, the British Library contains one copy of the Winchester *Quem Quaeritis* to which has been added an interlinear translation in Old English. This was no doubt made for teaching purposes – as also was the famous 'Latin primer' known as Aelfric's *Colloquy*. Aelfric, besides being a prolific writer, was a monk who (perhaps significantly from our point of view) lived in the monastery at Winchester until 987. In the *Colloquy*, under the guise of a teacher quizzing his pupils about their occupations, he gives the Latin equivalents for everyday Old English terms – of which several are of clear theatrical import.

Theatre historians have long been intrigued by this expectation of familiarity with the jargon of theatre, which is no less evident in continental works of a similar kind. So when, in the early twelfth century, Ailred, Abbot of Rievaulx in Yorkshire, warned that English priests who embellished the liturgical drama with gestures and mimicry were turning the church into a *theatrum*, and when Gerhoh of Reichersberg similarly accused German priests of turning their churches into theatres, what *kind* of theatres did they have in mind? According to etymological studies of the evidence, a 'theatre' in the Middle Ages indicated any kind of 'place for seeing' where an entertainment was being presented, and might even denote a brothel. Yet the scholar Mary Marshall cites a German glossary, probably dating from the ninth century, in which a *theatrum* is defined, quite explicitly and

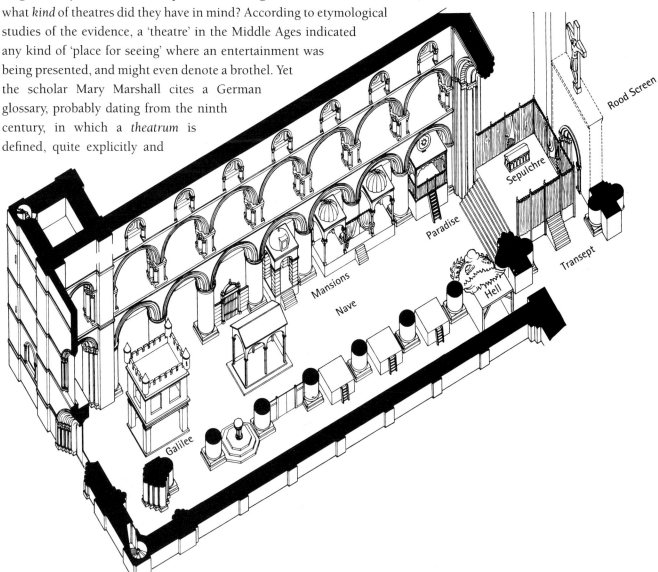

Cabinet of 'Terence masks' the first illustration (among nearly 140) in a twelfth-century manuscript of the comedies of Terence in the monastic library at St Albans – from which the picture on pages 24–5 of actors perform-ing Terence is taken. The tradition of 'Terence staging', whether or not adapted to actual performance, was clearly as widespread as it was deeply-rooted in western European medieval culture

unexpectedly, as a place 'built of wood where men play and create spectacles'. The present tense of those verbs clearly implies a continuing activity, and the wooden construction specified would explain why no trace of any such building has survived. Tenuous though such evidence may be, the thought of itinerant *mimi* setting up a trestle-stage in a purpose-built *theatrum* of this kind is intriguing.

In England, following the successful Norman invasion of 1066, the various dialects of Old English became the language of the conquered, and Norman French the language of the ruling classes – with Latin still functioning, of course, as a *lingua franca* for clerical and administrative use. The effects of this Norman hegemony, political and linguistic, must have been more devastating for the old Saxon gleemen, once the celebrants of their own patrons' conquests, than for the remnants of the *mimi*, long accustomed to being treated as underdogs. Now, the gleemen would have been supplanted by the likes of the legendary Norman minstrel Taillefer, who is said to have sung his heroic lays on the beaches at Pevensey in the vanguard of William's troops at the Battle of Hastings. Indeed, it seems likely that some of the gleemen would have sought to join forces with bands of *mimi* – for now they would have depended on audiences of the same humbled class.

THE ANGLO-NORMAN PLAYS

If we wonder what kinds of performance would most have appealed to the defeated Saxons, we have only to look at the extraordinary powers of survival of the various legends which speak of the people's ache for freedom from their new overlords – who had imposed upon them a feudal yoke that was cruelly tighter than of old. Whether in the freedom-fighting tales of Hereward the Wake, or the more allusive myths and legends concerning Arthur and his court, one suspects that the *mimi* and the gleemen would have found materials much to the taste of their audiences.

However, even Arthurian legend became caught up in the culture of the dominant Normans, from which the great bulk of the written evidence in the centuries following the Conquest inevitably derives. And so, as we find alongside the Latin liturgical drama of the Church the beginnings of a secular 'literary' drama, it is largely in the language of this new elite. An exception is the single play of English provenance among a group of Latin comedies of the twelfth century, all apparently conceived with 'Terence stages' in mind: called *Babio*, after its cuckolded 'smallholder' victim, it is also the best and bawdiest of the bunch.

Although there is no evidence that the play was intended as more than a literary exercise, it would have been almost perverse of its author – thought by some to have been the courtly gossip, Walter Map – to have structured his action so skilfully for performance were it not intended for some kind of staging. A performing dog is thus required – redundant in a 'reading play', but an expected feature if full use were to be made of the animal-training skills of a hired showman (his traditional talent still being exploited by Lance the clown with his dog Crab in Shakespeare's *Two Gentlemen of Verona,* and lingering at least into the nineteenth century, when one performer patriotically named his star attraction after Admiral Nelson).

Though its Latin is self-consciously convoluted, the earthy visual comedy of *Babio*, whether or not directed mainly at the illiterate, would have appealed to most classes – except, perhaps, the clerical. For when poor Babio is castrated (presumably of a phallus which had been tumescent in the property basket since the priapic rites of antiquity), he is told he'd better enter a monastery. Unlike the Latin plays of Hrotsvitha, *Babio* does not bother to be even perfunctorily didactic.

The illustration overleaf of actors in a play by Terence, presumably on a 'Terence stage' of the kind for which *Babio* may have been intended, is taken from the copy of the works of Terence owned by the Benedictine abbey at St Albans. So it may be no coincidence that a fragmentary saint's life of St Catherine, attributed to Geoffrey, a monk of that same abbey, is no less suited to this style of 'narrated performance'. The play, which was probably performed around 1100 before Henry I at nearby Dunstable, is also notable as being the first recorded non-liturgical religious drama written in the Norman French vernacular of the courtly elite.

A more considerable body of vernacular drama dates from the mid-twelfth to the late thirteenth century. The earlier of the two extant examples thought to have originated from the English side of the Channel, the anonymous *Jeu d'Adam*, comprises separate episodes dealing with Adam and Eve, Cain and Abel, and the Prophets (of which subjects only the last had been treated in the liturgical drama).

The fascinatingly detailed rubric with which the play opens may well have been added at a later date: if so, it presumably crystallizes an existing tradition of staging, and is remarkable in any case for its dramaturgical sophistication.

The playwriting, too, is evidently rooted in careful and conscious craftsmanship: in style, it modulates between the stateliness of the words of God and the colloquial idiom of Satan as he chats temptingly with Eve. The tone is further varied by Adam's lamentation over his fallen state, by choral interpolations in Latin – and, not least significantly, by sequences intended exclusively for mimetic action. Thus, the consigning of Adam and Eve to Hell contains no dialogue, but, as outlined in the very full stage directions, would have been well served by the talents of itinerant mimes (thought by some already to have infiltrated themselves into the 'showier' parts of the liturgical drama).

While it would have been quite feasible to perform the play inside a

Illustration (one of 140) from the St Albans manuscript of Terence plays. In this scene from the *Eunuchus*, the central pair are the courtesan Thais and the wily slave Parmeno, who is presenting gifts to her on behalf of his master – the slavegirl and the (supposed) eunuch on the right. The couple looking on from the left are Parmeno's envious rival Thrasso and his servant Gnato. Despite its presumed use of secondary visual materials, this illumination, like several others in the volume, is remarkable for its lively sense of movement and gestic signification, suggesting a handed-down if not an experienced stage tradition. Compare the 'cabinet of masks' pictured on page 22

church, the *Jeu d'Adam* seems best fitted for outdoor performance – the directions assuming an easy movement of characters from the specified *loci* or 'houses' into the generalized *platea* or 'place' which, with its proximity to the audience, was to become a favourite haunt for the likes of the attendant devils. A more complex form of 'simultaneous staging' is demanded for *La Seinte Resureccion*, which is thought to have been written towards the end of the twelfth century, though the manuscript in which the play most fully survives, probably from Canterbury, is rather later in date. This manuscript is apparently a reading version, but it is none the less clear from the introductory remarks of the Expositor that the staging requires seven well-defined 'houses', with no fewer than eight 'places' distinguished by separate acting areas.

THE THEATRICALIZATION OF ARISTOCRATIC BEHAVIOUR

Both these Anglo-Norman plays begin to employ the episodic format which we shall be discussing further in the next chapter, as it explodes into the great cycles of mystery plays. But *La Seinte Resureccion* is also notable for its ready assimilation of the role of the Expositor, who provides a linking narrative and, for us, a useful

Combat as performance. This was the *mêlée*, in which the assembled knights jostle around in the 'lists' – the enclosed jousting area immediately fronting the grandstand, from which the judges (left) and the ladies have an excellent view.

A sequence of miniatures like this, illustrating the progress of the tournament, appears in the *Livre des Tournois*, a classic work on the subject (*c.* 1450) by René, King of Anjou, who abandoned real-life battles to pursue the cult of chivalry as it became increasingly theatricalized

reminder that, all through this period, the epic or 'storytelling' mode continued to be a performing one. So, for that matter, did the medium of lyric poetry, which, since the twelfth century, had been flourishing in the vernacular verses of those nobly-born poet-musicians of southern France, the *troubadours*, their northern countrymen the *trouvères*, and their German counterparts the *Minnesinger.*

The amorous lyrics of the *troubadours* were largely responsible for the development of the cult of 'courtly love', which, while also originating in France, rapidly infected the nobility of western Europe – perhaps because its tenets seemingly reconciled the demands of feudal loyalty with those of the Christian faith. In essence, courtly love harmlessly formalized illicit heterosexual desires through a sort of chivalric role-play – a lover offering faithful service to his lady, despite all rebuffs and the fact that his love could not be consummated, or sometimes even declared.

By a similar process of conventionalizing its behaviour, the medieval aristocracy transformed the tournament from a bloody and mercenary miniature war into a forum for the expression of the values of courtly love – chivalric valour here sublimating a knight's sexuality through his 'defence' of the lady to whose favour he aspired. Disguises were frequent, and often drawn from the Arthurian legends now finding a literary form – as at the celebration of the marriage in 1299 of Margaret of France to Edward I, in whose reign the 'dramatizing' of tournaments became well established. By the fourteenth century, 'scenery' was used to illustrate the enacted scenario of a tournament, while a Herald served as 'narrator' of its mimetic action.

The phenomenon of courtly love, like the tournament which increasingly became its focus, contributed to the courtly cultivation of theatricalized behaviour – a *Theatre of Love and Honour*, to borrow the title of Favine's book, translated into English in 1623, which gave literary form to the legend of the *trouvère* Blondel, the reputed friend and saviour of Richard the Lionheart. Thus was created the climate in which mummings, disguisings, and the other more clearly dramatic activities which we shall discuss in the next chapter were later to flourish – but which, as early as the thirteenth century was already contributing to what Glynne Wickham has described as the 'rapidly widening horizons of theatrical activity'.

Wickham suggests two other, more mundane causes for this: the increase of trade, with the impetus it gave to the power of the merchant classes, and the founding in the previous century of the earliest English universities at Oxford and Cambridge, from which new recruits for the secular as well as the religious professions were increasingly being drawn. New audiences, based in the municipalities which were now rapidly developing both in size and economic importance, were clearly to be attracted from such secularly-minded sources.

University students, however, showed a chronic tendency to wander, and even to finance their travel by themselves joining the diverse ranks of the performing wayfarers collectively known as minstrels – a term often used generically to include such earlier performers as the *scops* and gleemen, but one which I have largely avoided until now, since it dates only from the twelfth century, as a derivation of *minister*, meaning simply a serving-man. In the context of performance, then, minstrels were, strictly speaking, those who entertained at the table of a particular lord. And it is at this time that we begin to see the names of such performers appearing in the account books of kings, courtiers, and religious houses.

MINSTRELSY, ARISTOCRATIC AND POPULAR

The 'Wardrobe Book' of Edward I records the extraordinary though apparently not exceptional number of 426 minstrels as present at the wedding of the Princess Margaret with John of Brabant in 1290. And a list of payments made later in the same reign to minstrels employed for a Whitsuntide feast hints at clear distinctions being made according to rank and origin. Thus, the highest payments, of five marks, went to those described as 'le roi', the veritable 'kings' among minstrels, while of the rest those with names of French origin appear to have been the most generously rewarded, and those with English-sounding names the least. This may reflect not only their relative positions in the social hierarchy, but also the differing respect accorded to 'higher' and 'lower' forms of the minstrel's wide-ranging art.

When, early in the fourteenth century, a future Archbishop of Canterbury, Thomas de Cabham, tried to categorize the various kinds of minstrels and other entertainers, he thus distinguished the bawdy *jongleurs* from the *joculatores*, who escaped his condemnation because they sang in praise of the lives of saints and great men. The *jongleurs*, with their masks, wanton songs, and indecent gestures, we may take to be the descendants of the *mimi*, while the *joculatores* were the 'true' minstrels of the new style, either courtly amateurs or thoroughbred profes-sionals domiciled with the King or some other great lord – the descendants of William of Normandy's Taillefer and his successor Berdic, who owned three villas in Gloucestershire during the reign of the Conqueror. Another of the best remem-bered is Rahere, the royal minstrel to Henry I who founded the priory and hospital in Smithfield dedicated to St Bartholomew – as also, in 1133, the fair whose revenues supported their upkeep.

During Lent, such well-to-do minstrels might exchange tricks of the trade and extend their repertoire by visiting one of the *scolae ministrallorum*, or schools for minstrels, held in France annually at this season, when public performances were forbidden. At other times, when not required by their royal masters, they might go on the road. But the regular itinerants, the *jongleurs* by Cabham's definition, were both more numerous and a good deal less affluent – their talents as finely-tuned to the market-place as to the baronial castle, whether the call was for a scurrilous satire or a courtly ballad, a comic *fabliau* or an epic lay. By the early sixteenth century, when minstrels were being employed by the larger municipalities to entertain on civic occasions, their duties might even include the piping of the nightly watch.

It seems that, despite the usual prohibitions, religious as well as secular houses employed the services of minstrels, and there are records of payments being made

Detail from a fifteenth-century illustration of minstrels performing at a feast. Where there was no separate gallery, it was usual for them to play, as here, before the banquet-laden table. The instruments appear to be a straight trumpet and a tabor

for their services in the account books of abbeys, priories, and clerical colleges. On occasion, apparently, religious lyrics were even set to popular, profane tunes – perhaps following the example of the friars of the mendicant orders, who first appeared in England early in the thirteenth century. Francis of Assisi actually described the friars of his own order as *joculatores domini*, or minstrels of the Lord – two of whom were turned out of an abbey in Abingdon when it was discovered that they were *not* the minstrels they had been taken for!

But so far as the influence of the friars upon the drama was concerned, most important was that they preached in the vernacular, returning to the gospel method of teaching by parable – in other words, by storytelling. And their stories, like the concurrently developing secular form of the comic *fabliau*, were both simple and immediate – their Jesus not a mysterious presence in wafer and wine, or for that matter a holy infant to be passively adored in a crib, or godhead conspicuous by his absence from an empty tomb, but an active, concerned human being, *imitable* in every sense. And such sermons cannot but have contributed to that 'humanizing' of the drama of Christianity which later distinguished the mystery cycles, with their great warmth and accessibility, from the liturgical drama, steeped in ritualized formalities.

THE NATURE OF 'CARNIVAL'

We have now touched briefly on the vernacular and secular elements which fed into the creation of these cycles: but, as ever, the purely *popular* element is the most elusive. To describe his own perception of popular celebration, the Russian critic Mikhail Bakhtin liberated the term 'carnival' from its strict definition, as the period of pre-Lenten merrymaking, using it instead to connote the whole calendar of activities of the common people at play – opportunities for which were fairly plentiful, to judge by Walter of Henley's calculation that by the fourteenth century, after taking out holy days and other 'hindrances', the working year amounted to just forty-four weeks.

A spirit of Rabelaisian topsy-turvydom marks out 'carnival' celebrations – as when the Christmastide Feast of Fools, often associated with the installation of a 'Boy Bishop', exalted the minor clergy and the choirboys above their superiors for a brief period of hungover Saturnalia. Since this occurred within the confines, physical and spiritual, of the Church itself, ample documentation has survived – often in the form of such scandalized protests as that made by the Dean of the University of Paris in 1445, which calls for corrective action by the bishops. Whether or not the relatively late date of this letter reflects an increasing tendency to licence in these 'sacred travesties', it certainly testifies to their powers of endurance.

The scholarly debate over the nature and function of such 'carnival' celebrations is often polarized between the belief that carnival was an expression of the counter-culture of the people, and the assertion that it was encouraged and carefully regulated by authority to serve as a safety-valve, thus reinforcing social decorum and hierarchy for the rest of the year. Probably those who argue that carnival owed its survival to the state of continuous tension in which it existed *between* these two models come closer to an elusive truth.

Certainly, authority, whether secular or religious, was always anxious to harness any potentially disruptive energies – either to ensure their regulated dispersal, or more subtly to utilize them for its own ends. And this, as we discussed in the previous chapter, the Church had already been doing for a millennium, through its Christianizing of the seasonal celebrations it inherited from the pagan calendar. The introduction in 1311 of the Feast of Corpus Christi was in this respect not only a formalizing of the new emphasis on 'the Word made flesh', but also an appropriation by the Church of the 'carnival' celebrations of summer, from May Day to the solstice. It also happens to be the most readily isolable 'cause' of the great mystery cycles of the fourteenth century.

Miniature from the fourteenth-century *Roman de Fauvel*, by Gervais du Bus, showing a variety of popular entertainers indulging in a 'charivari' to enliven the local widows – who look on disapprovingly while one of their number awakens to the dubious attentions of a cow. Other grotesque animal masks are worn by many of the fools, jongleurs, and goliards performing below

CHAPTER 3   *The Later Middle Ages*

Environmental and man-made disasters struck Europe on an unprecedented scale during the fourteenth century. The climate, after centuries of warming, became both colder and wetter, inflicting recurrent poor harvests upon the population, which had just reached a peak. In England, where the Thames froze over twelve times in the course of this 'Little Ice Age', famine was perhaps less severe than on the Continent, but the death rate none the less rose dramatically – as did thefts of food. No sooner had harvests started to recover than a sequence of epidemic diseases decimated livestock – and then, at mid-century, followed the almost unimaginable ravages of the Black Death, a spasmodic agony for the next few decades, heightened by further cruelties of climate and failures of crops.

In comparison, the effects on ordinary people of the events which preoccupy political historians – the Hundred Years War with France, and the overlapping civil

Illuminated initial from the Litlyngton Missal, *c.* 1383, illustrating part of a Corpus Christi procession. A bishop, sheltered beneath a canopy supported by choirboys, is bearing the Host – the bread consecrated to signify the body of Christ sacrificially offered, from which the Feast of Corpus Christi took its name

disturbances of the Wars of the Roses – were marginal, since war was essentially the concern of the nobility. But new weaponry, notably the longbow, and the centralized control over artillery this required, was already sapping the military prowess of the knighthood – whose feudal pre-eminence rested on the protection they supposedly provided for their underlings. Yet the Order of the Garter, usually considered to have set the pattern of chivalric behaviour, was not created until 1349, affirming that the tendency of chivalry towards 'theatricalization' accelerated just as its real-life importance was steadily diminishing.

Among a debilitated peasantry, discontent grew against a majority of overlords who, far from assisting their dependents in times of deprivation, were able to command inflated prices for food in a devalued currency. As depopulation took its toll, and labour became harder to come by, the survivors ironically found themselves in a better bargaining position. However, the secular power used every means at its disposal – typified by the betrayal of Wat Tyler during the Peasants' Revolt of 1381 – to maintain the subservience of the poor, whether villeins seeking commutation of their virtual slavery, or day-labourers exploiting their scarcity-value in defiance of the law. This was also a century of schism in the Church, culminating in rival popes at Rome and Avignon, while in England the 'heretical' Lollards, whose leader Wycliffe briefly enjoyed the support of John of Gaunt, posed a threat both to the political and the ecclesiastical order – as in the egalitarian preaching of John Ball, the 'mad priest of Kent'.

THE CHRISTIANIZING OF MIDSUMMER

One of the chief targets of the Lollards was the doctrine of transubstantiation, promulgated as recently as the early thirteenth century to affirm the 'real presence' of the body and blood of Christ in the bread and wine of the Mass. And this brings us back to the event which links the social and religious tensions we have touched on with the theatre of their times – the celebration of the new doctrine and of Christ's redemptive sacrifice on the cross through the introduction into the liturgical calendar of the Feast of Corpus Christi. This was proclaimed in 1311, but it was the introduction of a procession of the elevated Host, authorized seven years later, from which the dramatic potential of the occasion is generally thought to derive.

'By 1300', claims one well-known textbook of theatrical history, 'liturgical drama seemingly had developed as far as it could within the confines of the church, and consequently plays began to be given out of doors.' In truth, not only was liturgical drama still 'performed' within the church, but 'play', if not plays (the Latin term *ludus* was used indistinguishably for both), had long been associated with the churchyard outside. Thus, since the congregation had never taken an active part in the solemn drama of the liturgy, this was almost certainly of less experiential significance than the 'vigils' which preceded great feasts of the Christian calendar, when the church and its precincts became gathering places for the community. Song and dance were as inseparable from such occasions as gossip and good ale.

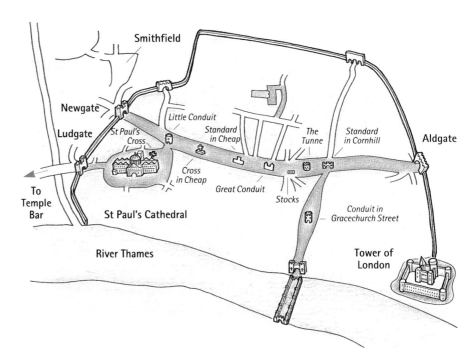

The City of London, with the chief processional routes of the later medieval and Tudor period shown in red. From the west, these proceed via Temple Bar and Ludgate (past old St Paul's) and via Smithfield and Newgate, converging along Cheapside and Cornhill to Aldgate; and from the south, across London Bridge (at this time the only river crossing). Along the routes, the principal 'stages' for civic pageantry are indicated by the labels in italics

Debate politely rages over whether surviving carols and round-dances, seemingly well-suited to such celebrations, were truly 'popular' – one assumption being that their written form marks them out as part of the 'official' culture. Yet a song-drama such as the enigmatically enchanting 'Maiden in the Mor Lay' has its roots deep in the pre-Christian lore of the people, and its mimetic possibilities seem more the stuff of village celebration than of noble feasting.

Other forms of 'play' were even more clearly pagan in origin, honoured by time though not by the Church – the rites associated with May Day and Midsummer among them. Thus, it can scarcely be coincidental, or merely because of a convenient gap in the calendar, that the first Thursday after Trinity Sunday was the date set aside for the Feast of Corpus Christi – ensuring its celebration, in late May or early June, as a proper Christian diversion from such pagan activities as still marked May Day and Midsummer. (In the event, not only did the May tree continue to flourish, but often to achieve a permanent erection, such as long cast its phallic shadow over the church of St Andrew Undershaft in the City of London.)

THE TASTE FOR CIVIC PAGEANTRY

Writing of the relationship between carnival and theatre, Michael D. Bristol suggests that in what he calls 'official' pageantry 'the social structure is made visible by allegorical representation through a display of ranks and categories . . . idealized in mythological, historical, or biblical images'. The established hierarchy is revealed as microcosmic of a larger, divinely-ordained pattern of authority. By contrast, the 'unofficial pageantry' of popular festivities 'represents the arbitrary transitoriness of all social forms': roles are inverted, exaggerated, made incongruous or ridiculous, while grotesque giants, transvestite figures, devils, or 'black men' assert what Bakhtin called 'the right to be "other".' Such a 'right' could not safely be encouraged amidst the turbulence and threatened transitoriness of the fourteenth century: and thus did the 'official' pageantry of the Church now seek to assimilate the 'unofficial' traditions of midsummer celebration.

Naturally, the Corpus Christi procession flourished best before audiences of the size that could be mustered in large towns – where its organization also provided an apt opportunity to express the civic dignity and power of the urban-based trades guilds. Just as the proclamation of the Feast was, then, in part an assertion of papal

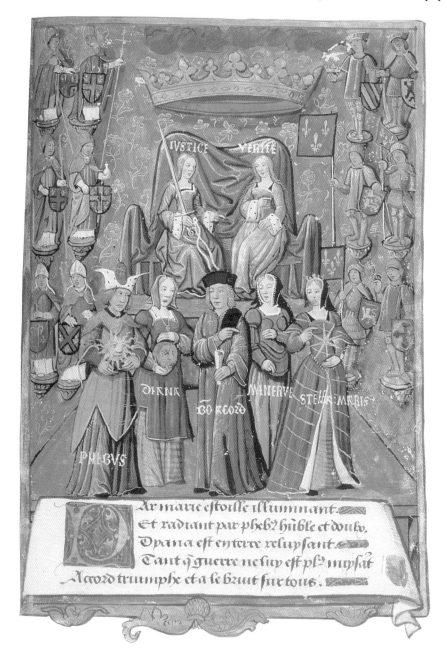

Civic and regal pageantry had many characteristics in common with the later medieval drama. In the pageant illustrated here, staged at Chatelet in Paris to celebrate the hastily-arranged marriage of Mary Tudor to the aged Louis XII of France in 1514, Justice and Virtue are enthroned, amidst other allegorical and mythological figures. Mary herself, who was widowed within eight months, shared the love of music and pageantry of her sometimes unsympathetic brother, Henry VIII

authority at a time when this was under threat – as much from divisions within the Church and from proto-nationalism as from the civil upheavals of the time – so also was its 'official pageantry' in part a demonstration of the wealth of the urban bourgeoisie, whose place in the social structure the procession made very visible indeed. Just a few years after its proclamation, in 1323, the Pope issued a papal bull denying that Christ and his apostles had owned no worldly goods: thus was property already beginning to supplant poverty as a mark of holiness.

The growing taste for civic pageantry had previously depended on happenstance for its satisfaction – the coronation of a monarch, the visit of a foreign prince, the celebration of a victory or a royal wedding. Such processional pageants, often known as 'entries', would adapt local architectural features as frameworks for appropriate decoration and display, usually of an emblematic nature – and the theatre historian Glynne Wickham cites an example of the craft guilds of London being associated with such an event as early as 1298, when the City celebrated a victory of Edward I over the Scots.

Within a century, the Lord Mayor's Show was becoming (in effect if not yet in name) a further annual excuse for pageantry, the City paying homage to the sovereign in its procession to Westminster, just as the King himself symbolically recognized the City's independence when, on his own royal 'entries' into the City, he took pause at the gates – which would, of course, have been suitably embellished for the occasion. In 1415, the triumphal entry of Henry V into the City after his

Three scenes from the Gospels (the Annunciation, the Nativity, and the Resurrection) are shown in this relief from the west front of the Chantry Chapel at the Church of St Mary's, Wakefield. The town's tradition of mystery plays may well have influenced the encapsulated, stage-like quality of these vivid tableaux

victory at Agincourt was celebrated with pageants which included a giant and giantess, St. George with a hierarchy of angels, twelve apostles accompanied by an equal number of 'kings of the English succession, martyrs, and confessors', and the sun enthroned with archangels.

ORIGINS OF THE MYSTERY PLAYS

The groups of plays dramatizing the Holy Scriptures which are now usually called the 'mystery cycles' probably had their origins, then, not in the secularization of the liturgical drama, as was once supposed, but, on the contrary, in this combination of the Christianizing of midsummer festivities and the 'making official' of their attendant pageantry – perhaps with a nod in the direction of the truly secular drama, since theatre historians now believe that early references to certain of the pageants suggest not plays but *tableaux vivants*, or living pictures, in which any form of action was mimed.

If the originating impulse behind the mystery cycles was, largely, evangelical – to save souls who would otherwise be damned – their determining techniques in effect theatricalized what the preaching friars already understood: that vernacular simplicity, a sense of humour, and a recognition of secular concerns were likelier to command the imagination in this direction than mystical solemnities in a dead language. That the Corpus Christi pageants should, in the medievalist William Tydeman's summary, successively have 'acquired a mimed element, a set of brief

speeches, and finally enough exchanges in dialogue form to be regarded as plays' seems consistent not only with this didactic impulse and the self-improving itch of civic pride, but also with other forms of medieval art. Thus, the episodic quality of the mystery cycles, so far from being detrimental to the purposes of their anonymous creators, was as integral to their methods as it was to their view of life.

The fourteenth century was, after all, the period of High Gothic, with its architectural apotheosis in York Minster, and in literature the great flowering of vernacular poetry represented by *Sir Gawain and the Green Knight*, *Piers Plowman*, the *Confessio Amantis* – and, of course, by Chaucer, whose *Troilus and Criseyde* the poet is himself seen 'performing' (as all such works were still 'performed') to a courtly audience in the illustration opposite. But while *Troilus and Criseyde*, like *Sir Gawain*, thus continued the tradition of the sustained epic, it is Chaucer's other great work, *The Canterbury Tales*, which better displays (as also, for example, does the *Decameron* of Boccaccio) the 'gothic' style in its narrative mode, as the mystery cycles do in the dramatic.

The claim of the art historian M. D. Anderson that the staging of the mystery plays may best be understood from the stained-glass windows of the time – their imagery supposedly being derived from performances witnessed by the artists – is probably overstated. But it does seem to me that the 'compilation pictures' or sacred comic strips offered no less by frescoes than in stained glass share the sense also to be found in the mystery plays of the cumulative yet *simultaneous* quality of experience. This reflected and perhaps also helped to reconcile the tensions felt by the medieval mind in its experience of time itself, whose ancient, cyclical quality was still celebrated in the Christian and the residual pagan calendar, yet which, as Christianity taught, was also moving irrevocably forward – to the imminent Second Coming of Christ, through which history would be brought to a close.

STAGING THE MYSTERY CYCLES

The cycle plays are also linked by their *figural* concern with the events they portray, exemplifying dramatically the contemporary belief that the ancient scriptures reveal a pattern of analogies or correspondences which foreshadow the events of the New Testament and beyond. That each guild performed a play in some manner appropriate to its craft (or 'mystery') was thus no mere whimsy, but itself of figurative significance – as were the modes of staging the plays, to which we now turn.

The cycles typically dramatized sacred history from the Creation of the World to the Last Judgement, with figural Old Testament stories, Nativity plays, episodes from Christ's ministry, plays of the Passion and Resurrection, and a Harrowing of Hell in between. They usually have in common not only the capacity to make contemporary – almost neighbourly – the events of sacred history, but qualities of bold characterization, broadly outspoken language, and visually compelling stage business. Instead of phoney pieties, here are homespun if often ribald truths. Of the four cycles still fully extant in English, that performed at York has forty-eight

Part of a thirteenth-century window in Canterbury Cathedral. It tells its stained-glass 'comic strip' story – of miracles experienced by visitors to the tomb of St. Thomas à Becket – in a pictorial style analogous both to the episodic drama of the cycles of mystery plays and to the discursive narrative of Chaucer's *The Canterbury Tales*

episodes, and probably dates from the beginning of the last quarter of the four-teenth century: it is now thought likely to be the earliest – though the manuscript in which we have it records, as do others, a version oft-revised and perhaps exten-ded over succeeding years. The nearby town of Wakefield apparently borrowed five of the York plays, while a further half-dozen of the thirty-two episodes of its own cycle are attributed to the 'Wakefield Master'. This is one of the few groups of plays in which a single and distinctive hand is discernible: but neither casual borrowing nor recognition of individual genius were matters of much concern in an age of collective consciousness and creation.

The Chester cycle, comprising twenty-five plays (of which one is now lost), is in some ways least typical, though no less resolutely anonymous: where the York and Wakefield cycles share a robust good humour and earthy realism, the tone of the Chester plays (copied late in their existence, and perhaps refined in the process) is often more austere and distanced – its effects, whether of Noah's wife with her gossips or of the

Chaucer 'performing' his *Troilus and Criseyde* to a courtly audience from a pulpit-like box similar to that of the Terence-narrator shown on page 15. Such late medieval forms as this and the window opposite, predicated upon a sense of art as an expression of its community, all bode forth the complex medieval perception of time – as at once a cyclical and cumulative yet also a simultaneous and all-embracing experience

merciful Christ with the suffering, being achieved no less forcefully but with greater simplicity and, where appropriate, pathos.

The other surviving group of forty-two episodes, once mistakenly attributed to Coventry but now considered to have been a touring cycle probably of East Anglian origin, is commonly known as the 'N-Town' plays. The term 'N-Town' derives from a reference in the 'banns' – a sort of extended, processional 'trailer' to the actual production – where the initial 'N' appears to be an abbreviation of the Latin *nomen*, 'a name', signifying that at this point the speaker would have filled in the intended place of performance.

The 'N-Town' cycle seems to have been conflated (not always very skilfully) from different sources, and the identity of its itinerant performers remains, well, a mystery. However, that they were professionals, for whom economic considerations counted, is suggested by the fact that only a single player is required for Christ, as for other characters who recur from play to play, whereas in the other English cycles the actor changed along with the responsible guild, professional involvement being limited to the hiring of musicians.

PAGEANT WAGONS AND THEIR USES

The method most familiarly associated with the production of cycle plays is now usually distinguished by scholars as 'station-to-station' staging, since it involved the manual hauling of 'pageant wagons' through narrow medieval streets from one 'station' to the next – this term deriving from the locations of the halts made along

Conjectural reconstruction by Richard Leacroft of a pageant wagon for one of the only two plays to have survived from the Coventry cycle. This cycle evidently bunched into one play incidents which were elsewhere given separate episodes – the Shearmen and Taylors' play, here illustrated, thus dramatizing events from the Annunciation to the Massacre of the Innocents. The action is shown as shared between the specific location represented by the wagon, and the generalized playing area, or *platea*, surrounding it

the route of the Corpus Christ procession for gospel readings. Sometimes, as at Coventry (where horse-power may have been employed) the plays were apparently all given in a single day – related incidents in this case having been grouped into ten or so longer plays (of which only two survive) for performance at just three or four stations. If, as some scholars argue, all the York plays were also performed in one day at as many as sixteen stations, this would have necessitated a start at 4.30 in the morning and a torchlight finish late in the evening.

Evidence concerning the Chester cycle (dating from 1596, when performances were already a memory) suggests that the plays there were given over three days at five different locations within the city. Wagons of two tiers were probably employed, the lower serving as a 'dressing room' and the upper being utilized for the actual performance. An even later source, of 1656, confirms that the pageant wagons were 'very large and high, and placed upon wheels': they were clearly not only costly to construct but also difficult to house when not in use, as records of the high rents paid for their safe-keeping attest. At Chester, two or three guilds, whose plays were performed on different days, sometimes cut their overheads by sharing the same cart.

We do not know how often each play was allowed to be performed when the 'station-to-station' method was used (an ambiguous record from York puts it as low as twice), or even if all were staged every year – those not chosen perhaps reverting to a processional *tableau* format. And we should always remember that the plays did not supplant the procession of the Host, but remained strictly subordinate to this, the central and most crucially symbolic event of the Feast of Corpus Christi. Thus, at York, when there was clerical pressure in 1426 against the plays overshadowing the procession, it was, very properly, the cycle performance which was moved to another day.

Even cycles now thought to have employed a stationary form of staging may also have required pageant wagons, if their occupants were to be shown to advantage in the main procession: the wagons would then have been drawn up around the town square or in another open space to provide one of several localized acting areas, perhaps supplementary to forms of fixed staging, and fronting an open *platea*, or generalized playing space – an elaboration of the 'mansion' tradition we have noted as descending from Ancient Rome to Hrotsvitha to the *Jeu d'Adam*. This form of staging, the more usual on the Continent around this time, is often described as 'simultaneous' – while the station-to-station method might no less aptly be called 'cumulative', since both in their different ways confront the paradoxes of the medieval sense of time.

Of the extant cycles, the Wakefield seems likeliest to have used a modified form of 'simultaneous' or 'place-and-scaffold' staging, while many of the N-Town plays also appear to have been adapted to its conventions. A lost Passion play from New Romney in Kent certainly used fixed staging, and the little that is known about the lost London cycle at least reveals its single regular location – Skinners Well, near

Carnival, ship-carts, and misericords

'Misericords' such as that along-side derived their name from the room in a monastery where the strict rule of the order was relaxed. Just so, below the narrow shelf in the choir stalls on which a monk might unobtrusively rest his long-suffering posterior, medieval carvers could exercise their imaginations freed from the normal constraints of a church setting – their fools, minstrels, acrobats, devils, and strange beasts coming into close and ironic contact with clerical rumps. This example is from Great Malvern Priory

One medievalist, William Tydeman, has suggested that the word 'carnival' derives not from the Italian carne levare, with its sense of the 'putting away of flesh' before Lent, but from the Latin carrus navalis – denoting a 'ship-cart' or wheeled ship, used not only in the Noah plays of the mystery cycles and in earlier civic pageantry but also in processional events going back at least to the worship of the Teutonic wood goddess Freya. The shipwrights, in constructing their often highly spectacular ark on wheels, seem to me, however, not so much to have been 'officializing' carnival (down to its very etymology!) as 'tensioning' the pagan against the Christian, the 'unofficial' against the 'official', in a manner of which other instances can be found in many of these plays.

Smithfield. It was here, as the Elizabethan chronicler Stow relates, that in 1409 'the parish clerks of London' presented a play 'which lasted eight days and was of matter from the creation of the world, whereat was present most part of the nobility and gentry of England'. At least one other, seven-day production, again by clerics, is recorded two years later.

So not only was station-to-station staging far from the invariable rule, but the evidence from London – despite the guilds being at their wealthiest and most powerful there – suggests that neither did the plays invariably come under the auspices of the craft guilds. Some were not even performed at Corpus Christi – Whitsun, as at Chester, being the usual alternative. This was probably to meet the clerical objections raised at York against attention being deflected from the procession of the Host. The mystery cycles were, for all their quotidian qualities, not carnival but 'official' pageantry.

It is no coincidence that the mystery cycles are now thought to date from a period which also saw the papal schism, the anti-clericalism of the Lollards, and the discontents which erupted into the Peasants' Revolt, when the 'official' culture may well have found it timely to inject the palliative properties of bread and circuses into their celebration of the miraculous powers of bread and wine. But it would, of course, be simplistic to consign the work of many different authors and actors over many years into a single ideological basket, despite the clerical approval the plays always required (and which, as we shall see in the next chapter, became the

Thus Mak the sheep-stealer (who threatens to steal the show besides, in perhaps the best known of all the mystery plays, the *Secunda Pastorum* of the Wakefield cycle) may not be quite so fully integrated into the 'official' reading of the piece as some scholars assert. Part, at least, of his presence is surely on the 'unofficial' side in that eternal, Brueghelesque conflict between Carnival and Lent which is also, I suspect, contested in many 'misericords' – curious carvings concealed beneath the seats of medieval choir-stalls, as illustrated on the opposite page. The easing of smug monastic rumps against these images of devils, imps, horned women, and strange creatures from the bestiary places (both literally and with an irony that is distinctly medieval) what Bakhtin called the 'other' as life's disreputable backside.

This dragon, an illumination from the Luttrell Psalter, owes less to images from the bestiary than to the pageantry of the streets. Such wheeled dragons may share an ancestry with the ship-carts of ancient Teutonic worship – while those of wood-strip and canvas construction, like the Norwich snap-dragon (operated by a man within), are closer to the hobby horses of the folk tradition

means of censoring them out of existence following the Reformation). Late-medieval life was too healthily complex for that, despite its perhaps corrective impulse to systematize experience into an encyclopedic straitjacket – an impulse reflected in the cycles themselves.

CLERKS' PLAYS AND SAINTS' LIVES

The mystery cycles did not, as was once believed, wither away like a failed evolutionary experiment: but their specific theological purpose linked them inextricably with Catholic doctrine, while their sponsors, the urban guilds, whose status within the towns was soon to be threatened by economic change, were probably none too anxious to retain connections (becoming ever costlier in inflationary times) with a forbidden Feast. In exploring the growth of a professional theatre, it is, then, to other kinds and conditions of performance that we must look: and, sure enough, all through the fourteenth and fifteenth centuries references to these recur in the records with increasing frequency.

We must, however, bear in mind the warning of the medieval theatre historian David Mills lest, 'thriving within a book culture, the modern reader may forget that dramatic activities uncontaminated by text were the medieval norm'. For the plays of whose existence we learn only from parish records and account books, and the many more which have been altogether obliterated by time, may well have been more representative than those few which have come down to us – and so been 'fixed' in what Mills describes as the 'authorized and official form' of the written word, as opposed to undergoing the potentially subversive process of oral transmission. Such an assumption must underlie the claim of one recent authority that medieval theatre was, 'in today's parlance, a mass medium . . . an important form of popular culture that spanned seven centuries' – for a scholar of no less repute, presumably relying on the written evidence alone, can assert with equal assurance that 'there is little to suggest a flourishing vernacular tradition' in the British Isles 'before the late fourteenth century'.

As so often, it depends what one is looking for. But the evidence does suggest that, for the authorities, theatre could be a constant irritant and a sometimes dangerous source of 'otherness'. As early as 1303, Robert Mannyng of Brunne is thus to be found including 'miracle plays' among many other manifestations of worldly error in his didactic poem *Handlyng Synne* – and since he goes out of his way to exclude plays of the Nativity and Resurrection within the church, it is clearly not to these that he objects but the unauthorized presentation of sacred matter.

Edward II, meanwhile, was condemned by the historian Ranulph Higden for consorting with actors – while elsewhere he is said to have preferred an Archbishop of Canterbury because he excelled 'in ludis theatralibus'. Around the same time, John Bromyard was deploring the preference for 'miracles' performed by 'foolish clerics' over sermons, and a 'Poem on the Evil Times of Edward II' from around 1330 refers as if generically to 'clerks' plays'.

Plays based on the lives of saints seem to have been what these critics had in mind: and such plays, which appear to have been popular both in England and in Scotland, turn out to be earlier in their origins than the mysteries – though at first, as we might expect, the evidence is anecdotal. Thus, we only know of the Dunstable staging of the early twelfth-century play of St Catherine mentioned in the last chapter because choristers' copes borrowed from the nearby abbey were destroyed by fire before they could be returned. But it is evident that the clerks of London were busy presenting such plays as early as 1170, if we are to judge from William Fitzstephen's description, prefaced to a life of his assassinated master, Thomas à Becket (as later reprinted by the Elizabethan historian of London, John Stow). Here, Fitzstephen is comparing the City favourably with Rome:

> London, instead of theatrical shows and scenic entertainments, has dramatic performances of a more sacred kind, either representations of the miracles which holy confessors have wrought, or of the passions and sufferings in which the constancy of martyrs was signally displayed.

Most 'saints' lives' were probably written for staging at the patronal festival of a church, and in this sense are perhaps more truly 'developments' of the liturgical drama than the mysteries ever were. The four such plays which remain extant are

The Cornish mystery cycle and the Cornish rounds

The Cornish cycle was a distinct tradition of mystery play not only in its use of the ancient Cornish tongue, rather than an English dialect, but also because it seems to have been staged in permanent theatres, of which remains have actually survived in the form of the so-called Cornish 'rounds'. The plays of this Cornish cycle, known as the Ordinalia, were performed over three days, the episodes within each part being much more closely integrated than in most of the English cycles, after the manner of continental Passion plays.

No fewer than eleven of the plays are without counterparts in the English cycles, but there is none dealing with the Nativity, and here the grand climax is the Ascension rather than the Last Judgement. The Cornish cycle is particularly strong in characters who flesh out the scriptural originals – the carpenters at work on the Temple, or the wife of the smith who is making nails for the cross, as she parries double meanings with one of the torturers.

Although there is evidence for as many as eighteen 'rounds' in Cornwall, only two sites are still visible – barely so, in the case of the remains at St Just. But the better-preserved Perran Round retains the clear form of an amphitheatre some 130 feet across, surrounded by a twelve-foot bank on which traces of seven tiers of seating may be discerned. (That this more accurately reflects one form of Roman theatre than any 'Terence stage' may or may not be connected with the fact that those Romans who did not depart with the legions fled to just such Celtic outposts of the British Isles as Cornwall.) This plen-an-gwary, or playing-place, has been found highly effective for modern performances.

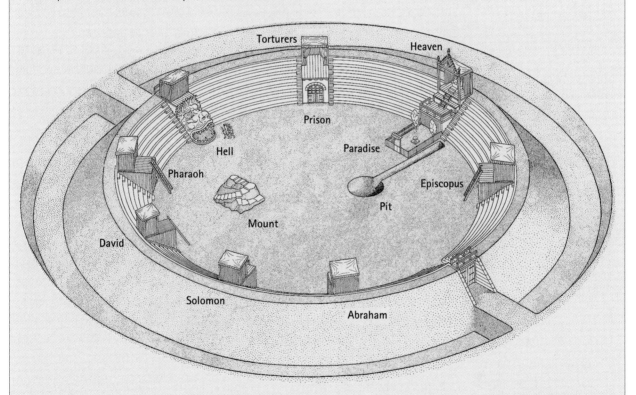

Perran Round set for the 'Origo Mundi', the opening day's plays of the Cornish Ordinalia. Richard Leacroft's reconstruction, based on diagrams in the manuscript of c. 1371, locates Heaven, as convention dictated, on the eastern and Hell on the northern side of the arena, which was some 130 feet in diameter. The manuscript describes its many fixed loci as 'tents' or 'pulpits'

all, however, of relatively late date, from the fifteenth or early sixteenth century – and when their subject-matter was drawn from the scriptures rather than from legend and hearsay, it no doubt proved more acceptable to the early protestant authorities, who were probably responsible for the extinction of other work in this elusive genre.

A play of *Mary Magdalene*, in over 2,000 lines, and the Cornish *St Meriasek*, of twice that length, were in the epic mould of the mystery cycles, and would have taken a full day or more to perform: but a *Conversion of St Paul* is less expansive, and closer in tone as well as in length to the 'moral interludes' which we shall discuss later. All these plays seem to have used 'simultaneous' or 'place and scaffold' staging: but whereas the *Conversion of St Paul* can be staged with perhaps only two 'stations' – a poet-persona linking the episodes and apparently leading the audience from one *locus* to the next – the *Mary Magdalene* requires at least ten scaffolds, these probably forming the perimeter of a *platea* which had Mary's castle at its centre.

A so-called *Play of the Sacrament* differs in that, while certainly commemorating a miracle, it does not deal with the life of a particular saint; and although associated by its 'banns' with the East Anglian region, the very purpose of those banns, as a 'trailer' to the actual performance, suggests that it was intended for touring. The medievalist .David Bevington has calculated that nine actors could have satisfactorily 'doubled' the roles between them, which is perhaps indicative of the limited resources available to itinerant companies. However, these, often comprising as few as four players, were more usually associated with the playing of the ambiguously-named 'interludes', to which we should now turn.

INTERLUDES, MUMMINGS, AND DISGUISINGS

'Interlude' is a word of elusive, even controversial etymology. It has been variously claimed to refer to playing 'between' the courses of a banquet, to forms of light relief provided 'between' episodes of a more serious nature – or simply to any dialogue 'between' two or more players, as distinct from a solo performance or mime. But a definition which would unite scholars such as Glynne Wickham with modern practitioners of popular theatre such as John McGrath assumes simply the 'compilation-format' characteristic of itinerant players, who would thus play these short dramatic pieces 'between' displays of other performing skills, rather in the later fashion of a music-hall bill.

In this sense, secular interludes, whether or not so-called, were as ancient as the mime troupes and as unlikely to have left more than the scantiest traces of their existence. Among such traces, a fragmentary Cornish text shares its theme, of a bawd assisting a young man to win a woman's favours, with both the *Interludium de Clerico et Puella*, a vernacular fragment from the thirteenth or early fourteenth century, and the better-known *Dame Sirith* – this latter usually regarded as a *fabliau*, but readily adaptable to staging, not least in its tell-tale deployment of a performing dog. There is even a collection at the end of *Dame Sirith*, which again points to a professional source – while the seducer is, as often in later pieces, a 'clerc feyllard', or (as the scholar Richard Axton succinctly translates it) a clerical drop-out.

A number of lost plays from the early fourteenth century, usually described as 'Pater Noster plays', evidently dramatized the petitions of the Lord's Prayer as defences against the Seven Deadly Sins – which were no doubt expected to make personal and properly flamboyant appearances. Such short plays of a religious character are often distinguished as 'moral interludes', and because these adapted better than the mystery cycles or saints' lives to the changed circumstances of the Reformation, and so continued to develop well into the sixteenth century, we tend to think of them as a later form. But in fact our earliest extant examples date from the period when the cycles began to flourish, the last quarter of the fourteenth century – and were arguably more in tune with those difficult times, in their pervasive preoccupation with life as a long, troubled journey towards death (whose macabre 'dance' dates from the same period), and with the loneliness of the struggle for salvation.

To the medieval mind, however, their common framework of an allegorized struggle between good and evil for the soul of a man, with his eventual salvation as its climax, would have been no great typological distance from the story of Adam's original sin and Christ's redemptive sacrifice. The medievalist David Bevington points out other shared characteristics between the moralities and, in particular, the N-Town cycle – while *The Castle of Perseverance*, from the early fifteenth century, shares its elaborate 'riding of the banns' with the East Anglian *Play of the Sacrament*.

The manuscript of *The Castle of Perseverance* includes one of the most fascinating and oft-debated pieces of illustrative evidence from the Middle Ages: the staging plan reproduced alongside, which indicates a circular *platea*, or 'place', surrounded by five scaffolds representing specific *loci*, with the eponymous castle dominating its centre. And this, of course, is more reminiscent of the *Mary Magdalene* just discussed than of other moral interludes – a useful reminder that, however we may choose to categorize medieval plays, they refuse to conform to mutually watertight generic or even geographical boundaries.

The study of the theatre of the Middle Ages, for long a worthy but rather dusty business of textual retrieval and archival burrowing, has only recently been enlivened by the work of scholars with a healthy interest in the practicalities of the form, and nowhere had this approach appeared more illuminating than in the case of *The Castle of Perseverance*, whose daunting length of over 3,600 lines had variously baffled and bored its earlier readers. Richard Southern focused a whole book on the form of in-the-round staging he envisaged for the play: and this turned minds to the possibility of utilizing Perran Round in Cornwall (described and illustrated on page 45) for an experiment in its staging.

However, no sooner had the resulting production been acclaimed as an unexpected demonstration of the play's vivid theatricality than scholars began to cast doubts on many features of Southern's reconstruction, and the present consensus is

The manuscript of the lengthy fifteenth-century morality play *The Castle of Perseverance* includes the diagram reproduced below, showing the five scaffolds required for its staging. As in the similar diagram accompanying the Cornish *Ordinalia*, discussed on page 45, the Devil ('Belial') is in the north (at the bottom of the diagram), and God ('Deus') in the east. Other scaffolds are assigned to three enemies of Man, 'Flesh', 'World', and 'Covetous'. The castle of the title, dominating the centre of the circular *platea*, is sacred space, for Man in a state of grace

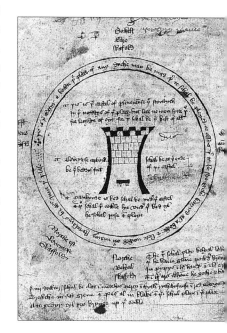

that the play was probably performed in a village square – and certainly closer to its East Anglian origins (shared with the N-Town cycle and the *Play of the Sacrament*) than to a 'Cornish round'. Yet Southern had, in effect, been responsible for restoring the play to theatrical life.

Moral interludes, with their uneven 'conflict' leading to a 'resolution' more theologically than dramatically appropriate, may not, indeed, be much in tune with typical twentieth-century sensibilities. Yet the sheer range of these plays is none the less considerable – from the elaborate and discursive battle of an isolated soul towards the discovery of an almost protestant God in *The Castle of Perseverance* to the brisk but thoroughly orthodox triumph of a church-mediated faith in the better-known *Everyman*; and from the distinctly medieval, almost chivalric tone of the fragmentary *Pride of Life* to the more 'modern' and sophisticated admixture of theology and popular dramaturgy which distinguishes *Mankind*. And, just as Elizabethan tragedy is prefigured by the struggle over the soul of a fallible mortal between the embodied forces of good and evil, so is its comedy in the figures of the 'vices' – those clownish devils who specialized in interacting amusingly (and often profitably) with their audience.

The interlude in its various guises thus assumes an increasing importance in the period covered by our next chapter, not least because its form was best-suited to the conditions of professional performance. Indeed, we may feel less surprise at the wide differences of topic and tone among the plays already mentioned if we bear in mind that an itinerant troupe would need to fit its repertoire not only to its audience – which might be clerical, 'respectably' secular, or cheerfully popular – but also to specific occasions, with solemn holy days making different demands from seasonal festivities such as May Day or Harvest Home.

The late-medieval interludes I have mentioned thus provide a link between the barely-glimpsed activities of the *mimi* in the Dark Ages and the professional touring companies who further energized the form as it proliferated into the early sixteenth century. And it is ironic, too, that the one kind of British drama which possibly pre-dated even the mimes, the semi-pagan performances of the folk, should now have emerged into the glare of courtly life through the plays of a figure who links the British theatre of the medieval and early modern worlds – not least in that, for the first time, we can attach an individual author's name to a body of dramatic work.

That author was John Lydgate, whose plays sustain and call to practical account the misconception of 'Terence staging' as a mimed performance accompanied by solo narration. Yet Lydgate's description of some half of his eight plays as 'mommynges', or mummings, connects them also with the ancient folk ritual of a silent performance *taken to* its audience. His other plays, termed 'disguisings', appear to have lacked the propitiatory gift-giving associated with mummings, and so looked not only backwards to the visitations traditional at New Year and Carnival, but also sideways to post-tournament festivities – the knights still in their jousting personae, but now the guests of the lady for whose favours they had earlier competed – and even forwards, to the fully-fledged masque as it was to develop during the late Tudor and Jacobean periods.

An earlier, anonymous 'mumming' of Christmas 1376–77 is described by Stow as a processional entertainment involving well over a hundred participants, who progressed through the City to Kennington, south of the Thames, where the future Richard II was spending the festive season. There, they silently invited the young prince to play at dice, rigged so that he and his family might 'win' plentiful gifts. The important element here, as the theatre scholar Glynne Wickham sums it up, is the assembly of courtiers, like-minded in their taste for spectacle and disguise, for an indoor entertainment – 'a magnet, drawing to itself the heterogeneous amateur and professional pastimes of earlier social recreation'.

Lydgate gave literary form to this tradition, although, as Wickham further points out, it is not in his plays but in his epic poem the *Troy Book* that we find a description – of an imagined performance in Ancient Troy – which suggests how his own dramas might have reached the stage. Written rather earlier than these, between 1412 and 1425, the *Troy Book* was commissioned by the prince who was to become Henry V, apparently from a desire to embroider the legend (which derived its 'authority' from Geoffrey of Monmouth's *History* of 1137) that London was the 'New Troy' settled by Brutus, a descendant of Aeneas, at the same time as Romulus and Remus were founding Rome.

The poem envisages a Homeric bard, whose recitation of the noble deeds of kings and princes is complemented by actors 'playing by signes in the peoples sight' while the poet sits on high – suggesting, again, some sort of variation on the elusive but persistent tradition of 'Terence staging'. After Lydgate, 'mumming' probably reverted to its folk roots, but the term 'disguising' continued in use to describe courtly entertainments until these merged into the 'masques' we shall describe in the following chapters.

The monarchs of the later fifteenth century, intermittently pruned by the Wars of the Roses, neglected the drama, and there are few records of theatrical activity at court while the dynasty fought out its remaining decades in civil war. The nobility, however, kept up its Christmas disguisings – John Blackham recording the shock of the fastidious Henry VI when confronted by bare-breasted women during one such seasonal show. More importantly, noble lords now began to take troupes of interlude players under their own protection.

A company had thus attached itself to the Earl of Essex by 1469, the Earl of Arundel by 1477, and the Earl of Oxford by 1490 – while as early as 1463 there were apparently enough players relying for their wardrobe on their noble patrons' cast-offs to require a statute exempting them from the usual penalties for rising above their sartorial station. Yet Richard III as king appears to have shown no interest in elevating the troupe to whom he had given protection as Duke of Gloucester, and it was left to the conquering Tudors to forge those strong links between the monarchy and the theatre that were to energize its development in the following century.

CHAPTER 4

The Shaping of a Professional Theatre

The early Tudor period has little to offer in the way of 'great drama': but it was a time of radical experiment and change which saw a great variety of theatrical activity, the extinction of old forms and the emergence of new. Elusively yet irresistibly, it was during these years that the theatre became aware of its power and potential as it had seldom and only sporadically been before – its 'official' forms often crossing the ill-defined boundary between pedagogy and propaganda, its 'unofficial' manifestations put at risk from wider recognition of their popular appeal. The dates of this chapter are thus staked out by political events – at its beginning, an act of usurpation which created the Tudor dynasty; at its end, an Act of Parliament which had the effect of

The 'Field of the Cloth of Gold', held on the Plain of Ardres, France, in 1520 – a theatricalization of summit diplomacy between Henry VIII and Francis I of France which took the tournament to the apotheosis of its decadence. As the dragon flying overhead suggests, the contemporary painting alongside is emblematic rather than exact – in effect, a 'composite' reconstruction of significant events. Thus, in the left foreground the King is riding towards his temporary palace, fronted by fountains, at centre right – while to the rear of the palace, before a golden tent, Henry is seen again, being greeted by the French king. On the extreme right is the 'Tree of Honour' on which the shields of the contestants are hung, and beside it is the tournament field itself – where the two kings reappear, now as observers of the jousting

sorting 'rogues and vagabonds' from legitimized companies of players. The theatre was caught up both in the expression and the attempted resolution of the many paradoxes of the period.

At last, a strong monarchy was setting out to contain and gradually to neutralize the factionalism of the nobility, creating a new breed of 'civil servants' from a grateful bourgeoisie: yet the monarchy was itself a product of regicide and rebellion, its survival dependent upon that propagandist rewriting of the recent past summed up by historians as the 'Tudor myth'. This the theatre helped to create, to sustain – and occasionally to challenge.

While the 'great chain of being' – that ordering of the medieval universe by strict hierarchies and degrees – remained ostensibly intact, its feudal rigidities were already fraying under the strain of capitalist individualism. Usury, supposedly outlawed, flourished, while hospitality, supposedly sacrosanct, withered away. Foreign entanglements and inflation impoverished the masses, while the wealth of the few

was hugely enhanced, whether through the dispersal of the lands of the monasteries dissolved by Henry VIII, or the more effective use of older estates – whose extent, once a sufficient measure of 'wealth', was now merely another kind of capital for exploitation. Often, this was to the detriment of rack-rented tenants as much as of wage-labourers, dispossessed by the profits to be made from less labour-intensive agricultural practices.

Political and economic impulses drove the Reformation under Henry VIII, whose objections were to papal authority rather than Catholic theology. But when doctrinal protestantism, its pace forced under Edward VI and put into sharp reverse by Mary, was finally repackaged into the 'moderate' Elizabethan settlement, the resulting compromises soon came under attack not only from the underground Catholic resistance, but from a more overtly aggressive puritan opposition. The relationship between the theatre and the puritans is more complex than was once allowed, but antagonism to the very idea of a theatre, whether in Calvinist or neo-platonic guise, encouraged that curious alliance between crown and players which helped to create the conditions for the 'golden age' to come.

THE RISE OF ACADEMIC DRAMA

While the mystery cycles were being censored out of existence, as described below, another form of amateur drama, under quite different auspices, began to flourish. As the 'new learning' associated with the Renaissance drifted westward into Britain, it brought with it a burgeoning interest in the work of the Ancient Greek and Roman dramatists. In the theatre this was reflected not, as in Italy, in the earnest application of supposedly classical rules (which, to the despair of such critics as Sir Philip Sidney, most dramatists cheerfully ignored), but in the new interest

An end to the mystery cycles

Religious reform had both an immediate and a longer-term effect on the Corpus Christi cycles, which could no longer function as an 'official' affirmation of shared faith and civic hierarchy. In some towns, they disappeared altogether soon after Henry VIII's break with Rome; in others (especially in the north) they wilted more slowly, as an unsympathetic higher clergy applied the pressures of excision and revision.

Whether or not the sponsoring city authorities and guilds wished to distance themselves from the celebration (and the increasing expense) of a feast expunged from the church calendar in 1548, the plays remained popular with the people, and it was not until the 1570s that they were finally censored out of existence. Thus, what had once been an instrument of orthodox instruction was now perceived as a potential focus for discontent – and it is no coincidence that the last performance of the 'amended and corrected' version of the York cycle

coincided with the abortive Northern Rebellion against Elizabeth of 1569.

One little-remarked effect of the severance of links with Rome was that the abolition of Corpus Christi (as of other, older feasts and saints' days) deprived the common people of many of their traditional holidays – an effect fully in line not just with reformist iconoclasm, but with what has become known as the 'protestant work ethic'. The process of keeping the worker to his task on almost every day of the year (except for joyless Sundays, on which sports and entertainments increasingly became taboo) was thus well under way: so another factor in the decline of the 'amateur' tradition, and of the increasing dependence on professional playing, may have been the lack of adequate time for its preparation, rehearsal – and even, in the case of substantial events such as mysteries, its performance.

taken in drama as an educational tool by teachers and men of letters. Editions of the extant works of the Ancient Greek and Roman playwrights had begun to appear within a decade of the introduction of movable type into Italy in 1465, and the canon was complete by 1518 – by which time the study of the classical drama, now also becoming available in English editions, was being assimilated into the syllabuses of schools and universities.

Nor was performance excluded: thus, Terence was staged at Cambridge as early as 1510, and Plautus a decade or so later, while Wolsey's players put on the *Menaechmi* of Plautus at court in 1527, and the boys of St Paul's gave Terence's *Phormio* there in 1528. With the Reformation, the links in the public mind between Latin and

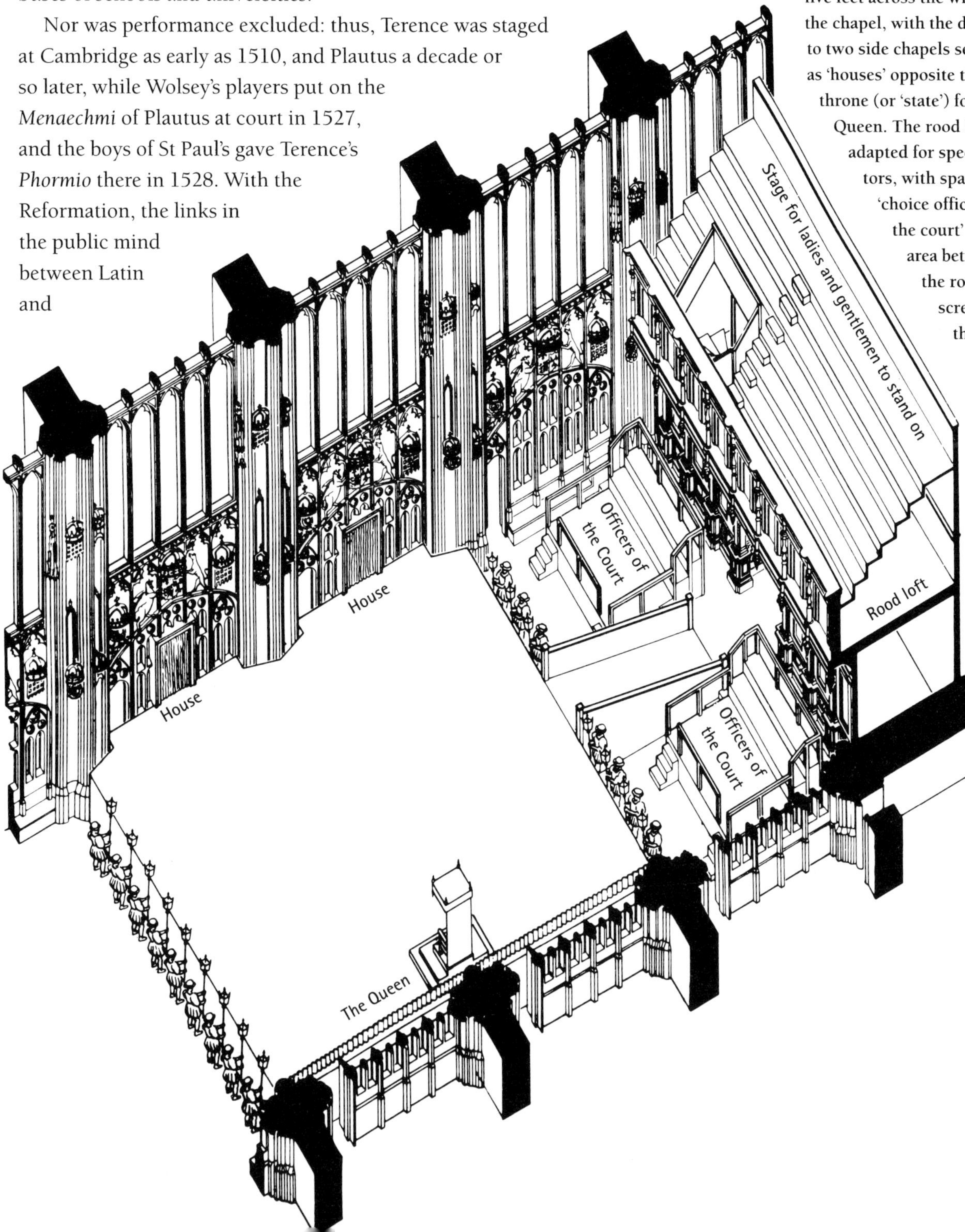

Reconstruction by Richard Leacroft of King's College Chapel, Cambridge, adapted for the staging of the *Aulularia* of Plautus in 1564 before Elizabeth I. The stage is raised five feet across the width of the chapel, with the doors to two side chapels serving as 'houses' opposite the throne (or 'state') for the Queen. The rood loft is adapted for spectators, with space for 'choice officers of the court' in the area between the rood screen and the stage

House

House

Officers of the Court

Officers of the Court

Stage for ladies and gentlemen to stand on

Rood loft

The Queen

Roman Catholicism brought it into some disfavour, and a compensatory boom in Greek studies led to performances of the plays of Sophocles, Euripides, and Aristophanes. As Ian Lancashire sums up from his own compendious records, 'by the 1540s, even as small a school as Hitchin had a large dramatic repertory', and 'by the 1550s both Oxford and Cambridge were staging Greek and Latin comedies and tragedies by all the major authors'.

Besides productions in the original, there were translations, adaptations – and, more important, new plays based on the formal models of the ancients. On the Continent, even Hrotsvitha's works appeared in print in 1501, inspiring other attempts at the Christianizing of classical models and the beginnings of a 'sacred drama' that was humanist rather than popularly orthodox in emphasis. As with Hrotsvitha's reworkings of Terence long ago, there were misunderstandings – notably over Seneca, who is today believed to have written 'closet' tragedies, never intended for performance. For the future of the drama, even following such a mistaken precedent mattered less than the sheer impulse to create plays of a new kind, which helped, however laterally, to nourish the native growth.

Nicholas Udall's *Ralph Roister Doister* (*c.* 1552), though geared to a schoolboy cast, was perhaps the best as it was certainly among the earliest of the comedies written in English on a 'Plautine' model – and included a native version of the 'braggart soldier' who was later to claim Sir John Falstaff among his distaff descendants. Udall was headmaster successively at Eton and Westminster, and enthusiasm for the comic repertoire was seemingly at its strongest in the schools – whereas the universities, and their legal equivalent the Inns of Court, appear to have catered more to the taste for tragedy.

It was thus at the Inns of Court that the earliest original tragedies on Senecan lines, Norton and Sackville's *Gorboduc* (1561) and Gascoigne's *Jocasta* (1566), found their audience. But the emergence of the robustly comic *Gammer Gurton's Needle* from Cambridge (*c.* 1553) would have to head any list of exceptions to this general rule – the more cosmopolitan atmosphere of the Inns of Court also making these the centre of a fashion for anglicized Italian comedies (including, in 1566, the play which became one of Shakespeare's sources for *The Taming of the Shrew*, George Gascoigne's *Supposes*).

It would be misleading to overstress the importance of the 'educational' and 'academic' drama. Its audiences were as limited as the pedagogic intentions of most of its practitioners, while its repertoire, ancient or modern, was not taken up by the professional troupes, whose visits proved increasingly worrying to the university authorities – as in 1575 at Cambridge, when the Vice-Chancellor complained to the Privy Council of players who lured scholars 'from the good course of their studies'. But a spirit of responsiveness to drama did emerge among the scholarly community: and this, as we shall see in the next chapter, meant that many of the pioneering dramatists of the late Elizabethan period were to be drawn from the academic milieu, and even to be singled out by their contemporaries as the 'university wits'.

Will Somers, Henry VIII's court jester: an illustration from the King's Psalter, *c.* 1540. Henry is playing a harp perched on what appears to be a sarcophagus, and Somers is facing away from him, with an expression of pained endurance. Both men are realistically portrayed – ageing, grizzled, and sallow-complexioned. Compare the more formal portrait on the opposite page

DRAMA AT COURT

Drama at court, neglected during the Wars of the Roses, also began to flourish under the Tudors. It was, however, probably from pragmatic considerations rather than personal preference that Henry VII, founder of the dynasty after his victory at Bosworth Field, encouraged its growth. A dour but dedicated monarch, he recognized the need to keep up appearances as well as to keep tabs on a nobility he was determined to tame – and 'splendour at court' furthered both ends.

Four 'players of the King's interludes' thus appear on his payroll at least from 1494, and tournaments, pageants, and disguisings stirred to new life. Henry VIII, for whom courtly extravagance conveniently combined policy and pleasure, increased the number of his 'interluders' to eight or ten; and in 1520 he took the tournament almost to the apotheosis of its decadence in that theatricalization of summit diplomacy with France, the so-called 'Field of the Cloth of Gold'.

Henry also shared his father's taste for the antics of court jesters, or fools, and his ministers took up the fashion. Sir Thomas More was painted by Holbein with his household jester, and Cardinal Wolsey handed over his own fool Patch to the King following his disgrace. Patch was evidently a 'natural' fool, one of those clowns who turned a slow brain or deformed body to the best account possible in an age amused by such defects – whereas the 'artificial' fool lived by his wits rather than the lack of them. One such was Will Somers, here portrayed – who, outlasting wives, ministers, and lesser royal favourites, from 1525 until the King's death in 1547 was probably closer to Henry than any other person.

Portrait of King Henry and his eldest daughter, the Princess Mary – with the jester Will Somers hovering like a morose apparition to the rear, his hand clenched towards his master's head. This wizened, stubbly, subordinate creature appears eminently more human in this strange composition than the regal figures in the foreground. Yet, despite the differences between this formal portrait and the illumination opposite, either 'version' of Somers could as readily suggest a court fool of King Lear's as of King Henry's – and half a century or so later it is likely that Somers might, indeed, have found a place as resident clown in a theatrical company

Both types of fool, natural and artificial, already feature as theatrical types in one of the most unusual moral interludes of the period, John Skelton's *Magnificence* (*c.* 1516), in which the clownish dwarf Fancy turns out to be brother to the clever and nimble Folly. Their dramatic function is that of tempters or 'vices' – those minor devils of the morality plays who specialized in subversive complicity with their early Tudor audiences (for whom the term 'vice' was more or less synonymous with 'fool'. Indeed, the contemporary critic George Puttenham, writing in 1589, likened jesters not only to 'counterfeit vices', but to the *pantomimi* of Ancient Rome.) Even Richard Tarlton, first of the great theatrical clowns, was sometimes called a 'vice' – but he began his career, according to evidence no less significant for being anecdotal, as the 'most famous jester to Queen Elizabeth'.

The role of a royal servant with a penchant for playacting thus merged into that of a specialist member of the fully-developed, late-Elizabethan acting company – nominally a household servant still, but in practice a professional actor, with a sideline now in playing on special occasions at court. And this was paradigmatic of an age in which the function of other actorly royal servants underwent a comparable transformation – choirboys achieving greater fame as boy players, and, most significantly, the 'interluders' becoming increasingly dependent on paying audiences rather than a nominal noble patron.

THE CHILDREN OF THE CHOIR SCHOOLS

Henry VIII, a famous lover of music, had increased the establishment of the choir schools, of which those attached to the Chapel Royal at court and to St Paul's Cathedral had the earliest performing traditions, with the boys at Windsor soon setting out to rival their prowess. The Children of the Chapel had performed at court at least since the early sixteenth century – in 1501 with an elaborate disguising to celebrate the marriage of the short-lived heir apparent, Prince Arthur, to the ill-fated Catherine of Aragon. The mastership of William Cornish, from 1509 to 1523, enhanced their reputation for drama, and later both Nicholas Udall and John Heywood appear to have written for them. After 1565, they played not only at court but also for the scholars of Lincoln's Inn.

The 'Children of Paul's' were especially well-placed within a cathedral precinct which, even after the Reformation, continued to function as much as a social centre as a place of worship. Heywood also wrote for this company, as did its successive masters, John Redford (*c.* 1531–47) and Sebastian Westcott (1547–82) – the former's *Wit and Science* (*c.* 1540) and the latter's *Liberality and Prodigality* (*c.* 1567) both being adapted for performance by adult players. Such entrepreneurs as these, who combined a measure of artistic attainment with a sound commercial instinct, were really the driving forces of the children's companies, arguably exploiting and certainly profiting from the talents of their charges – who by the end of the 1570s were offering a wide mix of plays, from moralities to mythological romances, and from classical comedies to pseudo-classical chronicles.

The boys had certain advantages over the adult players, a guaranteed subsistence not least among them. They also received a useful training in rhetoric, while their numbers were sufficient to make the logistics of doubling less troublesome – child companies averaging ten or twelve players, against the more usual eight adults. But, although they were able to call upon the wardrobe of the Revels Office for a wide range of costumes, they lacked resources for scenery or other effects, and for a long time had no adequate premises of their own from which to attract a wider metropolitan audience.

Earlier, it had probably been the Lollard inclinations of London's ruling elite which had prevented the 'clerks' plays' from taking root in the city: now, the opposition to the theatre of the City fathers was increasingly rooted in puritanism, disguised though it was as fear of the players' tendency to infect apprentices with idleness and disaffection, and everyone else with the plague. Indeed, all such places of popular assembly from which disorders might be expected to spring were kept if possible beyond the City's walls – notably on Bankside, across the Thames, where brothels and animal-baiting arenas had long flourished.

By 1575, however, Paul's Boys seem to have found themselves a playing place of sorts within the cathedral precinct, and in the following year the Master of the Windsor children, Richard Farrant, who had somehow manoeuvred himself into authority over the Chapel company as well, converted the buttery of the dissolved monastery at Blackfriars into a permanent theatre. For the City enjoyed no jurisdiction over such ecclesiastical 'liberties', and both troupes could thus boast premises which were not only conveniently situated, but impregnably so.

The period of the boys' greatest popularity, even notoriety, with public audiences followed: but that will be our concern in the next chapter. Their highest point of royal favour had, however, already been passed when, in the years since Elizabeth's accession in 1558, they gave 46 performances at court against only 32 by the adult players. Muriel Bradbrook has suggested that the Queen's subsequent loss of interest in the boy actors may have been due to the fading of her own prospects of childbearing: it would be ironic indeed if the return to pre-eminence of the adult actors at court should have hinged upon such a happenstance of royal gynaecology.

Be that as it may, what was to prove a permanent physical separation of 'interluders' from the court had already taken place. Apart from a single summons to play before the newly-crowned Elizabeth in January 1559, they spent most of their time thereafter on tour. Records of their provincial performances are extant for every subsequent year until 1573: but after one further glimpse of the interluders' activities in Ipswich in 1581, no more is heard of them, although a new itinerant troupe, Queen Elizabeth's Men, surfaces in the records two years later. This, coincidental or not, was typical of the change now overtaking the adult companies: glad as they no doubt were of the protection from charges of vagrancy afforded by noble or royal patronage, in the hard business of making a living they became increasingly dependent upon playing before the general public.

Early Tudor players – and plays in print

Who were the professional players of popular farce and romance? The companies whose performances and fees are recorded in the account books of civic authorities, and of royal, aristocratic, or religious households, were probably protected by the livery of a noble patron, and so had, almost by definition, achieved a degree of respectability.

Yet, as the critic and historian T. W. Craik rightly stresses, even noble patronage did not provide such companies with 'a sufficient salary and a continual playing place': it merely 'gave them the entrée to many places where they could play and be paid'. We know little about the lives of those who enjoyed no such entrée – and of how they were paid we know even less, though the traditional skills of the vice (as hilariously exercised in Mankind) included that of 'bottling', or parting an audience from its pennies.

It is notable that the earliest printed texts of plays seem to have been designed at least partly to serve as acting editions, if we may judge by the care with which the doubling (or, for that matter, quadrupling) of roles is worked out, or by comments such as that in the protestant moral interlude King Darius (1565) that 'six persons may easily play it'.

Print thus widened the repertoire of any company able to afford the price of a text: but it also narrowed the potential range of that repertoire, since no play regarded as subversive by the authorities was likely to reach print. Thus, an interlude presented at Gray's Inn at Christmas 1527 evidently infuriated Wolsey in its 'effect', as described by the chronicler Hall, 'that Lord Governance was ruled by Dissipation and Negligence'. Wolsey presumably felt himself satirized in the character of Lord Negligence, and had the author, one John Roo, thrown into prison: his play, unsurprisingly, is lost.

Print also provided a new means of livelihood for the descendants of the minstrels, who could now combine the singing of popular ballads with their sale in the form of broadsides – a vocation celebrated by Ben Jonson in Bartholomew Fair, and seemingly little changed when Henry Mayhew came to interview the 'patterers' and 'chaunters' singing and hawking ballads on the streets of nineteenth-century London – where, in due course, we shall be seeking them out.

For others, throwing in their lot with a company of strolling players was probably a better bet, especially since the numbers in these companies saw a gradual rise over the century – from the 'four men and a boy' (as recollected a century later, in a rehearsal episode of the late-Elizabethan play Sir Thomas More) to six or eight, and by the early years of Elizabeth's reign to as many as twelve. Some of these enlargements may have resulted from an opportune combination of smaller troupes.

MEDWALL, RASTELL, AND THE INTERLUDE PLAYERS

Not surprisingly, the nature of the adult repertoire also underwent a change, achieving a new flexibility and, gradually, a more secular emphasis. Even during the reign of Henry VII, with the court still the focus of dramatic activity, a new style of interlude was emerging – notably in the work of Henry Medwall, whose *Fulgens and Lucrece* (1497) is often described as the first English secular comedy. The play is structured in the traditional medieval form of a *débat*, here between a Roman father and his daughter – the first major female protagonist in English drama – over the relative merits as suitors of a profligate aristocrat and a self-made citizen.

Lucrece has virtually made her decision before the action begins. Unsurprisingly, it is in favour (as were the Tudors) of upward-mobility among the bourgeoisie. Of no less interest is the low-life sub-plot, in which the servants of the two suitors indulge in some parallel wooing, apparently stepping from the world of reality into the fictional action, and functioning in traditional interlude fashion as the links between the play and its audience.

Fulgens is unusual in its abandonment of allegorical characterization, but shares many features with other interludes of the period – its secular provenance, its

A lamentable tragedy

mixed ful of pleasant mirth, conteyning the life of
CAMBISES king of PERCIA, from the beginning
of his kingdome vnto his death, his one good deed of execution, after that many wicked deeds
and tirannous murders, committed by and
through him, and last of all, his odious
death by Gods Iustice appoin-
ted. Don in such order as
foloweth. By
Thomas Preston.

❧ *The division of the partes.*

Councel. Huf. Praxafpes. Murder. Lob, the 3.Lord.	*For one man.*	Prologue. Sifamnes. Diligence. Crueltie. Hob. Preparatio the 1.Lord.	*For one man*
Lord. Ruf, Commons cry, Cōmōs cōplaint, Lord fmirdis, Venus.	*For one man.*	Ambidexter Triall.	*For one man.*
Knight, Snuf. Small habilitie. Proof. Exccution. Attendance. fecond Lord.	*For one man.*	Meretrix. Shame. Otian. Mother. Lady. Queene.	*For one man.*
Cambifes. Epilogus.	*For one man*	Yung childe Cupid.	*For one man*

debate formula, its recurrent comic counterpoint and interplay with its audience, and its length of around a thousand lines, designed to fill an hour or so of playing time, perhaps as part of the entertainment at a banquet. Such overtly more traditional moralities as the anonymous *The World and the Child* (*c.* 1507), *Youth* (1513), and *Hickscorner* (1514), while showing due concern for the salvation of the soul, also display a humanist interest in how best to live on earth for the duration.

Most of these plays were carefully scripted so that they could be performed with doubling by a company of given size – usually, at first, the 'four men and a boy' mentioned a century later in the rehearsal episode of the late-Elizabethan *Sir Thomas More*. It was no mere whim that moved the authors of that play to show Henry VIII's doomed chancellor employing a troupe of strolling players: for the dramatists we know by name from the earlier part of the reign were almost all connected with what became known as 'More's circle'.

Medwall died in 1501, but More had been a member with him of the household of Henry VII's veteran chancellor, Cardinal Morton, and in his youth may well have seen Medwall's single other extant play, *Nature* (*c*. 1495). Declaring herself God's earthly representative, the female title-character of this play allots as companions to Man the personified shapes of Reason and Sensuality – an altogether more humanist pair than the Good and Bad Angels of *The Castle of Perseverance*. Sir Thomas himself wrote plays (of which all we know is that one concerned the legend of Solomon), and his great philosophical treatise, *Utopia*, was printed in 1516 by the man who married More's daughter, the playwright John Rastell – while a daughter of *that* marriage in due course became the wife of yet another playwright, John Heywood.

Rastell remains a fascinating figure, reminiscent of William Cobbett in his protean range of interests as also in his blunt integrity – his late conversion to protestantism, too, every bit as startling and as public as was Cobbett's to the radical cause. He is also – almost unnoticed by theatre historians, and half a century before James Burbage – the first person known to have constructed a permanent stage in London. This was sometime before 1526, but we know little about it beyond its location in Finsbury Fields, and the fact that it was still there when Rastell died ten years later.

The one surviving play of his certain authorship, *The Four Elements*, is an intriguing attempt to communicate within a morality format not only Rastell's common-sense view of salvation, but also the excitement of recent discoveries in geography and astronomy. A sturdy Taverner and a robust Ignorance, half way between vices and common men, provide comic interpolations, while the title-page pragmatically advises that the play may be enlivened by a disguising, 'if ye list'. *Gentleness and Nobility*, which may also be from Rastell's pen, politicizes both the form and the theme of *Fulgens and Lucrece*, its debate between a Knight, a Merchant, and a Ploughman coming to the Cobbettian conclusion that all are born to labour, gentility being a quality of mind and manners, not of wealth or rank.

To the printing business which John Rastell ran with his brother and son we owe the texts not only of his own work, but of Medwall's, Heywood's, and possibly of Skelton's – whose *Magnificence* is something of a 'sport' among these early Tudor interludes, in which it is difficult to disentangle the religious from the secular elements. Scholars have variously asserted that the play voices the fears of a conservative nobility as their young king flexed his autocratic muscles; that it displays an expected humanist concern with cultivating the balanced life; or that it is, after all, a moral interlude in the traditional mould, its other-worldliness overlain by Skelton's quirky prejudices and poetics.

Whatever its intentions (and they are probably mixed), *Magnificence* gives the impression of being a one-off – a poet's play, whose author is unaccustomed to dealing with actors, trusting them neither to present their characters without descriptive elaboration, nor to manage the mechanics of doubling without an authorial nudge. Yet there is something intrinsically theatrical about Skelton's skill in keeping his audience, like his readers, constantly on the alert; and the play's variegated verse forms, though often awkward in the reading, prove brisk and forceful when spoken – an attribute all too seldom put to the test by present-day critics, whose expectations, formed by the later ubiquity of blank verse, tend to be needlessly disappointed by the jagged metres and emphatic caesuras of the earlier Tudor drama.

Magnificence is unusual in its length, of some 2,500 lines – in which, however, it was to be exceeded by the massive 4,600 lines of another singular 'poet's play', Sir Robert Lindsay's *A Satire of the Three Estates*. This was first performed before the Scottish court of James V at Twelfth Night 1540, and was revived several times in varying versions and circumstances – the 'banns' for one later performance anticipating a start at seven o'clock in the morning, with a break for the audience to 'drink and make collation' at eleven, before settling down for an even longer second part.

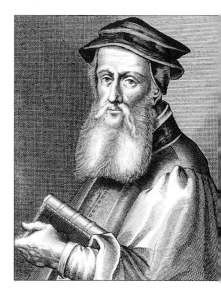

John Bale (1495–1563), protestant bishop and polemicist. He also wrote interludes which blended morality, history, and sermonizing into an early version of 'agitprop' for the protestant cause

In its sheer bulk, as also in its apparent suitability for some kind of 'mansion' staging, Lindsay's play may thus seem more akin to *The Castle of Perseverance* than to contemporary English interludes: yet its strong anti-clericalism is entirely of its times. True, in the first half all three of the 'estates' of the title – the Lords Temporal and the Burgesses, as well as the Lords Spiritual – refuse the advice of Good Counsel and ignore the virtues of Chastity, only to cower at the appearance of Divine Correction, just in time for the interval: but in the second part the attack is focused on the clergy, who alone are reluctant to reform, as if awaiting sterner retribution from the all-too-imminent John Knox. As the critic F. P. Wilson aptly describes it, the play is 'one vast Scottish *comédie humaine*. We have nothing like it in England.'

What we did have in England, with the coming of the Reformation, were moral interludes metamorphosed into instruments of protestant zeal – to the extent that Henry VIII, a notably more cautious reformer in his declining years, forbade their writers by an Act of Parliament of 1543 to venture any further upon the interpretation of the scriptures. But this act was repealed four years later, under Edward VI, whose protestant 'protectors' were only too happy that the drama should proselytize for the reformed religion.

The protestant dramatist of whom we know most is John Bale, a dispossessed clergyman who began writing plays, apparently for his own company, at the height of the reformist controversy of the late 1530s, in the interests of his ill-fated patron Thomas Cromwell. Bale's style has been characterized as dramatic sermonizing – an unhappy hybrid to modern minds, but one not uncongenial to sixteenth-century expectations. Sermons had, indeed, long been in the armoury of the religious reformers, whether mendicant friars in their first untainted enthusiasm or Tudor churchmen intent on explaining doctrine rather than presuming its absorption by liturgical rote. Good preachers could gather audiences no less avid than those for a play, and open-air venues for sermons, whether a rural market-place or Paul's Cross in the City, were focal points for their communities.

Bale's brief return to favour under Edward having taken him to Ireland, it was, aptly enough, at the market cross in Kilkenny that he is known to have presented three of his surviving five plays – *God's Promises*, *John the Baptist*, and *The Temptation of Our Lord* – for an all-day performance in 1553. Together, these constitute a sort of protestant mystery cycle in miniature, and their timing, to coincide with the coronation across the water of Mary Tudor, was an open provocation. Another of

Performing where they could

Companies had to perform when and where they could, from fit-up stages in market squares to the arenas normally used for baiting bulls or bears, and from the utilitarian yard of an inn to the sumptuous surroundings of guildhall or 'great hall' – that distinctive status symbol of the Tudor lord, where his guests and dependents could be lavishly entertained. In a few cases, inn yards in the Elizabethan style have survived to welcome jet-lagged tourists instead of weary travellers on horseback, while some of the remaining great halls have been scrupulously restored as part of the 'heritage culture' of the 'stately home' – as the pub scene opposite and the pictures of hall screens on pages 66–67 bear witness. Of the fit-ups, of course, no trace remains: if half-a-dozen mouldy ale casks made supports for the boards of a stage, it was as firewood that these would have ended their useful life. But the engraving below gives us an idea of their scale and typical ambience.

Alongside: fit-up stage, supported by barrels, at a village fair (detail from 'Temperantia', an engraving by the Dutch artist, Pieter Brueghel the elder). Opposite page: convivial corner of a surviving inn-yard, the Eagle in Cambridge, with its galleried first floor and narrow entrance-way – useful to control access from the street

Bale's extant works, *The Three Laws* (*c.* 1538), is a protestant version of the moral interlude, a type which figures prominently among his numerous lost plays, which also included, in addition to an earlier attempt at a 'reformed' mystery cycle, a piece which turned Thomas Becket from popular saint into papist stooge – thus, one can only conjecture, creating an anti-miracle play.

But Bale's work looked forward as well as back, and his single other surviving play, *King John*, has interested later generations for its seeming anticipation of the Elizabethan chronicle genre. Although probably performed at Ipswich before the young Queen in 1561, following Bale's return from exile, it actually dates from 1539, when it was played before Cranmer. John, reviled by Catholic historians, is here presented as a paragon of virtue surrounded by characters who shift between allegorical and historical functions as they contend for the England he rules as deputy for God – just like Henry VIII, whom this John of course prefigures.

Bale's dramatic qualities are difficult to assess in an age when preaching connotes at best a specialized form of doctrinal explication, at worst boredom to be avoided or endured. Perhaps he is most helpfully viewed not as a flawed predecessor of Shakespeare but as an early exponent of 'agitprop', setting out unashamedly to influence opinion through theatrical propaganda. Certainly, the middle decades of the sixteenth century saw an outpouring of similarly motivated drama, most of it now lost – including a play by the martyrologist John Foxe, in which Rome is naturally personified as the whore of Antichrist. There is nothing inherently undramatic or artistically improper about such work: it may not speak to our times, but it clearly spoke both for and to its own.

There are tantalizing hints of a lost drama of secular politics, as in a complaint laid by the Spanish ambassador in 1559 that his royal master Philip was being ridiculed in plays commissioned by no less a dignitary than William Cecil. But only a single Catholic riposte to the tidal wave of protestant playwriting has survived – *Respublica*, which was performed before Mary by boy actors in 1554. Here, the title-character, a widow of trusting disposition, is brought low by such successor-vices as Policy and Reformation until the old order is restored by Nemesis, on behalf of the watching Queen. Politically, the play is a mirror-image of *King John*, but, while also displaying some of the features of the educational drama, it has the more important quality of being funny – for both of which reasons it is often attributed to Nicholas Udall, author of *Ralph Roister Doister*.

FARCE AND ROMANCE

Textbooks seeking precursors to Shakespeare as a comic dramatist often plump for Udall, perhaps with a nod towards William Stevenson, the only contender for the authorship of *Gammer Gurton's Needle* (1575): but both writers, despite their neoclassical baggage, are themselves indebted to the native tradition of popular farce, which at one level they were also legitimizing. From this tradition, too, derive many of the comic elements in other works of 'elite' authorship, from *Fulgens and Lucrece* to *Respublica*. But it is the plays of John Heywood, of which only those written during the 1520s are extant, which perhaps show most clearly the way in which the popular comic heritage was now entering the 'official' culture.

The two-handed squabbles which recur so often in Heywood's *The Play of Love*, *The Four PP*, or the untitled piece known as *Wit and Folly*, are thus too often dismissed as a sort of debased, rhetorically incompetent form of *débat*, when they can more helpfully be understood as a sequence of 'double-acts' for what we would call 'stand-up' comic performance. Language which – like the behaviour it predicates – may appear stilted or nonsensical on the printed page is intended to take flight in the mouths of performers with a command of comic repartee.

A recent comparison might be with the wartime radio show *ITMA*, which displayed a not dissimilar delight in puns, *double-entendres*, and tongue-twisting word-play: again, the written script squats dully on the page, but at once springs to life on a scratchy recording through the skills and timing of Tommy Handley and his cast – most of whom were also, incidentally, experts in the art of doubling. In *The Play of the Weather*, Heywood even exploits that continuing comic standby, the English climate – the god Jupiter here functioning as a sort of divine meteorologist, wearied by selfish petitioners for a change in the weather.

It might be argued that the best known and most apparently accessible of Heywood's plays, *Johan Johan*, is also the least significant, since it is merely a free adaptation of a French farce: yet the tradition on which Heywood was drawing, of the topical-farcical *sotie*, is a product of transmission by the fifteenth century into the French literary repertoire of a popular comic form which was only to achieve 'official' cultural status in England in the sixteenth. Thus, a regular character of the *soties* – the *sot* himself, from whom the genre gets its name – was, sure enough, a French version of the secular vice, who now turns up in Heywood's plays, his head exploding with fireworks in *The Play of Love*, and always debunking the behavioural or linguistic pretensions of the other characters.

As ever, then, the scarcity of records should not allow us to forget the existence of a popular audience – least of all during the early sixteenth century, when, because the traditions were actively intermingling, we may fail to distinguish *what* is being influenced (for which we have evidence) from the influence itself (which remains elusive). One rightly respected authority on the period, Glynne Wickham, thus seems to me to over-simplify when he asserts that only 'two kinds of theatre' contributed to the 'essential stage and dramatic heritage of the Elizabethans' – 'that of worship, appealing to a universal audience; and that of social recreation, appealing to a small sectional audience'.

It would be surprising indeed if the 'universal audience' of ordinary people had not also felt the need to be entertained by a 'theatre of social recreation' – but, as so often, this can only be glimpsed through the ways in which it was absorbed into the official culture. Thus, as the adult players began to regain the ascendancy at court, there was a great vogue for the 'romances' so heartily despised by Sir Philip Sidney in his *Art of Poetry* – and these, almost certainly, had been uplifted and adapted by the adult companies from their roots in the 'recreational' theatre of the people. David Bevington argues that the typical pattern of the secular romance, of 'separation, wandering, and reunion', finds an echo in the morality formula of the 'fall from grace, temporary prosperity of evil, and divine reconciliation': but no less, of course, does this remind us of later popular forms, notably nineteenth-century melodrama – for the people, a theatre of necessary reassurance, for the elite, one of sentimental self-indulgence.

Very few theatrical romances have survived, and in these, as in melodrama, it is often uncertain whether we are supposed to be laughing at the characters or crying with them. The determining factor, one strongly suspects, is class loyalty. Certainly, the pair of would-be aristocrats from whom *Sir Clyomon and Sir Clamydes* (*c.* 1570) gets its title are both as daft as Don Quixote, albeit considerably defter at avoiding

The hall screen at Hampton Court Palace, built *c.* 1535. It may be that when a stage was erected for interluders in this large hall, it occupied only the area of the central screen, between the doors. 'Houses' may then have been set up at floor level in each corner. Alternatively, a wider platform, extending to the outside limit of each door, could have been pulled slightly forward to allow entrances to be made from the back or sides of the stage

imminent dangers. The women, though sympathetic, exist to be adored: and amidst all the turns of plot and place, the vice, Subtle Shift, manipulates and survives.

Of course, the ordinary people continued to entertain themselves through participating in folk performances, echoes of which reach us either through the veil of official disapproval (as of Robin Hood plays, thought to incite civil disobedience), or the cloak of professionalism, cast over forms as diverse as the stately masque and the lowly jig – to both of which we shall return. But, as the medievalist Richard Axton has persuasively argued, fragments of the folk tradition are also to be found scattered through many of the plays already mentioned in this chapter. These may be straightforward interpolations, like the wooing of a bisexual Bessy in *A Satire of the Three Estates*, or 'her' betrothal to Infidelity in Bale's *The Three Laws*; but often the influence is subtextual – in Axton's words, 'an exploratory way to test out feelings and entertain criticism without having to state it, to give shape and focus to attitudes which could not as yet be admitted as "official".'

Oak hall screen, completed 1573, for the Middle Temple, one of the four surviving Inns of Court (in effect, the universities of the legal profession). Plays, masques, and other entertainments were customarily held here, especially in the period from All Saints' (1 November) to Candlemas (2 February). The passage beyond the doors would have served as a tiring-house, with a raised platform stage probably stretching the full width of the screen, a traverse curtain being used for setting 'discovery' scenes. Candlemas 1602 was the occasion for a performance (probably not the first) of *Twelfth Night*

GREAT HALLS AS PLAYING PLACES

Of the formative influences upon the shaping of the permanent Elizabethan playhouse discussed on page 62, the fit-ups have long crumbled away, and the inn-yards gone out of fashion in favour of the great halls of the earlier Tudor nobility and gentry. Certainly, itinerant companies would have been accustomed to perform in these, and no doubt preferred the home comforts and assured returns they offered. But the greater accessibility of their physical remains has perhaps led to a disproportionate stress upon their relative importance.

Richard Southern argues persuasively that during the sixteenth century the great halls developed as playing-places in three stages: the whole available floor space was, he suggests, being used by the end of the 1520s, with the doors in the screens serving not only as entrances and exits but also as focal points to differentiate acting areas; then, during the next decade or so, the value of having some sort of 'retiring space' conjecturally led to the temporary placing of the 'traverse', a curtain on rods, between the screen doors; and finally, as first mentioned on the title-page of *Gammer Gurton's Needle* around 1553, a low 'stage' or 'scaffold' – a raised dais, fronting the traverse – provided a new version of the *locus*, an area in which parts of the action could be kept distinct and discrete.

Or was it new? Cannot the raised platform which, in Southern's view, *evolved* as 'a special development of the "differentiation" idea', be seen simply as an adaptation of the existing fit-up stage to a different environment? Again, Southern suggests that the positioning of the entrances and exits at the screen end of the great hall controlled the staging conventions of the interludes played there. But one might equally argue that players accustomed to 'clearing a space' in the market square, or in the tap-room of a tavern or alehouse (the local tippling places, that is: inns were meant for travellers), would naturally look to 'clear a space' upon entering a great hall. They would be imposing *their* convention upon their new surroundings – as the mummers still do today, calling for 'room' in which to perform.

Is this merely a difference of emphasis? If so, it touches even on our present-day tendency to think of plays in terms of 'acts' and 'scenes'. As Southern says of *Magnificence*: 'Every time a character comes in he arrives with a significant purpose and creates a significant (often deliberately contrived) effect in the development of the action and the maintenance of the interest. He does, in fact, initiate a new "scene".' We might, he goes on, 'had the convention been established so early', prefer to think of the opening section of the play as 'an act in six scenes'.

But the convention had *not* been established: more important, neither had the assumptions concerning 'development' on which it depends. During the early Tudor period, a play's units of action seem better understood in terms of 'entrances': and so, in *Magnificence*, we might rather think of the section Southern is describing as a 'scene in six acts' – understanding 'act' not as Skelton's first learned editor (like Shakespeare's) used the term, shoehorning the play into a neoclassical corset, but in the sense in which an 'act' or 'turn' still appears on a variety bill. Whether there are five acts in a play interests only scholars: if there are six good turns on a bill, they bring in audiences.

LEGITIMIZING THE THEATRE

All this is of more than academic interest because one of the processes at work in this period, as we have seen, was that of *legitimizing* theatre – a process which in some ways safeguarded its future as a profession, since it provided its practitioners with a measure of security, but which in other respects proved highly restrictive, since the boundaries delimiting what was *not* permissible became better defined, and punishment for transgressions that much easier to inflict.

The ultimate effect of the process was to consolidate control over the theatre in the hands of the Master of the Revels. This officer of the royal household was first appointed on a temporary basis by Henry VII in 1494, with responsibility for plays and other entertainments presented at court: but Henry VIII made the mastership a full-time post in 1545, whereafter its functions began to increase – and eventually embraced the censorship of plays. Ironically, Henry's order of 1543 forbidding the theatre to touch on matters of religion had been framed in a context careful to affirm the actors' right to present plays 'for the rebuking and reproaching of vices and the setting forth of virtue'. But an order of Edward VI in 1551 required the licensing of all plays by the King or the Privy Council, a task which an Elizabethan proclamation of 1559 reassigned to mayors, lords lieutenant, and local magistrates.

None of these restrictions affected the companies as such, only the plays they could perform, and with discretion few can have been seriously impeded. Quite distinct from these developments, however, a constant concern of Tudor government had been to control the increasing numbers of the itinerant unemployed: 'masterless men', as their status was so revealingly labelled. But, although the many strolling players who did not wear noble livery clearly fitted this category, they appear to have enjoyed reasonable freedom of movement in the early decades of the sixteenth century. They were presumably careful not to offend the civic authorities and others on whom, after all, their livelihood depended.

Then, in the wake of the Northern Rebellion and the Queen's excommunication in 1570, the Privy Council in 1572 set up the ecclesiastical commissions which eradicated remaining traces of the old religious drama. Also in 1572 a new act for the control of vagrancy was put on the statute book. Among its many provisions, this act gave legal protection to players – but only those who were 'servants of any Baron of this Realm', or 'any other honourable personage of greater degree'. Others were consigned to the punishable ranks of rogues and vagabonds.

Just two years later, the company which enjoyed the patronage of the Queen's favourite, the Earl of Leicester, was given royal 'letters patent' to perform in London on weekdays – a condition being that the troupe's plays should first be 'seen and allowed' by the Master of the Revels. The City fathers did their best to nullify the effects of the patent within their boundaries, and before long the leader of Leicester's men, James Burbage, saw the advantages of building a permanent home for the company well beyond the walls. The transformation of the theatre into a fully secular, largely professional, and carefully regulated institution was complete, with the Revels Office effectively its instrument of control – and, almost as a side-effect, instead of the theatre going to the people, the people of London were now able to go to The Theatre.

CHAPTER 5

The Era of the Outdoor Playhouses

It is ironic that, in an age when women were forbidden to act, their Queen was a great performer – and a lover of the pageants and other spectacles which variously portrayed her as Deborah or Judith, Diana or Cynthia, Gloriana or Belphoebe. She even went 'on tour', both as actress and audience, displaying herself to her people on those politic royal 'progresses', while her aristocratic hosts hoped to delight her with lavish entertainments – of which Leicester's nineteen-day wonder, the *Princely Pleasures* at Kenilworth in 1575, was the longest and most magnificent. But for the rest of the time she preferred men of wealth and influence to remain in London, within the ambit of the Court, where she could keep her eye on them, while teasing compliments for her latest regal-virginal pose.

LONDON'S THEATRE DISTRICTS

For ordinary people in the provinces, theatricality was becoming a matter less of regular participation, more of occasional visitation. The independent civic drama having been extinguished along with the mystery cycles, puritan pressures were mounting against the humbler folk celebration of holy days and seasonal festivals: thus, it is typical of the tensions (and class-alignments) of the time that Leicester allowed the local Hocktide play to be included among the festivities at Kenilworth, although the neighbouring clergy had been busily engaged in suppressing it. Even touring by professional players, though still an expedient for companies of lesser repute (and an economic necessity for all in times of plague), was often discouraged by the authorities, who in due course proceeded from bribing the actors *not* to perform to outright prohibition. And so, perforce, our history

Late-Elizabethan view of London from Westminster to the Tower, published in 1588 in William Smith's *A Particular Description of England*. The aerial viewpoint from south of the Thames gives prominence to the 'entertainments district' of Bankside, but although the first of the playhouses there, the Rose, had been erected in the previous year, the map shows only the bull- and bear-baiting arenas (in the foreground, slightly left of centre). To the north of the arenas looms old St Paul's, and not far eastwards lies St Saviour's church, now Southwark Cathedral, at the foot of London Bridge

Financing the Elizabethan theatre

The open-air 'public' playhouse, permanent and purpose-built, was the single innovation without which the so-called 'golden age' of the Elizabethan drama could scarcely have occurred. But its existence was not only dependent, as we have stressed, upon the relative security of the companies who had secured noble patronage. It also depended upon those companies being so organized that the members who had taken the financial risks should receive their appropriate share of the rewards – a matter, that is, of 'capital outlay' and 'returns upon investment', entirely consonant with the emerging capitalist spirit of the times.

When one man put up the money to build a theatre, as did Francis Langley for the Swan, he had a relationship with its occupants similar to that between landlord and tenant. But Philip Henslowe, who was notably in his close yet ultimately independent relationship with the Lord Admiral's Men at the Rose, acted rather as that company's 'banker', lending money for advances to playwrights, for the purchase of costumes, and even to players in personal difficulties, as well as receiving his landlord's share of the profits (calculated as a half-share in the takings from the galleries). He also seems to have had a share in certain plays, thrown in , in effect, with the lease of a playhouse to the company occupying it.

Henslowe's so-called 'Diaries', a record of these and other dealings with the theatres under his control, have survived for the years from 1592 to 1603, and afford fascinating insights not only into theatrical affairs, but also into his casual handling (probably typical of the times) of book-keeping and other financial matters. Recent studies have rather redeemed his reputation: although once scorned as an ignorant and grasping opportunist, he is now held to have combined good intentions towards his company and a relatively easy-going attitude to his creditors with a pragmatic determination that he and his family should prosper. They did.

begins to focus on London – already the centre of the nation's political and economic life, and now extending its magnetic pull into the social and artistic sphere.

So far as the theatre was concerned, not only were the largest audiences to be found in the ever-growing metropolis, but the sympathetic presence of the Court at Westminster counterbalanced opposition to the players within the square mile of the City. So it was that, fortified by the new security enjoyed by authorized companies, James Burbage chose in 1576 to locate his Theatre safely beyond the city walls, in the northern suburb of Shoreditch – where, within a few months and a few streets, a second speculative enterprise, the Curtain, had also opened its doors.

Plots, 'parts', and styles of acting

Ownership of a play was vested in the company, not the playwright, who sold his property outright. To avoid the poaching of popular plays by competitors, it was, therefore, in a company's interest to restrict the number of written or printed copies in circulation. Usually, just a single 'book' of each play was entrusted to the company's 'book-keeper', the official responsible for obtaining the necessary licence for its performance from the Master of the Revels, and for preparing each actor's 'part' – literally, no more than a set of his own lines, along with brief cues. His duty it also was to post backstage an outline 'plot'. This was a practical rather than descriptive document, as the rare specimen reproduced alongside affirms.

The actor thus had to learn his 'part' with only the playwright's customary reading to the company as a guide to its context and purpose. He needed, moreover, to hold a large number of such 'parts' in his head, for he might be called on to perform any one of them at short notice. He accordingly had to develop a 'line' of roles, suited to his talents and temperament – as it might be, hero, foil or hero's confidant, young man or lover, aged king or counsellor, villain, and of course clown. If he left the company or died

in harness, his replacement would thus need to take over in toto his particular 'line' of 'parts'.

With a rapid turnover of plays, and what must have been very limited rehearsal time, shorthand ways of conveying relationships, feelings, and states of mind must have been prominent among the acting conventions employed: but we need to remember that audiences had no expectation of psychological realism, or of 'development' in characters who, according to contemporary views of artistic 'decorum', were not expected to be strongly individualized, but typical or 'appropriate' to their class and kind.

Despite much earnest scholarly debate, there is insufficient evidence concerning Elizabethan acting style for any theory to amount to more than intelligent guesswork. But, at the very least, great virtuosity must have been required, if one compares, say, the swathes of extended speechifying in Kyd's The Spanish Tragedy with the quick idiomatic exchanges of Dekker's The Shoemaker's Holiday – or contrasts the out-front rhetoric and formal pace of Marlowe's Tamburlaine and Doctor Faustus with the conversational vigour and ready modulation of the same writer's Edward II and The Jew of Malta.

Perhaps significantly, the word 'acting' was originally used to describe the gestic component of the orator's art, and, at least in the early part of the period under discussion, the characters would probably have been 'presented' rhetorically rather than 'represented' dramatically. But around the turn of the century a new word was coined, 'personation', perhaps to describe the more subtle approach now required, in particular, for Shakespeare's plays – thus distinguishing Richard Burbage's 'natural' style from Alleyn's necessarily more 'presentational' way of playing the great Marlovian heroes.

One of seven surviving 'plots' (or, as here, 'platts') – the brief, functional summaries made by the book-keeper from the prompt-copy for the use of the actors and tireman backstage. This is the 'plot' for *The Second Part of the Seven Deadly Sins*, possibly by Richard Tarlton, as revived by Strange's Men, c. 1590. Note the square hole between the columns, where the card-mounted document was hung on a peg – also the casual way in which characters are referred to sometimes by their own, sometimes by their actor's name. 'R. Burbadg' thus accompanies King Gorboduc on his entrance in dumb-show

Whether or not the Theatre was the first permanent Elizabethan public playhouse (the claim of the Red Lion in Stepney to that distinction, in 1567, having recently been advanced), it was the first to house a resident acting company of distinction – a company which in the event was to survive all vicissitudes of plague and fortune until the closure of the theatres by the puritans in 1642.

James Burbage expired along with his lease in 1597, and two years later his son Richard and the company of Chamberlain's Men, by now including Shakespeare, made their legendary journey over the Thames, to recycle the timbers of the Theatre in the building of the first Globe on Bankside. Here, in 'the borough' of Southwark clustered around the southern end of London Bridge (still the only permanent river crossing), the 'liberties' were subject to the negligible jurisdiction of the Bishop of Winchester, whose other tenants included the proprietors of the bear- and bull-baiting arenas, glimpsed in the map on pages 70–1, and the brothels or 'stews' whose transpontine temptations had been on offer intermittently since Roman times.

The open-air playhouses remained closely linked with the 'sport' of torturing animals, and we may measure the confidence of their proprietors by their caution in making provision for this alternative amusement. Thus, when Philip Henslowe built the first of the Bankside theatres, the Rose, around 1587, he probably followed the example of the Theatre and the Curtain in making it adaptable to bear-baiting: but scholars believe that when, in 1592, he carried out extensive alterations to the Rose, he no longer needed to provide for such a contingency – so, as the excavations of 1989 (illustrated on page 88) appear to confirm, a permanent roofed stage now replaced a removable one supported on barrels or trestles. The capacity of the theatre was also increased, conjecturally from just under 2,000 to around 2,400 – as compared with the 3,000 or so spectators allegedly able to crowd into the Swan, built in 1592 by Francis Langley a little to the west of the Rose, and intended to function exclusively as a playhouse from the first.

Henslowe's own next enterprise, the Fortune – opened in 1600 beyond the northern boundaries of the City in Finsbury, perhaps to avoid the stronger competition on Bankside – was also built for use solely as a playhouse, as was the second Globe, on which work began in 1612 when pyrotechnics during a performance of Shakespeare's *Henry VIII* led to the old theatre's destruction by fire. But when, just two years later, the Hope presented *Bartholomew Fair* as its opening production, Jonson made a joke of the audience's leftover apples being saved as snacks for the bears. This playhouse was, in fact, built on the site of the old Bear Garden on Bankside, into which the wily Henslowe had already diversified his interests, securing a virtual monopoly over the 'sport'.

The Hope was the last new open-air theatre – or 'public' or 'common' playhouse, as the type was variously described – although the Fortune was rebuilt after a fire in 1623. As early as 1596 the elder Burbage had constructed at Blackfriars the first 'private' or indoor theatre intended for adult players – prematurely as it transpired,

Richard Burbage (c. 1569–1619) was leading actor with the Lord Chamberlain's (later King's) Men from 1594 until his death. The creator of such Shakespearean roles as Richard III, Hamlet, Othello, and King Lear, he was also known for his Hieronimo in Kyd's *The Spanish Tragedy* (the central character, of not dissimilar bearing, in the title-page woodcut on page 77). Whether or not the above is a self-portrait, Burbage was also known for his artistic skills, and later in his career is known to have been a scene-painter

since the actors were unable to take possession until well into the next reign. But such 'private' theatres, to which we shall turn our attention in the next chapter, then came quickly into their own, and the actors eventually deserted the Hope, pursued by bears.

It is not now fashionable to allow a direct descent of the open-air theatres from inn yards, such as those of the Bell and the Cross Keys in Gracechurch Street, the Bull in Bishopsgate, and the Bel Savage near Ludgate Circus, in which various companies undoubtedly performed. But it is none the less clear that at least two important theatres of the period, the Boar's Head in Whitechapel and the long-surviving Red Bull in Clerkenwell, were fully-fledged conversions of inns. The Red Bull did not become a playhouse until 1604, and was thereafter notorious for its rowdy audiences: but it outlived many of the other public theatres, even staging drolls during the Commonwealth closure. We shall return to it in later chapters.

THE PLAYERS AND THEIR COMPANIES

Within the Admiral's company, there was a distinction between, on the one hand, the 'sharers' – the leading actors who divided up the expenses and profits between them – and, on the other, the 'hirelings', who received wages by the week, and the boy apprentices, who played the younger female roles. But among the Lord Chamberlain's Men, following their move to the Globe, there was a further category of 'housekeepers' – actors who were also part-investors in the playhouse itself, to whom went the landlord's share of the gallery takings.

Surely no less important than this financial advantage, however, was the complete mastery that owning their own theatre gave the Chamberlain's 'housekeepers' over their own affairs – the Privy Council and the Master of the Revels permitting. Even aside from the acting genius of the younger Burbage and the playwriting supremacy of Shakespeare, this must have been of no small account in giving them the edge in their long-standing rivalry for metropolitan supremacy with the Admiral's Men. How that rivalry came about is a long and tangled story, which I shall necessarily simplify here.

Petitioning the Earl of Leicester to renew his protection following the Act of 1572, the half-dozen players who at that time constituted his company asked him 'to retain us as your household servants and daily waiters, not that we mean to crave any further stipend or benefit at your lordship's hands but our liveries'. Thus was a typical Elizabethan fiction maintained – for not least among the middle-class objections to the players was their pretension, as liveried servants, to the style of 'gentlemen'. In fact, Shakespeare was exceptional in inheriting rank and the coat of arms that went with it – his father's armorial motto, 'Non Sans Droict', jeeringly mistranslated by Jonson in *Every Man out of His Humour* as 'Not Without Mustard'.

The College of Heralds was, indeed, not above inventing impressive genealogies for those whom the Elizabethan meritocracy elevated from the middle or even the lower classes: for 'change' was perceived as the restoration of an older and assuredly better order, affirmed by ancient precedent. As the use of coats of arms in many plays of the period testifies, Elizabethan audiences were good at 'reading' the significance of heraldic as of other emblematic devices: but for the players their livery, whose retrospective symbolism made them servants of a noble household, conferred no privilege beyond statutory protection.

When Leicester's Men were granted their patent, they were probably playing at the Cross Keys in Gracechurch Street, but a new company of Queen Elizabeth's Men, formed in 1583, was evidently so large in size as to require two such inn-yard theatres as winter quarters, the neighbouring Bell, and the Bull in Bishopsgate. During these early years many of the companies were seemingly not much clearer about their immediate aims than their longer-term ambitions – and the Queen's Men certainly formed no model for later groups, although they could claim, in the clown Richard Tarlton, a figure whom the critic Muriel Bradbrook has aptly described as 'the first actor to achieve stardom'.

The wearers of the 'Queen's livery' appear never to have been formally incorporated, but were rather creamed off from other companies – who may or may not have basked in the favour so vicariously bestowed. One of the earliest (and longest-surviving) of the actor-playwrights, Robert Wilson, thus appears to have retained his links with Leicester's troupe, among whom we first hear of him in 1572, although he was also among the founding members of Queen Elizabeth's Men. Following the death of Tarlton in 1588, the fortunes of the Queen's company went into gradual decline: lacking a permanent playing place in London, and less frequently in demand at court, they suffered obscure extinction during the following decade.

The Earl of Leicester also died in 1588, and his dispersing company possibly formed the nucleus of a troupe then being reconstructed by Henry Strange and his son Ferdinando, successive Earls of Derby. But it was as a member of Worcester's Men, whose prestige at the time was probably second only to that of the Queen's, that, in 1583, we first come across Edward Alleyn – the actor who, though of a very different calibre and character from Tarlton, was destined to take his place in popular esteem. By the end of the decade, however, Alleyn was attached to the Lord Admiral's Men – a company which had been active since 1576, and was just beginning to achieve prominence.

In 1590 the Admiral's and Strange's Men underwent a form of amalgamation, but retained their separate liveries: they played as a united troupe in London, initially at Burbage's Theatre, but went their separate ways as smaller groupings in the provinces. Then a quarrel with Burbage in 1591 took the combined company to the Rose – the start of the long and mutually profitable association between Henslowe and Alleyn, who was to become not only his leading actor but his son-in-law and successful business partner.

For two years from the summer of 1592 a severe outbreak of the plague allowed little playing in London, and this led to a further shakeout and regrouping of the

Edward Alleyn (1566–1626) created the aspiring heroes of Christopher Marlowe's plays for the Admiral's Men, whom he joined in 1587, becoming a partner in Henslowe's enterprises after marrying his daughter in 1592. His style of acting is presumed to have been more rhetorical and presentational than his great rival Burbage's. He retired early, briefly in 1597 and finally by 1604, perhaps because this style was already going out of fashion – but also to concentrate on his interests in the entertainments business, which continued to flourish. The portrait below seems, indeed, intended to suggest a prosperous City father rather than an actor

companies. At first, when the plague began to abate in 1594, a consolidated company of Admiral's Men played in an obscure theatre in Newington Butts, alternating with a newly-formed troupe of Lord Chamberlain's Men, drawn from the old Strange's company: soon afterwards, the Admiral's were able to return to the Rose, and the Chamberlain's established their own base at the Theatre.

The clown Will Kemp was among the numerous Chamberlain's actors drawn from Strange's Men, as also conjecturally was Richard Burbage – but Shakespeare may well have come to the Chamberlain's from a broken company of Pembroke's Men, which seems to have been leading a troubled existence, mainly on tour, in the previous few years. Although Pembroke's had several of Shakespeare's earliest plays registered to their ownership, his earliest tragedy, *Titus Andronicus* – hugely popular in its own time though neglected in ours – passed through the hands of no less than three companies, from Strange's to Pembroke's, and thence to a group of Sussex's Men also found playing at the Rose in 1594. The drawing of characters from this play on page 81 is our only surviving visual evidence of how Elizabethan actors may have been positioned and costumed on stage.

When, in 1597, Francis Langley allowed a revived Pembroke's company to stage the 'seditious' *Isle of Dogs* at the Swan, this led not only to the imprisonment of the young Ben Jonson, one of its authors, but to the virtual eclipse of the playhouse itself. For the affair coincided with a proclamation by the Privy Council that *all* the London theatres should be destroyed – an order of obscure intent which, thankfully, was never carried out, but which resulted in the formalizing thereafter of a duopoly of the Admiral's and Chamberlain's Men. There followed a period of relative stability, until a new company of Worcester's Men, first authorized to occupy the Red Bull, began playing at the Rose in 1602 following the removal of the Admiral's Men to the Fortune. The subsequent history of these three surviving companies belongs to the following reign, and so to the following chapter.

During the later 1590s, the Admiral's company, whose work at the time is well-documented, thanks to Philip Henslowe's papers (the so-called 'Diaries' described on page 71), gave six afternoon performances each week during seasons which, in favourable circumstances, ran for over forty weeks of the year, the five weeks of Lent among those excepted. Not least because a stock of favourite pieces for revival could only be developed gradually, the appetite for new work was almost insatiable: and, out of the thirty to forty plays performed annually in the company's rough-and-ready repertoire, around half were new.

THE UNIVERSITY WITS

The demand for new plays supplied new playwrights, not least from among the younger and educated men looking for a congenial profession, who had perhaps served an informal apprenticeship in other kinds of literary hackwork. Among the 'university wits', as they were at first rather disparagingly dubbed by the players, the eldest, John Lyly, had already popularized the elaborate 'Euphuistic' prose style,

The Spanish Tragedie:

OR,

Hieronimo is mad againe.

Containing the lamentable end of *Don Horatio*, and
Belimperia ; with the pittifull death of *Hieronimo*.

Newly corrected, amended, and enlarged with new
Additions of the *Painters* part, and others, as
it hath of late been diuers times acted.

LONDON,
Printed by W. White, for I. White and T. Langley,
and are to be sold at their Shop ouer against the
Sarazens head without New-gate. 1615.

The Spanish Tragedy by
Thomas Kyd was among the
most popular of Elizabethan
plays: possibly written as early
as 1587, it first appeared in
print in 1592. On the left of
this woodcut on the title page
of the 1615 edition, the
revenger, Hieronimo, discovers
his son Horatio hanged (as his
'speech bubble' declares). On
the right (in an incident which
actually takes place slightly
earlier), the Duke's daughter
Belimperia is calling for
Hieronimo's help as the
murder is carried out – one
of the murderers, masked as
shown here, being her own
brother. Although the woodcut
makes no attempt to suggest
a stage performance, the contemporary costuming would
have reflected stage practice,
and the 'arbour' on which
Horatio hangs may have been
a stock property

adopted also by Thomas Lodge in his romance *Rosalynde*; and Thomas Nashe and
Robert Greene, who both experimented in what would eventually become the
novel form, were also notorious pamphleteers – in which role, incidentally, they
scorned such of their contemporaries as Kyd and Shakespeare, who lacked a university education.

   Greene, nevertheless, established a style of romantic comedy which Shakespeare
did not scorn to follow, while Lodge's *Rosalynde* became a source for Shakespeare's

Christopher Marlowe was born in 1564, the same year as Shakespeare – and when he was murdered in 1593 his theatrical career was arguably the more flourishing of the two. He had already created the 'over-reaching' roles – Tamburlaine, Faustus, Barabas – which Alleyn made his own, as well as personalizing the chronicle form in *Edward II.* Whether or not he was 'guilty' as accused of atheism, blasphemy, and sodomy (he was probably a government spy as well), his writings show him to have been a serious scholar and a hard-working craftsman-poet

As You Like It. Among the other members of this loosely-knit group, George Peele was an early exponent of dramatic pastoral, and Christopher Marlowe a pioneer of what was to become the distinctive dramatic idiom of the age – the unrhymed iambic pentameter, better known to us as 'blank verse'. This measure had been used by the poet Surrey for his translation of Virgil as long ago as 1557, and in 1561 was given a first, rather leaden theatrical tryout in Sackville and Norton's *Gorboduc.*

When, in 1587, Marlowe famously derided the 'jigging veins of rhyming mother wits' in the prologue to *Tamburlaine,* he was, then, quite possibly delivering not so much a manifesto in favour of unrhymed iambics as a piece of knocking copy on behalf of the Admiral's Men (who performed the play) against their rival author and actor from the Queen's, Robert Tarlton. However, the immediate success (as betokened by an almost instant sequel) of what Jonson later (maybe with irony aforethought) called Marlowe's 'mighty line' in *Tamburlaine,* together with the nearly simultaneous popularity of Kyd's blank-verse *Spanish Tragedy,* demonstrated the theatrical viability of the medium: and, over the next half-century, the range and flexibility of blank verse increased while its full expressive, rhetorical, and ironic potential came to be explored.

What, increasingly, was missing was the old religious impulse. Marlowe's *Doctor Faustus* proved to be the last play explicitly to show good and evil contending for the soul of a man, and even while it was being written, around the turn of the 1590s, Paul's Boys suffered temporary extinction, perhaps because John Lyly had tried to involve the company in counter-propaganda against the pseudonymous puritan pamphleteer 'Martin Marprelate'. No doubt the secular slant of the new drama was in part self-protection from official diapproval of such involvement: arguably, at least, it reflected also the simple fact that religion was now no longer so central to men's lives. Catholics and puritans might deplore this in the strength of their opposing faiths, but the 'middle way' of the Elizabethan settlement had proved so successful not least *because* it was a doctrinal patchwork – a comfortable and all-embracing cloak for those who were beginning to think more of man's place in this world than of his hopes for the next.

COMEDIES, HISTORIES, AND TRAGEDIES

What Marlowe did for tragedy in verse, John Lyly began to do for comedy in prose: but whereas Marlowe was working with and for the public theatre and adult actors, Lyly's use of boy players before courtly audiences was inbred as well as ingenious. Sexual confusions are exploited, even relished, as are the stylistic convolutions with which Lyly enlivens the old debate format – ironically aware as he is that courtly expectations seldom mesh with worldly realities. Unfamiliarly for us, his characters need to be viewed prismatically rather than developmentally, and his actions are often more emblematic than dramatic: but alike in his metalinguistic relish and his line of bantering romantic byplay – taken up by Shakespeare among others – he is quintessentially Elizabethan.

Both Lyly and Greene continued to exploit the theatrical self-awareness of the interlude, whether in Lyly's nudging reminders of the youth and confused sexual identities of the boy players for whom he wrote, or in the wider, metatheatrical framework within which Greene set his *James IV*. Indeed, theatrical self-awareness was a recurrent motif, whether in the final, fatal masque of *The Spanish Tragedy* (as in many more of its 'revenge play' moulds), in the many 'inductions' where actors played themselves or members of their audience, or in the 'play-within-the-play' – as used by Shakespeare for comic purposes in *The Taming of the Shrew* and in *A Midsummer Night's Dream*, and for tragic in *Hamlet*.

When Polonius commends the visiting company in *Hamlet* as 'the best actors in the world, either for tragedy, comedy, history, pastoral, pastoral-comical, historical-pastoral, tragical-historical, tragical-comical-historical-pastoral', his catalogue suggests aptly enough that most Elizabethan dramatists were unconcerned about such hybridizing of genres. But a conflicting urge to regularity is reflected in the very title of Shakespeare's posthumously collected works – not the 'First Folio', as later scholars distinguished it, but his *Comedies, Histories, and Tragedies*. And into one of those slots his first editors (two of his fellow-actors) duly fitted every play, with the proper exception of *Troilus and Cressida*. An educated self-consciousness about classical proprieties thus rubbed shoulders with a practical awareness of what worked on stage – and what an audience wanted.

Sir Philip Sidney, whose *Apology for Poetry*, published posthumously in 1595, is the major critical credo of the period, thus deplored the slapdash way in which English playwrights not only bred bastard genres such as tragi-comedy, but ignored the neoclassical 'unities' of time, place, and action. And so, with Ben Jonson as the sturdiest exception, largely and happily they did – though Shakespeare, at the beginning of his career in *The Comedy of Errors*, and at the very end in *The Tempest*, revealed both the possibilities and, some would say, the limitations of the 'rules'.

As it developed, late Elizabethan comedy tended to follow one of two strains. Mirth is secondary to matchmaking in Shakespeare's romantic kind, which is usually set in some never-never Illyria or Bohemia without benefit of geography, and often prescribes a pastoral sojourn (in Arden, perhaps, or 'a wood' near ancient Athens) as therapy for characters whose problems only exceptionally include a lack of money. For the more cussed inhabitants of Jonson's satiric comedy, money tends to outweigh love as chief motive-force: but there is, despite the didactic intent, a far higher laughter quotient, and the urban settings are rich in local colour. The comedies of Shakespeare would thus have pleased Sidney for arousing 'delight' rather than laughter – 'only a scornful tickling', rumbled the critic – whereas Jonson better answered Sidney's call correctively to ridicule 'the common errors of life'.

Of course such categories are too neat. Dramatists such as Peele and Lyly were already mixing a good deal of high jinks into their romances, while others, such as Thomas Heywood and Dekker, acknowledged that even romance might have a recognizably local habitation – not to mention an economic imperative. And George

COMEDIES,
HISTORIES, &
TRAGEDIES.

Published according to the True Originall Copies.

L O N D O N
Printed by Isaac Iaggard, and Ed. Blount. 1623.

Title-page of the first collected edition of Shakespeare's plays, published in 1623, seven years after his death, and known from its ample dimensions as the 'First Folio'. Its editors, Shakespeare's former fellow-actors John Heminge and Henry Condell, retrieved for posterity no less than half of his dramatic output, since of the thirty-six plays in the Folio only eighteen had already been published individually in the smaller, sometimes unauthorized 'quarto' format. The title emphasizes the division of the plays according to their genres

Elizabethan politics and the stage histories

As a distinct genre, the history or 'chronicle' form, although arguably anticipated by Bale and Gorboduc, began to crystallize in the late 1580s, in an ever-lengthening procession of medieval monarchs which included the anonymous two-part Troublesome Reign of King John, an unhappy Edward I from Peele, and Shakespeare's first history trilogy, Henry VI – while in the Edward II of Marlowe and the Richard III of Shakespeare the past was personalized and politicized in new and mutually challenging ways. Other historical figures given eponymous dignity included Jack Straw and Sir Thomas More – a fragment of whose multi-authored manuscript is reputedly in the hand of Shakespeare himself.

To the Elizabethan official mind, history was not understood as a disciplined study of the nature of the past – that, if anything, was antiquarianism: rather, it was a cautionary 'mirror for magistrates', and a means of demonstrating the rightful authority of present rulers. So when Tudor historians perpetuated the 'Tudor myth' – whereby the dynasty was presented as redeeming the nation from its guilt for the regicide of Richard II – this was not understood as a biased alternative to some other, more 'objective' version. Simply, it was what history was for.

The chronicle play, as further developed by writers from Shakespeare to Thomas Heywood, could, then, do no other than dramatize the 'official' version of events in its surface narrative – especially since the vogue for the genre in the late 1580s and throughout the 1590s reflected a chauvinistic response to the continuing war with Spain, which itself concealed the social and economic fissures caused by Elizabethan domestic policy, disastrous harvests, and worldwide inflation.

The mood is probably best captured in the high-patriotic reading of Shakespeare's Henry V – though even here 'official' history is constantly undercut, not least by the chronic reluctance of the crew from Eastcheap to be rallied to the breach.

At issue, as throughout Shakespeare's second tetralogy, is not, as some critics insist, the conflict between a hierarchical world order – the 'great chain of being' – inherited from the Middle Ages, and the forces making for its disintegration. On the contrary: the 'divine right of kings' (on which Shakespeare's Richard II so haplessly leans) was little asserted by actual medieval monarchs – but much called in aid by weak Mediterranean princelings of the Renaissance, who sought (as did Elizabethan actors of their liveries) a veil of antiquity to authenticate their power.

The matter of 'killing the king', a recurring theme in the historical sequence of plays from Marlowe's Edward II to Shakespeare's Richard III, thus brought false precedent into conflict with dangerous precedent: a clash of pragmatisms. And the issue remained potentially explosive, even before the Stuarts – the most fervent supporters of divine right – gave regicide a new cause, and eventually a new victim. When, in 1601, Essex contemplated, in effect, 'killing the queen', his supporters thus paid the Chamberlain's Men to perform Richard II the day before the abortive rebellion. No wonder Elizabeth continued to ban the scene of Richard's reluctant abdication – and no wonder that the chronicle genre was little exploited by playwrights under the Stuarts. The corrupt Italianate courts of Jacobean tragedy were to hold up a different kind of distorting mirror to that new breed of magistrates.

Chapman, while in spirit close to Jonson, was an even sterner classicist in his handling of plot, yet the more romantic in underlying mood. It remains true, however, that, if Jonson could not and would not have written *As You Like It* or *Twelfth Night*, no more could Shakespeare have created the characters or stage worlds of *The Alchemist* or *Bartholomew Fair*. Since tragedy gets by far the greater share of critical attention today, it's useful, too, to be reminded that comedies outnumbered tragedies by about three to one at this time – though calculations are confused by the difficulty of deciding whether, say, Shakespeare's *Richard III* should count as the tragedy it declared itself on its first title-page, or among the 'histories' where the Folio places it.

The most discursive of genres, the Elizabethan history play at one level sustained the tradition of story-telling theatre – indeed, 'history' continued to be used during this period in the same sense as 'story'. And in this respect it is significant that the two parts of Shakespeare's *Henry IV* range more widely through the classes and professions, the towns and the countryside, of his native land than his comedies or tragedies ever do.

Ironically, plays like *Richard II* and *Richard III* were, by Sidney's standards, purer tragedies than most of those unambiguously so described: for they contained (if

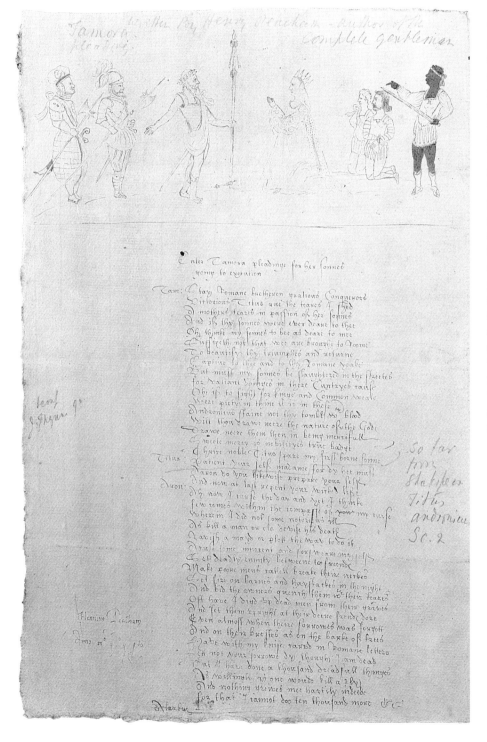

The only extant contemporary drawing of Elizabethan actors in performance, showing a scene from Shakespeare's early tragedy, *Titus Andronicus*. Tamora and two of her three sons, kneeling, are pleading for the life of her third son with Titus, who is standing with two soldiers on the left. Tamora's servant, Aaron the Moor, stands with drawn sword on the right. Scholars disagree over whether this is an authentic or imaginative reconstruction of actors in performance: possibly, in view of Aaron's curiously aggressive stance, aspects from different scenes have been deliberately conflated. The signature 'Henricus Peacham' identifies the writer of the text below, which is taken from the first and last acts of the play, and dated 1595 or 1599

Richard Gloucester's own vice-like ancestry be excepted) no clown or comic under-tow to bastardize the genre – or, as we might rather feel, to provide a telling counter-point. Many critics question whether Marlowe himself wrote the comic scenes of *Faustus*, and the textual history of the play is confessedly complicated. Yet, in truth, not only can these scenes be explicated as dramatizing the dross to be expected of a bargain with the Devil, but structurally as 'placing' the play within the less restrictive generic boundaries of the medieval tradition, with which it has so many other affinities. *The Jew of Malta*, in its very different way, also works best without being circumscribed as 'a tragedy' but given at times its farcical head.

The tragedies written during Elizabeth's declining years were, then, still tentative in their exploration of a form that had ill-suited the medieval temper. Most self-confident are the Senecan variety (Kyd's *Spanish Tragedy* their archetype), in which murder, after due delay, is avenged by much shedding of blood. But that a closet writer from Imperial Rome should have had so prevalent an influence itself suggests the poverty of accessible antecedents. Shakespeare's early *Titus Andronicus* falls into the neo-Senecan style, but *Romeo and Juliet* could equally well be a romantic comedy on the lines of *A Midsummer Night's Dream* until it is given formal

Richard Tarlton is best remembered as clown with the Queen's company from its founding in 1583 until his death in 1588. This drawing accompanies an elegy on his death, and may be compared with a slightly later description of him as 'attired in russet, with a buttoned cap on his head, a great bag by his side, and a strong bat in his hand'. Other references confirm the flat nose and squint – as also the tabor and pipe – here portrayed. He has been claimed as the original of Yorick in *Hamlet* – and was probably the author of *The Seven Deadly Sins*, whose 'plot' appears on page 72

Will Kemp, successor to Tarlton as best-loved clown of his times, joined the Chamberlain's Men in 1594, and is named in the First Folio as one of the 'principal actors' in Shakespeare's plays. A stage direction in the 1600 Quarto of *Much Ado* names him instead of Dogberry, his character: but by then Kemp had left the company, to dance his famous jig from London to Norwich, accompanied by his tabor player, Thomas Sly. Both appear in this woodcut from the title page of his account of the event, *Kemp's Nine Days Wonder*

direction by Mercutio's death. And Shakespeare's other tragedy of the 1590s, *Julius Caesar*, is as much Roman chronicle play as tragedy.

The failure (or theatrical repudiation) of religious faith now sets on their inexorable course towards destruction characters who, despite their sins, would have found repentance and salvation in the old moral interludes. And the ghosts who call for revenge from *The Spanish Tragedy* to *Hamlet* and beyond, from a purgatory which protestantism had technically abolished, are harbingers of an after-life unredeemed by predestination. It's as if tragedy needed the jolt into harsher Jacobean realities to make more sense of the conflicts that only death could resolve. *Hamlet*, which is usually dated 1601, was thus written on the cusp between two reigns – just as the play itself falls between two worlds. It took Shakespeare to transmute the uncertainty of direction of Elizabethan tragedy into its very essence, the eternally ambiguous tragic hero.

JIGS AND MASQUES

The tragedy was followed by the jig – or so Thomas Platter, a German tourist in London, reported of a visit to *Julius Caesar* at the Globe in 1599. And a little later, in 1613, Thomas Dekker, who should have known, affirmed that jigs were 'often seen after the finishing of some worthy tragedy'. Tarlton's formalizing of the jig from a vague species of bucolic song and dance, popular in village pastimes and itinerant performance, into a speciality playlet with the clown as protagonist had effectively converted a rustic farce into an urban afterpiece, which became highly popular with the groundlings.

The jig remained the special province of the clown, with the solo dance still among its many forms – as in Will Kemp's nine days' jig to Norwich, described above (the jig as jog, so to say). But, perhaps because so few scripts have come down to us, its prevalence also as an afterpiece remains one of the most widely ignored aspects of Elizabethan public theatre practice. It suggests a tantalizing analogy with the Ancient Greek tradition of following up each trilogy of tragedies with a satyr play: and those critics who, scrutinizing Aristotle, like to debate the cathartic effects of tragedy might do well to consider the effects of the jig upon the death of the hero.

If the jig had its roots in the country – the real, workaday country, not the cosy idyll of pastoral – so too, ironically, did the masque, now set to become the most elitist and allegorical form of courtly entertainment. But during the 1590s the 'Masque of the Nine Worthies' in Shakespeare's *Love's Labour's Lost* was still making metatheatrical use of the rustic and unsophisticated Elizabethan variety. What became of it was largely a development of the following reign.

PLAYWRITING AS A CAREER

Shakespeare, as we have seen, was and for long remained an actor as well as a playwright, intimately concerned with the affairs of his company, just as (in the absence of that distinctly modern intermediary, the director) he must have been closely involved with the rehearsal and staging of his own plays. But as his reputation grew more valuable to the company, he was no doubt able to choose roles which did not make too many demands on his writing time – whence the legend that he preferred small but memorable parts, such as that of the Ghost in *Hamlet*.

As what we would call a 'resident dramatist' with the Chamberlain's Men – their 'ordinary poet' in the parlance of the times – he would have been expected to produce a certain number of plays each year. The single extant contract with such a dramatist, though of a rather later date, stipulates two: so it may not be insignificant that in a playwriting career of more or less eighteen years (making due allowance for the plague), Shakespeare wrote more or less twice that number of plays.

At the other extreme, Thomas Heywood, who was in many ways a typical journeyman dramatist of the time, claimed towards the end of his long career (which spanned nearly half a century to the very brink of the closure of the theatres in 1642) to have had 'either an entire hand or at least main finger' in the writing of 220 plays – the most prolific *oeuvre* even of those lavishly productive days. There seems no reason to dispute his claim (significantly, nobody seems to have done so at the time) – for, while only some two dozen of his plays survive, this tells us more about the typical Elizabethan dramatist's casual attitude to the publishing of his work than about the true extent of Heywood's output. Indeed, as he declared: 'It never was any great ambition in me to be in this kind voluminously read.'

This reminds us that Shakespeare, although scrupulous in preparing for publication the verse with which he occupied himself in plague time, showed no concern to get his plays into print, and that half of his work would have been lost had others shared that disinterest. Even the busy Heywood took time to praise the printers for their helpfulness in according him 'all the rights of the press' over his prose polemic, *An Apology for Actors* (1612). But plays, unlike poems and pamphlets, were meant to be staged, not read.

John Webster, not a very prolific playwright, paid Heywood a back-handed compliment in his preface to *The White Devil* by bracketing him with Dekker and Shakespeare for their 'right copious industry'. Much of this Heywood exerted, at the peak of his career in the following reign, for the Red Bull – a theatre of ill repute, on whose lack of an 'understanding auditory' Webster blamed the failure of his own play. But in writing more to its tastes, Heywood evidently did not feel himself to be 'writing down'.

Heywood was a writer who could turn his pen to follow any fashionable taste, from chronicles in the 1590s to tragi-comedies in the 1600s and even to masques under Charles I; but he could also go his own highly individual way, as in his penchant for travellers' tales such as *The Fair Maid of the West*, and in that extraordinary sequence of five dramatizations of classical legend, from *The Golden Age* to *The Iron Age*, where old Homer himself is cast as link-man. In many ways, Heywood represents the continuing strand of Elizabethanism, adapting itself to the tastes of new audiences under new monarchs, but instinctively more at home with the old.

By contrast with Heywood, a model of low-key versatility, Ben Jonson was a high-profile writer who fully succeeded only in one form, that of satirical comedy, in the regular theatre. And by contrast with Shakespeare, he always remained a freelance, at first taking commissions as and when he could – notably as a hack for Henslowe, for whom he also acted early in his career (even, some say, being employed by him to write five new passages to flesh out that old favourite, *The Spanish Tragedy*, in the form in which it was published in 1602). But Jonson later disowned most of his work from the 1590s: and despite Francis Meres' description of him as among 'our best for tragedy' as early as 1598, he himself preserved nothing in that genre before *Sejanus* in 1603.

Nor has *The Isle of Dogs*, the first of the two plays which landed him in jail, survived, though one suspects that it must have been a topical satire – not least because it involved three writers working in collaboration, often a sign of the need for speedy composition. Thus, in 1599, the lost *Page of Plymouth*, written with Dekker, was based on a recent murder trial – evidently an attempt to wring domestic tragedy out of journalistic opportunism.

However, collaboration was quite common in all kinds of plays. The theatre scholar G. E. Bentley has calculated that, if we eliminate, as of unknown authorship, 370 of the 1,500 or so plays we know at least by name between 1590 and 1642, around twenty per cent of the remainder included a contribution from more than one writer. The actual proportion may well have been higher, for Henslowe's papers suggest that only one third of the plays presented by the Admiral's and Worcester's

Men were the work of a single playwright, and he records payments for up to five writers of a single play.

The market for freelances such as Jonson expanded late in the 1590s, with the return to fashion of the children's companies. Jonson may, indeed, have preferred writing for boy actors, since the tight managerial control exerted by their masters gave him a better chance of preserving the integrity of his texts – of which (unlike most of his fellows) he was always extremely jealous. The Children of Paul's began acting again in 1599, and in the following year the Chapel boys took the new theatre at Blackfriars which the Chamberlain's had been prevented from occupying by the City authorities – the increasingly nominal status of the boy actors as royal choristers, 'rehearsing' plays for their sovereign's delectation, enabling them to evade such restrictions in their 'liberty' of Blackfriars.

Perhaps because the emotional immaturity of the boy players better fitted them for pert comment than for the expression of profound feelings, they quickly gained a reputation for satire, recruiting not only the already experienced Jonson and Dekker but the youthful Marston and Webster to add contemporaneity to their left-over repertoires – which were full of what Marston, in one of the first plays produced by Paul's, described as 'musty fopperies of antiquity'. That play was *Jack Drum's Entertainment*, in which Marston took the opportunity of satirizing Jonson for a supposed slight in *Every Man out of His Humour* – the opening shots in an enigmatic affair that became known as the 'Poetomachia', or 'war of the theatres'.

Jonson responded with *Cynthia's Revels*, now adding Dekker to his satirical targets. Since both Marston and Dekker wrote for Paul's, while Jonson was working with the Chapel Children, the war, in which all combatants fired off further theatrical volleys, was as much between rival playhouses as rival playwrights. Yet it was the adult companies who felt the severest effects of the competition from the children – as Shakespeare reminds us in *Hamlet*, where they are blamed for the players having to tour so far afield as Elsinore.

It has, indeed, been suggested that the 'war' was no more than an elaborate publicity stunt to promote the interests of all involved. Certainly, by 1604 Marston was happily dedicating *The Malcontent* to his old enemy Jonson, and, along with Chapman, collaborating with him on the satire *Eastward Ho!* – which landed Jonson in prison again for its slurs on the new King's Scottish nationality (and his notorious sale of honours). But Jonson had soon redeemed himself in royal favour, and was able for long periods under James to make a better (and more prestigious) living from feeding the appetite for court masques which he now proceeded to create.

DEATH OF A CONSUMMATE ACTRESS

In the declining years of the old Queen's reign, her own revels continued at court, and in 1601 a permanent stage was finally constructed at one of their main venues, the Banqueting Hall in the sprawling Palace of Whitehall. But with the Queen's own

Miniature by Nicholas Hilliard of Queen Elizabeth playing a lute. A characterful portrait probably dating from *c.* 1580, it is (like the portrait of her father at his harp on page 54) unusual in showing a Tudor monarch playing a musical instrument. Here, there is a double celebration – of the Queen's actual musical virtuosity, and of her power to bring harmony to the 'body politic' besides. Such significance would readily have been recognized by the Queen's contemporaries, who were no less attuned to the emblematic import of paintings than to the purposeful use of verbal and visual imagery in plays

company in terminal decline by the beginning of the 1590s, the dramatic fare was largely imported from the repertoires of the established London companies – from 1594 until 1600 almost exclusively the Admiral's and the Chamberlain's Men, although in 1601 the reborn children's companies were again employed.

For many years the playing season at court had seldom been extended beyond Twelfth Night, but in 1603 the Chamberlain's Men received their final summons on 2 February, and the Admiral's on 6 March. Less than three weeks later, the old Queen was dead – a consummate actress to the last, commanding deathbed audiences from the great officers of state, and only at the very end letting slip the final piece of the plot, as she gave her voiceless blessing to James as heir. Over the previous five years there had been an average of just six plays over the Christmas season at court: in the first season of the new reign there were to be sixteen.

From the discoveries on the Rose site, seen below, we can reconstruct with some confidence the ground plan of that theatre. Its apparent fourteen-sided perimeter confirms the assumption that the pleasing but architecturally impossible evocation of the Elizabethan playhouse in Shakespeare's 'wooden O' was a poetic 'rounding off' of buildings which were actually polygonal in design. The Fortune, exceptionally, was square – and its successor was also unusual in that, although it reverted to a polygonal plan, it was built in brick, whereas most of the outdoor playhouses were of timber-frame construction. The Swan, however, was 'built of a mass of flint stones', according to the oft-quoted description of the theatre by a Dutch visitor, Johannes de Witt.

Rather than reproducing yet again de Witt's familiar sketch of its interior (as we have it, a copy made by a friend, but still the only contemporary visual evidence we have of the appearance of an Elizabethan stage), I have preferred the isometric reconstruction drawn by Richard Leacroft opposite, which gives a three-dimensional impression derived from this and other evidence. The general characteristics of the 'public' theatres, which may be recognized from this illustration, are well enough attested: a raised rectangular stage, sheltered to some extent by a sloping roof, its underside painted to resemble the 'heavens', with a dressing room or 'tiring-house' to the rear and some form of balcony or musicians' gallery above; a more or less circular yard, surrounding the stage on three sides, and providing standing room for the 'groundlings' who had paid their pennies for admission; the whole encompassed by three tiers of galleries which formed the outer perimeter of the building, and where, for further pennies, a better view, some shelter from the elements, and even a cushioned seat might be acquired.

One of the most intriguing discoveries at the Rose site, the apparent raking of the yard floor downwards to the stage, is thought by some scholars to be evidence not of an unexpected concern for sightlines, but merely of subsidence on the marshy riverside site. And so emerges another of the many points of

controversy surrounding the Elizabethan public theatre – of which probably the longest-running concerns the nature and function of the so-called 'inner stage'. Was this a playing space of significant proportions, or merely a curtained corridor to the tiring house, convenient for 'discoveries'? And what was the position and purpose of the 'lord's room': did it face the stage, where Leacroft locates it, to give the best view to a patron or other important visitors, or immediately overlook it, thus only becoming available when action 'above' was not required?

Stage directions and properties create their own problems of interpretation. What, for example, was meant by 'passing over' the stage – a mere circuit from one tiring-house entrance to another, or a procession through the yard, with opposing stairs needed for mounting and leaving the stage? Was the 'state', the great throne called for in so many plays as emblematic of princely power, lowered from a machine-room above the 'heavens', or trundled on from the tiring-house? Even the stage posts which held up the 'heavens' suggest aesthetic as well as architectural difficulties: were they awkward obstacles, at last happily avoided in the dual-purpose Hope, or valuable adjuncts to intimacy in the actor-audience relationship – at least as convenient leaning-posts for reflective soliloquys? Here, of course, the answer is probably 'both', since the players were surely adept at utilizing even the most functional of architectural features for their own purposes.

Pillars may also have been avoided when the second Globe was built in 1614, following the destruction of the first theatre by fire in the previous year. This and other aspects of its design may well have been influenced by the wish of the King's Men, who had been playing indoors at the Blackfriars during the winter months since around 1609, to incorporate the more advantageous features of their 'private' theatre – not to mention some of the scenic requirements dramatists expected when writing for it – in their summertime venue. However, the well-known contemporary map by Hollar suggests only that the sheltering hut may have extended the full width of the auditorium.

Left: Peggy Ashcroft, one of the leaders of the campaign to preserve the foundations of the Rose theatre, rests amidst the excavations. Revealed in 1989, during work on a new office block, these provided the first physical confirmation of our assumptions concerning the ground plan of the Elizabethan public theatre. Right: isometric reconstruction of the Swan theatre, based on a sketch made by a Dutch visitor, Johannes de Witt, previously the only extant contemporary evidence as to the interior appearance of the playhouse

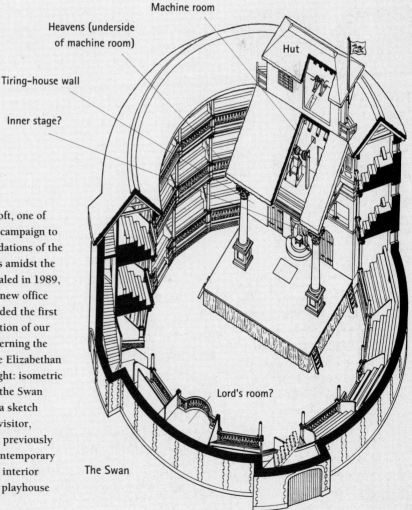

Machine room

Heavens (underside of machine room)

Hut

Tiring-house wall

Inner stage?

Lord's room?

The Swan

CHAPTER 6

The Jacobean Theatre

Despite the brief honeymoon between James I and a people thankful to have survived without strife a long-anticipated dynastic change, there was a perceptible shift in the national mood during the first few years of the new king's reign. Elizabeth, not least through her own fortuitous longevity, had come to personify stability in the religious and social order – perhaps even in the firmament itself. Ulysses in Shakespeare's *Troilus and Cressida*, written at the very end of her reign, might still proclaim his belief in the Ptolemaic order of 'degree, priority, and place': but by 1611 the poet Donne was expressing the discords of an untuned, Galilean universe, 'all in pieces, all coherence gone', while Flamineo, the anti-hero of Webster's *The White Devil*, goes not to heaven or to hell, but merely 'to study a long silence'.

Of course, Ulysses is not (as some critics can still be found to insist) Shakespeare's political spokesman, but a character in a play: his words not only contribute to a dialectic in which other speakers participate, but have to be contrasted with his own subsequent actions. And against the nihilism of Webster's Flamineo may be set his almost existential sense of a selfhood moulded by his own actions – a sense more positively asserted by the Duchess of Malfi, defiant in the face of death. Yet where only a decade earlier the drama had been expressing shared certainties and fears – the sense of emerging nationhood, say, in Shakespeare's history cycle – the triumphs were now those of individualism, the defeats endured in isolation and untempered by much spirit of community, or even faith.

That Jacobean tragedies were so often set in Italianate courts was no doubt calculated at one level to exploit their audiences' prejudices against papistry and to satisfy expectations of Machiavellian intrigue: but it spoke also of an endemic corruption that could not safely be identified nearer home. This had to do both with personality and policy. Where Elizabeth had been careful and parsimonious, James was reckless and extravagant; where she had made a cult of her own virginity, he was disarmingly brazen and openly concupiscent in his bisexuality; where she had been sparing in her patronage, and downright miserly about bestowing honours, he not only spent lavishly on his favourites but helped to subsidize his flamboyant tastes by putting knighthoods up for sale – and, having devalued those, proceeding to coin baronetcies for ready money.

The change of mood thus precipitated was clear and distinctive. If Elizabeth's studied equivocations had pent up change, James's self-righteousness and ineptitude now gave it added impetus: and even when he acted sensibly, as in making peace with Spain, good foreign policy only made for domestic grumbling at the absence of a proper enemy.

Unpropitiously, the reign was ushered in by a severe outbreak of the plague, which claimed some 30,000 lives in London, and also led to a closure of the theatres

Opposite: the major theatres and playing places of Elizabethan and Jacobean London, clustered around the old walled City – within which only inn-yard and private theatres are to be found. The dates given indicate the year of construction (or adaptation) and of course not all the playhouses were operating at any given time

for the best part of a year from March 1603. On this occasion the leading companies were sufficiently well-established to survive more or less intact – but with changed names, for within two months of his accession James required them to obtain royal rather than merely noble patronage.

THE PLAYERS AND THEIR PATRONS

James took the Lord Chamberlain's company under his own protection as the King's Men – a mark of their acknowledged supremacy – while Queen Anne, his long-suffering wife, gave her name to Worcester's Men. The Admiral's obtained the patronage of the heir to the throne, Prince Henry – and, following his premature death in 1612, that of the Elector Palatine, then betrothed to James's daughter, the Lady Elizabeth. She, a year or so earlier, had given her own name to a company which was just beginning to make a mark at court after playing largely in the provinces – whence a fourth London company had already emerged, with the bestowal of a patent in 1610 upon a troupe led by the clown-dramatist William

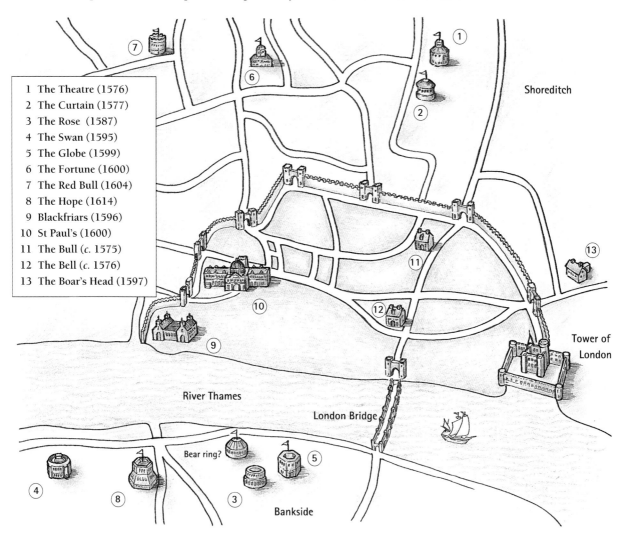

1 The Theatre (1576)
2 The Curtain (1577)
3 The Rose (1587)
4 The Swan (1595)
5 The Globe (1599)
6 The Fortune (1600)
7 The Red Bull (1604)
8 The Hope (1614)
9 Blackfriars (1596)
10 St Paul's (1600)
11 The Bull (c. 1575)
12 The Bell (c. 1576)
13 The Boar's Head (1597)

Rowley. Known briefly as the Duke of York's Men, this company came under Prince Charles's patronage when the King's younger son became his heir.

The boy players remained in fashion for a while, but an alleged abduction by the Master of the Chapel Children, Nathaniel Giles, and a succession of satires which touched too closely upon the personal and political susceptibilities of the King, caused the Children of the Queen's Revels, as Giles's company had become, first to lose its royal patronage and then, in 1608, to abandon its lease on the Blackfriars – by which time Paul's Boys had also ceased playing.

Although a revived company, established at a newly-converted theatre at Whitefriars in 1609, was soon restored to royal favour, its members were now verging upon adulthood: indeed, their leading 'boy' player, Jonson's protégé Nathan Field, was already twenty-two, and building a reputation as a competent dramatist as well as one of the leading actors of his day. In 1613 the remnants of this company joined forces with Lady Elizabeth's Men, now established in London and about to move into Henslowe's new Hope Theatre: but by 1616 Field had left them for the more prestigious roles the King's Men could offer him.

By that time, of course, the King's Men were well settled into the Blackfriars as their winter home, and would-be rivals were contemplating a similar 'move indoors'. And so, despite the opening of the Hope in 1614, and the rebuilding of the

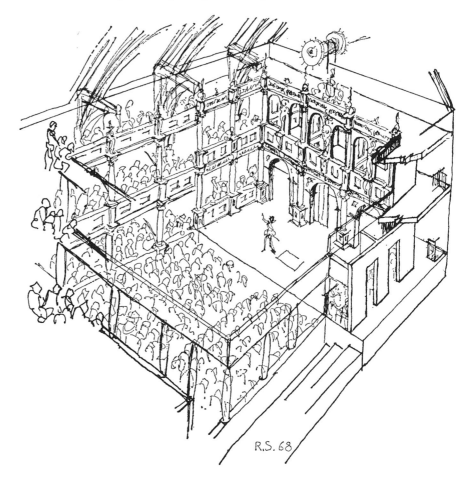

Impression by Richard Southern of the interior of the Blackfriars theatre, constructed for James Burbage in 1596, but occupied by boy players until the King's Men finally took possession around 1609. Boxes here run along both sides of the stage, which is raised above the pit area fronting it. Further tiers of boxes enclose the sides and rear of the auditorium. This drawing omits the candelabra which may have obscured the view from the boxes – the pit thus being considered the best part of the house. Note the curtained 'discovery space' – also the winding gear for flying effects

Globe and the Fortune, new theatres were increasingly planned as 'private' houses. The Cockpit – soon to be better known as the Phoenix, when it rose from the ruins of an apprentices' riot – was, however, the only indoor theatre of note to be built in James's reign: owned by Christopher Beeston, the leading entrepreneur to emerge during the period, it opened in 1616, with Queen Anne's the occupying company.

The first of the many theatres of Drury Lane, the Cockpit may or may not have been built to surviving but unattributed designs by Inigo Jones: certainly, the semi-circular auditorium envisaged by these designs suggests possible adaptation from a cockfighting arena. A few years after the King's death, the Salisbury Court, the last major theatre to be opened before the Civil Wars, was also built as an indoor playhouse: this was to survive, somewhat the worse for wear, into the Restoration, when it was reconstructed as the Dorset Garden.

INSIDE THE PRIVATE THEATRES

The received belief in a socially homogeneous Elizabethan audience – in which peers and plebeians responded with shared sensibility (though in varying degrees of comfort) to the same plays in the same buildings – has recently been called in question. However, in a London with the relatively small population of 200,000, the public theatres, with an average capacity of around 3,000, do bulk irresistibly large as evidence for a popular, broadly-based audience of some kind. The smaller capacity of the private theatres – the Blackfriars held fewer than 600 – made higher admission charges not only an economic necessity but a social deterrent, effectively pricing them beyond the reach of ordinary people.

Even the cheapest seats, in one of the two or three tiers of galleries, cost sixpence, while a further shilling was required for a share of a bench in the pit. Sixpence more would hire a stool, on which gallants and gulls alike (those who came not so much to see the play as to be seen) could perch along the sides of the end-on stage – despite popular legend, not a practice permitted in the public playhouses. No less than three contemporary illustrations, of which one is reproduced alongside, suggest that a low rail surrounded the stage, which was probably overlooked by side boxes, while some sort of 'discovery space', more functional than in the public theatres, opened off central double doors to the rear, with further doors on each side and a practical balcony 'above'.

The Blackfriars, at least, had windows which could be shuttered, offering a choice between natural and artificial illumination: but the windows at the Phoenix appear to have been designed to light the auditorium rather than the stage, while at the Banqueting House in Whitehall (designed by Inigo Jones for court performances, and opened in 1622) the ground-floor windows are known to have been boarded-up during theatrical performances. So candlelight, though dim by modern standards, may have been the norm: but the necessarily low-hanging candelabra must surely have created sight-line problems for those sitting in the galleries – perhaps the cause of the pit here becoming the most fashionable part of the house.

Vignette from the title-page of the 1632 edition of William Alabaster's tragedy *Roxana*. Unlike the stage of the Blackfriars, illustrated opposite, the stage here is apparently half-polygonal, and is fronted by rails. Members of the audience peer down from boxes in a rear gallery, below which curtains appear to stretch the full width of the stage. Although clearly out of scale and impressionistic, the basic form here is that of the 'octagon within a square' of a typical cockpit – a shape maintained (albeit to focus attention on the King rather than the actors) by Inigo Jones in his conversion of the Cockpit-in-Court, as illustrated on page 109

Among the public theatres, only the Globe continued to attract a fashionable audience – though for much of its summer season the aristocracy would have been out of town, and the students of the Inns of Court on vacation. The Red Bull and the Hope, in particular, gained reputations for rowdiness, and were mocked for their low fare – often, in reality, merely indicating their audiences' preference for the old Elizabethan favourites.

The 'coterie' audiences, who now made the private theatres their own, displayed more 'sophisticated' tastes. But from early in the reign the public theatres were trespassing upon the territory of the private: thus, in 1606 the King's Men staged a tragi-comedy which had originally been written for the boys, John Marston's *The Malcontent*, claiming that this was in retaliation for a children's company having

Jacobean clowns and comic style

Robert Armin (d. 1615)

With the new century, the King's Men had acquired a new clown – Will Kempe being succeeded by Robert Armin, for whom Shakespeare created the more reflective, sometimes even morose comic fools of As You Like It, Twelfth Night, and All's Well. And Armin's temperament was clearly more suited to the tragic variation upon the type in King Lear, with which the intimate, improvisatory genius of Tarlton and Kempe would have been mismatched.

But something had been lost, too: the older clowns spoke for and to their audiences in ways that Armin, despite his personal interest in the history of his craft, seems not to have attempted. He was, rather, the servant of the author, and now often found himself part of a comic team – Feste with Belch and Aguecheek as early in Armin's career as Twelfth Night, Caliban with Stephano and Trinculo as late in Shakespeare's as The Tempest.

But it was not, as one authority asserts, a case of 'an old-fashioned clown trading on a single personality' giving way before 'a sophisticated and versatile character actor'. One might as well claim that (say) Tony Hancock was more 'old-fashioned' or less 'sophisticated' than (say) Alec Guinness: one actor is, in truth, neither better nor worse than the other, just different – each a genius of his kind.

The Jacobean age continued to produce not only protean comic actors in the mould of Armin, but comic personalities in the tradition

NO-BODY, AND SOME-BODY.

With the true Chronicle Historie of Elydure, *who was fortunately three seuerall times crowned King of England.*

The true Coppy thereof, as it hath beene acted by the Queens Maiesties Seruants.

Printed for Iohn Trundle and are to be sold at his shop in Barbican, at the signe of No-body.

of Kempe: and one such was Thomas Greene, the clown of Queen Anne's Men. This company had moved in 1606 to the Red Bull, with Heywood as their 'ordinary poet': but it was a play of 1611 by another of their actor-dramatists, John Cooke, in which Greene's catch phrase, 'Tu quoque', came to be celebrated in

'stolen' a public theatre play – probably *The Spanish Tragedy* (than which, ironically, nothing could have been more old-fashioned). In any case, as the players in *Hamlet* attest, the adults had reasons enough to dislike the boys.

John Webster contributed additional material for the version of *The Malcontent* played at the Globe, and included an Induction which in its plentiful 'local colour' illuminates the differences between private and public theatre practice. Indeed, Webster's 'augmentations' were only necessary because plays for the children's companies were generally shorter, to allow for a preliminary musical entertainment and for further music between the acts – reminders of the *alter egos* of the boy players as choristers. Such music, as the Induction reminds us, was a 'not received custom' in the public theatres.

the very title. Characteristically of the time, Greene's character in the play, Bubble, is most dismissive about the talents of a clown – one Thomas Greene. Another famous clown, William Rowley, probably also began his career with Queen Anne's Men, but by 1609 had joined the company which was soon to become Prince Charles's, with whom he remained until moving upmarket to the King's Men in 1623. Rowley was also a prolific dramatist, usually in collaboration – at one time or another with most playwrights of his generation.

It was, however, in one of his few solo works, the tragedy All's Lost by Lust, that his own role was designated simply as 'Fat Clown', evidently an apt self-description. The scenes which fell to his share in collaborative writing normally included those in which he would also appear as clown: for example, in The Witch of Edmonton – a topical drama written in 1621 with Dekker and Ford, based on a recent trial for witchcraft – he carved out for himself the clown's role of Cuddy Banks. But Rowley's best-remembered collaboration was with Thomas Middleton on The Changeling (1622), in which he not only wrote his own scenes in the subplot, but topped and tailed the play as well, his contributions meshing intriguingly with his partner's in one of the most compelling tragedies of the age.

The woodcuts at centre left and centre right portray two comic characters – in effect, an early double-act – from a history-cum-morality play revised for Henslowe in 1602. To judge from the similarity of Nobody's costume to that in which the actor John Green was elsewhere drawn in the role, the comic attire is here correctly shown. Note the headgear characteristic of all the clowns on these two pages

Title-page of the play by John Cooke which celebrated Thomas Greene's catchphrase 'Tu quoque' ('You too!')

The neoclassical five-act structure of *The Malcontent* also distinguishes it from most plays written for the adult companies before the move indoors: indeed, many of the now-conventional act-divisions of Shakespeare's plays are no more than a notational convenience, hungover from the attempts of his eighteenth-century editors to tidy up their author. We simply do not know if and when intervals occurred in the public theatres, and although from the surviving texts it is clear that the scenic unit was more important than any act division, scenes were seldom

Playing the fair maid

The clown was not unique in his double-identity as character-type and actor. Today, the most difficult of all the character conventions of the Elizabethan and Jacobean theatre for us to assimilate is the absence of actresses in the female roles – which were numerous, often highly demanding, and of a dramatic weight and significance quite disproportionate to the actual subservience of the majority of women in society. Sadly, we know little of the actors – mature female impersonators as well as boys – who played parts as various as Shakespeare's virginal Isabella, compliant Cressida, and maturely knowing Cleopatra; as the swashbuckling Bess Bridges in Heywood's The Fair Maid of the West, the calculating, sensual, but elusive Vittoria in John Webster's The White Devil, and the casually vicious Beatrice-Joanna in Middleton and Rowley's The Changeling.

Some feminist critics have questioned whether today's actresses should attempt roles created exclusively by male playwrights for male performers: and even if one believes that they should (as in practice they generally do), we need to ask how our knowledge that the roles were written for males may affect their performance and our own response. The Jacobeans, as we have seen, were accustomed to such ambiguities of dramatic identity: but in what proportion, and in what plays were audiences responding, through their cultivation of theatrical self-awareness, to the performing skills of boy actors; and in what proportion, in what plays, through their no less ready acceptance of stage convention, to 'truly' female characters?

And how were both responses modified by the more complex, androgynous quality of multi-layered disguise – as when the boy actor playing Shakespeare's Rosalind in As You Like It disguises 'herself' as Ganymede, only to 'pretend' girlhood again in order to rehearse the techniques of courting for her lover (who, necessarily and conventionally, does not of course recognize her)? What controls were within the playwright's and the actor's armoury to manipulate so wide a spectrum of possibilities?

Title-page with woodcut of a topical play which rang yet another change – male playing mannish-female – on the varieties of transvestism in a theatre without actresses

numbered, their close being marked by the stage direction 'exeunt', indicating a complete clearance of the stage.

As a Chapel play, *The Malcontent*, in its original quarto text, not only numbers its acts and scenes, but follows the different convention for scene division employed in the private theatres (as also by Ben Jonson, in his attempt to lend neoclassical authority to all his work). In accordance with this method, a new scene in *The Malcontent* commences whenever there is a change in the composition of important characters on stage. This makes for no less than eight scenes in the first act, despite there being only two general clearances of the stage, and no apparent changes of location or other breaks in the flow of the action.

To stress this difference in convention is no mere bibliographical pedantry, since it relates to how players approached units of action – a typical Shakespearean 'scene' thus focusing on what 'develops' (and where), a Jonsonian 'scene' on an internal build-up of comic action, and a more static display of 'character'. And a Jacobean audience would probably have been more accustomed to 'character' and its modes of display as presented by Jonson – or Marston, or Middleton, or Webster – than with Shakespeare's (and Burbage's) new mode of 'personation'.

THE NATURE OF 'CHARACTER'

For example, in the set-piece which opens Tourneur's *The Revenger's Tragedy*, a duke and his family strut in procession across the stage, while the revenger Vindice (holding, after Hamlet, the *memento mori* of a skull) soliloquizes to the audience – a privileged communication, in which it is conventional to assume that he is revealing his true and heartfelt feelings. But he is also establishing the conventions of character by which the play proceeds to operate: and so, when Vindice proclaims his enemies 'four excellent characters', he is not intending an ironic reflection on their moral probity, but rather designating them perfect examples of their *types* – the ageing adulterer, the lecherous heir, the calculating stepmother, and the bastard.

Even Shakespeare, as witness Don John in *Much Ado* and Edmund in *King Lear*, did not expect bastards to behave other than according to their own 'unnatural' (or 'all-too-natural', selfishly instinctive) type: and it was the aim of most dramatists to catch not individuality but heightened typicality in their creations. Like Vindice, or Jonson's Sir Epicure Mammon in *The Alchemist*, many Jacobean characters even reflect this in their names – a convention which lingered to the very brink of naturalism in the nineteenth century.

A typical character-type of Jacobean drama, as much (or rather as little) at home in comedy as in tragedy, is the malcontent – the generalized, theatricalized version of the melancholic, whose ailment (we would get closest to it with 'depression') the age recognized as almost endemic. Jaques in *As You Like It* affects a comic melancholia, and Malvolio in *Twelfth Night* lards this with his own puritanical self-esteem, while Thersites in *Troilus and Cressida* rails against lechery and war in one of the period's least categorizable plays. More typically, the malcontent of Jacobean tragedy, such as Vindice in *The Revenger's Tragedy* or Flamineo in *The White Devil*, is a hanger-on at court, perhaps of noble birth but now impoverished: too proud or gentlemanly to work, too down-at-heel to be unemployed.

Yet in Marston's *The Malcontent*, Malevole's melancholia is a *disguise*, and his behaviour – like Hamlet's antic disposition – modifies the 'reality' of his railing against society. Richard Burbage, who had played Hamlet wearing the marks of a

Jonson at work: masques, anti-masques, shows, tilts

Jonson was unusual not only in asserting the value of plays as literature and the dignity of the playwriting profession, but also in his ability to exploit the full range of available performing media. Other writers might, like George Chapman, supplement their income from translating the classics, or, like Dekker, from writing pamphlets: but none spent so great a proportion of their careers as Jonson in 'irregular' playmaking – notably in the form which he virtually reinvented, that of the court masque. In increasingly rancorous association with Inigo Jones as his machinist and designer, Jonson transformed the masque (which even the puritanical John Milton did not despise) from a casual occasion of dressing-up and dancing into an elaborate allegorical or mythological compliment to the monarch or other noble patron.

Blending verse, music, dance, mime, and scenic splendours, and with the assembled nobility participating, the court masque, though essentially a pièce d'occasion, was to be of lasting importance in its introduction to the British theatre of the proscenium arch and its front curtain – behind which Jones would create his wonderful machines through which landscapes, mountains, castles, and artificial seas were created, or transformed one from the other, all with due attention to the illusion of perspective. And, as we shall see in the following chapter, the plays from the repertoire of the professional companies soon began also to utilize scenic effects when adapted for performance at court.

It was in The Masque of Queens, performed at the new Banqueting House in Whitehall in February 1609, that Jonson introduced (or, arguably, recovered from the mumming tradition) the 'anti-masque' – a sort of grotesque foil to the masque proper, in this case involving a dozen ugly witches

Costume sketch by Inigo Jones for Lucy, Countess of Bedford, in the role of Penthesilea in Jonson's *Masque of Queens* (1609)

malcontent, took the role of Malevole for the King's Men – but in Webster's Induction he also 'played' an actor named Burbage, who was about to play a deposed duke, Altofront, who is himself disguised as the malcontent Malevole. And at the end of the play the restored duke, who has just been 'playing' yet another character, assumed by Malevole for the climactic masque, turns out to be an actor named Burbage again, now asking for the audience's applause. The multiplicity of

from Hell, with whom the twelve gracious queens of the House of Fame might then (according to taste, and with typical Jonsonian ambiguity) either be favourably contrasted or ironically compared. As time went on, and to Jonson's personal concern, anti-masques assumed an ever increasing importance and popularity, until, in the grand climacteric masque of them all, Davenant's Salmacida Spolia, staged in the shadow of the Civil Wars in 1640, there were no less than twenty.

Ironically, the masque has been blamed for cutting off the actors from the audience, thus hastening 'the decline of the drama': yet it also united actors and audience, for not only were most of the performers courtly amateurs, but all joined hands with the spectators for the final, celebratory dance. More to the point, however, those spectators were drawn from an extremely limited social class, and the integration of masques and masque-like features into regular plays intended to appeal to the coterie audiences set these even further apart from the 'popular tradition'.

Shakespeare, though he is traditionally honoured among the 'popular' writers, also included masques or elements from them in his later plays (notably The Tempest and Henry VIII), presumably with a Blackfriars audience in mind. But Jonson himself kept his masque-writing separate from his regular comedies, in which he continued to rely on the actors' skills in repartee, comic timing, and double-take. Nor can a common moral or artistic vision be said to relate Jonson's stage comedies to the masques: thus, the masque Hymenaei, staged in 1606 to celebrate the ill-starred nuptials of Lady Frances Howard and the Earl of Essex, celebrates the married state as unequivocally as his regular comedy Epicoene three years later was to vilify its every aspect. (Ironically, another four years found Jonson duly celebrating the remarriage of Lady Frances, now divorced from Essex, to the King's favourite Robert Carr, in A Challenge at Tilt, played during the Christmas celebrations of 1613.)

Professional actors, almost always from the King's Men, were called in to play the unglamorous roles of the anti-masque, so Jonson's The Masque of Queens in 1609 provided some additional employment for the company which had presented his Volpone in 1606, and in the following year was to stage The Alchemist. And the 'boys' now playing at White-friars, Nathan Field among them, who performed Jonson's Epicoene there later in the same year, also benefited from the range of his craftsmanship when they were engaged for an entertainment which seems to have combined elements of what we would call environmental theatre with the Jacobean equivalent of a hypermarket opening.

James's hard-working Lord Treasurer, Salisbury – better remembered as Burleigh's son, the wily Robert Cecil – had used part of the gardens of Durham House, south of the Strand, which the King had confiscated from the disgraced Raleigh, to build the covered shopping precinct which came to be known as the New Exchange. But it was first dubbed 'Britain's Burse' by the King on the occasion of its opening in March 1609, and although Jonson's entertainment of that title is no longer extant, the Cecil family archives suggest that the building itself was employed as the 'stage', with a shopkeeper, his apprentice, and a key-keeper as main characters. Jonson and his designer, the inevitable Inigo Jones, both received £13 6s 8d for their labours.

Because of yet another plague-closure of the theatres in 1609, Jonson, reputedly a slow worker, could take his time over the writing of his next play, Epicoene, while planning a further royal entertainment. The investiture of the young heir as Prince of Wales (a title he was to enjoy for only two years) was to be commemorated by 'barriers' – strictly, the fencing separating the combatants in a tournament, but by then synonymous with the event itself.

The 'challenges' in this anachronistic affair were duly sent forth by Prince Henry to all the knights of the kingdom, and became part of an elaborate allegory in which the young heir adopted the name of Meliadus, mythical King of Lyonesse. For his Speeches at Prince Henry's Barriers, Jonson sustained this Arthurian motif, in the process celebrating the peace and moderation which supposedly characterized such 'golden ages' as the classical, the Arthurian – and, by implication, the Jacobean.

levels here deftly exploits that theatrical self-consciousness in which Jacobean audiences delighted, and which must surely have been reflected to a degree in styles of acting – about which, however, we have little evidence beyond what may be surmised from the texts themselves.

For example, we know that plays by certain dramatists tend to be strewn with *sententiae* – those pithy moral summations, often only a line or a rhymed couplet in length, sometimes lifted straight from the commonplace book. These were often distinguished in print by the use of italics or quotation marks: but what was the *spoken* or indeed gestic equivalent of such punctuation? Certainly, the actor here was stepping aside from his role, and may have spoken directly to his audience – but almost as authorial mouthpiece, and so in a style which would need to be distinguishable from that of the soliloquy.

As the title of *The Revenger's Tragedy* suggests, Vindice combines the character-type of the revenger with that of the malcontent: and we cannot fully understand Hamlet unless we acknowledge that he is a compound of these same types, however brilliantly individualized. Comparably, though less subtly, most of the dramatic 'characters' of the period were created by adding the slightest pinch of psychology to a veritable punchbowl of typology.

Satiric comedy, as decorum required, ridiculed those fixations or affectations which Jonson, with the barest of nods towards contemporary medical ideas, called 'humours' – as displayed by his Mammon, Morose in *Epicoene*, or Wasp in *Bartholomew Fair*. But in tragedy, too, typicality remained an aspect of personality – no less dooming Othello to be 'fixed' in his jealousy or Macbeth in his ambition than all those characters of Webster, Middleton, and Ford in the sexual and economic imperatives which drive them towards extinction.

Perhaps we need to remind ourselves that it is only since the romantic revival that special or individual characteristics have been more highly valued in art than those which are representative. Subsequently, psychology has given a semi-scientific gloss to this essentially aesthetic preference: so Jacobean characterization, which is also uncompromisingly non-naturalistic, is often wrongly regarded as being 'primitive' as well.

But other conventions which were derided in the age of the 'well-made play' – the narrative short-cuts offered by the soliloquy and the aside, for example – are now generally accepted as valid playwriting techniques. Amusingly, Shakespearean usage shunts any convention towards acceptability – even the 'bed trick', employed in *Measure for Measure* and *All's Well*, whereby one female character is secretly substituted for another between the sheets, in order to effect a desired union or avoid an unwanted one (a manoeuvre *never noticed* by the man involved). In Middleton and Rowley's *The Changeling* it takes a fire to separate the put-upon pair.

The arsonist, De Flores, is a malcontent whose lust for the unscrupulous Beatrice-Joanna is only satisfied when he agrees to murder the man to whom she is reluctantly betrothed. As a token of his success he shows her a ringed finger he has wrenched from the corpse – whose ghost eventually appears, identifying himself by the severed stump. Later, a troupe of lunatics from Rowley's sub-plot are brought on to rehearse a bizarre 'entertainment' to celebrate Beatrice-Joanna's subsequent marriage (hence the need for a maidservant's complicity in the bed trick, to avoid the discovery that Beatrice-Joanna is no longer a virgin). Scrupulous modern critics have deplored such elements of 'sensationalism' in Jacobean tragedy – the waxen corpses and bespoke coffin-making of Webster (Shaw's 'Tussaud laureate') another target for their scorn.

When, in Webster's *The Duchess of Malfi*, yet another malcontent, Bosola, is describing a stricken woman's attempt to scour away smallpox scars from her face, he declares that 'before she look'd like a nutmeg grater, after she resembled an aborted hedgehog'. Here, the visualizing of the macabre but precise image by verbal means is rightly acclaimed – yet the *theatricalizing* of just such images is decried. This is mistaken on two counts. Firstly, of course, these dramatists were writing not for the pages of some scholarly edition, but for the stage, and were able to calculate from experience the relevance and impact of visualized 'sensations': thus, even Hamlet is *seen* fondling that *memento mori* of a jester's skull and fighting over a suicide's grave.

Secondly, this was an age of close proximity to death and decay, in which the goriest of stage spectacles might be outdone on the streets outside by the agonies of a plague victim, or the sight of a traitor's head maggot-ridden on its spike at the foot of London Bridge. Unsurprisingly, the work of the Jacobean dramatists was rediscovered in our own century in the aftermath of the First World War, when even staid Oxbridge dons were haunted by memories of the slaughter and degradation of the trenches.

FROM THE RAW TO THE ROMANTIC

The play of Shakespeare's which most fully displays this 'Jacobean' rawness of sensibility is *Troilus and Cressida*, though it may even have anticipated the period by a year or two. It is no longer in critical fashion to surmise that the succession of such 'problem plays', all written around the change of reigns, indicate Shakespeare's personal unease with his life or his society, or that the great tragedies which succeeded them represent some sort of personal quest for reconciliation. Yet it is clear that he had broken the form of romantic comedy, to which after *Twelfth Night* he never returned, and that only reluctantly and belatedly did he bow to the demand for tragi-comedy – in which a serious, even tragic tone establishes expectations resolutely disappointed by a happy ending (*The Malcontent*, as we have seen, being an early example).

The romances which brought Shakespeare's career to a close proved that he *could* write in this vein if he wished, and *The Winter's Tale* is a model of the tragi-comic kind. But it was the partnership of Beaumont and Fletcher, writing tragi-comedies also for the King's Men, which by then was carrying all before it; and after 1610

John Fletcher (1579–1625), who with Shakespeare and Jonson formed 'the triumvirate of wit' in Jacobean London. Frequently a collaborative writer, in the first decade of James's reign he was largely responsible with Francis Beaumont for creating a vogue for romance and tragi-comedy, *Philaster*, *The Maid's Tragedy*, and *A King and No King* being among their joint successes. After Shakespeare's retirement, he worked with him on *Henry VIII* and *The Two Noble Kinsmen*, also following in his footsteps as 'ordinary poet' for the King's Men. Most of Fletcher's plays were written for this company – and so calculatedly adapted to the resources of the Blackfriars and to the taste of its audiences, who relished a blend of erudition, even-tempered emotion, and mild titillation. After Beaumont's marriage he most frequently worked with Philip Massinger – though *The Chances* (1617) and *The Wild-Goose Chase* (1621) are independent works, which stand up better in revival than most of his collaborations

there is a sense that Shakespeare wanted only to tie up enough artistic and economic loose-ends to get back to his beloved Stratford and a comfortable retirement. Beaumont, too, happily abandoned playwriting as soon as a good match enabled him to do so: but Fletcher carried on, even collaborating with Shakespeare before taking over as 'ordinary poet' for the King's Men in his own right, until his death in harness during the plague of 1625. Jonson, too, wrote on until he dropped – one suspects as much from an inner compulsion as from the destitution which dogged his final years.

These three – Jonson, Shakespeare, and Fletcher – were acknowledged, in the words of Sir John Denham in 1647, to be the ruling 'triumvirate of wit', and they alone achieved the dignity of having their output brought together into collected editions. But the dignity was posthumous in the cases of Shakespeare and Fletcher (harnessed not always accurately with Beaumont), whose editors followed the precedent set by Jonson when, in 1616, he oversaw the publication of his own collected *Works* – and suffered the jibes of those who would have reserved such a title for erudite writings in theology, philosophy, or natural science.

THE VOGUE FOR 'CITIZEN COMEDIES'

The sheer range of Jonson's work within a period of just over a year, as described on pages 98–99, usefully reminds us that, while fewer writers were now combining their profession with that of acting, a living might be made other than from the regular theatre. And while masques and barriers were, by their nature, the preserve of the aristocracy, other entertainments might celebrate humbler, civic virtues. Dekker, Heywood, Webster, and Middleton were among those who produced scenarios of pageants and other celebrations for the City of London – with which,

Ben Jonson (1572–1637), a painting after Abraham van Blyenberch, *c.* 1620. As a freelance writer of comedies, Jonson excelled in his own satiric, 'humours' mode, working both for the children's and the adult companies: he also virtually recreated the masque form and its antimasque variant, and wrote other entertainments to order, ranging from allegories for tournaments to openings for shopping arcades. While later generations have made him a rival of Shakespeare's, the two men were as different in the kinds of genius they displayed as they were in temperament – Jonson a Londoner whose plays remained rooted (as did he) in the City where he lived, drank, quarrelled, and died, disabled by a stroke but working to the last

as we know, the theatre had traditionally had at best an uneasy relationship. Opposite, an arch from one such pageant, devised to welcome James to London on the occasion of his Coronation, is illustrated and described.

Indeed, early in James's reign the vogue for what are sometimes called 'city' or 'citizen' comedies had satirized the values of the smug merchants and social climbers they portrayed. In the 1590s satire had been largely a matter of poetic imitation of classical models, but after the banning of such verse by the authorities in 1599 satire became increasingly a dramatic mode: and by 1605 those old or opportune enemies Marston and Jonson were collaborating with George Chapman on one of the most celebrated of the 'city comedies', *Eastward Ho!* One need only compare the London of this play, a city driven by the greed and corruption of the *nouveau riche*, with the almost heroic presentation of the bourgeoisie and artisans in Dekker's *The Shoemaker's Holiday* (1599) or in Heywood's *Four Prentices of London* (1600), to recognize, again, the shift in attitudes that had occurred over so brief a period.

Middleton continued to satirize the citizenry in such pieces as *A Mad World, My Masters* (1606) and *A Chaste Maid in Cheapside* (1611): but there is admiration and even affection, too, and by the end of James's reign the dramatist's sympathies seemed to be entirely with the bourgeoisie. *Women Beware Women*, probably written shortly after *The Changeling*, around 1623, has, indeed, been called a 'city tragedy', not because it scorns the citizens among its characters, but because it shows them as powerless before the whims of a great prince. Its 'hero', Leantio, is the Jacobean equivalent of a travelling salesman – and his tragedy is that Bianca, the woman he loves, is not only his social superior, but is betrayed into submission to the sexual demands of the Duke.

While Bianca is confronting her seducer, her supposed chaperons are playing chess: and in the nearly contemporary *A Game at Chess* of 1624 Middleton presents his characters as chess pieces, who play out, literally in black and white, the rights and wrongs of James's foreign policy. The staging of this unique and astonishingly daring play was only made possible by disagreements at court: even so, it was suppressed by the King after nine consecutive and wildly acclaimed performances – ironically by the King's Men, who, with the author, were brought before the Privy Council for the offence.

The play reflects the resentment of James's protestant subjects that their King had failed to go to the aid of his own son-in-law when the Elector Palatine had been driven into exile by Catholic armies – and, more recently and dangerously, that an alliance had been projected with the old enemy, Spain, through the marriage of Prince Charles and the Infanta. This had been encouraged by the deeply unpopular Spanish ambassador Gondomar, who was apparently 'counterfeited to the life' in *A Game at Chess*: but, more surprisingly, Charles, the King himself, and their canny favourite Buckingham also strutted among the chessmen – white pieces, confessedly, but none the less in breach of all protocol and prohibitions.

One of six elaborate designs by Stephen Harrison for the *Arches of Triumph* which welcomed James I on his progress to his Coronation in 1603–04. Writing the texts for such triumphal pageants provided work for dramatists – in this case Dekker, Middleton, and Jonson. It was Jonson who, in effect, 'directed' and wrote the words for this, the first arch, erected at Fenchurch Street, and celebrating the theme 'Monarchia Britannica'. Atop the arch is a carving of the entire City of London, while in the central section are the allegorical figures of Father Thames, the Genius of the City, and his six daughters. Divine Wisdom upholds British Monarchy in the central niches below. There were twelve performers in all, but only the Genius and Father Thames had speaking parts

The play itself, if viewed as an early experiment in satiric revue rather than as a static and inchoate regular comedy, seems to me to have greater intrinsic interest than many critics judge: but, coming as it did at the very end of James's reign, its theatrical importance is admittedly less than its political significance, for two related reasons. First, it showed that, given an exceptional opportunity, there was a vast and receptive audience in London for a politically alert play; and secondly, so far from meeting our expectation that the theatre was irrevocably tied by patronage to the cause of the monarchy, *A Game at Chess* presents the views of the political opposition – an opposition given ideological coherence by the puritans. Stuart politics were seldom simple: and recent researches have suggested that just as not all puritans were anti-theatrical, neither was the theatre invariably opposed to the puritan cause.

CHAPTER 7

The Caroline and Commonwealth Theatre

The accession of Charles I in 1625 was overshadowed by the severest outbreak of plague since 1603 – ironically, the year in which his father had come to the throne. Though the disease had remained endemic, prohibitions against playing during James's reign had generally been brief: now its more severe recurrence put the very survival of the weaker companies at risk. Apart from losing their 'ordinary poet', John Fletcher, in the outbreak of 1625, the King's Men were thus alone in weathering a closure of the theatres which lasted from James's death in late March until the following December. By then Charles had transferred his own protection, *ex officio* as it were, to the King's – whither the leading players of his former troupe, the Prince's, also found their way.

THE CAROLINE PLAYERS

As Shakespeare's near-contemporaries (and first editors) Heminges and Condell began to bow out of the company's affairs, its management fell increasingly into the hands of John Lowin – a stalwart member since 1603, whose speciality lay in bluff confidants and insidious malcontents – and a more recent arrival, John Taylor, who had taken on Burbage's 'line' of parts following the great actor's death in 1619.

Philip Henslowe had also died, in 1616, and Palsgrave's Men had barely recovered from this misfortune (ending an association which went back to their Elizabethan origins under the Lord Admiral) when the fire at the Fortune in 1621 consumed their precious prompt-books. For them the plague closure proved a fatal blow – as it did also for the Lady Elizabeth's Men, who had previously occupied Christopher Beeston's Phoenix (or Cockpit) theatre in Drury Lane. Beeston, having disbanded the company, proceeded to combine its best players with Queen Anne's to form a troupe headed by Richard Perkins, probably the best-known actor of the day. For this he successfully sought the protection of Charles's bride of a few months, Queen Henrietta Maria, who at the time was enjoying a honeymoon with all loyal subjects by virtue of being French – almost a White Queen for their new White King.

Measured by the frequency of their calls to perform at court, Queen Henrietta's went on to achieve a success second only to the King's, and were the only other troupe to be honoured with a grant of royal livery. But when a later, devastating outbreak of plague kept the theatres shut for an even longer spell, from May 1636 to November 1637, Beeston threw out the company in favour of a new troupe, in part composed of children, which became known simply as 'Beeston's Boys'. A new Queen Henrietta's thereupon began to play at the Salisbury Court – the latest indoor playhouse, built in 1629 just to the west of the Blackfriars, between Fleet Street and the Thames.

The second Fortune had reopened in 1625 with a company which united the remnants of the Palsgrave's Men with others of the Lady Elizabeth's, to become known as the King and Queen of Bohemia's. It thus revived and combined the patronage-in-exile of the popular couple, with whose distant troubles all good protestants felt common cause, despite the unbrotherly inertia of the King. The new company does not seem to have survived beyond 1629, when its manager Richard Gunnell went over to the King's Revels – a troupe created to open the Salisbury Court, with the declared aim of training boy players for the King's Men. Beset by financial problems, this company (by then composed mainly of adults) disappeared from view after the closure of 1636–37.

The birth of an heir to the throne led in 1631 to the creation of a new company of Prince Charles's Men, which also played briefly at the Salisbury Court. But Prince Charles's were later to be found either at the Fortune or the Red Bull, the surviving outdoor theatres beyond the northern City boundaries, where they alternated with a company of doubtful provenance known as the Red Bull-King's Men. Since the Globe was now the only theatre remaining on Bankside, the addition of the Salisbury Court to the Blackfriars and the Phoenix meant that there were now as many 'private' indoor theatres as there were outdoor playhouses – though the seating capacity of the 'public' theatres was of course far larger, since the indoor houses played to a self-limiting, wealthier clientele.

THE CAROLINE AUDIENCE

The received wisdom that a once-homogeneous Elizabethan audience became fragmented during the Jacobean period when the supposed elite defected to the private playhouses has, however, recently been disputed – one scholar actually contending that few of the 'unprivileged' even of Elizabethan London could have afforded either the time or money to visit a theatre. Yet, apart from requiring the 'privileged' to be almost fanatically frequent in their theatregoing, this view would make foolhardy the practice of the King's Men, after their move to the Blackfriars, of returning to the much larger Globe for the summer – when the legal profession was on vacation and most of fashionable society out of town. And, so far as the Caroline period is concerned, it also discounts derisive contemporary references to 'the meaner sort of people' said to attend the remaining outdoor playhouses.

What little we know of the repertoire of the public theatres does suggest an audience not only less upmarket but apparently less up-to-date – one which still relished the devils of *Faustus*, the battles of *Tamburlaine*, or the Machiavellian intrigues of *The Jew of Malta*, along with the easygoing certainties of the old chronicles, while also approving plays which portrayed the tribulations and triumphs of merchants and apprentices. The handful of new plays which have come down to us from these theatres also suggests their audiences' predilection for works of 'low life and roguery among brothels and prisons', as the theatre historian Martin Butler puts it,

Opposite: Richard Perkins (*c.* 1585–1650) was the first Flamineo in Webster's *The White Devil* at the Red Bull in 1612, and was singled out for praise by the author for his 'well-approved industry', which 'did crown both the beginning and the end'. Perkins had joined Worcester's (later Queen Anne's) Men in 1601, and after the death of Thomas ('Tu quoque') Greene in 1612 became their leading player. From 1625 he was with the new company of Queen's Men at the Phoenix, where his friend Heywood commended his performance as Barabas in Marlowe's *The Jew of Malta*

or even such a 'full-blown adventure packed with spectacle, devilry, and magic' as *The Seven Champions of Christendom* by John Kirke (*c.* 1638).

We should beware of taking at face value the glib dismissals of these theatres from contemporary writers who were, in truth, less concerned about their old-fashioned tastes than their new-fangled politics. As broadsides and pamphlets increasingly provided their own kind of outlets for popular discontents, the popular theatre – whose capacity for survival proved formidable – began to give these a dramatic focus. But the public playhouses, although the protests they voiced were the most radical, were not alone in offering a theatrical critique of the government – especially after 1629, when Charles began his ill-fated eleven-year experiment in personal rule, and the theatre became one of the many public forums for an opposition that was now, perforce, extra-parliamentary.

THEATRICALS AT COURT

To the ever-more-politicized theatre of the decade or so before the Civil Wars we shall return later in the present chapter. But the government, of course, already had its own theatrical mouthpiece, in London's 'third theatre' – that of Charles's court. When his father's Banqueting Hall in Whitehall had burned down in 1619, Inigo Jones was ready with plans for a new building within three months, and by 1622 this was in regular use. However, the installation of Rubens's ceiling panels in 1635 necessitated a change of venue to a temporary hall of similar size next door, lest the masterpiece be damaged by smoke from the thousands of torches and candles required for the masquing. Mainly for visiting professionals, Jones also built, in 1629–30, the 'Cockpit in Court', which is illustrated and described opposite.

Queen Henrietta Maria soon became the dominant influence over royal theatricals. At first, her great love was for pastoral – that curious idealization of supposed rustic innocence, of which Fletcher's *The Faithful Shepherdess* (*c.* 1608) had been a pioneering example in the English drama. For her first Christmas at court she outraged convention by requiring the ladies-in-waiting (who customarily combined their decorative presence with decorous silence) to take on speaking roles in the French pastoral *L'Arténice* – even persuading them into beards for the male parts.

In 1632 the Queen hired Joseph Taylor from the King's Men to rehearse her amateur cast (and herself) in another pastoral, *The Shepherd's Paradise*, which took some seven hours to perform. Taylor was rewarded with £100, which was more than generous for a common player – while the total of £2,500 given to the courtly author, Walter Montague, appears the more astonishing set against the fee of £10 for the outright sale of a play to one of the professional companies.

A few years earlier, in 1629, there had been great public outrage when a visiting French company, which included actresses, had tried to play a season at the Blackfriars; and it was probably this occasion which the puritan lawyer William Prynne had in mind when he attacked 'women-actors, notorious whores' in his anti-theatrical pamphlet *Histrio-Mastix, the Players' Scourge* – which, however, was published just ten days before the performance of Montague's play during the New Year celebrations of 1633. Prynne was savagely punished for his supposed libelling of the Queen, even to the painful indignity of losing his ears: and the Inns of Court, to which Prynne had belonged until debarred by his crime, made recompense by mounting James Shirley's Shrovetide masque *The Triumph of Peace*, processing to stage it at Whitehall, and later in the City, in the presence of the King and Queen.

With the ageing Ben Jonson out of favour, and no longer demonstrating and defending the literary potential of the masque, this became an ever more spectacular affair as Charles's reign progressed. Inigo Jones was now able to subdue the ambitions of more compliant dramatists to the whims of his scenographic genius – as he was still doing on the very eve of the Civil Wars, when Sir William Davenant's *Salmacida Spolia* (1640) paid its elaborate allegorical compliment to an all-wise King and a prudent, pregnant Queen for averting, through their 'secret power', the threats of 'Discord, a malicious Fury' and her malignant spirits.

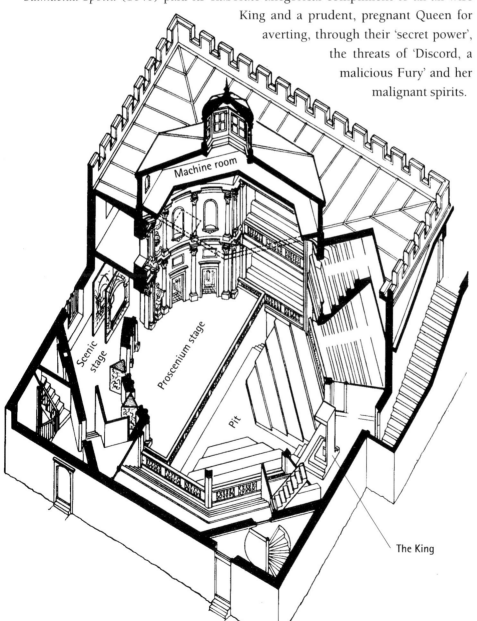

Reconstruction of the Cockpit in Court by Richard Leacroft, from the extant plans of Inigo Jones. Built in 1629–30 (and so-called to distinguish it from Beeston's theatre in Drury Lane), this was better suited than Jones's new Banqueting House to the twenty or so plays brought to court each year by the professional companies. Here, the King sat enthroned on a miniature stage of his own, directly facing the actors – the seating plan ensuring that no spectator could entirely turn his back on the royal presence

Design by Inigo Jones for the final masque of Charles's reign, Davenant's *Salmacida Spolia* (1640). This opens by acknowledging that the King has to 'live and govern in a sullen age' – but soon Concord and the Good Genius of Great Britain appear, to acclaim one whose 'secret wisdom' will outlast 'those storms the people's giddy fury raise'. It was during this last chorus that the pregnant Queen and her ladies descended from the 'huge cloud of various colours' here illustrated, costumed 'in Amazonian habits of carnation, embroidered with silver, with plumed helms'

Literary critics have tended to bemoan the triumph of decoration in the Caroline masque. Against this, it is argued that the masque was only now discovering itself as essentially a visual and musical medium – which, incidentally but crucially, was formative to the development of English scenography. Yet it must finally be conceded that the form came to mirror and even to encourage Charles's increasing detachment from political and social realities. If the pastoral prettified an actually discontented countryside, the masque became a substitute instead of a symbol for the King's relationship with his people – in both cases, theatricality as wish-fulfilment.

Among the other 'cavalier dramatists' of Charles's court were Sir John Suckling, Sir John Denham, and Sir William Berkeley, whose *The Lost Lady*, staged in 1637, celebrated the ideal of platonic love which the Queen had for some years been cultivating – a convenient cover for her political intrigues, which demanded the unswerving devotion of courtly male 'servants' without threatening the sanctity of her marriage with the King (which, in ironic contrast with his father's and his son's, remained a model of domestic harmony). Jonson had both imitated and parodied the dramatic possibilities of the emergent neoplatonic cult in one of his last plays, *The New Inn* (1629): unsurprisingly, it was a flop, for few beyond the charmed and self-deceiving circles of the court could make even satirical connections between the convolutions of courtly role-playing and the harsh actualities of life in an increasingly discontented kingdom.

Although the King's Men dutifully took a number of plays by the 'cavalier dramatists' from the court to the public stage of the Blackfriars, it is significant that these never seem to have survived the transfer for long – though the costumes that came with them were no doubt gratefully recycled by the tire-man. Indeed, in the two-way traffic between court and theatre, only Davenant proved equally competent and successful in both. In the single year of 1634, for instance, he was anticipating eponymously in *The Wits* the favourite character-types of Restoration comedy and in *Love and Honour* the heroic abstractions of its tragedy; and within another twelvemonth he had produced an old-style Jonsonian comedy, *News from Plymouth*, for the Globe, while accommodating the niceties of neoplatonism in *The Temple of Love* – one of the several court masques in which he submitted to the twin disciplines of allegory and Inigo Jones. But in other respects, as we shall see later, he was very much his own man.

THE PROFESSIONAL PLAYWRIGHTS

Among the professional dramatists who had learned their craft in the Jacobean theatre, Philip Massinger – who took over as regular dramatist for the King's Men following Fletcher's death – and his close contemporary John Ford were competent and prolific writers, whose skill lay in their ability to sense and give dramatic shape to the uncertainties of the new reign. As Charles's absolutist ambitions became clearer, 'opposition' began to imply independence not just of means but of ends – not only rejection of a monarch's advisors, but repudiation of the actions of the King himself. The average citizen was beginning to recognize that the patterns of court behaviour and morality were not necessarily either the best or even the most convenient: and the 'accepted order' began to appear neither very acceptable nor even (which to the middle classes was more threatening) capable of maintaining an appearance of social stability.

If Massinger's line of tragi-comedy was less fluent and easygoing than Fletcher's, this was, then, because the self-consciousness to which some critics have objected derived from an uncertainty of values which was entirely characteristic of the age. The alleged prurience of the incest theme in Ford's best-remembered work, *'Tis Pity She's a Whore* (c. 1632) reflects a similar sense that new rules might be needed for new situations: 'unnatural' love may only lead to self-destruction within the constraints of tragedy, but here it is allowed to speak for itself, and threatens to transcend generic as well as moral boundaries.

So Massinger and Ford, familiarly believed to represent a drama in its decadence, may alternatively be understood as theatricalizing their own astonishment at the world they were opening up. If their tragedies and tragi-comedies remain second-rate, as charged by the influential poet-critic T. S. Eliot, it is because the dilemmas

Portrait by Van Dyck of Inigo Jones (1573–1652). Appointed to the household of James I's young heir apparent, Prince Henry, in 1604, within a year Jones was using perspective scenery for the first time in the English court theatre. He introduced the proscenium arch to 'frame' his stage pictures, used elaborate continental devices for the transformation of scenes – and even experimented with coloured lighting, using candles ranged behind tinted glass. When, in 1619, he designed the Banqueting House in Whitehall, he had installed sophisticated devices for the raising and lowering of scenery. After the last of his many quarrels with Jonson over precedence, in 1631, he overawed other masque writers, and was approaching seventy when he produced his last designs, for *Salmacida Spolia* (see opposite). He died in poverty during the Commonwealth

they pose are not easily accommodated within the formulaic patterns of those genres – whereas their comedies remain alive (if largely ignored) because here the form gives bewilderment its own comedic dignity and slightly subversive triumph. Thus, Massinger's best-known work in the genre, *A New Way to Pay Old Debts* (1625), juxtaposes the conventional expectations of city comedy with the actual sympathies aroused for 'country' values – while *The City Madam* (1632) is as much a 'problem play' as a comedy proper, its resolution no less ambiguous than that of *Measure for Measure*. As with so much Caroline drama, one's response depends on whether one feels that the dramatist is purposefully *posing* the problem, or compounding it by evasion of the moral issues.

We look separately, on pages 114–15, at the social comedies of James Shirley and Richard Brome – whose usual theatre, the Salisbury Court, played host on occasion to companies otherwise to be found outdoors. Indeed, we find in its repertoire fewer plays calculated to appeal to courtly tastes than we might expect: and it was here in 1635 that Nathaniel Richards's *Messalina* reached the stage – a play that could be and was interpreted as downright puritanical in its critique of courtly extravagance and the self-indulgence of the rich. Audiences at the Phoenix, too, must have enjoyed the affirmation of mercantile and yeoman values to be found in the plays of Beeston's old colleague, the still prolific Thomas Heywood, who wrote regularly for Queen Henrietta's in the early 1630s.

THEATRE IN THE PROTESTANT CAUSE

Heywood achieved a modest success at court with *Love's Mistress* in 1634, and, perhaps in consequence, went on to spend two years with the King's Men, collaborating with Brome on the topical piece *The Late Lancashire Witches* and the lost but significantly titled *The Apprentice's Prize*. However, after the plague closure of 1636–37 Heywood seems to have written no more for the stage, though his prose output from then until his death in 1641 shows if anything a final flowering rather than any diminution of his prodigious energies. As titles of pamphlets such as *The Black Box of Rome Opened* and *The Jesuits Taken in Their Own Net* suggest, the stalwart old Elizabethan may have decided that pamphleteering was a better way of supporting the opposition. Not all dramatists felt that way, however, and in the course of the 1630s the theatre became increasingly responsive to the concerns of those who were critical of Charles's authoritarian rule.

Among extant plays of that decade, Henry Glapthorne's *Albertus Wallenstein* thus glorified the protestant cause in its struggles abroad, while an anonymous piece, *The Valiant Scot*, found an historical analogy for the presbyterian church's defiance of Charles's attempts to impose an Anglican liturgy in Scotland. And the titles of many among the numerous lost plays, particularly from the remaining public theatres – Dekker's *Gustavus, King of Sweden*, Heywood and Brome's *The Wars of the Low Countries*, the anonymous *Play of the Netherlands* – suggest that clear (if sometimes historically analogous) connections were being made with current events.

For a few years before the closure of 1642, it seemed almost as though the theatre was conspiring to offend the authorities. In 1639 the Red Bull company at the Fortune had been fined and some of its actors imprisoned for performing 'a new old play', now lost, called *The Cardinal's Conspiracy*, which was said to ridicule the Church – and they proceeded to compound their offence with a revival of *The Valiant Scot*. Later in the same year Prince Charles's Men were brought before the Privy Council when *The Whore New Vamped*, an attack on custom-farming, was claimed to have 'reflected upon the present government'. Then, in the following spring, Beeston's Boys at the Salisbury Court staged Brome's unlicensed *The Court Beggar*, perceived by Charles as an attack upon his expedition into Scotland. The actors, defying a royal command to cease playing, were eventually slapped into prison – along with their manager William Beeston, who had only just inherited the theatre on his father's death in 1638. The trusted Davenant was installed, unsuccessfully and briefly, as manager in his place.

The man responsible for Beeston's imprisonment was the Lord Chamberlain, the Earl of Pembroke – co-dedicatee with his brother of the First Folio of Shakespeare's plays. Symptomatically of the shifting loyalties of the times, Pembroke was himself dismissed in the following year for negotiating and recommending to Charles unacceptable peace terms with the Scots, and for subsequently supporting the impeachment of Strafford. The historian Margot Heinemann actually suspects Pembroke of complicity in Christopher Beeston's ousting of Queen Henrietta's Men, and identifies numerous other 'opposition' plays in the repertoire of his 'Boys'.

Even at the respectable Blackfriars, that cautious career-dramatist Shirley can scarcely have been unconscious of the parallels with Laud's downfall in his tragedy *The Cardinal* of 1641 – while in the same year and at the same theatre Jonson's last patron, the Duke of Newcastle, dared in *The Variety* not only to satirize courtiers but even to parody that last resort of Caroline self-deception, the court masque. By this time, not only were such plays alluding directly or indirectly to the current situation, but ever more explicit dramatic dialogues were appearing in profusion in pamphlet form.

Few of these, perhaps, were intended for performance, but Richard Overton's *A New Play Called Canterbury His Change of Diet* (1641), does bear marks of having reached the stage: thus, an engraving in the published text, reproduced alongside, not only depicts Archbishop Laud in company with a mocking stage clown, but imprisons him in a 'property' cage such as revivals of *Tamburlaine* would have left ready to hand. The 'play' has been aptly compared with the French proto-absurdist Alfred Jarry's *Ubu Roi* for its blend of broad but biting satire and surreal slapstick (part of the 'diet' that Laud is forced to change is his taste for human ears, poor Prynne's having proved an addictive morsel).

Despite the political confusion – to some extent because of it, in view of the loosening of the censorship it entailed – the season of 1641–42 looked propitious for the theatre. Brome was at the height of his powers as a truly exciting and

Title page of a pamphlet-play by the puritan satirist Richard Overton, *A New Play Called Canterbury His Change of Diet* (1641). The woodcut shows the third act, in which the impeached Archbishop Laud and a Jesuit priest are brought on in a 'great bird cage together, and a fool standing by, and laughing at them'. Although the piece is thought by some not to have been intended for the stage, its very brevity suggests its possible use as a jig. Such properties as are required would have been readily available – the cage, for example, from the ever-popular *Tamburlaine*

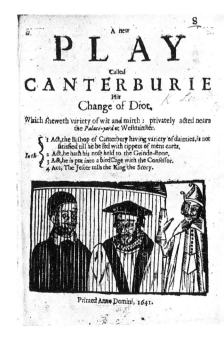

innovative dramatist, and, although Massinger was recently dead, Shirley was back in London and in harness for the King's Men. Most important of all, the theatre seemed set to exploit its recently discovered potential as an agent for change, not merely a mirror of its causes and effects. Had Charles been reconciled to the political compromise for which all but his extremest opponents were working, it seems at least possible that, so far from dwindling into decadence, the later Caroline theatre would have survived its necessary unshackling from past glories to emerge with a renewed and vigorous sense of purpose.

As it was, the theatres were ordered to be closed immediately after the outbreak of hostilities in August 1642 – 'while these sad causes and sad times of humiliation do continue'. As this phrasing suggests, it is unlikely that more than a temporary closure – expected by the players in times of plague and during periods of royal

Social playwrights of the Caroline theatre

The critic Margot Heinemann has usefully reminded us that the Mermaid collections which, from their first appearance in the late 1880s until the 1960s, remained the most accessible editions of 'the best plays of the old dramatists' for the average actor, teacher, or student, were at the time revolutionary in their editors' preference for plays which dealt frankly with sexual and emotional relationships. But the 'old Mermaids' often misrepresented a dramatist's full range, overlooking work which illuminated social or political themes – themes which, in the case of Caroline writers, tended better to suit the tight, 'well-made' plot construction of which James Shirley was perhaps the pre-eminent exponent.

Shirley began his theatrical career in 1625 as 'ordinary poet' for Queen Henrietta's Men at the Phoenix, worked in a similar capacity for the first permanent playhouse in Dublin during and after the plague of 1636-37, then returned to London after the death of Massinger in 1640 to fill the same role for the King's Men – a thoroughgoing professional, steadily productive and in continuous employment. Like Davenant, Shirley tends to look forwards rather than back, anticipating the Restoration in distilling the social 'manners' of his times into comedic form – and also, like Massinger, contrasting the values of 'the town' with those of 'the court' and 'the country', investigating and exploring all these modes of behaviour with a typically Caroline sense of polite shock that there should be alternatives in such matters.

At his best, as in The Example (1634), Shirley creates a chiaroscuro of local colour within the framework of a confessedly mechanical plot. In two plays of 1632, The Ball and Hyde Park, the very titles reflect his discovery and exploration of new venues for social (and dramatic) mingling, away from the conventional confines of City and Whitehall. He writes of a leisured society at ease with itself, but aware of the tensions between classes and sexes, of shifting allegiances – and of the threat to leisure itself as the mark of a gentleman.

Shirley's steady output averaged two plays a year – and when the reformed company of Queen Henrietta's Men went to the Salisbury Court in 1637, and Richard Brome took over as 'ordinary poet', we know from a lawsuit over his contract that this appears to have been a standard contractual

mourning – was intended. Often claimed to be the long-awaited revenge of rabid puritans, the closure was more probably the precautionary move of a still-moderate parliament concerned to secure the support of the respectable bourgeoisie, and worried by the new role of the public theatres as a mouthpiece for the people – thus potentially encouraging what would have been perceived as mob-rule.

Whatever the cause of the edict, its effect was the cessation of authorized playing for eighteen years. Very soon, this began to create problems for the members of what was now a well-organized profession, heavy with obligations to hirelings and landlords – a plight unavailingly described in a pamphlet of 1643 entitled *The Actors' Remonstrance*. As another, more satisfied source declared: 'They have beaten them out of their Cockpit, baited them at the Bull, and overthrown their Fortune' – and, it might have added, spun their Globe out of orbit, for its occupants, as befitted

expectation. Brome was less able to sustain such a pace – hence the necessity for the lawsuit – but his output, if less prolific than Shirley's, was in many ways more interesting, and intensely and consistently social in its range. In part for this reason, no doubt, Brome was not even accorded the passing immortality of a Mermaid edition, and his work remains extremely difficult to come by.

Brome was fond of directing satirical jibes not only at the cavalier playwrights and their tricksy staging techniques, but at the political system which the court, in the absence of a parliament, was increasingly assumed to represent. He blended the skill of his old master Jonson in the depiction of everyday London life with the softer realism of a Dekker, the love of intrigue of a Middleton – and, less expectedly, the capacity of a Shakespeare for showing characters changed by their experiences. Yet his works, so far from seeming derivative, are a highly personal synthesis of these elements – as of others which foreshadow trends instead of following them.

The multiple levels of action in A Jovial Crew (1641) thus anticipate Pirandello in their creation of a complex sense of theatrical illusion – even to the imaginary author who reveals himself at the end. And the therapeutic playacting in The Antipodes (1638) amounts to a seventeenth-century variation upon psychodrama, set in a topsy-turvy world of inverted behaviour. Here, beggars are courtiers, usurers give charity, and ladies learn parrot-fashion – from parrots. Not only does Brome display zestful ingenuity in these carnivalesque inversions, but the juggling of moral values in his anti-London has the purposeful ambiguity of Swift's Gulliver stranded in Lilliput or Brobdingnag.

Others of Brome's plays touch more closely on the immediacies of an actual London where civil war was now imminent – but, almost to the end, not in the least expected. Charles himself saw Brome's The Court Beggar (1640) as a satire on his recent, disastrous Scottish campaign, and the play's depiction of foolish and corrupt courtiers makes its own none-too-implicit comment upon the whole panoply of a personal government now in terminal decay.

Two hard-working professional playwrights of Caroline London. Left: James Shirley (1596–1666). Right: Richard Brome (*c.* 1590–1652)

Printed plays, closet dramas, and drolls

One expedient available to dispossessed actors and poets was to publish their plays – which, of course, they could now do free from fear of poaching by their rivals. The clause in Brome's contract that he should not publish his work without his company's consent appears to have been a standard one: thus, typically, none of the plays written by Shirley for the King's Men between 1640 and 1642 was published during those years, but all were brought into print in 1653. And it was presumably to alleviate the hardships of the King's Men that in 1647 they published a folio of plays attributed (with varying accuracy) to the marketable partnership of Beaumont and Fletcher – only the third time, following Jonson and Shakespeare, that writers had been so honoured. Ironically and fruitlessly, the volume was dedicated to the Earl of Pembroke, now firm for the parliamentary cause.

Numerous 'closet' dramas also found their way into print. Some, like those of the amiably eccentric Duchess of Newcastle, would have been unlikely ever to reach the stage – but others, such as those by Thomas Killigrew (whose long theatrical career began as a dramatist under Charles I), were published only as an unsatisfactory alternative to performance. However, one work which remained unpublished until after the Restoration was The Wits, a collection of brief and usually farcical pieces often taken from longer plays – as was Bottom the Weaver from A Midsummer Night's Dream. Such 'drolls' had come into their own during the interregnum, for they required only a clear space in a tavern or a fit-up stage hastily erected in a public place, and so were much less readily put down than regular plays.

The popularity of these pieces may have been in part responsible for the style and flavour of the propagandist playlets which continued to appear either in pamphlet form or in the newspapers or 'mercurys' that in the 1640s had begun to find a ready audience. Often reading like updated versions of the political moralities of a century earlier, these were probably written by authors who could also turn their hands to broadside ballads and chapbooks. Whether or not they were performed, outlets for them became severely restricted when unlicensed printing was suppressed in 1649, and only drolls on such age-old themes as sexual gulling and knockabout roguery survived. Although only briefly surfacing within the 'official' culture during this period of political and social ferment, the drolls derived from a popular tradition which predated the interregnum as surely as it was to survive it.

King's Men, had early volunteered for Charles's service, and by 1644 their old outdoor theatre had been demolished. In the following year the actors evidently found discretion the better part of loyalty, and threw themselves on the mercy of parliament: they were awarded their back pay, but given no hope for their future.

Yet playacting, despite its loss of legal sanction, did not altogether disappear. The Fortune was raided several times on account of illicit playing, and William Beeston was evidently active at the Salisbury Court at least until 1647, when soldiers broke up a performance of Beaumont and Fletcher's *A King and No King*. How many more such surreptitious occasions went undetected, and so unrecorded, we have no means of knowing – though the lull between the First and Second Civil Wars in 1647–48 evidently saw a more widespread resurgence of theatrical activity, necessitating a new ordinance to put it down. Eventually, this led to the demolition or wrecking of the interiors of all the old playhouses – except, apparently and inexplicably, the Red Bull, which, despite the regular intervention of the authorities, seems to have kept going intermittently almost until the Restoration.

Ironically, the performing art which eventually achieved an official seal of approval under Cromwell's protectorate was aristocratic rather than popular in its origins. Music had always been more acceptable to the puritan mind than the drama, and masques were still occasionally performed – Shirley's *Cupid and Death*, for example, before the Portuguese ambassador in 1653, and Thomas Jordan's *Fancy's Festivals* in 1657. Then, in 1656, William Davenant – who, following two years of imprisonment as an active royalist, was seeking to revive his fortunes through his old profession – became the leading and most successful exponent of a new kind of music drama when, in his own home, he staged the so-called *First Day's Entertainment at Rutland House*.

This served as a dry-run for what turned out to be the first part of his *The Siege of Rhodes* – usually dignified as the earliest English opera, which it accidentally was, since it differed from the masque in that its dialogue was sung throughout. Inigo Jones's pupil, collaborator, and successor John Webb designed the scenery for Davenant's stage in a style which in everything except its domesticated scale anticipated that of the Restoration – as also did the presence of a woman among the amateur cast.

That Davenant was not especially aiming at an operatic format, but at any performing mode which might overcome official objections to the spoken drama, is suggested by his next piece, *The Cruelty of the Spaniards in Peru*, for which in 1658 he actually obtained authority to refurbish the old Phoenix theatre. This contained juggling, acrobatics, dramatic monologues, and even tight-rope walking within what was in effect a compilation bill – but which won approval by making its political points in conformity with the anti-Spanish policy of the government. Eventually, by the time Davenant came to write *The Second Part of the Siege of Rhodes* in 1659, Cromwell was dead, General Monk about to make his move, and a Restoration expected: so Davenant simply reverted to the more traditional dramatic format of his past and many of his future successes.

Throughout the interregnum, there had been prominent support for a reopening of the theatres on reformed lines – most notably from the poet and parliamentary supporter John Milton, who even drew up a list of appropriate biblical and historical themes. These would have carried suitable moral messages, sweetened with a few scenes of spectacle and even mild titillation, but were essentially modelled along the neoclassical lines he himself later employed for *Samson Agonistes* (1671). The composer Richard Flecknoe, too, wrote his closet *Love's Dominion* (1654) as a 'pattern for the reformed stage', which he tactfully proposed as 'an humble co-adjutor of the pulpit'.

In the event, of course, 'reform' as it was understood by the returning monarch had to do not with the theatre's moral probity but with putting into effect the continental innovations which had impressed him in exile. As early as 1639, the ubiquitous Davenant had been projecting a scheme for a lavish new playhouse, where 'scenes', previously only utilized for court performances, might be set – and Charles himself, his reformist and sexual zeal neatly coinciding, was anxious that 'the evil and scandal' of boys appearing in 'the habits of women' should be remedied by the employment of actresses. And so, as the critic John Dennis was later to recall: 'They altered at once the whole face of the stage by introducing scenes and women.'

CHAPTER 8

The Restoration Theatre

Sir William Davenant, the only playwright of the first Caroline period to have succeeded in both the court and the professional theatre, peers out with serene confidence from beneath his laureate's crown of bays. Now, Davenant (1606–68) and Thomas Killigrew (opposite) were the patentees approved by Charles II to manage the only two theatrical companies to be permitted in Restoration London. Their portraits (both first used as frontispieces to their collected works) make very different 'statements', in keeping with their contrasting characters

Even before King Charles II entered his capital on 29 May 1660, pretenders to theatrical patronage were staking their claims. Hastily assembled companies began to put on old plays in the old ways at the old playhouses – among them, a troupe of young actors installed at the Cockpit by John Rhodes, an erstwhile prompter at the Blackfriars. When, on 18 August 1660, the diarist Samuel Pepys went there to see Fletcher's *The Loyal Subject*, he duly acclaimed Edward Kynaston in the role of the Duke's sister as 'the loveliest lady that ever I saw in my life'. Michael Mohun, himself a former boy player, was meanwhile leading a company at the Red Bull, and William Beeston was at the Salisbury Court. Actors and managers hoping to pick up the threads of their theatrical careers – not to mention Sir Henry Herbert, back in office as Master of the Revels – were clearly anticipating a restoration of the theatrical as of the political order.

OLD PRETENDERS AND NEW PATENTEES

Under the new dispensation, however, professional credentials had to be combined with courtly favour. Cannily, Thomas Killigrew had secured a place on board the ship bringing the King back into his own, and although Sir William Davenant had to work a harder passage of ingratiation, it was upon this pair of Caroline court dramatists that, within months of the Restoration, were bestowed the managements of the only two companies authorized to perform in Restoration London – the better-connected Killigrew heading the King's, while Davenant's company took the name of Charles's brother and heir presumptive, the Duke of York.

Another contender for patronage had been George Jolly, leader of a company of English actors on the Continent during the interregnum, so it was perhaps as a sort of consolation prize that he was permitted to run a 'nursery' for training young actors. But this enterprise, which crops up elusively at various venues and under various managements into the 1680s, seems to have produced few graduates of note – the outstanding exception being the comedian Joe Haines. Some unlicensed playing was also attempted, especially at the almost inextinguishable Red Bull, but this had been finally put down by 1663 – letters patent having by then confirmed the duopoly which was to form the legal basis of theatre regulation in London for almost two centuries. The Master of the Revels found his powers limited, in practice, to the censorship and licensing of plays – a matter in Charles's reign of protecting political rather than sexual or religious susceptibilities.

At first Killigrew and Davenant joined forces, leasing the Phoenix as a temporary base. Then, amidst the Guy Fawkes celebrations of 5 November 1660, the managers went their separate ways. Both planned moves to 'real' or 'royal' indoor tennis courts, which had proved suitable for theatrical use in France, and Killigrew quickly established himself at the former Gibbons's Tennis Court in Vere Street, off Clare

Market. But Davenant preferred to bide his time, taking a temporary lease on the Salisbury Court while Lisle's Tennis Court (in Portugal Street, Lincoln's Inn Fields) underwent a more thorough conversion – both to provide him with his own lodgings on the premises, and, more important, to accommodate 'scenes'.

Killigrew's company seemed set to outshine so tardy a rival. It was at his Vere Street Theatre on 3 January 1661 that Pepys – a notoriously anecdotal authority, but one of the very few we have for the early day-by-day activities of the two companies – records seeing actresses, as if for the first time. And not only did the King's players include Mohun and another Caroline veteran, Charles Hart, together with Kynaston the rising star, but they claimed the rights (as supposed successors to the King's Men of old) to an extensive pre-Restoration repertoire – which, bitterly for Davenant, even included works of his own.

Unexpectedly, perhaps, we find plays by Jacobean writers, notably Fletcher and Jonson, more prominent than those of Caroline writers among the revivals which necessarily dominated the early seasons. Shakespeare also held his own – his most popular plays being more or less equally distributed between the two managers in an agreement eventually imposed by the Lord Chamberlain which, while it restored to Davenant the rights to his own plays, left him with an altogether inferior share of the old repertoire.

However, in the event, the need to encourage new writers told in Davenant's favour, as did his dependence on younger players. These included Henry Harris, Thomas Lilliston, Cave Underhill, the Nokes brothers – and Thomas Betterton, who was destined to become the leading actor of his times. Davenant's agreement with his company survives, and is along traditional lines – the manager allocating himself a higher proportion of shares in recognition of his greater investment, but the ten leading players also becoming 'sharers' in the Elizabethan sense.

Pepys apparently did not see the Duke's company at the Salisbury Court until the end of January 1661, but his visits there soon became more frequent than to Vere Street. Then, in late June, Davenant took his players to their new theatre in Lincoln's Inn Fields – the Duke's house, as it became known – and chose to open with two plays of his own, *The Second Part of the Siege of Rhodes* and *The Wits*. Although, as described on page 122, the first actress on the Restoration stage had probably already appeared for Killigrew, it was at the Duke's that Mary Saunderson now made her name: and it was here that John Downes remarked upon seeing 'new scenes and decorations, being the first that were e'er introduced in England'.

By 1663 Killigrew evidently found it necessary to provide scenic effects of his own; and, abandoning his Vere Street theatre, he converted a former riding school in Bridges Street into the first of the long line of Theatres Royal, Drury Lane. Davenant died in harness in 1668, so when, two years later, the Duke's players also found themselves on the move – to the purpose-built Dorset Garden, between Fleet Street and the Thames – it was under the joint management of Betterton and Harris, acting on behalf of the widow.

Thomas Killigrew (1612–83), displays a worldly insouciance in the presence of his martyred monarch (who is gazing aptly heavenwards). Although Killigrew was quick to defend his monopoly – and, as supposed successor to the King's Men, to claim rights over their repertoire – he adapted less well than Davenant to changing circumstances, and by 1671 he had begun to leave the day-to-day affairs of the company to his son. Portrait by William Sheppard, *c.* 1650

Tradition attributes the design of the Dorset Garden, which impressed John Evelyn with the magnificence of its scenes and machines, to the leading architect of the period, Sir Christopher Wren – but although Wren was more assuredly responsible for the new Drury Lane theatre which opened in 1674, following the destruction of the Bridges Street theatre by fire in 1672, Dryden's prologue for the opening performance contrasted this 'plain built house' and 'mean ungilded stage' with the splendours of Dorset Garden. The Duke's had, indeed, become established as the superior company, and Killigrew's unpopularity with his actors forced him finally to relinquish his management to his son Charles in 1677. But he seems to have built the better playhouse: when in 1682 the companies united it was Drury Lane that they preferred as their regular home.

Wren's Drury Lane, which survived, with some modifications, from 1674 to 1791. Richard Leacroft's reconstruction shows the large forestage acting area, with a pair of proscenium doors on each side, the wings and shutters beyond, and the area for the display of 'vistas' furthest upstage. Nine rows of pit benches are surrounded on three sides by boxes, with two shallow galleries rising above

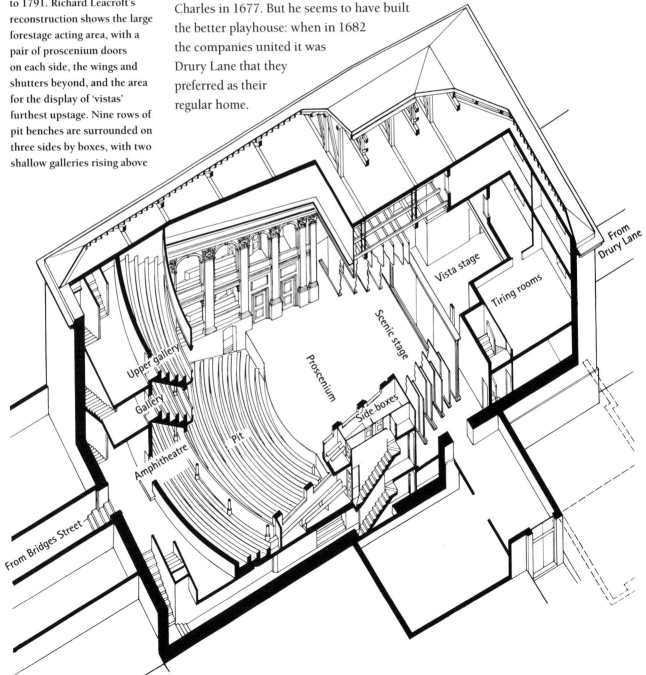

The Drury Lane stage, as set for the opera *Ariadne; or, The Marriage of Bacchus* (1674). In this reconstruction, based on a frontispiece to the printed libretto, a foreshortened apron adds depth to the street scene created by the receding perspective of the 'housefront' wings. These lead the eye towards a prospect of the Thames, along which three river nymphs are borne on a scallop while cupids fly above. One proscenium door has here been screened off, to direct the gaze into the scene beyond: but the acting area remains unencumbered by scenery

THE THEATRE ROYAL, DRURY LANE

With an initial capacity of perhaps 1,000, this theatre, which survived until 1791, was considerably larger than its predecessor, but shared its essential layout – itself a sound English compromise between native tradition and continental innovation. As Richard Leacroft's scaled reconstruction illustrates, rows of backless pit benches were surrounded on three sides by boxes, with two tiers of galleries rising above, all fronting the deep apron stage to which the acting was still confined. Beyond this, a proscenium arch framed 'scenes' set on changeable 'wings and shutters' – the most imposing scenes being painted onto the large flat 'shutters', divided down the middle so that they could be slid into position from each side along grooves in the stage floor. Here, they might either function as the back scene, or be drawn apart again to reveal a spectacular vista to the rear.

Several pairs of 'wings', painted to give the impression of receding into the distance, fronted the shutters. At first these were fixed, with the advantage that, set at a suitable angle, they created an illusion of three dimensions – the corners of buildings receding down opposite sides of a street, for example. Later, the wings, with matching 'borders' above, also commonly became changeable, sliding into position along grooves of their own. The actors made most of their entrances and exits through solid and highly practical proscenium doors – Drury Lane had two at each side – and, playing on the apron stage, did not (except for occasional tableaux or other special purposes) venture among the 'scenes', which provided a perspective background to their comings and goings. The proscenium curtain rose once only, to reveal the scene at the beginning of the performance.

FOREIGN INFLUENCES AND NATIVE GROWTH

As it had so often done before, plague closed the theatres (in the event, for the last time) for sixteen months from June 1665 – the fire that helped to sanitize the city in the following year also taking with it the old Salisbury Court. (Among the causes to which the puritans attributed this latest visitation of divine displeasure was, of course, the reopening of the theatres.) Before this further break in theatrical activity, the few new plays amidst the revivals were unremarkable, a number exploiting an easy, cavalier triumphalism. Unusually, Sir Robert Howard's *The Committee* (1662) outlived its topical anti-puritanism, while John Lacy's *The Old Troop* (1664) was less deservedly rescued from instant oblivion by its shrewd mix of cheerful smut and cheap chauvinism.

Unsurprisingly, after so long an interruption in playing, continental models remained popular throughout the decade, whether in attempts to domesticate the strict 'rules' of French neoclassicism or in variants on the easier-going Spanish tradition. Common to both, indeed, was a preoccupation with 'love and honour' – not only in serious dramas of the baroque Spanish school and in the more ascetic manner of Corneille, but also in comedies of intrigue after the 'cloak and sword' style of Calderón. Adaptations, more or less acknowledged, were plentiful in all these modes – though with an increasing tendency to understate moral intentions in favour of swiftly-paced action, often in a bastard genre.

Combining a tragi-comic 'high' plot with a coarsely comic 'low' level of action became a popular means of getting it both ways. Typically, Samuel Tuke's *Adventures of Five Hours* (1663) thus describes itself as a tragi-comedy and claims

The last 'boys', the first actresses

Edward Kynaston (*c.* 1640–1706), probably the last 'boy' player of women's roles – 'the loveliest lady that ever I saw in my life', according to Pepys

Immediately after the restoration of the Stuart line, former boy players such as Edward Kynaston and Michael Mohun, with their flowing locks and androgynous good looks, continued to act in women's roles. However, on 3 January 1661 Samuel Pepys the diarist – one of the very few authorities we have for day-by-day life in the Restoration theatre – mentions seeing actresses at the King's house, as if for the first time.

Margaret Hughes had probably been the first professional actress to appear on the Restoration stage when she took the role of Desdemona in The Moor of Venice (Thomas Killigrew's version of Othello) for the King's, at their Vere Street theatre in 1660. Actresses seem first to have appeared with the Duke's company late in June 1661 – among

them, in the role of Ianthe, Mary Saunderson, the woman who was to become the first leading professional English actress. She was one of eight actresses now employed by Davenant, male performers outnumbering them by two to one.

Mary Saunderson became Thomas Betterton's partner in married as in professional life. She was not alone in proving it possible for an actress to lead a life of untainted virtue at a time when chaste behaviour in such close proximity to the court must have seemed slightly eccentric. But, while the patents stressed that the introduction of actresses was a matter of morality, it was probably also inevitable that, in the absence of traditional routes for women into the profession, some actresses

to be 'taken from Calderón': but while at one extreme it pauses disconcertingly in its fast and furious action to debate the niceties of chivalric behaviour, at the other it cheerfully betrays these amidst the sub-plotting of the servants. In spite (or perhaps because) of this, the play achieved the then-unprecedented run of thirteen consecutive performances.

By the end of the 1660s, influenced by the superficially decorous but inwardly teeming townscapes of Molière, and anticipated by such Middletonian city comedies as John Wilson's *The Cheats* (1663), writers were producing a more locally-colourful line in comedies of London life, in which any residual moralizing finally gave way before farcical comedy of incident. Pepys, confessedly prone to such hyperbole, 'never laughed so in all my life' as at *Sir Martin Mar-All* (1667) – a play usually attributed to John Dryden, the leading professional playwright of the period, though the earlier claim that he had 'corrected' the Duke of Newcastle's original is now more readily admitted. The truth of the matter is unimportant, but the distinction it implies between a mere professional hack and an aristocrat of negligent genius is one which we shall again encounter.

By this time, too, the escapades of contrasting pairs of young lovers, overcoming all impediments to climactic unions, were being counterpointed by the posturings of a Restoration type with a greater propensity for boasting than for bedding – the fop. No fewer than four early varieties are to be found coxcombing their way through

in a licentious age should have achieved their positions through sexual patronage. The path of Elizabeth Barry was thus made smoother by the notorious rake Rochester – but she none the less became a remarkable tragic actress; and, Nell Gwyn, although she owed her early chances to being the protégée of Charles Hart, she achieved no less acclaim in comedy before she caught the eye of the King and endeared herself to the public as his vivacious mistress.

Nell Gwyn (1650–87) first appeared in Dryden's *The Indian Emperor* (1665). Two years later she had her greatest success in the 'breeches part' in his *Secret Love*

Shadwell's *The Sullen Lovers* in 1668 – all broad caricatures of real originals. The vogue for such personal satire soon fell out of favour – Edward Howard's long-lost lampoon upon the manners of the court, *The Change of Crowns* (1667), having been angrily suppressed by the King himself – but the fop survived, not so much fined-down as exultantly displayed by his typology.

The frank aptronyms for such characters as Lady Laycock and Lovemore in Betterton's *The Amorous Widow* (1667), or their equivalents Lady Cockwood and Courtall in Sir George Etherege's *She Would if She Could* (1668), suggest a similar process at work – here, the sex drive dramatized not as an attribute of personality but as its whole drift and purpose. Though critically explicable as in the tradition of Jonsonian humours, writ however large and lewd, this development may more pragmatically be viewed as a response to the increasing taste for bawdy in the aristocratic and elite circles from which theatre audiences were now largely drawn. It suggests a hardening of behavioural arteries, as if the known licentiousness of courtly life needed a theatrical mirror through which its jaded sensibilities might be titillated anew.

A little later, in 1672, Killigrew, who had been forced to borrow the recently-vacated Duke's house in Lincoln's Inn Fields after the fire at Bridges Street, tried to restore his fortunes by putting on three plays which were, as Pepys put it, 'acted all by the women'. In two of these, female characters need to adopt 'male' disguise – at once standing the Elizabethan convention neatly on its head (or perhaps its tail), and an early instance of the enduring taste for such 'breeches parts'. One of the plays was a revival of Killigrew's own late-Caroline comedy *The Parson's Wedding*, in which a pair of platonic lovers are outwitted by rakes who anticipate their Restoration equivalents by thirty years in their sensuality – and considerably exceed them in their cunning.

THE IDEOLOGY OF SELF-INDULGENCE

In truth, the supposed 'immorality' of the comic drama which flourished during the 1670s may be more aptly described as 'amorality'. For by contrast with Jacobean tragic heroes – who shape themselves existentially, through implementing active choices – the rakes of Restoration comedy tend rather to drift with the dictates of their appetites: and in this they are dramatic exemplars of the philosophy of Thomas Hobbes, who held that the ruling factors in men's lives are the pursuit of personal pleasure and the avoidance of pain. Although we may persuade ourselves that we are exercising free-will in deciding our actions, we are, according to Hobbes, only responding to external stimuli by 'choosing' what is best calculated to achieve these goals.

Yet if men can only act according to such external pressures, good and evil themselves become no more than appetites and aversions which we cannot but strive to pursue or circumvent. According to this fundamentally deterministic philosophy, human life resembles a race in which one never reaches the finishing post: as

Hobbes puts it, 'seeing all delight is appetite, and presupposeth a further end, there can be no contentment but in proceeding'. In considering the later drama of Charles's reign (as distinct from that vague 'Restoration' which critics allow to drift into the eighteenth century), we may usefully bear in mind its assimilation of these Hobbesian ingredients – behaviour perceived as an instinctive response to appetite, and the joy of the chase destined to culminate in anti-climax and ennui.

If Hobbes made a curiously English marriage between the laid-back pleasure principle long since embedded in Epicurean philosophy and the aggressive political pragmatism advocated by Machiavelli, so too, it seems, did his companionable pupil and sovereign – although, in the opinion of the contemporary historian Bishop Burnet, the King was too lazy to be a successfully despotic ruler in the true Hobbesian mould. For Charles had become accustomed in exile to the semblance of power and responsibility without having to confront the reality of either – a kind of role-play, we might call it, which was how he continued to regard life itself, once the immediacy of kingship was in his grasp.

As he strolled, supposedly incognito but recognized by all, into the House of Lords to listen to a debate, the King would thus declare the entertainment as good as a play, and join in the laughter at veiled references to himself. A regular visitor at the theatre, he is said to have lent a hand in the writing of plays, and interested himself in matters of casting. He allowed himself to indulge the open obscenities of Restoration behaviour and language as freely among women of good breeding as among his cronies or his concubines.

Aspects of the King's mercurial character are reflected in various plays of the period – especially those of William Wycherley, the most notable of the Restoration dramatists to have survived in the present-day repertoire. While Charles did not need to adopt the subterfuges of Horner in *The Country Wife* (1675), the workings of the 'double standard' were epitomized in his treatment of his own wife as sexually but not socially subordinate to the long line of mistresses his appetite consumed. And he was every bit as 'morally inconsistent' a character as critics have claimed to find Manly in Wycherley's *The Plain Dealer* (1676) – dour, cynical, and introverted at heart, yet capable of a wit that could be by turns callous or kindly, pretty or obscene.

As for the leading courtiers – such men as the notorious Earl of Rochester, Wycherley's mentor Buckingham, and his fellow-playwright Charles Sedley – they were a clever and highly-literate but promiscuous and hard-drinking set. The spirit of the times was such that Rochester and Sedley could with impunity attempt to rape an heiress in broad daylight, while the King himself instigated an assault upon a parliamentarian who dared to criticize one of his mistresses. These were men to whom such violence came as casually as a well-turned epigram, and in their everyday behaviour they walked that uneasy tightrope between rape and seduction, as between brutality and the defence of honour, which is an aspect of so many plays of the period.

It was seemly and witty to write plays, as even the Duke of Buckingham condescended to do – but not with any appearance of industry. It thus became a matter of some labour to appear casual, in art as in personal behaviour. And by the time that Wycherley began writing in the early 1670s even the self-indulgence which had at first seemed a spontaneous, almost patriotic repudiation of defeated puritanism had become to a degree formulaic – the theatre by that time not so much emulating the calculated decorum of courtly behaviour as involved in a complex process of interaction with it.

COURTIER PLAYWRIGHTS – AND PROFESSIONALS

There was thus a 'theatricality' in the everyday life of the court that was in part mirrored by and in part fashioned by the plays its frequenters saw and wrote. Most people in fashionable society appear to have behaved in public as if they were act-ing – while actors, frequently, were 'playing' characters from fashionable society. When Charles Lamb, well ahead of Victorian prudery, described Restoration comedy as 'artificial', he meant to explain away its excesses by suggesting that they did not reflect a real world: on the contrary, it would seem that the 'real world' of the courtly elite constructed itself in accordance with an 'artificial' code.

If the comic drama of the 1670s often appears uncritical of the social evils of its times, it theatricalizes them with a frankness that is no less devastating for such 'artificiality'. So, just as Etherege lays bare the sexual ethics of the Restoration with utter clarity in *The Man of Mode*, Wycherley in *The Plain Dealer* displays the misogyny that lies behind much of the behaviour of the court circle. The characters in *The Plain Dealer* have all just been to see *The Country Wife*, and the whole play has curious echoes of Shakespeare's *Twelfth Night* – the resulting metatheatrical tensions being used both to reveal and conceal the dissociation between language, social behaviour, and sexual experience in Wycherley's ever-lengthening theatrical hall of mirrors.

The puzzled and uncertain audience at the first performance of *The Plain Dealer* took their cue from the 'loud approbation' of Buckingham, Rochester, Dorset, and their cronies to decide in the play's favour. If the court wits approved, that was enough to launch what John Dennis called the play's 'sudden and lasting repu-tation'. Yet this was Wycherley's final play in a canon of four, and *The Man of Mode* the last of Etherege's meagre three. By contrast, John Dryden produced nearly thirty plays between 1663 and 1694, and Aphra Behn at least sixteen in a shorter active career from 1670 to 1682.

The difference was, of course, that between courtly amateurs – and professionals, whose livings depended upon their writing. Dryden owed his first preferment at court to the whim of one of the King's mistresses, and, despite his prestigious succession to Davenant as poet laureate, could never expect the treatment as an equal that Sedley and Etherege enjoyed by rank – and Wycherley alone, it seems, earned by virtue of personality and presence rather than by pedigree. Buckingham

Two great professional writers for the Restoration stage. Aphra Behn (left), was Britain's first woman playwright. Born in Kent, brought up in Surinam, and widowed at twenty-six, she worked as a spy during the Anglo-Dutch wars and turned to writing only after being imprisoned for debt. Her popular and racy plays, mainly in the comic form, included *The Forced Marriage* (1670), *The Rover* (1676), and *The Lucky Chance* (1686). John Dryden (right), was a poet, satirist, and critical theorist as well as a prolific playwright. His dramatic output ranged from comedies such as *The Rival Ladies* (1664) and *Marriage-à-la-Mode* (1673), to plays in the briefly fashionable 'heroic' mode, including *The Indian Queen* (1664) and the two-part *The Conquest of Granada*, and to blank verse drama – notably *All for Love* (1678), in which, as described on page 132, he set out to 'regularize' Shakespeare's *Antony and Cleopatra*

was thus free to ridicule Dryden as Bayes in his burlesque play *The Rehearsal* – but when the disputatious poet was suspected of a satirical attack upon Rochester, he was beaten up in a back alley by masked hirelings.

Dryden had hoped to achieve a measure of security in 1668 by contracting to write three plays a year for the King's in return for one and a quarter shares in the company – but the pace proved too demanding. John Crowne appears to have had a similar relationship with the Duke's, and Mrs Behn also wrote almost exclusively for this company, though no evidence of a formal agreement has survived. But freelance writers had to make do with the profits of the third night, and sometimes the sixth – the beginnings of the benefit system, which will demand further notice in the next chapter.

While both Dryden and Mrs Behn thus needed to accommodate public taste, both would have preferred to change it – Dryden artistically, and Behn in terms of its sexual *mores*, which were ostensibly 'liberated' but in practice thoroughly exploitative of women. So in *The Rover* (1676) Mrs Behn duly marries off her rakish reprobate to an heiress, but leaves as a notorious 'loose end' the forceful, acronymic courtesan Angelica Bianca – who has, in very truth, nowhere to go. Seized upon as a defect in construction, such a 'loose end' is all that Mrs Behn dared dangle before an audience disdainful of the lot of women such as herself, who sought independence in a society which demanded the rights but respected few of the obligations of patriarchy. Her 'intrigue comedy' is now rightly reclaiming its place in the permanent repertoire, following its author's own reclamation by feminist criticism.

It is a mark of Mrs Behn's consummate professionalism that the modern critic Robert Hume should single out her work as providing a 'striking index to changes of taste' in the 1670s, during which time she moved from serious intrigue dramas and tragi-comedies, through lighter comedies with foreign settings, to *Sir Patient*

Discovery of the villain, impaled on spikes, during the last act of Elkanah Settle's heroic drama, *The Empress of Morocco* (1673). The published text – a rare source of visual evidence concerning scenic design in the Restoration – includes an illustration for each act of the play, suggesting that the wings and borders for this spectacular production were appropriately but expensively changed during the action. Note the elaborate proscenium arch 'framing' the scene. Apart from such 'discoveries' as here pictured, and similar set-piece spectacles and tableaux, the actors would have been confined to the forestage area, here just visible between the proscenium doors in the foreground

Fancy in 1678 – 'a low London comedy of cuckoldry, vigorous, farcical, and dirty'. The same might be said of Dryden's *The Kind Keeper; or Mr Limberham*, also written in 1678, and replete with a rake who – not content with Willmore's two women in *The Rover* or Dorimant's three in *The Man of Mode* – dallies with the affections of no less than four ladies, all fairly compliant but tending to get in one another's way.

The difference between such plays and Wycherley's *The Country Wife*, with its apparently similar theme of multiple cuckoldings, is that between high-spirited farce, which recognizes at once the ubiquity and the ultimate absurdity of sexual desires, and comedy of manners, with its distinctive Restoration interplay between 'real' and artificial behaviour. It is needful thus to stress such differences between Restoration comic forms because only the 'mannered' comedies get much noticed today – although the sexual farces should be equally to the taste of a society that appreciates Joe Orton no less than Alan Ayckbourn.

The stern moral absolutes upheld in that seldom-revived but much-debated genre, 'heroic tragedy', seem hard to reconcile with the sexual caperings of Restoration comedy. Perhaps we can best consider their apparently equal appeal to the same audiences by calling the form, more properly, heroic *drama*. Its intention was thus to induce 'admiration' rather than Aristotle's 'fear and pity': 'serious' plays in consequence might enjoy 'happy' endings, and the stylized, 'artificial' nature of the language and actions offered the same kind of theatrical endorsement of the higher instincts of the age as comedy provided for the lower.

In heroic drama, however, the stylization lagged even further behind the behaviour, for here was a form which set out with deliberation to dignify a war well over by finding epic analogies for its conflicts – most notably, the conflict between the demands of public and private life. 'Love and valour ought to be the subject of it', as Dryden famously proclaimed of the genre in 1672 – a thematic opposition complemented by the distinctive verse idiom employed, the 'heroic' couplet or rhymed iambic pentameter. This replaced the increasingly unruly blank verse of the former age (as the Restoration mind perceived it) with the balanced dialectics and careful closures theoretically encouraged by the couplet form. In practice, however, the discipline could prove a corset from which bombast burst irresistibly forth, while the need for rhyme often reduced noble sentiments to bathos.

Titles such as Settle's *The Empress of Morocco* (1673) and Crowne's *The Destruction of Jerusalem* (1677) suggest well enough the exotic settings and lavish spectacles which were the usual requisites of the form – in which, as in its operatic elements, it was indebted to Davenant's earlier experiments. Not only in these technicolour tendencies, but also in its highly individualistic, Hobbesian sense of 'honour' – as a matter more of self-image than of service to others – heroic drama was scarcely 'epic' in the classical sense to which it aspired: indeed, we might more aptly acknowledge its distant ancestry to 'epic' as understood by Cecil B. De Mille.

The separate existence of the form dates from 1664, when Dryden collaborated with Sir Robert Howard on *The Indian Queen*, and its popularity was longer-lasting than is usually assumed – Buckingham's burlesque *The Rehearsal*, first staged in 1671, providing a sort of alternative *en travestie* at its peak of popularity, rather than precipitating an early decline. Dryden's other heroic plays included *The Indian Emperor* (1665), *Tyrannic Love* (1669), and *The Conquest of Granada* (1670) – but although, in the phlegmatic prologue to his last heroic play of 1675, *Aureng-Zebe*, he announced his intention of abandoning rhyme, heroic drama continued to flourish in revivals, as well as in new works by such writers as Elkanah Settle and Nathaniel Lee.

In 1672 Dryden had argued that, since the 'dramatic poetry of the last age', there had been 'an improvement of our wit, language, and conversation', which was attributable, 'freely and without flattery', to 'the court, and in it, particularly, to the King, whose example gives a law to it' – an influence we may well regret, severing as it did the link between drama and the common people. But there is a distinction between the veneer of politeness Dryden is here identifying and the stern principles of neoclassicism with which this is sometimes confused. Not least, heroic dramas could betray Aristotle's supposed 'unities' with as cheerful abandon as those of 'the last age', and display with no less relish the violence which neoclassicism would have kept offstage. The effects on Shakespearean drama are discussed on page 132.

'CITY END' AND 'TOWN END'

The dependence of the theatre upon courtly favour was never clearer than in the rapidity of the decline which followed its slackening of interest. By 1678 the King's company was already in difficulties: its leading members were growing old and infirm, while the bickering which broke out over misappropriations of costume spoke of chronic mismanagement and growing debt. In the same year, the 'popish plot' distracted royal attention from theatrical matters, and the subsequent 'exclusionist crisis' – the attempt to bar Charles's brother, a known Catholic, from the succession, in favour of one of his illegitimate offspring – further diverted the energies and attentions of the courtly audience.

For the King's, this was the start of a terminal decline. In April 1682, Charles Killigrew closed the Theatre Royal in Drury Lane, and began to negotiate a merger of the two patent companies with Davenant's son Charles – who had by now entered into his inheritance at Dorset Garden, where Betterton and his friend and fellow-actor William Smith were assisting him in the management. In truth, it was a takeover – of playhouse, playbooks, and all. Killigrew's entitlement to act without consulting his fellow-sharers was challenged, but in the end he succeeded in cutting his losses and securing what would today be called a golden handshake: and in the event the 'United Company', which opened at Drury Lane in November 1682 just a week after the Duke's played for the last time at Dorset Garden, was found sufficient for London's theatrical needs for the following thirteen years.

Dorset Garden continued in use as a theatre, but largely for the more lavish kind of entertainments – which apparently suited not only its technical resources but

'Triple portrait' of John Lacy (d. 1681) by Michael Wright, painted in 1662 to the commission of Charles II. The favourite comic actor of his generation, Lacy is here shown in three of his most admired roles – Teague in *The Committee*, Scruple in *The Cheats*, and Galliard in *The Variety*. In 1667, however, Lacy infuriated the monarch (and was briefly imprisoned) on account of satirical touches (through which he appeared to reflect on court corruption) in *The Change of Crowns* (1667), by Edward Howard. Famous also for his Falstaff, Lacy reputedly caught Dryden to the life in the role of Bayes in Buckingham's *The Rehearsal* in 1671. He was the author of *Sauny the Scot*, based on Shakespeare's *The Taming of the Shrew*

also the tastes of an audience increasingly drawn from the nearby City of London, whose denizens were said to prefer spectacle to wit. Since this was the judgement passed upon them by writers and courtiers living in 'the town' – that is, the emerging West End, now rapidly creeping down the Strand towards Whitehall and the Palace of Westminster – it is clearly prejudiced. But it does at least confirm that members of the middle and merchant classes who lived and worked in the square mile of the City of London (citizens observed the protestant work ethic, while gentlemen defined themselves by their leisure) were beginning to make their presence felt in theatre audiences.

Indeed, on the evidence of Pepys's *Diary*, and the many prologues and epilogues which had now became almost *de rigueur* in their solicitations of approval from the various sections of the audience, it seems that as early as the end of the 1660s citizens and even apprentices had begun to infiltrate back into the auditorium – though since the total daily capacity of the theatres at that time amounted to little more than a thousand places, their numbers cannot have been very large. Certainly, 'the cits' from the City were already featuring as attendant characters in plays – at first as targets for satire, cuckoldings, and contempt, but sometimes actually making the milieu their own.

Thus, Thomas Shadwell was putting distinctly bourgeois concerns into a distinctly bourgeois setting in *Epsom Wells* (1672) long before he delved into the murk of London's underworld (ironically, by courtesy of Terence) in *The Squire of Alsatia* (1688). And Dryden's *The Kind Keeper* had been largely set in a boarding house. But as the 1680s dawned in a climate of continuing crisis, old animosities against the citizens – prominent now amongst the exclusionists, just as they had been quick to declare for parliament not so long before – broke surface: and two plays which vent these animosities exemplify the continuing contrast between the 'mannered' and farcical comic modes.

Thomas Otway's brief dramatic career is best remembered today for the tragedy *Venice Preserved* (1682), in which, at the very end of the period covered by this chapter, he combined passion, elementary psychology, and pace in a manner interestingly anticipatory of melodrama. Even in this play – one of the very few Restoration tragedies that revive successfully today – Otway could not resist creating, in the figure of the corrupt, lecherous, and largely irrelevant old senator Antonio, a cruel caricature of the leading exclusionist politician, the Earl of Shaftesbury.

But it had been in his earlier comedy, *The Soldier's Fortune* (1680), that, in place of the conventional 'mannered' contrast between witty courtiers and silly cits, Otway had set a noble but penniless captain against a wealthy old cit, Sir Davy Dunce – now married to the woman he loves, who needs the money and security Sir Davy can offer. The play ends with a basis for complaisant cuckoldry established: but meanwhile the nature of the new economic relationship between 'town' and 'city' has been revealed with acute and sardonic realism.

By contrast, Edward Ravenscroft's *The London Cuckolds* (1681), a sprightly sexual farce, is significant for the prominence given, in plotline as in title, to three rich city merchants, all of whom have married young wives and are made to share their favours with sprightlier admirers. There is little direct political content to the play – indeed, one of the rakes is himself a merchant – and it continued to be revived on Lord Mayor's Day for almost a century, evidently greatly enjoyed by the classes it mocked. Yet perhaps this is itself significant: for the theatre, as it saw its courtly audiences shrink, had soon to acknowledge that it needed the cits; and once the cits had come politically as well as economically into their own, they could afford to laugh at themselves in the theatre, because they knew that in real life the last laugh would be theirs.

ronically, when John Dryden 'disencumbered' himself from rhyme in 1678, the play in which he chose to do so, All for Love, perfectly exemplified the heroic drama's characteristic conflict between love and valour: but it also observed the 'unities' of time, place, and action – thus making a properly neoclassical, blank-verse tragedy out of its Shakespearean original, Antony and Cleopatra, which had preferred to sprawl purposefully in 46 scenes across the ancient world. In style, nevertheless, Dryden claimed to have imitated 'the divine Shakespeare' – remarking that the models of the ancients, though 'regular . . . are too little for English tragedy, which requires to be built in a larger compass'.

In the same year, 1678, the critic Thomas Rymer, while brooding on the defects of The Tragedies of the Last Age, came up with the concept of 'poetic justice', which heroic drama already tended to observe. This held that moral propriety must always be observed in art, the wicked duly being punished and the virtuous rewarded – a principle which Nahum Tate proceeded to put into effect in the upbeat climax to his King Lear of 1681, in which the King comes into his own again (as all Kings should), but abdicates in favour of those reunited lovers, Edgar and Cordelia. The Fool, incidentally, is quietly abolished, as he had been in the Restoration theatre at large.

Though authors might dignify such reworkings in preface or prologue by reference to neoclassical rules or poetic justice, in practice most were responding pragmatically to changing fashions and theatrical possibilities. Indeed, when William Davenant was granted his share of the Shakespearean canon in 1660, it had been on the condition (not imposed on Thomas Killigrew) that the plays be 'reformed' – and reform them Davenant did, according to his own and, it seems, his audience's preference for spectacle, music, and vivid incident.

Details of two frontispieces from the first 'scholarly' edition of Shakespeare (1709), edited by Nicholas Rowe. The 'closet scene' from *Hamlet* (left) is said to portray Thomas Betterton in the title role. His ungartered stocking suggests Hamlet's 'madness', while the overturned chair signifies alarm. The actor strikes an 'attitude' of unbalanced terror which he would presumably have held for the audience's appreciation and applause. The Ghost's feudal armour consorts rather oddly with the unequivocally 'modern' dress of Hamlet and Gertrude. Right: Banquo's ghost (behind the witches) displays a procession of Stuart-lookalike kings to Macbeth (again reputedly Betterton), who, in his full-bottomed wig, long-pocketed waistcoat, and square-toed shoes looks every inch a gentleman of Queen Anne's reign. The witches, whose half-sunken cauldron is emerging from the stage trap, are now comic hags, played by men

When, in 1667, Davenant and Dryden 'polished' The Tempest, one of the few plays in which (as it happened) Shakespeare already observed the unities, they thus chose to flesh it out with an extraneous sub-plot, providing sisters for Miranda and Caliban and a female counterpart for Ariel. As for violence, in 1678 Edward Ravenscroft managed to make his version of Titus Andronicus even gorier than the original, while in the following year Dryden's count of corpses was higher than Shakespeare's in the last act of Troilus and Cressida. By 1681, Nahum Tate was even adding a dash of comedy to Coriolanus – the only one of the great tragedies in which Shakespeare himself had resisted such bastardy of genre. As for Macbeth, Davenant's long dominant version included machine-flown witches and music by Matthew Locke.

Bearing in mind that most of Shakespeare's plays are themselves reworkings of other people's originals, there is nothing reprehensible or even unusual about the way in which Restoration (and later) writers reshaped them to reflect their own tastes. Recent generations have done so in different ways, typically imposing a heavy layer of directorial 'interpretation' even while restoring the 'integrity' of the text – a text which, it is now increasingly argued, derives any 'authority' from theatrical practice rather than the author's unmediated genius.

We might also bear in mind that this was the first period in which the British theatre had available a repertoire of past 'classics' – though it did not yet regard them as such. That it restored them to the stage, however selectively and with whatever interventions of its own, contributed in part to the good state of health enjoyed by the drama during the decade from 1668 to 1687 – the originality and formal range of the new comedies and tragedies, as discussed in the main text, further suggesting a craft in a state of creative ferment.

CHAPTER 9

The Birth of a Bourgeois Theatre

As bare statistics affirm, the repertoire of the United Company at first leaned heavily towards revivals. Thus, during the early 1680s, when the King's company was still active, around twelve new plays a year had been reaching the London stage. The remainder of that troubled decade saw the death of Charles, the brief but divisive reign of his brother James, and the 'bloodless revolution' which paired James's protestant daughter Mary with her husband William of Orange as supposedly 'constitutional' monarchs: it also saw, on average, barely four new plays a year reaching the stage of Drury Lane.

The theatre had been quick to respond to the politically-charged atmosphere of the times. Now, tragedies were often heavy with historical analogies – Tate's adaptation of *Richard II*, with its theme of the deposing of a legitimate monarch, having caused trouble for the King's company in 1680 just as Shakespeare's

William III in triumph, escorted by Flora and Britannia. The ladies at the bottom left of this picture were identified by Horace Walpole as Mrs Barry and Mrs Bracegirdle, the leading actresses of the late seventeenth century. The original Millamant in Congreve's *The Way of the World*, Anne Bracegirdle (1671–1748) had a preference for comic or pathetic roles, whereas Elizabeth Barry (*c.* 1658–1713) excelled in tragedy – especially of the nobler or more heroic kind, in which, according to Cibber, she could 'pour out the sentiment with an enchanting harmony'. Bracegirdle was reputedly the greater beauty of the two, and vivaciously expressive where Barry tended to sonorous intensity. The painting by Sir Godfrey Kneller celebrates the 'constitutional' monarchy which followed the deposition of James II in 1688

original had done as an unwitting apologia for Essex's rebellion in 1601. There was outspoken Whig propaganda in Lee's *Lucius Junius Brutus* – its celebration of the toppling of the tyrannic Tarquin and the founding of the Roman republic leading to the play's prohibition after a few performances in 1680. But there were also Tory counterblasts, which in the same year ranged from Southerne's *The Loyal Brother* (1682), with its eponymous tribute to the waiting, Catholic heir, to Dryden's *The Spanish Friar* – which actually tagged an anti-Catholic sub-plot to its central theme of a monarch divinely-inspired against illegitimate overthrow.

In other tragedies, such as Lee's *Caesar Borgia* (1679) or John Crowne's *Thyestes* (1680), old heroic certainties seemed to be giving way before the merely horrific. If Otway's *The Orphan* (1680) was an early and superior response to the developing taste for pathos, this was more often and more lazily met by adding an extra dose of tears to conventional tragi-comedy, as in Southerne's *The Disappointment* (1684) or D'Urfey's *The Banditti* (1686). On occasion, as in Settle's *Fatal Love* of 1680, horror and pathos collided in a single play, with generally unfortunate consequences.

John Banks had his eye on one influential section of the audience for pathos when he described *The Unhappy Favourite* (1681) as a 'ladies' play', and in the following year he wrote the first of his true 'she-tragedies', *Virtue Betrayed; or, Anna Bullen.* The tastes of the 'fair sex' had now to be properly respected, not because the upper and middle reaches of society were becoming any less patriarchal, but because leisure, though no longer an invariable gentlemanly attribute, remained the certain mark of a lady.

NEW KINDS OF COMEDY

In comedy, Aphra Behn had tried her hand at political playwriting early in the decade, savaging the old puritan enemy in *The Roundheads* (1681) and the new whig opposition in *The City Heiress* (1682) – one character being a thinly disguised Shaftesbury, gulled into promoting himself as heir to the Polish crown. But when, in the epilogue she wrote for the anonymous *Romulus and Hersilia* (1682), she advocated the execution of an illegitimate son who intrigued against his father – a clear reference to the pretender Monmouth – she outraged the King's curious sense of family honour, and probably found herself briefly in jail.

Turning increasingly to fiction for her living, Mrs Behn wrote only a few further plays – and the contrasting fates of two of these in the thin seasons of 1686 and 1687 are instructive. Thus, *The Lucky Chance* (1686), though successfully revived as a roistering sex comedy in our own age, was by now too blatantly immoral for its original audience, and Mrs Behn found it expedient to add a defensive preface to the published version. She then tried a complete change of direction, and in *The Emperor of the Moon* (1687) wrote a spectacular musical farce which was zany in the most precise sense – foreshadowing as it did the fashion for anglicizing the types of the Italian *commedia dell'arte*. The actor

William Mountfort tried to repeat the great success of this farce with his *Life and Death of Doctor Faustus* in 1688, but the fashion for the *commedia* style was not to flourish fully until the new century.

Aphra Behn, with the consummate timing of a professional, died in 1689. By then, of the old courtly crew, Rochester was also dead, and Buckingham 'worn to a thread with whoring', while among Mrs Behn's playwriting friends Etherege had gone into exile with his erstwhile king, Otway was buried in a pauper's grave, Wycherley was in a debtors' prison, and Nathaniel Lee was on public exhibition in a madhouse. James during his brief reign had had more important things on his mind than theatre – and neither William or Mary showed more than a perfunctory interest. So the theatre finally lost its function as a focus of courtly activity – and, needing instead to cater to the tastes of the bourgeoisie, it had to become responsive to the market forces they increasingly controlled.

To judge from Sedley's preface to his *Bellamira* (1687), in this case it was not the play's immorality that offended its audiences, but an edge of sardonic wit too sharp for middle-class comfort. The huge success of Shadwell's *The Squire of Alsatia* (1688) revealed that simpler preferences now prevailed – for a plotful romp, set (despite its Terentian origins) in a recognizable ambience, in language that was racy without being indecent, and (not least significantly) in which virtue, as well as receiving its climactic reward, should consistently be preferred to vice. From this time onwards, as new plays began to reappear in the repertoire in greater numbers, a fair proportion were just such swift-moving comedies of local colour, whose authors hoped to emulate Shadwell's success – not to mention his initial run of thirteen nights.

Prologues and epilogues, which by now were expected appendages to a play, needed to calculate with some precision their regular appeals for an audience's applause. During the earlier part of Charles's reign, these had regularly identified the pit as the haunt of the wits, the young gallants, and the fops. The side boxes were seen as the special preserve of the 'fair sex', while in the 'upper boxes' to the rear sat the 'great people', as Pepys described them – or 'all that keep coaches', in Dryden's nicer definition. In the middle gallery the worthy but despised 'cits' seem to have been jumbled together with whores, their bullies, and their clientele – while in the topmost tier sat the footmen and the lackeys, awaiting the bidding of their betters below.

BETTERTON DEFECTS FROM DRURY LANE

The changes towards the century's end are subtle but irresistible, and complicated by a streak of masochism among the middle classes – who appear to have found a measure of theatrical insult acceptable, so long as it was prompted by a due recognition of their power. The critic John Dennis, writing just after the century's turn, mourned not so much the lack of breeding as the inattentiveness of the new audiences. 'Tumbling and vaulting and ladder-dancing' and other such *entr'acte* entertainments had now begun to fill out the bill: and Dennis attributed this to audiences themselves filled out with 'younger brothers', the newly-rich, and a 'considerable number of foreigners'. He also remarked that 'there are ten times more gentlemen now in business' than there had been in King Charles's reign – apparently objecting not to the class origins or commercial associations of such 'gentlemen', but to the probability that their political and business worries would prevent them from concentrating properly on a play.

Just as dramatists were coming to terms with the tastes of their new audiences, another development was threatening the livelihoods of the players. The last and least of the theatrical Davenants, Alexander, had deprived Betterton and Smith of their cautious but knowledgeable management of Drury Lane in 1687, and proceeded to milk the company financially at a difficult time. When he was eventually forced to flee, his affairs passed into the hands of his chief creditor, one Christopher Rich – who preferred to employ cheap beginners to the experienced actors with which the ageing company was now weighed down. In December 1694, Betterton and most of his fellow veterans laid their grievances in a formal petition before the Lord Chamberlain – and when the death of Queen Mary halted playing later in the same month, the rebels seized their opportunity to consolidate plans for an independent future.

This King William himself authorized in March 1695, whereupon the new company raised a subscription to restore Lisle's Tennis Court in Lincoln's Inn Fields. The end of royal mourning enabled Drury Lane to reopen in the same month (with a revival of Mrs Behn's passionate tragedy *Abdelazar*, which was poorly received). But although the Lincoln's Inn theatre was not ready for another three weeks, Betterton's company had secured the loyalty of the young William Congreve, whose first play, *The Old Bachelor*, had been the success of the season in 1693: now, not only did his *Love for Love* achieve a comparable first run of thirteen performances, but the company 'had seldom occasion to act any other play' in their opening season. So Congreve's new style of mannered comedy also inaugurated a new 'war of the theatres' – to both of which we shall return.

At first, then, the breakaway troupe at Lincoln's Inn Fields benefited from their seniority. Betterton, although approaching sixty – and, for all his protean range, apparently plain in appearance and a trifle plump – was now more than ever at his best in tragic and heroic roles, but he also continued to take youthful male leads such as Congreve's Valentine. He had Cave Underhill, cast in the 'humours' role of Sir Sampson, as his 'heavy', while the young but lugubrious character comedian Thomas Doggett won huge acclaim as Sailor Ben. Mary Betterton having just retired, the chief female lead was now Elizabeth Barry, whose hard-headed and worldly-wise women seem better to have reflected her character than her tragic line in high-sounding heroines. The younger Anne Bracegirdle – already a veteran in her early twenties – took the ingénue role of the vivacious Angelica.

Cave Underhill (*c.* 1634–1710), a character actor who excelled in strong supporting roles. He is pictured here as the pompous puritanical clerk, Obadiah, in Sir Robert Howard's *The Committee* – one of the few topical plays of the immediate post-Restoration period which established itself in the continuing repertoire. The 'committee' was that set up by Cromwell to redistribute royalist estates – the play's two cavalier heroes not only holding on to their own but securing heiresses besides. From the same play, John Lacy's comic but kindly Irishman, Teague, is portrayed on page 130. This mezzotint by R. B. Parkes is after a painting by R. Bing

THE RISE OF THE BENEFIT SYSTEM

In 1692, William Mountfort had been killed while defending Mrs Bracegirdle from the unwelcome attentions of Lord Mohun – the light punishment meted out to the offenders indicating not only the low regard in which the players generally were held, but the presumption that any actress was fair sexual game. However, Barry, Bracegirdle, and Mountfort's widow, Susannah – by then Mrs Verbruggen – achieved the distinction of being named as equals with the men on the licence granted to the Lincoln's Inn company, though when only the first two were made full sharers the neglected Mrs Verbruggen returned in disgust to Rich's camp.

This partial emancipation of women at least as financial equals within an acting company corrected an inequality that had been recognized as far back as the 1660s, when performances were, as Pepys put it, set aside 'for the women's

Portrait by Giuseppe Grisoni of Colley Cibber (1671–1757) in probably his most famous role, that of Lord Foppington in *The Relapse*. Having himself created this callous coxcomb, as the unelevated Sir Novelty Fashion, in his own play, *Love's Last Shift* (1696), the pragmatic Cibber was as happy with Vanbrugh's cynical sequel as he was proud of his own sentimental original. In life he seems to have been a more self-aware and self-fashioned version of the fops he played on stage: but though his execrable verse as poet laureate offended Pope, who made him Prince of Dullness in the final version of his *Dunciad* (1743), as a man of the theatre Cibber was an astute and thoroughly professional all-rounder. His autobiography, the *Apology* of 1740, is a rich source of astute comment on his contemporaries – and a curious mixture of the self-opinionated and the self-depreciating concerning his own long stage career

sake' – thus putting them on the same charitable footing as the younger players, who were allowed similar 'benefit' performances. By the 1680s, the youngsters were being given the privilege of playing their own repertoire during the slack summer months, and the 'benefit system' – of allocating the profits from one performance for a particular purpose – had become an individual perquisite.

As we have noted earlier, for many dramatists the receipts from their third day's benefit became a chief source of revenue – though sometimes as much effort might be required to prevent a play being damned at its opening as to ensure a house packed with generous friends three days later. Slowly, as play-writing became more professional and as first runs also lengthened, a further author's benefit was awarded when a play reached its sixth performance, and eventually even its ninth.

Mrs Barry is said to have been the first player to have been granted a benefit, sometime during the 1680s, and references in the actors' petition of 1694 suggest that it had by then become an expected annual bonus for senior members of the company. Following Betterton's defection, the sharing arrangements at Lincoln's Inn at first made the practice redundant there, but at Drury Lane Rich is said to have given his actors an average of sixty benefits a year between 1696 and 1704, 'to prevent their desertion and mutining'. By the following century, the privilege had hardened by custom into an expected right.

THE RISING GENERATION

Betterton's defection from Drury Lane paradoxically left the 'Old House', as it was called, in the hands of predominantly youthful (and cheaper) players, such as George Powell, to whom Rich had already been making over some of Betterton's parts, the 'unpolished hero' Jack Verbruggen, and the comedian William Pinketh-man, who excelled as Harlequin. By the turn of the century, William Bullock, Robert Wilks, Henry Norris, and Anne Oldfield had all joined the company.

The influence of this new generation upon acting style will concern us in the next chapter. Meanwhile, as one of its leading members was to recall many years later in his autobiography: 'Betterton's people . . . were most of them too far advanc'd in years to mend; and tho' we, in Drury Lane, were too young to be excellent, we were not too old to be better.' This young actor, who had made his debut at Drury Lane in 1690, was Colley Cibber, and he demands our earlier attention here – for, having first made his mark by stepping at short notice into a leading role in a court performance of Congreve's *The Double-Dealer* in 1694, he was soon and successfully trying his hand at creating roles on his own behalf.

In 1696 Cibber was accordingly cast as the foppish Sir Novelty Fashion in the hit of the season at Drury Lane, his own *Love's Last Shift* – a play which is sometimes accorded the dubious distinction of being the first 'sentimental comedy'. Indeed, although its rake undergoes only a perfunctory conversion – having, as his creator cheerfully acknowledged, been 'lewd for above four acts' –

the piece did sting Sir John Vanbrugh into writing, as his first play to reach the stage, a no less successful 'sequel', *The Relapse*, in which the climactic repentance of Cibber's play is seen as prelude to a marriage lacking in fidelity or love, but from which no escape is possible.

Despite its wit and sheer vivacity, Vanbrugh's play was in many ways old-fashioned, not least in its easy assumption of the superiority of town over country ways – and in Miss Hoyden it even made a belated contribution to the misogynistic sexual typology of Restoration comedy. However, the pragmatic Cibber was delighted to play Vanbrugh's version of his fop, now elevated to the peerage – and the Drury Lane audiences were seemingly no less responsive to

Formulating the 'rules' of acting

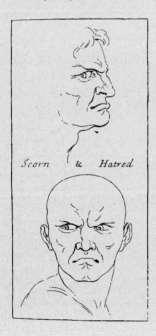

Lebrun's's profile and full-face expressions for scorn and hatred (1701)

The acting style of the late seventeenth century had, of course, been shaped at a time when rituals of behaviour – the conventionalizing of self – were of great importance to everyday courtly life, and its 'presentational' quality thus reflected the formality of elite intercourse.

Although the relationship between the theatre and the court was now changing, many books of the period continued to offer instruction in social behaviour based on the assumption that its everyday manifestations – the recurrent ceremonies of greeting and parting, bowing and complimenting, and asserting or acknowledging precedence, not to mention all the subtle significations of sexual response – were governed by forms of expression so formalized as to be in themselves 'theatrical'.

Even fashion accessories could now be made to encode a wide range of meanings. When Harriet is given an 'acting lesson' in Etherege's The Man of Mode, much of it has to do with the many ways of holding her fan – a visual aid to social and sexual discourse of some intricacy, since its signals could variously affirm, contradict, or modulate the spoken word.

In an essay in The Spectator in 1711, Addison imagined an academy for 'handling the fan', whose syllabus would cover the many ways in which the object might be tapped, opened, unfurled, discharged,

and 'fluttered' – this latter exercise including fine distinctions between angry, modest, timorous, confused, merry, and amorous emotions. So what Mrs Loveit is 'saying' when she 'tears her fan in pieces' in The Man of Mode is only half-expressed by the 'hell and furies' she flings verbally at Dorimant.

Rhetoric already had its 'grammar' of gestic accompaniment, illustrated in the diagram opposite (prepared for the deaf) by John Bulwer; and by 1701 Charles Lebrun was formulating a similar set of rules for facial expression – such as those for 'scorn' and 'hatred' also illustrated alongside. Betterton himself (according to his first biographer Charles Gildon, writing in 1710) believed in a relationship between human behaviour and its many forms of physical expression that was no less precise:

> Every passion or emotion of the mind has from nature its proper and peculiar countenance, sound, and gesture; and the whole body of man, all his looks, and every sound of his voice, like the strings of an instrument, receive their sounds from the various impulses of the passions.

Such beliefs could result in an extreme stylization of individual performances, but the added expectation of kinetic and even

Vanbrugh's fluently cynical view of life than to what Cibber called the 'moral delight' on offer in his own play. Little over a year later, the publication of *A Short View of the Immorality and Profaneness of the English Stage*, by a nonjuring clergyman, Jeremy Collier, was to make such casual equivocation more difficult.

In the first part of the *Short View* (which was actually of considerable length) Collier gave chapter and verse for his charges that the theatre was immodest and obscene, that it ridiculed the clergy, and that it not only portrayed vicious persons as its heroes but rewarded them, in violation of poetic justice – whose desirable extension from tragedy to comedy Collier did not invent, but to which he now gave general currency. When, in the second part of his book, he

pictorial refinement probably made for an even greater formality in stage groupings.

Holding a pose, moreover, had the purpose not only of signalling a particular emotional mood, but also of soliciting applause. As Jocelyn Powell has pointed out, in an age long before theatre directors were thought of (but with playwrights far less closely involved in the rehearsal process than in Shakespeare's day), the dancing-master would almost certainly have been prominent in 'designing' poses and tableaux, and may well have helped with other conventionalized stage movements – as indicated by stage directions to 'come forward', 'retire', or 'converse apart'. This approach to acting almost certainly survived the changing generic, stylistic, and moral qualities of the plays presented, simply because the actors who had entered the profession at the Restoration, and who by the early 1690s were senior members of the only surviving company, continued to exert a dominant influence over the limited number of new entrants to the profession.

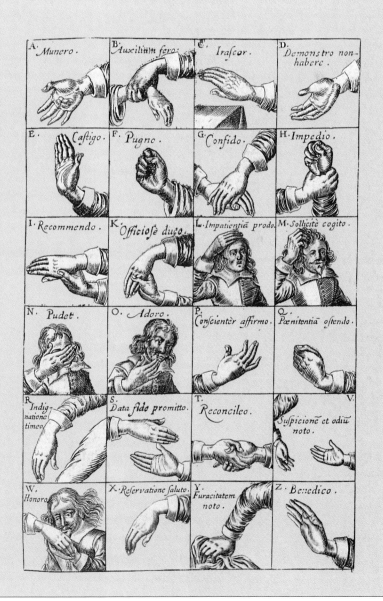

Mimetic gestures from
Bulwer's *Chirologia* (1644)

proceeded to mount an attack on the theatre as such, citing authorities ancient and modern in his support, he justified his opponents' charges that, while posing as a reformer of the stage, he was actually seeking its destruction.

However, although Collier's strictures upon theatrical obscenity and blasphemy were in themselves often naive, pedantic, and humourless, they struck an immediate chord. And the scores of 'amendments' and 'answers' which poured from the presses in the wake of the *Short View* (amongst, however, twice as many 'defences' and 'vindications' in its support) shared the disadvantage that, in the terms of the debate dictated by Collier, many of the plays of the previous forty years were very difficult to defend.

Several issues touched on earlier in this chapter now begin to come together. In truth, Collier did no more than identify and articulate a changing social mood, and the theatrical response to his strictures could only be to accommodate more openly those changes in the composition and expectations of audiences which in practice had already been acknowledged. Conversely, the need of the theatre to build an audience base among the merchants and money-men of the City of London was as much a recognition of the increasing economic power of the bourgeoisie as it was the result of stray gunfire from a pamphlet war.

'HARD' VERSUS 'HUMANE' COMEDY

The middle classes were now dictating the terms of the economic as of the moral debate – to the extent that making a profit from the handling of money, once condemned as the sin of usury, was now not only recognized but institutionalized. Thus, the economic life-lie of the National Debt had been created along with the Bank of England in 1694 – the Bank being legally entitled to issue paper money and so to raise further funds by recycling capital already 'loaned' to the government. When the Goldsmiths' Company, with a vested interest in more traditional forms of security, had tried to break the Bank in 1697 by demanding payment upon an amount assembled in excess of its 'real' reserves, the government stepped in to prevent this: wealth, for so long measured in the possession of land or at least in material goods, could thus be safely amassed in promises written on pieces of paper.

In this respect, the dramatic canon of the tragically short-lived George Farquhar, newly arrived in London from Dublin's Smock Alley Theatre in 1697, is exemplary. As late as 1699, in his highly successful *The Constant Couple* at Drury Lane, we find him still pouring scorn on the bourgeois 'cits' – their representatives portrayed either as selfish hypocrites like Vizard (who ironically quotes Hobbes in his vindication), or as duplicitous crooks in the mould of Alderman Smuggler, whose profits are made from illicit dealings with the French. Yet the economic strains of the intermittent war with France, which made Smuggler's activities so treacherous, paradoxically reinforced the need for new forms of credit – and within a few decades, as we shall see, those who controlled

The 'female wits' and the drama of sensibility

By the early years of the seventeenth century, the 'humane' style of comedy was in the ascendant, with such plays as Richard Wilkinson's Vice Reclaim'd of 1703, Sir Richard Steele's The Tender Husband of 1705, and Cibber's The Lady's Last Stake of 1707 laying their eponymous claims to virtue. In the last of these, incidentally, the ever-opportunistic author took up at Drury Lane the debate on divorce which Farquhar had initiated with Betterton's company earlier that year in The Beaux Stratagem – plays of very different dramatic qualities, yet alike portraying sexual incompatibility, for so long regarded merely as an enabling device for cuckoldry, as a cause of mutual misery and despair.

Although the new 'drama of sensibility' did not often present its female characters as other than sexual targets (however elusive), it did accord them an intellectual stature of sorts, as well as a greater degree of moral integrity. A group of women writers had already begun to seize such ground as their own: thus, despite their declared discipleship to Aphra Behn, it was in their anticipation of the new morality that the 'female wits', as they have become known, achieved success with audiences.

Ironically, The Female Wits was originally the title of an ill-tempered burlesque upon their work – staged at Drury Lane when Mary de la Riviere Manley, whose comedy The Lost Lover had been presented there in March 1696, defected a few months later to Betterton's new company with her tragedy The Royal Mischief.

Also emerging as 'female wits' at this time were Mary Pix and Catherine Trotter, both of whom acknowledged Mrs Manley's lead: but the most successful of their number, Susannah Centlivre, did not begin writing until 1700 – by which time no fewer than nine women writers (confessedly not all playwrights) could be assembled to offer a verse memorial to Dryden, who had died in that year. Feminist criticism has now properly retrieved many of their number from neglect, though probably only the works of Mrs Centlivre – whose The Busy Body (1709), The Wonder (1714), and A Bold Stroke for a Wife (1719) all remained popular for a century or more – would challenge the rich output of Mrs Behn in their appeal to more modern audiences.

The historical significance of the 'female wits' is none the less for its brevity: for they struck the right moral note for the right audiences at the right historical moment. In the 1690s, moreover, the theatre was the medium to which any aspiring writer would naturally turn, and even as late as the 1720s it was as a dramatist that Eliza Haywood began her career: but, following the earlier example of Defoe, Mrs Haywood soon turned to the periodical and the emergent novel – as did most leading female writers until well into the present century. So far as women were concerned, the stage was abandoned to the actresses – while the actresses, in polite society, were assumed to be already abandoned.

Susannah Centlivre (1669–1723), the leading figure among the so-called 'female wits' of the early eighteenth century, for whom the drama rather than the novel was briefly the genre of natural choice. Mrs Centlivre was author of nineteen plays, largely in the intrigue comedy style: among these, *The Wonder* owed its first success to Anne Oldfield, and was later to provide a strong role for Garrick, while the role of the multiply disguised hero in *A Bold Stroke for a Wife* continues to offer a challenge to actors of mimetic resource

the national purse-strings, so far from being portrayed as the villains of plays, had become models of dramatic propriety.

Farquhar's later style, as struck in *The Recruiting Officer* (1706) and *The Beaux Stratagem* (1707), is distinguished not by an abandonment of 'mannered' comedy as such, but by its transplantation into new kinds of social and geographical milieu – to which the traditional class warfare between 'town end' and 'city end' was happily irrelevant. In the process, his characters gain a capacity for experiencing subtler nuances of pleasure, and (perhaps more significantly) also for experiencing real pain. The modern critic Robert Hume has made an apt distinction between the 'hard' comedy of Congreve and Vanbrugh, as late exponents of the Restoration mode, and the 'humane' school which, with Collier's assistance, was soon to provoke both writers into abandoning the theatre: in the work of Farquhar alone do we find the broader sympathies of the new mode combined with the wit and verve of the old.

THE NEW WAR AND THE NEW UNION

In the 'war of the theatres' between Drury Lane and Lincoln's Inn Fields, Rich's company struggled along on the strength of a single lucky success in each of their early seasons – the first, Southerne's adaptation of Mrs Behn's novel, *Oroonoko* in 1695, being followed by *Love's Last Shift*, *The Relapse*, and another, less well-remembered comedy in two parts by Vanbrugh, a dramatic version of *Aesop* from the French of Boursault, in which Cibber took and evidently relished the title role.

Then, with Farquhar's *The Constant Couple* in 1699, the Drury Lane company hit their stride – their leading player, Robert Wilks, being just half the age of Thomas Betterton when he created the role of Sir Harry Wildair. Opposite Wilks, as Lady Lurewell, Mrs Verbruggen was in her early thirties – but Anne Oldfield was already a juvenile member of the company, and more than ready to step into Mrs Verbruggen's shoes upon her death in 1703. Indeed, her success was soon to drive Mrs Bracegirdle into precautionary retirement.

Not only was the age of the rival Lincoln's Inn company starting to tell, but its 'co-operative' structure was increasingly giving rise to internal dissensions, and in 1700 the Lord Chamberlain required Betterton to assume the sole management. By then a gout-ridden 65, in the same season the veteran player stepped sideways into the slightly less demanding though still-youthful part of Fainall in Congreve's last play, *The Way of the World*, with Verbruggen playing Mirabell opposite Mrs Bracegirdle's Millamant – and Mrs Barry in the role of Marwood, which she virtually prefigured. Although the play is now regarded as Congreve's masterpiece, it achieved only a moderate initial run. The company's dependence upon Betterton was highlighted by his subsequent triumph as Falstaff in both parts of *Henry IV*. It provoked a flurry of revivals and adaptations of Shakespeare and Jonson at both houses.

Wittily but defensively, both Congreve and Vanbrugh had written their responses to Collier in 1698: but Vanbrugh's *The Provoked Wife* of the previous year turned out, as now did Congreve's *The Way of the World*, to be not only his best but also his last work of significance for the stage. This was a pity, for both writers were now beginning to stretch characters beyond the limiting confines of the traditional Restoration typology. Vanbrugh thus presents with a measure of psychologically-realized pain the problems of incompatibility in marriage, while Congreve, in the relationship between Millamant and Mirabell, suggests possible ground-rules for compatibility – painting, too, the many faces of sensuality, and tensioning sexual desire against dynastic and economic imperatives. His plot, however, becomes at times so dense as to require more constant attention than his first audiences were probably inclined to pay.

The uncertainty as to what would now 'take' with audiences was also reflected in experiments with farcical double-bills, an increase in afterpieces, and various kinds of musical attraction, from ever more elaborate *entr'acte* diversions to full-scale operas. Davenant had, of course, whetted the English appetite for opera before and during the Restoration, and occasional productions continued to find an audience. Much of Purcell's sadly limited operatic output had thus been presented at Dorset Garden in the days of the United Company – *The Fairy Queen* costing some £3,000 to stage in 1692, a not untypical figure which suggests the potential drain of a failure on limited resources. However, it was not English but Italian opera which became suddenly fashionable early in the new century – its popularity soon to be boosted by the arrival of Handel in London, where his *Rinaldo* was staged in 1711.

It was in part to accommodate Italian opera that in 1705 a new playhouse, the Queen's, was built to the designs of Vanbrugh. This was also intended to serve as a long-awaited permanent home for the company from Lincoln's Inn Fields, whose management Vanbrugh now assumed: but its location in the Haymarket, while sensibly anticipating expansion of the West End, at first deterred audiences by its distance, and its acoustics proved unsympathetic to regular drama.

Both companies, hoping to profit from the new vogue, interspersed opera with the spoken drama until the spring of 1706, in which year Vanbrugh sold out his interest at the Queen's to Owen Swiney. Although Swiney seems at first to have acted in covert alliance with Rich, the ill-tempered Drury Lane manager soon succeeded in alienating not only Swiney but most of his own company – and he eventually allowed Cibber to lead a mass defection of actors to the Haymarket, on the understanding that the company there would present its plays unadorned by the entertainments in which he now felt it expedient to specialize.

It was this company which presented Farquhar's *The Beaux Stratagem*, at the Queen's, in March 1707 – in the event, one of the last new plays to be staged there, for in the same month Rich was 'silenced from acting' at Drury Lane on the orders of the Lord Chamberlain – who proceeded, at the end of December, to order a new union of the two companies. The actors were then redistributed according to their skills, the singers going to the Haymarket, where Swiney launched a full-scale operatic endeavour, and the actors to Drury Lane. So, with Farquhar a dying man even before *The Beaux Stratagem* reached the stage, our chapter ends as it began: with a single company of actors at Drury Lane, and a singular dearth of good new plays in prospect.

CHAPTER 10   *The Actors Ascendant*

Plaster bust of a world-weary
Colley Cibber, attributed to
Roubillac, *c.* 1750, when
Cibber would have been in
his late seventies: contrast
his ebullient fop on
page 138. Although
long retired from
management,
Cibber
had been
acting as
recently as
1745, in his
own *Papal
Tyranny in the
Reign of King
John* – inspired,
after Shakespeare,
by the Jacobite
rebellion of the
same year

The new union of the companies did not long survive. In June 1709 Rich was again silenced by the Lord Chamberlain following a dispute over benefits, whereupon his actors decamped to the Haymarket to play under Swiney. Following the forcible seizure of Drury Lane from the squatting Rich by William Collier, a Tory MP and court favourite, Aaron Hill was installed as manager, but barely survived the season. However, he achieved greater success at the Haymarket in 1711, not least as librettist for *Rinaldo* – thus confirming the theatre's loss to the 'legitimate' drama, and also initiating its long association with Handel (who was soon to settle in London along with his patron, the Elector of Hanover, already in waiting for the English throne).

Much wheeling and dealing followed. Led by Cibber, Wilks, and Doggett, the actors returned to Drury Lane under the management of Swiney (which they begrudged), while Collier took over at the Haymarket. Then, after changing places again in 1712, both disappeared from the scene – Swiney in flight from his creditors, and Collier an early victim of the long Whig ascendancy affirmed by the accession of George I in 1714. In the following year Sir Richard Steele – who was already more successful as an essayist than a playwright – was made patentee of Drury Lane, presumably in return for his early espousal of the Whig cause. Wisely, Steele contented himself with a share of the profits, and the effective management reverted to Cibber, Wilks, and (in disputed succession to Doggett) their fellow-actor Barton Booth – ironically a high Tory, who, no less ironically, had taken the title-role in the success of 1713, the pseudo-classical tragedy *Cato*, by the staunchly Whig Joseph Addison. This had been a true *succès d'occasion* – its month-long run owing more to the political temper of the times than to its scrupulous observation of poetic justice and neoclassical 'rules'. Of course, both sides espoused its declarations of liberty as their own.

Occasional disputes with the Lord Chamberlain notwithstanding, a long period of relative stability and modest financial success now set in at Drury Lane, and the triumvirate of actor-managers even secured the patent for themselves upon Steele's death in 1729. By that time, as their own careers drew to a close, their various styles had come to epitomize both the qualities and the defects of early eighteenth-century acting – in so far as it is possible to recapture these from contemporary sources. Thus, although the beginnings of theatre criticism and early attempts at theatrical memoirs at last begin to provide us with evidence that is more than circumstantial, unfamiliar assumptions about the nature of theatre – and, indeed, about the meanings of words – often complicate our interpretation of that evidence.

The *Roscius Anglicanus* of Betterton's 'book-keeper and prompter' Thomas Downes became the first attempt at a history of the English theatre, albeit only of the period from the Restoration until its publication in 1708. By that time, the insertion of notices of the day's play in London's first regular newspaper, the *Daily Courant*, founded in 1702, had become as important a medium of publicity for the theatres as was the customary posting of 'great bills' in prominent places in central London. And numerous essays on subjects related to the drama also appeared in the periodicals which now began to spring up in some profusion.

Among these was Steele's rather misleadingly titled *The Theatre* (1720), which succeeded by several years his better-known collaborations with Addison on *The Tatler* (1709–11) and *The Spectator* (1711–12). None of these ventures, however, was journalistic in the modern sense: rather, they were what we might regard as 'part-works' which built into collections of belletristic essays. Similarly, Charles Gildon's *Life of Mr Thomas Betterton* (1710) was anecdotal and discursive well beyond what we would regard as the biographer's range.

To judge from one of Addison's essays in *The Spectator*, George Powell, Rich's 'heavy' tragic lead at Drury Lane until he was supplanted by Wilks, was especially prone to the fault of bombast, in 'those particular speeches which are commonly known by the name of *rants*'. This was bad enough, Addison suggests, when Powell 'raised himself a clap' by his 'violence of action' in tragedies meant to be performed with moderation: but other writers actually encouraged the fault, 'adding vehemence to words where there was no passion, or inflaming a real passion into fustian'.

WILKS, BOOTH, AND THE 'RANTING SCHOOL'

Thus were actors encouraged to deliver 'such sentiments as proceed rather from a swelling than a greatness of mind'. And such calculated 'ranting' could, it seems, woo applause from audiences rather in the same way that expressive stage tableaux had done during the Restoration. But bombast was not the invariable tragic manner, if we are to take at face value the opinion of Cibber's son, Theophilus, that Barton Booth, for one, 'scorned to purchase applause at the expense of his lungs, to the disgrace of his judgement'. 'In his grief' as Othello, 'he never whindled, whined, or blubbered', and 'in his rage he never mouthed or ranted'.

However, when two apparently knowledgeable sources reach resolutely opposite conclusions, the problem of dealing with such impressionistic evidence becomes clear. Thus, while even Wilks, according to Downes, could not resist the opportunities offered by 'unnatural rants', his overall verdict on the actor was that Wilks's 'elevations and his cadences' were 'just' and 'congruent to elocution' – 'especially in genteel comedy', but 'not inferior in tragedy' – while the 'emissions of his words' were 'free, easy, and natural'. According to Cibber, however, Wilks tended to 'dart' his words 'with too quick and sharp a vehemence', and he was prone to 'break into the time and measure of the harmony, by too many spirited accents in the line'.

While Cibber's judgement here seems more detailed and considered than that of Downes, it is also some thirty years less fresh – and whereas Cibber was comparing Wilks unfavourably with Mountford, Downes declared him 'the finished copy of his famous predecessor, Mr Charles Hart'. From an even longer retrospect, Thomas Chetwood pronounced Wilks the master of 'manly sorrow': but his assumption that 'moving the passions is a great art in acting' perhaps speaks more of an audience's settled expectations in 1749, when Chetwood was writing, than of 1709, when Wilks was at the very height of his powers.

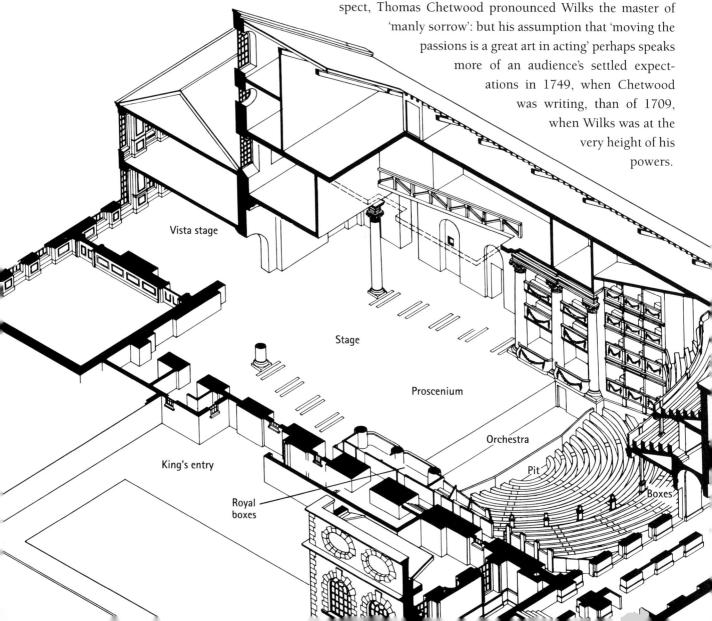

Vista stage

Stage

Proscenium

Orchestra

Pit

Boxes

King's entry

Royal boxes

Actors, acoustics, and the apron stage

Colley Cibber, recollecting the hopeful arrival of Betterton's company at the new Queen's theatre in the Haymarket, resorted to a slightly smug rhetorical question: 'What could their vast columns, their gilded cornices, their immoderate high roofs avail, when scarce one word in ten could be distinctly heard in it?' No plan of Vanbrugh's original playhouse has survived, but its acoustic flaws were apparently inherent in his attempt to create a formal Palladian style by means of a high-arched proscenium. This feature made the ceiling of the auditorium into an echo chamber. 'The articulate sounds of a speaking voice' thus came to resemble, in Cibber's words, 'the gabbling of so many people in the lofty aisles in a cathedral'.

When the practically-minded Owen Swiney closed the theatre in 1707 in order to lower the ceiling (probably by some fifteen feet), he also took the opportunity to squeeze more spectators into the empty corners which had surrounded Vanbrugh's semi-circle of pit benches. The isometric drawing opposite shows the theatre after these alterations – in which Swiney was following the precedent set by Christopher Rich at Drury Lane. Here, by 1696, Rich had increased the seating capacity by trimming four feet from the depth of the apron and reducing its width, in order to install boxes in place of the original stage doors. The result, according to Cibber, a perceptive judge

of such matters, was that the actors, forced also to compensate for poorer sight-lines, were drawn some ten feet further back from the audience than before, to the serious detriment of the intimacy which they had previously enjoyed:

> When the actors were in possession of that forwarder space . . . the voice was then more in the centre of the house, so that the most distant ear had scarce the least doubt, or difficulty in hearing what fell from the weakest utterance. All objects were thus drawn nearer to the sense: every painted scene was stronger; every grand scene and dance more extended; every rich, or fine-coloured habit has a more lively lustre: nor was the minutest motion of a feature (properly changing with the passion, or humour it suited) ever lost, as they frequently must be in the obscurity of too great a distance.

The withdrawal of the actors beyond the proscenium arch thus set under way – and so frequently remarked upon and regretted by modern critics – was not, however, due simply to the continued nibbling away of the forestage area to accommodate larger audiences. Indeed, Cibber as a manager and playwright could not but encourage a development that as an actor he might deplore: for the 'larger', less subtle acting style of the early eighteenth century was as much a product of new kinds of plays being written for a new audience as it was of larger theatres with poorer sight-lines. These in turn were a by-product of the more complex class structure of the audience itself, which was no longer drawn mainly from the courtly elite and its dependents. The loss of intimacy had other than physical dimensions: none the less, a good view of the stage became just a negotiable commodity, which the better-off might purchase and the poor could only envy.

Opposite: a reconstruction of Sir John Vanbrugh's Queen's theatre in the Haymarket, after Owen Swiney's alterations of 1707–08. The pit seating is now arranged in a semi-circular, 'fan-shaped' fashion, with the large orchestra as its focus. Pillars support a first gallery which is proportionate to the pit – but the deep upper or 'footman's' gallery extends over the lower entrance foyer. The tiers of boxes splaying slightly outwards from the pit were Swiney's addition

Such are the difficulties of attempting to reconstruct an acting style even from superior anecdotage.

When it came to actresses, the exclusively male breed of critics remained more concerned to convey sexual allure than to analyse professional skills. The assortment of adjectives chosen by an anonymous correspondent of 1747 is thus evocative in its comparisons between the male performers of the earlier decades of the century – Booth being 'majestic', Porter 'correct', Wilks 'agreeable', and Cibber 'many-gifted'. But Anne Oldfield, although acknowledged to be the greatest actress of her time, is merely and unhelpfully 'bewitching'. Downes's reference to her 'potent and majestic charm' and the tribute in a verse obituary to her 'comely form and grave majestic mien' are not much more illuminating.

Mrs Oldfield's triumph in Cibber's *The Careless Husband* had established her reputation in 1704, and although she won acclaim in 1712 for her Andromache in

Anne Oldfield (1683–1730), whose fame is said to have driven Mrs Bracegirdle into an early retirement. Slow to blossom after a Drury Lane debut in 1692, she made her name in Cibber's *The Careless Husband* of 1704, and was the original Silvia in Farquhar's *The Recruiting Officer* and Mrs Sullen in his *The Beaux Stratagem*. Thus excelling in comedy, she was at first reluctant to put on a 'tragedy face', but later won acclaim for her 'majestical dignity'. According to Walpole she was 'an agreeable gay woman of quality, a little too conscious of her natural attraction'. She made her final appearance in 1728 in Henry Fielding's first play, *Love in Several Masques*

Ambrose Philips's adaptation from Racine, *The Distressed Mother*, as she did two years later for her playing of the eponymous heroine of Rowe's 'she-tragedy' *Jane Shore*, her lifelong preference remained for comic parts. In these, Cibber suggested, she could capture 'the different humours' of real life – whereas the 'lofty disregard of nature' in 'the tragic strain' resulted in its 'manner of speaking' varying 'as little as the blank verse it is written in'. Yet, while it is true that comedy remained rooted in prose, its rhythms were beginning to take on a somnolence not too far removed from the routine iambics censured by Cibber (arguably not unconscious of his own inadequacy in tragic roles). In performance, incidentally, comedies continued to outnumber tragedies, by around three to one.

PATHETIC TRAGEDY, REFORMED COMEDY

The pall of poetic justice was now settling over both genres, so that the distance between the pathetic impulse of such tragedies as *The Distressed Mother* and *Jane Shore* and the 'reformed' comic mood discernible in *The Careless Husband* – as in *The Lady's Last Stake*, also by Cibber (1707), or Charles Johnson's *The Wife's Relief* (1711), or Steele's *The Conscious Lovers* (1722), to name some other successes of the time – was now perceptibly narrowing. Though Cibber determinedly included a role for Lord Foppington in *The Careless Husband*, there are few laughs in the main plot of *The Conscious Lovers*, and Sidney would have approved of Steele's prefatory claim that an audience's pleasure might be 'too exquisite for laughter' – this response now being reserved for the subsidiary action below-stairs. The outcome is deserved 'happiness and success' for the consistently virtuous pair whose ultra-sensitivity towards their own fine feelings is summed up in the play's title.

For Colley Cibber's forgiving wives, other dramatists now substituted forgiving husbands – as, of course, did Rowe in *Jane Shore*, where at least history upheld poetic justice in requiring the fallen heroine's pathetic end. To begin to understand the positive response such plays received from their original audiences, we must allow their force not only when they happen to soothe our own sensibilities, as in Jane's reflections on the sexual 'double standard', but also when they offend them, as in the fear lest gentility be tainted by contact with the manners of the working class. Thus, while Mrs Centlivre avoided the worst pitfalls of the pathetic by continuing to work the vein of intrigue comedy, she was careful to excise proletarian pertness as well as Restoration bawdy from her plays: 'reform' thus involved not only moulding one's dramatic morality to the values of a Jeremy Collier, but validating the sense of self-worth of the middle class.

However, if the phenomenon of 'sentimentality' was more complex in its causes and effects than was once believed, so also was it less pervasive. Even during the early decades of the century, when pathos in new writing was in the ascendant, not only was its influence in the repertoire counterbalanced by a high proportion of 'unreformed' revivals, but few regular plays, comic or tragic, would have been performed without *entr'acte* diversions, or the addition of a farce or pantomime.

Barton Booth (*c.* 1680–1733) joined Betterton's company in 1700, but did not come into his own until he was able to take over some of Betterton's 'line' of roles at Drury Lane after 1610. He created the title part in Addison's *Cato* in 1713, and with Cibber (opposite) and Wilks (portrayed in role on page 160) he became one of the triumvirate of actor-managers who steered the theatre's fortunes until his retirement in 1728. Although renowned for his carefully posed 'attitudes' and sonorous delivery, according to Aaron Hill his 'secret' lay in his 'adaptation of his looks to his voice' so that 'the variation in the sounds of the words gave propriety to every change in his countenance'

(1725)

For the Benefit of Mrs SAUNDERS

By His Majesty's Company of Comedians.

1725

AT THE

THEATRE ROYAL

In *Drury-Lane* :

On MONDAY the 14th Day of *April*,
will be presented, *(In the Time of Wilks,
and Mrs Oldfield)*

A COMEDY call'd,

Rule a Wife, *and Have a* Wife.

With Entertainments of Singing and Dancing,
as will be Express'd in the Great Bill.

To begin exactly at Six a-Clock.

By His Majesties Command, No Persons are to be admitted behind the
... ney to be Return'd after...

Indeed, the development of the so-called 'multiple bill' bears witness to the desire of respectable bourgeois humanity to be entertained between the acts even as its social and economic integrity was didactically asserted within them.

While critics are less dismissive than they once were of the coming of 'the whole show' to the London stage, they still tend to explain it away in terms of rivalry between the houses, without explaining *why* the inclusion of assorted dancers, singers, contortionists, jugglers, and impersonators should have provided such a competitive edge. But if we look back to the itinerant performers of the Middle Ages, who displayed similarly wide-ranging skills, and forward to the triumph of the multiple bill in the music-hall and 'variety' – as since in television schedules the world over – we may rather wonder at the strength of the neoclassical purism which, since the Restoration, had so narrowed the focus of an audience's attention.

FARCE AND THE MULTIPLE BILL

If neoclassicism demanded five acts to a play, it thereby provided four interstices to fill with tempting extras. But an alternative was to offer a double-bill – perhaps a three-act tragedy followed by a two-act farce, or, more often, a one-acter offered as 'afterpiece' to a full-length play. Whether one considers this the more obvious course depends on how one assesses the force of habit – but it was certainly cheaper, since it did not entail the hiring of speciality acts. In the absence of a recent English tradition of farce writing, Molière and other French exponents proved a convenient source to plunder – ironically, since until late in the seventeenth century the form had usually been derided, in Dryden's words, as a 'damn'd dull' French import.

Various comedies had, however, already been so described – Pepys's reference to *The Old Troop* as a 'farce' back in 1668 being one of the first uses of the term in its modern sense recorded in the *Oxford English Dictionary*. The extensive use of physical comic 'business' in Lacy's play, as in Ravenscroft's *The London Cuckolds*, was certainly to become one of the features of the developed form – for which Nahum Tate was an early apologist, so-describing his own *A Duke and No Duke* upon its publication in 1693 (it had been first acted nine years earlier). The ensuing popularity of farce may have been as much cause as effect of the development of the double-bill: at least, it provided a healthy counterweight to regular comedy, where verbosity was winning out over physical action as surely as morality was dampening wit.

Farces had been employed as 'vehicles' for the talents of low comedians as early as 1672, when Nokes had enjoyed a personal triumph in Edward Ravenscroft's *The Citizen Turned Gentleman* (based on Molière's *Le Bourgeois gentilhomme*, and later performed as *Mamamouchi*). Now the increased demand for farcical afterpieces led to full-length plays being filleted of their sub-plots to the same end, as in Doggett's conversion of his own *The Country Wake* of 1696 into the one-act *Hob* of 1711, and in Christopher Bullock's adaptation of Marston's Jacobean city comedy, *The Dutch Courtesan*, into the three-act *The Woman's Revenge* in 1715.

Opposite: playbill for a benefit performance at Drury Lane on 14 April 1718. (As the mistaken handwritten date reminds us, such bills did not include the year until *c.* 1760.) Note the now familiar addition of 'entertainments of singing and dancing' to the main piece, details of which are promised in the 'great bills' to be displayed poster-like nearer the date (this small bill, more like a leaflet, is reproduced close to its actual size). The benefit is for Mrs Saunders, a lively comic actress who has here chosen to display her talents in a comedy of Beaumont and Fletcher's: allowing for house charges of around £40, she might, with a good audience, net around twice that amount. Despite the practice at some theatres, the warning at the bottom (here half-torn) reads: 'By His Majesty's command, no persons are to be admitted behind the scenes, nor any money to be returned after the curtain is drawn up.' The announced starting time of six o'clock is usual for this period

Statistically-minded historians have observed that early peaks in the incidence of such afterpieces coincided with periods when rivalry between the companies was at its height. One such spurt is evident in the bills for the season of 1709–10, when the Queen's and Drury Lane were both briefly offering 'legitimate' fare; and another occurs in 1714–15 – by which time the King's (as the theatre in the Haymarket was now called) was given over entirely to opera, but fresh competition for Drury Lane had emerged with the opening of a new playhouse in Lincoln's Inn Fields.

Theatre at the fairs

Theatrical offerings formed a regular attraction at the great annual fairs. Early in the century the regular playhouses even closed for the week of May Fair, where acting was banned in 1709 – however, the far stronger traditions of Bartholomew Fair rendered such prohibitions ineffective. Its timing in late August, moreover, meant that it neither created nor suffered any competition, and actors from established companies (unpaid when not actually performing) were recruited to play in the traditional 'great booth' at Bartholomew Fair. The yard of the George Inn was a favoured location, from which the proprietors could then transplant their booths to Southwark, whose fair followed in September.

Provincial fairs saw similar if more obscure flurries of theatrical activity. They had a time-honoured calendar which enabled the itinerant companies to plot them regularly into their perambulations. We know little of the portable theatres such companies used, though it seems likely that the wagon needed for their equipage – costumes, basic backcloths, and props – would also have served as a stage, often with some sort of canvas shelter for the audience (and to keep out non-paying spectators).

While popular successes and the stock repertoire of the London theatres would have been pressed into service in much abbreviated versions (to permit a good turnover of audiences), an older, underground repertoire based on folk tales, interludes, jigs, and drolls probably also survived, and interacted with the stuff of the chapbooks and the broadside ballads. Companies would have been skilled in adapting such material to local circumstances and topical events: but because it was transmitted orally, we have little evidence concerning this kind of playing until it resurfaced for detached middle-class observation in the penny gaffs of the nineteenth century.

Southwark Fair, held for around fourteen days every September, as pictured by Hogarth, 1733. Note the prize-fighter, rope dancer, performing horse, tumbler, giant, waxwork show – and, of course, Lee and Harper's theatrical booth, where *The Siege of Troy* is playing

This had originally been put in hand by the dispossessed Christopher Rich, who, however, died a few months before its completion. The playhouse – which was built along the now-conventional lines, with a capacity of up to 1,400 – therefore opened under the management of his son John, who not only inherited the old Davenant patent, but, as it turned out, proceeded after a shaky start to make a personal success of the new venture. This he did by exploiting his own genius in a form whose pedigree was as doubtful as its subsequent history was curious, but whose

popularity during the 1720s often meant that, in effect, the afterpiece became the main attraction. That form was English pantomime.

THE BIRTH OF ENGLISH PANTOMIME

Some scholars trace the genealogy of pantomime in England back to the presence of a *commedia* troupe at the Earl of Leicester's entertainment before Elizabeth at Kenilworth in 1575; but there were very few further visits from Italian companies, and in the native drama of the succeeding century little trace of the influence of *commedia* is to be found. However, its importation into France during the seventeenth century probably inspired the occasional attempts at domesticating Harlequin we noted in the previous chapter, and it was no doubt as a result of the temporary ban placed on the Comédie Italienne in Paris in 1697 that the first decade of the new century found *commedia* companies playing at London fairs – in the dumb-show to which the ban on dialogue in the Paris fairs had habituated them.

So-called 'Italian night scenes' – balletic *commedia* scenarios transposed into native English settings – then began appearing as afterpieces at the regular theatres. The dancing-master John Weaver probably mounted the first of these at Drury Lane in 1716 (much later than he was wont to claim), but he was quickly imitated at Lincoln's Inn Fields by John Rich, who played the title role in *Harlequin Executed* under his stage name of Lun. In March of the following year Weaver presented *The Loves of Mars and Venus* – and, in pronouncing it 'after the manner of the ancient pantomime', he displayed that creative confusion of classical and *commedia* elements which came to characterize the English style. A month later Rich transplanted Harlequin into a native setting, with *The Cheats; or, The Tavern Bilkers.*

Typically, English pantomime opened with a mythical or legendary scene in dumb-show, its significance being conveyed in arias burlesquing Italian opera. A 'transformation scene' then served as a mechanically spectacular link into the longer second half, where the familiar masks from *commedia* mimed their boisterous anglicized antics to music. The intention was often vaguely satirical, as when, in April 1717, *The Jealous Doctor* at Lincoln's Inn parodied the recent Drury Lane comedy *Three Hours after Marriage* – itself notable as being Pope's only attempt at a stage play, in collaboration with his Scriblerian colleagues Arbuthnot and Gay.

This was not, however, the first or last theatrical endeavour of that clubbable writer John Gay, whose two-act 'tragi-comi-pastoral farce' of 1715, aptly enough entitled *The What D'ye Call It*, long remained popular in the Drury Lane repertoire. But although Cibber was given first refusal of Gay's later masterpiece, *The Beggar's Opera*, he rejected it, and it first reached the stage in 1728 at Lincoln's Inn Fields, where Rich already enjoyed a reputation – a rather doubtful one among the orthodox – for dramatic experiment, and had long been acknowledged as the leading producer of pantomime.

In pantomime, Drury Lane thus followed where Rich led – his enormous success with *The Necromancer; or, Harlequin Dr. Faustus* in 1723 (for which he is attired in

Opposite: John Rich (c. 1682–1761), in his Harlequin guise as 'John Lun'. His genius in a silent pantomime role may have had its roots in the illiteracy which made it difficult for him to learn lines: but, having inherited his father Christopher's patent in 1714, he also proved himself an astute manager, successively at Lincoln's Inn Fields and, after 1732, at the new Covent Garden, where James Quin headed the company. Rich's pantomimes were annual events from 1717 to 1760, their 'serious' mythological openings soon giving way to the antics and transformations of Harlequin as he overcame all obstacles in his pursuit of Columbine

the engraving alongside) duly being imitated by the rival company, as was his *Harlequin Sorcerer* two years later. Pantomime audiences, not unlike their medieval counterparts, greatly enjoyed such descents into Hell – for which Rich's *Orpheus in the Lower Regions* provided a further opportunity. According to a foreign visitor, Rich spent £4,000 on this show, which was 'full of wonderful springs and clockwork machinery', and 'altogether the most surprising and charming spectacle you can imagine'.

Cibber at first acknowledged the pleasures of pantomime, which he described as 'a connected presentation of dances in character, wherein the passions were so happily expressed and the whole story so intelligibly told by a mute narration of gesture only, that even thinking spectators allowed it both a pleasure and a rational entertainment'. But he competed with caution and against his own artistic judgement in the 'succession of monstrous medleys' which followed, and maybe the half-heartedness showed. Certainly, the popularity of pantomime, despised though it was by literary men like Pope, made accessible to ordinary theatregoers a theatrical experience not all that different in its composite kind (however different it may have been in descent) from the elitist court masque of the previous century.

PATTERNS OF PERFORMANCE

With two companies operating in lively competition throughout the 1720s, and newspaper advertising now providing a more consistent source of information, we can risk a few generalizations about their patterns of performance. Both continued to employ around twice as many actors as actresses – 28 men to 16 women at Lincoln's Inn Fields in the season of 1724–25 – during a season which ran from September to June. *The London Stage*, that compendious record of eighteenth-century theatre, tells us that during the 192 nights of the season of 1721–22 Drury Lane drew upon an active repertoire of 70 different full-length plays – one out of four afterpieces being added on 15 of those occasions. On 163 nights at Lincoln's Inn Fields, only 46 different plays were performed – but on the notably higher number of 62 occasions one out of no fewer than ten afterpieces was on offer.

At Drury Lane, John Mills – little remembered today, but evidently of protean range and prodigious memory – was advertised in the bills to play 50 different roles in the 70 plays acted, and he probably had smaller parts in another ten besides. Mills followed up one successive run of twelve different roles in twelve days (Sundays excepted) with a further eleven roles, nine of which were different again, in the next twelve – and although this was at the start of the season, when revivals were to be expected, the company would also have been rehearsing new plays during the day. The demands made on Mills were perhaps exceptional – he was acknowledged by a contemporary writer to be 'the most useful actor that ever served a theatre' – but even a 'star' such as Robert Wilks acted at least 140 times during the season, despite the additional calls upon him as a member of the triumviral management.

Although a new playhouse built in 1710 in St Martin's Lane had foundered after only one or two inauspicious seasons, ten years later the opening of a second theatre in the Haymarket – usually known as the Little, to distinguish it from the King's – offered more sustained if not at first serious competition to the two patent houses. First occupied by a visiting French troupe, it was thereafter used either by other foreign companies, or for amateur performances and similar one-off ventures. Initially, then, the significance of the Little theatre lay simply in its capacity to survive without (apparently) either a patent or a licence – but in the 1730s, as we shall see, it demonstrated that giving offence to politicians was to incur greater danger than a mere downmarket challenge to the theatrical establishment.

Theatres were now also beginning to be built in the suburbs, and the accessibility of Greenwich, a pleasant river trip away from the West End, no doubt tempted Londoners as well as local audiences during the light summer evenings from 1709 to 1711, when William Penkethman mounted seasons there – his slightly earlier starting time of 5.30 enabling visitors to return home 'before night'. The royal associations of Greenwich no doubt helped – as did the residence of the Prince of Wales at Richmond in Surrey, where Penkethman played in two theatres between 1718 and his death in 1725 (making the most of royal neighbourliness with celebrations of every Hanoverian anniversary). A theatre was also built at Hampton Court for command performances, and the Drury Lane company is known to have played there in 1718.

THE FIRST PROVINCIAL PLAYHOUSES

Although fit-up stages continued to be used almost into our own times, it was in the early eighteenth century that some of the more respectable of the itinerant companies – notably those with a licence or old-style patron to legitimize their activities – began to acquire sufficient confidence in their audiences and in themselves to build the first permanent playhouses outside London. Thus, purpose-built theatres were opened in Bath in 1705, in Bristol in 1729, in York in 1734, and in Ipswich in 1736, as the early theatrical 'circuits' gradually took shape – embracing those towns within an area to which a company, usually operating from a conveniently central or populous base, could viably tour its products from year to year.

During the 1720s, such companies began to take their names from their 'home' towns rather than from the noble patrons of old. Thus, troupes of the 'Duke of Norfolk's Servants' and the 'Duke of Grafton's Servants' clashed to command the 'Norwich circuit', which came to number Bury, Colchester, Ipswich, and Yarmouth among many smaller East Anglian towns; while the York circuit included Doncaster, Hull, Leeds, Pontefract, and Wakefield. The heyday of the provincial circuits was yet to come: but in their origins they were products of the creation of that broader class-base of theatre audiences we have noticed in the metropolis – rooted in the middle-class prosperity and self-confidence so approvingly observed on his travels by Daniel Defoe.

Delivering Play Bills in the Country.
My first Appearance, 'pon my honour,
Sir, in Hamlet the Great Prince of Denmark.

SHAKESPEARE — IN THE STUDY AND ON THE STAGE

The Shakespearean scholar Gary Taylor has argued that these audiences increasingly formed part of what he calls 'the Whig consensus' – into whose service the bard himself was now being posthumously pressed. Symptomatically, Shakespeare's name thus appears in the first, last, and numerous intervening issues of *The Tatler*, edited by the chief literary spokesman of the Whigs and patentee-in-waiting, Sir Richard Steele: but Shakespeare's fellow immortals in the Restoration pantheon were ignored or dismissed, for neither the aristocratic tastes and ambitions of

Robert Wilks (1665–1732), pictured here as the original Harry Wildair in Farquhar's *The Constant Couple*. Also the first Archer in his *The Beaux Stratagem*, Wilks was well known for his portrayals of such gentlemanly lovers, and his much-admired Hamlet was evidently played in the same negligent manner. According to Cibber, he was, however, generally better suited to tragic roles expressive of 'sorrow, tenderness, or resignation'. Comparing him with Barton Booth (portrayed on page 151), Cibber claimed that whereas Booth 'often contented himself with too grave a dignity', Wilks 'had sometimes too violent a vivacity': neither 'the exclamatory rage or jealousy' of Wilks nor the 'plaintive distresses' of Booth 'were happily executed or became either of them', but 'in the contrary characters they were both excellent'

Fletcher nor the unfortunate dabbling in low-life eccentricities of Jonson offered suitable sops to middle-class morality or pretensions.

But if during the Restoration it had been Shakespeare's plays that were recast into a neoclassical mould, there now began the long process of what Taylor calls 'reinventing' the playwright himself. When Colley Cibber came to adapt *Richard III* in 1700, it was not in the interests of propriety, but in the interests of Colley Cibber – yet for Nicholas Rowe the impulse was to imitate rather than to amend. And if he made the attempt – and, by his own lights, succeeded – only in the tragic vein, this was because Shakespeare was now remembered essentially as a tragic writer. Thus, of the seven most revived of his plays between 1700 and 1728, five – *Hamlet*, *Macbeth*, *Julius Caesar*, *King Lear*, and *Othello* – were tragedies (the others revealing a continuing taste for spectacle in the operatic *Tempest*, and a properly unquenchable affection for Falstaff in *Henry IV Part 1*).

It was from Nicholas Rowe that the publisher Jacob Tonson commissioned the first 'critical' edition of Shakespeare's plays. This duly appeared in 1709, along with a prefatory 'Life' (also the first of its kind), which for many generations 'placed' Shakespeare in the public mind – as a good citizen, of habits both orthodox and kind (not least to an ungrateful Jonson), and as full of wise investments as of wise saws. Rowe's place as Shakespeare's first editor may thus have ensured his lasting influence, but he was, of course, to be the first in a very long line indeed. Almost within a decade, the canny Tonson had appropriated Pope's name for Shakespeare – and Shakespeare's name for Pope – just as he had Rowe's: and Pope duly repudiated Rowe's work, just as Theobald was to repudiate Pope's. And so the wheels of the Shakespeare industry began to turn, and the captains of that industry to compete in the creation of the perfect Shakespeare, as it might have been the perfect mousetrap.

At least Rowe was a man of the theatre, and his editorial decisions and revisions derived from a sound knowledge of stage conventions (his edition was also replete with engravings which, while scarcely masterpieces of their craft, did derive from theatrical practice – as our discussion of two examples on pages 132–3 suggests). Later in the century, too, came the publication of humbler but functional sets of single plays, based on contemporary stage practice – notably Bell's Shakespeare of 1773. But Pope was a man of the study, not of the stage, and it was from the study that his own, like most subsequent scholarly editions, emerged – and for whose shelves they were intended. Thus opened the breach between the academic and the theatrical approach to Shakespeare, which in many respects remains unhealed even today.

It is therefore ironic that one of the known if uncredited collaborators on Pope's edition of Shakespeare was his friend John Gay, who within two or three years of its appearance in 1725 had happily conceived the idea for a play which was entirely original rather than imitative, and which – uncircumscribed by any rules other than those of thumb – was to initiate a decade of theatrical freedom and experiment. That play was, of course, *The Beggar's Opera*.

CHAPTER 11

Opposition and Oppression

The transition from the Stuart to the Hanoverian dynasty in 1714 saw the beginning of a Whig ascendancy which was destined to endure for half a century – and which reached right down to the ranks of the magistracy, for even such lowly but influential offices had to be resigned upon a monarch's death. After the abortive Jacobite rebellion of 1715, those Tories who had been ineptly intriguing for a continued Stuart line could even be accused of treachery, and by 1727 the Whigs were sufficiently entrenched for the succession of the second George to the first to pass without incident. And so the traditional Tory values of church, hierarchy, and land continued to give way before Whig beliefs rooted in the 'protestant work ethic', prioritizing social mobility, cash and credit, and the expansion of trade.

Even the internal struggle for leadership among the Whigs was by then resolved, albeit almost by default. In 1717 the creation of a 'Sinking Fund' to pay off the National Debt (hung over from the wars of the turn of the century) had raised hopes that this was a temporary expedient – for no more than the Tories did the Whigs fully comprehend the capitalism they were struggling to control. Then, in 1720, the South Sea Company's agreement to take over the debt in return for a trade monopoly led to the notorious speculative 'bubble' – which, however, burst to disastrous and legendary effect in August.

Robert Walpole rose to unchallenged power as one of the few Whig politicians untainted by the scandals of the 'bubble' – and in due course he became, in effect if not yet in name, the nation's first prime minister. Meanwhile, those seeking a more secure investment turned to the 'Sinking Fund' itself: but since it was a far easier option for the government to meet expenditure by raiding this readily available resource than by increasing taxation, the national debt, so far from being paid off, continued its steady, inexorable growth.

THE VOGUE FOR BALLAD OPERA

As we have seen, while political sympathies did count in theatrical affairs, neither the Whig-inclined management at Drury Lane nor John Rich at Lincoln's Inn Fields, unobtrusively Tory, could afford to offend any section of their audience: so it is unlikely that, in accepting *The Beggar's Opera*, Rich had felt himself to be taking a stand for his party – and Colley Cibber's rejection of the piece was probably motivated by his distaste for novelty rather than from fear of giving offence to the government. But its author, John Gay, was himself an 'out-of-office' Tory in the sense that his politics now deprived him of patronage: and when, forced back on his own devices, he had done well from publishing a collected edition of his verse in 1720, only to lose his profits by investing them in South Sea stock, his distaste for the system which had produced the debacle – and for those in power who had corruptly encouraged it – could only have been increased.

John Gay (1685–1732) spent a long career as a working dramatist and poet before the success of *The Beggar's Opera* brought him belated fortune. A close 'Scriblerian' friend of Swift and Pope, and a Tory lacking friends at court or in high office, he had no great liking for Walpole: but the satire in *The Beggar's Opera* is laughingly allusive rather than direct. However, when Gay attempted a sequel, *Polly*, in which his highwayman hero Macheath is exiled to the West Indies, Walpole banned its performance outright

However, in so far as *The Beggar's Opera* targets Walpole and his Whig administration (a matter which has absorbed more subsequent scholarly annotation than it did, at first, audience attention), it does so tangentially, through a consistent comic inversion of expected values. The womanizing highwayman Macheath is set up as a 'great man' and hero, while the values of the thieves' den, the prison, and the brothel become the criteria for the play's ironic morality. The prevailing dramatic assumption that vice should invariably be punished and virtue rewarded is thereby happily inverted – not least in that topsy-turvy combination of decorum and poetic justice which requires that the condemned Macheath be granted a climactic reprieve.

How far the ballads set to traditional English airs were an indirect satire upon the still-fashionable Italian opera is also open to question: but that Gay had here crafted a new and distinctive kind of music theatre is indisputable. His play is not, perhaps, the 'Newgate pastoral' which Swift (according to tradition) had proposed: rather, it is a theatrical equivalent of the Hogarthian print – so rich in incident, interpolation,

Painting by Hogarth of *The Beggar's Opera*, illustrating an air from Act III, 'When My Hero in Court Appears'. The actors, still downstage of the proscenium, are cramped between the stage boxes occupied by casually interacting spectators. The 'scene' of the prison is created by the upstage wings, back shutter, and gallows – the downstage satyr being a permanent feature at Lincoln's Inn

and low-life impropriety as to upset conventional expectations of dramatic art, but, like the best caricature, thought-provoking in its simultaneous likeness and unlikeness to life, even as it delights with its detail and dark corners. Appropriately, it is Hogarth himself who provides the illustration on the previous page of a contemporary performance.

The immediate success of the play, which enjoyed an initial run of thirty-two nights and notched up an unprecedented sixty-two performances during the season, encouraged a heavy crop of imitations which, inferior though they undoubtedly were, at least lent variety to what had become a highly predictable repertoire. For by 1728 any new play, let alone one of such original virtues, had become a rarity, both patent houses relying on a diet of tried-and-tested revivals – few being products even of the previous twenty years. Rich was notorious for his dismissal of hopeful playwrights with a peremptory 'It will not do', while Cibber likened his own treatment of aspiring writers to 'the choking of singing birds'.

The one great success of the early 1720s, *The Conscious Lovers*, had thus been written for Drury Lane by its own patentee, and that theatre's afterpieces were almost entirely the work of its salaried dancing master, John Weaver – the role of the 'ordinary poet' having long since disappeared. Such new names as came up on the bills – James Moore Smythe, say, or Leonard Welsted in comedy, and Philip Frowde or David Lewis in tragedy – did not recur, and, like their one or two plays, have now sunk without trace. As the theatre historian Robert Hume sums up: 'no one was making a living from writing plays in the mid-1720s.'

Since actors received no extra pay for rehearsals, the diminishing number of new plays meant a welcome lessening of their workload. At the same time, however, opportunities for career advancement had been restricted by the establishment in 1722 of a virtual cartel between the managements of the patent houses, who agreed neither to poach each other's actors nor to accept their services if offered. Salaries, lacking a competitive edge, could thus be held down – while audiences might also find themselves deprived of choice, since during the quieter parts of the season the theatres arranged to play only on alternate nights.

Such, indeed, was the situation at the start of the season of 1727–28, until the Coronation of George II in October 1727 brought audiences flocking back to London to fill both houses. Then, on 10 January in the New Year, Drury Lane premiered what turned out to be Colley Cibber's last regular comedy, *The Provoked Husband* – an adaptation of Sir John Vanbrugh's *A Journey to London*, which the playwright-turned-architect had left unfinished at his death two years earlier. The play achieved a surprising enough first run of 28 nights, and played a further nine performances later in the season: but its success was soon to be overshadowed by the phenomenon of *The Beggar's Opera* – in comparison with which *The Provoked Husband*, though competent and craftsmanlike, is indeed conventional stuff.

The sustained success of these consecutive offerings undermined the expectation on which both managements had previously based their policies – that all but the most exceptional play would have exhausted its initial audience after half-a-dozen or at most nine performances. Now, as the vogue for pantomime had also begun to reveal, popular fare could draw audiences from a far wider social and geographical spectrum than had been assumed, or indeed encouraged – a double-edged discovery for Cibber and Rich, since it not only sparked interest among potential rivals, but also alerted the politicians, wary of anything that threatened to arouse 'the mob'.

Political muscles were soon being flexed. In 1715 Sir Richard Steele had success-fully challenged the need for the Master of the Revels to license plays mounted by the patentees: but when, late in 1728, it became known that *Polly*, Gay's sequel to *The Beggar's Opera*, was about to go into rehearsal, the Lord Chamberlain forcefully reminded Rich of his authority, and banned it outright. (As it happened, the resultant notoriety gained its author, or so he claimed, four times as much from publication as he could have expected from the performance of this more openly satirical but theatrically less challenging piece.)

The threat (or from an audience's viewpoint the promise) of increased competi-tion was also becoming clear. Just five days after the 'positively' last performance of *The Beggar's Opera* at Lincoln's Inn Fields on 19 June 1728, a new production of the same play had opened at the Little theatre in the Haymarket – in open breach of the gentlemen's agreement that an originating company had undisputed title to what it staged. No less significantly, well over half the new season's repertoire at the Little consisted of new plays, of which three were outstanding successes of rather different kinds – *The Humours of Harlequin*, a pantomime; *The Beggar's Wedding*, one of the many ballad operas written in emulation of Gay; and *Hurlothrumbo*, a highly original piece of creative nonsense by one Samuel Johnson of Cheshire.

THE EMERGENCE OF HENRY FIELDING

The solid but unspectacular four performances which a new young playwright, Henry Fielding, achieved at Drury Lane with his first effort, *Love in Several Masques*, in February 1728 had not attracted much notice at the time. After a year or so at university abroad, Fielding now returned intent on a stage career, and his second intrigue comedy, *The Temple Beau*, ran for a more satisfying nine nights in January 1730 at the new theatre in Goodman's Fields, described overleaf. But that theatre's manager, Thomas Odell, was generally no more adventurous in his repertoire than the patentees, and it was to the Little in the Haymarket, with its openness to new and experimental work, that Fielding took his next venture – the lack of a conven-tional managerial structure at the Little perhaps also allowing him greater control over its staging.

The Author's Farce is a high-spirited account of a young author's travails at the hands of thinly-disguised caricatures of Rich, Cibber, and Wilks: it is replete with a play-within-a-play and a climax which elevates its mock-author, Luckless, to the Kingdom of Bantam. Following Gay's example, several other playwrights were now

Henry Fielding (1707–54) is now better-known as author of *Joseph Andrews* and *Tom Jones* than as a playwright. But he turned to (and helped to shape) the still-emergent novel form only after being driven from his first career as a dramatist by the Licensing Act of 1737. As well as writing over two-dozen plays in less than ten years, Fielding guided the fortunes of the Little theatre in the Haymarket, where many of them were first performed. His regular comedies were less successful than his 'illegitimate' comic pieces – which included not only quick-moving farces but witty burlesques of tragic pomposity and experiments in a new style of dramatic satire, which prefigured many of the ingredients of present-day revue

New theatres – and a new threat to the theatre

By 1729 the Little was attracting ever larger audiences from the West End, whose further reaches were at last lapping its doorstep. But another theatrical entrepreneur, Thomas Odell, understood that many members of the audiences who had flocked to The Beggar's Opera must have travelled from the middle- and working-class districts to the east: and thus it was that in October 1729 Odell opened a new theatre converted from a warehouse in Goodman's Fields, Whitechapel – just outside the jurisdiction of the ever-suspicious City fathers.

A pamphlet published to oppose the venture warned that it would 'draw away tradesmen's servants and others from their lawful callings', and encourage 'great numbers of loose, idle, and disorderly persons... to infest the streets'. But Odell, apparently on legal advice, defied the Lord Chamberlain's prohibition thus invoked, and so made the short-term future secure for his own and other unlicensed theatres.

In 1731 the actor Henry Giffard was confident enough to purchase the Goodman's Fields theatre from Odell, and even to raise capital for its rebuilding. And no sooner had Giffard's new theatre opened than Rich's plans for a new playhouse in Covent Garden, first laid in 1730 (anecdotally funded by his profits from The Beggar's Opera), had also come to fruition. Both theatres were designed (by the same architect, Edward Shepherd) in the fan-shape made familiar from the King's in the Haymarket, illustrated on page 149. Rich's house had a capacity of around 1,400, while Giffard's seated perhaps half that number. From the first, the new Covent Garden was a success with audiences, its elegance of proportion and excellence of acoustics being generally remarked: but by 1735 neither Rich nor Fleetwood was anxious to do more than add a very judicious sprinkling of new work to repertoires still dominated by revivals, and there is even evidence that, as a form of mutual insurance, they experimented with profit-sharing.

In the same year a bill was put before parliament which would have had the effect of once more limiting the number of theatres, and of abolishing playing in the provinces altogether. It fell, not apparently owing to any lack of support but to an ill-advised attempt by Walpole to add a clause strengthening the Lord Chamberlain's powers of censorship over plays. Despite its wide scope, the bill seems to have originated in the continuing desire of the City fathers to rid themselves of the proximity of the Goodman's Fields theatre: so the reprieved Giffard was no more anxious than the patentees to rock the boat by mounting risky work.

Engraving by Hogarth of Rich's 'triumphal entry' into the new Covent Garden theatre (1732)

abandoning neoclassical niceties in favour of generic novelties, and in the spring of 1730 *The Author's Farce* was competing for audiences with such pieces as *Bayes's Opera*, a satirical pot-pourri by Gabriel Odingsells at Drury Lane, and James Ralph's *The Fashionable Lady* at Goodman's Fields, a comparable mix of ballad opera, farce, and rehearsal play.

An entirely distinctive contribution from Fielding soon revealed his mastery of an older if neglected form, that of the self-contained burlesque. *Tom Thumb*, a still-hilarious send-up of inferior tragedy, was intended as an afterpiece to *The Author's Farce* in April, but the tail at once began to wag the dog: the Prince of Wales himself attended the second night, and by June the piece was not only playing daily but 'entirely new dress'd' – an almost unheard-of expense for a play in its first season. Fielding later expanded the piece into *The Tragedy of Tragedies*, and added a mock-scholarly apparatus to the printed text, solemnly identifying the authors of bathetic lines he had taken over from actual plays, as if they had themselves been 'borrowed' from this supposed masterpiece of early English drama.

In the same month, the Little offered yet a third play by Fielding, *Rape upon Rape*. Although the piece won him two benefits, Fielding's attack upon corrupt justice sits

a little uneasily within the framework of a romantic plotline: but he was sufficiently encouraged to set to work on *The Modern Husband*, a further 'comedy of social purpose', as it has been aptly dubbed, which in the event did not reach the stage until 1732. For Fielding personally, these plays proved to be false starts – but it is worth noting that his attempt to infuse 'serious' social comment into a comic format foreshadowed the 'plays unpleasant' of Bernard Shaw (who was to acclaim Fielding as the greatest dramatist since Shakespeare) by over a century and a half.

The Beggar's Opera had thus created or revealed a taste for plays which presented topical issues within new and unconventional generic modes, and Fielding and others were now sustaining this. But most authors remained wary of taking up an overt oppositional stance – for to do so was to court either the outright banning which had been the fate of *Polly* (and which seems to have deterred Rich from any further ventures in support of the Tory cause) or retaliation such as fell upon the Little when, in the summer of 1731, it staged an adaptation of *King Edward III* (attributed to Mountfort, and first published in 1691). Although *The Fall of Mortimer*, as it was now called, clearly equated Walpole with the 'villain-statesman' of this new title, it somehow got through fifteen performances before being suppressed – but the actors were then arrested and their playhouse closed. The Little did not reopen until the New Year of 1732.

Such consequences of open opposition to the government may have been behind the abandonment of Fielding's plan to expand his satirical afterpiece, *The Welsh Opera*, which had also opened in April, into the three-act ballad opera advertised for June as *The Grub-Street Opera*. Certainly, the play's identification of Robin the butler with Walpole is clear enough: equally certainly, Fielding now withdrew for several seasons from direct engagement in political playmaking. His motives were probably mixed, with discretion and ambition chief among them – but intimidation and bribery have also been surmised, since, although it was published, *The Grub-Street Opera* never reached the stage in its revised form.

TRAGEDY DOMESTICATED

At Drury Lane, the management continued to follow where the success of others led. However, during the summer season it was Colley Cibber's custom to allow his younger players their heads, and in June 1731 they gave the first performance of a tragedy by George Lillo, *The London Merchant* – a dramatized version of the chap-book tale of George Barnwell, the weak apprentice who, though corrupted by a scheming woman into betraying his master and murdering his uncle, undergoes a model repentance before he meets the hangman. The play thus promoted a common man to the role of tragic protagonist, and tested him not against the code of love and honour – let alone against the whims of fate – but according to the values of mercantile probity, as personified by his master, the aptly-named Thorowgood.

The London Merchant is not the first 'domestic tragedy': even in such anonymous Elizabethan plays as *The Yorkshire Tragedy* and *Arden of Faversham* bourgeois characters had been infiltrated into a genre supposedly reserved for their betters – and both old plays were now duly dusted off and revised. But in its revolutionary choice of a prose idiom (however rhythmically elevated) as well as in its middle-class milieu, Lillo's play set in motion the long and slow process whereby the formal stylization and noble trappings inseparable from tragedy were to give way before the intended realism in style and social setting of the nineteenth-century problem play. *The London Merchant* was an immediate success, and remained a stock piece in the repertoire for many years.

No more than had Steele in *The Conscious Lovers* did George Lillo in *The London Merchant* take up an explicit political position. However, his identification of virtue with the values of the merchant classes firmly aligned his play with the Whig philosophy – although its setting in the Elizabethan past allowed Lillo not only to attack Spanish perfidy but also to glorify the wise counsels enjoyed by the old Queen. In both these respects the play could thus be taken as an attack on Walpole from his own side – for the minister's non-interventionist policy in foreign affairs, at first seen as assisting the stability of trade, was now increasingly felt to be hindering its aggressive expansion.

This new imperialistic drive led to the strengthening of the alliance between Hanoverian Tories and out-of-office Whigs which, with the support of the City of London, now began to threaten Walpole's position – leading in 1732 to the defeat of his plans for an excise duty on tobacco and wine, and so to further depredations on the Sinking Fund. 'The patriots', as they predictably proclaimed themselves, favoured a war of commercial aggrandisement, and they found a natural spokesman in William Pitt, who echoed alike the rhetoric and the rhythms of Lillo's Thorowgood in his repudiation of compromise with Spain: 'When trade is at stake it is your last retrenchment – you must defend it or perish.'

Fielding was himself a disaffected Whig, and, with the future of the Little theatre still in doubt, his return to Drury Lane in the autumn of 1731 was unsurprising. Cibber and Wilks, pragmatically swallowing the insults of *The Author's Farce*, could no more reject the services of the most important playwright of his generation than he himself could fail to be tempted by the theatre's potentially greater rewards. But although seven new plays by Fielding duly reached the stage of Drury Lane in the following two seasons, in the main these were along conventional lines – the little-recognized exceptions being his now-completed dark marital comedy *The Modern Husband* and the blank-verse burlesque *The Covent-Garden Tragedy*, which was damned for being set in a brothel.

POWER STRUGGLES AT DRURY LANE

In the event it proved an unfortunate time for Fielding to have tied his fortunes to Drury Lane, for momentous events were occurring offstage. The old triumvirate had been belatedly accredited as patentees in succession to Steele: but Booth, who had retired from acting in 1728, now sold half his share to the dilettante socialite John Highmore, and within a month Wilks was dead – in harness almost to the end, his role in *The Modern Husband* his last. When his widow appointed another outsider, the painter John Ellys, as her representative, Cibber decided to revert to being a salaried player, and rented his own share to his son Theophilus, who had been serving an apprenticeship as manager of the summer seasons for four years.

Despite (or because of) Theophilus's initial success in securing increased salaries for the actors, Highmore then persuaded old Cibber secretly to sell him his share over his son's head. Told that his services would no longer be required in the new season, Theophilus retaliated by forming a primitive actors' trade union, and in May 1733 managed to obtain a lease on the theatre from the shareholders of the building itself – whereupon Highmore, unable to profit from his patent without players or playhouse, forcibly seized the theatre. The actors then exiled themselves to the Little, which Highmore, in expedient alliance with Rich, duly tried to silence by invoking the old vagrancy laws – even getting one of the rebel actors committed to Bridewell, irreparably damaging his own public relations in the process.

Eventually snubbed and censured by the Lord Chief Justice himself, Highmore decided to abandon his managerial ambitions, and in January 1734 sold out to

Charles Fleetwood, a landed gentleman who, having secured his position by purchasing Wilks's old share, entered into negotiations with the actors. The company returned to Drury Lane in March under what proved to be a relatively stable management of eleven years duration – with Theophilus Cibber at first serving as Fleetwood's acknowledged deputy.

Fielding thus found himself on the losing side, having only that January created an unsympathetic Theophilus-persona when revising *The Author's Farce* for what the prologue frankly described as 'this poor deserted place'. So it was now Fielding's turn to be forced back to the Little theatre – ironically, taking with him the makeshift company which Highmore had recruited for Drury Lane. And here, in April 1734, he staged his first political play for two years, *Don Quixote in England* – a ballad opera full of satirical references to the general election then in progress, whose outcome was considerably to weaken Walpole's control over the Commons.

By the New Year of 1735 a reconciliation at least of mutual convenience had evidently been effected between Fielding and Drury Lane, where he enjoyed a great success in January with *An Old Man Taught Wisdom*. This was one of a number of afterpieces Fielding wrote as vehicles for Kitty Clive, who was now emerging as a successor to Anne Oldfield, at least in the broader comic range – while appearing in the minor role of the lawyer Wormwood was a more recent recruit to the Drury Lane company from Ireland, the late-maturing but long-enduring Charles Macklin.

In the following month, however – and despite the presence in the cast of both Cibber and James Quin – the failure of Fielding's *The Universal Gallant* again demonstrated the public distaste for his attempts at comedy of social purpose: and it may, therefore, have been more as a last resort than a gesture of self-confidence that he decided to form his own company – 'the Great Mogul's' – and to return to the Little theatre for the season of 1735–36.

Although Fielding seems to have begun to build a repertoire there – with a new domestic tragedy by Lillo, *Fatal Curiosity*, among the new season's offerings – he soon recaptured the favour of the town with a play of his own. Billed as a 'dramatic satire', *Pasquin* is, like *The Author's Farce*, structured on the rehearsal formula, but in this case there are not one but two plays-within-the-play. The mock-comedy, *The Election*, is fairly even-handed in targeting Whigs and Tories; but the burlesque tragedy, *The Life and Death of Common-Sense*, focuses on Walpole in its attack on government corruption. *Pasquin* achieved upwards of sixty performances, latterly with *Tumble-Down Dick; or, Phaeton in the Suds*, a lampoon of a recent Drury Lane pantomime, as afterpiece on the same bill.

Fielding seems to have returned late to London for the season of 1736–37, and so not to have been involved in the early productions at the Little. Indeed, his first offering of the New Year was another afterpiece for Kitty Clive at Drury Lane, an updated operatic travesty, *Eurydice*, in modern dress, which was undeservedly extinguished by a riot in the footmen's gallery. Although there is evidence that Fielding was now trying to raise capital to build a playhouse of his own, in the

Charles Macklin (1699–1797) found success relatively late in his long career, with a performance of Shylock at Drury Lane in 1741 which portrayed the character not as a figure of fun but of serious, even tragic stature. After returning to the stage from an ill-advised retirement, Macklin was still playing the role some twenty-five years later, when the German artist John Zoffany painted this portrait. In the view of his contemporary John Hill, Macklin had 'a saturnine cast of countenance, sententious utterance, hollow-toned voice, and heaviness of deportment'. But if not an agile he was evidently an expressive performer, especially in roles which called for psychological subtlety – such as his Iago (to Garrick's and Barry's Othello) and, after 1774, his 'old Caledonian ' Macbeth. Macklin's own plays included *Love à-la-Mode* (1759) and *The Man of the World* (1781) – in which, well into his eighties, he also played the 'heavy' lead, the social-climbing Scot Sir Pertinax MacSycophant

meantime he returned to the Little, with a repertoire mainly of new plays, most of them now lost or understandably forgotten. The attempt was none the less a brave mark of confidence in his contemporaries, at a time when Fleetwood, Rich, and Giffard (who had now moved his operations to Lincoln's Inn Fields) were keeping firmly to their policy of playing safe.

One new play which outlived the season was *The Dragon of Wantley*, a sprightly musical romp by Henry Carey, a farceur of rare originality whose *Chrononhoton-thologos* had worked an individual vein of burlesque nonsense at the same theatre three years earlier. But again it was a play of Fielding's own which outran all competition – *The Historical Register for 1736*, a sequence of sketches on current political, social, theatrical, and literary topics, loosely-linked as a dramatized version of the reference work from which the play takes its unlikely title. In this artistically innovative piece, which opened in March and achieved 34 performances, Fielding virtually invented the form of the satirical revue: but, dangerously, the attempt at even-handedness in *Pasquin* was now abandoned, in favour of a sustained attack on Walpole and his administration.

THE LICENSING ACT

Fielding was now staging political plays not only with almost predictable success, but also with impunity – and this finally bestirred his competitors into action. Also in the spring of 1737, Giffard put on Francis Lynch's opposition polemic *The Independent Patriot* and William Havard's dangerously allusive *King Charles I*, while even Fleetwood risked Robert Dodsley's gentler comic essay in good government, *The King and the Miller of Mansfield*. Then, on 25 May, Fielding advertised, of all things, a production of Gay's banned *Polly* – but this never reached the stage, probably because the Little theatre's usually quiescent proprietor, one John Potter, was promised a pay-off by Walpole. Potter then proceeded not only to eject his tenant, but also (as his extant accounts attest) to claim government compensation for 'taking down scenes and decorations so that the theatre was rendered incapable of having any play or other performance'.

Already a bill against 'rogues and vagabonds' had failed during the parliamentary session, and Walpole now wished to be certain that any measure permanently to silence his theatrical opponents would stick. His opportunity came when Giffard showed him *The Golden Rump*, a seditious play he had allegedly been offered, and from which the prime minister read choice extracts to the House of Commons. Working on the resulting outrage, Walpole sneaked in a repressive bill at the tail-end of the parliamentary session (and, for that matter, of the theatrical season), securing its eventual passage by 185 votes to 63. It received the royal assent on 21 June, and passed into law and theatre history as the Licensing Act of 1737.

Whether *The Golden Rump* was written as a calculated provocation, and to Walpole's own orders, we do not know – nor how far Giffard was complicit in the matter. By re-establishing the monopoly of the two patent theatres, the act terminated both Giffard's own career at Lincoln's Inn Fields and Fielding's at the Little: and by also requiring the Lord Chamberlain's prior approval of any play intended for performance, it effectively extinguished at one stroke the use of the stage as a forum for public controversy. Surviving the breaking of the patent houses' monopoly by the Theatres Act of 1843, the Chamberlain's powers of censorship, systematically and resolutely exercised, exerted their stultifying influence over theatrical innovation and freedom of expression for the next two hunded and thirty years.

Fielding's surprising silence in the face of this mortal blow to his livelihood has tempted some scholars to suggest that he must have been bought off by a lavish bribe, perhaps in the guise of compensation. Be that as it may, at the early age of thirty his career as a playwright was at an end, just as he was starting to build on its strong foundations a solid edifice of mature achievement. As with Farquhar's death thirty years earlier – ironically, also in his thirtieth year – the loss was not merely of an individual genius, but of the direction in which the theatre might have been encouraged to flourish.

The abrupt termination of this remarkable decade was an oblique testimony to its challenge. It had begun with Gay's virtual invention of ballad opera, and flourished with Fielding's experiments in other 'illegitimate' forms such as burlesque, dramatic satire, and revue – as also in his tentative exploration of a new, socially-critical comedy. Meanwhile, Henry Carey and the 'other' Samuel Johnson had been actively expanding the boundaries of farce, and George Lillo finding his way towards a tragedy of contemporary relevance. All this, moreover, had been in the face not only of government suspicion but of the indifference or hostility of the patentees.

ACTORS AND ACTING

An increased number of actors and theatre staff had, of course, been needed to serve the larger number of playhouses, and a combined strength of around 150 before 1728 had doubled within the decade. The proportion of women among the acting members at the patent houses rose slightly, with around twent-five female to thirty-five male actors in companies which, including front-of-house and backstage staff, altogether numbered between eighty and ninety at each theatre.

The breakdown of the cartel led to considerable movement between the houses, and Giffard and Fielding seem to have given serious attention to training the younger performers who figured largely in their companies. In part, no doubt, this was because Fielding at the Little had enjoyed the services of few well-known players – apart from Colley Cibber's cross-dressing daughter Charlotte Charke, who had deserted to him from Drury Lane, but whose promising career thereafter declined into a succession of one-night stands and booth performances, eventually as a puppeteer.

Charlotte's disputatious brother Theophilus also defected from Drury Lane after a few seasons as Fleetwood's deputy, and as his successor – effectively in control of the theatre's artistic as distinct from its administrative affairs – Fleetwood chose Charles Macklin. Having by now established himself in solid but secondary comic parts, Macklin went on to find more enduring fame in 1741 when, playing the role of Shylock for the first time, he shook off its low comic traditions in favour of revealing its tragic potential.

But the times were, as we have seen, more propitious to varieties of comic than to tragic acting, and James Quin – after Booth's retirement the leading serious actor of the times – might have done better to build on his Falstaff than so determinedly to strive for the tragic weight on which reputations turned. Writing of Quin in 1733, one critic (whose incidental commendation that he was always perfect in his lines suggests that this was by no means to be taken for granted) thus complained that 'the calm stoic, Cato, the jealous, furious lover, Othello, the debauched drunken Sir John Brute, speak in the same tone; a hoarse monotony goes through them all'. (Quin's costumes remained as resolutely old-fashioned as his acting style.)

In 1734 Aaron Hill founded *The Prompter*, the first magazine to be mainly devoted to matters of the stage, in which he made a similar point – warning Quin that his 'pausing, solemn significance, and that composed air and gravity of your motion', was becoming stultified: 'though dignity is finely maintained by the weight of majestic composure, yet there are scenes in your parts where the voice should be sharp and impatient, the looks disordered and agonized, the action precipitate and turbulent.' And the playwright Richard Cumberland later recollected Quin playing Horatio in Rowe's *The Fair Penitent* 'with very little variation of cadence, and in a deep full tone, accompanied by a sawing kind of action'.

Cumberland went on to claim that Quin 'rolled out his heroics with an air of dignified indifference, that seemed to disdain the plaudits that were bestowed upon him'. According to Aaron Hill, such indifference was not confined to the speaking actor, since he singled out for praise 'that impressive attention' with which Samuel Stephens 'listened, while spoke to, and the direction of your eye to its proper object, on the stage; whereas it is common among modern actors to bestow their looks and language upon the audience'. One suspects, however, that so far from being a characteristic of the 'modern' actor, this was in part a hangover from the presentational tradition of the Restoration, not yet quite unlearned.

But some actors showed that learning was possible. Another of the Cibber clan, Theophilus's wife Susanna, appears to have followed Quin's lead in her early years, chanting rather than speaking her lines. Thus, Richard Cumberland recalled her Calista in *The Fair Penitent* as 'extremely wanting in contrast', in a manner which 'wearied' the ear: 'when she had once recited two or three speeches, I could anticipate the manner of every succeeding one.' Yet within a few years, according to Thomas Wilkes, audiences were 'surprised at the wild exertions of her powers in the sudden transitions she makes from love and grief to the extremities of rage and despair'. The transformation was wrought by the experience of working with the man who was to bring English acting style into a more congruent relationship with its times: David Garrick.

GARRICK AT GOODMAN'S FIELDS

Garrick's first appearance on the London stage exploited a loophole in the Licensing Act, whose provisions actors and managers soon sought to evade. Thus, James Lacy, a stalwart of Fielding's company, had apparently mounted one-man shows in 1738, while Tony Aston twice advertised 'Serious and Comic Oratory' in tavern venues – and Charlotte Charke turned to her puppets. But it was Henry Giffard who first engaged a full company and mounted regular performances, at his old theatre in Goodman's Fields, through the device of promising a concert of 'vocal and instrumental music' – between the two parts of which 'will be presented a comedy, gratis, by persons for their diversion'. This 'concert formula' must have enjoyed at least tacit government approval, since the plays were even submitted to the Lord Chamberlain, as his powers of censorship now required.

Garrick, fresh to the town as a law student turned wine merchant, was evidently on good terms with Giffard, for whose benefit he had written an entertainment at Drury Lane in 1740: then, in October 1741, Garrick appeared anonymously in the title role of *Richard III* at Goodman's Fields. In the same year, a general election had returned a majority favouring the vigorous pursuit of the war which – already in progress against Spain – was soon to involve all Europe. And in February 1742 Sir Robert Walpole resigned, giving way to a 'broad-bottomed' Whig ministry dedicated to imperialistic expansion. As it turned out, the art of the new actor was ideally suited to the temper of the new age.

Opposite: portrait by Hogarth of Garrick as Richard III, on the restless night before the Battle of Bosworth Field. Painted in 1745, only a few years after Garrick's creation of the role at the Goodman's Fields theatre in 1741, this picture suggests the facial and gestic stress through which Garrick conveyed emotion for a pre-romantic theatre. However, the untheatrically sumptuous trappings also warn us against too literal a reading of such portraits, through which Garrick hoped to immortalize his genius: for the conventions are those of historical painting rather than of the theatre

That Garrick's acting style was famously 'natural' does not, of course, mean that it was 'naturalistic' according to our own expectations. His great strength was apparently in his 'turns', or transitions from one mood to another – an ability to modulate the emotions in a subtler manner than the formal style had ever permitted. To this continuity in the rendering of characters was harnessed a richer sense of their complexity, capable of breaking down old generic expectations to reveal the comic or grotesque in tragedy and the absurdity in high comedy – thus making his Abel Drugger in The Alchemist, or his Sir John Brute in The Provoked Wife, as renowned as his Lear, or his Hastings in Jane Shore. Despite – or perhaps because – of this scrupulous concern with emotional minutiae, Garrick was sparing of stage movement. As John Hill put it in The Actor, one of the earliest attempts at a technical analysis of the histrionic art, published in 1750:

David Garrick (1717–79), here portrayed in engravings from the 1770s as (left) King Lear, and (right) the cross-dressed Sir John Brute in Vanbrugh's *The Provoked Wife*. These sketches, less posed than the formal paintings on pages 174 and 178, better capture the fluent mobility and no less expressive tranquility of Garrick's acting. A fellow professional, Arthur Murphy, remarked of Garrick that '*off* the stage he was a mean sneaking little fellow. But on the stage . . . oh, my great God!' Egocentric, envious, and ever hungry for admiration, he was not only the greatest and widest-ranging actor of his generation, but a dramatist in his own right, and an effective if not a well-liked manager during his twenty-nine years at Drury Lane. Here he judiciously balanced popular demand against his perception of the dignity of the profession – and of himself

He will stand in his place on the stage, with his arms genteelly disposed, and without once stirring hand or foot, go thro' a scene of the greatest variety. He will in this single posture express to his audience all the changes of passion that can affect a human heart; and he will express them strongly, so that tossing about of the arms and strutting from side to side of the stage, is not his business.

As a French critic also implied, in rebuking Garrick for eliciting laughs in comedy 'more by the grimaces of his face than the proper modulation of his voice', Garrick evidently recognized the power of the age-old art of mimicry. Indeed, Theophilus Cibber, criticizing him in 1756 for an 'over-fondness for extravagant attitudes . . . a set of mechanical motions in constant use', actually described this as a 'pantomimical manner of acting': and Cibber pointed out of Garrick's soliloquizing Gloucester, that holding such 'extravagant attitudes' not only served as a powerful clap-trap, but, worse, involved 'unnatural pauses in the middle of a sentence' and a 'wilful neglect of harmony'. Even a friendly writer remarked in an open letter to Garrick of 1772 that 'your perfection consists in the extreme; in exaggerated gesture, and sudden bursts of passion. . . . Where the extensive powers of voice are not required, you are inimitable.'

The anecdote concerning the deaf and dumb child who none the less claimed to understand every nuance of meaning in Garrick's performance is no less significant whether it be apocryphal or true – but it is doubtful whether such concern with conveying visualized meaning would be regarded as 'natural' in today's mainstream theatre, where verbal skills are routinely analyzed but movement is generally understated and often goes unremarked. The style would, however, have been well suited to an age when, although artistic fashion dictated a new openness to sensibility, Hogarth's urban art of moral caricature was probably better appreciated than were Gainsborough's attempts to transplant portraiture into a rustic landscape; and Hogarth's engravings, not unlike Garrick's acting for the deaf and dumb child, could sustain their 'narrative' without the use of words.

It is also instructive to remember that the contemporary encyclopedist and critic Denis Diderot called

upon Garrick's art to illustrate his point that acting was not a matter of emotional identification but of artifice consciously applied. And Thomas Davies, recollecting Hannah Pritchard playing opposite Garrick's Macbeth, suggests that this artifice could to some extent be taught – his 'distraction of mind and agonizing horrors' being 'finely contrasted by her seeming apathy, tranquillity, and confidence. The beginning of the scene after the murder was conducted in terrifying whispers. Their looks and actions supplied the place of words.' Mary Ann Yates, too, was commended by Francis Gentleman for her skill in 'judicious transitions of voice, happy variations of countenance, and picturesque attitudes'.

CHAPTER 12

The Garrick Years

'If this young fellow be right, I and the rest of the players have been all wrong.' The reputed verdict of a bemused James Quin on David Garrick's acting style might as aptly have been Walpole's on the political style of the elder Pitt. For the period which began with Garrick's first appearance at Goodman's Fields and ended with his departure after almost thirty years as actor-manager of Drury Lane also saw Walpole's cautious foreign policy overtaken by a drive for colonial expansion, in which Pitt's was the moving spirit. In consequence, this was an epoch when the nation was either at war or preparing for war – and although Pitt, 'the great commoner', only briefly became prime minister, his influence remained pervasive.

European 'theatres' were found for the conflict, successively in the War of the Austrian Succession and the Seven Years War, but its real battlegrounds were in the Indian sub-continent and in North America – and its ultimate aim was imperial supremacy over France. Appropriately, perhaps, American independence was proclaimed in 1776, the same year as Garrick's retirement: and within three more years the actor and the statesman, now Earl of Chatham, were both in their graves.

At home, Jacobitism finally flared out in the uprising of 1745 – less a genuine threat this time than an opportunity seized to eliminate all Scottish resistance at Culloden. *Henry V* was duly brought on to stimulate patriotic fervour at the theatres, while in September 1745 the National Anthem for the first time accompanied the performance at Drury Lane – inaugurating a tradition which was to have audiences shuffling to their feet for well over two hundred years. And so, whereas the theatre of the 1730s had been, if not the hotbed of opposition sometimes alleged, at least a constant irritant to officialdom, during Garrick's long ascendancy it tended rather to reflect the prevailing chauvinistic mood.

THE ECONOMICS OF RESPECTABILITY

Although there is no doubt at all that Garrick was a great actor, part of his strength lay in his capacity to create a theatrical complement to this mood: and, something of a snob himself – with a great need for the respect and admiration of others – he not only achieved but enjoyed the power to impose the greater measure of respectability he felt requisite. This was made manifest not so much in flag-waving fervour as through his managerial drive towards a higher moral tone on stage and a compliant order in pit and gallery – ambitions which his audiences did not invariably share. Yet if respectability was a patriotic duty, even more surely was it an economic imperative – for the emergent novel was already offering an alternative and securely domestic kind of entertainment. Thus in 1740 had appeared Samuel Richardson's pioneering and sensationally successful work in the genre, *Pamela* – a masterpiece of sentiment in which a serving girl defends her virginity and subdues her would-be seducer into marriage.

Revealingly, in the following year, while yet billed at Goodman's Fields as 'the young gentleman who played King Richard', Garrick took the role of Jack Smatter in a stage adaptation of the novel – whose high moral tone, in Henry Fielding's view, ill-concealed its titillating sexuality. That the novel survived his satiric onslaughts in *Shamela* and *Joseph Andrews* was in no small part due to an increasing public squeamishness which by 1743 had rendered Fielding's own earlier comedy *The Wedding Day* unacceptable to the Lord Chamberlain, simply on the grounds that its heroine was a whore. Fielding duly subjected her to a retributory carting, whereupon the play was allowed its licence – but was none the less damned by its audiences for supposed immorality. By then, however, Fielding was beginning to build as a novelist the more responsive and tolerant audience which the combination of censorship and self-censorship denied him in the theatre.

Opposite: painting by Francis Hayman of David Garrick as Ranger in Benjamin Hoadly's intrigue comedy *The Suspicious Husband* (1747). Playing opposite him is Hannah Pritchard (1711–68), who had first appeared at Drury Lane in 1733, but moved to Covent Garden from 1743 to 1747 before joining Garrick for the remainder of her career. Extending her range beyond such light comic roles as Hoadly's Clorinda and Mrs Oakly in Colman's *The Jealous Wife* (1761), she played Lady Macbeth opposite Garrick and was also Gertrude to his Hamlet. She was favourably compared with Mrs Cibber both by Richard Cumberland, who claimed that she had 'more change of tone, and variety both of action and expression', and by Charles Dibdin, who declared: 'Mrs Cibber's acting was delightful, Mrs Pritchard's commanding. One insinuated herself into the heart, the other took possession of it. . . . It made acting like a picture, with grand breadths of light and shade'

Meanwhile, Garrick's popularity at Goodman's Fields had provoked Fleetwood and Rich to combine in securing the theatre's closure. By way of consolation, Fleetwood not only signed up Garrick for the following season at the then astonishing salary of 600 guineas, but took on the dispossessed Giffard and his wife as well. At the tail end of the 1742 season, therefore, Garrick tried out his three most successful roles at Drury Lane: and thus it was that in May he found himself playing Lear opposite the Cordelia of Peg Woffington – herself a newcomer at the playhouse, but already winning a reputation as the most exuberant actress since Nell Gwyn. It was with Peg Woffington that Garrick proceeded to spend the summer season in Dublin – and the next three years in shared lodgings. But the itch for respectability led him eventually into marriage with a lady of more reticent disposition – while the less vivacious and perhaps less threatening Susannah Cibber, now divorced from Theophilus, became his preferred partner on stage.

By May 1743 Fleetwood's patent at Drury Lane was, in effect, mortgaged to his gambling debts, and, following visits to the theatre from the bailiffs, Garrick and Charles Macklin led a walkout of nine of the leading actors. Failing to secure the independent licence they sought from the Lord Chamberlain, they were forced into an accommodation with Fleetwood in September, whereby Garrick alone achieved an increase in salary, and some players were even forced to return on inferior terms – while Macklin was refused employment at any price, and, feeling himself betrayed, induced his sympathizers to disrupt performances. On this occasion Fleetwood got the better of 'the mob' by hiring prizefighters to eject them: but when he tried to ease his problems by raising prices in 1744 the resulting riots were more successfully sustained, and he was forced to capitulate.

Fleetwood then decided to cut his losses by selling out to his creditors, who offered James Lacy from Covent Garden a one-third share in the patent to manage the theatre for them – only to retreat into bankruptcy themselves as a result of the breakdown of banking confidence during the Jacobite uprising of 1745. As the crisis mounted, Garrick, with characteristic caution, absented himself in Dublin, eventually returning to play the summer season of 1746 at Covent Garden under a profit-sharing agreement with John Rich – the mutual success of which tempted Garrick into remaining at Covent Garden, and the pragmatic Rich to subdue his pantomimic inclinations by launching a full season of straight plays.

THE LEADING ACTORS AND THEIR STYLES

The company assembled by Rich and Garrick included Mrs Cibber, Quin, Lacy Ryan, John Hippisley, Harry Woodward, and Hannah Pritchard, while Lacy, in opposition at Drury Lane, had induced Macklin to return, in company with Kitty Clive and Peg Woffington, Richard Yates, Henry Giffard, and the latest prodigy from Ireland, Spranger Barry. Garrick and Quin, as the leading exponents respectively of the formal and the 'natural' styles, now found themselves not only acting in the same plays but sometimes alternating in the same roles – to Garrick's clear

Opposite: A cartoon by Gillray of backstage hostilities between contending leading ladies. This incident is said to have arisen from the ill-concealed delight of Kitty Clive (right) at the indifferent reception given to Peg Woffington's Lady Percy in *Henry IV*. While Kitty Clive (1711–85) remained loyal to the Drury Lane company, she learned to distrust Garrick no less than Peg Woffington (c. 1714–60), whose equivocal position as his former mistress led to her intermittent withdrawal to Covent Garden – on whose stage she fought with Anne Bellamy during a performance of *The Rival Queens*

advantage as Richard III and Lear. However, Quin apparently had the edge as Cato, and Garrick's Hotspur was quite outshone by the Falstaff of Quin when the two rivals acted together in *Henry IV*. But in Rowe's *The Fair Penitent*, as soon as Quin's laboured, mechanical Horatio gave way to Garrick's Lothario, 'young and light and alive in every muscle . . . it seemed', or so Richard Cumberland remembered, 'as if a whole century had been stepped over in the transition of a single scene'.

With the exception of an Othello from Spranger Barry which acted Garrick out of a part to which he never returned, Drury Lane had come off worse from the unwonted competition, and Lacy was anxious to secure Garrick's return. The Lord Chamberlain having promised him a renewal of the patent, he therefore bought out his backers and on 9 April 1747 entered into a partnership with Garrick which, in the event, was to last until his death in 1774, just two years before Garrick himself retired. Despite a few altercations, the division of labours they agreed seems to have worked well – Lacy controlling finances and attending to the wardrobe, Garrick dealing with authors, actors, and all the other practicalities of production.

After some mutual suspicions were allayed, Garrick hired both Mrs Cibber and Hannah Pritchard to play opposite him in tragedy, with Spranger Barry to share the

Samuel Foote (1721–77), with his leading comedian Thomas Weston (left), in *The Devil upon Two Sticks* (1768). In this play the actor, manager, and dramatist satirized his own loss of a leg following a horse-riding accident – as well as the attempts of the medical profession to treat him. Foote's career in some ways paralleled that of Henry Fielding – for not only did he also find the Little theatre a convenient base, but became, within the new constraints of the censorship, the most experimental comic dramatist of his day. His revue-like dramatic satires varied from *The Diversions of the Morning* (1747) to the less successful but aptly titled *Taste* (1752)

leading roles. For the broad comic leads there were Ned Shuter and Dick Yates – while Macklin had a famously protean range. Dennis Delane, William Havard, and Isaac Sparks lent stalwart support, and within a year or two Henry Woodward – soon in contention with his mentor Rich as Harlequin – together with the young Tom King, later to become Garrick's assistant, had further strengthened the company. Among other actresses, the fast-living George Anne Bellamy came to rival Mrs Cibber in tragedy, while in comedy the 'nimble pertness' of the eternally coquettish Kitty Clive contrasted with the more conventionally honed beauty and poise of Peg Woffington, whose strength lay not only in her well-loved 'breeches parts' but in such genteel leads as Millamant and Lady Townly. Later, Frances Abington, though a lesser personality offstage, was perhaps the truer professional, with the full comic spectrum at her command from ingenue to hoyden, and from witty young lady to frustrated old maid.

While Garrick's reputation, discussed and illustrated from the views of his contemporaries on pages 176–7, cast a long shadow over other actors of his generation, Spranger Barry could reputedly outshine him as Mark Antony as well as Othello, and was evidently a sexier if not a more soulful Romeo. Thomas Sheridan gave Garrick great unease in *King John*, and some preferred him as Hamlet – while the veteran Quin retained the advantage in the more sonorous ranges of the repertoire, until a retirement in 1751 from which he hoped but failed to be tempted back by Rich. Significantly, Garrick was less open to competition in comic roles – even Woodward failing to prosper in his own right when he went to Dublin with Barry in 1758. But the Abel Drugger of Thomas Weston revealed him capable of providing more than his accustomed low comic support, while Ned Shuter excelled in the heavier eccentric roles – not least those created for him just a few years before his death by Goldsmith and Sheridan.

FOOTE AT THE LITTLE, COLMAN AT COVENT GARDEN

Macklin, who long outlived Garrick and was still acting in 1789, his ninetieth year, complemented his successes in 'psychological' realism as Shylock and Iago – the latter, calculatedly, to Barry's Othello – with comic roles written by and for himself. A friend and disciple of Macklin's, and a no less individual actor-playwright, was Samuel Foote, who came closest to sustaining the satiric tradition created by Henry Fielding – also following in his footsteps to the Little theatre, where he played inter-mittently after 1747, finally obtaining a patent for summer seasons in 1766. These he gave with his own company until a year before his death, in 1777.

Like Fielding, too, Foote experimented with comic miscellanies which antici-pated revue – but it was with his full-length satirical pieces that he enjoyed his greatest success. Among many and various targets, he attacked artistic pretensions in *Taste* (1752), lampooned Methodism (and provided no fewer than three parts for himself) in *The Minor* (1760), and mocked the medical profession – and the loss of his own leg, which had led him to suffer its ministrations – in *The Devil upon Two Sticks* (1768). Foote's contemporaries regarded him as 'the English Aristophanes', but his reputation has suffered alike from Garrick's professional jealousy and from the restrictions of the Licensing Act – which never much obstructed Garrick's altogether blander and safer managerial style.

Nevertheless, as dramatist as well as manager Foote found himself in com-petition with the ubiquitous Garrick, whose playwriting was prolific, highly professional – sometimes even mildly experimental. The satirical *Lilliput* (1756), thus capped its Swiftian credentials by being cast with children, while *The Male Coquette* (1757) boasted a transvestite heroine as well as a homosexual gallant, and *A Peep behind the Curtain* (1767) charmingly fulfilled its promise in the form of a rehearsal play. However, Garrick's most successful pieces were those which made least demands on his audience's sensibilities – the early but perennial *Miss in Her Teens* of 1747, for example, or *The Guardian* of 1759, both adapted from the French.

Garrick's most enduring success came with *The Clandestine Marriage* of 1766, written in collaboration with George Colman. The play, a pleasant and never ill-tempered satire upon bourgeois values, is a seamless piece of craftsmanship, in which each writer corrected the other's faults while displaying his own virtues to advantage. Unhappily, the friendship between the two men was soured by disputes over their respective shares in the writing – and was soon to be put to the further test of professional rivalry. After John Rich's death in 1761, Covent Garden had briefly flirted with opera: however, in 1767 Colman began his stormy but fruitful managerial partnership at the playhouse with Thomas Harris, restoring regular drama to its stage, and in the following decade, as we shall see in the next chapter, introducing the work of both Goldsmith and Sheridan.

The Shakespeare industry gathers pace

While always ensuring that his own character was displayed to best advantage, Garrick salvaged some of the plays of Shakespeare from their Restoration 'improvements': but he cheerfully gutted others, to create a sort of refined version of the old drolls, transforming The Taming of the Shrew into the tamer Catherine and Petruchio and filtering out The Fairies from A Midsummer Night's Dream. Meanwhile, Shakespeare's editors continued to justify their more or less scholarly endeavours by vilifying their predecessors – the 'refinements' of Warburton's edition of 1747 being worthier of vilification than most.

That his eight volumes were soon being sold at a discount was due less to the undoubted deficiencies of the texts than to the perspicacity of Sir Thomas Hanmer in decorating his own otherwise unremarkable edition with illustrations by Francis Hayman. In describing his edition of 1744 as 'another small monument . . . to Shakespeare's honour', Hanmer was giving due precedence to the memorial statue which had been erected in Westminster Abbey four years earlier – and by the end of the decade the dramatist's effigy in his Stratford birthplace had also been carefully restored. Garrick, as ever in tune with his times, duly acquired a taste for such bits of Shakespearean statuary, and commissioned Louis François Roubillac to sculpt one for his home near Hampton Court. This he installed in a domestic temple dedicated to the poet, alongside a chair carved from the mulberry tree supposedly planted by Shakespeare in Stratford, but since heretically lopped. A protestant nation had, it seemed, found a secular saint whose relics might be consecrated, and whose graven image might be acceptably worshipped.

Jubilee Amphitheatre.

It had been in a prologue written for the first night of Garrick's management at Drury Lane that Samuel Johnson famously coined the dictum: 'The drama's laws the drama's patrons give, / For we that live to please, must please to live.' Ironically, Johnson's own single dramatic effort, the tragedy *Irene* (1749), was very clearly the work of a man of letters: but Garrick, Foote, and Colman, all actor-managers as well

Left: the memorial amphitheatre constructed for the Stratford jubilee of 1769. Above: the procession of Shakespearean characters, as planned for the jubilee (and illustrated prematurely in contemporary prints), but in the event washed out by rain. It was later profitably reassembled by Garrick for *The Jubilee* at Drury Lane

Boswell well recognized, harnessed his own social advancement to the semi-divine status of the 'immortal bard' – an epithet which Garrick was among the first to employ. The jubilee ended without a single scene from a play being performed, since pageantry and portraiture were much preferred (indeed, it is to Garrick's faith in the immortalizing powers of canvas that we owe all the portraits which capture him in Shakespearean roles).

However, Garrick eventually managed to capitalize on the Stratford celebrations by recreating The Jubilee as a dramatic spectacle for Drury Lane. With its lavishly costumed procession protected from the elements, and an 'outer play' devised gently to mock both the bemused natives of Stratford and their visitors, this 'devilishly lucky hit' (as Lacy called it, with grudging admiration for his partner) ran for ninety-two performances. Thus did the consummate showman in Garrick recoup both the money and the dignity he had laid out by converting a pretentious pageant for the provincial few into a lavish entertainment for the metropolitan many.

In 1768 Garrick acquired another hunk of sacred mulberry, this time in the form of a chest presented to him by the Corporation of Stratford along with the freedom of the Borough. Flattered according to plan, Garrick agreed to mount a belated jubilee celebration for the town in the following summer. A memorial theatre to Shakespeare was duly constructed on the banks of the Avon – a wooden octagonal playhouse which yet constituted, according to Garrick, a 'sacred...shrine' to a playwright translated into a 'demi-God'.

Garrick emerged none too happily from the ensuing rain-sodden affair, which, as observers from Samuel Foote to James

COMEDY in the COUNTRY.

TRAGEDY in LONDON.

Pub.ᵈ May 29ᵗʰ by Thoˢ Tegg N° 111 Cheapside — One Shilling colour'd 1807

Rowlandson Sculp.

as playwrights, fulfilled the dictum to the letter, and wrote largely and undemandingly to please. Colman's greatest solo success, *The Jealous Wife* of 1761, is thus filled with long-familiar character types – their sexuality muted, as contemporary morality required.

COMEDY, TRAGEDY — AND SENTIMENTALITY

Benjamin Hoadly was one of the few dramatists who, although forgotten today, achieved success in comedy from outside the enclosed theatrical world. His *The Suspicious Husband*, staged at Covent Garden in 1747 during Garrick's brief engagement there, was even described by the later dramatist Arthur Murphy as 'the first good comedy from the time of *The Provoked Husband* in 1727' – 'a long and dreary interval', in Murphy's debatable judgement. Significantly, the play's good-natured rake is drawn along the lines of Fielding's hero in his *Tom Jones*, published two years later – both embodying a 'benevolist' alternative to the scrupulous sentimental hero, their fallible natures prey to weakness but, come the crunch, replete with hearty warmth.

The stock situations and characters of melodrama are not very far away – and another of its easy assumptions, that love conquers all, had already become the premise behind many of Isaac Bickerstaffe's popular musical afterpieces. Thus, his *Thomas and Sally* (1760), set to music by Thomas Arne, was an early variation on what was to become the familiar theme of the simple country girl resisting the evil squire until her sailor lover's return; and he followed up the success of his pioneering comic opera *Love in a Village* (1762) with *The Maid of the Mill*, a reconstruction of Samuel Richardson's *Pamela* demonstrating the democratizing effects of love – a motif which recurred in his long-successful *Lionel and Clarissa* (1768).

The philosophical origins of this theatrical benevolism are less interesting from our point of view than the consequences of setting its character typology against that predicated upon sentimentality. Two plays of 1768 exemplify the polarity of possibilities – in *False Delicacy* Hugh Kelly more or less abandoning comedy to the endless moral scruples of sensibility, while in *The Good-Natured Man* Oliver Goldsmith took them to hilarious excess, rewarding virtue in hard cash (as, without tongue in cheek, did Richard Cumberland in his *The West Indian* of 1771).

In an essay published in 1763, Goldsmith claimed that sentimental comedy was in truth 'a species of bastard tragedy': certainly, the original of that species was apparently in terminal decline – most works of interest which laid claim to the genre proving in retrospect to anticipate the imminent split between the more realistic and the more melodramatic tendencies of the form. Edward Moore's *The Gamester* (1753), for example, was written in prose, had a contemporary setting, and some psychological insight into its protagonist's obsessive and fatal vice – while his destruction is presented as self-driven rather than a requirement of poetic justice. By contrast, and despite its greater outward regularity, John Home's *Douglas* (1756) conjures the foreboding atmospherics and the fraught, darkly elliptic emotions of

Opposite: 'Comedy in the Country,' and 'Tragedy in London'. This cartoon by Thomas Rowlandson, though not published until 1807, pictorializes a long-established urban presumption – that audiences in the country are unsophisticated both in manners and in their response to a play. It is instructive, therefore to contrast the view of the experienced Tate Wilkinson, in his *Memoirs* of 1790: 'A farce, if it possesses true humour, in London will be greatly relished and applauded. In the country, very possibly the same . . . shall be termed vile, low, vulgar, and indelicate.' And mannered comedies which 'are in London attended to as plays of wit and merit' in the country are 'not permitted, or if permitted to appear, not upon any account fashionable, which is just as bad'

what was to become the gothic style of melodrama – even then taking shape in the fertile, febrile imagination of Robert Walpole's fourth son Horace, ensconced close by Kitty Clive in his own 'little gothic castle' at Strawberry Hill.

If sentimentality was nothing like as pervasive in the theatre as is sometimes claimed, this is because literary historians not only tend to ignore new writing of a less 'regular' kind, but also to forget that the theatrical repertoire was heavily weighted with revivals made of sterner stuff – especially at Drury Lane, where Lacy, if not Garrick, tended to view the mounting of any new work as an unnecessary financial risk. But the effects of sentimentality were none the less felt in the way that those revivals were tempered to the changing times – not only in the neutering of Restoration ribaldry, as typified in Garrick's toning down of Wycherley's *The Country Wife* into his own innocuous *The Country Girl*, but in the regularizing of Shakespeare himself, who during these years was elevated by Garrick into a figure of patriotic as well as dramatic dignity.

DE LOUTHERBOURG AND THE NEW SCENOGRAPHY

In 1761, Garrick had discommoded his audience when, mounting a theatrical celebration for the coronation of George III, he had flung wide the back doors of Drury Lane, so that the stage procession might merge with the real-life revelling beyond – only to let in the suffocating smoke from the bonfires in the street. But both this and *The Jubilee* (described on pages 184–5) suggest well enough the new appetite for stage spectacle which was now enhancing the importance of the scene-painter within the production process.

Thus, whereas opera had from the first been decked out with settings and costumes as lavish as financial and technological resources allowed, in the regular drama only limited changes had generally been rung upon the same old sets of wings and shutters. Once a novelty, the stylized perspective these simulated had come to be regarded with affectionate scorn – not least since actors, now increasingly required to play within the scene, appeared to grow larger the further they moved upstage, and to shrink as they strode back down.

For most purposes a dozen or so sets of stock scenery had sufficed. These might represent, in the inventory of one contemporary writer, temples, tombs, city walls and gates, the outside and inside of palaces, streets, chambers, prisons, and gardens, together with prospects of groves, forests, and deserts. While regularly revived plays might enjoy dedicated sets, and scenic 'pieces' and properties would also lend an appearance of variety, most new work from the mid-century appears to have required only a couple of settings, typically an interior and an exterior. No doubt their authors were disinclined to make technical demands which might deter a frugal and conservative management from mounting their work.

None the less, foreign visitors seem to have been impressed by the sheer rapidity of scene changes in the London theatres – especially admiring the nifty trickwork involving traps and transformations that was the special preserve of pantomime.

'The Theatrical Steel-Yard of 1750', a print depicting the rivalry between Garrick at Drury Lane and the outfaced Rich at Covent Garden. Garrick, brandishing his helmet from the right-hand end of the steel-yard, does not need the added weight of his own Harlequin, Woodward, who stands ready to place Queen Mab (subject of the successful Drury Lane pantomime) on the scales. On the left, Rich, an overcoat half-concealing his Harlequin costume, is distraught that the combined weights of Peg Woffington, Spranger Barry, James Quin (as Falstaff), and Mrs Cibber cannot outweigh Garrick *solus*

Though ostensibly despising 'the pomp of show', Garrick mounted a moderately successful challenge to Rich's primacy in this form, with Henry Woodward as his usual Harlequin following the immense and oft-repeated success of *Queen Mab* in 1750. (The cartoon below celebrates Garrick's triumph.) But it was another Drury Lane actor, Tom King, who startled the town by first giving this conventionally mute character a tongue, in the equally successful *Harlequin's Invasion* of 1756.

By the later 1760s 'new scenes' were increasingly being advertised as an attraction at both patent houses, and some exciting drop-scenes were evidently being painted. But it was during the ten years spent at Drury Lane from 1771 by the Alsatian scenic artist and technician Philip James de Loutherbourg that scenographic techniques underwent there a startling reformation. *A Christmas Tale* of 1774 thus not only displayed a succession of extravagant prospects, transformations, and illusions, but employed licopodium to give the illusion of a palace in flames, while the leaves of a forest were made to turn seasonally from green to a bloody red.

De Loutherbourg did not abolish the old wings and grooves, but used ground-rows to fill the often-yawning space between: thus, in *Omai*, a lavish production

prepared by John O'Keeffe for Covent Garden in 1785, one observer counted no less than 42 separate pieces, intended cumulatively to create an illusion of frozen seas. And during the 1770s Drury Lane had begun to carpenter practicable doors and stairways into its interiors, even topping them out with roofs or ceilings – an early intimation of the 'fourth wall' convention which was to culminate in the box set of the following century.

Such representational trimmings may, according to one's taste, be viewed as a necessary nudge towards naturalism or mere decorative pedantry. Equally, De Loutherbourg himself may be considered a first mover in establishing the creative integrity of scenic design – or as a craftsman properly and professionally most concerned with accommodating rather than creating artistic fashions. Certainly, these were about to undergo a radical change, in favour of that individualizing of experience and heightening of its most mundane manifestations which in poetry found sublime expression in the work of the great romantics. In the theatre, the new taste was to be made more humbly manifest – in the necessary but sometimes trite emotional shorthand of melodrama, whose early audiences tended to relish precisely the elaborate, atmospheric, and often exotic settings which De Loutherbourg's technical innovations made possible.

Whether the accompanying changes in acting style were cause or effect of the imminent increases in playhouse capacities will be a concern of our next chapter. Meanwhile, it is sufficient to note that Garrick's success was in no small part due to the socially stable composition of his relatively small audiences, whose roots, like his own, were in the affluent but still aspirant middle classes. Thus, although Garrick made 'improvements' to Drury Lane on no less than nine occasions, gradually increasing the capacity of the house from perhaps 1,400 to 1,800, the only significant effect of these changes was the final elimination of spectators from the stage, achieved by an enlargement of the pit in 1762. At Covent Garden the audience probably lingered on the stage for another twenty years, especially at benefits – while minor alterations here, as at the two theatres in the Haymarket, were largely cosmetic.

Not only were no new permanent playhouses built in London during the period, but an act of 1752 which required the licensing of all sorts of entertainments struck a mortal blow to the fairground theatres of the metropolis. And although concert rooms, pleasure gardens, and other leisure resorts flourished, the competition they offered to the regular playhouses was not in kind – except, perhaps at Marylebone Gardens, where numerous operettas were performed on an apparently large and well-equipped stage. However, that ordinary people were becoming accustomed to paying for an informal musical entertainment cannot but have helped to prepare the ground for the free-and-easies and saloons, the ancestors of the music halls of the following century.

THEATRE IN THE PROVINCES

Performances outside London had, of course, already been prohibited by the Licensing Act of 1737, and that they continued to occur was at first a matter of tolerance rather than regulation – a concert often providing cover for the enjoyment of a play 'rehearsed' gratis. Players on the northern and eastern provincial circuits were forced to lead a constantly itinerant existence, but the southern seaports seem to have offered more regular employment, and fashionable resorts were singled out in season. While the focus of a 'season' might be a race meeting or court of assize, for the fashionable it increasingly involved the taking of medicinal waters: and the pre-eminence of Bath among the spa resorts led, in 1750, to the building of a permanent theatre in Orchard Street, which after a lengthy campaign secured a royal patent in 1768.

Opposite: model of a prison scene by Philip James de Loutherbourg (1740–1812), the innovative scene painter at Drury Lane for a decade from 1771. Garrick himself may be said to have begun the revolution in stage lighting when, in 1765, he replaced the huge chandeliers over the stage with smaller sets of candles or oil lamps in the wings, equipped with reflectors to vary the intensity of the light. But De Loutherbourg was the first scenic artist to make fully creative use of illumination, achieving subtly realistic effects by employing coloured silks as filters, and thus perfecting (though not, as John O'Keeffe claimed in 1826, inventing) 'transparent scenery – moonshine, sunshine, fire, volcanoes, etc.' De Loutherbourg also, in effect, theatricalized the art of landscape painting, bringing to life the beauties of nature through creative lighting in such spectacles as *The Wonders of Derbyshire* (1779)

A precedent thus created, further patents were granted to playhouses in Norwich later in 1768, and to York in the following year – these three cities being accounted the most important provincial centres, whence players often graduated to the London stage. Theatres in Hull, Liverpool, Manchester, Bristol, and Newcastle were all granted patents over the next two decades, while Brighton, Windsor, and Richmond, as royal residences, held licences from the Lord Chamberlain. A boom in building smaller theatres for the touring circuits followed an act of 1788 which empowered local magistrates to grant their own licences for seasons not exceeding sixty days.

The regulation by licensing of provincial theatres has been interpreted as part of the process which, by 1843, had led to the success of the so-called 'struggle for a free stage' in London. However, it may also be understood as one of the ways in which the state was extending its power over the lives of the people, thereby not only dispossessing Londoners of the booth theatres of the fairs, but also increasingly eroding the old pattern of holidays, feasts, and other popular celebrations in the countryside. Pre-industrial society, of which this period is usually seen as marking the final phase, was no carefree idyll for those who suffered its privations: but it did permit the pursuit of individual pleasures and pastimes in ways that the drift to the towns of the 'industrial revolution' was soon so brutally to extinguish.

The steady movement of the population into urban areas was, of course, to grow from a trickle to a flood in the following half-century – though in the case of

The Theatre Royal, Bristol, as viewed from the stage. This was built in 1766 on the model of Drury Lane, with a capacity of around 1,600. This house and the Georgian at Richmond (opposite) are the two oldest working theatres in Britain. They are nicely contrasting examples of different provincial styles

The Georgian theatre at Richmond in Yorkshire, built in 1788, abandoned for almost a century from 1848, and fully restored and reopened in 1963. This has a humbler capacity – an intimate 250 – than the Theatre Royal, Bristol, which is pictured opposite

London the population of the 'square mile' actually declined, and it was the slums of Westminster and the jerry-built parishes 'outside the bills' that almost burst their bounds. Theatrically, the need thus began to emerge for amusements which were not only more locally based but also more responsive to the needs and experiences of the poor than the old, bourgeois repertoire of the West End houses – where, perpetuating the traditional typology, the working classes were still largely presented as either pert but subservient or lazy and parasitic.

The heads of the Jacobites executed after the rebellion of 1745 still hung from Temple Bar some thirty years later – a gruesome reminder of the cheapness of life and the proliferation of capital crimes in an age when property and patriotism were sacrosanct. Yet steadily, with the demand for more broadly-based political power rooted in the grim realities of economic deprivation, the voice of 'the mob' grew ever louder on the streets – sometimes venting an easy chauvinism, as in the early popular support for Pitt or in the anti-Catholicism of the Gordon Riots, but also capable of expressing a new and proto-democratic radicalism.

As we have noted earlier, a surge of feeling in support of the American revolution coincided with the year of Garrick's retirement, 1776: and this was closely contemporary with the emergence for the first time of a political 'party' which favoured reform – around a dozen of whose supporters actually won seats in the election of 1774, despite widespread corruption and a severely limited franchise. The relationship between the theatre and the burgeoning movement for reform is a tenuous one, but it must command our attention – not least because the period covered by this chapter is the last in which any discussion can be mainly confined within the geographical or social boundaries of the West End, or dominated by a single personality such as Garrick, able to read and so to shape its concerns. For the next century, the theatre was arguably to become the first medium of mass communication.

CHAPTER 13

From Manners to Melodrama

Theatre Royal, Drury Lane, in 1808: 'A wilderness of a place', according to Sarah Siddons, this huge house had a capacity of over 3,600, and was never much liked by actors, who, said the playwright Richard Cumberland, had great difficulty making themselves heard. He added that 'the splendour of the scenes, the ingenuity of the machinist, and the rich display of dresses, aided by the captivating charms of music' now superseded 'the labours of the poet'. It burned down in 1809

It was largely on borrowed money that Richard Brinsley Sheridan bought out Garrick, and went on to acquire the other portions of the Drury Lane patent. Like the speculative capitalists whose factories and sweatshops were now beginning to spread across the newly urbanized landscape, Sheridan remained blithely confident of earning more on his enterprise than he need repay in interest: but since he believed that he could better serve his own and his country's needs in parliament than the theatre, the fortunes of Drury Lane were destined to remain precarious throughout his semi-detached management.

THE SHERIDAN PHENOMENON

As a Whig sensitive to premonitions of the new liberalism, Sheridan remained to the last in almost permanent opposition – though he was renowned for his forceful oratory, notably in defence of the oppressed Indians during the protracted impeachment of Warren Hastings. For this was a period when, under the younger Pitt, the nation's electoral pulse took on a chauvinistic Tory beat – quickened

first from fears of revolutionary contagion, then by the more tangible threat of invasion as the wavering democratic spirit in France turned its energies abroad under the Napoleonic dictatorship.

Ironically, it had been at Covent Garden, in 1775, that Sheridan's earliest plays reached the stage: a farce, *St Patrick's Day*, a comic opera, *The Duenna*, and the first of the comedies for which he is best remembered, *The Rivals*, with its casually convoluted plotting and multi-faceted mockery of the cult of sensibility – not forgetting the immortal if not entirely original Mrs Malaprop. By the end of the decade, in charge at Drury Lane, Sheridan had produced for that playhouse his later comic masterpiece, *The School for Scandal*, and, in *The Critic*, a burlesque which briskly revamped Buckingham's *The Rehearsal*. Both were rapturously received.

Together with Oliver Goldsmith's equally well-loved *She Stoops to Conquer* (1773), these classic comedies of Sheridan's represent a final, ironic apotheosis of the twin traditions of mannered and humours comedy – ironic because, while they look back sometimes with nostalgia to the stable social order which pro-vides their necessary sounding-board, they were written for a theatre which no longer socially *mattered* (or was legally allowed to matter) in quite the same way. Pitt was thus at his most effective in putting down Sheridan's political oratory when he scornfully likened it to a theatrical performance. Sure enough, the endur-ing strengths of Sheridan's comedies lie not in their 'literary' qualities, but in their capacity to capture the idiomatic patterns and nuances of the spoken word.

Such colloquial vigour was notably absent from the single further play Sheridan wrote following his election to parliament in 1780. This was *Pizarro* (1799), an adaptation of *Die Spanier in Peru* by August von Kotzebue – the German dramatist whose prolific and widely-influential output is usually seen as transitional between the sentimental and the melodramatic modes. Yet although *Pizarro* did not outlive its huge initial popularity, its very different rhetorical codes were no less fully understood and appreciated by its early audiences. And, just as the throwing down of the screen in *The School for Scandal* exemplified Sheridan's consummate sense of traditional stagecraft, so the exotic settings and strange rituals of *Pizarro* exploited newer scenographic techniques and tastes to the full. The play is, in effect, a spectacular political melodrama.

Not unlike the Indians of the subcontinent, whose sufferings under colonial rule had so engaged Sheridan's parliamentary sympathies, the American Indians of his *Pizarro* are noble savages ignobly exploited – as had been earlier portrayed, for example, in *Inkle and Yarico*, a stage adaptation by George Colman the Younger of a story by Richard Steele, seen at the Haymarket in 1787. And here, almost incidentally, we already have cause to question the deduction of Ernest Bradlee Watson, an early but still respected theatre historian of this period, that – since 'evil-working influences' ensured that 'the masses had soon made the theatres almost exclusively their own' – 'of the nation's political life, almost nothing is traceable in the drama'.

John Philip Kemble as Rolla, the brave commander who opposes the ruthless title-character of Sheridan's *Pizarro* (1799). Here, despite his wounds, Rolla is escaping with the rescued child of his beloved Cora – having earlier saved its father, his honour-able rival in love. In the two decades since *The School for Scandal*, Sheridan had thus moved from a social comedy reminiscent of the Restoration mode to a proto-melodrama, replete with an exotic setting and the characteristic romantic themes of savage nobility and selfless renunciation

Opposite: two contrasting
impressions of Richard
Brinsley Sheridan – on the
right the urbane and charming
subject of a portrait by Joshua
Reynolds; on the left, in a
detail from a cartoon by James
Gillray, the mismanager of
Drury Lane, brandy-nosed and
gloating over the proceeds
from *Pizarro*, in whose
costume he is portrayed
proclaiming the lines:
'Honour? Reputation? A mere
bubble! Will the praise of
posterity charm my bones
in the grave? O Gold! Gold!'

It is, however, no less possible to propose that the theatre and politics were now becoming inextricably intertwined, and in consequence that the drama was perhaps more responsive to the social conditions of the mass of the people than ever before. That such conflicting judgements are possible is itself a reflection of the complex nature and manifestations of the relationship between the theatre and an emerging industrialized society – as of the way in which the authorities attempted to regulate it. Not least is it difficult, for example, to disentangle cause and effect in the matter of the great increase in the physical capacity of the leading theatres which now began to occur.

In 1792 Covent Garden, under the continuing management of Thomas Harris, was thus restructured and enlarged – to the designs of Henry Holland, who two years later also oversaw the rebuilding of Drury Lane, as pictured on page 194, to seat over 3,600 spectators. The new Covent Garden burned down in 1808 – and even before its successor, with Richard Smirke as architect, sprang up in the following year, Drury Lane had also fallen victim to the flames.

A ruined but resigned Sheridan thereupon quit the scene, and it was thanks to the brewing magnate Samuel Whitbread that the fourth, surviving theatre, designed by Benjamin Wyatt, finally reoccupied the site in 1812. Both playhouses continued to seat over 3,000 spectators: but did this enormous increase in capacity lead to or follow from the democratization of the drama, with its allegedly attendant loss of 'naturalness' in acting style? *Pizarro*, for one, no less required a scaled-up acting style than a scaled-up Drury Lane demanded it.

Many other theatres, old and new, were by then also flourishing – but still only one other was authorized to stage legitimate drama. In 1776 George Colman had emerged from retirement to take over the summer seasons at the Little Theatre in the Haymarket from the dying Foote, but himself suffered a stroke in 1789: it was thus effectively under his son, the younger George, that the theatre continued to prosper. 'Little' indeed, by comparison with its older rivals – a third tier of boxes being the only enlargement undertaken – this was, according to Hazlitt, 'the most sociable of all the theatres'. Its success was in no small part due to the considerable playwriting skills of Colman himself, who trod carefully between the calculated liberal sympathies of *Inkle and Yarico* and the conservatism of a man of property and a patentee – who, as Examiner of Plays from 1824, was to become a strict official censor during a period of acute social tension.

That new, albeit so-called 'minor' theatres now began legally to be built was a consequence of the act of 1752 which, as we have seen, was primarily intended to prevent the proliferating popular resorts around London from becoming 'disorderly houses'. But the act also made it possible for any place of entertainment within twenty miles of the capital to obtain a magistrates' licence, so long as it did not infringe the monopoly of the patent houses: and thus it was that, in 1765, the old music house at the Islington spa of Sadler's Wells was replaced by the grand new theatre pictured overleaf, seating 2,600; and by the early 1780s

two amphitheatres on the Surrey side – Astley's and the Royal Circus, to both of which we shall return – had been fitted out for theatrical use.

In 1794, the Lyceum, which had previously functioned as an exhibition hall, also became a playhouse. Situated in Wellington Street, at the eastern end of the Strand, this was almost on the doorsteps of the patent houses – whose jealousy of their monopoly had already been demonstrated when, in 1787, John Palmer from Drury Lane opened the first Royalty Theatre in Wellclose Square, in the shadow of the Tower of London (from whose governor, Palmer cannily obtained his licence). He mounted productions of *As You Like It* and of Garrick's

A Miss in Her Teens, but quickly found himself in prison at the behest of the patentees – the theatre duly resorting to a diet of pantomime, juggling, rope-walking, dancing, and other such irregular but permissible fare.

THE ORIGINS OF MELODRAMA

Opposite: Sadler's Wells theatre, 1815. This originated as Sadler's Music House as long ago as 1683, but it was in the new stone theatre constructed in 1765 that the clown Joe Grimaldi made a youthful first appearance in 1792. Under Charles Dibdin's management from 1804, the Aquatic Theatre, as it was briefly known, specialized in nautical dramas and marine spectacles of the kind here portrayed – its location at the New River Head in Islington guaranteeing plentiful water for its supply tank, which covered an area of 100 by 40 feet. Bills for *The Siege of Gibraltar* (1804) boasted of ships built and rigged 'by professional men from His Majesty's dockyards', with 'the whole space of the stage real water' for the closing scene, in which contending fleets engaged in a full-scale naval battle. Later, the early work of Douglas Jerrold was seen here, and in 1844 Samuel Phelps inaugurated the Shakespearean seasons discussed in Chapter 15

In 1796 Charles Dibdin moved his Sans Souci, opened some five years earlier, to a slightly different, superior location in Leicester Square – where this 'elegant little theatre' housed Dibdin's own one-man entertainments and other small-scale shows, including an acrobatics display which featured the juvenile Edmund Kean. The Sans Pareil was opened in 1806 by a doting John Scott for the display of his daughter's histrionic skills. The playhouse became sufficiently successful for a gallery and new frontage to be added: but it was as the Adelphi that it was to make its lasting name in the 1820s, by exploiting the newly popular form of melodrama – to whose earlier history we must now turn.

'Mélodrame' was not perceived as a mass entertainment when the term was first used by Rousseau in 1775 – to describe his technique in *Pygmalion* for expressing by musical means the emotions of a silent character. But when, under the influence of Kotzebue and his fellow German Friedrich Schiller, romantic ideals and proletarian realities were blended with dialogue ripe for musical counterpoint, this mix became potentially explosive. Schiller's *The Robbers* (1781) was hugely popular in revolutionary France – but banned in England, where the minor theatres were none the less quick to customize a form which, while it demonstrably engaged with popular feelings, also gave artistic purpose to the music prescribed by law.

Again, it is difficult to disentangle cause from effect – or to judge how far the rise of melodrama may be attributed to the ironic convenience of its inherently 'illegitimate' form; how far to its popularizing of the known capacity of operatic music and balladry to heighten emotions; and how far to the need of new audiences for a drama which seemed to take seriously their own concerns and sense of self-worth. Nor did melodrama wait upon influences from abroad, for various native types anticipated aspects of its content or style – the naval drama, the topical spectacle, and the gothic drama being the earliest of these.

Plays with a tang of the sea were thus enjoying a vogue well before 'nautical melodrama' had become an acknowledged type – for the Jolly Jack Tar, already the hero of tavern songs, broadside ballads, and many a chapbook tale, enjoyed the advantage of being both patriotic and proletarian: and he could be admired whether doing his duty against pirates and foreign foes, or assuming the mantle of Robin Hood on his return home, to protect the weak against the strong, the poor against the rich. His adopted element also offered plenty of scope for aquatic spectacle – Thomas Morton's *Thomas and Sally; or, The Sailor's Return* having seen its hero step from a boat onto the stage as early as 1760.

Before long, Charles Dibdin had created an acceptable, 'official' stage version of the common sailor in such nautical dramas as *The Friendly Tars* at Sadler's

Wells in 1777 and *True Blue; or, The Press Gang* at the Haymarket in 1781. *England's Glory; or, The British Tars at Spithead* followed in his wake at Covent Garden in 1795. (Dibdin was even awarded a government pension in 1803 for championing the sailor's cause – within the safe confines of his service to the ruling elite.) Also in the 1790s, at the Royal Circus, John C. Cross had begun to mount his 'serious pantomimes' – native equivalents to the French variety, among the most successful of which was *Blackbeard; or, The Captive Princess* of 1798, which even boasted a breeches part for its 'narrator' Nancy, who defeats piracy on the high seas in drag, with the aid of sword, songs, and scrolls bearing such assured clap-traps as 'The Enemy Is British and Will Die or Conquer'.

When the appetite for current affairs seemed to offer similar opportunities for lavish spectacle, an outcrop of 'documentary' plays resulted. Thus, *Paris in an Uproar; or, The Destruction of the Bastille* and *The Triumph of Liberty* reached Astley's and the Royal Circus respectively in 1789, the year of the French Revolution they portrayed. Just as plays set in distant climes enabled the poor to travel by the only means they could afford, so such topical spectacles fed not so much a lubricious taste for sensation as a desire for vicarious participation in an age of momentous discoveries and great events.

Sadler's Wells specialized in dramatizing such events. The changing political mood required a sympathetic portrayal of *The Royal Prisoners* of France in 1793, while the desire to celebrate British victories against Napoleon at sea stimulated a whole sequence of naval engagements during the watery management of the younger Charles Dibdin, illustrated on pages 198–9. The equestrian potential of land battles was meanwhile being exploited at Astley's, where such epic conflicts as *The Siege, Storming, and Taking of Badajoz*, *The Battle of Vittoria*, and *The Siege of Salamanca* were all re-enacted on stage, and where, in 1815, *The Battle of the Nile* was fought while Wellington was busy with the Battle of Waterloo. The Royalty went on to mount a dramatized version of this, the climactic victory against Napoleon, within five months of its occurrence.

In 1797, at Drury Lane, George Colman's *Blue-Beard* had combined the appeal of the aquatic with the emerging taste for the gothic – one of whose earliest exponents in the novel form, M. G. 'Monk' Lewis, enjoyed a theatrical success in

the same year with the dungeons, 'drear forests', and ghostly apparitions of *The Castle Spectre*. And in 1801 Lewis's *Adelmorn the Outlaw* proceeded 'to deluge the town with such an inundation of ghosts and magicians as would satisfy the thirst of the most insatiable swallower of wonders'. But the master of the gothic form was probably the French writer René Charles Guilbert de Pixérécourt, many of whose sixty-odd plays were freely plagiarized in the London theatres. In 1802 an adaptation by Thomas Holcroft for Drury Lane of Pixérécourt's *Coelina* as *A Tale of Mystery* was apparently the first play in English to lay claim to the designation 'mélo-drame'.

Thus, the many varieties of melodrama, though embryonically abundant, were by no means invariably so described: but features of what were to emerge as its distinctive sub-genres could already be distinguished early in the century. The 'dog drama' was anticipated by Frederic Reynolds's success at Drury Lane in 1803 with *The Caravan; or, The Driver and His Dog* – and, although the form was not to

'Melos', tableaux, and 'poses plastiques'

However accidental the native origins of melodrama in the need of the minor theatres to legitimize their fare, what became the shared defining characteristic of this highly diverse form was its use of music to heighten emotional effect. As time went by, it was found that particular chords and musical phrases, recurring at analogous moments from play to play, could stimulate emotional reactions on demand, rather like 'clap traps'

of old – as it might be, feelings of horror, admiration, pathos, or patriotic fervour.

Often, following the example of the French writer Diderot, such 'melos' would also signal the sculpting of the action into a tableau, to be held for the duration of the applause it solicited. These tableaux vivants, as the historian Martin Meisel has clearly demonstrated, were often based on popular paintings, whose message and (increasingly) moral purport were carried over into the play itself. Douglas Jerrold's The Rent Day (1832) thus incorporated tableaux emulating didactic paintings on the rackrenting theme by David Wilkie.

Not least in Wilkie's own hands, the creation of such 'living pictures' became a minor art form in its own right. Emma Hamilton, Nelson's future mistress, was an early and famous exponent. Her Andromaches and her Cassandras were discreetly draped, but classical statuary remained a favoured model for poses plastiques in view of the artistic licence it gave the performers to freeze into a nude or semi-nude display.

This ancestor of strip-tease was much in demand, needless to say, at the song-and-supper rooms which were becoming increasingly popular resorts for male audiences in search of conviviality rather than edification. But the form still had its more respectable side, and in 1833 David Wilkie found himself 'directing' a programme of tableaux based on Scott's novels for no less a bastion of the establishment than the Duke of Wellington.

A display of *tableaux vivants* and *poses plastiques* offered in 1845 by Professor Keller's company of 'unrivalled artistes'. Although many of the 'Professor's' subjects were respectably scriptural, his 'Ancient Hall of Rome' sheltered more decadent statuary. The ambiguity was typical of an age when 'art' was one of the few permissible excuses for the public display of nudity – or more often (as a writer in the *Art-Union* felt called on to explain) 'a dress fitting the person nearly as closely as the skin itself'.

However, many *poses plastiques* achieved respectability while still satisfying a voyeuristic middle-class: thus, when 'General' Tom Thumb visited the Egyptian Hall in 1844 his poses were cast in the heroic mould, and he was reported by Douglas Jerrold to have claimed that 'the 'Ercles a-stranglin' the Nimmin Lion was, arter the 'Pollo, the special favourite'

reach its peak of fashion until the mid-century, most of its characteristics were already present by 1814 in Barrymore's *The Dog of Montargis*, in which a faithful hound avenges the murder of his master.

Meanwhile, the elements of what was eventually to become the most familiar form of melodrama, the domestic, were also beginning to fall into place. In 1800

From pantomime clown to circus clown

While the catch clubs and glee clubs of a previous generation had catered largely for musical tastes, the 'long rooms' for concerts now often attached to taverns and pleasure gardens appear to have offered what we would today describe as 'variety' – that is, a 'compilation bill' of entertainment, including comic, mimetic, and acrobatic acts as well as singers – long before the emergence of music hall proper. So also, apparently, did the mutual diversion of pub customers that went by the name of 'Comus Courts', though their history is elusive and unreliably documented. Meanwhile, other acts which were to appear on future 'compilation bills' were emerging, at first as speciality performances in their own right.

Philip Astley, a retired cavalry officer, had thus first capitalized on his equestrian skills in 1768 by exhibiting his 'Little Learned Military Horse' in an open field. But by 1770 he had secured the land in Westminster Bridge Road on which he proceeded to build (and name after himself) the first modern circus ring. Within ten years or so this had been converted into a full-scale amphitheatre, with its own stage, plus pit, boxes, and gallery – and soon dramatic entertainments as well as circus skills were on display. By the early 1800s, a typical bill at Astley's might comprise first a 'hippodrama' featuring a performing horse, such as The Brave Cossack or The Blood Red Knight, then three-quarters of an hour or so of 'scenes in the circle', or circus acts as we would now understand them, and finally a pantomime or burletta – the whole show having lasted from 6.30 until midnight or even later.

Charles Hughes emerged as Astley's chief rival, opening his own Royal Circus – the first modern amphitheatre to be thus described – in 1782. Both transpontine arenas proved

Alongside: the Royal Circus, Lambeth, as rebuilt in 1806. Though by now becoming better known as the Surrey, this was the first modern 'circus' to be so-named; and the availability of both stage and amphitheatre facilitated either pantomimes (as here pictured) or equestrian entertainments – to which other acts familiar in present-day circus were gradually added. These, of course, included clowns – although, ironically, the father of modern clowning, Joseph Grimaldi (opposite page), never worked in a circus ring. Both food and (as here) drink supplied Joey's voracious persona

Prince Hoare's *Indiscretion* at Drury Lane thus cast a pioneering unmarried mother out into the snow – while in Kenney's *Ella Rosenberg*, seven years later, a villain intent on seducing a married woman succeeds in having her husband wrongfully cast into jail. Dimond's Haymarket piece of 1809, *Foundling of the Forest*, made its villain more hateful for his peerage, and to the staple ingredients

susceptible to fire, new buildings being opened respectively in 1804 and 1806 – by which time Robert Elliston had re-named the Royal Circus the Surrey, and gone over largely to dramatic fare. Astley, after establishing his new style of entertainment throughout Europe, was back for the reopening of what he now called the Royal Amphitheatre, and a vintage period of spectacular equestrian melodrama ensued.

By this time, a white-faced clown would often be brought on to cover scene changes and indulge in banter with the ringmaster – an oblique tribute to the popularity of Joseph Grimaldi, a harlequinade Clown who, paradoxically, never himself appeared in a circus arena. Probably the greatest exponent of his art in the modern age, he first found fame at Sadler's Wells (whose company he had joined in the early 1790s), playing Clown in Dibdin's panto-mime of 1800, Peter Wilkins; or, Harlequin in the Flying World. Exchanging Clown's traditional rosy complexion for a white face with scarlet half-mooned cheeks, his best remembered success was to be Harlequin Mother Goose; or, The Golden Egg, first played in 1806 at Covent Garden – the theatre at which Grimaldi remained, apart from occa-sional guest returns to Sadler's Wells, from 1805 until his virtual retirement (as it appears, from exhaustion) in 1823.

Clown was the only character in the English harle-quinade not directly descended from an original mask in the commedia dell'arte: but as characterized by Grimaldi, who made him a creature of inordinate appetite as well as infinite resource, his ancestry was arguably much older than that. The medieval zanni who, in Dario Fo's version, emulated a hunger so intense that the performer 'eats' first himself, then the spectators, then the surrounding mountainside, and finally God chimes with Grimaldi's pre-occupation with the miraculous qualities of food and drink. Deprivation and hunger were now experiences to which audiences drawn from the new urban slums were as sub-ject as a peasant society of the Middle Ages.

With the Dibdin brothers, Charles and Thomas, and Charles Farley as his chief authors, Grimaldi thus meta-morphosed the harlequinade into a vehicle not only for Clown himself as chief propagator of mischief, gluttony,

Mr GRIMALDI, as Clown.

chases, and transformations, but for a good deal of social satire besides – evidently adding to the pantomime character some of the qualities of the age-old mimus and others from the rustic 'natural' of native tradition. And while it must be remembered that, for Grimaldi, Clown always remained a character in pantomime, it was his own supreme artistry in the role which encouraged others to translate it into a circus 'act' in its own right.

This kind of process was typical of an exploratory age in which many and diverse kinds of entertainment began, however uncertainly, to compete for new mass audiences, and to find appropriate stage formats within which best to do so. Even film may be said to have begun its prehistory here, with the invention by De Loutherbourg in the 1780s (following his retirement from Drury Lane) of a device he dubbed the Eidophusikon: this transformed and enlarged the traditional peep-show, displaying apparently moving pictures by means of cunningly lit transparencies within a miniature cinema-like auditorium.

of the gothic style added hired assassins, a rightful heir restored – and a cottage in the woods.

Already, then, a rustic emphasis was beginning to displace the gothic – perhaps unsurprisingly, at a time when many workers in the cities could still look back on a rural past, its undoubted deprivations perhaps taking on the appeal of lost pastoral innocence when contrasted with the harsher realities of urban life. By 1813, the scenic emphasis of Isaac Pocock's *The Miller and His Men* – in which a band of villains abduct an honest peasant's beautiful wife, and a virtuous count assists in her rescue – had shifted from castles and dungeons to the humbler surroundings of the labourer's cottage.

URBANIZATION – AND CONFLICTING IMPULSES

Sheridan and Goldsmith aside, few of the native authors named in this chapter are ever mentioned in histories of dramatic literature – the likeliest exceptions being the two most successful playwrights of the turn of the century, the younger Colman and his close contemporary Thomas Morton, whose *Speed the Plough* of 1800, probably the best of his many pieces for Covent Garden, made the person of Mrs Grundy so memorable in her absence. Although one standard theatrical history goes so far as to begin its section on the nineteenth century with a sort of supernumerary chapter on all the plays laboriously attempted by the great poets and novelists of the period, it necessarily has to concede that the majority of these even when they reached the stage scarcely deserved to do so.

Rather than nodding apologetically towards such 'classic' writers, it might be more relevant to consider the indebtedness of the drama to the resurgence in ephemeral street literature – the broadside ballad and the chapbook tale. These had never entirely disappeared, but urbanization now provided a huge new market, much easier to tap than of old; and publishers such as the astute James Catnach, based on the fringe of the notorious 'rookery' of Seven Dials, churned out cheap literature in vast quantities – in effect, commercializing what had previously been a more genuinely popular form. (A typical street balladmonger, as drawn to illustrate an interview with the Victorian reformer and pioneer of 'oral history', Henry Mayhew, is pictured on the opposite page.) The tension between the real needs of the underclass from which a growing proportion of the 'drama's patrons' was now drawn, and the compromises, artistic and ethical, whereby professional writers and impresarios might exploit these for profit may also be felt in the theatre – and not least in the convoluted moral universe inhabited by the characters of melodrama.

In many respects, then, the drama of the period covered by this chapter was as transitional as the society it reflected – and this is not least true of its development of a new decorum affecting the relationship between a character and his or her mode of speech. Thus, lower-class speakers were no longer necessarily reduced in linguistic status, but might lay claim to a rhetoric no less articulate

Opposite: 'long-song seller', as drawn for *London Labour and the London Poor*. In this three-volume work, published in 1851, the socially-conscious Victorian journalist Henry Mayhew interviewed, among all the other denizens of the slums and rookeries of his city, a large number of street entertainers and their hangers-on. Street ballad-singers or 'chaunters' might accompany themselves on the fiddle, while other 'running patterers' sold the street literature of the day. Other performers whom Mayhew encouraged to tell their own stories, more or less in their own words, included peep-show impresarios, street conjurers, sword and knife swallowers, penny-gaff clowns and circus jesters, tight-rope dancers and stilt-vaulters, trainers of dancing dogs, an 'exhibiter of mechanical figures' – and a fairground figure known as 'Silly Billy', evidently a mixture of 'natural' fool, child impersonator, and singer of comic songs

and high-flown than that of their supposed betters – especially at moments of high emotional tension. And this was not a lapse of craftsmanship, but one of the ways in which melodrama articulated the feelings of its audiences – just as it also offered them vicarious victories over enemies, such as the unscrupulous factory owners or rack-renting landlords whose economic power enabled them in real life invariably to prevail.

As with 'carnival' of old, it can be argued with equal fervour that such an inversion of everyday expectations aroused in audiences a greater openness to the possibility of change – or that, by providing a brief and sublimated discharge of anxieties, it helped to resign them to their lot. In any case, throughout the ensuing century the conflicts we have already identified – commercial instincts poised against popular need, the tendency to induce catharsis confronting the impulse towards remedial action – continued to operate dialectically in melodrama, and so to modify the nature of the 'reality' which the emerging 'realistic' drama was now attempting to mirror.

So far in this chapter I have, then, been mainly concerned to describe those forms which clearly signify the transitional nature of the period: but we must also, of course, consider the ways in which the leading players at the patent houses served the 'legitimate' repertoire, new and old – while remembering that, to the disgust of the critics, they often followed the fashion for 'illegitimate' entertainments on their own stages. Covent Garden appears to have been the more open to new plays, from writers who included Morton, Frederic Reynolds, Elizabeth Inchbald, and John O'Keeffe – whereas the managers of Drury Lane under Sheridan's proprietorship relied more heavily on the stock classics. According to the invaluable *London Stage* (whose records, however, end with the old century), Fletcher, Otway, Congreve, Cibber, and Farquhar were among the favourites – after the inevitable Shakespeare.

THE KEMBLE RELIGION

Of course, this difference was in part due to the initial good fortune of Drury Lane in becoming the shrine of 'the Kemble religion' – whose origins go back as far as Garrick's last season, in which the young Sarah Siddons was inauspiciously tried out in the company. She failed to impress, and although the conventional wisdom has it that she 'learned her craft' for seven years in the York and Bath companies before making her sensational return to Drury Lane in 1782, it is possible, too, that in the meantime public taste had caught up with the idiosyncrasies of her style, which was surely better suited to the dawn of romanticism than to the neoclassical twilight.

Sarah's brother, John Philip Kemble, joined the Drury Lane company for the following season, and in 1788 took over the management of the theatre from Tom King, who refused any longer to endure Sheridan's capricious style. Eventually Kemble, too, despaired of his proprietor – having even found himself under arrest for one of Sheridan's debts – and in 1803 bought a third of the Covent Garden patent, taking himself and his sister off to lead the rival company, at first in partnership with the veteran Harris. Whatever his strengths as an actor, Kemble was also a consummate showman – as witness his exploitation of the brief craze for the pre-pubescent prodigy Master Betty, whom he equally allowed to drive both himself and Mrs Siddons from the Covent Garden stage almost as soon as they had arrived there, while the star of the boy genius burnt itself out in a blaze of androgynous glory.

Just as it is difficult to assess how far the rise of melodrama was a cause and how far an effect of changing tastes and audiences, and how far the sheer size of the rebuilt theatres determined the broader and more declamatory acting style that now prevailed, so also is it difficult to judge how far the natural qualities of the Kembles shaped their approach to acting, and how far they were responding to audience tastes and acoustic necessities. Nor are critical comments always helpful: thus, the essayist William Hazlitt's reference to Kemble playing Hamlet 'like a man in armour' has misled many into assuming he was a static performer – yet a newspaper commentator of 1789 likened his performance as Henry V to 'the flailing of a windmill'.

What Hazlitt was trying to suggest was Kemble's *intensity* – his working up of a character through a single 'line' of thought or characterization 'and never letting it go'. Not for him the 'transitions' which had so delighted Garrick's audiences, but rather the steady shading-in of a character conceived as already and essentially *there*. Macready thus compared his predecessor's art to that of a 'Rembrandt picture' – his performances remarkable 'for most brilliant effects worked out with wonderful skill on a sombre ground'. Conversely, Sir Walter Scott found his close analysis of each sentiment pedantic – 'a peculiar emphasis' being given 'to each word of the sentence' – and compared Kemble's anticipation of an imminent effect to 'the warning, as it is called, given by some time-pieces that they are about to strike the hour'.

If such a conscientiously detailed approach was appropriate, however, Scott was unstinting in his admiration – as for Kemble's Macbeth, with its 'exquisitely and minutely elaborate delineation of guilty ambition, drawn on from crime to crime'. Where – as here, or with Coriolanus or Cato – Kemble could seize a character by the scruff of its neck, and drag it undeviatingly along in its course, he was evidently unmatchable in his generation. But Hazlitt objected to his 'lowness' as Brutus – by nature a less stoically resolute, even equivocal character, whose course of action could less persuasively be reduced to a stylistic 'given'.

The style of Sarah Siddons seems not so much to have contrasted with Kemble's as to have been complementary to it. Thus, brother and sister were both excellent in dumbshow: but whereas Kemble struck poses or provided a portrait study for an audience to applaud, Siddons, absorbed to the exclusion of onlookers, created creatures in movement, her countenance expressing every

Opposite: 'The Trial of Queen Katharine' by G. H. Harlowe (1787–1819): the Kembles in *Henry VIII*, which John Philip Kemble (1757–1823) first produced at Drury Lane in 1788, his opening season there as manager. He himself played Wolsey (seated on left), with his sister Sarah Siddons (1755–1831) as Katharine. Their brother Stephen Kemble (1758–1822) played the King (enthroned behind table), while the youngest of the siblings, Charles Kemble (1775–1854), took the role of Thomas Cromwell (writing at the table)

modulation of emotion her body moulding itself to each change of mood – seeking, in short, not to corset her character but to work with the dramatist's evolving conception. The historian of tragic acting Bertram Joseph conjectures that she 'must have made her own emotions the source of her moving representation': and, indeed, she seems to have anticipated what the great Russian theorist of acting style Konstantin Stanislavsky described as 'emotion memory' – admitting to Thomas Moore in her retirement that she had always found in the stage 'a vent for her private sorrows, which enabled her to bear them better'.

The talents of both Siddons and Kemble were better suited to the classical range, and for them tragedy tended to prevail – although Kemble as a manager was responsible for broadening the live Shakespearean repertoire to include more of the comedies and histories, and in the latter employed 'set scenes' painted by William Capon to special advantage. Interpretations of the best-loved classics were, however, so far entombed in amber that the successive innovations of leading players had accumulated into an anthology of 'points', eagerly anticipated by audiences and altered at the actor's peril. Sarah Siddons dared famously to reject one such 'point' – the curious convention that Lady Macbeth should hold a candle throughout her sleepwalking scene – only to replace it with a 'point' of her own, the handwashing business which became no less *de rigueur* for succeeding generations.

Significantly, the change derived from Siddons's psychological study of the role – for she attempted (aptly, in an age which first recognized that individual psychology might be rendered into art) to allow her character to emerge from a web of human motives rather than dramatic conventions. Brother and sister, in short, were, in their very different ways, both subject to the creative tensions of this transitional period – Kemble responding to an impulse for representation which sprang not from the neoclassicism of the eighteenth century but from the desire for emotional certainties of the nineteenth, and Siddons to the romantic concern with the nature and limits of the human psyche.

KEMBLE AND THE OLD PRICE RIOTS

When, in 1809, Kemble opened the rebuilt Covent Garden –'the house that Jack built' – he had hoped to meet the costs of the rebuilding and of the slight loss of audience capacity by raising seat prices and converting the third tier from a public gallery into private boxes. These measures precipitated what became known as the Old Price (or OP) Riots, which continued for 66 days, until Kemble was forced into capitulation.

In truth, these were not what we would today call 'riots', but demonstrations – and with their special badges, banners, hats, an 'OP dance', and even an OP version of the National Anthem, they soon became celebratory as much as recriminatory. Although there were certainly elements of class antagonism, what the 'riots' made most fully manifest was a sense that the theatre belonged to its

The first week of the Old Price Riots: engraving by Isaac and George Cruikshank, dated 18 September 1809. The threat of the Riot Act here portrayed served only to exacerbate deeply felt grievances, and in a year which the radical reformer Francis Place recalled as one 'of considerable agitation', protests against Kemble's new charges at Drury Lane must be seen as part of a broadly-based popular discontent which (as here) mingled protest and festive celebration, concern for a better future with respect for traditional rights

new patrons – that audiences, however lowly, were not mere customers but full participants in the theatrical event. There was, it is important to note – and we shall return to this theme in the next chapter – very little violence, and no damage to property.

Kemble never recovered financially (or, perhaps, emotionally) from the twin blows of the fire and the riots; and by 1812 the diarist Crabb Robinson was recording sadly of Siddons that her voice 'appeared to have lost its brilliancy (like a beautiful face through a veil)'. Within a month followed a dismal verdict: 'she labours'. In June, she retired, her farewell performance in *Macbeth* ending with the sleepwalking scene.

Sarah Siddons's own career had briefly and inauspiciously overlapped with that of the actor whose dressing-room at Drury Lane she had inherited: now Drury Lane, too, was in severe financial difficulties – from which it was to be rescued, at least temporarily, by the arrival of a fiery, erratic, but brilliant young actor, able to communicate with his audiences on the visceral level which Kemble never understood but which Siddons to a degree anticipated. His name was Edmund Kean.

Acting MAGISTRATES committing themselves being their first appearance on this stage as performed at the National Theatre Covent Garden Sep.r 18. 1809

On Edmund Kean, the verdict of Coleridge that his acting was 'like reading Shakespeare by flashes of lightning' is over-familiar, but it does convey a good deal about the actor in a few words. The success of his first appearance as Shylock in February 1814 (a debut which must have been all the more startling for the actor's half-starved state at the time) propelled him at once into the roles of Richard III, Hamlet, Othello, and Iago – the tragic heroes, significantly, outnumbered by the scheming villains, to whose number in 1816 Kean added that of Overreach in Massinger's A New Way to Pay Old Debts. This performance is said not only to have reduced Byron, among others, to convulsions, but, more revealingly, to have disturbed Kean's fellow actors with the sheer energy of its communicated evil.

Vocally, Kean seems to have been somewhat erratic, veering from the grand manner to the colloquial – often to startling effect, but on occasion with more ease than justification. Yet he could be oddly impressive at his least articulate – choking or calculatedly fumbling on an emotion rather than verbalizing it. Seeking to express physically the existential moments of a character's dramatic life, his lithe but compact frame would twist itself into 'the picturesque expression of an outward emotion': thus, even his death scenes could be more physically than rhetorically revealing, as when, in Crabb Robinson's description of the dying Richard, 'his sword beaten out of his hands, he continues fighting with his fist as if he had a sword'. Hazlitt sums up:

> In a word, Mr Kean's acting is like an anarchy of the passions, in which each upstart humour, or frenzy of the moment, is struggling to get violent possession of some bit or corner of his fiery soul and pygmy body – to jostle out and lord it over the rest of the rabble of short-lived and furious purposes.

Kean lived out his life in a rather similar frenzy of anarchic passions and furious purposes, and as an actor, according to Hazlitt, his powers began to decline within a few years of their being recognized. By the early 1820s he was already a spent force, though he struggled on, dying on stage as Othello to his son's Iago only a few weeks before his actual death in 1833.

Kean probably despised a public that as eagerly deplored his decline as it had lionized his success. He was insatiably dependent upon drink and sex to fire his energies on stage, and his excesses surely contributed to the rapidity with which those energies burned out: yet Mrs Siddons, sober and resolutely modest in private life, had also been unable to sustain an approach to acting which drew so deeply on inner resources. It is no wonder, perhaps, that Byron swooned, recognizing in Kean a mirror-image of his own erratic genius – that romantic doppelganger which consumed the life it briefly illuminated. Thus died Shelley and Keats so painfully young, and thus dwindled Wordsworth and Coleridge into mentally recumbent maturity.

The eyes have it in both these images of Edmund Kean (1789–1833). Hamlet (left) was one of his roles during his first, triumphant season at Drury Lane. Whether descending into chaos with Othello or in the final frenzy of the mad Sir Giles Overreach (right) in Massinger's dark comedy, A New Way to Pay Old Debts, which he first played in 1816, Kean depended for his effects on moments of emotionally epiphanic transition. Fanny Kemble offered a cogent summing-up – of an actor of 'particular physical qualifications: an eye like an orb of light, a voice exquisitely touching and melodious in its tenderness, and in the harsh dissonance of vehement passion terribly true.' He had an 'amazing power of concentrating effect', which gave him 'an entire mastery over his audience in all striking, sudden, impassioned passages, in fulfilling which he has contented himself, leaving unheeded what he could not compass – the unity of conception, the refinement of detail, and evenness of execution.' Thus, even early on Kean made a limp Romeo, and in his decline a disastrous Henry V

CHAPTER 14   *The End of the Monopoly*

Between 1736 and 1848, according to figures assembled by the historian George Rudé, 'rioting' crowds in London killed at most a dozen people – 'while, on the other side, the courts hanged 118 and 630 were shot dead by the troops'. Today, such figures would lead to public outrage at the use of police or military force out of all proportion to the provocation: yet so firmly is the 'official' version of events etched into our consciousness that theatre historians can still casually refer to 'mob rule' in the theatres on the assumption that it reflected 'mob violence' on the streets. So against the casual condemnations of audience 'debaucheries' by contemporary writers such as Sir Walter Scott, we should all the more carefully set the judgement of William Hazlitt that any 'noise and quarrelling in the gallery' at the patent houses was due to the impatience of its inhabitants 'at not being able to hear what is passing below' – whereas the 'gods' (the uppermost galleries) at the minor theatres were, he declared, 'the most quiet and attentive' section of the audience.

THE THEATRE AND POLITICAL REFORM

The theatre managers aimed to preserve some elementary social distinctions, maintaining both the six o'clock start which had been common for nearly a century and the concession of half-price entrance at eight or half past. The 'respectable' classes to whom the mainpiece most appealed could thus turn up for it in good time, while the toiling masses, thought to prefer the later appendages to the programme, had not only their longer hours of work allowed for, but also their emptier pockets. In consequence, a varied programme of entertainments, four or five hours

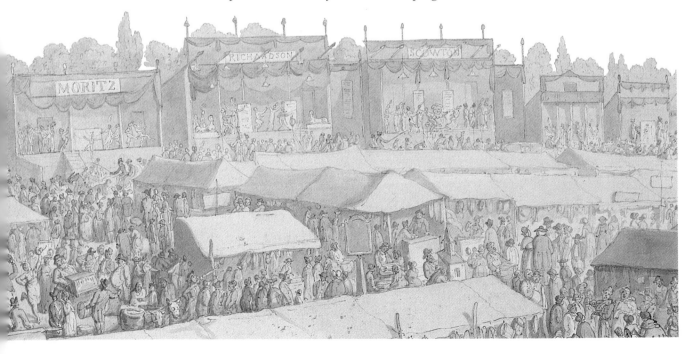

in length, was becoming the norm. We should bear in mind, too, that for the urban working classes, their lot worsened by the severe depression which followed the Napoleonic wars, length was in itself an attraction: for the theatre was the only place other than the tavern where good company, light, and warmth – if only the warmth of body heat – might be found on a bleak winter's evening, when 'home' for many was a corner of a crowded room in an ill-lit, unventilated, and insanitary slum.

The prevalence of such conditions, and the oppressive policies of a Tory regime which presided over the suspension of *habeas corpus* and the Peterloo massacre of 1819 (when an open-air meeting in Manchester was charged by the hussars), made this a period of radical protest – and of agitation for the reforms later consolidated into the 'charter' from which the Chartist movement got its name. The disfranchised middle and working classes at first made common cause: and although their alliance did not survive the Liberal election victory of 1830 and the limited enfranchisement of the bourgeoisie by the Reform Bill two years later, the early consensus was reflected in the theatre, where the movement for electoral reform enjoyed its share of dramatic attention.

Thus, in 1831 alone, Moncrieff's *Reform; or, John Bull Triumphant* was staged at the Coburg, and the anonymous *More Reform! or, The Bill! The Whole Bill!! and Nothing But the Bill!!!* at Sadler's Wells – while a topical pantomime, *Harlequin Reformer*, reached the Surrey for Christmas. The programme for the opening of the new Strand Theatre in the New Year even boasted a transparency which caricatured the King, and bore the explosive legend, 'Reform it Altogether' – that is, presumably, the monarchy along with parliament and the patent-house monopoly. Certainly, the parliamentary Select Committee appointed in the same year 'to enquire into the laws affecting Dramatic Literature' appears to have been more worried by the theatre's potential for political than moral subversion, declaring: 'political allusions appear to be much more popular to the frequenters of the theatres than any licentiousness'.

Sweated factory conditions also became a topical issue in 1832, with the failure in parliament of a bill setting a ten-hour limit to the working day, and the publication of a report from a committee under Michael Sadler's chairmanship which revealed, for example, that fourteen hours or more of daily work were common for children employed in the mills. And so, just as plays by Colman and Sheridan, among others, had lent theatrical support to the anti-slavery agitation of the turn of the century, factory conditions now became the subject of dramas meant not only to shock the working classes into recognition, but the middle classes into sympathetic support.

In October 1832 the early death through exhaustion of young girls in the cotton mills was thus dramatized in Douglas Jerrold's *The Factory Girl* at Drury Lane, while at the Surrey John Walker's more overtly politicized *The Factory Lad* had an Owenite (at times even a Luddite) ring. Indeed, the advertising of the acting edition of Walker's play in the radical newspaper *The Poor Man's Guardian* suggests that it may have been used in the working men's reading circles which were flourishing at the time. A well-intentioned but only partially effective Factory Act followed in 1833.

Opposite: Brook Green Fair by Thomas Rowlandson, *c.* 1818, showing the theatrical booths of Moritz, Richardson, Scowton, and others. The early nineteenth century proved a high water mark for such fairground booth theatres. By 1825, one of the most famous, Richardson's, was some 100 feet long by 30 feet high, and lit by 1,500 lamps. From Greenwich at Easter until Bartholomew Fair in September, Richardson and other booth proprietors went 'on the road', with an itinerary of up to sixty regular locations, as far afield as Oxford and Winchester. Richardson sold up in 1826, perhaps recognizing that the rise of the minor theatres was rapidly providing poorer and suburban localities with a year-round alternative. And, already, the authorities had set about suppressing the fairs themselves, fearful of their disruptive effects upon a production-line economy. Southwark had thus lost its fair as early as 1763, and even Bartholomew Fair had gone by 1855

It remains uncertain how far such activity represented the tip of an iceberg in the political use of theatre on a smaller scale. But these were years of exceptional political consciousness, and it is known, for example, that Owenite lectures were regularly enlivened with professionally orchestrated if not professionally performed entertainments – one such being billed by the *The Poor Man's Guardian* in 1832 under the title of *Political Comicalities*. Theatrical entertainment was, after all, now becoming a 'mass medium', no less open to political and social use or abuse than its printed and broadcast equivalents in the present day.

NEIGHBOURHOOD PLAYHOUSES

If, by buying off the support of the bourgeoisie, the Reform Act of 1832 ill served the interests of those it kept disfranchised, so the Theatres Act of 1843, conventionally greeted as a desirable outcome of 'the struggle for a free stage', also created as many problems as it resolved. Arguably, it merely regularized the *de facto* situation: but its subjection of the theatre to new and more enforceable kinds of regulation restricted the development and stratified the class appeal of the medium. The effects of this will concern us in the next chapter: meanwhile, it is worth anticipating the bare statistic that, while three new playhouses were built in London during the 1820s and no fewer than fourteen during the 1830s, no new theatres at all opened in the

How well-behaved were the occupants of the 'gods' – a theatre's topmost gallery, where the poorest spectators were crowded together on backless benches? The critic and essayist William Hazlitt argued that any rowdiness – as illustrated and no doubt exaggerated in the Cruikshank cartoon below – was often due to the failure of the actors to make themselves heard. Contrast the well-mannered galleryites pictured opposite

BOXING-NIGHT——A PICTURE IN THE NATIONAL GALLERY.

central district between 1843 and 1870, and few of importance in the suburbs –
while one by one the fairs with their booth theatres were suppressed.

But in the three decades or so before 1843, the 'minor' theatres were well set
to enjoy a boom – and not least because they could offer comfort as well as entertainment. When the canny actor-manager Robert William Elliston acquired the
lease of the Royal Circus in 1809, he thus made no attempt to compete with Astley's
equestrian supremacy, but converted the circus arena into his pit – and from the old
stabling created front-of-house facilities for refreshment and recreation unmatched
in London. Renamed the Surrey, the theatre opened with a production of *The
Beggar's Opera* in recitative, with accompanying music and mimed action. *Macbeth*,
billed as 'A Ballet of Music and Action', soon followed, and a version of Garrick's
The Jubilee, with seventeen mimed scenes from the plays.

The popularity of Elliston's Surrey was due not only to this combination of
excellent facilities and enterprising programming, but also to its convenient situation at St George's Circus, where a delta of roads branched out towards the three
new Thames bridges of Blackfriars, Waterloo, and Westminster. However, while the
theatre was thus readily accessible to travellers from across the Thames, the Surrey
was also, and more significantly, among the first of the 'neighbourhood playhouses'
which set out quite calculatedly to serve the densely-populated perimeter of the
metropolis, whose lower middle- and working-class citizens had neither the cash
nor the inclination to venture into the West End.

Also south of the river, the recently rebuilt Astley's lay towards Westminster
Bridge, while the Coburg – later the Royal Victoria, and still with us as the Old Vic –
opened in 1818, within a year of the construction of Waterloo Bridge. Towards
Blackfriars, the Rotunda, built as a museum, was converted for theatrical use as the
Globe around 1830 – and also became, as the theatre scholar Clive Barker has
pointed out, the headquarters of the National Union of the Working Classes.
Although it was later to become known as a music hall rather than a theatre, the
Bower in Lambeth, built in 1837 to the plans of a scenic artist from the Surrey, was
among the earliest of the saloons to boast a fully-equipped stage and orchestra pit.

In the East End, the old Royalty burned down in 1826, but the Pavilion,
Whitechapel, was opened two years later. The short-lived City Theatre, Cripplegate,
followed in 1830, and the Garrick in Leman Street, Whitechapel, in 1831. Then in
quick succession came the Standard in Shoreditch in 1835, the City of London
Theatre, Bishopsgate, in 1837, the Eagle Saloon in the City Road with its Grecian
Theatre in 1838, and the Britannia in Hoxton in 1841. Even the sparser western
suburbs were catered for: the Regency (later known officially as the Prince of
Wales's, but familiarly as the Dusthole) opened off Tottenham Court Road in 1814,
to be followed in 1830 by the Marylebone, as it became best known, a popular
melodrama and pantomime house in Church Street, off the Edgware Road.

The full histories of these neighbourhood theatres (unless, like Sadler's Wells
and the Old Vic, they were later absorbed into the official culture) have yet to be

The gallery is raptly attentive
in this contrasting view by
Durand of 'Saturday Night
at the Victoria Theatre'. No
doubt the artists' differing
perceptions were as subject
as Scott's or Hazlitt's to the
political or social point they
were trying to make

Looking glass 'curtain', reflecting a full view of the auditorium, installed a few years after the opening in 1818 of the Royal Coburg (later Old Vic) Theatre. Made up of sixty-three pieces, the curtain was not only clumsy and difficult to move, but found to be placing an undue strain on the roof, so it was not long retained once its novelty value had declined – though tradition long insisted that a particular dressing room mirror was a relic. An Indian juggler, Ramo Samee, is the performer here portrayed. The theatre was at first in hot competition with the nearby Surrey, but it suffered a slow decline in status, and in 1858 sixteen lives were lost in a false fire alarm. It closed down in 1880 after a short period as a music hall, but was then purchased by the social reformer and temperance advocate Emma Cons, who aimed to offer family entertainment at cheap prices. Emma Cons's niece, Lilian Baylis, took over in 1912, and the Shakespeare seasons – destined to continue until the Old Vic gave the National Theatre its first home in 1963 – began two years later

Theatrical Reflection.
or a Peep at the Looking Glass Curtain at the Royal Coburg Theatre.

written – and of the fairground booths, saloon stages attached to pubs, and make-shift penny gaffs even less is known, beyond the reports of a few earnest middle-class observers on cultural safari. Such enterprises often flourished none the less, and the later history of some will concern us in the next chapter.

COMPETITION IN THE WEST END

In the central district, there was, of course, already competition for the patent houses. The Lyceum, rebuilt in 1816 as the English Opera House, was burned down and replaced with the present structure in 1834. At the Adelphi the early melodramas of the young James Robinson Planché enjoyed some success soon after the major reconstruction of 1819 – but in 1821 Moncrieff's *Tom and Jerry* out-did them all, achieving the first recorded run of over a hundred performances, to be followed as the theatre's staple fare by nautical melodramas and adaptations of the novels of Sir Walter Scott.

In Wych Street, off the Strand, the Olympic – which had been built by Astley in 1806, to be taken over and later (as pictured on page 219) rebuilt by Elliston – became surprisingly fashionable in the hands of an enterprising young singer known as Madame Vestris, who, between 1830 to 1838, staged there a succession of elegantly designed comedies and extravaganzas by the prolific Planché, latterly in partnership with her second husband, the comedian Charles Mathews. While Vestris's popularity in breeches parts owed much to her legendary legs, at least as a pioneering woman impresario she could *choose* to exploit her own charms, at a time when ill-paid girls were elsewhere being ogled in *tableaux vivants*, or in the flesh-ings and tutus of the dancers in the recently-popularized romantic ballet.

Among new West End theatres, the short-lived and unsuccessful Westminster, on the site of the present Central Hall, opened in 1832, as did the first Strand Theatre, near Somerset House: this was taken over four years later by Douglas Jerrold, and went on to house a successful series of dramatizations based on the novels of Charles Dickens. The St James's, on the very doorsteps of the Lord Chamberlain's palace, followed in 1835, to cater largely for the inexplicable vogue then being enjoyed by visiting French companies. Further afield, and much less auspiciously, the Royalty in Dean Street, Soho, and the Princess's in Oxford Street both opened in 1840.

Thus, even before the legal ending of their monopoly, Drury Lane and Covent Garden had become just two among a growing number of competing playhouses in central London: and, while the 'minors' had by 1843 found ways of evading the restrictions upon their performing 'legitimate' drama, the patent houses, only irregularly availing themselves of their supposed privilege, were no less dependent than their rivals upon the popularity of 'illegitimate' fare. The brief histories which follow trace their dying fall, as they tried to tempt fashionable audiences through what Engels described as 'some of the worst streets in the whole metropolis . . . in which the houses are inhabited from cellar to garret exclusively by poor families'.

In 1817 Kemble had handed over his interests at Covent Garden to his brother Charles, under whom Planché – who was a heraldic expert and art historian as well as a playwright – made his first attempt at creating historically 'authentic' Shakespearean costumes for *King John*. Charles Kemble's own daughter, Fanny, proved an attraction against her inclinations from 1829 to 1831, but for two years from 1833 the theatre passed into the hands of Robert Elliston's stage manager, the egregious Alfred Bunn, who tried to manage it in tandem with Drury Lane. This 'Great Grand Junction', as Bunn called it, enabled him not only to reduce salaries at will, but to organize his actors on a shift system, so that they were forced to shuttle between the playhouses to perform different roles on the same evening.

From 1837 to 1839 the great actor William Charles Macready (see pages 226-7) took charge at Covent Garden, and from 1841 to 1842 Madame Vestris and Charles Mathews. Both managements had more success artistically than financially – although in 1841 the production of *London Assurance*, which introduced the writing of Dion Boucicault to the London stage, gave Vestris a welcome breathing

Vestris, Mathews, and Liston at the Olympic

John Liston (1776–1846), one of the earliest 'cockney' comics, at first specialized in 'low' parts, but his comic genius was better exploited when he left Drury Lane in 1823 for Covent Garden. In the following year, at the Haymarket, he memorably created the title character in John Poole's *Paul Pry*. At the Olympic, he further extended his range in 'character' roles, where his rich personality could aptly complement the elegant manners of Mathews. He retired in 1837

During their management of the Olympic (1831–38), Vestris and Mathews, in addition to staging the ingenious extravaganzas of J. R. Planché, stretched their 'burletta' licence (which supposedly restricted a minor theatre to musical entertainments) to its now permissive limits with Planché's one-act versions of French comedies. For these they created realistic flats with practical doors and windows surrounding three sides of an interior setting, which was then topped out with a ceiling cloth. Not only wall and ceiling coverings, but furnishings too (previously limited to the barely functional) were chosen to match the style of the apartment. The 'box set', as it became known, had earlier pioneers: but it was during this period that it became an accepted, almost expected style for domestic interiors.

Mathews, his acting style well suited to Planché's adaptations from the French, must have made a happy contrast with the 'low comedian' of the company, John Liston. Probably the greatest comic actor of the preceding generation, Liston was best known for his success in 1825 in the title-role of Paul Pry, which ran for 114 performances at the Little. Pry's aptronym – and his catchphrase, 'I hope I don't intrude' – fixed the prevailing passion which Liston evidently caught with a mix of cultivated physical extravagance and laconic cockney humour. Mathews, a practised mimic and master of patter, lacked Liston's comic reach, but, with his wry elegance of manner, excelled in that laid-back wit which was to become the hallmark of the masculine presence in 'drawing-room' comedy.

space. Covent Garden was only intermittently in use between 1842 and 1847, then reopened as the Royal Italian Opera. Burned down in 1856, it was rebuilt (its capacity halved in the process), and an Opera House it has remained ever since.

The upturn in the fortunes of Drury Lane following the debut there in 1814 of Edmund Kean – his virtual deification quite driving out the 'Kemble religion' – did

Left: the Olympic Theatre in 1818. This theatre made pioneering use of gas lights, which can be seen suspended from the brackets mounted along the top gallery. As lessee here between 1831 and 1838, Madame Vestris presented the comedies and extravaganzas of J. R. Planché with a company which also included Charles Mathews (seen with Vestris below) and John Liston (opposite)

Right: Charles Mathews (1803–78) and Madame Vestris (1797–1856) in J. R. Planché's comedy *Court Favour; or, Private and Confidential*, staged at the Olympic in 1836. By this time 'box sets' such as the one illustrated here – replete with three walls, ceiling piece, tasteful furnishings, and practicable doors and windows – were the norm for the Olympic's more domestic pieces. The couple married in 1838, and after an American tour took over Covent Garden for a three-year management, during which Mathews scored one of his greatest successes as Dazzle in Boucicault's *London Assurance* (1841) – as usual combining elegant languor with the deft delivery of an inveterate 'patterer'. However, both this venture and the couple's management of the Lyceum from 1847 to 1855 ended in bankruptcy, and Vestris, her health broken, died in the following year. Mathews never again ventured into management, but rebuilt his acting career as a master of classical and contemporary comedy

not survive the onset of that actor's early decline, and in 1819 Elliston took over the lease. At first, he endeavoured to restore the theatre's legitimacy by asking major writers in other genres to try their hands at a play, rather as George Devine was to do at the Royal Court in 1956 – but those who complied (in both cases, as it happens) showed only that they had little understanding of the practicalities of theatre.

A great comic actor in an age when comedy attracted much revival but little attention, Elliston was fully at his ease even with a recalcitrant audience – not least when confessing to failures and to personal defects (chronic alcoholism among them) which he managed to present as almost endearing traits. He seems to have inspired the same mixture of respect and contempt as, in an earlier generation, had Colley Cibber – and to have combined self-importance and self-deprecation to rather the same degree. Although he has not been kindly treated by theatre historians, many of his own contemporaries, from Charles Lamb to Madame Vestris, found him 'a most delightful companion'.

The death of the mad George III in 1820, and the succession of the son whose regency had scarcely tempered his flamboyant hedonism, gave Elliston the opportunity to stage the Coronation procession in facsimile at Drury Lane, with himself bestowing the sovereign's blessing upon his subject audience. A skilled publicist, he organized a parade to accompany Kean back to the theatre after his American tour of 1820. Continuing to spend his money like water – a real waterfall being among the effects on which, in 1823, he allegedly spent £5,000 for Moncrieff's *Cataract of the Ganges* – Elliston had bankrupted himself by 1826.

When Edmund Kean stalked off to Covent Garden in 1827, Elliston's successor for four seasons, the American Stephen Price, hired Kean's sixteen-year-old son Charles as replacement. He also became the first impresario to send his stars, almost as a matter of course, on transatlantic tours. Alfred Bunn oversaw the season of 1832, during which Kean and Macready battled it out for supremacy on the same stage, and by the next year his ill-fated attempt to run the patent houses in double-harness had begun. Bunn tried to keep Drury Lane afloat after this scheme collapsed, but succumbed to bankruptcy in 1839: seemingly irrepressible, he bounced back four years later, when Macready abandoned the ambitious plans for the theatre which, in the intervening years, had proved his own financial undoing.

CANTILEVERED BALCONIES – AND THE COMING OF GAS

Before this period, the many alterations to the old patent houses had been partly of sheer scale and partly of proportion – the familiar horseshoe of the early Georgian auditorium gradually bulging into a circle as ever more boxes were built around its perimeter, and the ever-widening pit also slowly encroaching upon the fore-shortened apron. The new century saw the relics of Restoration intimacy finally made redundant or swept away: when the new Drury Lane reopened in 1812, the actors were thus disturbed to find that the proscenium doors had disappeared, and, although they were briefly reinstated after protests, by 1822 they were gone for good.

Although Colman, celebrating their loss, mocked a convention that might variously represent 'Palace, Cottage, Street, or Hall', it was, of course, in their very non-specificity that the stage doors had proved their value. Now, if entrances and exits had to be made from within the scene, could the apron itself, a point of acknowledged contact between actors and audience, much longer survive? Textually as architecturally, such contact was no longer felt desirable, and so, within the next few decades, even prologues and epilogues began to disappear – Planché, or so he claimed, pioneering their abandonment.

Cantilevered construction, first used at the Adelphi in 1819, now made it possible to support overhanging balconies instead of the tiered galleries of old: and since spectators, previously overlooked in the pit below or the boxes opposite, were now out of the line of vision, attention was focused downwards and inwards, towards the fictional reality on the stage. Towards the end of the period even the pit itself began to ebb, as the more comfortable and expensive front stalls began their slow encroachment: and the acting, responsive as much to atmosphere as to price differentials, narrowed its focus accordingly – an experience to be shared with the customers cosily ensconced in stalls and 'dress circle' rather than pitched presentationally towards the boxes, above the heads of the sociable throng in the pit.

The Lyceum was the first theatre to instal gas lighting, in 1817. Next year the newly-built Olympic followed suit, and Drury Lane was also converted for gas. At first, the convenience of the new source seems to have been better appreciated than its creative potential – indeed, it was only towards the very end of this period that house lights began to be lowered for the duration of the action. By this time, too, limelight had become available, and was even tentatively employed by Macready, though its emphatic powers were not yet being fully exploited.

For exterior scenes, the use of varied backcloths, of panoramas and dioramas, and of other effects gained through lighting (often in combination with the increasingly imaginative use of gauzes), could create realms far wider and more realistic than the old stock sets of wings and shutters, though these of course continued extensively in use. But for interiors there was a growing sense that a room ought, well, to resemble a room – 'of which the audience compose the fourth wall', as Leigh Hunt was apparently the first to put it, around the time our present chapter begins.

ENTER THE CRITICS

In the features on Kean and Macready between which this chapter is sandwiched, it will have been noticed that we are now beginning to draw upon the contemporary responses of a growing number of theatre critics. Even today, the enthusiasm of reviewers seems either to thrive on accumulated experience or to be quickly surfeited: just so, Leigh Hunt, whose appointment as dramatic critic of the *News* in 1805 was arguably the first in the modern sense of the term, was still writing knowledgably about the theatre in 1832, while William Hazlitt, although he contributed essays to a variety of newspapers between 1813 and 1818, was declaring by 1820 that he preferred 'to be a hundred miles off from the acted drama in London'. Charles Lamb also wrote extensively on the theatre – but irregularly, since (another common cause for abandoning the craft) he 'could not write to time'.

Arguably, Hazlitt and Lamb remained by instinct essayists of the old school rather than critics of the new. But, in good form, both could be no less astute than Hunt in their technical analysis of a performance – and that three perceptive writers of such widely varying opinions and backgrounds should have been close contemporaries begins to enable us to build up pictures of actors, and even of particular performances, by comparing and contrasting views (and by testing them against known preferences and prejudices) rather than being forced to accept or reject outright a single impressionistic voice.

THE FLOURISHING 'MINOR FORMS'

However, all these critics were concerned mainly with the classical and the legitimate repertoire, and have little helpful to say about the many flourishing 'minor' forms. So one looks in vain in the writing of the time for a more than perfunctory analysis of pantomime – or of equestrian drama, though this now found a new virtuoso in Andrew Ducrow. Much of Ducrow's early career was spent in France, but in 1824 he returned to Astley's, now the Royal Amphitheatre – where the revival of Planché's *Cortez; or, The Conquest of Mexico* must have played much more

Andrew Ducrow (1793–1848), who took over the management of Astley's old amphitheatre from 1830 until it burned down in 1841. Like John Rich just a century earlier, he made up for illiteracy by combining a silent mimetic genius with an astute business sense. Most famously, he staged in 1831 a version of Milner's melodrama *Mazeppa* which was to hold the stage for half a century – eventually providing a breeches (some said, lack of breeches) part on horseback for the American actress Adah Isaacs Menken. He also added an equestrian dimension to *poses plastiques*, and is here seen in classical pose as Mercury, the messenger of the gods

MR DUCROW AS MERCURY.
Pub. by M.&M.SKELT. 11 Swan St Minories London.

effectively in the circus ring than on the confined stage of Covent Garden. Ducrow did not relish speaking parts, and a mute central character, as in *The Factory Assassin; or, The Dumb Boy of Manchester* of 1837, thus suited him admirably. (In melodrama, handicapped heroes or heroines encouraged instant empathy.)

Ducrow did not long survive the burning down of the old amphitheatre in 1841, but his fame lived on in folk memory – not least because of his policy of touring widely, well before the coming of the railways had made this commonplace. It was thus in Edinburgh that Sir Walter Scott watched Ducrow in a dramatized version of *Ivanhoe* – one of a dozen or so adaptations of that novel. The rest of Scott's prolific fictional output also became grist for the melodramatists' mill, and a whole school of Scottish melodrama spun off its popularity – an early example, C. E. Walker's *The Warlock of the Glen*, long surviving in stock after its Surrey opening in 1820. A little later, adaptations of Dickens's novels were no less numerous – three of the many versions of *Oliver Twist* reaching the stage in 1838, the same year in which the serial publication of the novel was completed.

When Elliston returned to the Surrey in 1827, he made it the home of nautical melodrama, and it was here that probably the best-known of the type, Jerrold's *Black-Eyed Susan*, enjoyed a run of some 400 nights following its opening in 1829 – an unprecedented success, even during this period when the 'long run' was establishing itself as every manager's noblest aim. One of the pleasures of this piece is that it does not have to be taken too seriously – but Jerrold was deeply serious in his exposure of the evils of flogging in *The Mutiny of the Nore* in 1830. Two years later came not only his attack on unjust landlords, *The Rent Day*, at Drury Lane, but also R. B. Peake's *The Climbing Boy* at the Olympic, condemning the cruel exploitation of child chimney sweeps. And by the close of that radical decade, G. D. Pitt, in *Simon Lee* (1839), had created the prototype of the sympathetic poacher, who continued to embody resentment against the game laws throughout the century.

An early standby of what was to become the dominant style of melodrama, the domestic, was William Moncrieff's *The Lear of Private Life* at the Coburg, in which a daughter with her illegitimate child, wandering through a forest in the snow, discovers her father – driven mad by a shame that is naturally cured when her seducer marries the girl after all. Later, at the Adelphi in 1826, the brave British sailor was pressed into the service of domestic melodrama, to save a family from the wicked squire and the eponymous hired ruffian of Buckstone's *Luke the Labourer*. Luke is not an entirely unambiguous character, however, since his actions are seen to stem from the drunkenness to which he is driven by impoverished despair. Two years later, Jerrold's *Fifteen Years of a Drunkard's Life* became one of the first of many melodramas overtly to espouse the temperance cause.

Despite – and because of – a decline in the financial rewards for dramatists, several seasoned writers numbered their plays in hundreds, and could churn out as many as a dozen pieces in a single season. Here, we can barely scratch the surface of the dense mass of 'illegitimate' material which reached the stage in a bewildering

Andrew Ducrow in France. Followed his early success at Astley's as the dumb boy in *The Dog of Montargis* (1814), he built a career as a performer in continental circus before returning to Astley's to mount equestrian dramas such as Amherst's *The Battle of Waterloo* (1824) – of which each act ended in a 'general contest' of foot and horse

W. G. Ross (d. 1876) was one
of the earliest performers to
make his name in what later
became known as music hall.
Having enjoyed some success
in harmonic meetings in his
native Glasgow, his journey-
ing south brought him to the
Cider Cellars in Maiden Lane,
where he was billed as a serio-
comic vocalist. But there was
little comic about the song
which made his name, 'Sam
Hall' – the gallows reflections
of a condemned murderer on
his last journey from Newgate
to execution at Tyburn, with
its mordant refrain, 'Damn
your eyes!' For a decade Ross
drew the crowds – even to
Vauxhall Gardens – with this
song, but he never repeated
its success, and following an
attempt to go legitimate under
Buckstone at the Haymarket
he took his own company into
the provinces and obscurity

variety of forms, many of them original or crossbred. Brewer's *Reader's Handbook* of
1898 thus conscientiously assigns each drama it lists to one of no fewer than 120
different kinds, which range from the simple 'play' or 'pastoral tragi-comedy', which
Polonius would have understood, to such portmanteau formulae as 'Great Eastern
melodramatic spectacle' or 'nautical comic operetta' – not to mention the perplex-
ing 'solemnity' and 'spasmodic tragedy'. While some of these descriptions reflect
either authorial whimsy or the Victorian urge to impose scientific order upon the
unscientific and disorderly, the sheer range does also hint at the generic confusion
which, in the 1830s, still had important legal implications.

Among the more distinctive of the newly-emergent forms, the extravaganza
became, under Planché's guidance, a gentle mockery of human affairs transposed
into a fairyland of puns, doggerel verse, and topical allusions, while W. B. Rhodes's
Bombastes Furioso as early as 1810 anticipated the new style of burlesque – no
longer conceived, as from the pen of Buckingham or Henry Fielding, as a formal
satire upon a particular dramatic mode or pretension, but striking a vein of solemn
incongruity closer to the well-mannered nonsense tradition of Lewis Carroll or
Edward Lear.

However, the term 'burletta', which in the previous century had signified a farce
with interpolated music, now confusingly became a catch-all label for any play
which might legally be performed at a minor theatre – which was thus said to have
a 'burletta licence'. During the 1820s, George Colman, as Licenser of Plays for the
Lord Chamberlain, solemnly laid down 'five or six' as the number of 'songs in a
piece of one act' needed to make it acceptable as a burletta – provided that the songs
were 'a natural part of the piece' and, in Colman's own italics, '*not forced into
an acting piece*, to qualify it'. However, well before 1843 a scattering of songs and a
due proportion of emphatic 'melos' were taken to excuse almost any amount of
spoken dialogue – anecdotally, *Othello* being transformed into a burletta by the
simple expedient of 'having a low piano accompaniment, the musician striking a
chord once in five minutes, but always so as to be totally inaudible'. Even greater
liberties were taken by Madame Vestris at the Olympic, as described on page 218.

A wide social mix of influences went into the creation of that most enduringly
illegitimate of forms, the 'music hall'. Such all-male resorts as the Cider Cellars in
Maiden Lane or the Coal Hole off the Strand, which now interspersed their
convivial sing-songs with professional entertainers – such as W. G. Ross, with his
lugubrious rendition of 'Sam Hall' – attracted a bohemian or raffishly professional
clientele, whereas the more traditional pleasure gardens were rapidly becoming the
preserve of the bourgeoisie – the last of any consequence, the Cremorne, having
opened in 1831. But it was largely a working-class audience which attended the
tavern concerts which, as they outgrew the confines of the bar, began to be held in
adjacent 'saloons' with their own stages – some of which by the 1830s were already
calling themselves 'music halls', probably because, before the term acquired its later
connotations, it sounded vaguely respectable.

THE THEATRES ACT — AND THE RIOT ACT

The subsequent rapid development of the 'halls' was hastened by that same Theatre Regulation Act of 1843 which abolished the monopoly of the patent houses – ten years after a similar measure had passed through the House of Commons, but been defeated by the Lords. In the interim, a new Lord Chamberlain, Lord Conyngham, had proved highly sympathetic towards the minor theatres, not only extending the scope of their licences and encouraging the boom in new building, but also, ironically, demanding that the patent houses should confine themselves to plays with spoken dialogue.

Under the new act, which ended the old monopoly outright, the Lord Chamberlain's powers of censorship were affirmed and strengthened, in the form in which they were to survive for well over a further century. But of greater immediate importance was the provision that any theatre might now obtain a licence from the Lord Chamberlain to perform the spoken drama – so long as it did not purvey refreshments within the auditorium. If a manager wished to serve food and drink, he could only obtain a music-hall licence, which prevented him from staging regular plays. And so, as one theatrical great divide was abolished, a new one opened up, between the theatres and the music halls. Some of the consequences of this we shall explore in the next chapter.

The year before the Theatres Act became law, the full force of the economic depression that led to the deprivations of the 'hungry forties' produced a wave of Chartist-inspired strikes against massive unemployment, and the starvation wages to which those still in work were being reduced. The strikes were savagely repressed. Then, in 1845, the great famine struck Ireland – a nation on whose resources the English had become so parasitic that the failure of a single crop, the potato, now made a whole population destitute. Many, in the wave of emigration that followed, fled to the United States – one of the areas in which the Irish exiles congregated being the Bowery, in New York.

In 1849, two years before Macready, longing for retirement, felt financially secure enough to leave his detested profession, he undertook an American tour, with performances at the Astor Place Theatre in New York planned as its climax. His great transatlantic rival, Edwin Forrest, established himself at another theatre – the Bowery. The ensuing demonstrations both inside and outside the Astor Place were encouraged by the opportunistic Forrest – but aroused such passions only because, for the Bowery Irish, Macready stood for the whole English nation, which had driven so many of them from their homeland.

Even so, no physical injury was done to Macready, and very little to the theatre. Yet, in the words of one recent 'authoritative' work of reference, which appears to endorse the judgement it describes, 'Apart from a handful of radicals, most New Yorkers applauded Mayor Woodhull's firm handling of the rioters.' In consequence of this 'firm handling', between twenty and thirty unarmed 'rioters' were shot dead by the forces of law and order.

The generation which succeeded Kean's, and witnessed the accession of Queen Victoria in 1837, preferred its artists to ripen into old age, exuding the respectability with which her long reign (however misleadingly) soon became synonymous. Thus did Macready, the 'eminent tragedian', strive to make himself and his profession no less socially acceptable than were his novelist friends Dickens and Thackeray – who, observing all the proprieties, concealed painful private lives behind distinguished public faces. Macready, as his journals reveal (those that escaped the flames to which well-intentioned descendants consigned them), was similarly self-torturing in private. Fuelled, no doubt, by a controlled release of pent-up energy, he was capable on stage of a violence largely kept bottled-up in his life – though one exasperated blow at the insufferable duopolist Alfred Bunn cost him £150 in damages, and no doubt a good deal more in self-esteem.

Macready's style is as elusive as the man. Seeking through varied stress and the thoughtful use of the blank-verse caesura to avoid Kemble's orotund delivery, like Siddons he subjected his roles to intense study – but unlike her, it seems, in search of their intellectual rather than their emotional core. With Kemble he thus shared a certain austerity of manner – not to mention an incapacity for comedy – yet he was also capable of sustaining pathos as well as power in the great tragic roles. Indeed, what Leigh Hunt called this 'expression of domestic tenderness' fitted him better for the title-roles in Knowles's Virginius (1820) or Bulwer-Lytton's Richelieu (1839) than for Shakespeare.

However, especially during his managements of the patent theatres between 1837 and 1843, Macready did his duty by the bard. Perhaps most notably, he sought to purge his Shakespearean texts of the worst accretions and deletions – restoring the Fool to Lear, while Charles Mathews and Madame Vestris were rediscovering the tragic ending of Romeo and Juliet and Love's Labour's Lost in its entirety. Assisted by the scenic artist Clarkson Stanfield, he also strove for a greater degree of scenic authenticity, thus complementing Planché's concern for accurate costuming. In later years, however, he regretted the initiative, feeling that others building on his example had taken decoration to excess, and were 'willing to have the magnificence without the tragedy'.

Some have discerned in Macready the first director in the modern sense: certainly, he discontinued the old practice of hiring actors for a 'line' of parts, and required leading players occasionally to undertake minor roles. And when he urged his fellow-actors to act during rehearsals, rather than merely recite and block, amused disbelief was apparently their first response, confirming that this was not at all the expected practice. Though he remained contemptuous of the 'beasts' that were his colleagues, his productions were models of unselfish orchestration: conversely, the only matter of concern to Edmund Kean was ensuring that attention remained rivetted upon Edmund Kean (this quickly becomes clear from the American actor James Hackett's attempt to annotate Kean's Richard III, which reveals the subtle or not so subtle self-focusing of his choices).

Left: Macready as Shylock, 1841. William Charles Macready (1793–1873) had been as reluctant to embark on a stage career as he was eager to retire from it, but bankruptcy, following his doomed attempts to manage first Covent Garden and then Drury Lane between 1837 and 1843, intervened. Right: diorama by Clarkson Stanfield for *Henry V* at Macready's Covent Garden, 1839. Lending irony to the Chorus's confession that the theatre could ill suggest 'the vasty fields of France', this gives an aptly desolated air to the battlefield after Agincourt. Prince Hal's triumphant return to London was among other designs for this production

CHAPTER 15

Towards a Respectable Theatre

William Charles Macready has been much applauded for his ambition to make the theatre, like himself, acceptable in good society. But since no activity could really be deemed respectable which was not conducive to hard work and support of the established hierarchy, good society was reluctant to embrace theatre. In so far as moral seriousness can be distinguished from self-interest in the writings of the time, an economy based on low wages, long hours, and an efficient production line was perceived as good for the labourer's soul as well as for the employer's pocket: and the period saw not only the acceleration of the movement to deprive the poor of their traditional holidays, but the banning of most secular pleasures on the single, biblically-prescribed day of rest. Even the prohibition of animal-baiting 'sports' in 1835 was probably due as much to the feeling that these wasted the worker's time as to concern for animal welfare – a concern from which 'game' hunted by the rich was accordingly exempt.

BEGINNINGS OF THE MUSIC HALL

The theatre and the tavern were thus the only amusements readily accessible to the poor – and since both made inroads upon scarce leisure time and scarcer cash, it is not surprising that music hall should so successfully have combined their attractions. Of course, live entertainment had been a happy adjunct to alcohol from the mead hall to the Cider Cellars: and the street entertainer or 'chaunter' of ballads, who had recently found a welcome in glee club, free-and-easy, or harmonic meeting, formed part of a tradition stretching back to the *scop*, the minstrel, and the jongleur. (As illustrated on page 205, in Henry Mayhew he now also found a sympathetic interviewer.) But the passing of the Theatres Act now enforced a choice upon the saloons: some, like the Britannia in Hoxton and the Grecian in Islington, 'went legitimate'; others kept their drinking licence by becoming music halls – setting under way that slow and subtle change whereby food and drink became incidental to such entertainment rather than the reverse.

Opposite: The 'great halls' of the Tudors democratized? Not only the decorations but also the social pretensions of the Canterbury music hall, Lambeth, rebuilt by Charles Morton in 1854, were clearly of a high order: yet the feeling is still that of a large dining hall rather than a theatre

Thus it was that the sing-songs in the 'long room' at the Grapes in the Southwark Bridge Road came to be superseded by the more formal entertainments offered in a purpose built music hall alongside, known first as the Surrey and then as the Winchester. This hall – unlike such concert rooms as the Yorkshire Stingo in Marylebone – was kept discreetly separate from the bars of the pub, the better to attract a family audience. And thus it was that, within four years of its opening in 1847, the Mogul saloon at the top of Drury Lane had also been transformed – into the Middlesex Music Hall, though in the affections of its customers it would always remain the 'Old Mo'.

The so-called 'father of the halls', Charles Morton, was able to learn from such earlier ventures when, having taken over the Canterbury Arms in Lambeth in 1848 and successfully conducted 'harmonic meetings' in its parlour, he built the separate Canterbury Hall alongside in 1852. This held 700, but proved so popular that a new hall with twice that capacity had to be erected within two years – during which short period, according to London licensing records, the totals of four separate music halls and 22 integral to pubs had increased to seven and 92. It was Morton, too, who took the important step of making a separate charge for admission rather than redeeming part of this – the 'wet money' – against the purchase of drink.

Operatic as well as popular music was on offer at the Canterbury, and in an effort to appeal to a would-be cultured clientele Morton even opened a 'handsome picture gallery' and reading-room alongside the hall – while elsewhere miniature museums of natural history or scientific curiosities were assembled, as managers sought to appeal to the appetite for painless education which the Great Exhibition of 1851 had decisively demonstrated to exist. In this, the great age of

TPACKER

the museum, the Alhambra in Leicester Square had thus enjoyed an original existence in 1854 as the Panopticon of Science and Art before being converted into a music hall seating 3,500 just four years later.

The first London Pavilion, at the top of the Haymarket, opened in 1861, a few weeks before Morton's new venture, the Oxford – which was situated, aptly enough, on the site of an old coaching inn, at the junction of Oxford Street and Tottenham Court Road. And it was during this decade that two of the longest-surviving and best-remembered of the halls, the Bedford in Camden Town and the Metropolitan, Edgware Road, began their existence – while in the humbler halls of the East End the 'twice-nightly' system began to operate, in emulation of the almost continuous performances still offered by the penny gaffs (as once by the booth theatres of the fairs). Although, in most of the larger halls, the balcony running round three sides of the auditorium gave the feel of a theatre, the stage as yet was no more than a raised platform; and the area below, as the illustration of the Canterbury on page 229 suggests, rather resembled a dining hall than a pit. However, at the Oxford the tables first gave way to the promenade pictured opposite, then to rows of seats, backed with a shelf on which to rest one's food and drink.

In many ways, this period saw the heyday of the halls as popular institutions. Stringent safety regulations imposed in 1878 not only killed off hundreds of the smaller venues, but led to the erection of more luxurious, highly-capitalized halls, with all the constraints of businesses run for the profit of shareholders. This led to a decline in the working-class orientation of the halls, whose performers, often themselves of humble origin, had expressed in song their solidarity with the grievances and aspirations of the poor. Indeed, that complex balance characteristic of the best in music hall – between social criticism and chauvinism, between proud self-sufficiency and ironic envy – was sustained by the singers long after comic turns more concerned with 'character' than comment began to win equal or higher billing.

By the late 1850s music halls existed in Birmingham, Blackburn, Manchester, and Sheffield, and before long as far afield as Plymouth and Aberdeen. Thornton's Varieties, which opened in Leeds in 1865, outlived them all, and, as the City Varieties, was until recently the venue for that nostalgic music-hall simulacrum on television, *The Good Old Days*. But for the 'legitimate' theatre in the provinces this was a period of mixed fortunes. A reference book of 1827 lists 41 provincial managements, most of them still systematically working the regular 'circuits', with eight further companies operating more or less as strolling players: but many were already suffering the effects of the post-war depression, and when the Theatres Act of 1843 freed companies from the sixty-day restraint of the old magistrates' licence, many of their managers opted to settle permanently in the larger centres, leaving theatres in the smaller towns abandoned or unoccupied for years at a time. In nonconformist strongholds, too, the Methodists were taking a resolute stand against theatregoing.

Opposite: the first Oxford music hall, built for Charles Morton in 1861, as pictured on a song-sheet cover for 'The Oxford Galop'. It will be noticed that the dining tables seen in the picture of the Canterbury on page 229 have already given way to a promenading throng, and theatrical-style seating was soon to follow. The Oxford was three times rebuilt – after fires in 1869 and 1873, and yet again in 1893. George Robey and Harry Tate both made their first London appearances in the hall, but by 1870 Morton himself had moved on to manage the Philharmonic in Islington, and was later associated with the Palace, the Alhambra, and the Gaiety. He died in 1904. The Oxford eventually became a 'legit' theatre under the management of C. B. Cochran, before making way for a Lyons Corner House in 1926

THEATRE AND THE COMING OF THE RAILWAYS

With the railway boom of the 1850s – which saw the laying down of a far wider network than has survived to this day – most parts of the country were brought within easy and relatively inexpensive reach. This necessitated, among other things, standardized timekeeping, so that villages whose church clocks had for centuries kept their own appointments with the noonday sun now found themselves shunted sideways to the Greenwich meridian. But if the coming of the railways necessitated this change, it was a quite different invention which facilitated it – the electric telegraph, by means of which the Royal Observatory sent its time signals down the wires that by 1852 ran alongside all main lines. The age of the mass communication of information, as of the mass transportation of peoples, had begun.

Already, during the 1790s, the practice had become widespread of importing a leading player from London, to perform his or her favourite roles at the head of

skimpily-rehearsed local players. But now the London managers could send out entire companies (eventually as many as three) with touring versions of West End successes – and could later try out productions in advance. This development helped first to weaken and then to destroy the old stock companies in the provinces – while the long London run on which it depended no less surely saw the demise of their metropolitan equivalents.

Thus, the closely-knit group of players which could trace its ancestry back to Shakespeare's day – based at a single theatre, where each actor had a 'line' of parts and prior claim to similar roles as new plays entered a bulging repertoire – gave way to the ad-hoc company assembled for a single production and led by one or two fashionable stars. The hope, however hard of fulfilment, was for a long run. Thus, to notice only plays by authors we shall be mentioning later, the 165 performances notched up by Dion Boucicault's *The Colleen Bawn* in 1860 were soon to be outstripped by the 314 of Tom Taylor's *Our American Cousin* at the Haymarket in 1862 – and while Tom Robertson's *Caste* accumulated over 350 performances during successive runs at the Prince of Wales in 1867 and 1869, H. J. Byron's *Our Boys* broke all records with an astonishing 1,362 performances at the Vaudeville between 1875 and 1879.

For established players, this encouraged more closely observed and developed characterizations, since they were now cast and rehearsed for specific roles rather than having to keep roughly-and-readily in their heads every character in a particular 'line'. And just as stage managers could devote more time to their preparations, so might scene painters now pay more individual attention to their sets and technicians plan lavish effects – the costs of which could hopefully be recouped over a long period. The apprentice actor, however, who, under the repertoire system, would in a single season have cut his teeth on a wide range of small parts across the whole generic spectrum, might now be reduced to carrying the same spear in the same play for a single mind-numbing run – and then perhaps be condemned to travel with it on tour. Inadequate experience on the job was in this way compounded by the stresses of an itinerant existence: and although this led to calls for a better trained and better organized profession, both demands were to take several decades of campaigning to accomplish.

The railway boom which made it possible for provincial audiences to see London productions on tour made it still easier for audiences to come into the West End from that ever-widening suburban sprawl which the railways at once serviced and encouraged (for shorter journeys horse-drawn omnibuses were introduced in 1855). And since 'respectable' audiences could thus be drawn from further afield, central London theatres aiming to attract a fashionable clientele might not only ignore but actively discourage their poorer potential customers. Clustered aplenty though these probably were in some adjacent rookery, for them the penny gaff or the music hall now provided a cheaper and often more congenial alternative.

Opposite: returning from the pantomime, Charing Cross station, 1871. This engraving by J. M. L. Ralston bore the caption: 'Half past eleven o'clock at night is too late for such little ones to be knocking about in town. For those who live in Sydenham or Blackheath, and trust to the last railway train, at midnight, for their return . . . the necessity of catching a cab and driving fast to Charing Cross station, with a party of tired or excited youngsters, is rather an anxious affair'

THE NEW QUEST FOR RESPECTABILITY

Opposite: A sketch of the duel
scene from Boucicault's *The
Corsican Brothers*, made in her
own journal by Queen Victoria
– who saw the play five times
following its opening at the
Princess's in February 1852.
She wrote that this tableau, in
which Louis (Charles Kean)
lies dying at the feet of his
triumphant antagonist (Alfred
Wigan), 'was beautifully
grouped and quite touching.
The whole, lit by blue light
and dimmed with gauze, had
an unearthly effect and was
most impressive and creepy. . . .
We both, and indeed everyone,
was in admiration at the whole
performance and much struck
by it. We told Kean so, when
he accompanied us downstairs'

In its striving for such socially-exclusive respectability, the West End theatre was much heartened by the patronage of the young Queen Victoria, a far livelier lady than the staid empress in perpetual mourning of later popular image. As a girl, she had risked her reputation by attending the Olympic to see Vestris and Mathews, and she continued to follow their fortunes at Covent Garden – while the proximity of the St James's to Buckingham Palace facilitated her visits during the 1840s to its supposedly 'refined' French fare. However, the continental revolutions of 1848 provoked demonstrations against foreign plays and companies, and in that same year Charles Kean was appointed to oversee 'Windsor theatricals' – in effect, command performances of London productions, transplanted (in an echo of the traditions of an earlier era) to the palatial ambience of the royal family's Christmas retreat.

But behaviour in West End theatres was now becoming more conducive to the royal presence, and by 1859 a contemporary observer, J. W. Cole, was able to remark, with evident surprise, that audiences 'sit, for the most part, in silent admiration' – a reverential response which, while it certainly owed something to the disciplined delicacy of the Victorian sensibility, was also promoted by such factors as the lowering of the house lights during a performance (by now the common procedure) and the narrowing of attention upon the stage itself.

In an era when the domestic hearth was becoming sacrosanct, theatre managers were also concerned to offer comforts comparable to those of the home. Plush stalls seats thus continued to encroach upon the foreshortened pit, and it became a matter of note when, in 1855, Marie Wilton had a carpet laid in the stalls at the Prince of Wales. Then, towards the end of our period, the first gallery began to give way to the 'dress circle', with all the sense of occasion that the term conveys – not to mention the exclusion of the inadequately attired which it also clearly implied.

Unlike the spectators at music halls and neighbourhood playhouses, the new breed of West End audience did not demand or require a full evening's entertainment. Indeed, they were concerned to fit their theatregoing into a pattern of social activity which at the very least would include dinner around six o'clock, necessitating the pushing back of the starting time till eight. And it was at the Prince of Wales that Marie Wilton and Squire Bancroft were apparently the first to abandon the long-surviving curtain-raiser, limiting their evening's offering to a single play – a practice preferred, one suspects, less from considerations of artistic unity (or even economy) than for its supposition of a more 'refined' taste.

Then, at the very end of the period covered by this chapter, the matinee performance crept in, catering especially to well-bred ladies who had never lacked the leisure but would earlier have lacked either confidence or inclination to attend a theatre in daytime. The increasing financial risks involved in mounting a new play meant also that many an unknown playwright, desperate for attention,

II.ᵈ act *Corsican Brothers.*
Louis de Franchi (C. Kean) Château Renaud (A. Wigan.)
Feb: 28: March 23.
1852.

was happy to take advantage of the innovation by hiring a theatre for a special matinee performance of his brainchild. The lack of an adequate law of copyright led to agitation for proper remuneration should a play be revived – a point we should bear in mind when we come to discuss the Shakespearean productions of Samuel Phelps and Charles Kean, their man having the advantage of not only being good box office but long dead besides. Those new plays which did reach the fashionable stage tended, moreover, to come from an ever-narrower circle of writers who were already well established.

Slowly, then, the West End repertoire was adapting to the 'respectable' but in many respects limited tastes of its new audiences. And so, while the careers of Planché in extravaganza and of Bulwer-Lytton in the more traditional forms of comedy and romance pursued their courses, that prolific writer of more radical inclinations, Douglas Jerrold, largely forsook the theatre for journalism, following his involvement in the creation of *Punch* in 1841 and the *Daily News* in 1846 – the latter at first under the editorship of Dickens. As his writings in both suggest, Jerrold's angry sympathy for society's outcasts might, in a differently inclined theatre, have led him to sustain a tradition of dramatic satire in the footsteps of Henry Fielding. Although he died (in 1857) still a passionate advocate of social reform, like his erstwhile colleague Thackeray he had become increasingly cynical about the chances of its achievement.

DION BOUCICAULT AND TOM TAYLOR

Opposite: Dion Boucicault (1820–90), characteristically flamboyant as Conn, the title-character of his own play *The Shaughraun*. He played Conn during the first production in New York in 1874, at Drury Lane in the following year – and all over the world until 1888. This pose was, of course, held for the camera – the long exposure times then necessary accounting for the stilted, glazed-eyed quality of many such early 'production photographs'

The pragmatic and almost apolitical Dion Boucicault became, unsurprisingly, altogether more successful by pleasing many and offending few. Shot to fame as a dramatist by the success of *London Assurance*, Boucicault went on to become an actor and manager, at his most appealing in the creation and performance of his own breed of loveable Irish rogues. He spent several fortunes and married three wives in the course of a long theatrical career during which a naturally acerbic temperament often conflicted with a professionalism seemingly no less innate.

The early encouragement of Charles Mathews taught Boucicault a good deal – not least how to sustain the relaxed, drawing-room manner which gave a modern flavour to dialogue and situations which in other respects drew heavily on tradition and nostalgia. His avoidance of the harsher realities of the present (not least those of his native Ireland) no doubt advanced his popularity with audiences – as did time profitably spent in Paris, where a bounteous crop of boulevard fare was regularly picked over by dramatists from across the Channel. When, in 1850, Boucicault became, in effect, 'house' dramatist for Charles Kean at the Princess's, it was judicious use of such Parisian gleanings that led to the success there two years later of *The Corsican Brothers* (in which, as illustrated on the previous page, he was sketched by no less exalted an observer than Queen Victoria).

The association with Kean proved short-lived – for Boucicault proceeded to fall in love and elope with his young ward Agnes Robertson, prompting an expedient American exile during which Agnes became practised in the pathetic roles she regularly played opposite her husband. Among Boucicault's plays from this period, the flamboyant pyrotechnics of the collaborative melodrama *The Poor of New York* (1857) set new standards of spectacular realism, while in *The Octoroon; or, Life in Louisiana* (1859) he equivocated judiciously over slavery – his head shaking with the abolitionist audiences of the north, his heart lost to the parasitic but picturesque gentility of the south.

Boucicault's first American exile reached an apogee in 1860 with the success of *The Colleen Bawn*, a tightly-plotted piece in which the Victorian taste for earnest renunciation is crossbred with comic stage Irishness and celtic whimsy. Tempted back to London in 1860 to present the play at the Adelphi for the veteran actor-manager Benjamin Webster, Boucicault proposed a profit-sharing arrangement – and from this he eventually secured no less than ten thousand pounds. While the popularity of the play made this an exceptional figure – indeed, as late as 1870 many authors were still accepting a flat fee of two or three pounds per performance – it was thanks to this precedent that the royalty system gradually became established, usually allowing authors a more equitable ten per cent of the gross receipts. *The Colleen Bawn* was also of note as the first play for which two companies were rehearsed and sent out simultaneously on tour.

Boucicault then entered into active partnership with Webster, bowed to popular demand by giving *The Octoroon* a substitute happy ending, plunged into bankruptcy in an attempt to legitimize Astley's, and scandalized the town with an inadequately discreet adultery. In 1864 he tried to repeat the success of *The Colleen Bawn* with *Arrah-na-Pogue*, here blending a pinch of nationalistic sentiment into the Irish roguery: but it was with his frankly opportunistic transposition of *The Poor of New York* into *The Poor of Liverpool* (which he proceeded further to 'localize for each town') that he began to recover his fortunes. A decade of hackwork ended with his return to New York and the triumph of his last great Irish play, *The Shaughraun*, in 1874. Boucicault himself took the role of Conn – the boozy but benign Irish itinerant pictured alongside, who at once embraces and transcends his melodramatic type of the 'comic man'.

Credited with a whole or part share in nearly 200 plays, Boucicault, who remained in harness until his death in 1890, learned his craft in an earlier age, but had the flexibility at once to stretch and confine his talents to the tastes of the new. A more typical writer, his theatrical career virtually coterminous with the period of this chapter, was Tom Taylor – a Professor of English and editor of *Punch* as well as author of some seventy plays. Taylor could produce a proficient burlesque, pantomime, or extravaganza as readily as turn his hand to orthodox melodrama. He worked hard also to win himself a 'serious' reputation with plays on historical themes, some unhappily in blank verse, but these revealed even more decisively than his comic pieces an indifferent talent for dialogue.

In so far as Taylor is remembered today, it is for his collaborations with the novelist Charles Reade, among them *Masks and Faces* (1852), a period piece which prettified the manners and purified the morals of the times of Peg Woffington and Kitty Clive; for *Still Waters Run Deep* (1855), a domestic drama in the 'well-made' style; for the comic role of Lord Dundreary created by E. A. Sothern in *Our American Cousin* (1858) – during an American revival of which Abraham Lincoln was assassinated; and for *The Ticket-of-Leave Man* (1863), a thoroughgoing melo-drama with a social conscience which also, in the character of Hawkshaw, happens to boast a pioneering stage detective.

'Costume drama' was now entering upon its long period of popularity, and Taylor was an early exponent. His adaptation for the Strand in 1850 of Oliver Goldsmith's novel *The Vicar of Wakefield* already typified the style – updating the typology and social assumptions of the original, while evoking a purely impres-sionistic sense of 'period'. The novels of Dickens continued to be widely drama-tized, as did those of other best-selling novelists: thus, Harriet Beecher Stowe's *Uncle Tom's Cabin* inspired at least nine stage versions hard on the heels of its publication in 1852, while the prolific John Oxenford's adaptation for the Surrey in 1866 of Mrs Henry Wood's popular tear-jerker *East Lynne* was only the first of fourteen to reach the stage before the century's end.

The prolific H. J. Byron specialized in exploiting the popularity of extrava-ganza, tending to rely rather more heavily than the veteran Planché on the appeal of fleshings – Marie Wilton captivating most of her male spectators with the stunning androgyny of her breeches part in *The Maid and the Magpie* (1858). But he also introduced Buttons into *Cinderella* (1860), and many another staple ingredient into Christmas pantomimes which included *Ali Baba*, *Robinson Crusoe*, *Whittington and His Cat*, and *Beauty and the Beast* – the harlequinade, however, usually still surviving. And he ridiculed the excesses of melodrama to provide a more contemporary focus for burlesque – his success no doubt building on the mild contempt with which the transpontine variety was beginning to be viewed by the better-educated.

VINTAGE YEARS OF FARCE

Many minor forms thus continued to lean heavily upon music and spectacle – ironically, since the Theatres Act had removed the legal necessity for them to do so. But one clear consequence of the lifting of the old restrictions upon a purely spoken drama was that Victorian farce now entered upon its vintage years, the only hindrance to the onrush of swift and energetic action it required being that addictive polysyllabic loquacity (my phrase exemplifies it) with which Victorian jokes were wont to be not so much cracked as lugubriously masticated.

Yet there is still a pleasing freshness about the best work in the genre of Charles Selby, Mark Lemon, J. S. Coyne, and William Brough, to name just a few of the many unremembered mid-Victorian farceurs: and this is due not only to their inventiveness and lack of pretension, but also to the very ordinary, even working-class characters they confront with ordinary, even everyday problems – which are then escalated by fate or coincidence into nightmares of logistic convolution and personal crisis management.

Whereas, in the eighteenth and early nineteenth centuries, farce, like comedy, had tended to work towards climactic matrimony, by the Victorian era marriage was more often where the troubles began. French farceurs such as Labiche and later Feydeau worked from the assumption that extra-marital affairs were no less natural for having to be kept under cover: but their English counterparts preferred to put any interruption of connubial bliss down to some sexually innocent misunderstanding, or to the intervention of an unsympathetic third party – *My Wife's Mother*, it might be, as Charles Mathews revealingly entitled his extended mother-in-law joke of 1833. And domestic harmony, not to mention the dignity of the patriarchy, was normally restored.

Such farces, which threaten but never finally disrupt sexual proprieties, tend, if taken seriously, to seem at best simplistic, at worst downright hypocritical in their moral assumptions. By contrast, those which deal in threats to economic and social stability are readier to transgress taboos – at least, as ready as the average situation comedy of today, which satisfies a rather similar appetite for threatening but ultimately harmless adventures in familiar surroundings. John Maddison Morton's *Box and Cox* (1847) exemplifies the type, and is one of the few to have survived from the huge mid-Victorian output.

Opposite: so popular was John Maddison Morton's farce *Box and Cox* (1847) that it enjoyed a renewed lease of life twenty years later in a musical version – its title (like its characters) transposed. The *Punch* writer F. C. Burnand wrote the words, and the young Arthur Sullivan the music – his first venture into light comedy. Also in the Adelphi audience for the first, amateur production in May 1867, as critic for *Punch*'s rival, *Fun*, was W. S. Gilbert, who remarked that his future collaborator's music was 'in many places, of too high a class for the grotesquely absurd plot to which it is wedded'. The poster is for the professional production which followed, at the 'Royal Gallery of Illustration' – a short-lived venue for one-person and small-scale entertainments aimed at families who still found the idea of attending a theatre beneath their dignity

As the critic Michael Booth points out, such farces often worked up a degree of complicity with their audience which was otherwise quite out of fashion. Thus, when actor-playwrights such as Mathews and J. B. Buckstone created vehicles for their own talents, they would employ extended exposition and even interpolated soliloquys in order to chat directly with their audience, for all the world like Elizabethan clowns from beyond the proscenium arch. John Maddison Morton thus opened his *Grimshaw, Bagshaw, and Bradshaw* (1851) with a two-page comic monologue for Buckstone – while in *Little Toddlekins* (1852) Mathews wrote for himself three pages of what, to us, reads like a script for a stand-up comic. Books of comic monologues for hearthside amateurs also flourished.

Farce usually had the added virtue of brevity, in which case it would be presented within the framework of a double or triple bill. At the Strand, in accordance with the winning formula established by W. G. Swanborough in the 1850s, the evening's farce would thus have been paired with a short comedy, one of

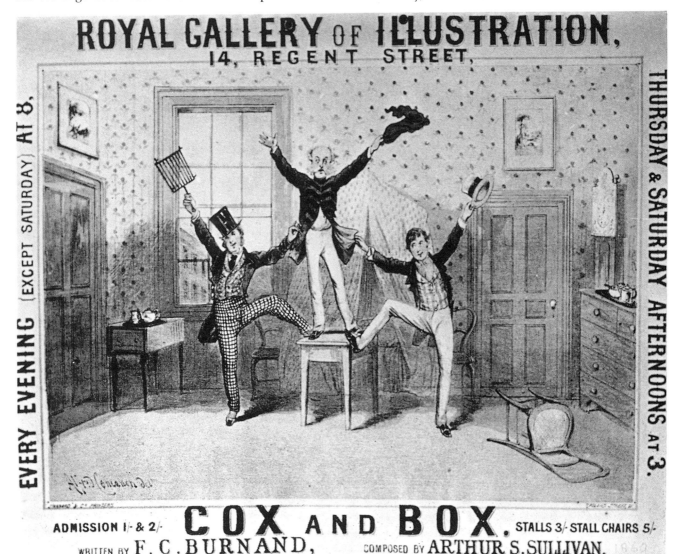

Byron's burlesques bringing the evening to its close. Among other theatres which excelled in particular kinds of fare, the Adelphi, under the long management of Benjamin Webster, was famous for its melodramas and also for accommodating the new style of 'well-made' play, after the manner of the French dramatist Eugène Scribe. And over the road at the Lyceum, Planché renewed his association with Mathews and Vestris during their managerial swan-song from 1847 to 1854 – while from 1863 to 1867, at the same theatre, the Anglo-French actor Charles Fechter succeeded in making the romantic drama virtually his own.

BRITANNIA THEATRE,

HOXTON,

Stage Boxes, 1s. 6d. Boxes, 1s. Slips and Pit, 6d.

No person admitted to the Boxes unless suitably attired. Omnibusses from all parts of London stop within Two Minutes Walk of the Britannia every Quarter of an hour. Children under Seven Years of Age, Half-Price to Boxes and Pit.

Gallery, equal to the Boxes at any other Theatre, 4d. Back Pit, 3d.

Half-Price at Half-past Eight, to Boxes and Pit. Private Entrance, open at a Quarter-past Five, no extra charge to the Boxes. Performances to commence at half-past Six.

Celeste Stephan — every Evening !

On Monday, January 29th, 1855, and all the Week, will be presented
The Gorgeous Glittering Pantomime, entitled

EGYPT! 3000 Years Ago

A Dream in the

CRYSTAL PALACE.

The Extensive and Gorgeous Scenery of the Opening by

MR. JOHN GRAY,

THE OPENING Written by Mr. W. ROGERS. THE COMIC SCENES written by Mr. W. CUSHNIE, and Painted by Mr. C. BULLER.

King Cambyses....Guardian of the Princess—a model for young Kings, a little too fat perhaps, & certainly too good for this vile world..Mr. W. ROGERS, afterwards *Clown*..........Mons. LOUIS
Prince Rhadamanthus ....his Son—a fast young Man, in love with Polyanthus, who having no idea of bridling his appetites, ought to be sent to BRIDEWELL, afterwards *Harlequin*..MR. W. SMITH
Old Nick, or Nicholas....the Incarnation of Evil, who like a certain Emperor, his namesake, scruples not to set half the world by the ears, Mr. C. PITT, afterwards *Pantaloon* Mr. W. H. NEWHAM
Mandoo....a powerful Magician—supposed to be wandering about the Crystal Palace at midnight, no man living having ever seen him there by day ....Mr. C. WILLIAMS
Amos Shortweight.................Mr. J. CLEMENTS   Ephraim Grindcorn....Mr. SACKFILL
Zekiel Clover ....a Farmer, who would not for the world keep up the price of corn ....Mr. Mangel Worzel
The Four Statues....Guardians of the Tomb of Abou Simbel—somewhat tired of sitting 3000 years, and speculating on a rise ....Messrs. Dean, Lucas, Clarke, and Hawkins
The Princess Polyanthus (A Dulcet Warbler) Miss CLARA ST. CASSE
Whose notes "—— Come o'er the ear like the sweet South—That breathes upon a bank of Violets—Stealing & giving odours." And who, in the course of the Pantomime, will sing a New Song Written expressly for her :—The Popular Canzonet, called "THE LADIES' NO!" and the Comic Ballad of "THE GIRL WITHOUT A BEAU," afterwards *Harlequina*.................Miss C. BORROW
MRS. S. LANE....afterwards Queen Cleopatra, a lady who—(but who does not know Mrs. S. Lane !) a Manageress, seeking Materials for a Christmas Pantomime, in the Crystal Palace, with Parodies on the Popular Airs of "Bid the ruddy nectar flow," "Stop that knocking," "The rose shall cease to blow," "Far at sea," "'Red, white, & blue," & an air from "Puritani,".MRS. S. LANE
Rhodope. ..an Egyptian Lady, who would dance all night, if she might, "By the bright moonlight," Miss Green, afterwards *Columbine*......Mdlle. CELESTE STEPHAN

Sc. 1. Model of the Tomb of Abou Simbel in the Crystal Palace
Sc. 2. Egypt (as it used to was 3000 years ago) Pavilion of Queen Cleopatra !
IN THE GARDEN OF CEDARS, & DISTANT VIEW OF THE CITY OF PALACES, (by Sunrise)
Scene 3.   Great Pyramid of King Cheops !
Allegorical Representation of the Triple Alliance—ENGLAND, FRANCE, & TURKEY.
SCENE 4.   THE NILE & ENTRANCE TO THE PORT OF PHARAOH RAMESES
Sc. 5. Pyramids of Gizeh & Pilgrims Encamped in the distance
SCENE 6.   MYSTIC APARTMENT IN THE GREAT PYRAMID.
Sc. 7.   Illuminated Point Lace Grotto !
GRAND METEMPSYCHOSIAN TRANSFORMATION !
Clown..Mons LOUIS   Pantaloon..Mr W.H.NEWHAM
Harlequin   Mr. W. SMITH
Sprites ....   Messrs. TALLIEN, BROTHERS,
Harlequina..Miss C. BORROW   Columbine..Mlle. Celeste STEPHAN
Sc 8-Stunningrog's Gin Palace & Smallcomb's a Wig-maker
TRIP..PAS DE TROIS D' AGREMENT..HARLEQUIN, COLUMBINE & HARLEQUINA..The jolly fat Boniface of 1854..PANT..'my first is appropriate ; my second is one to 'one if you guess it; and my whole elevates the sole above the earth," what's that? CLOWN..."Why a Patten."
Sc. 9—BATHS AND WASHHOUSES for the MILLION
TRIP..LA POLKA..HARLEQUIN, COLUMBINE & HARLEQUINA..PANT. takes a warm bath, and CLOWN does his week's Washing..The Roushans are coming.."Kornified and Nacified both off, who'll be next off ! let us hope Romanoff."

FORTRESS OF SEBASTOPOL

Sc. 10=Chickenheart's the Poulterer and Chokemcheap's Manufactory !
TRIP..LA TARANTELLE..HARLEQUIN AND COLUMBINE..PANT..My first is always, m second's durable, and my
Sc. 11---FURNISHED APARTMENTS
TRIP..THE UNITY PAS DE TROIS..HARLEQUIN, COLUMBINE, AND HARLEQUINA
Scene 12.   Caius's Juvenile Stage Repository !
AND ROYAL PENNY GAFF !
TRIP—Pas de Trois de Genre—Harlequin, Columbine & Harlequina
Walk up here, walk up, my little dears, No advance in the Prices, only a penny !
SCENE 13.   THE PYRAMID OF BRITANNIA PANTOMIME !!
LAST SCENE.   MR. J. GRAY'S GRAND PANTOMIME ANNUAL.
Interior of the Temple of Memnon in the Land of Egypt! Brilliant Transformation—
Britannia Presents to her Children,

THE CHRISTMAS TREE!

Illuminated by 1000 Christmas Candles.
Opening of the Shells of the Ocean. Mystic Growth of the Tree.

After which, every Evening,

MR. HENRY SMITH,

Will give a portion of his celebrated

Vocal Entertainment

Introducing a Selection of those Dramatic, Descriptive and Comic Ballads, in rendering of which, he stands unrivalled.

To conclude with an entirely New, Interesting, Instructive and Didactic Drama, adapted from an admired Tale which recently appeared in "Reynolds' Miscellany," "Family Herald," and "London Journal," and Licensed expressly for this Establishment, to be entitled

Fashion and Famine!

William Leicester..Mr. W. R. Crauford   Robert Otis..Mr. Dean   Benjamin Wilcox..Mr. J. Reynolds
Nicholas.........Mr. W. Rogers   Magistrate of Police Court..Mr. C. Williams
Jacob Strong...Mr. C. J. Bird
Mr. Acunem ....Mr. C. Pitt   Mr. Smoothly...................Mr. F. Wilton
Judge of the Criminal Court......Mr. Bedella   Jailor....Mr. Lucas   Jim....Mr. J. Clements
Mulatto Woman.............Mr. Clarke   Crespigny................Mr. Hawkins
Julia.................Miss C. Borrow   Ada Leicester....Mrs. E. Yarnold
Maude Wilcox...Miss Richardson   Florence....Miss Green   Widow Gray......Mrs. Atkinson
Widow Leicester....Mrs. Mackney   Lilly Clark...Mrs. B. Ware   Sally....Miss Pettifer
Rosana....Miss Davis   Market People, Constables, Ladies and Gentlemen, &c.

The Lone Mansion and its Mistress !
THE VILLAIN & HIS VICTIM. TABLEAU OF EXCITEMENT.
The Old Homestead & Home Memories.
THE STRIDES OF DESTINY. The Last Link Broken. Death of the Betrayed One. EXAMINATION BEFORE THE MAGISTRATES
HALL OF JUSTICE. THE CONDEMNED CELL
The Prisoner under Sentence. The Last Hour—

DEATH OF THE AGED VICTIM

NEIGHBOURHOOD THEATRE

On the neighbourhood theatres of the inner suburbs there is very little helpful contemporary comment. However, a scarce, privately-printed volume by T. W. Erle, *Letters from a Theatrical Scene-Painter*, published in 1880, gives us some colourful glimpses of such playhouses as the Royal Effingham and the Pavilion, both in Whitechapel, the Marylebone, the Britannia in Hoxton, the Victoria and the Surrey south of the river, and the Grecian off the City Road, 'as they were twenty years ago' – that is, around 1860. In a tone of affection mingled with condescension, Erle suggests that most of these continued to subsist on a diet of melodrama, all decked out with old-fashioned stock settings, scanty properties, and primitive effects, regardless of changes in dramatic fashion, acting style, and staging techniques in the West End.

However, recent research into the repertoire of the Britannia – managed throughout this period and well beyond by the Lane family – suggests not only a far higher degree of technical proficiency but an audience devoted and numerous enough almost to guarantee a twelve-week run for each Christmas pantomime, as tantalizingly advertised opposite. And in Sarah Lane, the actress wife of the manager, the Brit had its own local star, for whom house dramatists would bespeak the eccentric comedy roles in which she excelled. One such long-serving hack, Colin Hazlewood, wrote around half of the sixty or so new plays presented at the theatre between 1863 and 1874 – many of them, confessedly, adaptations of earlier works or from best-selling novels, with *Lady Audley's Secret* out-distancing the rest in popularity.

It is true that, as Erle suggests, outside the panto season (and give or take an occasional burlesque) melodrama was the staple diet: indeed, it was at the Brit that George Dibdin Pitt's splendid prototype of the criminal melodrama, *Sweeney Todd*, had first been played in 1847. But following its rebuilding in 1858 the theatre appears to have been second to none in technical resources: it was the first to use the famous 'Pepper's Ghost' effect in 1863, while volcanic eruptions, shipwrecks, and flights of angels were other specialities of the house. And alongside the exotic pieces which luxuriated in such trimmings were dramas of East End life which stressed the divisions between rich and poor – especially the pressures of poverty upon virtue. Hazlewood's *The Work Girls of London* pressed hard on Lady Audley's heels among the most popular plays of the period.

'ARCHEOLOGICAL' ACCURACY IN SHAKESPEARE

Shakespeare did not figure much in the Brit's repertoire, and although a number of the newly legitimized theatres tried out favourites from the canon, few had flourished in the attempt. The major and unexpected exception was at Sadler's Wells in Islington, where Samuel Phelps, during a management of the theatre that lasted from 1844 until 1862, mounted all but four of Shakespeare's plays – including even such still-elusive pieces as *Timon of Athens* and *Pericles* – in texts

Opposite: playbill for the Britannia Theatre, Hoxton, for the week of 29 January 1855, advertising a 'glittering' pantomime on an Egyptian theme. As the reference to 'a dream in the Crystal Palace' confirms, the exotic foreign location is a hung over influence from the Great Exhibition four years earlier. Even so, there is a traditional transformation scene, featuring Clown, Pantaloon, Harlequin, and Columbine – played by Celeste Stephan, who tops the billing. (Note that the typography for Scene 7 is 'transformed' as well.) Throughout, a tone of familiarity is struck with the neighbourhood audience, whose children are promised a climactic Christmas tree with a thousand candles. Yet to come are a solo vocal entertainment and a sombre-sounding 'didactic drama', leading to the condemned cell

which for the times were relatively unadulterated. Though less innovative as an actor than as a manager, Phelps was equally adept in tragic and comic roles, with a special affection for such broader character parts as Falstaff, Shallow, Jaques, Malvolio, and Bottom the Weaver.

During his management of the little Princess's from 1851 to 1859, Charles Kean was also to call Shakespeare in aid to make this one of London's most fashionable theatres. Among his innovations were 'folding curtains of magnificent velvet' which were drawn to cover scene changes – the more traditional use of act-drops alone, with intervening scenes changed in full view of the audience, apparently continuing elsewhere into the 1880s. In an otherwise varied repertoire, Kean's major productions of Shakespeare, though they won him huge contemporary acclaim, scaled new heights and plumbed new depths in their striving for archeological accuracy.

Antiquarian absurdities abounded. For *A Midsummer Night's Dream*, for example, the furnishings and tools in 'the workshop of Quince the Carpenter' were all 'copied from discoveries at Herculaneum'. (Perhaps such pedantry was better suited to a revival of Byron's *Sardanapalus*, for which the elaborate scenery was based on the recent excavation of Nineveh.) As an irritated Jerrold put it: 'We claim a higher rank for Mr Phelps's management than for Mr Kean's. We do this on the same principle that we should pronounce Shakespeare in a plain sheep's skin a better book than Kotzebue in gilded morocco.' And more cuttingly

still: 'The little importance that Mr. Kean attaches to good acting needs no further proof than the fact of his generally taking the principal character himself.'

Thus Kean's willingness virtually to relearn his art as an actor during his years at the Princess's, under the subduing influence of the drawing-room drama, was not universally appreciated. Some critics denounced his conversational style, objecting with *Punch* to the 'dissociation of rhythm from meaning' which resulted, or with W. B. Donne that 'ever since Macready's day tragedy has become more homely' and 'utterly devoid of heroic proportions'. The Irish actor Barry Sullivan was an earlier exponent of the new style, noted especially for a vocal range expressing 'subtle and varied shades of meaning': but it was the Hamlet of Charles Fechter in 1861 which was revelatory for many in the elegance of its low-key approach.

Fechter's Hamlet was said to transform a hero into an individual – which in itself is suggestive of the expectations of psychological realism in acting which were now emerging alongside a concern for greater realism in playwriting. But realism is as realism does – or as those demanding it do. And so, in the unlikely setting of the old Dust Hole – now dignified in the royal presence as the Prince of Wales's Theatre – Marie Wilton and her future husband Sir Squire Bancroft, sustaining the tradition of Vestris and Mathews, almost accidentally defined 'realism' for the 1860s by providing for their audiences plays which reflected their own view of themselves and their ambitions.

Diorama designed by Thomas Grieve for the woodland scenes in Charles Kean's production of *A Midsummer Night's Dream* at the Princess's in 1856. A 'diorama' comprised two long canvases, one set behind the other, moved along by rollers so that cutouts in the frontmost gave a three-dimensional impression of the passing scene. Kean also employed a ballet of Amazonian soldiers, and an arched avenue of flowers held up by fairies. In other productions, no less care was lavished on more literal details, such as the palace interior for *A Winter's Tale*, or on topographical precision, as in William Telbin's practicable bridges and boats moving along canals, for *The Merchant of Venice*

Squire Bancroft and Marie Wilton (who married in 1867), largely assisted by Tom Robertson as 'house dramatist' to the Prince of Wales, well understood that a theatre seeking to attract a fashionable audience needed to provide models of decorum for the aspirant or the uncertain as well as mirrors of behaviour for the self-assured. They perceived, too – as had Davenant and Killigrew during the Restoration – that in Victorian high society behaviour was becoming codified and artificial to a degree that 'acting' could not only mirror but modulate. However different in moral values and social origins, the audiences of both eras were alike in their ostensible self-confidence – though the Victorian, perhaps less inwardly secure, also sought opportunities for further upward mobility, and a code of instant etiquette which would assist them in achieving it.

And so, as the middle classes began to reclaim their theatre, they were happy to patronize plays which helped them to acquire as well as to witness the manners of their supposed betters. If such a writer as Tom Robertson was, truth to tell, no better than themselves, at least he had the imagination to believe he was. Robertson's career had developed slowly and unpropitiously: even his first success, David Garrick, in 1864 was a highly derivative costume drama, however good the acting part he provided for the title role. His subsequent popularity was in large measure due to his capacity (whether from calculation or ignorance is arguable) to redraw the upper echelons of society not realistically but in terms which seemed realistic to its middling orders – and perhaps to himself. During the Bancrofts' tenancy of the Prince of Wales, Robertson thus not only wrote but stage-managed (in effect directed) such plays as Society (1865), Ours (1866), and Caste (1867), in all of which the characters and situations only just transcend the melodramatic, but in which the polite overlay offers an appearance of 'realism' attractive to their audiences – an attraction heightened by the Bancrofts' due concern for the accuracy of their drawing-room settings.

That a species of domestic play discernably different from melodrama, and 'realistic' at least to the class for which it was written, now began to separate itself out was not, of course, due simply to some unspoken need for theatricalized codes of protocol. Rules were in philosophical fashion, and the scientific cast of the age, with its confidence that all knowledge and experience would in time be systematized, was earnestly seeking the rule-book that must surely regulate human nature – encouraged by the belief that the code governing its heredity had just been cracked. Thus Darwin's Origin of Species was published in 1859, and Marx's Capital in 1867.

The struggle between the interests of scientific accuracy and moral dignity, as derived from religious belief, that was precipitated by Darwin's theory of evolution meant that there was much that neither the drama nor (despite its more flourishing condition) even the novel could properly explore. It was not

politically or morally acceptable to draw the face of the evil that kept so many entrapped in misery. Even Dickens, who knew its lineaments well, could only sketch it allusively – merely hinting, for example, at the horrors that lurked in the shadows as Little Dorrit scurried anxiously round a night-time London from which even the Marshalsea prison was a place of refuge.

Audiences at the Britannia, Hoxton, brushed daily against evils from which those at the Prince of Wales could turn aside: but while a Brit melodrama like The Dark Side of the Great Metropolis might thus deal more openly with the economic causes of prostitution, its effects are shown upon an individual who is eventually rescued from them – just as happy accidents remedy the effects of the workhouse for Oliver Twist. The need for larger social remedies may be assumed, but is not seriously explored – least of all in the drama, which at this time was supposed only to show, not tell, and so lacked even an explicit authorial voice. The drama's rulebook, too, awaited rewriting.

Squire Bancroft (opposite page) as the condescending Captain Hawtree and George Honey (right) as the 'loveable rogue' Eccles in Tom Robertson's *Caste* at the Prince of Wales (1867). In this, his best play, Robertson created a wide range of nicely contrasting characters, who at least stretched the conventions from which they sprang. However, a clear plotline, ostensibly colloquial dialogue, and a good deal of simple but attractive comedy lead only to the unsurprising conclusion that 'Caste's a good thing if it's not carried too far'

Left: also in *Caste,* John Hare and Marie Wilton (soon to become Mrs Bancroft) played the good-hearted working-class pair, Sam Gerridge the plumber and his sweetheart Polly Eccles. Embodying the Victorian virtue of 'self-help', the couple strive hard to 'better themselves' – but not too far above their station. Originally in partnership with H. J. Byron, Marie Wilton set out to create at the Prince of Wales a home-from-home for the Victorian middle classes, remaining there until 1879. For Robertson, John Hare's roles ranged from foreign diplomats and suavely dissolute MPs to cunning gamblers and doddering old aristocrats

CHAPTER 16

The Speculative Theatre

Impressions of characters from *Babes in the Wood*, Augustus Harris's Drury Lane pantomime of 1888. These were drawn for the *Illustrated Sporting and Dramatic* – the journalistic conjunction reminding us of the strong links between the stage and the turf at this time. Dan Leno is shown here in the 'dame' role of the wicked aunt, with Harriet Vernon (she of the redoubtable thighs) as the 'principal boy', Robin Hood. The two babes ('of forty or thereabouts', as the *Sporting and Dramatic* reminds us) are older music-hall stars, Herbert Campbell and Harry Nicholls

However clear-sighted may have been Karl Marx's diagnosis of the ill-effects of nineteenth-century *laissez faire* capitalism, his prognosis, especially if misread as a programme for continuing action, was deeply flawed. He acknowledged the skill of the English ruling classes in deflecting revolutionary tendencies through timely concessions: but he recognized less well their capacity to assimilate or, where necessary, to cauterize the traditional culture of the proletariat – the breeding ground of effective subversion.

At the lowly level of recreation, the process of assimilation had been accelerating since mid-century. Many of the sports which, though played for generations according to vague but locally recognized oral codes, had been banned as disruptive in their 'unofficial' forms now began to be 'officially' resuscitated – replete with printed rulebooks, top-hatted regulating bodies, and all the class ramifications of 'amateur' and 'professional' status. However, those popular customs which threatened profits as well as peace of mind had, necessarily, to be put down rather than merely contained. And so it was, for example, that the diverse ways in which midwinter had traditionally been celebrated were now tidied up and at first confined to Christmas Day itself: the addition of Boxing Day (following the act of 1871 which established Bank Holidays) was thus made to appear a benevolent concession rather than a grudging acknowledgement of a far ampler ancient right.

Not only were the twelve days reduced to two, but a once-communal feast was turned inward upon the family and the domestic hearth – even the raucous street music of the waits being suppressed in favour of the 'rediscovery' of carols, so much more reverent and demure. And all those charitable ladies who, on Christmas Day, massaged their consciences by doling out to those incarcerated in prisons and workhouses their one decent meal of the year had now, in the cause of temperance, to concede that their healths be drunk in water instead of good ale – while the annual treat was, of course, preferably to be confined to the 'deserving' rather than the recalcitrant poor.

Despite all these tendencies, Epiphany long kept its hold on the popular imagination, although its traditional inversions had become largely symbolic – practical jokes, typically, rendered down to cardboard as the subjects of Twelfth Night cards (which long predated Christmas cards as we know them). Stubbornly, however, seasonal topsy-turvydom did survive – not least in traditions of cross-dressing, an indecorous ebullience which disturbed not only the smug religiosity of the makers of the Victorian Christmas but the discreeter hypocrisies of their sexual habits.

And so it was that the subversive transvestism of old became a sanctioned form of sublimation, made manifest in the rituals of pantomime – which, although often a Christmas offering in the past, was now becoming exclusively so. In the process, most lingering associations with the old *commedia* masks were purged, as Harlequin and Columbine gave way to a transsexually titillating principal boy and principal girl, backed up by a chorus line in fleshings. The Clown was cut down to the likes of Buttons, and Pantaloon unsexed to become the Dame – a male in drag, usually a music-hall favourite drafted in to boost the box-office, as pop stars and television personalities are today.

Drury Lane, notably under the management of Augustus Harris from 1879 to 1896, restored its drifting fortunes by specializing, for ever-lengthening Christmas seasons, in pantomimes of the most spectacular kind – filling out its year with sensation dramas similarly dependent upon extravagant effects, for which the theatre's technical resources as well as its sheer size made it well suited. Such effects ranged from the sinking of the Birkenhead in *Cheer Boys, Cheer* (1895) to August Bank Holiday on Hampstead Heath in *The Great Ruby* (1898) and a full-scale horse-race in *The Whip* (1909).

A NEW BOOM IN THEATRE BUILDING

That the ruling classes were now showing some readiness to alleviate the harshest excesses of the industrial revolution had to do in part with enlightened self-interest, in part with a calculated appeal to class allegiances. Thus, because factory owners tended to be free-trading Liberals, an imperialist Conservative government might embark upon industrial reforms without offence to its supporters in the rural shires – while in the process wooing those newly enfranchised by the Reform Acts of 1867 and 1884, which gave the vote to virtually all male householders. No less

Augustus Harris (1852–96), under whose management from 1879 Drury Lane interspersed its regular diet of spectacular dramas with an annual 'Christmas' pantomime which might run past Easter. Although condemned by traditionalists for his recruitment of music-hall performers into panto, Harris retained many of its older features, including the Clown and the harlequinade – which duly featured in *Babes in the Wood*. Dan Leno, whom Harris introduced to the West End in this production, remained teamed with Herbert Campbell in pantomimes at the Lane until both died in 1904. This cartoon was one of the long sequence published in *Vanity Fair* by 'Ape' and (as in this case) 'Spy', otherwise Sir Leslie Ward

important, the Ballot Act of 1872 kept secret from employers and landlords alike the way in which a man cast that vote: and although no woman was yet able to cast hers, the Married Women's Property Acts of 1870 and 1882 marked a first step towards greater economic independence.

Although the Elementary Education Act of 1870 was passed by Gladstone's first Liberal administration, it was thus his successor Disraeli – the first to deplore 'two nations' living in mutual ignorance – who as leader of the Conservative government of 1874 enacted a programme of reforms which one of the first two Labour MPs then elected declared to have 'done more for the working classes in five years than the Liberals in fifty'. Factory legislation significantly loosened the shackles of long hours and insufferable conditions, while trades unions were freed from criminal penalties for strike action and peaceful picketing. Under a Public Health Act, sewage systems were built which have only recently begun to show their age. An Enclosures Act not only brought the private absorption of common land virtually to an end, but increased the provision of public recreation grounds and allotments.

The vintage Victorian theatre

Our illustration shows some typical features of the vintage Victorian theatre: its fully-formed and ornately gilded picture-frame stage, from which any residual trace of apron and stage doors has been eliminated; its rich but highly (and sometimes confusingly) eclectic embellishments; its pit foreshortened or (as here) abandoned before encroaching stalls; and upper tiers ever-extending towards the stage, as new techniques of canti-levering removed the necessity for so many supporting pillars. Other less immediately obvious characteristics were dictated by considerations of safety: these included, besides improved ventilation, a new tendency for the pit to be sunk below ground so that the dress circle was at entrance level, and a requirement that the theatre should be isolated from sur-rounding buildings by passageways.

Since rooms could no longer be built above the auditor-ium, the fly-tower now became a dominant external feature, while new scenographic techniques were encouraging the in-ternal improvement and development of the flying space. However, overriding commercial considerations meant that, in comparison with continental practice, front-of-house facili-ties in the new theatres were meagre, with box-office, cloak-room, and refreshment areas often so cramped as not even to be adequately functional. As, in many such theatres, they remain.

But the most enduringly important innovation in theatre construction to occur during this period lay, of course, in the use of electric lighting. Richard D'Oyly Carte led the way in 1881, his new Savoy not only the first theatre but the first public building of any kind in London to be so lit: and later in the 1880s two disastrous fires within two years at the Theatre Royal, Exeter, accelerated a nationwide conversion from gas which was virtually complete by the end of the century. But D'Oyly Carte continued to illuminate the auditorium as well as the stage during performances, and this hungover habit at first limited the artistic potential of electricity – at a time when Henry Irving was insisting not only on the lowering of the house lights at the Lyceum, but on the retention where possible of gas, which he believed to permit subtler control over his effects.

Irving was, indeed, entirely modern in deploying light not merely for illumination but for dramatic emphasis, a diffusion and variation allowed more readily by the banks of individual gas taps and valves than by the initially more limited controls over the new source. Famously, Irving relished, too, the resources of limelight – not merely for its mellow brilliance in tracking his own actions like a modern follow-spot, but for the varying impressions of moonlight and directional or waning sunlight it facilitated.

The Empire music hall, Newcastle, pictured in 1891, and probably much as it had been for the previous half century. Note the cane chairs for the orchestra, the plush seats in the 'front stalls' – and the hard benches in the slips. Flock wallpaper and pictures lend a homely touch to the auditorium, which contrasts with the fantasy world conjured up on the stage

And local authorities were encouraged to build 'artisans' dwellings' – thus creating the very system of council housing that more recent Conservative governments have been anxious to dismantle.

Although conditions for ordinary working people thus began slowly to improve, the 1870s saw also the start of a severe trade depression which, with only two brief intermissions, persisted almost until the end of the century. But since some of the causative factors – tariff barriers abroad, the end of the railway boom at home – left investors with spare capital, the theatre, as an alternative focus for speculation, ironically benefited, and it was during this period that an 'entertainment industry' effectively emerged.

However, the tale of the two London theatres known as 'the rickety twins' suggests that this development could have its pitfalls. On a site between the churches of St Clement Dane and St Mary le Strand were thus constructed in 1868 and 1870 the back-to-back playhouses best remembered as the Globe and the Opera Comique. Slum clearance in the area to make way for the Aldwych and Kingsway

development was already being actively planned, and the speculative builder Sefton Parry therefore erected both theatres of the flimsiest materials in expectation of their imminent demolition – and his own hefty compensation. They were considered serious fire hazards, although in the event both managed just to outlive the century.

Two sturdier products of the new boom in theatre building also opened in 1870 – the charming Vaudeville in the Strand, and the first Royal Court, whose situation in Sloane Square testified to the ever-westward drift of fashionable London. On Regent (soon to be Piccadilly) Circus, the subterranean location of the Criterion Theatre, built in 1874 beneath the restaurant of the same name, bore witness to the spiralling land values in the heart of the West End. Even further west, if never quite so fashionable, Hammersmith saw its Lyric Opera House go up in 1888. And in 1881 had opened both the Comedy, in Panton Street between the Haymarket and Leicester Square, and the first Savoy (pictured on page 256), midway along the Strand. The Playhouse, which followed a year later, was anecdotally another of Sefton Parry's gambles, owing its obscure situation off the Embankment to an anticipated extension of the Charing Cross railway, from which he hoped in vain to profit.

In 1884 the Prince of Wales's opened in Coventry Street, off Piccadilly Circus – and then, in 1887, were completed the slum clearances which now drove Charing Cross Road north towards Oxford Street from Trafalgar Square, and Shaftesbury Avenue south-west from Holborn down to Piccadilly. The very heart of theatreland now underwent a rapid transplant, fed by these wide, well-lit, and accessible arteries. In 1888 the first Shaftesbury Theatre went up near Cambridge Circus, where the two roads crossed, to be closely followed by the Lyric, just a little further west: and then, in 1891, arose the great sprawl of the Palace, at first as the Royal English Opera, to dominate the Circus itself. The Garrick had already staked a first claim for the theatre along Charing Cross Road in 1889, and three years later arose the almost abutting Trafalgar, now known as the Duke of York's, with its frontage on St Martin's Lane.

IRVING AND THE LYCEUM YEARS

In view of the modernity of his approach to lighting (described on page 248), it is ironic that in other respects the period's leading actor-manager, Henry Irving, was a rather old-fashioned player with a preference for an old-fashioned repertoire. Indeed, in 1877 there even appeared a small, anonymous pamphlet entitled *The Fashionable Tragedian* – a 'criticism with ten illustrations' which set out to prove that, for all his then burgeoning influence, Irving was, in truth, 'a very bad actor'.

Unlike much of the critical sniping to which he was subjected, this squib in brown paper wrappers merits attention because its authors, William Archer and Robert W. Lowe, were to become respectively the leading critic and theatre historian of their generation. And both clearly sensed, as early in their own careers as in

Irving's, that the grip this charismatic performer was already exerting would encourage (as it also exemplified) a spirit of conservatism which for some time yet would insulate the British theatre from the new drama of Europe. For while Irving was not a 'very bad actor', he did, as Shaw perceived and complained, choose to contour his greatness within a corset of very constraining trim.

Having served an old-style extended apprenticeship in the provinces, Irving spent five inconspicuous years in London before being noticed in 1871, at the age of 32, in the role of Digby Grant in James Albery's *Two Roses* – a role which, ironically, was also to be among the most modern he ever attempted. Albery, whose dilutions of what Archer described as the 'flippant and feebly sentimental small talk' of the 'Robertsonian school of playwriting' kept the new Vaudeville full for 294 performances, was briefly hailed as the natural successor to Tom Robertson – who, already in ill-health, died in the following year. However, Robertson proved to have no natural successor – although his widely imitated knack of making dialogue trip with seeming ease from well-mannered tongues made this an era when affluent amateurs encouraged themselves to believe that acting was an accomplishment easily acquired.

Thus arose a new breed of superior supernumeraries – 'extra ladies and gentlemen' who duly got their billing, but seldom in other than walk-on roles. And among the fond (though in this case not so foolish) parents who encouraged their offspring in their histrionic ambitions was one Hezekiah Bateman, who, also in 1871, had gone so far as to take the lease of the old Lyceum Theatre – which was still finding it hard to live up to the pretensions of its portico – as a showcase for the talents of his four daughters.

Bateman duly recruited Irving to the company: but neither the opening play by his own wife nor the stage adaptation of Dickens's *Pickwick Papers* which followed caught the imagination of audiences. And so it was very much as a final fling that Bateman agreed to let Irving take the lead in an adaptation from the French by Leopold Lewis of a melodrama entitled *The Bells*, in which Irving was to take the role of the haunted burgomaster Mathias. The opening night of 25 November 1871 not only rescued Bateman's fortunes but, in the words of Clement Scott – a critic as traditional in his tastes as Archer was innovatory – lifted Irving 'at one bound above his contemporaries'.

That same night, Irving, returning home, is said to have stepped down from his cab and out of his marriage when his socially ambitious wife asked irritably if he was going to go on making a fool of himself all his life. His subsequent career was dedicated to showing that making a fool of oneself might be no bar to social advancement: and in 1895, at the second time of asking, he duly accepted a knighthood – the first such honour for services to the theatre, which could from then on regard itself as officially respectable and respectably official. A knighthood for Squire Bancroft followed in 1897, and for Charles Wyndham, aptly an Edwardian creation, in 1902.

Henry Irving's Mephistopheles in W. G. Wills's version of Goethe's *Faust* (Lyceum, 1885). Against massive costs of over £15,000, the production (five years in the planning) took in nearly £70,000 in its first year and £57,000 in its second. By then Irving had added the grotesque splendours of a scene in the Witches' Kitchen to the climactic Walpurgisnacht revels on the Brocken Mountain, in which (according to Clement Scott) a 'shrieking, gibbering crowd' of witches, goblins, and apes from hell made a terrifying contrast with 'shadowy greys and greens' suggestive of Gustave Doré

A rare photograph of Irving in performance – in Sardou's *Robespierre*, on tour to New York in 1900 (cameras were banned at the Lyceum, where the production had opened in the previous year). Irving as Robespierre is here addressing the hall of the revolutionary Convention in the last act of the play. The picture is, of course, posed, but begins to suggest Irving's concern for the careful orchestration of his crowd scenes

Meanwhile, in September 1872, began Irving's long association with the hack dramatist W. G. Wills, whose reincarnation of the martyr king in the actor's own image for the historical romance *Charles I* led to his appointment as house dramatist to the Lyceum at £300 a year. Wills's talent, like Lewis's, was mediocre, but in every sense adaptive – and subservient to Irving's requirements, as in his mangling of Goethe's *Faust* in 1885, in the interests of the actor's Mephistopheles (pictured on the previous page). Even the poet Tennyson, then entering his dotage, permitted Irving to shape the part of Philip of Spain in *Queen Mary* (1876) as a vehicle for his talents; and while the laureate lay dying, Irving went to work on *Becket* (1893), reconstructing the role of the archbishop and a good deal else besides.

Irving's first Shakespearean production at the Lyceum, judiciously chosen, was his *Hamlet* of 1874. He played the title role 'like a scholar and a gentleman', wrote Clement Scott: Irving was 'not acting', but 'talking to himself . . . thinking aloud'. During the run of 200 nights, then unprecedented for a Shakespearean revival, Bateman died, and his widow, after briefly toying with the reins of management, amicably resigned them to Irving in 1878. Irving continued to extend his Shakespearean range, a mannered *Othello* (1876) and a curiously unromantic *Romeo and Juliet* (1882) easily outweighed by triumphs as Richard III in 1877, as Shylock in 1879, as Wolsey in *Henry VIII* in 1892, and as Iachimo in *Cymbeline* in 1896.

Despite scenic embellishments of a kind which had driven others into bankruptcy, incidental music often specially composed for an orchestra of thirty, and ambitiously choreographed crowd scenes, Irving managed to make more money from Shakespeare, and to play him for lengthier runs, than had ever proved possible before. He took no less trouble over lesser plays: his biographer Alan Hughes has thus calculated that the formidable number of 639 people were employed to work on *Robespierre*, including 355 performers and musicians, 236 technicians (the lighting crew alone numbering 38), and 48 administrative staff. That was in 1899: later in the same year Irving gave up his management of the Lyceum, which he had recently turned into a limited company. He died six years later, during what he had already declared to be his farewell tour.

As an actor, Irving seems to have exerted a force of will which not only infused his role but took command of his audience. An unusual mixture of the protean and the idiosyncratic, he was physically adept at shrinking, extending, and otherwise disassembling his spidery limbs into a new character, while deploying mannerisms of speech and gait which made him, unmistakably and with deliberation, Irving. An eccentric showman who wooed his audiences rather as Disraeli wooed his Queen, he sustained the dying tradition of a permanent acting company, but not in the spirit of interdependence on which Richard Burbage or even David Garrick had built: rather, Irving was the undisputed first among unequals.

Only his leading lady, Ellen Terry – whose hiring was one of the first acts of his independent management – was permitted to complement rather than challenge his supremacy, and even she had to confine herself to roles which would reflect Irving's brilliance. As Beatrice and Benedick, Portia and Shylock, or Imogen and Iachimo the pair could thus work on an equal footing: but she was unable to play, for example, Rosalind in *As You Like It*, because there was no role of equivalent stature for the 'partner' who was also the boss. Terry's Imogen, which was much to the taste of virtuous Victorians, is pictured on page 264.

As a manager, Irving well understood his respectable Lyceum audiences and was always responsive to their predictably limited tastes: but within these limits his productions were rigorously rehearsed by disciplined companies, and their polish scrupulously maintained during long runs which would otherwise have fallen apart. And to be found among the names of his company were such harbingers of the theatrical future as George Alexander, Johnston Forbes-Robertson, and John Martin-Harvey.

PROSPERITY IN THE WEST END

Irving not only brought commercial and (by his own and his audience's standards) artistic success to the old Lyceum: he also did much to create a climate in which other West End managements might prosper – though all, confessedly, were assisted by favourable economic conditions. Thus, the increase in middle-class incomes consequent upon falling prices and stable salaries after 1873 allowed them not only to shunt many patrons of the pit to a more fitting place – well out of sight in the upper gallery – but also to risk increases in seat prices, thereby boosting profit margins.

And so, despite Tom Robertson's death in 1871, the Bancrofts continued to prosper at the old Prince of Wales's, prettifying safe classics from Shakespeare to Sheridan with what Bancroft called 'elaborate illustration'. In 1880, following the retirement of the veteran Buckstone, they moved to the Haymarket, which he had left largely unrefurbished: they proceeded to refurbish it thoroughly, gilding the picture-frame of their proscenium arch, cunningly concealing the footlights and orchestra, and, to howls of impotent protest, pioneering the total abolition of the pit. Meanwhile, their protégé John Hare, in partnership with Madge Robertson and her husband W. H. Kendal, was winning the public's initially uncertain favour for the new Court Theatre, the same team later moving successively and successfully to the St James's and the Garrick.

In 1875 Charles Wyndham began his long association with the underground Criterion, where at first he specialized in vasectomized adaptations of French farces, before becoming his own matinee idol in middle age. Augustus Harris was soon to begin his long reign over pantomime at Drury Lane, and Richard D'Oyly Carte to take Gilbert and Sullivan's light operas in triumph from the Opera Comique to the Savoy – whence George Edwardes crossed the road to help John Hollingshead keep 'the sacred lamp of burlesque' burning at the Gaiety. J. L. Toole, taking on the little Charing Cross Theatre in King William Street in 1879, reflected the prevailing managerial self-confidence by renaming it after himself – an American fashion which found few other followers.

The promenade of the **Empire**, Leicester Square, **in 1902**. A youthful Winston **Churchill** was among those opposed to the attempts led by **Mrs** Ormiston **Chant** to close down the promenade **in 1894** (on the grounds that it **was a** haunt of 'ladies of the **town**'). Later, the theatre **housed** revue, and, after the **First** World War, musicals were performed there, until it was demolished **in** 1927 to make way for **a cinema**

Music Hall as big business

When, as the spectacular centrepiece to *A Life of Pleasure* (1893), the promenade at the Empire Theatre in Leicester Square was recreated on the stage of Drury Lane, a back-handed compliment was being paid to the famous music hall. As the notoriety of the Empire promenade confirms – it was allegedly a favoured haunt of prostitutes – music hall continued to offend the bourgeoisie, though its appeal (like that of horse-racing) united the more raffish elements of the aristocracy with the generality of the working class. This was in spite of the endeavours of those would-be respectable music-hall managers who banned alcohol from the auditorium – an auditorium in which the old, convivial clusters of tables and chairs were giving way before regular rows of fixed seating, and where performers once welcomed with the raised glass of the chairman were now identified by numbers slotted into the invasive and alienating proscenium arch.

Such palatial West End establishments as the Empire, the nearby Alhambra in Leicester Square, and later the surviving Palace on Cambridge Circus were, of course, aiming to attract customers of a different class from those who attended the humbler halls down in the East End, and there were many gradations of neighbourhood hall in between. But after 1878 all had to obtain a Certificate of Suitability by meeting minimum legal standards of safety and sanitation: and the cost of the necessary reconstruction work often required a major injection of capital. Companies were therefore floated to build new halls as well as to rebuild old – often to the designs of 'legit' theatre architects such as the prolific Frank Matcham.

Some managements also began to accrete first a local chain of halls, and then a larger circuit – the beginnings of the music-hall empires of the likes of Oswald Stoll and Edward Moss. At the same time, a divide began to open up between the top-billing stars who were able to command huge salaries to work the new circuits – Dan Leno and Marie Lloyd being probably the most familiar to emerge during this period – and their lowlier brethren, whose dispensable services were open to exploitation. A long struggle for better conditions began with the formation of the Variety Artists' Association in 1885, well before 'legitimate' players had successfully formed themselves into a union – a right at last acknowledged by the social reforms of the 1870s.

Opening bill for the New Cross Empire in 1899. Designed by the prolific Frank Matcham, this typical suburban hall had a capacity of around 2,000. Note the 'credentials of the organizers', whose capital investments are listed along with their 'present market value'

"'Tis not in mortals to command success, but we'll do more—deserve it."

THE NEW CROSS EMPIRE

NEW CROSS ROAD, S.E.

Proprietors	THE LONDON DISTRICT EMPIRE PALACES, LIMITED
Chairman	H. E. MOSS	Managing Director	OSWALD STOLL
Acting Manager	HENRY RAYMOND

ON JULY 31ST 1899

THE ABOVE PALATIAL ESTABLISHMENT

WILL OPEN TO THE PUBLIC

CREDENTIALS OF ORGANIZERS

Chairman, H. E. MOSS, is Chairman and Managing Director of similar Theatres in Glasgow, Liverpool, Birmingham, Leeds, Sheffield, Edinboro', Bradford, Hull, and the New London Hippodrome, now in course of erection, in Charing Cross Road and Cranborne Street.

The Managing Director, OSWALD STOLL, is Managing Director of similar Theatres in Nottingham, Cardiff, Swansea, Newport, Stratford, and Holloway.

The Board of Directors control the properties comprised in the following Companies:

	Capital
The Birmingham Empire Palace, Limited [Issued and Interior Capital]	£57,000
Cardiff, Newport, and Swansea Empire Palaces. Limited	£86,000
The Edinburgh Empire Palace, Limited	£60,000
The Glasgow Empire Palace, Limited (Owning the Metropole Theatre also).	£80,000
Liverpool, Leeds, and Hull Empire and Palaces, Limited (including the Bradford Empire and Alexandra Hotel).	£170,000
The London District Empire Palaces, Limited	£132,000
The London Hippodrome. Limited	£210,000
The Newcastle Empire Palace, Limited	£63,000
The Nottingham Empire Palace, Limited (Also owning the Nottingham Theatre Royal).	£76,000
The Sheffield Empire Palace, Limited	£65,000

REPRESENTING A TOTAL CAPITAL OF £999,000

THE PRESENT MARKET VALUE OF WHICH EXCEEDS

ONE MILLION AND A QUARTER, £1,250,000

THE BUILDING

From the Plans of the Eminent Architect, FRANK MATCHAM, Esq., Warwick Court, Holborn, is Handsomely Designed, Constructed upon the Latest Principles, Luxuriously Furnished, Electrically Lit, provided with Heating Apparatus, Sliding Roof, and all the Appointments that Safety, Comfort, and Elegance dictate. A Coloured Sketch of the Interior adjoins this paragraph.

METHOD OF WORKING. In these days of hurrying through life with many things to do and little time to do them in, compression becomes a desideratum. The pithy paragraph is our popular form of reading, and it is thought that the pithy programme is to be a popular form of Entertainment. It has been decided therefore to introduce

WITH WEST-END LUXURY OF SURROUNDINGS AND QUALITY OF ENTERTAINMENTS the method of

TWO COMPLETE and DISTINCT PERFORMANCES NIGHTLY.

People can often spare half an evening that can seldom or never spare a whole one, for the relief-giving lighter side of life.

THE EARLY PERFORMANCE provides distant residents with an Entertainment of satisfying length, whilst it enables them to reach home at a convenient hour. It also meets the views of those in the more immediate vicinity who prefer early hours.

THE LATE PERFORMANCE answers the requirements of persons detained late at business and who have hitherto had to pay whole prices for half Performances or forego those Entertainments altogether.

THE METHOD OF TWO PERFORMANCES NIGHTLY enables the Company to make exclusive engagements by paying to Artistes in one week as much as the Artistes earn at a combination of several Variety Theatres at each of which they appear nightly by travelling from one to another; and thus, with its associations, being in a position to engage Artistes for ONE WEEK AT EACH OF MANY ESTABLISHMENTS instead of MANY WEEKS AT ONE ESTABLISHMENT, it can present

AN ENTIRE CHANGE OF PROGRAMME EVERY WEEK.

Moreover, by punctuality and permitting no intervals or delays to steal away time, it has been found that a Programme, equal to what is usually presented at a Performance occupying a whole evening, may actually be gone through twice, and that the rapidity of so working it invests it with greater Brightness and Entertaining Power, and that this system economises the time and the money of the public without diminishing their amusement.

QUALITY OF ENTERTAINMENTS.
As an index to the standard aimed at it may be mentioned that the prospective engagements include MISS CISSIE LOFTUS, MISS VESTA TILLEY, MISS MARIE LLOYD, MISS HARRIET VERNON, MISS LOTTIE COLLINS, DAN LENO, BIONDI, EUGENE STRATTON, R. G. KNOWLES, GEORGE ROBEY, T. E. DUNVILLE, G. H. CHIRGWIN, GUS ELEN, PAUL CINQUEVALLI, and LITTLE TICH, with Leading Specialities from THE CONTINENTAL CIRQUES AND HIPPODROMES, the Stage being Spacious and Well Equipped.

THE SCENERY is specially painted by WALTER HANN, Frederick Fox, & J. B. Parker.

BOX OFFICE OPEN from July 27th, for Booking Reserved Seats.

	FIRST PERFORMANCE.	SECOND PERFORMANCE.
TIMES & PRICES	Doors open at 6.30. Curtain rises at 6.50 Curtain falls and audience leave at 8.50	Doors open at 8.55. Curtain rises at 9.10 Curtain falls and audience leave at 11.10

Private Boxes, 10/6 four persons. Extra Seats, 2s 6d. 7/6 three persons. Extra Seats, 2s.	Fauteuils, Numbered and Reserved.	Grand Circle, Numbered and Reserved.	Stalls, Highly Carpeted and fitted with Tip-up Seats.	Pit, Upholstered Seating.	Balcony, Upholstered Seating.	Gallery,
	2/-	**1/6**	**1/-**	**6d.**	**4d.**	**3d.**
Seats not guaranteed.	No money returned.	The right of refusing admission reserved.				

Oswald Stoll

New writing – and a new style of operetta

Managements in the 1780s required new writing to provide vehicles for the acting talent at their command and to satisfy the expectations of their paying public. Indeed, by the 1880s the problem of the English drama was not particularly the absence of a 'literary' output of intellectual substance – none such had existed for over a century – but rather the presence of a deeply bourgeois audience which, scornful of the hearty affirmations of melodrama, had come to prefer the enervated emotional shorthand of the 'society' style. Writers now seen as harbingers of a 'new drama' could and did get their work staged in the West End – just so long as their innovations titillated but did not seriously disturb their audiences.

The production of original work was encouraged by the international copyright agreements which now began to stem the flood of foreign imports and adaptations. The five years of protection from unauthorized translation given to foreign writers in 1852 was extended in 1875 to cover adapted pieces, and in 1887 the Berne Convention strengthened copyright arrangements between most European countries – the most important non-signatory, the United States, following with its own legislation in 1891. Some doubts remained until 1911 as to how far prior publication of a play might endanger performing rights, and this led to numerous one-off 'copyright performances': but the new arrangements did help to encourage reading editions, alongside the ubiquitous acting texts of Lacy and French – whose technical jargon and abbreviations proved forbidding to the uninitiated.

As commissions to adapt foreign plays began to dry up, some writers unwisely made bids for posterity by attempting those five-act historical tragedies in blank-verse for which posterity was presumed to have an unquenchable thirst. As Irving wryly observed in 1880, many of the unknown authors who submitted such works to him by the score 'proudly claimed that they made a point of never going near a theatre'. Even such a piece as Joan of Arc (1871), by the thoroughly professional veteran Tom Taylor, has not only failed to impress posterity ever since, but owed such notoriety as it enjoyed in its own day to the realism with which the saintly maid was burnt at the stake.

Among the few writers who achieved both an immediate and more enduring fame, W. S. Gilbert occupies a special place. His 'fairy' comedies for the Kendals at the Haymarket in the early 1870s were, improbably, satiric burlesques in blank-verse in which Gilbert made audiences laugh at their own hypocrisies by transplanting them to fairyland. Despite a prolific early career (in 1872, for example, no fewer than five

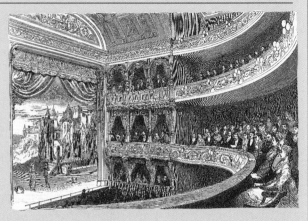

The Savoy Theatre, during the opening production, *Patience*, in 1881. So closely were Gilbert and Sullivan's light operas associated with Richard D'Oyly Carte's new theatre that they are often known collectively as the 'Savoy operas'. The theatre was the first to incorporate electric lighting, and in its decorations and colouring it was more subdued than earlier Victorian houses. It was to the Savoy that

J. E. Vedrenne and Granville Barker moved in 1907 from the Court, staging the first London production of Shaw's *Caesar and Cleopatra*. Between 1912 and 1914 Barker staged here his innovatory productions of Shakespeare, further described on page 271. The theatre was reconstructed in art deco style in 1929, but severely damaged by fire in 1990

of his plays were running in London theatres), at first he won more respect than acclaim. His satirical edge was a touch too sharp for comfort, needing not so much to be blunted as to be melodically honed to the music of Arthur Sullivan.

Although John Hollingshead first teamed the pair in the over-erudite Thespis at the Adelphi in 1871, it was only when Richard D'Oyly Carte, in search of a native equivalent to the French opera bouffe, persuaded Gilbert to adapt his Trial by Jury for a musical setting at the Royalty in 1875 that the long, symbiotic association began, finding a first permanent home at the Opera Comique from 1877 to 1881. Then the team transferred along with their latest production, Patience, to the new Savoy Theatre, a slight but salubrious step westwards along the Strand. G. K. Chesterton described the characteristic tone of what have ever since been known as the 'Savoy operas' as capturing that 'half-unreal detachment in which some Victorians came at last to smile at all opinions including their own'.

THE LEADING WRITERS

Arthur Wing Pinero, whose later 'problem plays' contributed to the theatrical debate over the 'woman question' (to which we shall turn in the next chapter), made an earlier and arguably more deservedly enduring reputation as the writer of a string of successful farces, largely for the Court Theatre. From *The Magistrate* in 1885 through *The Schoolmistress* and *Dandy Dick* to *The Amazons* in 1893, he rang proficient changes on that distinctively British pattern whereby would-be adultery and its exposure are secondary to the dread of embarrassment and social gaffes – a dramatic emphasis also happily inoffensive to the Lord Chamberlain.

Unlike many other farceurs, Pinero gave the impression of being almost fond of characters who were often only a degree or so offset from reality. George Rowell compares the types with those of the Aldwych farces of the 1920s – among them a 'pure and persecuted husband', a 'knowing man of the world' with his 'vacuous companion', and a 'formidable matron'. These were played respectively by Arthur Cecil, John Clayton, Fred Kerr, and Mrs John Wood – a team whose regular 'lines', well-developed sense of ensemble, and consummate timing must have endowed Pinero's writing with the same ring of confidence that Robertson Hare, Tom Walls, Ralph Lynn, and Mary Brough were later to give Ben Travers.

Among those considered leading writers at the time, Henry Arthur Jones cuts the least appealing figure today. The equivocal stance of his 'problem plays' – and their no less equivocal solutions – must, like Pinero's, await later discussion: meanwhile, in his early work his success depended upon combining an old-fashioned melodramatic instinct – well-matched to the temperament of the actor-manager Wilson Barrett at the Princess's – with a solid storytelling technique and a good ear for dialogue. However, such structural skills were too often blighted by a pervasive and invasive social snobbery – perhaps inspired by contempt for his own petty-bourgeois origins – as early exemplified in *Saints and Sinners* (1884).

Jones went on to specialize variously in dramas of thwarted or distorted passion, such as *Judah* (1890), and old-fashioned intrigue comedies of which *The Triumph of the Philistines* (1895) is a typical and *The Liars* (1897) a rare superior example. Unfortunately his satire was not only heavy-handed, but betrayed an almost clinical detestation of the common people – also evident in his distaste for 'The Theatre of the Mob', as Jones dubbed it in one of his numerous polemics for a higher drama. Elsewhere, a shrill anti-clericalism sits oddly with an awed reverence for high society – any intended criticism of which is effectively muted by his insistence that those of lowly origins, inhabiting 'the dark places of the earth', are beneath the notice of art. Later, he was to prophesy that 'the epitaph on . . . all this realistic business will be – it does not matter what happens in kitchen-middens'.

Oscar Wilde was outraging and amusing fashionable London by strutting his aesthetic stuff as early as 1881, when Gilbert parodied such greenery-yallery decadence (as it was viewed by the properly grey majority) in *Patience*. Although, with nice incongruity, Wilde was a cousin of W. G. Wills, it was only with *Lady*

Arthur Cecil as Posket, *The Magistrate* in Pinero's farce of that name. Seen at the Court in 1885, this was one of the sequence of plays at that theatre with which Arthur W. Pinero (1855–1934) consolidated his early reputation as a farceur. After flirting with a seduction theme in *The Profligate* (1890), he turned, most famously in *The Second Mrs Tanqueray* (1893), to social dramas and 'problem plays': but these have generally worn less well than either the farces or such later comedies as *Trelawny of the 'Wells'* (1898) and *The Gay Lord Quex* (1899). He wrote inextinguishably on, but was out of touch with the style and values of the post-Victorian world

George Alexander as Jack
Worthing, in mourning for his
pretended brother Ernest, in
the first production of Wilde's
The Importance of Being Earnest
at the St James's in 1895. In
an interview published one
month before the opening in
February, and four months
before the libel action which
changed the course of his life,
Wilde declared of the play: 'It
is exquisitely trivial, a delicate
bubble of fancy, and it has its
philosophy . . . that we should
treat all the trivial things of life
very seriously, and all the
serious things of life with
sincere and studied frivolity'

Windermere's Fan (1892) and *A Woman of No Importance* (1893) that he found
his own, very different kind of theatrical voice: for within the ostensibly well-made
structures of these plays social norms are obliquely questioned by means of that
calculated confusion of satire, cynicism, and delight in paradox which was already
shaping the Wildean inverted epigram.

Wilde's masterpiece, *The Importance of Being Earnest* (1895), which pushed this
technique to its comic limits, is a farce rooted in the native stock of situation and
mistaken identity rather than in threatened adultery – though here sublime aristocratic insouciance substitutes for the precarious poise which Pinero's middle-class
characters strive to maintain. The play is, indeed, in part a parodic reaction to the
Robertsonian style of understatement, still dwindling into the drawing-room mini-
aturism of the likes of James Albery: but where those authors believed that their
neatly-turned phrases aspired to some ultimate truth, Wilde delighted in ultimate
paradox, avowedly aiming at an 'art divorced from life'.

Wilde was the first in a line of homosexual dramatists whose legally prescribed
distance from accepted social and sexual norms lends ironic weight to their latter-
day comedies of manners. In *Earnest*, his own delight in outraging the proprieties
gave us an inimitable slice of art divorced from life – but, as life divorced him so
cruelly from art, it was also to enmesh him in the scandal and imprisonment which
(compounded, it is now believed, by the debilitating progress of syphilis) led to his
premature death.

The would-be successful social critic had to find a more protective persona: and
it was through his genius in creating just such a persona that Bernard Shaw secured
his dominance over the drama of the ensuing decades. Shaw was, of course, a novelist and critic well before he found success in the theatre – and by the time he pitched
himself into the critical front-line in the early 1890s two of his contemporaries,
Clement Scott and William Archer, had already staked out positions as heads of the
opposing forces in a new battle of 'ancients' versus 'moderns'.

ANCIENTS VERSUS MODERNS

Scott, the theatre critic of the *Daily Telegraph*, who also edited the leading general-
interest theatre journal of the day, *The Theatre*, headed the traditionalists, while
Archer had sounded his optimistic clarion call for the new in *English Dramatists of
To-day* as early as 1882. Writers such as Robert Lowe and Percy Fitzgerald were at
the same time introducing some scholarly discipline into the writing of theatre
history and biography, which in the past had been largely impressionistic when not
unashamedly anecdotal. Lowe also produced his massive *Bibliographical Account of
English Theatrical Literature*, the first serious attempt to review everything
published about the theatre – as valuably distinguished from treatments of the
drama as if it were a branch of literature.

Even the theory of acting, which had not much concerned either the profession
or its critics of late, began to be debated with some liveliness. As long ago as the

1770s the French encyclopedist and playwright Denis Diderot had written in defence of objectivity as opposed to emotional identification in acting: now, Walter Pollock's translation of Diderot's work as *The Paradox of Acting* (1883) became central to a dispute which found Diderot's fellow-countryman and disciple, Constant Coquelin (who had published his own study of intellectually controlled acting technique in 1880), ranged against no less an authority than Henry Irving. The issues – and the opinions offered by these and numerous other actors – were summarized and analyzed in Archer's aptly titled *Masks or Faces?* in 1888.

Thanks to ever-speedier means of transport, this international interchange of ideas was increasingly complemented by the cross-fertilization of theatrical activity. Irving and Wyndham took full companies to America where earlier they would have taken only themselves, while Sarah Bernhardt with the company of the Comédie Française visited London from Paris. From the USA came Edwin Booth to play Othello (to an Iago which far better fitted Irving's temperament than his earlier Moor), from Italy the great tragedian Tomasso Salvini, and from Germany the company of the Duke of Saxe-Meiningen – often regarded as the first director in the modern sense, whose meticulous concern with ensemble playing certainly influenced Irving's treatment of his Lyceum crowd scenes (illustrated on page 252).

Then in 1891 a visit from André Antoine's Théâtre Libre from Paris inspired the creation of a similar experimental art theatre in London, the Independent Theatre, by the critic J. T. Grein. This provided a living platform on which the 'moderns' might focus their attack against the 'ancients' through their promotion of the already ageing Norwegian dramatist Henrik Ibsen – among whose champions were both Shaw, whose *Quintessence of Ibsenism* also appeared in 1891, and Archer, whose first complete edition of his works in translation was then in preparation.

However, for most British audiences Ibsen remained merely an obscure dramatist from an obscure country whom such intellectuals had made it their business to promote well above the heads of their good selves – and who might therefore consider himself lucky to have had his *Doll's House* redeemed by the use of its happy ending in Henry Arthur Jones's version of 1884, coyly retitled *Breaking a Butterfly*. Janet Achurch acted in Archer's more faithful translation in 1889, and this was duly pronounced 'ibscene' by Scott – who two years later was scandalized beyond such punning put-downs into his legendary scream of outrage against the first English performance of Ibsen's *Ghosts*. Staged as the opening production of the Independent Theatre at the Royalty, on 13 March 1891, this was at once condemned by Scott as 'an open drain; a loathsome sore unbandaged; a dirty act done publicly' – and anything phoney about the war between 'ancients' and 'moderns' was clearly over.

Wilde's 'studied frivolity' as ironic liberation: Janet Achurch as Nora Helmer, dancing the tarantella in the middle act of Ibsen's *A Doll's House*. This pen and ink drawing was made when the play was staged for thirty performances at the Avenue Theatre in 1892 – one of no fewer than five London revivals during the 1890s

CHAPTER 17 _Romance and Realism_

Opposite: the fall from the tower of the title character in The tension between Victorian verities and Edwardian frivolities was already perceptible when, in 1901, the portly Prince of Wales belatedly succeeded to the throne. A world ever more closely resembling our own had been ushered in as much by the arrival of primitive film and popular halfpenny newspapers in the 1890s as by the activities of trades unionists and the suffragettes at home and intimations of revolution abroad in the following decade – which also saw the parliamentary struggle of the last great Liberal government to lay the foundations of a Welfare State. Already the rights and wrongs of the Boer War, bridging the old century and the new, had divided the nation, and soon the First World War (by present-day standards a conflict somewhat short on technology, but profligate of suffering and death) was to cast its long, engulfing shadow.

Opposite: the fall from the
tower of the title character in
The Master Builder, by Henrik
Ibsen (1828–1906). This
illustration (from the _Pall Mall
Budget_) is of the first British
production at the Trafalgar
Theatre in 1893. Watching
Herbert Waring's Solness is
his youthful hero-worshipper
Hilda Wangel, played by the
anglicized American actress
Elizabeth Robins (1862–1952),
who held the British stage
rights to most of Ibsen's plays.
Among other of his leading
female roles, she played
Martha Bernick in _Pillars of
Society_ (1889), Mrs Linde in
A Doll's House (1891), the title
role in _Hedda Gabler_ (1891),
Rebecca West in _Rosmersholm_
(1893), Asta Allmers in _Little
Eyolf_ (1896), and Ella
Rentheim in _John Gabriel
Borkman_ (1896). Controversy
over the true merits of the
Norwegian dramatist
dominated critical discussion
during this period. Though
his cause was championed
both by his first translator
William Archer and by the
young Bernard Shaw, he was
virulently attacked by such
conservative writers as the
ageing but influential theatre
critic of the _Daily Telegraph_,
Clement Scott

THEATRE AS A 'SOCIAL LUXURY'

In the face of all this, commercial theatre remained cosily complacent, concerned to insulate the class interests it served. An Italian observer, Mario Borsa, writing in 1908 in _The English Stage of Today_, summed it up: 'The entire organization of the theatre reflects that special and aristocratic conception of its status which is the point of view of its patrons.' In consequence, although London was 'overrun with theatres', there was, in Borsa's judgement, a pervasive 'intellectual apathy' behind the 'lack of good prose drama' – or, as even that most Anglophilic of immigrants, Henry James, had to concede, the theatre in England was 'a social luxury and not an artistic necessity'.

Such contemporary comments should serve to caution us against the selective recall to which some theatre historians have been prone as they earnestly trace the ascendancy of a 'new drama'. This, although it undeniably existed, was in truth written by and for a mere handful of intellectuals – while the West End theatre continued to cater to audiences who were either unconcerned with or actively seeking diversion from political and industrial struggles symptomatic of profound social discontent. Ibsenism may have been as quintessential to Bernard Shaw as socialism: but neither was considered a fit subject in polite conversation.

The nation was becoming no less intellectually than it was socially divided. The 'moderns' in the theatre, as in all the arts, were by and large radical in their political as in their artistic beliefs, just as they not only held but were now able to propound a rationalist philosophy which would have been unmentionable (if not unthinkable) a bare thirty years earlier. Yet they still sought to storm the citadels of that 'special and aristocratic' theatre, with little thought of reaching a popular audience through its own forms of art – of which the music hall, as we shall see, was enjoying a proud heyday before its fall – or of touching the habits and tastes of other than the well-to-do.

Johnston Forbes-Robertson (1853–1937) in the role of Hamlet – which he first played, at the age of forty-four, in 1897. Seeing this performance is said to have inspired Shaw to write *Caesar and Cleopatra*, in which Forbes-Robertson eventually played in 1907. Generally recognized as the inheritor of Irving's mantle, Forbes-Robertson, like Lewis Waller (opposite) had a 'fallback' role, in his case that of the Stranger in Jerome's mystical melo-drama *The Passing of the Third Floor Back* – although, perhaps to the envy of Waller, Forbes-Robertson could count no less on the enduring popularity of his *Hamlet*. According to Hesketh Pearson, biographer of *The Last Actor-Managers*, Charles Wyndham could similarly rely on reviving *David Garrick*, Hare on *A Pair of Spectacles*, Alexander on *The Importance of Being Earnest*, Tree on *Trilby*, Martin-Harvey on *The Only Way*, and Fred Terry on *The Scarlet Pimpernel*

In the West End theatres, the curtain generally rose at eight o'clock, to permit patrons to dine beforehand, and was down in time for 'carriages at eleven' and a late supper. Evening dress was *de rigeuer* except in the residual pit and the gallery, whose lowlier patrons were generally assigned their own entrances in adjoining alleyways – and so discouraged from joining the fashionable foyer throng. Certainly, they were not expected to have much to contribute to the plays themselves: thus, Arthur Pinero claimed that 'a certain order of ideas expressed or questions discussed' was simply beyond the powers 'of the English lower-middle and lower classes' to articulate. And it is ironic that even Bernard Shaw, for all his declared socialism, in practice seemed to concur – his occasional working-class characters being drawn either from the long typology of clever servants, such as Enry Straker in *Man and Superman*, or conceived as good-natured but indolent buffoons, as when Alfred Doolittle in *Pygmalion* fulfils the expectations of his charactonym (a convention now rare in the 'realistic' drama).

THE ACTOR-MANAGER AS MATINEE IDOL

Often, when dramatists strayed from idealizing the respectable classes in their contemporary drawing-rooms, it was to transplant their value system into the realms of romance: and the last great generation of actor-managers increasingly found it expedient to cast themselves in the choicest romantic leads. It was George Alexander who began the trend in 1896 when, in the face of scepticism from his contemporaries, he accepted Edward Rose's adaptation of Anthony Hope's *The Prisoner of Zenda*, himself doubling the roles of Rudolf Rassendyll and the King – thereby restoring the fortunes of the St James's Theatre, which he managed from 1891 until his death in 1918.

But sometimes actors found themselves trapped within the romantic personae they created. Lewis Waller, for all his personal modesty and classical ambitions, thus came to be increasingly identified with just two parts – those of D'Artagnan in the most successful of numerous adaptations of Dumas's *The Three Musketeers* (1898), and of Booth Tarkington's eponymous *Monsieur Beaucaire* (1902). To Waller is usually given the doubtful credit of becoming the first matinee idol – his faithful followers even wearing badges proclaiming that they were 'Keen on Waller' (a slogan which quickly gave way to its unfortunate acronym).

Among his fellow matinee idols, none was a better physical embodiment of the 'interesting' romantic type than Johnston Forbes-Robertson. This 'dreamy, poetic-looking creature' – as he was described by Ellen Terry, who had played opposite him as early as 1874 in *The Wandering Heir* – was already in his forties when, in Irving's absence, he triumphed as Romeo to Mrs Patrick Campbell's Juliet in 1894: and three years later he gave what was generally acclaimed as a definitive Hamlet for the *fin de siècle* generation, causing Irving to forswear acting the part again.

Forbes-Robertson's last great success was as the enigmatically beneficent Stranger in Jerome K. Jerome's *The Passing of the Third Floor Back* (1908), a sort of bourgeoisified Bloomsbury equivalent to the mysterious vagrant in Maxim Gorky's *Lower Depths*. The self-denial personified by Jerome's Stranger was approved as a vicarious virtue by audiences not much given to its practice: thus, no less popular was the role of the selfless Sydney Carton which John Martin-Harvey had carved for himself at the Lyceum (again while Irving was on tour) in a dramatization of Charles Dickens's *A Tale of Two Cities*, retitled *The Only Way* (1899). Unfortunately the character so overwhelmed Martin-Harvey's reputation that, to borrow Bryan Forbes's apt metaphor, 'his many journeys to the tumbrel led to a guillotining of what might have been a more varied and distinguished career'.

Towering above all these, with his usual deceptively indolent air, was Herbert Beerbohm Tree, who managed the Haymarket from 1887, just eight years after his professional debut, until he built the new Her Majesty's Theatre across the road in 1897. Tree produced Shakespeare with a legendary extravagance to which we shall return, while as an actor he preferred larger-than-life characters ranging from Falstaff to Fagin. Even when he found himself bowing to the new taste for romance, he usually managed to tune-in a character to his own temperamental wavelength – as with his Svengali in Paul Potter's adaptation of George du Maurier's *Trilby* (1895).

Tree was also prepared to take occasional risks on less formulaic stuff, with varying degrees of success. When he staged Ibsen's *Enemy of the People* in 1893 it barely graduated from matinees to evenings, achieving a mere seven performances: but in 1914 it was Tree who gave Shaw his first great commercial success with *Pygmalion* – in which Mrs Patrick Campbell, playing Eliza, completed an unholy trinity of creatively tensile personalities. However, among the actor-managers it was George Alexander who most consistently preferred new British plays, and who staged at the St James's Wilde's *Lady Windermere's Fan* (1892) and Pinero's *The Second Mrs Tanqueray* (1893). Both plays raised and, in the end, ducked the issue of the sexual 'double standard' – which brings us to the one serious issue with which West End audiences did (as it were) flirt: the 'woman question'.

THE 'WOMAN QUESTION'

As pursued in the drama, the debate over the 'woman question' largely reflected a patriarchal concern to give the matter serious attention and then to come down solidly in favour of the status quo. Sydney Grundy (a dependable churner-out of overly well-made plays after the manner of the French boulevardist Sardou) thus wrote an eponymous put-down of *The New Woman* for the Comedy Theatre in 1894, the year in which the phrase entered popular usage, in the clear expectation that his audience would share his own conclusion – that she was really 'as old as Eve, and just as hungry for the fruit she plucked'.

Of course, the prevailing sexual hypocrisy touched the theatre no less than the rest of society. In *The Case of Rebellious Susan* (1894), another of that topical cluster of plays of the early 1890s which deigned to notice the 'woman question',

Lewis Waller (1860–1915) as d'Artagnan in *The Three Musketeers* (1898). Waller was embarrassed by his reputation as supposedly the first of the great 'matinee idols': he much preferred Shakespearean or light comedy roles, but found himself (like several other of the great actor-managers of the period) inescapably identified with the romantic leads his fans preferred. ('Will no one', he is said to have pleaded, 'rid me of these turbulent priestesses?') He was also greatly admired in Booth Tarkington's *Monsieur Beaucaire* (1902), playing the even-tempered Frenchman of the title, whose exquisite, debonaire wit gallantly puts down ill-bred English rivals

Henry Arthur Jones, while calmly affirming the inevitability of male philander-ing, set out to show how a wife who tries to pay back her husband in kind comes to grief, repentance, and acceptance of the woman's role – to 'forgive the wretches till they learn constancy'. The manager of the Criterion, Charles Wyndham, refused to allow his leading lady, Mary Moore, to utter the one line which would have confirmed Susan's adultery: but in real life, though very unobtrusively, Wyndham had long been committing adultery with Mary Moore. Like Wyndham, Tree managed to acquire a knighthood while at the same time breeding children faster with his mistress than his wife, and personifying the ideal of the Edwardian male described by Frank Harris as 'adultery with all home comforts'.

Ironically, the profession of actress was meanwhile becoming, if not exactly respectable, at least a good deal more acceptable than it had been – although no less an actress than Ellen Terry had bolstered all the worst Victorian expectations of her calling by strewing an estranged husband, a lover, and illegitimate children in her wake. (Careless of the respectability vicariously restored by her association with Irving, she took a third husband half her age in her sixtieth year, and was duly made to wait until three years before her death in 1928 – thirty-three years after Irving's knighthood – to be created a Dame.)

Successive census returns reveal that whereas in 1851 there had been around half as many actresses as actors, by 1881 women were outnumbering men in the profession, as they have continued to do ever since: precisely, their numbers rose from 891 in 1861 to 3,696 thirty years later. However happily such figures may reflect the improved social standing of the profession as a whole, and a wider acceptance that actresses were not instantly to be identified as whores, it was, none the less, largely the male dramatist's typology of womanhood which deter-mined the parts they were permitted to play.

When Robertsonian society dramas had begun both to emulate and to educate in polite behaviour, the public tendency to confuse manners displayed on stage and off encouraged the assumption that a socially acceptable role reflected an actress's 'real' nature. So while the American Adah Isaacs Menken, in achieving a *succès de scandale* with her notorious breeches role as Mazeppa, was behaving as might be expected of a foreigner, English actresses wishing to advance their social standing had followed the lead of Helen Faucit – who had made a 'good' marriage and been able to retire early by specializing in roles which identified her with the Victorian ideal of demure, domesticated womanhood. Even Ellen Terry enjoyed one of her greatest successes, as Imogen in *Cymbeline*, in part because the role embodied the untainted female virtue deemed desirable by the Victorian patriarchy.

And so, when Clement Scott, nearing his dotage in 1898, warned that 'it is nearly impossible for a woman to remain pure who adopts the stage as a profession', the collective outrage of the London managements secured the old man's dismissal from his influential position on the *Daily Telegraph*. But male playwrights continued to assume that in the serious affairs of life their sex was, as of right, cast in the decision-making role: thus, in such products of the patriarchy as Jones's later plays *The Liars* (1897) and *Mrs Dane's Defence* (1900), young reprobates are saved from the clutches of 'women with a past' in order to fulfil their destinies as the providers and legislators of society.

Thoughtful actresses were well aware that the roles they were given to play made them haplessly complicit in the way that their sex was presented on stage. Even the vaguely supportive Pinero deeming it necessary to convert his title-character in *The Notorious Mrs Ebbsmith* (1895) from a 'woman agitator' with 'original independent ideas' (as her creator, Mrs Patrick Campbell, described her) into a creature of 'Bible-reading inertia' in the last act.

So a growing number of women began to write their own plays – a task few had successfully attempted since the early eighteenth century, despite (or perhaps because of) the pre-eminence of women in the less public form of the novel. And, with the predominantly male breed of actor-managers unsympathetic (as much on account of the absence of central roles for themselves as from ingrained prejudice), women had also to involve themselves in management – as did Lena Ashwell, when she took over the Kingsway Theatre in 1907.

In the following year was formed the Actresses' Franchise League, which offered active – and activist – support to the campaign for women's suffrage. As in the days of Chartism, sympathetic performers would sugar the propagandist pill at meetings and rallies – at first with solo acts, then with specially written plays. One of the best of these, a collaboration between Cicely Hamilton and 'Christopher' St John, female partner to Ellen Terry's daughter Edith Craig, was a swift-moving farce entitled *How the Vote Was Won* (1909), which fulfilled the anticipatory promise of its title by showing women taking men at their word – and completely overwhelming them with demands for the 'protection' they claimed as their prerogative.

A more conventionally prestigious outcome of the League's activities was its members' reluctantly-conceded participation in the gala celebrations of 1911 for the Coronation of King George V – in which, ironically but imaginatively, they presented a masque by Ben Jonson, *The Vision of Delight*. And some women prominent in the movement went on to form permanent companies – most notably Inez Bensusan, who mounted a successful women's season at the Coronet in 1913, and Edith Craig, whose Pioneer Players, formed in the following year, managed to survive beyond the First World War.

PROBLEM PLAYS – AND POPULAR PLAYS

Other women's plays were more orthodox in structure if not in theme, and probably neither Cicely Hamilton, whose *Diana of Dobson's* was staged by Ashwell at the Kingsway in 1908, or Githa Sowerby, whose *Rutherford and Son* enjoyed a full season's run at the Vaudeville in 1912, would have objected to her

Opposite: Ellen Terry (1847–1928) as Imogen in *Cymbeline*. Playing opposite Irving's Iachimo in the Lyceum production of 1896, she had to embody a Victorian ideal of constancy in the face of doubts and temptations – to become, in Swinburne's words, 'the most adorable woman ever created by God or man'. Terry's genius added some mercurial spirit to the character, but the patriarchal expectations which confined her were as much part of Irving's acting style as of her audience's life style. Shaw warned her of 'an idiotic paragon of virtue produced by Shakespeare's *views* of what a woman ought to be'

work being labelled a 'problem play' – though it was with malice aforethought that Grundy had coined the term in the 1890s to describe the collision between the belated British discovery of naturalism and that discussion or illustration of a specific social 'issue' which so often distinguished its dramatic expression.

Of the continental 'slice-of-life' realism of Zola – as more immediately of Gerhard Hauptmann's *The Weavers* or Gorky's *The Lower Depths* – there was very little trace in the British theatre: indeed, such rare examples as spring to mind were products either of the women's movement or of the more down-to earth provincial theatre (to which we shall shortly turn). And so it was, for example, that D. H. Lawrence's vivid depictions of a coal-mining community in *A Collier's Friday Night*, *The Daughter-in-Law*, and *The Widowing of Mrs Holroyd* – all of which were written before 1912 – remained unperformed for over fifty years.

Predictably, the box sets which entrapped the characters of the 'new drama' more often than not represented domestic or business interiors not dissimilar from those in which their audiences passed their lives – or aspired so to do. So while Bernard Shaw wryly acknowledged that the 'problems' identified in his *Widowers' Houses* or in *Mrs Warren's Profession* – respectively slum landlordism and prostitution – qualified them as 'Plays Unpleasant', not one of their scenes is set in a slum or a brothel. Rather than in any closer visual (or for that matter verbal) approximation to the 'real' – or, more precisely, much sense that it should be other than bourgeois in its dramaturgic boundaries – it was largely in a changed perception of character that naturalism in the new drama was now manifesting itself

In melodrama (as indeed in society drama) character had been largely a function of plot – the product of changes rung, often arbitrarily, upon a set of immutable traits. The assumptions behind the received rules which governed this socio-dramatic decorum were either duly fulfilled, or simply inverted – as when aristocrats are turned into villains, or labourers are endowed with nobility of spirit. Naturalism, on the other hand, presented character as it presumed it to be formed in life – as a composite *effect* of heredity and environment. In this it became, however, a mode not much less deterministic than classical tragedy.

Thus, while it is clearly more 'realistic' that past actions rather than plot mechanics should be seen as the driving force behind present events, man's destiny appears no less inescapable when it is governed by birth and social circumstance than when ruled by an implacable fate. And so a sense of inevitability pervades even the choicest products of the new naturalism – whether twisted towards tragedy as by Ibsen in *Ghosts*, or towards comedy as by Shaw in *Man and Superman*. Despite the best intentions of the dramatists, this could not but bolster an audience's feelings that, however imperfect the world might be, there was not much that they personally could do about it.

It is not surprising, then, that in the works of such writers as Alfred Sutro, St John Hankin, and the emergent Somerset Maugham, native naturalism should have integrated itself so soon and so seamlessly with the old 'society drama'. And even while the freer-spirited among the new dramatists were trying to broaden its horizons – Granville Barker, for example, through the unresolved dilemma of *The Voysey Inheritance* (1905), or Galsworthy through the egalitarian concerns of *Strife* (1909) and *Justice* (1910) – on the Continent the creative energies of the style were already on the wane.

Henrik Ibsen had thus written his last play in 1899, by which time Alfred Jarry had strangled individual psychology almost at birth in the proto-absurdist *Ubu Roi*, August Strindberg was already moving into his expressionistic phase, and Maurice Maeterlinck was sparking symbolism into fitful dramatic life. The closest counterpart the British theatre could muster was Stephen Phillips – whom William Archer, with what proved to be undue optimism, acclaimed as a new Milton for his high poetic dramas such as *Herod* (1900), *Ulysses* (1902), and, most notably, *Paolo and Francesca* (1902). Both Alexander and Tree briefly took him up, but his work soon floundered into high-sounding incoherence.

The theatrically enduring plays of the period often tell us truths in their authors' despite. Thus, Brandon Thomas skilfully energized that most perennial

Poster for the first production of J. M. Barrie's perennial Christmas show, *Peter Pan*, at the Duke of York's Theatre, 1904. Barrie (1860–1937) wrote other, more 'grown-up' whimsies, such as *Quality Street* (1902) and *Mary Rose* (1920), but these have weathered less well than his gentle social satires, notably *The Admirable Crichton* (1902) *What Every Woman Knows* (1908), and *Dear Brutus* (1917), where his chronic sentimentality is redeemed by imagination and an insistent, insidious charm

of farces, *Charley's Aunt* (1892), by blending mild sexual titillation into his even milder satire upon social and mercenary ambitions: while this was sufficient to ensure the play's contemporary success, today we can relish, too, its understated, perhaps sublimated uncertainties over gender role and the ageing process.

Other uncertainties, social rather than sexual, lie beneath the mannered surface of James Barrie's *The Admirable Crichton* (1902), whose titular paragon of a butler, his household marooned on a desert island, assumes the master's role only to withdraw into his 'proper place' with the return to normalcy. Even so, Squire Bancroft, as recorded by A. E. W. Mason, was surely not alone in feeling that such a 'juxtaposition of the drawing room and the servants' hall' was 'a very painful subject'. And the even more enduringly successful *Peter Pan* (1904) is, for all its whimsical pleasures, no less painful in the truths it tells, whether about Barrie's own psyche – or about a patriarchal society which was already gearing up to fight a world war according to the ethics of the preparatory school.

The relative popularity of writers we might today consider of greater importance is instructive. Figures collated by the critic Ian Clarke indicate that although plays by Shaw enjoyed 2,568 performances between 1890 and 1919, Jones notched up a total of 3,690, and Pinero no fewer than 4,834 – while Galsworthy and Barker managed a mere 290 and 231 respectively. Shaw, who actually overtook his rivals in the final decade, was thus alone among the 'new' dramatists in breaking into the commercial sector, and so making an impact upon an audience beyond the intellectual elite: but it took him well over a decade after his first play reached the stage, and a good deal of conscious self-publicizing – not to mention the staking out of acceptable boundaries – to establish a platform from which to do so.

THE SELF-FASHIONING OF BERNARD SHAW

All through the 1890s Shaw had thus remained more influential as a critic than as a dramatist, while meanwhile calculatedly fashioning himself as a cross between a socialist *enfant terrible* (albeit in early middle age) and a prototype of what we would today call a media celebrity. In 1898, when only two of his seven *Plays Pleasant and Unpleasant* had been performed, he also took the then unusual step of publishing them in a nicely-presented reading edition, apparently as the only way of guaranteeing them a reasonable circulation. For his fortunes as a performed playwright were at first inseparable from the activities of the little play-producing societies which, since the creation of the Independent Theatre by J. T. Grein in 1891, had been attempting to emulate the work of the 'free theatres' of continental Europe – and which played (in borrowed theatres) to audiences which, however critically receptive, were usually very small indeed.

For most of its six-year existence the main concern of the Independent Theatre was with the work of little-known foreign dramatists (Ibsen of course among them), but it had also launched Shaw's belated dramatic career in 1892 with a production of *Widowers' Houses*. Its mantle was inherited first by the New

From the first production of Shaw's *Man and Superman*, staged in 1905 during the Vedrenne-Barker management of the Court: Ann Whitefield and Jack Tanner, the couple drawn irresistibly together by the 'life force', were played by Lillah McCarthy (also seen as Viola on page 271) and her future husband, Granville Barker – here in distinctly Shavian guise. Barker only adopted the more familiar hyphenated form following his second marriage, when, at his new wife's instigation, he abandoned the stage – but produced the valuable series of *Prefaces to Shakespeare*

Century Theatre, formed in 1897 by Elizabeth Robins, a pioneer of the Ibsenite as of the women's movement, and then, more enduringly – indeed, until the very eve of the First World War – by the Stage Society, which gave Shaw renewed exposure with its opening production of *You Never Can Tell* in 1899. In the following year came the premiere of *Candida* – in which the role of Marchbanks was played by the then rising actor and aspirant playwright Harley Granville Barker.

It was when Granville Barker entered into managerial partnership with J. E. Vedrenne at the Court Theatre from 1904 to 1907 that Shaw's work began to reach a wider public. No fewer than eleven of his plays were produced, firmly establishing his reputation as a 'new' but entertaining comic dramatist, while the Vedrenne-Barker seasons also presented work by Barker himself, Galsworthy, and Hankin – not to mention Euripides, three of whose tragedies (in new translations by Gilbert Murray) were restored to the live theatre after centuries of confinement to the study. Somerset Maugham followed in Shaw's footsteps, though not his politics, making his name with productions first by the Stage Society and then at the Court – whence *Lady Frederick* transferred to the West End in 1907, to be joined within a year by three more of Maugham's finely-honed yet hollow-centred society dramas.

Shaw himself had by now entered heartily into what was to prove his lifelong role as licensed jester to a social system which, as a self-proclaimed communist, he supposedly despised. Since he also believed that the sex drive was controlled by 'creative evolution' (which he theatricalized as the 'life force') any love interest in his comedies tends towards coyness and the encouragement of good breeding – understood as a matter not of armorial bearings but of eugenic engineering. In this as in other matters the Shavian 'tone of voice' is inimitable: but so far from filling his plays with spokespeople for himself, as popular legend asserts, Shaw gives the devil considerably more than his due in the dramatized debates which flesh out his plots, serious issues all too frequently being reduced to rhetorical diversions in the process.

Shaw's topical satire upon the Irish question, *John Bull's Other Island* (1904), was thus greatly enjoyed by most of its supposed targets – the Prime Minister, Arthur Balfour, actually paying a return visit. And although in *Major Barbara* (1905) Shaw dared to delve so far into the sanitized lower depths of London as a Salvation Army hostel, his delight in dialectical paradox ensures that he ends up apparently in favour of armament production as a species of social service. Only in *Heartbreak House*, written during the First World War when armament production was no longer a laughing matter, does a raw nerve of honesty seem touched within himself, creating a more contemplative, bittersweet mood which the English later came to insist on regarding as Chekhovian. Thus far, however, few had so much as heard of Anton Chekhov.

The little play-producing societies were believed, by virtue of their club status, to enjoy immunity from the Lord Chamberlain's continuing powers of censorship. It is not simply that *Ghosts* would not have been produced in the commercial theatre: it *could* not have been, since the Examiner of Plays in the Lord Chamberlain's Office had made it clear that he would refuse a licence – as he later refused one for *Mrs Warren's Profession* in 1902 and for Barker's *Waste* in 1907. An intensive and widely-supported campaign against the censorship resulted in a parliamentary Committee of Enquiry in 1909, which took voluminous evidence from the great, the good, and the opinionated before deciding to leave things more or less as they were – to the relief of the commercial managers, who had no wish to second-guess an audience's tastes, and who valued the protection a licence seemed to afford.

THE REPERTORY MOVEMENT

In other respects, attempts to 'organize the theatre', if not quite as irresistible as the late-Victorian critic Matthew Arnold had proposed, met with mixed success. The opening in 1904 of what was to become the Royal Academy of Dramatic Art owed much to the energy and generosity of Beerbohm Tree – incongruously, since he had always claimed that acting could not be taught. RADA was only the first of many such schools of acting, and the improved standards of training which resulted were to affect entry into the profession almost as profoundly as the formation in 1905 of the Actors' Union – whose efforts to secure better pay and conditions remained largely unrealized until, ironically, it ceased to be a union in name and, as Actors' Equity, became one in practice in 1929.

In 1904, William Archer and Granville Barker had published an elaborate *Scheme and Estimates for a National Theatre* which, despite some premature laying of foundation stones, was to take even longer to reach fruition. Their advocacy of performances playing in 'true repertoire' on the continental model went beyond the limited-run system which was then being employed at the Court: but when it was put into practice following the move of Vedrenne and Barker to the Savoy in 1907, its expense led to the dissolution of their partnership. In 1910, Charles Frohman also tried to run a repertory season of ten plays at the Duke of York's: and while it was surely significant that so wily a commercial manager should make the attempt, even more so was its failure, which bore Darwinian witness to the way in which the long-run system, the survival of the theatrically fittest, had reshaped the habits of West End audiences.

Outside London, however, a typically British compromise between the limited run and 'true' repertoire, whereby single productions were played (often twice nightly) for a single week, began to be adopted as a preferable, locally-based alternative to the touring system. The earliest theatre to be run on such lines was set up in Manchester in 1907 by Miss Annie Horniman, heiress to a tea fortune, and between 1908 and 1913 further 'rep' theatres were established in Glasgow, Liverpool, Birmingham, and Bristol. From 1908 at the Gaiety, Miss Horniman's Manchester company worked with particular success to reflect local attitudes and concerns – which, though arguably just as class-ridden as those of the West End, now seem less exclusively and claustrophobically so.

The most notable exponents of the 'Manchester school' of playwriting were Allan Monkhouse, with *Reaping the Wind* (1908) and *Mary Broome* (1911); Stanley Houghton, with *The Younger Generation* (1910) and *Hindle Wakes* (1912); and Harold Brighouse – a writer of more than neighbourhood naturalism, whose *The Northerners* (1914) is almost as expressionistic in its exploration of a Luddite theme as is *Hobson's Choice* (1916) in its more recognizable workaday mould. Unsurprisingly, *Hobson* – its plot hinging upon a strong woman who stands up for 'her' man – was alone in finding favour in London, where 'provincial' had long been favoured as an appropriate epithet of abuse for Henrik Ibsen.

Earlier, in 1904, the munificent Miss Horniman had taken a lease on the Abbey Theatre in Dublin, where, the poet W. B. Yeats, Lady Gregory, George Moore, and Edward Martyn had been sustaining the Irish Literary Theatre since 1899. While Yeats was able to tap into the mythic roots of the Irish consciousness in plays which, further afield, have remained a rather specialist taste, Lady Gregory was more at home with an anecdotal, almost domesticated approach to her resurgent nation's folklore: then, in J. M. Synge, the new Abbey company found a voice of naturalistic genius, as readily expressed through the tragic dimension in *Riders to the Sea* (1904) as in the peasant comedy of *The Playboy of the Western World* (1907).

Owing to his premature death in 1909, Synge's plays were sadly few in number, and some met with hostility from audiences over-sensitive to supposed affronts to their national dignity – most famously during the '*Playboy* riots' which marred both the Dublin and New York premieres, but also on account of the wry anti-clericalism of *The Tinker's Wedding*, which opened in London in 1909 since it was considered 'too dangerous' for the Abbey. In truth, Synge gave a vital, poetic expression to the Irish national character and new cause for its reviving cultural pride no less than had Shakespeare for his own countrymen three centuries earlier.

APPROACHES TO SHAKESPEARE

Shakespearean productions during this period ranged across an ever-widening stylistic spectrum. After 1897 the showcase for the established (indeed, expected) spectacular approach shifted from the Lyceum to the new Her Majesty's, where Tree followed Irving in cutting his texts and rearranging his scenes in the cause of decorative convenience. Long waits during all the complicated scene changes were none the less common, though Tree did eliminate two intervals by reducing the conventional five act divisions to the three which were becoming the norm in new plays.

Tree's elaborate and top-heavy style was to attract ridicule soon enough: but if he took both his naturalism and his symbolism a touch too literally, the aim was often similar to that of his revered near-contemporary, Stanislavsky, in his

Lillah McCarthy as Viola in Granville Barker's production of *Twelfth Night* at the Savoy (1912). Norman Wilkinson's formal and stylized permanent set contrasted with the lavish embellishments (and real grass) employed by Tree. While best remembered for her roles in Barker's productions (which included many of Shaw's female leads), Lillah McCarthy (1875–1960) also went into management on her own account, at the Little Theatre in 1912 and at the Kingsway in 1919 – a year after the divorce from Barker which was effectively to bring both their careers in the live theatre to an end

legendary productions of Chekhov for the Moscow Art Theatre during the same period – even down to the twittering of attendant birds, arguably no less super-fluous in Konstantin Stanislavsky's *The Cherry Orchard* than in Tree's *Much Ado About Nothing*. Again, Tree's live rabbits on stage for *A Midsummer Night's Dream* and his terraces of real grass in *Twelfth Night* have passed into theatrical folklore as examples of misconceived straining after verisimilitude: yet they suggest an instinct not that different from Stanislavsky's when he commended the filling of hollow oars with water for realistic splashing along Venetian canals in *Othello*.

From 1905 Tree invited fellow Shakespeareans to participate in annual festivals to commemorate the bardic birthday: and so directors – as we can now unreservedly begin to call those who saw it as their function to give artistic cohesion to a production – as different as F. R. Benson and William Poel both found themselves working at His Majesty's (as the theatre had duly become). Benson had for some thirty years been touring Shakespeare round the provinces with one of the last stock companies worthy of the name – and from 1886 had also been responsible for mounting the annual festivals at the new Shakespeare Memorial Theatre in Stratford-upon-Avon (opened in 1879), where bardolatry was just beginning its acceleration from the light fantastic to the light industrial.

As a director, Benson's approach seems to have varied between the highly athletic, jogging *Henry V* along at a welcome pace, and the sonorously funereal, stretching out his *Hamlet* to six hours excluding an interval for dinner. William Poel was more consistent in seeking to recover the 'swiftness and ease' which he believed to have characterized Elizabethan acting, in the wider interests of replicating the manner in which he believed the plays had first been staged. No less pioneering than his *Hamlet* of 1881, based on the First Quarto in a seminal conjunction of scholarly and theatrical disciplines, was his restoration to the living repertoire of the works of Shakespeare's contemporaries. His revival for the Independent Theatre of Webster's *The Duchess of Malfi* in 1892 coincided, moreover, with the popularization of the 'minor' Elizabethans and Jacobeans through Havelock Ellis's launching of the influential, bravely unexpurgated, Mermaid Series of 'The Best Plays of the Old Dramatists'.

A year later, again for Grein, Poel staged *Measure for Measure* in a would-be facsimile of the original Fortune. Then, in 1895, he formed his own Elizabethan Stage Society, which for the next ten years mounted what Poel proclaimed to be 'authentic' Elizabethan productions – with Jonson's plays, among others, happily featuring alongside Shakespeare's. Although subsequent scholarship has cast doubt on some of his beliefs – and he himself often vitiated the intimacy he sought by pitching his Elizabethan platform beyond a host proscenium arch – Poel's was a leading influence in the clearing away of centuries of accumulated clutter, both physical and metaphysical, from Shakespearean production.

Rhetorically Poel revealed, in Lillah McCarthy's words, that it was possible 'to keep the exquisite rhythm and cadence of the verse even whilst the drama was hurtling along its swift tempestuous course'. Lillah McCarthy is herself best remembered as the creator of the earliest of Shaw's female leads – in which she was directed by Granville Barker, who became not only her husband but her collaborator on a series of Shakespearean productions mounted at the Savoy Theatre between 1912 and 1914. In these the lessons of Poel's work were assimilated, but its niceties adapted to the conditions of contemporary staging and the expectations of a contemporary audience.

Barker thus built an apron stage out over the front stalls of his theatre, and replaced its footlights with a batten mounted across the front of the dress circle. His eclectic approach even extended to incorporating some of the revolutionary design ideas then being propounded by Ellen Terry's son, Gordon Craig – a curious, lonely figure, whose monumental columns and sweeping swathes of steps had little to do with Elizabethan staging, but did begin to meet the need for single settings conducive to a play's atmosphere and properly uninterrupted pace.

Spending his long life largely in self-imposed exile, Craig enjoyed more influence as a theorist than a practitioner, his view of actors as super-marionettes tending to attract frustrated directors but to deter the profession at large. Yet he remained devoted to the memory of Irving – not only as a surrogate father, but

Opposite: the forum scene from the production of *Julius Caesar* (1911) by Herbert Beerbohm Tree, showing his characteristic concern for the scenic and actorly detail of the stage picture. Here, Tree, playing Antony, is standing with his back to the rostrum. While taking risks on productions of Ibsen and Shaw, Tree (1853–1917) was also ruthless in establishing his own stage presence, whether as Svengali in *Trilby* (1895), Falstaff in *Henry IV, Part 1* (1896) – or (against a no-less-determined Mrs Patrick Campbell) in Shaw's *Pygmalion* (1914). Tree managed the Haymarket from 1887, then personally oversaw the building of Her Majesty's, which became his base from 1897 to 1915

for the kind of mesmeric power with which as an actor he had, in *The Bells*, transcended melodrama. However, as a theatrical force melodrama had virtually died along with its last traditional exponent, William Terriss – struck down in 1897 at the stage door of the theatre with whose very name it had become synonymous, the Adelphi.

DEVELOPMENTS IN MUSIC HALL

While the increasingly diverse nature of the music-hall bill now made it 'variety' indeed, many of the stars of the pre-war years remained true to the proletarian tradition of the older 'halls' – not least Marie Lloyd, prohibited from appearing before royalty as much on account of her risky double meanings on stage as her unconventional private life. The period saw many other such legendary acts at peak form and peak popularity – varieties of comic experience ranging from the 'character' acts of George Robey and Harry Tate to the 'eccentric' Dan Leno and Little Tich, from the the 'grotesque' comedy of Nellie Wallace to the 'coster' comedy of Albert Chevalier and Gus Ellen, from the stylized Scots of Harry Lauder to the stylish males of Vesta Tilley – glimpsed in characteristic military mode on the song-sheet cover opposite.

Honourably, most such bill-topping acts showed solidarity with their humbler brothers and sisters in the music-hall strike which followed the formation of the Variety Artists' Federation in 1906, and which secured a slight improvement in conditions. Then, in 1912, a long-standing dispute over the inclusion of 'dramatic' material was resolved with the legalization of sketches up to thirty minutes in length. However, an earlier advance was by then proving double-edged – the music-hall managers having at first welcomed the arrival in the 1890s of the first short moving pictures, which they hired for 'ciné-variety' bills on the grounds of novelty and relative cheapness. But within a decade feature-length movies had arrived along with purpose-built cinemas to exhibit them, and film had become a dangerous competitor – not only for audiences, but also for performers. Charlie Chaplin and Stan Laurel, both graduates of Fred Karno's slapstick company, were just two of those who deserted the halls as also their native land for the lure of boom-town Hollywood.

A leading music-hall singer of a slightly earlier period, 'the Great Macdermott', otherwise G. H. Farrell, had achieved a hit at the time of the Russo-Turkish War of 1877 with 'We don't want to fight, but by Jingo! if we do', a patriotic ditty which added the word 'jingoism' to the language – and continued, 'We've got the ships, we've got the men and got the money, too.' By the time that the jingoism which fuelled the First World War had been purged, nearly a million men from Britain alone lay dead, some in the still-disciplined ranks of the war cemeteries, some scattered disorderly and dismembered across the poppy fields of Flanders – one million of the ten million who died in a war which left wounded twice as many more, to devastate a generation and sow only the seeds of renewed conflict.

Opposite: Vesta Tilley, (1864–1952), most famous of music-hall male impersonators, pictured on a song-sheet cover in typically jingoistic mood. Even before the First World War, Tilley's strutting soldierly personae were no less popular and only a little less plentiful than her gallery of would-be dandies and elegant young men about town. Unambiguously female in her personal life, on stage Tilley created gamine males who combined the centuries-old appeal of 'breeches parts' for the men in her audience with an unthreatening image of an asexual Adonis for her many female admirers. During the First World War, Vesta Tilley made forceful appeals for recruitment in numbers such as 'The Army of To-day's Alright' and 'Jolly Good Luck to the Girl who Loves a Soldier'. Her act, in the words of Elaine Aston, thus 'moved away from satirical comment on social behaviour towards prescribing or instructing people on how to behave' – men, in short, being urged to volunteer for the trenches, and women to permit them the sexual licence their heroism merited. She made her farewell appearance at the London Coliseum in 1920

Burlesque had been kept artificially alive through the dedication of John Hollingshead and the genius of his leading players, Fred Leslie and Nellie Warren: but its dual attractions of sexual display and gentle satire now began to find distinct outlets in the rapidly developing forms of musical comedy and revue.

'Musical variety farce', as Hollingshead's partner and successor at the Gaiety, George Edwardes, dubbed it, was at first quite decorous, hinting at rather than disclosing the femininity of The Gaiety Girl – a species that bred generically from the show so-titled in 1893 to spawn The Shop Girls and other girls decoratively packaged for decades to come. Of course, impresarios soon saw the potential for exploiting the fleshlier reaches of the 'chorus girl', who thus found herself supplanting the 'legit' actress as a lady-in-waiting for the 'stage door Johnny' – in whose company she entered many a smart restaurant, just occasionally the peerage, and the reach-me-down demonology of the censorious.

The more intimate style of revue began hesitantly to find itself in Under the Clock at the Court in 1893, and was fully formed by 1899 when Potpourri opened at the little Coronet in Notting Hill. Its genealogy having been interrupted along with Henry Fielding's theatrical career, this now blended topical skits, songs, and parodies of fashionable plays into political satire rather less barbed than Fielding's – although one title appearing to claim direct descent from his Historical Register for 1736 did open at the Crystal Palace just two days before Potpourri: called, intriguingly, A Dream of Whitaker's Almanack, it appears, alas, to have sunk without trace.

Revues on a more lavish scale became increasingly popular after the turn of the century. At the Empire in Leicester Square the shows ranged from Venus 1906, which vaguely celebrated womanhood, to By George! in 1911, which even more vaguely celebrated the new King. And at the Coliseum in St Martin's Lane, purpose-built as a variety theatre in 1904, Oswald Stoll celebrated his own large debt to the French style – a debt which later extended to his titles, as Stoll nudged customers into the refurbished Middlesex Music Hall with C'est Bon! and Cachez Ça! and C'est Chic!

In 1912 Everybody's Doing It at the Empire duly acknowledged the arrival of ragtime, fresh from the USA. In the same year Albert de Courville set out to become the Londoner's Ziegfeld with the first full-scale spectacle after the American manner, Hullo, Rag-time! at the Hippodrome – while at the Alhambra André Charlot arrived from Paris to present Kill That Fly! Then, in 1914, C. B. Cochran began his management of the new and intimately proportioned Ambassadors, and two years later also took on the adjoining St Martin's (where his opening Houp La! exploited the more relaxed wartime attitude towards female flesh on display). By this time Charlot had moved to the Vaudeville, along with such coming names as Binnie Hale, Beatrice Lillie, and Gertrude Lawrence.

Thanks to longer holidays and cheap railway excursions, the seaside resorts had entered upon their boom years with the new century, and troupes of pierrots from many a beach and pier-head drew from and fed into revue, and music hall besides – Pelissier's Follies most successfully venturing inland to appear in variety, as also by royal command at Sandringham. King Edward's tastes had lowered a little the class barriers that once separated music-hall audiences from their 'betters', and the inauguration in 1912 under his successor of an annual Royal Variety Performance (aptly enough at the Palace Theatre) accelerated this legitimation. But Marie Lloyd, more on account of her doubtful morals then her double meanings, was not invited.

The presumed naughtiness of all things French was exploited by Oswald Stoll with a sequence of French-titled revues at the Middlesex. On the left, the spelling-out in the cause of modesty of one such offering, *Cachez-Ça* (1913), is an oblique reference to the banning of a poster for the earlier *C'est Chic* – on account of its excess of pink flesh. As the illustration on the right attests, American influence was no less strong: here, the chorus dances down the 'joy plank' used in *Hullo, Rag-time!* at the Hippodrome (1912)

CHAPTER 18

The War and the Long Weekend

Entering the Hippodrome, 1922 – the couple in evening dress taking as their due the obsequiously opened door. The picture sums up a socially and politically divided era, aptly deconstructed by the poet Robert Graves as *The Long Weekend*

As a precautionary measure following the outbreak of the First World War, the West End managements patriotically reduced the salaries of their actors by up to a half – though those in Martin Harvey's touring company, offered a profit-sharing deal instead, found their pay packets fuller than before. Soon every night (and every proliferating matinee) was a 'khaki night' in theatres which quickly learned to cater to the presumed tastes of the boys in battledress. *The Man Who Stayed at Home* (1914), by Lechmere Worrall and Harold Terry, cultivated the early preference for militaristic melodrama, guttural German spies and all, while by the following year plays with such titles as *The War Baby*, *Brave Women Who Wait*, *The Enemy in Our Midst*, and *Are We Downhearted? No!* were busily exploiting the facile chauvinism of the times.

More honourably, if a touch portentously, some dramatists and producers sought an allegorical angle on the conflict. Tree revived the historical pageant *Drake* by Louis N. Parker, a past master of decorative populism, while Granville Barker, venturing further upmarket, staged exemplary British victories from Thomas Hardy's intractable dramatic poem *The Dynasts*. 'Phantom Intelligences' figured in Hardy's cast list, while Stephen Phillips, in his ramblingly patriotic *Armageddon*, even recruited the Spirit of Joan of Arc to her old enemy's cause, along with Beelzebub, Moloch, and, inevitably, the Shade of Attila the Hun.

But an increasingly exhausted and disillusioned soldiery quickly tired of sanitized or historicized versions of a war which, however briefly, it only wanted to forget. And so, alongside the relatively tasteful intimate revues of Cochran and Charlot, such provocative titles as *Hot Lips* and *High Heels and Stockings* soon began to hint at altogether different kinds of intimacy. Escapist musicals also enjoyed a boom. *Chu Chin Chow*, which opened at Her Majesty's in 1916 during Tree's absence in the USA, went on to achieve a run of 2,238 performances, which remained a record until *The Mousetrap* overtook it in 1958, and *The Maid of the Mountains* enjoyed a more regulated success at Daly's in the following year. Farces, too, were popular – Walter W. Ellis's long-running *A Little Bit of Fluff*, which occupied the Criterion for 1,241 performances from 1915, eponymously suggesting the mild naughtiness and cotton-wool substance it delivered.

The government ungratefully repaid all this work for the war effort by imposing an Entertainments Tax in 1916. In the same year the military authorized the fighting men to organize their own kinds of entertainment, and by the Armistice of November 1918 some ten companies were playing to the troops in 'garrison theatres'. The first of these, built out of the soldiers' own funds at Oswestry, was the inspiration of a young producer named Basil Dean who (like others as various as J. B. Priestley, Jack Hylton, and Dodie Smith) went on to achieve success in the post-war theatre. Dean himself was later to mastermind the far more substantial provision of entertainment for the troops by ENSA (the Entertainments National Services Association) during the Second World War.

For the heroes returning after the Armistice, expectations of jobs, let alone homes, were swiftly disappointed – as were hopes for the better regulation of international affairs through the League of Nations, set up to ensure that 'the war to end wars' lived up to its propaganda. Following the defection of the wartime Prime Minister, Lloyd George, from the Liberals, the government which got itself elected on an opportunistic 'coalition' ticket was in essence and philosophy Conservative: and, apart from two brief intervals of minority Labour rule, Britain remained under Conservative domination until a more genuine coalition confronted a resurgent Germany when Chamberlain was ousted in favour of Churchill in 1940.

The inter-war epoch divides naturally into two, before and after the economic recession precipitated by the Wall Street crash of 1929. Throughout the whole period, however, Britain not only remained a socially divided nation but was increasingly self-aware of its divisions – as measured, for example, by reactions for or against the Russian Revolution of 1917, for or against the General Strike of 1926, and (though not always along the same lines) for or against the appeasement of fascism in Germany after Adolf Hitler's rise to power in 1933. The self-appointed elite, fearful for its continuing hold on wealth and leisure at the expense of a no longer quiescent working class, closed ranks in defence of its uncertain certainties: and in its service the West End theatre became ever more myopic in its social assumptions – and in an increasing narrowness as much of sensibilities as of cultural horizons.

Against this drift towards exclusivity, new technologies – first in the form of radio broadcasting, then of a cinema which found its voice midway through the period – were shaping mass modes of performance which could not but transcend social barriers, albeit sometimes at the expense of reinforcing other kinds of stereotype. Meanwhile, those who recognized the potential of theatre as a force for change sought to employ it for their own ends in clubs, halls, and other arenas far beyond Shaftesbury Avenue – the expansion of whose elastic boundaries tellingly ceased after the first decade or so of our period.

About the plays themselves there was all too often a pervasive, calculated sense of detachment – the snobberies rooted in insecurity about social roles compounded with an awkward, English uptightness about matters of sex, typically contained within an atrophying 'well-made' structure and prone to drift into a laconic mode of sub-Shavian debate. The terse and tight-lipped dialogue of these plays perhaps speaks as much of repression – a refusal of too close encounters with one's own emotions – as of mannered naturalism, and, viewed charitably, can in part be accounted for by the strains of war: a necessary blunting of responses in the face of what men had done and been calmly ordered to do by

George and Ira Gershwin's *Lady, Be Good!* (1926) was the first great West End hit in the jazz-influenced transatlantic idiom. Although the Viennese-Ruritanian style was still enjoying a final fling with *Rose Marie* (1925) and *The Student Prince* (1926), the future lay with such shows as Jerome Kern's *Sunny* (1926), the Gershwins' *Funny Face* (1928), Jerome Kern's *Show Boat* (1928), Rodgers and Hart's *A Yankee at the Court of King Arthur* (1929), Irving Berlin's *Face the Music* (1932), and Cole Porter's *Anything Goes* (1935). The style gained a wider currency with the arrival of the talkies, and was given a new energy when Rodgers and Hammerstein achieved a happier integration of book, lyrics, and choreography in *Oklahoma!* and *Carousel*

EMPIRE THEATRE
LEICESTER SQUARE, W.C.2.
MANAGING DIRECTOR · · · · ALFRED BUTT
MANAGER · · · · · · OSCAR BARRETT

FRED and ADELE ASTAIRE

in "LADY BE GOOD"

| EVENINGS, 8-15 | MATS. : WED. & SAT., 2-15 |

Noël Coward (1899–1973), with Lilian Braithwaite, in the controversial last-act confrontation of his own play *The Vortex* (1924), in which Nicky Lancaster forces his mother to confess her affairs, and himself admits to drug-taking. As a playwright, Coward in the 'twenties captured both the hedonism and the brittle sensibilities of the 'bright young things': as an actor, and frequently his own director, his clipped and consciously mannered delivery suited an age accustomed to emotions being deflected into defensive ironies. Later, his work reflected the chauvinistic mood of the thirties, and the more purposive patriotism of the war years

their fellows. In life they called it being 'hard-boiled', and those too young to have experienced its causes replicated its effects in the desperate striving after superficial gaieties of the 'bright young things'.

OLD DRAMATISTS AND NEW

In these circumstances, it is unsurprising that few plays offered a serious analysis of the war itself. R. C. Sherriff's *Journey's End* (1928) – a curious combination of distaste for militarism and regret for lost comradeship – was the only British play of note successfully to attempt a depiction, however diluted, of the reality of the trenches: and this, as its date suggests, was the product of a period when the war could be recollected with rationality if not tranquillity. It was left to an Irish writer, Sean O'Casey, to employ in *The Silver Tassie* (1929) the harsher vocabulary of expressionism to illuminate the dark horrors of the battlefield as well as its lingering scars – just as, in his earlier plays for the Abbey in Dublin, he had shown that heightened naturalism was still capable of delivering a vivid picture and criticism of life.

Writers such as Allan Monkhouse – who, in *The Conquering Hero* (1924), wrote with bitter truth rather than bland palliatives about the aftermath of war – were few and generally unsuccessful. Even such an established dramatist as Somerset Maugham failed to sustain an audience for his *For Services Rendered* (1932), described as 'a *Journey's End* of the post-war years'; while *Post-Mortem*, in which a dying soldier at the front returns to visit the London he died to save, went unperformed until 1968 – though it had been written in 1930 by Noël Coward, a new dramatist then at the very height of fashion.

Significantly, Coward later wrote of the play as 'hysterical', while defending its 'utmost sincerity' – as though the one were an unhappy consequence of the other. He was learning that his craftsmanship was best kept at a distance from all but the superficies of feeling – a distance which for him, as also for Maugham, was increased by the need, both social and legal, to dissimulate homosexuality. Maugham, in plays like *Home and Beauty* (1919), *The Circle* (1921), *The Constant Wife* (1927), and *The Sacred Flame* (1928), had been continuing carefully to tailor his work to a tight-buttoned West End cut; but he was beginning to chafe at such restrictions, and when, a year after the failure of *For Services Rendered* in 1932, *Sheppey* – a study of a middle-aged barber who comes into money and tries to live like Jesus – was also indifferently received, he deserted the stage for good in favour of the novel.

Coward, always a performer and a showman as well as a writer, kept more constantly attuned to his audience's tastes. Early on, in *The Vortex* (1924) – a depiction of a neurotic mother-son relationship with a dash of modishly 'degenerate' drug-taking – he revealed that any capacity in him for deep feeling was muted, like his audience's, by an elliptic uptightness of expression; and soon, with a consummate professionalism ever honed by pragmatism, he retreated, in

Fallen Angels (1925) and *Private Lives* (1929), to the safer 'modern' territory of guarded sexual dalliance in high society. Yet, as the depression set in, Coward was among the first to scent the coming retreat into nostalgia, and by 1931 was wowing Drury Lane audiences with a sweep of domestic and national history intertwined in the spectacular *Cavalcade* – its sentimentality the flip side of his more usual veneer of cynical wit.

Many of Coward's comedies of superficial modern manners have proved too formulaic (and the manners too ephemeral) to survive. But when, as in his farces, moral conventions are observed with an apparently straighter face, only to be outraged to good comic effect, he strikes a more enduring vein, and works like *Hay Fever* (1924) and the wartime *Blithe Spirit* (pictured and discussed on pages 300–1) stand alongside the vintage work of Ben Travers in that underrated form.

Travers, like Pinero before him, was able to draw upon a regular acting team at a regular theatre – in his case, Ralph Lynn, Tom Walls, Mary Brough, and Robertson Hare at the Aldwych – for a sequence of vintage farces which included *A Cuckoo in the Nest* (1925), *Rookery Nook* (1926), and *Thark* (1927). His *Plunder* (1928) even received the imprimatur of a production at the National Theatre in 1978 – three years after Travers, by then in his ninetieth year, had enjoyed a final West End success with the less obliquely titled *The Bed Before Yesterday*.

Rookery Nook (1926), one of a series of farces, mostly by Ben Travers (1886–1980), which kept the Aldwych Theatre full for ten years from 1923. All featured Tom Walls and Ralph Lynn (lounging, third and fourth from left), with Robertson Hare (bald, below the chandelier) and Mary Brough (bending over the sofa on the right) also regulars in the team. The scene here, of incipient tumult fed by a commodious stairway and lots of practical entrances, is characteristic of a genre whose no less incipient (but usually just avoided) combination of social and sexual disasters Coward (opposite) had also exploited in *Hay Fever* (1924)

Advisedly, those few dramatists who enjoyed any success with 'problem plays' tended to address sexual rather than social issues: but their ostensible daring was usually thermostatically-adjusted to an audience which already fancied itself 'advanced' in such matters. And so, in Miles Malleson's *The Fanatics* (1927), any threat of titillation is cold-showered in earnest debates about the merits of free love as opposed to marriage, while Clemence Dane's plea for easier divorce in *A Bill of Divorcement* (1921) is on the already uncontentious ground of insanity. This play, however, elicited a performance of reputedly painful intensity from Meggie Albanesi, whose death two years later at the age of 23 robbed the theatre of an actress of outstanding potential.

Dane's other work covered a varied assortment of literary, historical, and topical themes, and St John Ervine was no less eclectic in range, though he now seems clearly at his best in the plays set in his native Ulster, which were often first staged at the Abbey. Apart from Ervine, Frederick Lonsdale and A. A. Milne were among the most prominent of the numerous practitioners in undemanding comedies of modern manners – typically, almost mythically, set in the drawing rooms of small country houses exuding french windows, unsullied leather bindings, and expository domestics.

Of the two, Lonsdale, notably in *Spring Cleaning* (1925) and *The Last of Mrs Cheyney* (1925), had the sharper satirical edge, Milne the quirkier sense of character. However, Milne's gentle irony, at its best in *Mr Pym Passes By* (1919), was prone to modulate into the merely fey – as in *The Dover Road* (1921), in which young lovers in mid-flight are benignly dissuaded from elopement (a propensity for which Maugham, in *The Circle*, rather pompously put down to

The expansion of Shaftesbury Avenue

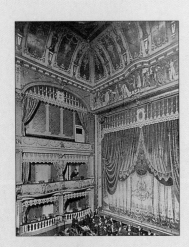

The Adelphi Theatre, as reconstucted in late-Victorian style in 1901

A last cluster of theatres that, in atmosphere and architectural style if not in chronology, were late-Victorian, had opened during the first decade of the century – surviving among them the rebuilt Adelphi, pictured alongside, and the Apollo (both 1901), the New (1903), the Coliseum (1904), the Waldorf, now the Strand, and the Aldwych (1905), the Globe, originally Hicks's (1906), the Queen's (1907), the Palladium (1910), and the Prince's and the Victoria Palace (1911).

The Ambassadors' (1913), together with the neighbouring St Martin's, which had been under construction at the outbreak of war and opened three years later, were the first to be built in a trimmer, neo-Georgian style, often with art deco embellishments. The style would predominate in a renewed spurt of building a decade or so later when the Fortune (1924), arose, along with the Piccadilly (1928), the Duchess (1929), the Phoenix, the Cambridge, the Whitehall, and Prince Edward (1930), and the Westminster, Saville, and Windmill (1931). In 1931 Sadler's Wells underwent a complete reconstruction.

Although the Prince of Wales's was also rebuilt in 1937, no other major new theatre was to be opened in central London until the Mermaid, itself far from Shaftesbury Avenue, opened its doors in 1959. Give or take the odd conversion to a cinema (and, more recently, back again), the map of the West End theatre in the 1930s was thus very much as it was to remain into the 1990s.

heredity). Milne's regularly revived adaptation of Kenneth Grahame's *The Wind in the Willows* as *Toad of Toad Hall* (1929) suggests the affinity for childhood he shared with Barrie – and which was, of course, soon to take on fabulous proportions in the stories and verses of Christopher Robin and Winnie the Pooh.

Eden Phillpotts sustained an idiosyncratic but utterly safe west-country version of pastoral in such plays as *The Farmer's Wife* (1924), while Laurence Houseman and Clifford Bax were the most craftsmanlike of those who offered the different kind of security and solace offered by the costume drama. Significantly, John Drinkwater's more serious investigation of the lessons of history and the qualities of leadership in *Abraham Lincoln*, which had enjoyed a timely success in 1919 when it came to London from Barry Jackson's Birmingham Rep, was never repeated as the age rapidly lost faith in heroic solutions to the intractable problems of the peace.

The so-called 'golden age' of the detective novel – which, unsurprisingly, coincided with the invention of the cryptic crossword puzzle – had its echo in the theatre, even William Archer achieving a box-office success as he neared his dotage with a most un-Ibsenesque oriental thriller at the St James's, *The Green*

The Queen's Theatre in the 1930s. Built in 1907 at the opposite end of a Shaftesbury Avenue block to Hicks's (now the Globe) Theatre, the Queen's staged a typical inter-war mix of light comedies, musicals, and historical dramas – interrupted in 1929 by John Gielgud's *Hamlet*, and again by his longer classical season in 1937. Dodie Smith's archetypal domestic drama, *Dear Octopus*, played here a year before the theatre was bombed in 1940. The Queen's was rebuilt in 1959, with a modernist frontage now in marked contrast to its one-time 'twin', the nearby Globe

Set design by Augustus John for the second act of Sean O'Casey's *The Silver Tassie* (1929). Despite its 'realistic' labelling – 'Somewhere in France' – the set embraces in expressionistic fashion a critical iconography of the First World War: a crucifix askew, a monastery in ruins, barbed wire, big gun and gun-wheel, the glow on the horizon eerily illuminating a veneer of mud and rain. In the first act a Dublin lad has been seen revelling in his small-time fame as a football hero – then, in the last act, he is shown like so many of his comrades, crippled and impotent in the aftermath of war

Goddess (1923). But the master of the genre was the perennially proficient Edgar Wallace, whose career reached its theatrical apotheosis in 1928 when three of his plays were running simultaneously in the West End. His best, *The Ringer* (1926), adroitly manipulated the now slightly foxed device of revealing the master criminal to be one of the investigating detectives. By 1933, Anthony Armstrong's *Ten Minute Alibi* (1933) had taken the dramatic thriller about as far towards applied mathematics as it could be expected to go.

FROM ACTOR-MANAGER TO DIRECTOR

Plays were now being plentifully published as well as performed, but few would warrant disturbing from their dusty immortality on secondhand bookshelves. Among the exceptions are, of course, the works of Bernard Shaw – which also serve usefully to illustrate the changes which were taking place in the artistic control of a production. Thus, the pre-war battle of the titans over the staging of *Pygmalion* – with Shaw as author-director, Tree as actor-producer, and Mrs Patrick Campbell as, well, Mrs Pat – may be contrasted with the creative collaboration between Shaw and Lewis Casson in 1924, when they served, in effect, as co-directors of *St Joan*, with the young and inspirational Sybil Thorndike in the lead. But already, in 1923, under Barry Jackson's benign management, a relatively unknown and entirely unflamboyant young director, Henry Ayliff, had assumed independent control over Shaw's elephantine *Back to Methuselah*, securing for it, as six years later he did for *The Apple Cart*, a success *d'éstime* if not of the box office.

Of actor-managers in the traditional mould, Tree, Alexander, and Hare were dead by the end of the war, and only a few theatres – notably Wyndham's, where George du Maurier's cigarette had become as subtle a semiotic indicator as any Restoration fan – were still run in their extrovert proprietorial fashion. Forbes-Robertson had retired, and other surviving actor-managers of the old school, such as Cyril Maude, Charles Hawtrey, Seymour Hicks, and Oscar Asche, were generally more peripatetic – while many of the newer arrivals, their ambitions and talents not so much histrionic as economic, became commercial impresarios after the modern manner.

Among these, the likes of Alfred Butt, who in 1923 took over from Arthur Collins at Drury Lane, had no greater ambition than to keep a theatre filled with whatever pleased the public. Butt was astute enough to recognize that his predecessor's love of spectacle had to give way before the public's preference for musical comedy – and further to concede, with the arrival of the jazz-based style described on page 279, that the Americans were now doing this sort of thing rather better, at least in the grand manner well suited to his stage. Butt continued to alternate such imported products with the home-grown variety, as first cultivated for him by Coward and then, in the years before the Second World War, as almost monopolized by Ivor Novello.

It took more imaginative impresarios to take risks in broadening their own as well as their audience's horizons. Charles B. Cochran was thus prepared if not happy to lose the profits from the sure-fire revues featuring his 'Young Ladies' on the first London production (*Anna Christie*, in 1923) of a play by that first genius of the American theatre, the energetic but erratic Eugene O'Neill. Cochran was canny enough to recoup his fortunes by snapping up the talents of Noël Coward, but also brave enough to bring to London, among others, Pavlova, Diaghilev's Russian Ballet, Eleanora Duse – and the Marx Brothers.

Cochran it was who also dared to stage the premiere of O'Casey's *The Silver Tassie* when the Abbey turned it down, imaginatively casting a young actor called Charles Laughton in the role of the war-wounded Heegan – but also hiring Raymond Massey actually to direct the play. And it was in part thanks to the likes of Cochran – who had first staged Reinhardt's mystical spectacular, *The Miracle*, in the great open spaces of Olympia in 1911, and who brought the Pitoëffs to London in 1930 – that the British theatre was gradually accommodating itself to the director's role as the guiding creative force in the production process.

Even before the war the director had been finding his way into the 'legitimate' theatre from the musicals and other spectaculars where his existence was first acknowledged among the programme credits – though in name he was still the 'producer', as in his humbler incarnation he had been the 'stage manager'. From

Poster for the revival of
Congreve's *The Way of the
World* at the Lyric Theatre,
Hammersmith, in 1924. Nigel
Playfair's production featured
a vintage Millamant from
Edith Evans – and designs by
Doris Zinkeisen, one of several
scenographers of the period
who blended their own and
their production's period style
with the suave, symmetrical
elegance of theatricalized 'art
deco'. Such a combination
also distinguished George
Sheringham's Lyric set for
The Duenna (1924) – and, of
course, that of Claude Lovat
Fraser for *The Beggar's Opera*
(opposite)

1902 to 1915 Charles Frohman had thus employed Dion Boucicault, the dramatist's son, as his resident producer at the Duke of York's: but the true shaping
genius of the profession in Britain was, of course, Granville Barker – who after
the war suffered not only the hyphenation of his name but the termination of his
theatrical career at the whim of an hypergamous second wife.

Basil Dean, a graduate of Miss Horniman's company, was perhaps his closest
successor, at first through the 'Reandean' management he formed with Alec Rea.
More concerned than Barker with the externals of behaviour, Dean had a formative
influence in the inter-war years on the mannered, slightly phlegmatic realism
which came to distinguish English acting style: he thus excelled in the orchestration of casual conversational encounters – whether intimate or, as in his famous
handling of the party scene in *The Constant Nymph*, in apparently aimless mass.

Both Dean and another former actor-manager turned director, Leon M. Lion,
kept before the public the work of John Galsworthy, whose post-war successes
included Dean's production of *The Skin Game* (1920) and Lion's of *Escape* (1926).
Dean also directed Galsworthy's *Loyalties*, paired with an unfinished curiosity by
Barrie, *Shall We Join the Ladies?* (1922) – in which the merging of detective-drama
and metaphysical conceit anticipated the tricks with time played by J. B. Priestley
in the thirties. Although Dean directed Coward's *Easy Virtue* in 1924 and his *Home
Chat* in 1927, in the main Coward served as his own director, contributing his terse
yet insouciant style of evasive interchange to the ranges of theatrical Englishness.

There is, perhaps, a distinction to be made between managers of vision and
directors in the modern sense – a distinction which would not have seemed very
important at the time, but which was to become so as the two breeds increasingly
went their separate ways. Thus, although Barry Jackson continued to shape the
policy behind the Birmingham Rep, and in 1929 created the Malvern Festival
dedicated to the work of Bernard Shaw, he himself only directed occasionally, and
so falls clearly into the former category, as an 'artistic director' before the currency
of the term – whereas such a personality as Nigel Playfair was far more immediately and regularly involved in shaping the overall style of his productions.

THE SUBURBS, THE PROVINCES, AND THE NEW SCENOGRAPHY

Playfair had taken over the old 'blood-and-flea pit' which was the Lyric Theatre,
Hammersmith, in 1918, and throughout the twenties created there a series of
productions which combined his own distinctive vision with the spirit of the
decade. Best remembered for his revival-cum-reworking of Gay's *The Beggar's
Opera* (1920), which ran for nearly 1,500 performances, Playfair refurbished
many other neglected classics, in which he took cheerful liberties alike with text
and context – rendering *The Importance of Being Earnest* into severe shades of
black and white, outfacing the bawdy of *The Way of the World* with more artifice
than Lamb could ever have imagined, or using *The London Merchant* as a vehicle
for replicating in pastiche the lost art of the Crummles from *Nicholas Nickleby*.

Among the leading set designers who collaborated with Playfair at the Lyric, the most influential, despite his early death, was certainly Claude Lovat Fraser, whose economical designs for *The Beggar's Opera* evoked an elegant, toyland version of the eighteenth century entirely in tune with Playfair's frankly prettified production. Playfair also used George Sheringham and Norman Wilkinson, both of whom, along with the waywardly idiosyncratic Russian emigré Theodore Komisarjevsky, went on to become part of the regular team at Stratford during the thirties.

At the Birmingham Rep, Paul Shelving's work for Barry Jackson embraced an eclectic range of styles from symbolism (for the exotic musical *The Immortal Hour*) to cubism (for Georg Kaiser's sternly didactic *Gas*). And in Cambridge, where Terence Gray converted the eighteenth-century Barnwell playhouse into his own Festival Theatre in 1926, the non-illusionistic settings were of striking modernity, many employing a set of two-dozen or so geometric shapes in various combinations upon the open stage of multi-levelled platforms. Although Basil Dean had promoted the importance of stage lighting after his own more realistic inclinations, it was also for Gray in Cambridge that Harold Ridge – for the first time in England – consistently applied the techniques advocated by Adolphe

Set design for Gay's *The Beggar's Opera*, which opened in 1920 at the Lyric, Hammersmith, and ran in all for 1,463 performances. The original budget was tight, and Claude Lovat Fraser (1890–1931) designed a single basic set, suggesting specific locations by means of backdrops and curtains. Such 'permanent sets' now became artistically fashionable – as well as making sound economic sense

Appia for creating atmosphere through diffused and deflected light, as long since practised for Wagnerian productions in Bayreuth.

During this period of scenographic innovation it is, then, a telling reflection upon West End standards that only a few one-off designs of brilliance were conceived within its confines – Charles Ricketts's sets for *St Joan* for example, or Erté's realization of the Aztec ballet for *It's in the Bag*, Cecil Landeau's Saville revue of 1937. By and large, drawing-room comedies remained firmly plonked down in those improbably open-plan drawing-rooms so characteristic of the genre, replete with out-front sofas, multiple entrances, and oddly located stairways – all lit with the apparent intention of replicating a hundred-watt centre pendant, which was duly switched on or off with a resounding backstage clunk.

Cochran's productions were, as so often, the honourable exceptions. He regularly used modern artists of the calibre of Rex Whistler and Christian Bérard, and for the second act of *The Silver Tassie* employed Augustus John to create a set (as pictured on page 284) which powerfully combined the emblematic and the terribly real. Even for Cochran's revues, Oliver Messel's sets were reliably original and expressive, and Messel it was who also memorably designed A. P. Herbert's adaptation of Offenbach's light opera *Helen!* for which Cochran brought Max Reinhardt back to London in 1932.

THE CHALLENGE OF THE 'OTHER THEATRE'

The efforts of such enlightened producers and directors apart – in 1923, for example, Playfair followed up Dean's production of the Capek brothers' *RUR* (which gave the word robot to the language) with their *The Insect Play* at the Regent – there was little concern to explore the more experimental reaches of the continental repertoire. Chekhov was belatedly beginning to breach this insular smugness, albeit largely on account of being thought to conceal a decent English reticence behind a melancholic Russian facade ('all shadows, all despair', as Hannen Swaffer bemoaned in 1929). But few British plays of this period show much awareness of, let alone responsiveness towards, the expressionist experiments of the German theatre, the constructivist ideas of the early Soviet era, the futurism of Italy, or the surrealist and dadist movements in France.

Apart from Gray, only Peter Godfrey – who opened his little Gate Theatre in 1925, moving it from a Covent Garden warehouse to a former skittle-alley alongside Charing Cross Station two years later – made it a matter of policy consistently to bring innovative Europeans before English audiences; and it was no doubt an accurate reflection of the limited appetite for such work that neither of his houses had a capacity of more than ninety. Another pioneering director, Norman Marshall, took over in 1934, judiciously leavening his foreign imports with the less elusive attractions of the famous Gate revues.

The Gate was formed as a club theatre in order to avoid fire regulations rather than censorship, but its precedent was followed when, in 1927, the opening of the Arts Theatre, off the Charing Cross Road, gave what Marshall later dubbed the 'other theatre' a permanent toehold in the West End. The glory days of the Arts were yet to come: meanwhile, hiring commercial theatres for the occasion, various groups (the surviving Stage Society and Edy Craig's briefly revived Pioneers, the new Three Hundred Club, and later the London International Theatre) dedicated themselves to the production of uncommercial but worthwhile drama for Sunday-evening, subscription audiences. Other, actor-based organizations – the Repertory Players, the Play Actors, the Fellowship of Players – set out rather to 'package' potentially more commercial productions in the hope of finding backing for a full-scale run.

Also prominent among the 'other theatres', the Phoenix Society worked valiantly between 1919 and 1926 under the leadership of Allan Wade to resuscitate the lesser-known Renaissance and Restoration drama. Mainstream Shakespearean revivals during the twenties were relatively few, and largely undistinguished: but Barry Jackson, whose *Cymbeline* of 1923 and better-noticed *Hamlet* of 1925 were the first in a line of modern-dress productions, thus restored a long-enduring tradition of playing (rather than making the revolutionary gesture it was presumed by some); while Terence Gray, despite shocking Cambridge audiences with the listless Portia of his inaugural *Merchant of Venice* in 1927, reasserted for the plays the right to a single, flexibly unlocalized setting – a fashion anticipated, albeit on economic grounds, by Lovat Fraser's set for *The Beggar's Opera*.

At Stratford, Frank Benson – knighted in costume during the tercentenary commemoration of Shakespeare's death in 1916 – gave way three years later to W. Bridges-Adams, who was installed with a view to forming the nucleus of a National Theatre company. That aim was never realized, but in 1922 the company

Colin Keith-Johnston as Hamlet in the famous modern-dress production – 'Hamlet in plus-fours', as it was popularly known – brought to the Kingsway Theatre, London, in 1925 by Barry Jackson's company from the Birmingham Rep. His *Cymbeline* had been the first such 'experiment' (in fact a return to the eighteenth-century tradition) two years earlier. This *Hamlet* was the work of the regular Birmingham team, with Henry Ayliff directing and designs by Paul Shelving. *The Outfitter* condescendingly noted that 'there were few sartorial errors of real importance'

was the first of its kind to become (at least by intention) non-profit making, with a policy of ploughing back all revenues into the theatre. However, the original Memorial Theatre burned down four years later, enforcing upon Bridges-Adams a retreat to a local cinema until the new, present building opened in 1932 – its broad but intractable proscenium stage belying the modernity of its riverward facade. Two years later Bridges-Adams, under whom the season had been extended from three weeks to five months, was succeeded by Ben Iden-Payne.

Not strictly of the 'other theatre', yet distant from the West End in situation as in sensibility, the Old Vic, continuing under Lilian Baylis's management, was now recognized as the main London venue for the production of Shakespeare's plays – the project for producing all 37 plays in the First Folio, initiated in 1915 under the direction of Ben Greet, reaching completion in 1923 under Robert Atkins. After 1931 Miss Baylis ran the theatre in tandem with Sadler's Wells, at first alternating opera and drama at both theatres, but soon making the Wells the base for opera in English – and for the company that was to become the Royal Ballet.

VINTAGE YEARS OF ACTING

The dearth of challenging new writing meant that actors too often found themselves caught between those prolix stage directions with which, following Shaw and John Galsworthy, lesser writers were increasingly prone to pin down their

Romeo and Juliet at the New Theatre, 1935. John Gielgud began a three-year association with this theatre in 1933, and his Hamlet was seen there in 1934. In this picture, Gielgud's Mercutio (right) and Laurence Olivier's Romeo flank Edith Evans's Nurse – but later in the run of 186 performances (a record for the play) they exchanged roles. The critic James Agate commented that the resulting 'clash of magnanimities is almost embarrassing, Mr Gielgud going to the length of not letting us see what he thinks of Mr Olivier's diction in the Queen Mab speech, and Mr Olivier tempering Mercutio's death agonies to permit us a glimpse of Romeo's contrition'

characters in the script, and the director's tight and too-often preconceived plotting of every movement – almost, the actor's very stage presence. And so it was largely in Shakespearean and other classic revivals – and, of course, in meeting the new challenge of the talking pictures – that the actors who came into prominence between the wars established their reputations. Thus, although Sybil Thorndike was the first to achieve stardom with the Old Vic company, during the 1920s and 1930s its members included most of the rising names of modern English acting, among them John Gielgud, Laurence Olivier, Ralph Richardson, Edith Evans, Michael Redgrave, and Peggy Ashcroft.

During the 1930–31 season at the Old Vic, Bryan Forbes has calculated that Gielgud and Richardson played twenty roles between them, Edith Evans no less than thirteen. Olivier was a later arrival: already, in the West End, he had achieved a quiet success as Stanhope in *Journey's End*, and a rather noisier one in *Private Lives* (during which Coward trained him not to giggle at awkward moments). By 1935 Gielgud was installed at the New Theatre, where (as pictured on the opposite page) he invited Olivier to play Romeo to his own Mercutio, the pair exchanging roles as the season progressed – an early example of the blend of rivalry and reciprocity that was to characterize their long subsequent professional relationship.

While temperamentally best suited to high comedy, Gielgud had first achieved fame as Hamlet in 1929 – and his second attempt at the role, during his 1934

View from the stage at the new Shakespeare Memorial Theatre, Stratford-upon-Avon, designed by Elizabeth Scott and opened in 1932. Despite the modernity of its riverward frontage, and a functional internal appearance, its spatial relationships were firmly cast in a nineteenth-century mould – a yawning orchestra pit separating the actors, on a wide proscenium stage, from the spectators in a large fan-shaped auditorium seating around 1,500. In 1944, a forestage was built out over the orchestra pit. Further alterations were carried out when the theatre became home to the Royal Shakespeare Company after 1961: but an uneasy tension persists between the theatre and the staging concepts of many of its directors and designers

season at the New, was recognized as definitive for a rising generation that was sharply articulate and self-aware, yet also desperately uncertain of its bearings. Two years later, Olivier came to the Old Vic to play Hamlet in a production by Tyrone Guthrie (who by that year of Lilian Baylis's death was already master-minding the policy of her theatre). Characteristically, Olivier explored the role with as meticulous attention to subtext as to text – absorbing himself in the Freudian interpretation of Hamlet's Oedipal impulses (as put forward by Ernest Jones), and so evidently rendering his character truer to this 'essential' psyche than to his audience's times.

Of the two, Gielgud's genius was seemingly more demonstrable, yet in truth the more elusive – a mercurial quality charging with an edge of danger his none the less precisely-honed and ultimately cerebral technique. Olivier relished emotional complexity, where Gielgud mastered a role intellectually and drove a straight line through its demands. Gielgud commanded attention through the power of speech, usually at its most mellifluous, while Olivier wrestled to communicate all the non-verbal signifiers of feeling, then wrought speech to their service – often more roughly-hewn. In Olivier's own comparison, he and Gielgud were 'the reverse of the same coin', Gielgud 'all spirituality, all beauty, all abstract things', himself 'all earth, blood, everything to do with earth, humanity if you like – the baser part of humanity'.

Of the period's great actresses, Sybil Thorndike had already been working before the First World War – during which, with actors in short supply, she had taken on Shakespeare's males, from Prince Hal to Lear's Fool, as readily as his females. This wondrously vital, charismatic performer brought to her work an inner warmth which was of herself – yet, because it partly derived from an openness of sensibility towards others, also allowed her characters to be demonstrably themselves. Her stately impishness was utterly right for St Joan, Candida, or Major Barbara – but no less surely could she scale the sublime tragic peaks of Hecuba and Medea, or tread the gentler foothills as Aase to Richardson's Peer Gynt.

Edith Evans, whose own aptitude was for pronouncedly comic performance, remained prouder of her Nurse to Peggy Ashcroft's Juliet in Gielgud's *Romeo*, and of her ravishing if rather overwhelming Millamant, than of her Lady Bracknell in *The Importance of Being Earnest* (1940), with which she became distractingly identified. But a 'character actress' in the best sense she remained – as Olivier was a 'character actor', while Ralph Richardson, for all his clutch of character parts, was in essence a brilliant eccentric comedian.

From Falstaff to Peer Gynt, from Uncle Vanya to the title-role in Priestley's *An Inspector Calls*, Richardson was peerless in conveying the concealed depths beneath a character's blustering, bland, or professional facade. If Gielgud was the consummate master of verse speaking, Richardson at his (admittedly less consistent) best could command all the nuances of prose – while if Olivier excelled in demonstrating the ordinariness beneath the heroics, Richardson, sensitive and

Opposite: Arthur Askey and Richard Murdoch playing to the BBC microphone in *Band Wagon*, which ran for three series from 1938. This show was highly innovative in its time, presenting the two resident comedians (under their own names but with distinct radio identities) in a regular weekly slot and ambience – a fantasy 'top-floor flat' in Broadcasting House. The formula, with supporting comic regulars and musical interludes, became a popular one, later deployed for such comic domestic sit-coms as *Ray's a Laugh* (1949–61) and even *Hancock's Half-Hour* (1954–59). But Tommy Handley's *Itma* (1939–48), *Take It from Here* (1948–59), and *The Goon Show* (1952–60) soon found more inventive ways of filling a half-hour radio comedy slot

almost shy behind a sort of roisterous innocence, demonstrated that ordinariness could conceal a heroism of its own.

While even Olivier could flounder as well as flourish in the talkies, Charles Laughton, like many others, came consistently to prefer the new medium, which was coming into its own just as the brittle brightness of the twenties was giving way to the anxious thirties of depression at home and dictatorships abroad. But as film found its voice, it lost something of the stylistic flair of the silent era, replacing an embryonic vocabulary of speaking eyes, lips, and hands with dialogue which often remained all too stagey, and expressed a good deal less.

THE COMING OF 'THE WIRELESS'

The creation of the British Broadcasting Corporation in 1926 ensured that, for the immediate future at least, radio would grow as a public service, not (as in the USA) in response to the needs of advertisers; and by the outbreak of war the BBC had developed from a novelty into a national institution, mocked sometimes for its stuffiness but also genuinely respected.

A side effect of the arrival of radio was the pervasive influence of the 'official' broadcast voice as the embodiment of the 'received' accent. Conversely, variations from this norm became regarded not merely as regional characteristics but as class signifiers – as of course to some extent they had always been. The close-drawn boundaries of the official culture may be illustrated at their laziest when actors with voices trained to speak 'properly' proved ill-equipped to offer any other accents beyond the limited spectrum of the mock-cockney, the broad mummerset, and the generic northern.

The first play in the world to be written for and broadcast by radio – Richard Hughes's *Danger*, in 1923 – exploited the 'limitations' of the medium by taking as its setting a coal mine during a power-cut: and only slowly did writers begin to exploit the potential of radio with a less literal-minded dedication. With Tyrone Guthrie as an honourable exception, too many radio writers worked within an aural equivalent of the box-set, using obtrusive sound effects and awkward exposition to apologise for the lack of vision – instead of creatively exploiting it. And Val Gielgud, John's brother, who remained Head of Drama at the BBC for over thirty years, was – despite the urging of the likes of Guthrie – notably unresponsive towards such experimental work as came his way.

It is thus significant that the most creative use of radio in the 'thirties came not from the drama but the 'features' department, where experiments with the blending of words and music, dialogue and narrative, actuality and invention, led the way (with the availability after the war of the early portable tape recorder) to the creation of the 'radio ballads' of Charles Parker and Ewan MacColl, to which we shall return in the next chapter. Variety performers, too, used radio to let the imagination off the leash – from Stainless Stephen, with his bizarre spoken punctuation, to A. J. Alan with his unique storytelling style; from Arthur Askey and Richard Murdoch, with their lodgings and pet goat on the roof of the new Broadcasting House, to Gillie Potter with his monologues of resonant pomposity.

The sheer range of material on offer – news and sports coverage, live broadcasts of music from opera to swing, talks and documentaries, as well as drama, features, and variety – created a 'compilation bill' of the fireside which nibbled away at the old audience for live theatre perhaps more insidiously but no less effectively than did the coming of the talking pictures. But there was also a strong pedagogic impulse behind early public-service broadcasting, and while this did not create the strong movement towards self-education which had already been discernible in the twenties, it certainly encouraged its now determined stride.

This burgeoning desire for knowledge among the more aspirant sections of the working and lower middle classes manifested itself not only in the queues for Shakespeare at the Old Vic and opera at Sadler's Wells, but in informal gatherings dedicated to listening to and discussing classical gramophone records and wireless talks; in full classes for the lecturers of the Workers' Educational Association and university extra-mural departments; and in self-imposed devotion to reading

which saw the flowering not only of the public libraries but of inexpensive series – classics in the old Everyman's Library, new writing in the startlingly successful Penguin paperbacks, instructional non-fiction in the companion Pelicans.

THE AMATEUR THEATRE – AND THE WORKERS' THEATRE

Even popular newspapers were fighting the circulation wars then raging with bribes not only of free insurance but of sets of the novels of Charles Dickens – and also of the plays and even the prefaces of Bernard Shaw (at a time, too, when 'collected editions' of such writers as Galsworthy, Barrie, and Ashley Dukes sold by their thousands). Ill-fed though it was by the classbound commercial sector, there was a huge appetite for the drama, and this found its outlet in part through a proliferation of amateur theatre, which was both consolidated and further encouraged by the creation of the British Drama League in 1919.

One manifestation of this boom in amateur theatre was the new popularity of the one-act play, for which there had been a steep decline in demand since the death of the multiple-bill. In part this renaissance had its origins before and during the First World War, when, following the loosening of the old restrictions on the presentation of dramatic material in music halls, the more bookable of the actor-managers had lowered their dignities to display their genius on the halls – in

Cinema wins the provincial heart

The fantasies offered by film, and its capacity for creating spectacle and vicarious thrills, made up in liberally applied gloss, glamour, and sheer technical proficiency what the medium lacked in subtlety and imagination. In this respect, film took over the function of melodrama – and even bred up new audiences for it, in the Saturday morning children's shows whose cliffhanging serials ensured the habit-forming of a new generation of 'fans'.

Cinemas were now sprouting even in towns too small ever to have boasted their own theatre. Expectations of dress and behaviour were more relaxed – but the sheer physical luxuriance on offer was classless, and the dreams a twice-weekly compensation for the drabness of impoverished lives.

Provincial theatre lost out not only to the superior comforts of the cinema but to the tempting splendours of its bill of fare in an era when, with few exceptions, 'weekly rep' offered only a pallid aftertaste

of an already largely insipid West End diet, while touring attractions seemed tacky beside their cinematic equivalents. If we allow Terence Gray in Cambridge and J. B. Fagan at the Oxford Playhouse as special cases, in view of their captive university audiences, we have also to concede that the example of the Birmingham Rep, however worthy, was also exceptional – even the Gaiety having abandoned the struggle in Manchester in 1921.

Music hall, too, was suffering, and it is notable that most of the stars of these, its declining years – Maurice Chevalier, Sid Field, George Formby, Gracie Fields, Max Miller – achieved fame less through the halls (keep faith with them though they did) than through their wider exposure in films, and, of course, through the new medium of radio broadcasting, which now made its own stars. Such rare exceptions as the knockabout Crazy Gang, indubitably live and alive, only went to prove the rule.

Opposite: entrance to the Granada, Tooting, a typically opulent inter-war picture palace. The entrance foyer, with its soft-carpeting, candelabra, swathes of mirror-glass, and sweeping stairways, sustained the luxurious welcome offered to all-comers – at a time when poorer theatregoers were still consigned to side-street entrances and narrow concrete stairs. The number of cinemas in the UK, already at 3,170 before the First World War, rose to 3,760 by 1928, and had reached a peak of 4,900 in 1939. By 1964 the number was down to 2,057, and in 1990 had further shrunk to 1,561

suitably regulated doses. Now amateur societies, too, wanted plays tailored in length to the requirements of competitive festivals, or to the need to offer as many acting opportunities as possible to their members through double- or triple-bills.

Still-flourishing survivors from that vintage period of amateur theatre include the galleried Maddermarket Theatre in Norwich, where Nugent Monck mounted productions of neglected classics; the Tower in Islington, opened by Duncan Marks; and the Questors in Ealing, the brainchild of Alfred Emmet. But such culturally aspirant groups were less representative than the mass of smaller societies, many of which were no more (though no less) than social gatherings with a sense of purpose – that purpose generally being, honourably enough, the amusement of themselves and their audiences.

Sometimes, however, there was also a political imperative, and this became more overt as the 'popular front' of left-wing opposition to fascism sought theatrical aid. The Workers' Theatre Movement, which held its first national conference in 1932 and at one time or another included over sixty affiliates, was thus in part a product of the wider enthusiasm for do-it-yourself theatre – but also a product of that alternative lifestyle in which Socialist Sunday Schools, the

Woodcraft Folk, union branches, working men's clubs and institutes, the Co-op 'divi', and later the Left Book Club were all compounded.

Stalwarts of the movement included Tom Thomas, who founded the pioneering Red Radio in London's East End, and Ewan MacColl, who, with the young Joan Littlewood, developed the Salford group the Red Megaphones into Theatre of Action. Finding little inspiration in the class-ridden contemporary British drama, the WTM groups looked for models amidst the creative chaos of Weimar Germany; from the theatrical ferment of the twenties in the Soviet Union, before the dead hand of Stalin and socialist realism descended; and, most accessibly, from the work of the Federal Theatre Project, which had been created by the Roosevelt administration in the United States to alleviate unemployment in the acting profession. Later, Littlewood in particular began to explore forms of popular drama and clowning in Elizabethan England, and the *commedia* style of Renaissance Italy.

Thus, although 'conventional' plays (including Joe Corrie's *In Time of Strife* and Thomas's adaptation of Robert Tressell's novel *The Ragged Trousered Philanthropists*) were presented by the WTM groups, more characteristic was the influence of the politicized cabaret the Blue Blouses, and the Soviet technique of agitational propaganda or 'agitprop' – short, sharp, topical sketches combining elements of revue and polemic suited to factory-gate or other informal modes of presentation. Mass chanting, tableaux, and political pageantry were also employed in the more ambitious pieces developed for rallies and demonstrations.

By 1937 the Rebel Players of St Pancras had opened their own permanent theatre, the first Unity in Goldington Street – and by the following year its members could look back not only to a guest appearance by Paul Robeson, but to the creation of their first living newspaper, *Busmen*, and (inaugurating a long tradition) a political Christmas pantomime, *Babes in the Wood*, which took as its focus the betrayal of Czechoslovakia during the Munich crisis of that autumn.

POLITICAL POETRY, ESCAPIST HISTORY

It was left to the left-wing poets of the thirties, products though they were of the public schools and Oxbridge, to inject politics into mainstream playwriting. The Group Theatre, formed by Tyrone Guthrie in 1933, staged plays by W. H. Auden and Christopher Isherwood, Stephen Spender, and Louis MacNeice, in which moral archetype was set against immoral archetype in the cause of the proletarian revolution – the style often an odd mix of medieval morality and expressionist polemic. In the event, this movement remained of minority interest – though MacNeice's later role as a BBC producer gave it a wider audience on the radio. The Group also performed the first verse play, *Sweeney Agonistes* (1935), by the innovative but politically conservative poet T. S. Eliot, who went on to achieve wider theatrical acclaim with *Murder in the Cathedral* (1935). To the brief renaissance of poetic drama inaugurated by Eliot and the Group writers we shall return in the next chapter.

Opposite: The production at Unity Theatre of *Waiting for Lefty* (1936), by the American dramatist Clifford Odets. This play became a classic of left-wing propagandist theatre, combining naturalistic and agitprop techniques towards a climax which embraced its whole audience in a demand for strike action. Later in the thirties, 'living newspapers', first created by a unit of the Federal Theatre Project, also exerted a seminal influence on British left-wing theatre: these were dramatized documentaries on current themes, which could be updated in the light of a developing situation

With very few exceptions – honourable among them Walter Greenwood's *Love on the Dole* (1935), adapted with Ronald Gow from his successful novel, and Emlyn Williams's *The Corn is Green* (1938) – the West End theatre continued to disregard the problems of the lower orders, let alone the causes and social consequences of the depression. Thus, the division in the country between those who advocated confronting the fascist threat and those who preferred to ignore it – or to buy it off by appeasement when it could be ignored no longer – was reflected in the commercial theatre only in so far as chauvinism and escapism continued to prove a profitable combination.

Often, this took the form of a retreat into the glories and reassuring certainties of the past – Coward's *Cavalcade* providing a confessedly superior case-study for imitation. Certainly, its example was taken to wild excess in the phenomenon of *Young England* (1934), a patriotic melodrama which ran for 278 performances. Written in all seriousness by the elderly Walter Reynolds, the play was good-naturedly ridiculed by loudly participatory audiences who liked to think themselves less ingenuous than its outraged author – but in truth were no less susceptible to the chauvinistic verities it propounded.

Exotic or historical settings provided ready escapist routes. Thus, while S. I. Hsiung's *Lady Precious Stream* (1934) offered pleasant distraction through what the critic J. C. Trewin aptly called its 'willow-pattern charade', a whole cluster of 'portrait plays' did so by distancing their audiences in time from the disturbing present. Reginald Berkeley's *The Lady with a Lamp* (1929) created a sanitized Florence Nightingale, Rudolf Besier portrayed the Brownings in love in *The Barretts of Wimpole Street* (1930), Gordon Daviot (actually Elizabeth Mackintosh) gave Gielgud a star-vehicle as *Richard of Bordeaux* (1933), and Napoleon in exile figured in R. C. Sherriff's *St Helena* (1936).

Versions of the Brontës, Cromwell, and Samuel Pepys were also popular, and Laurence Houseman created whole omnibuses of dramatic vignettes from the lives of Queen Victoria and St Francis. Although, as censor, the Lord Chamberlain was not amused at the portrayal of a monarch scarce thirty years in her grave, Houseman's playlets had an enduring appeal for amateurs – prompting one to wonder if village-hall performances long ago rejoiced the childhood heart of Margaret Thatcher, that she should later invoke so unlikely a pair in her vicarious support.

Interestingly if less influentially, James Bridie, a pseudonymous Scottish doctor, pursued his own quirky line in a prodigious output usually (unlike the work of his fellow-countryman Barrie) aimed at and first seen in his native Scotland – where, in 1943, he was also to found the Glasgow Citizens' Theatre. In such plays as *Tobias and the Angel* (1930), *A Sleeping Clergyman* (1943), *Mr Bolfry* (1943), and *Daphne Laureola* (1949) he combined an eye for character with a harsh critique of hypocrisy (not least in the learned professions), often adding a refreshing dash of the surreal. This was escapism still, but of a superior, intellectually tantalizing kind.

Opposite: J. B. Priestley's *Johnson over Jordan* (1939), performed (like *Music at Night* in the same year) by his own Mask Theatre company at the Westminster. Using music, ballet, and the masked allegorical characters here portrayed, the play concerned a very ordinary businessman coming to terms with his own recent death. Priestley (1894–1984) was a prolific novelist and dramatist, who infused a common-sense radicalism into the naturalistic vein he more usually worked – also utilizing a variant on the relativity theory as a successful dramatic device in his self-styled 'time plays'. Two of his wartime plays are discussed in the caption on page 303: later, in *The Linden Tree* (1947), he gave rare expression on the West End stage to the political climate of the immediate post-war period

For all the contemporary success of John van Druten's many polished comedies of the 'thirties, only his earlier *Young Woodley* (1928), a sensitive evocation of adolescent passion, has proved enduring – while of Dodie Smith's output, her canonization of the domestic verities in *Dear Octopus* (1938) has alone survived. J. B. Priestley's portraits of solid, often industrial middle-class England, rendered no less fully through its smug hypocrisies than its hard-working self-sufficiency, have better withstood the test of time, whether in the broadly comic vein of *When We Are Married* (1938) or the serious mode through which, in *Eden End* (1934), he rebuked the nostalgia of his audiences with some troubled truths about the supposedly idyllic England of their dreams.

Priestley also wrote a sequence of 'time plays', from *Dangerous Corner* (1932) to *I Have Been Here Before* (1937), in which he made dramatically palatable the fashionable theories of serial time propagated by Ouspensky and J. W. Dunne. Then, following the experiment in allegory of *Johnson over Jordan* (1939), came the more clearly articulated political vision of *They Came to a City* (1943), which offered hope for a better future rather than reconciliation with the past. But by then Priestley was reaching far wider audiences, through his brilliant use of radio as spokesperson for a nation at war – a role in which he found himself at once a willing collaborator and an unlikely competitor with another, more overtly theatrical performer, the wartime prime minister Winston Churchill.

CHAPTER 19   *The Utility Theatre*

It was the worst of times, it was the best of times. The nation stood, for one brave and battered year alone, against the fascist tide which had already engulfed continental Europe, and whose evil nature was even then scarcely understood – only the liberation of the death camps in 1945 exposing the full horror of the holocaust that had been Hitler's 'final solution'. Then, just a few months later, the destruction of Hiroshima, though it ended the war in the Far East, demonstrated the terrible potential of nuclear conflict – the threat of which cast its shadow over the breakdown of the alliance with the Soviet Union, as Eastern Europe found enforced shelter behind the 'Iron Curtain'. At home, the privations of war were followed by continuing shortages of food and power, especially during the bleak winter of 1947, the worst for a century. Even the weather, it seemed, was conspiring to crush the hopes raised by the election two years earlier of the first majority Labour government.

On the other hand, the sense of common purpose created by the need to defeat the nazi powers did linger for a while into the peace. The wartime coalition had been practising economic intervention of the kind advocated by Maynard Keynes, and exploring the provision of a state system of social security on the lines of the Beveridge Report, well before the Labour government made these the twin pillars of its plans for reconstruction: and, although opposed with virulence at the time, the creation of a mixed economy and a fully-fledged Welfare State helped to shape a political consensus which was to be sustained until the end of the 1970s. The state now accepted among its responsibilities the elimination of mass unemployment, the avoidance of the worst extremes of poverty, and the alleviation of ill health.

Infant mortality thus continued steadily to fall, war babies from all classes remaining well nourished thanks to the fair rationing of scarce resources. And, as this history begins to mesh with my own experiences, I can only say that, despite being born into one of the poorest-paid sectors of the community, my own childhood memories are not of impoverishment and shortage, but of the small astonishments of bananas, ice-cream, and dinky toys. For my parents, a free Health Service was a more solid assurance of a better future – as was the arrival of electricity in the countryside, allowing farm workers like my father to rise a little later in the mornings now that the cows could be milked by machine. And educational reforms were making it possible for poor children to receive a 'good' if still class-ridden schooling, and even to win their way to university with state support.

The theatre reflected all these social changes and the tensions which accompanied them – sometimes directly, in a new counterpoising of state involvement with commercial interests, sometimes indirectly, in necessary accommodations to changing times and conditions. Some temporary wartime expedients, such as the abandonment of evening dress by patrons of the dress circle and front stalls, proved symbolically permanent – and even the new West End starting time of six o'clock, designed to allow audiences to arrive straight from work and get home early, has never crept back to the 8.30 norm of pre-war days, with its presumption of a leisured clientele dining out before the performance and going on to supper afterwards.

THE THEATRE IN WARTIME

During the periods of bombing some theatres played matinees only – and even lunchtimes became an enclave for cultural as well as bodily refreshment when the last of the old barn-storming actor-managers, Donald Wolfit, brought his company to London with a programme of pre-prandial Shakespeares. But the only two theatres to carry on playing nightly throughout the blitz were, famously, the Windmill – whose long-standing boast to that effect, 'We never closed', was inevitably if inaccurately amended by its patrons to 'We never clothed' – and, almost unnoticed by posterity, the Unity, where a new topical revue had been written and mounted within forty-eight hours of the outbreak of war.

The Shaftesbury, Queen's, and Little Theatres were destroyed and the Duke of York's, the Royal Court, and the Old Vic were among those theatres badly damaged during the blitz: but gradually managements and audiences learned to live with the bombing, and by the summer of 1941 the worst seemed over – until flying bombs in 1944 posed a new and stealthier threat, at one time closing all but eight of the remaining West End theatres. Ironically, two of the established successes which continued their runs regardless of the rockets were farces concerned, as were their audiences, with outfacing the ultimate taboo of death – Noël Coward's *Blithe Spirit*, and that masterpiece of the comic macabre, Joseph Kesselring's *Arsenic and Old Lace*.

Among the abundance of acronymic organizations which flourished during the war, three – ABCA, ENSA, and CEMA – had some kind of theatrical significance. The first two of these were military in origin and the last civilian, but in some respects (exchanges of personnel and bureaucratic demarcation disputes among them) they worked on common lines, hoping to bring theatrical experience to new kinds of audiences. ABCA, in line with its full title of the Army Bureau of Current Affairs, was most sternly didactic of purpose: yet it is a tribute to influences as diverse as the Federal Theatre's Living Newspapers, the wartime boom in documentary film-making, and the Features Department of the BBC that ABCA should have been persuaded to create its influential Play Unit, and seek for dramatic means to put across its educational propaganda.

Michael Macowan (remembered for a *Troilus and Cressida* at Stratford whose message of the futility of war had coincided momentously with the Munich crisis) headed the Play Unit, and also directed the play Priestley wrote especially for ABCA, *Desert Highway* – a semi-mystical celebration of hopes and fears for

In Noël Coward's *Blithe Spirit* (1941) Margaret Rutherford (opposite) played the hearty rustic medium employed to exorcise the garrulous ghost of Elvira (Fay Compton, right), seen below with her successor-wife, Ruth (Kay Hammond). Next year from Broadway came Joseph Kesselring's *Arsenic and Old Lace*, making mass-murderers out of a prim and proper spinster pair. Both long-running wartime farces pushed the boundaries of the form to accommodate death – without reference to the war

the future which, ironically, moved into a West End theatre in 1944. But more typical of its output were such dramatic collages and semi-documentaries as *United We Stand* and *It Started with Lend-Lease* – or on the down side *What's Wrong with the Germans?* and *The Japanese Way* – which involved writers, directors, and actors of the calibre of Ted Willis, André van Gyseghem, Bridget Boland, and Stephen Murray.

ENSA – popularly supposed to stand for 'Every Night Something Awful', but properly the Entertainments National Services Association – was effectively the brain-child of Basil Dean, who became its long-serving director, with Henry Oscar eventually taking charge of the drama programme. From its unlikely headquarters in the historic Drury Lane Theatre, ENSA's far-flung operations involved it as much in building mobile cinemas, and touring Shakespeare, symphony orchestras, and ballet, as in mounting the variety shows for which it is best remembered – some replete with end-of-pier acts signed up for the duration, others prestigious vehicles for top-billing performers whose battledress was a temporary bureaucratic expedient.

ENSA not only took out such shows into the furthest-flung 'theatres' of war, but backed the touring of independent London productions to garrison theatres or Royal Ordnance hostels at home: and here its work overlapped with that of CEMA, the Council for the Encouragement of Music and the Arts. This had been formed under the private charitable auspices of the Pilgrim Trust soon after the outbreak of war, with the state assuming at first shared and after 1942 sole financial responsibility for its work of bringing theatre to factory canteens, community centres, and even bomb shelters in areas otherwise ill-served by the living arts, from Cumbria to the wilder reaches of the home counties.

At one time, CEMA was responsible for no less than sixteen productions touring simultaneously. And when, in 1940, the Old Vic had suffered extensive damage from wartime bombing, it was under the auspices of CEMA that companies in exile were formed, with bases in Burnley and Liverpool – whence touring productions were sent out northwards into County Durham and southwards into the mining areas of Wales. CEMA also helped to establish an alternative London home for the Old Vic, at the New Theatre – from 1944 to 1949 under the leadership of Olivier, at first in a sparkily incongruous collaboration with Richardson.

By then, the company was routinely employing the system of 'true' repertoire, whereby the productions on offer were alternated throughout the season, rather than each playing for an uninterrupted spell – a welcome change after a century of increasing subservience to the long run. A pioneer in making this change was the young Alec Clunes, who, having taken over the Arts Theatre Club in 1942, mounted a Festival of Comedy in high classical style in the following year. An actor of ascetic appearance and wry authority, Clunes also directed much of the work which, over the next decade, was to sustain a glittering reputation for himself and his theatre.

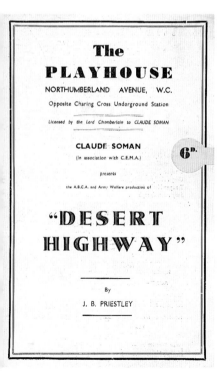

The
PLAYHOUSE
NORTHUMBERLAND   AVENUE,   W.C.
Opposite Charing Cross Underground Station

Licensed by the Lord Chamberlain to CLAUDE SOMAN

CLAUDE SOMAN   **6ᴰ.**
(in association with C.E.M.A.)

presents

the A.B.C.A. and Army Welfare production of

"DESERT HIGHWAY"

By
J. B. PRIESTLEY

A season of five plays by Shaw played in 'true rep' at the Lyric, Hammersmith, in 1944, and in the same year companies under John Gielgud at the Haymarket and Donald Wolfit at the Scala also alternated their bills throughout the season. The public, so far from being puzzled by the system as many of the commercial managers had warned, found it convenient to book for several productions simultaneously. More to the artistic point, alternating rep encouraged the creation of at least semi-permanent acting companies – sometimes with a degree of greater equity in the distribution of leading and minor roles, but in any case freeing members from the tyranny of playing the same part night after night until audiences or energies were exhausted.

THE ARTS COUNCIL AND THE COMMERCIAL MANAGEMENTS

CEMA had been active in the creation of the Citizens' Theatre, Glasgow, in 1943, and in the same year took over the Theatre Royal, Bristol – which three years later, as the Bristol Old Vic, passed into local control under the direction of Hugh Hunt. For a while after taking on its peacetime guise as the Arts Council in 1946, the organization continued in theatrical management on its own account, in pursuit of its policy of decentralizing the British theatre. Now it was authorized to give capital grants as well as guarantees against loss, and was soon concentrating its limited funding on support for the leading repertory theatres, in Birmingham, Cambridge, Liverpool, Sheffield, and Glasgow.

At first its seemed probable that such direct subsidies would gradually be superseded by grants from local authorities, who were enabled by a provision in the Local Government Act of 1948 to levy a rate of up to sixpence in the pound for artistic and cultural provision. In the event, however, civic pride was to be made manifest less through support for existing theatres than in the making of plans for new ones – purpose-built (as the dwindling stock of cavernous regional touring theatres clearly was not) to meet the requirements of the age. These plans, as we shall see, began to bear fruit in the ensuing decade.

Among its other powers, the Arts Council was now able to recommend that productions of cultural or educational value should be exempted from paying Entertainments Tax – which, at ten per cent of gross profits, had come to constitute by 1948 over a quarter of the price of a theatre ticket. This led to a boom in the creation of not-for-profit companies, some formed by commercial managements to present tryouts of potentially profitable productions with some claim to cultural credibility: thus, the earliest London productions of plays by the two leading post-war American dramatists, Arthur Miller's *Death of a Salesman* and Tennessee Williams's *A Streetcar Named Desire*, were both accorded such 'tax free' status in 1949. But there were charges that the system was liable to abuse, and Arts Council support for commercial managements ceased in 1951.

When Basil Dean mounted a season of productions from state-supported regional theatres at the St James's in 1949, London audiences were, with due

Programme for J. B. Priestley's *Desert Highway*, written for performance in army camps by the Play Unit of ABCA (the Army Bureau of Current Affairs), and brought to the Playhouse Theatre in February 1944 'in association with CEMA' (the Council for the Encouragement of Music and the Arts). This play is a deeply serious exploration of the ways in which the crew of a stranded tank confront the imminence of death: but the play Priestley wrote for ENSA (the Entertainments National Services Association) was a lighter though no less topical piece, *How Are They at Home?*, portraying the effects of billeting, Land Army girls, and ration books upon a staid English country house

condescension, surprised both by their quality and their variety. But the lowlier weekly reps were by then struggling for survival, in the face not only of continuing competition from the cinema but of the new and at first more insidious threat from television – the BBC's service having been relaunched in 1946 after its embryonic beginnings before the war. Viewing figures grew only sluggishly at first, but accelerated after the televising of the Coronation service in 1953 and with the arrival of a second, commercial channel in 1955 – by which time the touring circuits, too, were in a parlous state.

For this, the causes lay not only in competition from films and television, but in the 'rationalization' of an investment portfolio now in the hands of an effective monopoly. Throughout the war, when town centre properties were often available at almost giveaway prices, the impresario Prince Littler had thus been busily adding to his already extensive theatre interests, his takeovers including both the former Stoll Theatre chain and the old Moss Empires. The critic John Elsom has calculated that, by 1945, the interconnected companies comprising 'the Group' (as it came to be known in the industry) owned 57 of the theatres which formed part of the residual touring circuits, including 34 of the 53 which offered 'number one' dates. By the end of the 1950s, following developments or conversions into shops, offices, dance halls, bingo parlours, and bowling alleys, out of an

Ralph Richardson is seen here with Meg Jenkins in *A Day by the Sea* (1953), a quintessentially post-war play by N. C. Hunter (1908–71). Staged at the now-prestigious Haymarket, and with John Gielgud, Sybil Thorndike, Lewis Casson, and Irene Worth also in its cast, the action took place beneath a sturdy, emblematic oak and along a seashore doubly symbolic of permanance and ebb and flow. A similar atmosphere of wistful nostalgia for an unfulfilled past had been evoked in Hunter's earlier *Waters of the Moon* (1951), in which Edith Evans cut a sophisticated swathe through a staid west-country guest house, leaving residents and staff (Thorndike and Wendy Hiller among them) with an aching longing for the unattainable

original total of 150 provincial theatres owned by the Group, a mere handful, around thirty, survived.

Littler's Howard and Wyndham organization also controlled 18 out of the 42 active London theatres, and had a majority shareholding in H. M. Tennent Ltd, the leading play-producing management in the capital. Although the West End theatres were more secure from threats of conversion or demolition, they were thus coming increasingly under the sway of Tennent's powerful managing director, Hugh 'Binkie' Beaumont, then at the height of his long and legendary influence. Beaumont's tastes were not so much bad as blinkered – his choice of plays calculated either to affirm an old audience's old prejudices, or to offer vicarious refuge from the egalitarianism which the middle classes now felt to be steadily diminishing their prosperity and status.

Despite the brief flurry of new Russian plays which had marked the Soviet entry into the war, communism was of course perceived as the ultimate threat, and soon its exponents might once more be snubbed in decent society. So when, in 1948, Priestley chaired a three-day theatre conference, to which the Chancellor of the Exchequer lent his presence and support, its proceedings were boycotted (and, in retrospect, effectively scuppered, despite high hopes at the time) by the Group managements – on the grounds that its organizers were communists. (One of them, Ted Willis, went on to create on television that epitome of well-regulated subservience to the capitalist system, PC Dixon of Dock Green.)

IN THE WEST END

Only rarely, then, were West End audiences disturbed by plays which presented the radically changed social conditions of those years with a degree of honesty rather than evasion. J. B. Priestley, in *The Linden Tree* (1947), did engage with the real problems and concerns of a middle-class family (a provincial one, at that) who felt themselves dispossessed and undervalued: but more usual were pieces which combined wish-fulfilment with a sort of sublimated revenge upon the proletariat – a combination typified in William Douglas Home's *The Chiltern Hundreds* (1948), where a socialist aristocrat is defeated at a by-election by a butler who represents, in every sense, the Conservative interest.

Most writers appear to have been pragmatically resigned to the limitations under which they wrote. For his own over-crafted models of English understatement, Terence Rattigan even immortalized the typical audience member for whom he had to cater – that 'nice, respectable, middle-class, middle-aged lady' Aunt Edna, whose sensibilities no playwright, he claimed, dare offend. So Rattigan confined himself to innocuous light comedies such as the precocious *French without Tears* (1936) and *Love in Idleness* (1944) – or, in serious vein, to safely private problems – although *The Winslow Boy* (1946), in which a naval cadet is vindicated from a charge of theft at the cost of financial ruin for his family, now seems almost allegoric of its audiences' belief that they, too, were being bankrupted in defence of their social standing.

Dorothy Tutin (b. 1931), one of the outstanding 'discoveries' of an otherwise transitional period of British acting. Later to establish herself as a leading but always individual player of classical roles, here she is seen with Eric Portman as the priest in *The Living Room* (1953), the first of a clutch of half-a-dozen or so plays with which Graham Greene added a brief theatrical fame to his more enduring reputation as a novelist. While Greene's fiction achieved a free-flowing movement of ideas and action, his plays were stuck in the still-prevailing 'well-made' tradition, and often reworked themes familiar from the novels – in this case, the guilt felt by a Catholic girl, played by Tutin, over an adulterous affair, pitched against the chance of happiness it offers. The conflict is resolved, with a neatness more dramatic than moral, by the further 'sin' of suicide

Alec Guinness (b. 1914) as the Unidentified Guest, with Eileen Peel and Robert Flemyng, in T. S. Eliot's *The Cocktail Party* (1949) – a blandly authoritative role which well suited his often understated genius. The early comedic progress and protean range of this supreme mimic may still be traced on film through the 'Ealing comedies', in whose profusion of simple but subtle character parts – no less than eight in *Kind Hearts and Coronets* (1949) – he often seemed at his happiest. Perhaps this was because the camera was better able to capture every nuance of Guinness's quiet, often self-effacing presence – his apparent lack of stage charisma making unwonted demands on the audiences of live theatre, who had been encouraged into lazy responses by the usual diet of enervated naturalism

Rattigan was good at suggesting the emotional depths below the surface of English bourgeois reticence – an elderly schoolmaster's in *The Browning Version* (1948), a whole hotel-full of shabby-genteel failures in *Separate Tables* (1954). Of the other writers acclaimed in those years, the polite melancholic nostalgia of N. C. Hunter in such plays as *Waters of the Moon* (1951) has not worn well, while the more original Peter Ustinov, eternally compromised by his own eclectic cleverness, was at his best when bending his wit to the light fantastic, as in *The Love of Four Colonels* (1951) or *Romanoff and Juliet* (1956). The novelist Graham Greene also entered upon a theatrical phase relatively late in his career with *The Living Room* (1953), as did Enid Bagnold with *The Chalk Garden* (1956) – both well structured plays with solid acting parts, and now well-nigh forgotten.

As so often in theatre history, farce remained a law – even a lore – unto itself, with 'Whitehall farce', its ensemble led by Brian Rix, creating an instant tradition for the financially and politically insecure post-war years as 'Aldwych farce' had for the emotionally and socially insecure inter-war era. Experience of conscription for National Service thus helped to set *Reluctant Heroes* on its long run in 1950, while the love of a 'flutter' ensured a similar success for *Dry Rot* in 1954.

Whitehall farce also appealed to different *kinds* of audiences, building its long runs on block bookings from what became known as the 'coach-party trade', whereby local clubs or pubs would get together sufficient numbers to fill a coach and qualify for a discount at the box-office. It was largely through this trade that another phenomenon of the period, Agatha Christie's run-of-the-mill 'whodunit' *The Mousetrap*, laid the foundations for its apparently interminable success after a critically undistinguished opening at the Ambassadors in 1952.

The false dawn of poetic drama

In The Cocktail Party (1949), T. S. Eliot's first post-war play, his verse was already becoming overlaid with the prosaic mannerisms of drawing-room drama, while religious mysticism hovered close to a surface below which erudite parallels with Greek tragedy lay buried at ever more elusive depths. Eliot wrote two further plays, both of which, like The Cocktail Party, were first seen at the Edinburgh Festival in the productions by E. Martin Browne – who in 1945 had set out to make Ashley Dukes's little Mercury Theatre in Notting Hill a home for the supposed 'renaissance' of poetic drama.

Here were produced such plays as Ronald Duncan's This Way to the Tomb (1945) and Donagh MacDonagh's Happy as Larry (1947), both of which transferred successfully to the West End. The play with which Christopher Fry first attracted notice in 1946, A Phoenix Too Frequent, went on from the Mercury to the Arts – whence two years later his gentle meander around a medieval moral maze, The Lady's Not for Burning, found its way to the Globe, with Gielgud in the leading role. Fry's annus mirabilis was 1950, when Olivier played the Duke of Altair in his Venus Observed at the St James's, Burton starred in Gielgud's production of The Boy with a Cart at the Lyric, Hammersmith, and Brook directed Fry's translation of Jean Anouilh's 'charade with music', Ring Round the Moon, at the Globe.

Although Fry's name is often linked with Eliot's as a twin-pillar of the verse drama movement, and the writers did share Browne's belief in the Christian purpose of their work, their plays have little in common either in verbal style or theatrical effect. Fry was the less overtly 'poetic' of the two: but in place of Eliot's recondite references and rather lumpen colloquialisms, he worked up his oblique plotlines – often far more actable than logical – through dialogue of uninhibited lyricism and dancing metaphors. His work went decisively out of fashion in the late fifties, but although he was generally considered a less 'serious' dramatist than Eliot, we may now recognize the more intrinsically theatrical (and, simply, speakable) qualities of his plays.

Set design by Oliver Messel for Jean Anouilh's *Ring Round the Moon*, translated very much in his own idiom by Christopher Fry, and directed by Peter Brook at the Globe Theatre in 1950, with Margaret Rutherford and Paul Scofield in the cast

ACTING STYLE IN AN AGE OF AUSTERITY

When 'star vehicles' did not present themselves, and with few new British plays offering challenges beyond those of home-fired naturalism, it is unsurprising that leading performers should have looked to the far wider range of acting opportunities available in the classical repertoire – which also had the economic edge, from a manager's viewpoint, of qualifying as culture and so escaping the

Laurence Olivier as Puff in Sheridan's *The Critic* – described by the rising young critic Kenneth Tynan as a 'leisurely . . . undressing of the eighteenth-century tragic muse'. Wearing a nose felt by Tynan to be 'foolishly *retroussé*', the elegantly coiffured Olivier is here seen with Ralph Richardson, who played the cameo part of the enigmatic Burleigh. In a double-bill for the 1945–46 season of the Old Vic company, exiled by wartime bombing to the New Theatre, Olivier famously combined the comic demands of this burlesque role with the high tragedy of the title-part in Sophocles' *Oedipus Rex*

Entertainments Tax. The period was thus rich in stylish revivals, not only at the Old Vic under Laurence Olivier and at the Arts under Alec Clunes, but also in the West End – from John Gielgud's *Love for Love* at the Haymarket in 1943, through *The Rivals* at the Criterion in 1945 with Edith Evans as a resounding Mrs Malaprop, to *The Beaux Stratagem* starring Robert Eddison, John Clements, and Kay Hammond at the Phoenix in 1949.

With Gielgud's policy of accommodating himself modestly within a company of acting near-equals may be contrasted Donald Wolfit's preference for shining brightly against a lacklustre background. Antipathetic though such an approach has become to the temper of modern acting, it can work with the grain of a play like *King Lear*, in which Wolfit's lonely grandeur remained, for all its hubris, naggingly heroic against a landscape peopled by pygmies. Edward Bond, for one, has an epiphanic childhood recollection of Wolfit's *Macbeth* when it was revived during a season in 1949 at the old Bedford music hall in Camden Town – with Ibsen's *Master Builder* included, almost symbolically, amongst the Shakespeares.

While Gielgud during these years was perhaps more influential as manager than as performer, Olivier was at the peak of his powers. For a memorable Old Vic double bill of 1945–46, in a single evening he descended deliciously to the comic depths as Sheridan's pompous Mr Puff and soared to the tragic heights of Sophocles' Oedipus, in the same season playing the youthful, abrasively heroic Hotspur in the First Part of *Henry IV* and the senile old pragmatist Justice Shallow in the Second. This delight in his own protean range was further displayed when, in 1949, Olivier went into management on his own account at the St James's, playing opposite his then wife, Vivien Leigh, in Shakespeare's *Antony and Cleopatra* back to back with Shaw's *Caesar and Cleopatra* – the couple also demonstrating in *A Streetcar Named Desire* that they were no less capable of taking on 'the Method' and winning.

Olivier and Leigh were only the most famous and devotedly worshipped of the many who during this period combined marriage and stage partnerships – others including Clements and Hammond, Jack Hulbert and Cicely Courtneidge, Michael Denison and Dulcie Gray, John Mills and Mary Hayley Bell, Roger Livesey and Ursula Jeans, and Rachel Kempson and Michael Redgrave. Such

Festival year – and after

Although the structured fragility of Oliver Messel's permanent set for Ring Round the Moon (pictured on page 307) now seems slightly quaint, it clearly struck a chord with audiences (who gave it its own round of applause) during a period when icons as various as Rowland Emett's precariously articulated rustic railways, drawn for Punch, and that soaring taper of metallic ambiguity, the skylon, were also helping to fashion a mood of whimsical fantasy for a tired but resolutely cheerful nation.

Emett's cartoon railway popped into three dimensions in the Pleasure Gardens at Battersea, not far from where the skylon made its thrusting phallic point alongside the great didactic womb of the Dome of Discovery, as part of the Festival of Britain of 1951 – a nationwide civic pageant whose blend of the pleasurable and the pedagogic was at once an affirmation of historic roots and a declaration of optimism about the future. Much of the spirit of all these manifestations of their times is captured in the first play to reach the stage by that temperamentally isolated dramatist John Whiting, whose comic epic of the English preparing their domestic defences against Napoleon, A Penny for a Song, was directed by Brook at the Haymarket in March, 1951.

The darker, indeed obscurer side of Whiting was controversially recognized six months later with the award of first prize in the Arts Theatre's festival play competition to his Saint's Day, regarded by some as a precursor of the new drama, but in truth a compelling, claustrophobic study of meta-couplings, which tended to exude a very English self-perception of urbane charm combined with emotional restraint (some would say uptightness), meshed neatly with the many plays of this period structured around subtle or unsubtle threats to the domestic verities.

This cerebral and pragmatic although (increasingly) inbred and mannered acting style can, of course, still be retrieved from films of the period – after making necessarily complex allowances not only for the different demands of the medium, but also for changes in our own aesthetic and moral expectations. The brittle yet brusque performances of Celia Johnson and Trevor Howard in *Brief Encounter* (1945) perhaps best recapture the manner – in part because the film originated as a one-act play by Noël Coward, and remains relatively stage-like in its focus, characterization, and narrative line. This is the very antithesis of the Method – that distinctively American harnessing of Freud and Stanislavsky, of gut instinct with emotional insight, which was already working its way like a gritty irritant into the oyster-shell of English actor training.

The analytical approach at its coolest and most detached, exemplified in the work of such actors as Emlyn Williams and Eric Portman, could even make the stern but benign headmasterly manner of the likes of Robert Donat appear emotional in comparison – and the dominant and monumental Frederick Valk seem positively explosive. While excellent younger actors were emerging who were beginning to break this mould – the lithe and sweetly fluent John Neville, the more ruggedly handsome Alan Badel, the moodily compelling Richard Burton – they seem in retrospect to have lacked the self-confidence, not to say the sheer staying power of their seniors. The fault was less in them, however, than in the changed mood of the British theatre after the mid-1950s, when all

self-hatred and its consequences which is as much an individual 'sport' of the theatre as was Wuthering Heights of the novel. Soon after the failure of Marching Song three years later Whiting abandoned the theatre, as he thought for good. The Devils in 1961 suggested a renewed potential, but his premature death two years later left this unfulfilled.

Design by Rowland Emmet for *A Penny for a Song*, John Whiting's festive comedy of 1951 which portrayed the English preparing with eccentric haphazardness to confront the threatened Napoleonic invasion. Note the manservant Humpage keeping watch from atop his tree, while the aeronautically inclined Sir Timothy ascends in a requisitioned circus balloon

such polished acting found itself challenged not only by the Method, but by the demands of the new kinds of play we shall be considering in the next chapter.

Already, a few insightful directors were working for change. Some, like Peter Brook, responded intuitively, from their own sense of what each particular production demanded. Others were exploring alternatives with a more fully articulated sense of purpose – in the case of Michel Saint-Denis, under the influence of the French director Copeau, who had advocated a spare and ascetic but what we might now call holistic approach to his art. Saint-Denis it was who created the Old Vic Centre in 1945, based in the bomb-damaged premises off the Waterloo Road, which embraced both a school of acting under Glen Byam Shaw and a Young Vic company under George Devine. Despite internal dissensions which led to its dissolution in 1951, the Centre exerted a strong influence both on training methods and in shaping the as-yet-embryonic ideal of the acting ensemble.

Comic acting, with its tendency towards the larger than life, has always been better placed to transcend constricting fashions – not least in the work of those last giants of the music-hall tradition, Max Miller, Frank Randle, and Sid Field, each of entirely individual and inimitable genius. In 'legit' comedy there were the angular eccentricities of Joyce Grenfell and Alistair Sim, and the more rotund, not to say orotund roles fleshed out by Robert Morley and Margaret Rutherford (whose Madame Arcati is pictured on page 300). All these actors were, of course, also associated with the vintage comedy films now emerging from Michael Balcon's Ealing Studios, which both reflected and became part of the post-war British zeitgeist.

VINTAGE YEARS OF RADIO

It was during the Festival year that the BBC loosened its corporate corsets to accommodate *The Goons*, an anarchic radio show of engaging surrealism largely scripted by Spike Milligan. In the same year a young comic actor named Tony Hancock was hired to play tutor to a ventriloquist's dummy in *Educating Archie*, and went on, in *Hancock's Half Hour*, to create his own classic comic persona – a seedy, suburban Walter Mitty, see-sawing between bouts of Sunday-afternoon enervation and flurries of entrapment in the small-time schemings of Sid James, who played that archetype of post-war self-interest, the spiv. Quite other kinds of comic frisson were created when the staid and straight Kenneth Horne was teamed with the (for his time) outrageously camp Kenneth Williams in *Beyond Our Ken*, while the sublimely awful Glum family surfaced in *Take It from Here* to create an anti-sitcom way ahead of its time. Radio comedy's golden age was enjoying a glorious sunset.

Family life was also at the epicentre of that curiously durable domestication of melodrama, the British soap opera – which took its generic label but little else from its less quotidian but more disposable American counterpart. Thus did the pre-war family saga of the Robinsons now spawn the Dales and the Archers – while the genre soon demonstrated that it could be no less indestructible on television, as the human scale of that imaginary Salford terrace, Coronation Street, outlasted the vogue for tower-block redevelopment. *The Archers* and *Coronation Street* have, at the time of writing, run in their regular programming slots, adding up to an hour or more of airtime a week, respectively well in excess of forty and thirty years.

Often dismissed as trivial audience fodder, such long-running 'soaps' constitute a phenomenon unique in the annals of performance – epic dramas which continue in 'real time' alongside the lives of their audiences. The more settled rustic ambience of *The Archers*, and the capacity of radio to replace retiring or dying actors with soundalikes to which the ear soon gets accustomed, means that story-lines now feature the matrimonial upheavals of the children of the children of the original village patriarch. The scriptwriting – and indeed the acting – has varied from the devastatingly awful to the sociologically trendy and the comically astute: and there seems no reason why the series should not go on indefinitely, its semi-therapeutic purpose of offering vicarious sociability to its more lonely and frustrated listeners perpetuating the function of melodrama, whose stock characters and situations it reproduces in carefully measured doses.

A reshuffling of radio networks in the aftermath of the war saw the creation in 1946 of the Third Programme, an unashamedly 'highbrow' enclave for 'good' music, speech, and drama. Easy now to mock for its seemingly elitist pretensions, its aim – not altogether unrealistic in the light of the wartime thirst for culture – was simply to encourage wider audiences for more demanding fare. Early on, it even offered experimental comedy – in *Third Division* bringing together for the first time three of the four comedians who went on to become the Goons. So far as radio drama was concerned, 'the Third' found airtime for plays less dependent on threadbare stage conventions than those which filled the regular drama slots on the middlebrow 'Home Service' and the no less revealingly named 'Light Programme'.

The eery evocation of Welsh soldiery fighting ancient and modern wars in David Jones's *In Parenthesis* (1946) thus employed formalized verse idioms far from the contemporary colloquialisms utilized by Louis MacNeice in his allegory of an artist's quest, *The Dark Tower* (1946): but both sought to capture the intrinsic poetry of voices in a soundscape, and to make this their dramatic focus as well as their controlling structure. Dylan Thomas's *Under Milk Wood*, with its rich medley of voices evoking the inner worlds beyond the daily rounds of Llaregyb (which fortunately no one in authority at the BBC tried to pronounce backwards), was not broadcast until 1954, after the poet's death: but it, too, was a product of the boozy ideamongering in the BBC's 'local', the George, through which this celtic fringe of writers became an innovative mainstream in radio drama. At last, words, sounds, and challenges to the collaborative imagination were achieving primacy over the old, laboured attempts to construct a bakelite proscenium arch.

As early as 1942, MacNeice had been integrating words with William Walton's music in *Christopher Columbus* – which, like much 'dramatic' work of this period, was actually a product of Laurence Gilliam's Features Department. And Francis Dillon's *Rumpelstiltskin* was a true sound opera – an imaginative equivalent to the series of 'radio ballads', in which, thanks to the arrival of the first portable tape-recorders in the 1950s, Ewan MacColl and Charles Parker collaged the voices of ordinary people with written narrative and folk song to celebrate in entirely fresh and appropriate ways the lives and heroisms of fishermen, railwaymen, and coalminers. By this time the quirky interior worlds of Giles Cooper and the erudite parodies of Henry Reed were revealing yet more of the potential of drama on radio – which (though, as we shall see, it continued to flourish) was doomed to relinquish its primacy as the mass medium of communication just as it was finding its distinctive dramatic voice.

JOAN LITTLEWOOD AND THEATRE WORKSHOP

Many of the radio writers mentioned had been on the staff of the BBC, especially during the war years – when both MacColl and his partner in the pre-war Theatre Union, Joan Littlewood, were among a lively group of pioneers working out of Manchester under the inspirational Archie Harding. After the war MacColl became, in effect, resident dramatist for Littlewood's new company, Theatre Workshop – for which he wrote, among much else, *Uranium 235*, one of the very few plays of the time to confront the threat of the atomic bomb.

Theatre Workshop spent the early post-war years combining intensive in-service training with touring from a variety of makeshift regional headquarters. Leading a hand-to-mouth existence of two- or three-night stands, and ignored by the national press, they none the less created their own distinctive style, combining new plays, largely by MacColl, with works from the European repertoire: and they further expanded their range when, in 1953, they secured a permanent base at the ageing but intimate Theatre Royal in Stratford, East London. The critics were reluctant to travel in so unfashionable a direction down the Central Line – until their curiosities were aroused by the enthusiastic reception of two Elizabethan revivals (the anonymous *Arden of Faversham* and Jonson's *Volpone*) which the company took in 1955 to the new Théâtre des Nations festival in Paris.

Soon after returning from France, Workshop played a three-month season at the Comedy Theatre with *The Quare Fellow* – a play by that charming, boozy Irish ex-con, Brendan Behan, about life in prison on the eve of an execution. This loose-knit but emotionally compelling piece exhibited typical Workshop qualities – getting across its social message through clowning rather than preaching; creating vivid local colour at the expense of expounding a well-made plot; and played with cheerful reciprocity as if by a group of close friends. Indeed, often the impression was of actors improvising as they went along – which, thanks to the acquired skills of a training which included *commedia* techniques, most were perfectly

Opposite: scene from the Theatre Workshop production of the anonymous Elizabethan thriller, *Arden of Faversham*, which, together with Ben Jonson's *Volpone*, the company took to the second Théâtre des Nations festival in Paris in 1955, and then to the Edinburgh Festival. Both plays were directed by Joan Littlewood (b. 1914), who in 1953 had settled her band of previously itinerant but highly trained 'scholar clowns' at the Theatre Royal, in Stratford, East London. Belated critical recognition led to a string of West End transfers – which were necessary to the company's financial survival, but a drain on its creative energies and sense of cohesion. Joan Littlewood left in 1961, but – failing to create her intended 'Fun Palace' in the East End – returned two years later to direct Workshop's greatest popular success, *Oh! What a Lovely War!* She has not directed in Britain since 1973, but her vision of a theatre which would attract genuinely popular audiences with an Elizabethan mix of energy and erudition has remained an inspiration to like-minded directors ever since

capable of doing. Already, Workshop was showing that such ensemble acting with a heart could work: already, too, the need simply to keep going was hinting at the dangers of the company losing its soul to the temptations of a West End run.

The no-less committed Unity had arguably already lost its soul, a post-war decision to go professional soon proving ill-advised – though not before splitting the membership down the middle. But other 'little' and club theatres – able to avoid West End overheads, and often owning their own premises in less expensive areas – seemed at first to be quietly flourishing. In addition to the Arts and the Mercury, there were the Boltons and the Lindsey (both of which were best known for their revues), the Players (with its nostalgic recreations of Victorian music hall and Christmas pantomime), the Chepstow, the Gateway, the Torch, the Irving, and the Watergate, not to mention such suburban outposts as the 'Q' at Kew Bridge and the Intimate Theatre, Palmer's Green.

Anthony Quayle, with Barbara Jefford as Desdemona, in the title-role of the 1954 revival of *Othello* at the Shakespeare Memorial Theatre, Stratford-upon-Avon. Quayle was very much an actor of and for his own generation, with a distinct if muted classical 'manner' and a sure-tongued authority in the modern roles for which he seemed temperamentally better suited. Taking over the management of the Memorial Theatre in 1948, Quayle brought stars to Stratford – a policy which led to a period of greater financial than artistic success, laying firm foundations for Hall's establishment of the Royal Shakespeare Company in 1960

BECKETT AT THE ARTS, BROOK AND HALL AT STRATFORD

However, of the dozen or so such theatres operating in the late 1940s, by 1955 the only notable survivors were the Players and the Arts – from which Alec Clunes had bowed out in the early 1950s. In 1954 the new management brought in a young director, Peter Hall, who quickly established his reputation with a mix of European and American imports – and then, in 1955, staged the English premiere of a first play by an already elderly Franco-Irishman, unpromisingly featuring two tramps and a withered tree.

The play was, of course, *Waiting for Godot*, and its author was Samuel Beckett, who, like so many of his fellow-countrymen, wrote from exile: for the Irish theatre was in the doldrums. The Abbey in Dublin had already driven its only major inter-war discovery, Sean O'Casey, across the water, and, although its pioneering role had in part been taken over by the Gate Theatre under Micheál MacLiammóir and Hilton Edwards, the only active Irish writer of importance still working from his native land was Denis Johnston – who, following the rejection of his first play by the Abbey in 1929 had retitled it *The Old Lady Says No*. The old lady largely continued to do so.

None the less, Beckett – like his early master Joyce – remained profoundly influenced by the *mores* and the idiom of his native land, though while establishing his early reputation as a novelist he had written largely in French. Now, in *Waiting for Godot*, which had been first produced in Paris in 1953, he created one of the seminal plays of the post-war years – following it in 1957 with the stark apocalyptic vision of *Endgame*, and continuing to refine his dramatic art, as it sometimes seemed almost out of existence. But those two tramps – in eternal expectation of the arrival of Godot, and who in their waiting run through a sort of inverted paradigm of the conventions of comedy as of life itself – have remained the most enduring of Beckett's metaphors for the ways in which humankind tries to reconcile itself to its absurdity, and to its no less absurd mortality.

In 1956 Hall left the Arts, and was invited to the Shakespeare Memorial Theatre in Stratford to direct *Love's Labour's Lost* – which, with nice symmetry, had also been Peter Brook's inaugural production there, just ten years earlier. Brook had cut his Shakespearean teeth in 1945 with a *King John* for Barry Jackson in Birmingham – in which the role of the Bastard had been played by Paul Scofield. Now, the ageing Jackson, newly appointed to the management of the Memorial Theatre, brought both these young protégés with him – Scofield to play Armado in what a contemporary critic famously described as the 'Watteauesque *fête champêtre*' through which Brook effectively restored *Love's Labours Lost* to the regular repertoire after centuries of benign neglect.

Jackson, beset by inherited problems (though on the way to resolving many of them), was forced into retirement early in 1948, having already appointed just two young directors, Michael Benthall and Anthony Quayle, to share out the coming season's plays between them. This they did, with some brilliance – which, of course, reflected on their reputations rather than on Jackson's foresight. Quayle, also continuing to act as well as direct, was then appointed to manage the theatre, and soon established Stratford as a sort of scenic branch-line from the West End, relying on star performers, glittering sets and costumes, and a directorial style that was bright and elegant without making too many demands on the audience.

Brook had been brought back in 1949, to direct Gielgud as Angelo in his now legendary *Measure for Measure*, and the Festival year of 1951 was celebrated with (astonishingly) the first-ever attempt to play Shakespeare's second history cycle in its full chronological sequence, with Redgrave as Richard II, Burton as Prince

Laurence Olivier's headlong
plunge to his death in the title-
role of Shakespeare's seldom-
revived Roman tragedy,
Coriolanus. This was one of
two productions by Peter Hall
in the season before he was to
take over as artistic director.
The other, *A Midsummer
Night's Dream*, was generally
considered more fully to
anticipate the coherence of
style and interpretive drive of
his later tenure, while
Coriolanus was more typical of
the 'old' Stratford in its
dependence upon a star-laden
cast – Edith Evans proving
mismatched as Volumnia –
and in a set which seemed at
odds with the flow of the
action. But the stoic, dictatorial
Coriolanus was, in the critic
Kenneth Tynan's view, 'All-
round Olivier. We have the
wagging head, the soaring
index finger, and the sly,
roaming eyes of one of the
world's cleverest comic actors,
plus the desperate, exhausted
moans of one of the world's
masters of pathos. But we also
confront the nonpareil of
heroic tragedians… . A more
shocking, less sentimental
death I have not seen in the
theatre; it is at once proud and
ignominious, as befits the
titanic fool who dies it'

Hal, and Quayle himself as Falstaff. The apogee of the company's success under Quayle came in 1955, with a season which included Olivier playing Macbeth alongside his astonishing, athletic, and revelatory Titus Andronicus, in a production by Brook full of intense but formalized horror.

By now, leading players were ready to give up a season's metropolitan homage for the deferent centrality they were accorded in Stratford – and it was the Old Vic, weakened by internal wranglings, which was being perceived as dowdy and provincial. Quayle's regime thus achieved its own pragmatic ends, providing the impression of glamour and opulence on budgets which were at first exceedingly tight or even in deficit. In 1953 he was joined by Glen Byam Shaw and George Devine – who brought with them fresh acting blood from the Old Vic school. A second, touring company was established, reserves began to build, and when Devine left in 1956, to establish a new, playwrights' theatre in London, the youthful Peter Hall became an initially informal but already highly influential member of the triumvirate which, now under Shaw's leadership, continued to govern the company for a few more years.

Hall had come into the theatre straight from Cambridge, Brook from Oxford, the universities now being a frequent route into the profession – just as they were also beginning to accord due academic status to the theatre, with the opening in Bristol of the country's first Drama Department in 1946. Another highly influential post-war graduate was Kenneth Tynan who, in 1954 – at 27 already theatre critic for *The Observer* – had bemoaned the 'peculiar nullity' of the contemporary drama, declaring that, 'apart from revivals and imports, there is nothing in the London theatre that one dares discuss with an intelligent man [*sic*] for more than five minutes'.

That there were foreign imports worth discussing was thanks not only to Hall's work at the Arts, and indeed to Brook's earlier introduction of the plays of Anouilh, Sartre, and other contemporary French writers, but also to the enthusiasm and insight of one of the unsung heroes of the British theatre, a young impresario named Peter Daubeny. Taking on single-handedly the task of creating an English equivalent to the Théâtre des Nations, by 1956 Daubeny had already brought work by Spanish, French, Indian, and Russian companies, among others, into the West End: and now, for an international season at the Palace, he took the daring step of inviting an East German company largely unheard of in England, though already acclaimed by Tynan – the Berliner Ensemble, under the direction of the playwright Bertolt Brecht.

Tynan had ended his lament of two years earlier with the rueful wish that he might 'rather be a war correspondent than a necrologist'. Thanks to the groundwork laid by the likes of Littlewood, Brook, and Hall, and the plans even then being made by both Hall and George Devine, the visit of the Berliner Ensemble turned out to be only one of the many events of 1956 which were to give Tynan battles aplenty to report.

CHAPTER 20   *Anger and Affluence*

In the election of 1951 the outgoing Labour government received the highest popular vote for any party before or since – but the quirks of the electoral system gave a small parliamentary majority to the Conservatives. That they so far consolidated their position as to remain in office for thirteen years was in part due to their conceding rather than attempting to dismantle the domestic reforms of the post-war period: but in foreign policy older, imperial ambitions at first prevailed, and the clamour of many colonial nations to be granted the independence achieved by the Indian sub-continent under Labour was firmly and often bloodily resisted. Then, in 1956, came a watershed caused by the convergence of two crises, which effectively destroyed old allegiances and gave greater coherence to new.

Among the anachronistic relics of colonial rule was the continuing ownership of the Suez canal by an Anglo-French company – which the Egyptian president, Nasser, now determined to nationalize. Not only did he remain unperturbed by the sabre-rattling this action provoked, notably from the British prime minister Eden, but demonstrated, against all dire predictions, that his own people were perfectly capable of running the waterway. Finally, in late October, British and

French forces were sent in to reoccupy the Canal Zone, under the pretence of policing a 'coincident' but in fact collusive invasion of the Sinai by the Israeli army. The brief ensuing war aroused not only the expected opposition of the eastern and neutral blocs, but American hostility as well: and an abject withdrawal in a matter of weeks was brought about less by threats of Russian military intervention than by fear of American economic sanctions.

However, by that time the Suez conflict had provided a convenient cover for the crushing by the Red Army of a rebellion against the Soviet-backed regime in Hungary – a brutal action which destroyed hopes that the death of Stalin in 1952 might be leading to a thaw in the Cold War. In Britain, the prompt replacement of the humiliated Eden by the pragmatic Macmillan produced a reluctant recognition by the Conservatives of what their new leader dubbed a 'wind of change' in foreign as in colonial affairs – while on the left a new alignment emerged between disillusioned Communists and old-style Socialists, energized by their party's forceful opposition to the Suez adventure.

There followed a flourishing of single-issue groupings, from the Movement for Colonial Freedom and Anti-Apartheid to the better-remembered Campaign for Nuclear Disarmament – whose four-day Easter marches from the Aldermaston nuclear weapons research establishment to Trafalgar Square in London combined mass demonstration and instant ritual in an often highly theatrical manner. This was scarcely surprising, for in the theatre, too, 1956 had seen a change of direction no less profound than in the nation at large, and theatre people were soon at the forefront of most forms of political protest.

THE NEW DRAMA AT THE ROYAL COURT

It was thus ironic that Jimmy Porter, the central figure of the play which, in May 1956, heralded the coming theatrical revolution, should have been bemoaning the lack of 'a little ordinary human enthusiasm', and of 'good, brave causes' for which to fight, at precisely the moment when events on the world stage were about to generate just such causes and enthusiasms. The play was, of course, John Osborne's *Look Back in Anger* – and in the conclusion to his influential *Observer* review of its Royal Court premiere, Kenneth Tynan anticipated the extremes of emotion it was to arouse. 'I doubt', he declared, 'if I could love anyone who did not wish to see *Look Back in Anger*.' Somerset Maugham dismissed all such as 'scum'.

No matter that the play now seems a fairly orthodox psychological drama about a mixed-up marriage: the fact that it drew for its characters upon the dropped-out young, and that it was set in a scruffy provincial bed-sit far from the borders of Belgravia or the stockbroker belt, gave its subject-matter a freshness that redeemed its conventional style. Then, later in the same year, the visit to Britain of the Berliner Ensemble provided a jolt of a different kind – to accepted attitudes concerning the relationship between a play's form and its content,

Opposite: Kenneth Haigh and Mary Ure as Jimmy Porter and his wife Alison in the original Royal Court production of *Look Back in Anger* (1956). Although the play now seems old-fashioned in construction, and less about social anger than personal angst, at the time it startlingly revealed the possibilities of theatre for a new generation of writers, some of working-class origins. George Devine had declared the Court a 'writers' theatre', and he and his directorial associates continued to encourage dramatists in whom they believed – such as John Arden and Edward Bond – against initial critical hostility and incomprehension, while providing a London showcase for those who, like Arnold Wesker, achieved an earlier breakthrough. Osborne himself long remained associated with the theatre, achieving the West End transfers needed to boost the Court's always precarious finances with *The Entertainer* (1957), *Luther* (1961), and *Inadmissible Evidence* (1964). Later, Osborne became disaffected from the 'good, brave causes' Jimmy Porter had sought – as *West of Suez* (1971) and *A Sense of Detachment* (1972) clearly signalled. Eventually the mythically angry Jimmy Porter was transformed into the grumpy, middle-aged reactionary of *Déjàvu* (1992)

between its performers and their audience. In the explosion of energy which followed, the Royal Court and Theatre Workshop were at first the twin epicentres, though there were shock waves, too, from the regions, where new civic theatres were coming steadily on stream amidst the relative affluence of the late 1950s and early 1960s.

When George Devine founded the English Stage Company at the Royal Court in 1956, he first sought plays beyond the West End rut by approaching writers who had already made their names as novelists. Thus, it is testimony alike to the seminal influence of *Look Back in Anger* and to the sure instincts of Devine and his directorial associates – who included Tony Richardson, John Dexter, Lindsay Anderson, and William Gaskill – that they responded with sympathy and flexibility to the flood of manuscripts now pouring in from previously unheard-of authors, who sensed that theatre was again becoming a medium through which matters of importance to their lives might be expressed.

Devine proclaimed 'the right to fail', but created the circumstances for success. He assembled a Writers' Group in which promising but unpractised playwrights could discuss and try out their work in a sympathetic ambience, and in a series of Sunday-evening 'productions without decor' he found slots for plays which did not warrant a full run. Later, the club membership necessitated by Sunday theatregoing provided a good audience-base for plays which were refused the

Theatre Workshop – crippled by success

Down in the East End, Theatre Workshop developed its own, earlier-established and perhaps freer-flowing tradition in parallel with the Royal Court. Apart from the burnt-out Behan, who enjoyed a final, exuberant fling with The Hostage (1958), the most promising Workshop writer of these years was Shelagh Delaney, whose A Taste of Honey (1958) – legendarily written in disgusted reaction to a play of Terence Rattigan's – displayed with raw authenticity and genuine poetry the facts of life and love in a northern industrial slum. Deeply influential, the play remained Delaney's only major work – which raises the question of how far both she and Behan owed their success to the collectively creative reshaping which often characterized Joan Littlewood's rehearsal process.

It was through such working methods that Theatre Workshop fostered a whole school of minor demotic dramatists – both the title and the tempo of the cockney musical Fings Ain't Wot They Used T'Be (1959) suggesting the breezy if slightly self-conscious style which was later rough-hewed by Joan Littlewood into the unpolished perfection of Oh What a Lovely War! in 1963. That show divided Workshop aficionados over whether its rendering

of the First World War into an end-of-pier entertainment sharpened its political points through vivid stylistic juxtapositions, or, as the now estranged Ewan MacColl claimed, blunted their force by merely encouraging the classless camaraderie of singalong nostalgia.

This was also, to all intents, the end of the road for Littlewood, who effectively broke with the company after the production, a few one-off revisits notwithstanding. Sadly, her alternative vision of continuing her work on the broader canvas of a popular 'Fun Palace' never left the drawing board – and while Wesker's no less grandiose scheme for trades union involvement in the arts, focused on his 'Centre 42', did get as far as securing a permanent base at the Round House in Chalk Farm, and playing a few provincial festivals, this too eventually foundered. It must remain a matter of debate how far this was due to a lack of cash, and how far to an incapacity to tap the working-class audiences Wesker like Littlewood sought.

All the Workshop plays I have mentioned, and more besides, transferred into the West End, often for long runs – and this created the additional problem that a company trained and consolidated over many years, and

Lord Chamberlain's licence, as was Osborne's *A Patriot for Me* in 1965 – a main objection being to the drag ball scene, which featured a radiant Devine in what proved to be his final appearance, a few months before his untimely death and Gaskill's succession as artistic director. As we shall see, such small stupidities of censorship now only served to hasten its demise.

John Osborne continued to write for the Royal Court with more or less success throughout the period, though his talent was increasingly recognized as highly individual rather than representative of his generation. Sometimes his rather casual craftsmanship proved out of sync with the invective-laden dialogue and instinct for strong situations which continued to characterize his work – as in the quasi-Brechtian epic style of *Luther* (1961), which proved (despite a compelling performance from Albert Finney) ill-suited to a psychologically-based portrait of the protestant reformer. His best plays were those in which form accommodated subject almost by instinct – notably *The Entertainer* (1957), a timely allegory of the empire declining in step with a mediocre music-hall comic, and *Inadmissible Evidence* (1964), a close-knit, claustrophobic study of a small-time solicitor in the tightening grip of a nervous breakdown.

While Osborne gradually subsided into an ill-tempered, old-bufferish rural retreat, Arnold Wesker, whose career was from the first more in tune with the 'commitment' favoured by the times, in his own way better sustained a humanist

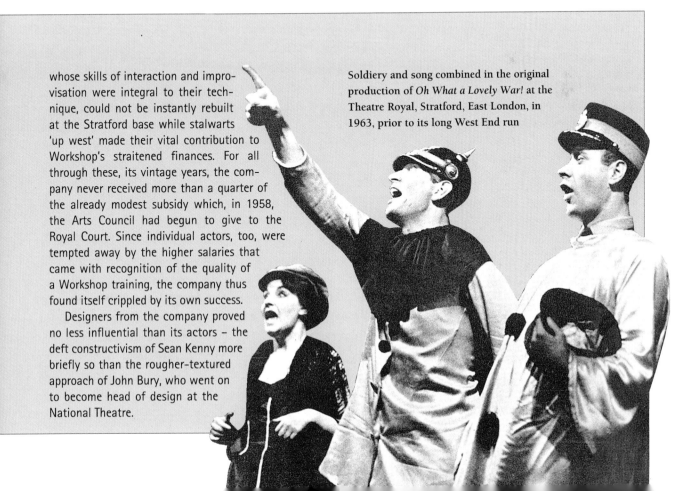

whose skills of interaction and improvisation were integral to their technique, could not be instantly rebuilt at the Stratford base while stalwarts 'up west' made their vital contribution to Workshop's straitened finances. For all through these, its vintage years, the company never received more than a quarter of the already modest subsidy which, in 1958, the Arts Council had begun to give to the Royal Court. Since individual actors, too, were tempted away by the higher salaries that came with recognition of the quality of a Workshop training, the company thus found itself crippled by its own success.

Designers from the company proved no less influential than its actors – the deft constructivism of Sean Kenny more briefly so than the rougher-textured approach of John Bury, who went on to become head of design at the National Theatre.

Soldiery and song combined in the original production of *Oh What a Lovely War!* at the Theatre Royal, Stratford, East London, in 1963, prior to its long West End run

Opposite: from the Royal Shakespeare Company's *The Wars of the Roses* (1963–64), Shakespeare's first history cycle as heavily adapted by John Barton. David Warner is the ingenuous, ever-tentative Henry VI, with Peggy Ashcroft his vehement and plotful Queen – her steadily ageing, vengeful presence dominant as the sequence developed. In the productions by Barton and Peter Hall, a sense of the shifting but ineluctable politics of power was rendered through a cool, precise control alike of verse structures and of the stage picture – stylistic qualities which came to characterize the company's early work. By the time Terry Hands came to direct the cycle again, in 1977, a more passionate, even romantic flavour pervaded the plays: personalities rather than politics were dominant, and the sequence was sustained by the actors' quest for feeling rather than by a sense of the 'grand mechanism' of history, through which power is gained, exercised, and lost

if not radical temper. First associated with Coventry's new civic theatre, the Belgrade, Wesker quickly gravitated to the Royal Court, and, like Osborne, at first wrote – within three-act, naturalistic confines – plays which were simply, startlingly fresh in their subject-matter. The 'Wesker Trilogy' (1958-60) thus constituted an elliptic, semi-autobiographical history of two generations of an East End family of working-class Jewish socialists, seen from three very different angles. But Wesker had already shown a greater alertness than Osborne towards other formal possibilities – as early as *The Kitchen* (1959), then in *Chips with Everything* (1962), experimenting with an almost expressionistic blending of action, environment, and the flow of time.

In such later plays as *The Friends* (1970), *The Old Ones* (1972), and *The Merchant* (1976), Wesker shifted the emphasis if not the underlying ideology of his writing from public affairs to private pain – whereas the third major writer to emerge from the Royal Court at this time, John Arden, was almost alone in his generation in moving from the scrupulous dialectic balance of his early work towards a more polemical, avowedly socialist viewpoint – also becoming, especially in collaboration with his partner Margaretta D'Arcy, among the first to show a creative recognition of the recurring 'troubles' in the North of Ireland, and of their roots in past oppression and neglect.

Arden had been remarkable from the first for striking out in widely varying stylistic directions – these ranging from the episodic modern mythmaking of his first play to reach the main stage, *Serjeant Musgrave's Dance* (1959), through the council estate naturalism of *Live Like Pigs* (1957) and the updated *commedia* conventions of *The Happy Haven* (1960), to Aristophanic farce in *The Workhouse Donkey* (1963), poetic epic in *Armstrong's Last Goodnight* (1964), and historical chronicle in *Left-Handed Liberty* (1965). No more than Wesker has Arden suffered from any falling-off in creative energies, but rather from a combination of changing fashions, rigid critical expectations – and managements which have insisted on 'doing things properly', rather than with the asymmetric imagination his later plays have required.

THE ROYAL SHAKESPEARE COMPANY

The issue of how a true ensemble of actors could be artistically and economically sustained was the subject of lively debate, in public through the pages of the lively 'little' theatre magazine *Encore*, which kept step with all these developments – and in private through the discussions which Peter Hall was already having with the powers behind the Shakespearean throne at the Memorial Theatre. In 1960 Hall not only took over the direction of the Royal Shakespeare Company, as it was soon rechristened, but found a metropolitan base for its work at the Aldwych Theatre – which in the event it was to occupy for twenty years, while plans for a purpose-built London home for the RSC at the Barbican began to grind their slow way along.

Determined to create an ensemble by attracting players with more than passing loyalty, Hall introduced a system of long-term contracts for his actors. In choosing 'big names' he went for those who seemed most sympathetic to the needs of ensemble playing; and occasionally, as with Peter O'Toole – a resolutely individual Shylock in the opening season – he mistook his man. But most of that first generation of long-term contract artists – Max Adrian, Peggy Ashcroft, Vanessa Redgrave, Dorothy Tutin – relished the chance both to extend the range of their acting, and to develop it in depth. More important for the future, lesser-known actors from within the RSC ranks – like Tony Church, Ian Holm, Ian Richardson, Norman Rodway, David Warner, and later Glenda Jackson – began to win an acclaim to which the concept of 'stardom' seemed irrelevant.

Hall abandoned the old, 'balanced' Stratford programme of five plays a year in favour of putting on a related group, beginning with a season of comedies – which produced no instant insights, but helped to develop the in-depth perceptions which led to a magical *As You Like It* with Vanessa Redgrave in the following year. The approach worked triumphantly in 1963-64, when a *Wars of the Roses* sequence was expanded for Shakespeare's quatercentenary to include the full sweep of the history plays. Peggy Ashcroft's Queen Margaret, ageing almost before our eyes, David Warner's ingenuous Henry VI, Ian Holm's Prince Hal, and Hugh Griffith's Falstaff were among performances which were not meant to be 'outstanding', but which crucially contributed to the development of the intermeshing, politically-focused action.

John Bury, who designed *The Wars of the Roses* and whose long association with Hall now began, came to the RSC from Theatre Workshop, where he had worked miracles on a shoestring – often creating his typically tensile settings, full of latent energy and suggestive purpose, from findings on a scrapheap. The new constructivism of Sean Kenny, another Workshop alumnus, opened up contrasting, more purposefully cluttered possibilities, especially well adapted to the complex needs of musicals, while at the Court Jocelyn Herbert had led the way in realizing Devine's wish to 'let in light and air' to the tiny stage, allowing the design to serve 'the actor and the text'.

Jocelyn Herbert's was accordingly a minimalist, object-centred approach, stylized or realistic as the play required, whereas John Bury, serving the RSC's classically-focused repertoire – and so needing to complement the actor's imagination and the director's interpretation as much as the writer's long-written words – created a style in which texture took precedence over colour, while resonance and what Hall called 'archetypal' qualities supplanted decorative grandeur or irrelevant realism. The feeling for a less 'busy', more atmospheric yet aptly 'textured' design was already lending its own sort of strength to Paul Scofield's doggedly humane King Lear in Peter Brook's production of 1962.

One of Hall's chief artistic aims in securing the Aldwych had been to explore the ways in which Shakespeare's plays could be cross-fertilized with the work of

The Royal Shakespeare Company's 1967 revival of *The Taming of the Shrew*, with Janet Suzman as Katharina firmly in control of her father (Roy Kinnear's Baptista) and her sister (June Watts's Bianca). As director, Trevor Nunn allowed the characters from the Induction (in which a drunken tinker, Christopher Sly, is haplessly transformed into a lord) to observe and even intervene in the subsequent action – a device which stressed that a play often seen as misogynistic works at several removes from the 'real' world. In 1978, also for the RSC, Michael Bogdanov allowed his Sly to demolish the Italianate setting before the play had even begun, the later action showing Petruchio (Jonathan Pryce), as a leather-clad chauvinist biker, eventually himself tamed by the over-the-top transformation of his bride (Paola Dionisotti)

other dramatists, classic and contemporary: and the opening production there in 1960 – Webster's *The Duchess of Malfi,* with Max Adrian and Eric Porter as tormentors to Peggy Ashcroft's duchess – at once affirmed the value of testing Shakespeare against the more oblique cutting edge of his contemporaries. A touch too obviously, however, the first plays by modern writers to reach the Aldwych were costume-dramas of one kind or another – though these ranged from Jean Anouilh's *Becket* to John Whiting's final play, *The Devils,* and the very first RSC experiment in finding a style for Bertolt Brecht, William Gaskill's production of *The Caucasian Chalk Circle.*

An experimental season mounted in 1962 at the little Arts Theatre Club more fully vindicated Hall's approach, introducing the company to the work of dramatists ranging from Thomas Middleton, whose *Women Beware Women* had a rare revival, Henry Livings, David Rudkin – whose *Afore Night Come* transferred to the Aldwych as the RSC's first truly modern success – and Maxim Gorky, whose *Lower Depths,* included in the Arts season, was later to become one of four plays by the Russian writer to be directed for the RSC by David Jones.

Although in that same year, 1962, Hall at last won his battle for a small Arts Council subsidy, continuing financial stringencies enforced an end to the work at the Arts just as its value was becoming clear. And although Hall now persuaded Michel St Denis and Peter Brook to join him as associate directors, St Denis, in spite of a moving, moody *Cherry Orchard* for the first Aldwych season, remained more of an *eminence grise* than an active participant – while the influence of Brook, who followed his *Lear* with an exploratory 'Theatre of Cruelty' season which led towards the controversial *Marat-Sade* of 1964, remained, however potent, occasionally eruptive rather than a pervasive guiding force.

But the younger Clifford Williams was already part of that group of directors, some of whom have worked with the company over three decades, who have been quietly instrumental in shaping our often kaleidoscopic impressions of 'RSC Shakespeare'. His first success came in 1962 with a rip-roaring *Comedy of Errors*, rehearsed as a stop-gap but destined to ride high in the repertoire for four years. And he rescued an even more 'impossible' play in 1965, revealing how Marlowe's *Jew of Malta* could be made to work by accepting that farcical elements were inextricably blended with the tragic.

John Barton had been an associate director of the RSC from the first, and his responsibilities soon widened from concern with the company's verse-speaking to active direction. Early on he worked in some notable collaborations with Hall, including a 'sandpit' *Troilus and Cressida* which traumatically spoke its anti-war message at the very height of the Cuban missile crisis in 1962. Like Williams, Barton also achieved an early, 'accidental' success – with his compilation on king-ship, *The Hollow Crown,* intended for a single performance, but revived on all sorts of occasions since. Barton has continued to lend an unobtrusive authority to the company's work, with explorations ranging from Greek tragedy to the proto-feminism of Aphra Behn.

Hall's own production style with the RSC probably reached its apogee in the mid-sixties – variously expressed in the subtle orchestration of Harold Pinter's scrupulously paced *The Homecoming*; through the feeling for contemporary Shakespearean relevance of his *Hamlet,* in which David Warner somehow pinned down the drifting, ambiguously angry mood of a generation; or in the joyous handling of ensemble work which set off Scofield's dithering comic gem of a Khlestakov in *The Government Inspector.*

Though still youthful himself, Hall was anxious to encourage a new generation of directing talent into the now maturing company. Trevor Nunn arrived in 1966 with a four-square, zesty *Revenger's Tragedy* whose cast, which included Alan Howard and Ian Richardson, rang with the names of a rising RSC generation – of which Janet Suzman and Michael Williams, teamed for Nunn's *The Taming of the Shrew* in the following season, were already leading members. That same year saw two other new names, of Terry Hands and David Jones, appearing among the directing credits.

A NATIONAL THEATRE AT LAST

As if heeding his own warning that a theatre company should find some means of self-renewal every seven years or so, in 1968 Hall chose to resign as artistic director of the RSC – already in waiting, some said, to succeed Laurence Olivier at the National Theatre. This had at last come into existence in 1963, and during the long planning and construction of its permanent, three-stage home on the South Bank had been operating from the Old Vic – where, under its last director, Michael Benthall, the now-displaced resident company had recently completed a 'five year plan' for a second presentation of all the First Folio plays.

However, despite some excellent one-off productions – such as the revival of Ibsen's *Peer Gynt* with Leo McKern in its closing season – Benthall's Old Vic had appeared somewhat adrift in the wake of the invasion from Stratford: and there was widespread unease that, since Peter Hall appeared to be creating a National Theatre in all but name, Olivier's efforts would also turn out to be replicative and

redundant. In the event, the approach of the two men and the companies they shaped proved complementary. Hall's was essentially a directors' theatre, with the works of Shakespeare as its focus and *raison d'être*, while Olivier's was an actors' theatre – freed by the very existence of the RSC to build a wider, more eclectic repertoire.

As a sort of trial run for the National, in 1962 Olivier had directed the inaugural summer season at the new Chichester Festival Theatre – an exciting sweep of a playhouse with a hexagonal thrust-stage in a rather somnolent setting. Building some of the Chichester productions into the first year's work at the Old Vic, Olivier also drew heavily but wisely on personnel imported from the Royal Court, including a number of actors as well as his chief directorial associates, Gaskill and Dexter. Kenneth Tynan, chief critical champion of the Court's work, was variously to prove a useful irritant and a creative catalyst as the National's 'dramaturg' – the first such appointment in Britain.

George Farquhar's *The Recruiting Officer*, in the production by William Gaskill in 1963 during the opening season of the National Theatre at the Old Vic. Gaskill stressed that his production was strongly influenced by Brecht's adaptation of the play as *Trumpets and Drums* – not least in its setting, by the French designer René Allio. Taking the play out of the stuffy closet of 'mannered' comedy put the focus instead on its strong social drive and healthy sensuality. Maggie Smith took the 'breeches part' of Silvia, the magistrate's daughter who dons male attire because of her love for the charming but unscrupulous Captain Plume (played by Robert Stephens, with Laurence Olivier as his fellow-officer Brazen). Here, confronting Colin Blakely's Sergeant Kite, Silvia is observed by the country wench Rose (Lynn Redgrave, with her back to the door), who has the misfortune to fall in love with this debonair *alter ego*, 'Jack Wilful'

Below and opposite: The four satirists of the apocalypse – from left to right, the original *Beyond the Fringe* team of Jonathan Miller, Peter Cook, Alan Bennett, and Dudley Moore. The 'fringe' was that of the Edinburgh Festival, whence this innovative revue – wide-ranging in its satire, but with a declining government the ripest target for ridicule – came to the West End in 1960. Comic acting sustained the subsequent careers of Cook and Moore (sometimes in tandem, as 'Pete and Dud'), but Miller went on to gain a separate reputation as a director, and Bennett as a writer of quirky plays which celebrate the unobtrusive eccentricities of the English as they seek to preserve the niceties of culture and class

Thus began a vintage period. A new and illuminating approach was taken to 'Restoration' comedy, notably with a colourful yet socially-realistic *Recruiting Officer* from Gaskill and a more sombre *Love for Love* from Peter Wood. A varied range of work from the classical and continental repertoires was on offer, from Marston and Lope de Vega to Ibsen and Brecht. And even lowly farce was revalued and rejuvenated – the French variety with a Feydeau adaptation, *A Flea in Her Ear*, the native breed with Coward's own production of his *Hay Fever*, and a contemporary British sport in the genre, Peter Shaffer's *Black Comedy*, transposing light and dark to dazzling comic effect.

In its occasional homage to Shakespeare, the company blended scholarship with an older actorly tradition – not too successfully with another attempt to cut Peter O'Toole to ensemble cloth in the opening *Hamlet*, but memorably in the following season's production of *Othello* by John Dexter, with Olivier himself giving a compulsively mimetic performance as the Moor. Anticipated accusations of 'poaching' from the commercial sector were largely avoided by a choice of new plays which required elaborate technical and casting resources, such as Peter Shaffer's ambitious epic of the conquest of Peru, *The Royal Hunt of the Sun* (1964), and John Arden's *Armstrong's Last Goodnight* (1965). The company also took rewarding risks on then-unknown writers, as when, in 1967, they brought Tom Stoppard's *Rosencrantz and Guildenstern Are Dead* straight from the fringe of the Edinburgh Festival. The continuing loyalty of Shaffer and Stoppard was thus ensured.

The fairly narrow directing base had been broadened from the first by a regular use of guest directors, including several from abroad. But whereas in the first ten seasons, during which 40 or so different directors had been employed, as many as 25 were brought in for a single production only, many actors remained with the National over long periods – ensuring the company's stability, but also extending their own range and reputations. From Albert Finney and Joan Plowright to Colin Blakely and Geraldine McEwan, from Frank Finlay and Lynn Redgrave to Robert Stephens and Maggie Smith, from Robert Lang and Derek Jacobi to Ronald Pickup and Anthony Hopkins, the roll-call reads as impressively now as it seemed innovative and often type-challenging then.

The opening seasons having almost instantaneously established a stature appropriate to a truly National Theatre, the following four or five years sustained a level of excitement which, in retrospect, made some falling away almost a due process of nature. Although Frank Dunlop, Michael Blakemore, and Jonathan Miller were brought into the directorial team, internal disagreements led to Tynan's effective sidelining, and Olivier himself was eventually and not very happily eased out in Hall's favour in 1973 – this, despite his triumphant return from cancer to play Tyrone in a production by Blakemore of O'Neill's *Long Day's Journey into Night* which, two years earlier, had marked the beginning of a renewal in the company's fortunes.

Olivier had been responsive to the new drama as early as 1957, when he played Archie Rice in Osborne's *The Entertainer*, and it was curiously fitting that his final role for the National, in 1973, should have been as John Tagg, a grizzled upholder of Trotskyist verities in *The Party*, by an even younger dramatist, Trevor Griffiths. Despite such early forays into live theatre, Griffiths himself soon preferred to aim his work at television – where the arrival of the independent companies during the 1950s and of BBC2 in 1964 had combined with new technological developments to spur major changes in traditional thinking.

DRAMA AND SATIRE ON TELEVISION

Until the early 1950s, television plays had almost invariably been rooted in dialogue rather than intrinsically visual, and were normally transmitted live from studio sets, shot from three or four cameras, and mixed according to a pre-arranged script. With videotape techniques still fairly primitive, it was at first the greater flexibility and cheapness of 16 mm over the old 35 mm film which permitted the pre-recording of plays, unlimited location shooting, and more sophisticated editing – television drama thus moving from a stage-based to a film-based grammar, some said without ever quite claiming a creative vocabulary of its own.

The BBC's Head of Television Drama from 1954, Michael Barry, encouraged some of the earliest innovatory work, notably the three science-fiction series which began with *The Quatermass Experiment* – whose author, Nigel Kneale, went on to stimulate more earthbound tremors with his adaptation of George Orwell's *1984*. Sydney Newman arrived from Canada in 1956, just in time to see *Look Back in Anger* and to infuse its spirit into the work he produced in the 'Armchair Theatre' slot for ABC. Moving across to the BBC, he initiated a distinguished line of 'Wednesday Plays' – under which guise he encouraged Tony Garnett to evolve that distinctive style of drama-documentary of which *Cathy Come Home* and *Up the Junction* remain the best-remembered. It was under the heading of 'documentary', too, that Ken Russell began, with *Isadora*, his free-form explorations of the lives of artists and musicians.

Soon, certain dramatists were beginning to create distinctive television styles – David Mercer revealing the capacity of the medium for conveying the interior world of the imagination in *A Suitable Case for Treatment*, Alun Owen evoking a poetic sense of the grimmest urban characters and settings in such plays as *No Trams to Lime Street* and *Lena, Oh My Lena*, John Hopkins cross-cutting times and moods as well as locations in *Talking to a Stranger*, and Dennis Potter combining political comment with private pain in *Vote, Vote, Vote for Nigel Barton*. Other leading writers for television at the time included Clive Exton, Philip Mackie, Fay Weldon, Jack Rosenthal, and Julia Jones.

Even crime and thriller series were now crossing the old conventionalized boundaries. John McGrath and Troy Kennedy-Martin thus revolutionized the television perception of police work through the nitty-gritty but elliptic realism of *Z Cars*, while at the other extreme there was the stylish, even-tempered fantasy of *The Avengers*. And in so-called 'light entertainment' the broad-based appeal of *The Army Game* and *Bootsie and Snudge* rubbed shoulders with the comic oedipal claustrophobia of *Steptoe and Son*.

Then, in 1962, Ned Sherrin produced a late-night series of live satirical shows for the BBC, *That Was the Week That Was*, which (with the tacit approval of a new Director General, Hugh Greene) cheerfully breached many of the po-faced rules forbidding near-the-knuckle allusions in matters of politics, religion, and sex. The show, while distinctive in its own right, also reflected the prevailing 'satire boom' – itself in part a condemnation, in part a celebration of the decadence of the last, scandal-ridden years of the Macmillan government. While the magazine *Private Eye* had thus been launched only a few months earlier, live theatre had got there first – when, in 1960, a group of four Oxbridge graduates wrote and presented the revue *Beyond the Fringe* at the Edinburgh Festival. Transferred the following spring to the Fortune in London, its mix of topical and cultural satire with a dash of inspired surrealism survived even the departure of the original cast for New York.

THE SECOND WAVE

Beyond the Fringe not only gave a new lease of life to revue, but launched its alumni into distinguished though very different futures in the world of entertainment. Jonathan Miller thus became one of the most eclectic directors of his generation, while Peter Cook and Dudley Moore pursued joint and several careers in comedy acting – and the more retiring Alan Bennett wrote a wide range of closely-observed, gently satiric plays both for television and the stage, to become part of that 'second wave' of new dramatists which had begun to emerge around the turn of the decade. Bennett's first full-length work, *Forty Years On* (1968), was a discursive spoof as much on the values of inbred Bloomsbury culture as on those of the public school it portrayed, with Gielgud splendidly self-mocking as its bemused, chronically beset headmaster.

Some writers who had first been persuaded of the potential of theatre by the work of the Royal Court – John Mortimer springs to mind – received their first productions there, but went on to write mainly for the West End and television. David Mercer, however, moved in the opposite direction, building on his television work and on the commercial success of *Ride a Cock Horse* (1965) to become a sort of unofficial 'house dramatist' for the RSC, where his stern old-fashioned socialism rubbed shoulders with Laingian psychology in a series of psycho-political plays which stretched from *Belcher's Luck* (1966) to *After Haggerty* (1970), and from *Duck Song* (1974) to *Cousin Vladimir* (1978).

Robert Bolt, after his West End successes with *Flowering Cherry* in 1957 and two years later with *A Man for All Seasons* – one of several plays of the period in which Brecht was pasteurized for bourgeois consumption – was among those whose later career lay largely in films. Shaffer, after a period of mixed fortunes in the West End, returned to the National with the phenomenally successful *Equus* (1973) and *Amadeus* (1979). And a writer with a background in television drama, Peter Nichols, followed the same route when his first play for the stage, *A Day in the Death of Joe Egg*, came down from the Citizens' Theatre in Glasgow to commercial success at the Comedy in 1967. This serio-comic, flippantly presented but deeply-felt piece, about the parenting of a severely handicapped child, was followed two years later at the Old Vic by *The National Health*, in which the feelings were, for me, too often saturated in the flippancy.

Stoppard continued to combine metaphysical high jinks with cunningly crafted plots and slightly cardboard characters in *Jumpers* (1972), *Travesties* (1974), and beyond. That an easygoing conservatism underlay his digestible erudition and undoubted wit naturally endeared him to West End audiences, who, though of much the same social composition as ever, came over time to assimilate the less politically threatening innovations they at first despised. Even Joe Orton thus enjoyed enormous posthumous success after his murder in 1967, as the very taboos he had calculatedly outraged in *Entertaining Mr Sloane* (1964) and *Loot* (1966) lost some of their sanctity. These sexually freebooting farces owed something of their impish energy to the tradition of Ben Travers, while their distinctive dialogue yoked Congreve in unlikely harness with the jargon of the civil service, Wilde with the bathos of copywriting overkill.

The very different verbal ingenuities of N. F. Simpson belonged to a native, Lewis Carrollian tradition of eccentric nonsense rather than to the 'theatre of the absurd' in which some critics tried to locate him. For the tendency of the times was to pigeonhole writers either as politically committed or as exponents of this largely French school, which had been assembled not by its supposed members but in a book by the influential critic Martin Esslin. As the new Head of Radio Drama, Esslin was doing valiant work in introducing such continental styles to BBC audiences, as also in giving airtime to new British writers, including Arden, Stoppard – and the most widely discussed, analyzed, and explicated of them all, Harold Pinter.

The disastrous reception of Pinter's *The Birthday Party* in 1958 – a *Sunday Times* rave by Harold Hobson apart, as its author made a habit of reminding us – soon gave way to critical acclaim for *The Caretaker*, which transferred for a long West End run after its 1960 opening at the Arts. There followed the radio plays for Esslin, new work on television – and revue sketches which amounted almost to imagist playlets. Pinter's long association with Hall began in 1965 with *The Homecoming*, and continued four years later with *Landscape* and *Silence*. Though it was perhaps inevitable that Pinter, too, should first have been labelled an 'absurdist', in truth his style has long paid off whatever debts it owed to Beckett, becoming increasingly terse and mannered, yet continuing to orchestrate for actors a rhetoric of language and notated silences that exerts over audiences a seemingly compulsive power.

The most important 'second wave' writer to emerge from the Royal Court during the early 1960s was Edward Bond, whose vision was uniquely his own, but whose hard-edged socio-ecological concerns foreshadowed those of the coming decade. From the first, his plays blended high seriousness of purpose with an acute sense of theatrical potential – and a gift for interdependent verbal and physical imagery unequalled since Brecht. Like Arden, Bond also displayed a capacity to fit style to subject, in forms ranging from episodic social realism, steeped in street argot, in *Saved* (1965) to the baroque comic-strip formalism of *Early Morning* (1968), and from the austere, poetic drift of *Narrow Road to the Deep North* (1968) to the broad, mythic canvas of his rich, resonant, and highly politicized reworking of *Lear* (1972).

Orton, Pinter, and Bond all found themselves engaged in disputes over censorship with the Lord Chamberlain – paradoxically, at the very time when London was supposedly 'swinging' and the 'permissive society' getting its act together. It is curious, then, that although the Royal Court made itself temporarily into a club in Bond's defence, as it had earlier in Osborne's, the older-style club theatres were now in something of a decline. But the Mercury did find a new identity for itself as home for the International Theatre Club, giving over its pocket-handkerchief stage to experimental work both from the continent and the USA – whence came rumours of revolutionary new styles being developed by the Becks' Living Theatre, Peter Schumann's Bread and Puppet Theatre, Joseph Chaikin's Open Theatre, Ronnie Davis's San Francisco Mime Troupe, and Ellen Stewart's Café La Mama.

In a similar spirit, around 1966 the People Show began to create strange events, rooted as much in the company's art training as in theatre, in the shop basement of Better Books in the Charing Cross Road. And such cross-bred disciplines were clear also in the vogue for 'happenings' – organized but seemingly spontaneous disruptions, often intended to explode unexpectedly into non-theatrical environments, as when the first had shocked (not least with the nudity of its performer) a drama conference at the Edinburgh Festival in 1963. Not entirely coincidentally, in the same year an American expatriate, Jim Haynes, had created the tiny Traverse Theatre, which became a centre of innovative activity in the Scottish capital outside the overflowing three weeks of its festival.

Together with his fellow-American Charles Marowitz, Haynes tried in 1967 to create a London Traverse within the rather anaemic ambience of the recently-built Cochrane Theatre in London's Southampton Row. The ramshackle Soho sprawl which, in the following year, Haynes opened under the name of the Arts Laboratory was to prove a more sympathetic environment for experiment, while Marowitz went his own way to create the Open Space Theatre in a basement in Tottenham Court Road. This is to take us, however, from manifestations of the

Opposite: the Belgrade Theatre, Coventry, opened in 1958 – the first newly-built playhouse of post-war Britain. The theatre was typical of the civic playhouses which continued to flourish for the next decade, with a wide proscenium stage and removable apron, and accommodating its modest audience capacity of 910 in a broad swathe of stalls and a single balcony. Originally, members of the company lived in flats forming part of the theatre complex, and efforts were made in this as in other respects to make the theatre part of its community – notably through the establishment in 1965 of the first theatre in education team, which enabled actor-teachers to take specially conceived plays into local schools. An early success for the Belgrade was the virtual discovery of Arnold Wesker, whose first plays were staged here before being transferred to the Royal Court

dying fall of the 'little' theatre movement to intimations of the spirit of 'alternative' theatre, which will occupy us largely in the next chapter.

THE CIVIC THEATRES

New theatres of a more conventional kind, in London at least, were taking an unconscionable time to spring from the institutional drawing boards of the National and RSC. And of the few new commercial houses (the first since the early thirties), the much-vaunted Royalty (on the site of the old Stoll Theatre off the bottom end of Kingsway) and the Prince Charles (with a rather unobtrusive presence near Leicester Square) both soon found themselves turned over to films. Only the Mermaid, converted from a riverside warehouse through the drive and inspiration of the comic actor turned impresario Bernard Miles, made an immediate and distinctive contribution to the London scene.

The airy, single-tier auditorium of the Mermaid, with its versatile, end-on open stage, adapted well to the multiplicity of minor classic revivals and reworkings in which the theatre tended to specialize – from mystery plays to the minor Elizabethans, and from Fielding to lesser-known Shaw and O'Casey. No less significantly, the Mermaid also became the first theatre in London to offer a truly all-day welcome, with a spacious foyer, bars, and restaurant areas which appeared more than concessive afterthoughts – a concept of theatre as a sociable gathering place which was already taking stronger root in the regional centres.

In part, confessedly, this was because of the less cramped building conditions and lower overheads outside London: yet it was also because the new purpose-built civic theatres had from the first been conceived as part of a whole range of community activities. There remained flashes of entrepreneurial spirit in the regions: the Pitlochry Festival Theatre in Perth, for example, had been running its summer festival since 1951 largely (if often precariously) as a commercial enterprise. The Chichester Festival Theatre, too, had sprung from the vision of one man, Leslie Evershed-Martin, while the Yvonne Arnaud in Guildford and the Thorndike in Leatherhead were also products of creative private enterprise. Outside such affluent areas of the south east, the Octagon Theatre in Bolton was a rare example of a northern rep which was individually inspired (by its director Robin Pemberton-Billing), though later sustained from local and national funding.

But most of the energy behind the thirty or so new regional theatres which followed the Belgrade, Coventry, into existence in the decade after 1958 was the product of a collective, civic pride. The flip side of their consequent reliance upon municipal and Arts Council subsidy was, of course, that its withdrawal or significant reduction could enforce a rapid fading into obscurity of once proud names: such was to be the fate, despite its early achievements, of the Ashcroft in Croydon – which, like the Forum in Billingham, was perhaps the more at risk for being part of a larger leisure complex.

Others among the new playhouses (including the Northcott in Exeter, the University Theatre in Newcastle, the Gardner Centre near Brighton, and the Gulbenkian in Hull) were more or less integral to the campuses of the new universities which were also proliferating during this period of economic expansion – and, sure enough, were to feel the countervailing pressures of later squeezes on academic funding. Others again were part of smaller-scale arts centres, as in Birmingham, Warwick, and Hull. In all, the number of repertory companies during this period increased from around twenty to over one hundred – while the touring theatres continued their seemingly inexorable decline.

In terms of human resources, some regional directors regarded their appointments as an apprenticeship en route to London: others displayed a fine loyalty to their areas, and made enduring reputations and careers in a single post. Thus, Peter Cheeseman remained at the Victoria, Stoke-on-Trent, to create a style of regional documentary, based on local history, characters, and accents, which has been widely admired and copied. And in 1969 Giles Havergal went to the then-troubled Citizens' Theatre in Glasgow, soon to be joined by Philip Prowse and Robert David MacDonald – this team going on to pursue for over two decades a brave but successful policy of mounting uncompromising and unparochial productions at prices accessible to working-class Gorbals audiences.

Others who more temporarily abandoned metropolitan fame included John Clements, who succeeded Olivier as director of the Chichester Festival in 1965, and John Neville, who directed the new Playhouse in Nottingham from 1963 to

1967, when he departed in protest at the level of Arts Council funding – the more limited support from the local council being, not untypically, more than cancelled out by rent and loan repayments.

MONEY FOR THE ARTS

Already, then, strains in the system were showing – one problem, not unique to the regions, being that bricks-and-mortar require resources for maintenance before a single production can be mounted. However, by and large this was a period when, under governments of both parties, there was confidence that the state's commitment to the arts was steadily increasing. Thus, in 1956 the Arts Council had a mere £820,000 at its disposal: by 1964, when Labour was returned to office, this had risen to £3,205,000 – and in the course of the six years of that administration to £9,300,000. This was in part thanks to the presence (for the first time in Britain) of a Ministry for the Arts – whose first, forceful incumbent, Jennie Lee, also inaugurated the appositely named Open University.

State funding for the Arts Council went along with an affirmation by both parties of the 'arm's length' principle – that the allocation was as free from political strings as should be the Council's own relationship with its proliferating clients. Desirable as this seemed, with its apparently final recognition that the arts required assistance from public funding (which, incidentally, they more than repaid as a tourist attraction), it began to create a dependency among companies and artists which, in a less sympathetic climate, could destroy long-developed plans at the stroke of a civil servant's percentage cut. Also left unresolved was the question of who should be responsible for sharing out the resources, and there were complaints that the Drama Panel – the voluntary committee of specialists whose recommendations were largely endorsed by the Council itself – was at best unrepresentative, at worst self-perpetuating and perhaps self-serving.

But so long as funding went on increasing, such questions were not pushed too hard or too often, and by 1968 the future of British theatre appeared rosy. Even its traditional insularity was beginning to break down – the RSC's regular programme of touring thus leaving the inexhaustible Peter Daubeny free to occupy the Aldwych each spring from 1964 to 1975 with his World Theatre Seasons. These annual feasts of international drama helped to broaden the minds of British theatre people beyond the vague axis stretching from Brecht to the absurd along which their opinions had previously been formed.

Other events abroad were also beginning to shape domestic opinion and argument, and so to impinge upon a politically-conscious theatre. Most divisive of these was the steady escalation (a term much abused at the time) of the undeclared American war in Vietnam, which was becoming the focus of student protest on college campuses across the USA. The coincidence of these protests with events in Paris and Prague was to make 1968 another turning point in European political history – and in British theatre history besides.

CHAPTER 21   *Alternative Theatres*

Staying in the north-east on the way to the Edinburgh Festival in August 1968, I first heard on Newcastle railway station the news that Soviet troops had been sent in to crush the revolutionary movement in Czechoslovakia. For all its hopes of fashioning 'socialism with a human face', the short-lived 'Prague Spring' was, it seemed, destined to prove no more successful in humanizing the communist system than, in that same season of hope, had been the barricades on the streets of Paris in denting (let alone destroying) the capitalist.

A few days later, I left a dignified, peaceful protest outside the Usher Hall in Edinburgh, where the Russian State Orchestra was making an ill-timed appearance, to join an audience of the dead – as the spectators watching *Acropolis* were supposed to be, silent witnesses of the desperate fantasies through which the victims of a nazi concentration camp were creating a kind of meaning from the preparations for their own extinction. There was deep poignancy in watching a company from Poland (near neighbour to Czechoslovakia not least in suffering) dramatizing at that moment in history the stubborn resistance of the human spirit. Retrospectively, it seems no less of a coincidence that this should have been the first production in Britain by the Laboratory Theatre of Jerzy Grotowski, whose style of 'poor theatre' came for many to exemplify the 'spirit of 1968'.

Less than a week later, the mounting tide of protest against American involvement in Vietnam reached a peak outside the ruling Democratic Party's presidential convention in Chicago, where the city's police reacted with repressive violence. On the following day I watched a brilliant production by Michael Blakemore for the Glasgow Citizens' Theatre of Brecht's *Resistible Rise of Arturo Ui* – a cautionary comic allegory tracing Hitler's path to power in terms of feuding protection racketeers, with Leonard Rossiter as the comic-strip führer and a little-known young actor named Steven Berkoff as his seedy henchman. The play, written almost three decades earlier, was set in a mythical but uncannily apposite Chicago.

Leonard Rossiter as the title-character in *The Resistible Rise of Artuo Ui* at the Saville Theatre in London. En route to this successful transfer, Michael Blakemore's production for the Glasgow Citizens' Theatre had been playing at the Edinburgh Festival at the time of the police suppression of anti-Vietnam demonstrations at the Democratic convention in Chicago – the city in which Brecht had made his Hitler-figure a gangland boss

In such ways did the politics and the plays of 1968 continue to mesh for me, as for so many in that unnervingly eventful year – when radical action worldwide continued to express, arguably in the face of all the evidence, a belief that the times were ripe for change. In the theatre, the 'spirit of 1968' manifested itself in the wish of many emerging young companies to respond to human needs before economic imperatives: indeed, there was a belief that such a driving force could only operate from the bottom up, not from the top down – rather as the 'fringe' of the Edinburgh Festival had for some years been proving that grass-roots, 'unofficial' theatre had more on offer, in quality as well as sheer quantity, than the 'official' variety. In the weekly column in which I reviewed that year's festival, I remarked that London had venues aplenty in which a fringe theatre (soon to dub itself 'underground' and then, more enduringly, 'alternative') might mount its challenge on a sustained, year-round basis.

Already, pioneering spirits were hacking out a new, lunchtime niche for their work – the Quipu company, created by the writer David Halliwell, finding an eventual home at the truly-named Little Theatre off St Martin's Lane, and the Ambiance, under the socio-cultural entrepreneur Ed Berman, operating in a variety of premises until it was transformed in 1972 into the Almost Free Theatre (whose audiences were asked, in the true spirit of the times, to pay only what they could afford).

PRECURSORS OF THE FRINGE

Other precursors of the London fringe – notably the People Show, whose work since 1965 had often been scripted by Jeff Nuttall – were already reflecting a closer convergence between theatre and the visual arts. In June 1968 such a collaging of talents was on display at the (by now normally staid) Unity Theatre, where John Arden and his wife Margaretta D'Arcy had joined forces with the London-based collective CAST, and with students from the Bradford College of Art under the direction of John Fox (who went on to form the community theatre group, Welfare State), to create a sprawling, critically derided, but in many ways seminal piece of propagandist theatre, *Harold Muggins Is a Martyr*.

CAST, the 'Cartoon Archetypical Slogan Theatre', described its style not so much as agit-prop as 'agit-pop' – since its brief 'get-in and get-out' playlets, performed at any and every available venue, owed less to Marx (despite the put-downs of capitalism) than to the youth culture and proliferating do-it-yourself music of the times. For now rock groups as powerful yet as various as the Beatles, the Rolling Stones, and the Who, all at the peak of their creative powers, were spawning a host of imitators, and giving definition *through performance* not only to the aspirations but to the sexual awareness and (less definably) the 'style' of a generation largely untouched by regular theatre.

This youth culture provoked such media clichés as 'swinging London' (with its epicentre, Carnaby Street, epitomizing a new, calculated sartorial ease) and the 'permissive society' – whose other manifestations included a rather more relaxed attitude towards the use of 'soft' drugs, and a considerably more relaxed attitude towards sexuality. The sexual 'liberation' of the sixties was 'permitted' as much by more liberal divorce laws as by the availability of the female contraceptive pill and the apparent control of sexually-transmitted diseases: it was lubricated, too, by the confidence and cash of continuing full employment – while remaining as yet uncomplicated by the insights of feminism, which was to

Mick Jagger, lead singer of the Rolling Stones, one of the many sixties rock groups who theatricalized their stage acts. In the USA, the calculated self-advertisement on stage of Jim Morrison and The Doors pioneered this brand of 'rock theatre', while other 'performing' British bands – by then establishing their dominance of the medium – included The Kinks and, most notably, The Who. Rock artists of the time who created vivid stage images included Pete Townshend of The Who, Jimi Hendrix, Lou Reed and The Velvet Underground – and of course Bob Dylan, who took rock into the Newport heartland of folk music. He established for 'rock culture' a claim to the 'serious' consideration which the Beatles were the first to receive in Britain

recognize its largely unconscious servicing of male fantasies of dominance, and of promiscuity untrammelled by responsibility.

CELEBRATING THE ABOLITION OF CENSORSHIP

Following the unsuccessful prosecution of Penguin Books for their publication of an unexpurgated edition of D. H. Lawrence's *Lady Chatterley's Lover* in 1963 (the year in which, according to the poet Philip Larkin, 'sexual intercourse began'), a loosening of most forms of censorship was at least passively encouraged by the Labour government which remained in office from 1964 until 1970. In 1968 (when else?) the theatre thus benefited from the efforts of an individual MP, Michael Foot, who successfully steered through Parliament a Private Member's Bill which at last abolished the powers of the Lord Chamberlain to censor or even ban a play. Henceforth, the theatre was to be subject simply to the laws of the land rather than to the whims of an archaic official of the royal household. The occasional *cause célèbre* apart, the laws of the land remained largely unconcerned.

Although the Chamberlain's moral pedantry in taking his blue-pencil to the scripts of prominent playwrights – Osborne, Pinter, and Bond recently among them – had largely ensured his demise, at first it was the greater visual liberty

The Arts Lab and other new spaces

Back in uncomplicated 1968, sex was being happily compounded with drugs and rock'n'roll – at least in the public perception of Jim Haynes's Arts Laboratory, which, in a brief but explosive existence of twenty-one months from that January, offered a home sometimes to its audiences as well as to the performers and visual artists who cluttered its rambling Drury Lane premises (and its equally rambling schedules) in an explosion of often inchoate creativity.

Some early 'fringe' shows were to be found in more conventional settings – the Brighton Combination's brashly, brightly innovative Rasputin Show thus making its London home in the lush surroundings of the Arts. But this was a time when numerous new 'spaces' – notionally more flexible and certainly less luxurious – were being created or adapted for theatrical or multi-media use. Examples might include the Combination's own base on the Sussex coast, the Arts Centre in York – and Oval House, opened by Peter Oliver in Kennington, south London, in 1967, to offer probably the most sustained (and incidentally the best organized) of welcomes to the many itinerants of the fringe.

Another long-surviving venue was the Theatre Upstairs, which was converted – in 1968, of course – from a former rehearsal space in the attic of the Royal Court (two years later Bill Gaskill gave over both theatres to the 'Come

Together' festival, which for many conventional theatre-goers was a first vicarious sampling of the fringe). Also in 1968, the Round House, a former railway turning-shed in Chalk Farm, opened as a centre for larger-scale experimental activity – having remained previously unused by Wesker's Centre 42, in the mistaken belief that it required extensive rebuilding rather than the rougher adaptation to which its unique resonances now responded.

There was (and is) an even greater turnover in theatres attached to pubs as in the landlords who run them: but the King's Head in Islington, which opened in 1971, and the Orange Tree in Richmond, which followed a year later, managed to survive most vicissitudes of trade and times. This largely transient category apart, new venues divided roughly between 'receptive' spaces, such as Oval House and the Cockpit in Marylebone (1970), and dedicated though often diminutive playhouses which tried to sustain a consistent policy if not a permanent company.

Among the more notable of these were the Soho Theatre and the Young Vic off Waterloo Road (1970); the Pool in Edinburgh (1971); the Half Moon in Aldgate (1972); and the experimental theatre attached to the new premises in the Mall of the Institute of Contemporary Arts (1973). Several of these theatres, including the Soho and the Half Moon,

now permitted which the theatre began to exploit. Thus, in *Harold Muggins* Arden had incidentally featured a female nude – and that her presence *was* incidental, almost offhand, was very much to his point. In *Squire Jonathan and His Unfortunate Treasure*, presented in the same month by the Ambiance, he made a fulsome naked lady the highly visible object of the impotent musings of a squire incarcerated in his own treasury – her 'objectifying' again part of the play's proto-feminist intention.

This was over three months before the American 'love-rock musical' *Hair* – which, like many manifestations of the youth culture, was destined speedily to metamorphose from an urgent, hip celebration of the 'age of Aquarius' into a fashionable event – was hyping its own nude scenes, safely distant and discreetly lit though these were in the cavernous Shaftesbury. Soon, no less hyped but brightly illuminated, came shows such as the girlie-magazine-on-stage which was *Pyjama Tops* (1969), and Tom Eyen's slightly more pretentious *The Dirtiest Show in Town* (1971), both now lurking in very obscure corners of the memory. Probably better remembered is *Oh! Calcutta!* (1970), an ostensibly erotic but actually slightly limp revue assembled with surprisingly prestigious support by Kenneth Tynan.

eventually shifted to new sites – as did the Open Space, which was at first situated in a basement in the Tottenham Court Road, but later moved upstairs and up the road, alongside Warren Street Station. Directed by Haynes's fellow-expatriate American and erstwhile collaborator Charles Marowitz, the Open Space opened (yes, in 1968) with John Herbert's Fortune and Men's Eyes – not only one of the first plays to feature male nudity in the aftermath of the censorship, but one of the earliest with an overtly homosexual theme.

Tim Curry as Frank N. Furter in *The Rocky Horror Show*. Beginning its long life at the Royal Court's new studio, the Theatre Upstairs, in 1973, this took a fresh, tongue-in-cheek look at the Frankenstein theme and other vintage movie clichés, in the form of a gothic rock'n'roll fantasy musical which itself became a theatrical (and later a cinematic) cult. It transferred from the Court for a seven-year run in Chelsea cinemas and at the Comedy Theatre

All these exploited their titillation potential by appearing to venture respectably upmarket of the sleazy offerings of the then-booming Soho strip clubs. Yet it was to such specialist catering that the sexually explicit theatre largely returned when attitudes towards 'permissiveness' began to change – under the impact on the one hand of the women's movement and the assertion of gay and lesbian rights (which encouraged a fuller sense of the infinite complexity of human behaviour), and, on the more sinister side, of the threat to active, uncomplicated sexuality posed by the spread of the Aids virus. To the new kinds of awareness such forces produced, we shall, of course, return.

CRUELTY AND COLLECTIVE CREATION

By now, Charles Marowitz had infiltrated the mainstream theatre as director with Peter Brook of an experimental RSC company, whose exploration of the theories of Antonin Artaud gestated into the influential 'Theatre of Cruelty' season, presented at the recently completed, adaptable LAMDA Theatre in 1964. Out of this season grew not only Marowitz's various 'collage' versions of Shakespeare, but Brook's production later in the same year (for the RSC at the Aldwych) of Peter Weiss's *Marat-Sade* – a quasi-Brechtian, Marxist-driven, verbose historical epic, which Brook transformed into an exercise in Artaudian 'cruelty'. Two years later, in similar vein, he directed the self-flagellating *US* – ostensibly a collectively-created theatrical statement against British attitudes towards the war in Vietnam, but an experience which seemed to me to feed and also feed upon the very liberal masochism it purported to despise.

Like Gordon Craig, the French anarcho-surrealist Antonin Artaud was an erratic genius little honoured or understood in his own country. His concept of 'cruelty' had less to do with sadism than with a kind of perceived rigour which would draw largely upon an actor's non-verbal resources – and which probably had its origins as much in the expressionist silent films in which Artaud had himself acted as in the Balinese dance which famously influenced him at the Paris Exhibition of 1931. In part thanks to Brook's sometimes misdirected homage, Artaud's influence became part of a wider tendency to question – and on the director's part sometimes to usurp – the 'authority' of the dramatist's text, in favour of collective creation directed towards 'total' theatricality.

In practice, such subordination of verbal elements tended less to encourage challenging new theatrical forms than new hierarchical relationships – in which the role of the playwright was duly diminished. Thus, within a few years both Wesker and Arden found themselves involved in disputes with the RSC (briefly democratized in the 'spirit of 1968') over the acceptability or interpretation of their work. The experience must have contributed to the failure of both writers, despite their continuing productivity and diversity, to find a niche in the changing theatre: but some of the younger playwrights now emerging were in sympathy with the new mood, and there were even a few attempts at 'collective' playwriting – resulting in such multiply-authored, slippery-styled curiosities as *Lay-By* (1971) and *England's Ireland* (1972).

Several of the authors who contributed (on rolls of wallpaper, as one recalled) to such endeavours were also involved in Portable Theatre and its offshoot Paradise Foundry. That scripts from Portable have, unusually, survived in print was due to the company happening to embrace no less than three playwrights of major promise – Howard Brenton, David Hare, and Snoo Wilson, to whose fortunes we shall return. And, exceptionally, the London Theatre Group made a single writer, Steven Berkoff (albeit also the company's director and leading man) its focus of activity, as Berkoff learned with a sort of brazen suavity to mesh his distinctive personal idiom of compulsive doggerel with ping-ponging patterns of movement and interaction.

Among other groups and receptive venues which from the first gave considered encouragement to new writing, the Wakefield Tricycle and the Foco Novo companies, the Half Moon Theatre, and a veteran of the pub theatre movement, the Bush on Shepherds Bush Green, spring to mind. But for many groups, the prevailing mode, at least until the early seventies, was of 'collective creation' – a script, if any, being evolved through group improvisation rather than individual inspiration.

Hull Truck, formed in 1971 by Mike Bradwell, who had worked with the leading improvisational *auteur*, Mike Leigh, enjoyed a unique success in evolving recognizable 'plays' by improvisational means – plays, that is, which employed a fairly conventional, quasi-naturalistic structure dependent upon verbal underpinning, though their thematic concerns were those of a previously undramatized social group, the rootless and often ostensibly classless young. But most such groups were working, consciously or unconsciously, in reaction against the

Opposite: the assassination scene in Peter Brook's Aldwych production for the Royal Shakespeare Company of Peter Weiss's *Marat-Sade* (1964). The play's full title – *The Persecution and Assassination of Marat as Performed by the Inmates of the Asylum of Charenton under the Direction of the Marquis de Sade* – also serves as a plot summary for a piece which, in its German original, was richer in Marxist dialectics and Brechtian 'distancing' than in the Artaudian 'cruelty' with which Brook infused his production – the outcome of the experimental 'Theatre of Cruelty' season he and Charles Marowitz had earlier mounted at the new LAMDA Theatre. Here, Patrick Magee as de Sade looks on while Glenda Jackson, the inmate playing the assassin Charlotte Corday in the 'play-within-the-play', raises her knife to kill Ian Richardson's Marat. The production achieved some spectacular effects in the asylum bath-house (designed by Sally Jacobs) which served as de Sade's theatre, and the actors responded heartily to Brook's injunction 'to dig out the madman' in themselves. As Glenda Jackson – one of the actors introduced into the company through the 'Theatre of Cruelty' season – succinctly put it: 'We were all convinced that we were going loony'

Opposite: *Dogg's Hamlet*, by Tom Stoppard, as played at the Collegiate Theatre, Bloomsbury, in 1979. This short 'entertainment' was one of several pieces originally written by Stoppard for the Dogg's Troupe, created by Ed Berman as part of the small, benevolent empire he sheltered under his 'Inter-Action' umbrella during the sixties and seventies. Other constituent parts included the Ambiance Theatre Club, the Almost Free Theatre, The Other Company, and the Fun Art Bus – from which an earlier version of this playlet was performed before its more conventional staging by Berman's last theatrical enterprise, the British American Repertory Company. All, as Tom Stoppard later put it, were 'phenomena of a decade which was simultaneously playful and desperately serious'. Later, Berman diverted most of his considerable energies into urban regeneration projects

'primacy of the word' and so towards a more broadly-based semiotics of performance – though they would not yet have recognized such terminology.

Inspiration came not only from Grotowski, whose company paid a second visit in 1969, and from other visiting continental gurus – notably Ariane Mnouchkine with her Théâtre du Soleil, and Jérôme Savary with the Grand Magic Circus – but (more accessibly for most) from American groups already probing the further reaches of innovation. The Becks' Living Theatre had thus played in London as early as 1964, and came again, more influentially, in 1971, while the La Mama Experimental Theatre Company visited in 1967 and 1969, Joseph Chaikin's Open Theatre in 1967 and 1973, and Peter Schumann's Bread and Puppet Theatre annually from 1968 to 1970. A London-based La Mama group was founded in self-evident discipleship in 1968, from which the Freehold soon split away to concentrate on work which was strong in physically disciplined movement.

Moving Being, as their name suggests, also focused strongly upon dance- and movement-based work – while, in contrast, the eponymous founder of the Roy Hart Theatre combined theatrical and therapeutic intentions in exploring the use of voice. But few companies were dominated by a single expansive personality such as Berkoff or Hart – though another exception was the Ken Campbell Road Show, with its compelling line in raucously dramatized shaggy-dog stories. For most fringe groups had their origins in a coming-together of like-minded and ideologically equal associates, often from the art schools or universities which (now opened up to their fullest intake of students from all walks of life) had been a centre of creativity as well as of discontent in 1968. Even the Pip Simmons group, though named after its director, remained in spirit a collective – its infusion of rock music, 'psychedelic' lighting, and pop-art into an up-front confrontational performing style having much in common with the pop festivals also burgeoning at this time.

Most fringe companies employed such 'mixed media' effects in one way or another: but it was practitioners in the new mode of 'performance art' who brought actorly and painterly instincts into their closest conjunction. Though formed relatively late, in 1976 – and more sparing in its output than (for example) the pioneering and prolific John Bull Puncture Repair Outfit – the IOU company perhaps most fully exploited the potential of this medium. For me, its displays of performance art were sometimes irritatingly elliptic, but they could also achieve a powerfully kinetic, often lyrical synthesis of visual imagery, light, music, and flowing, ritualized action.

EXPERIMENTS IN ENVIRONMENTAL THEATRE

IOU was a spinoff from Welfare State, whose mystical aspirations – of connecting people to their communities through celebrations which are largely 'invented', though seeming to emanate from profoundly pagan roots – ushered in a theatrical 'New Age' long before its time. The ebullience and ingenuity (not to mention resolute cheerfulness) of these 'engineers of the imagination' in adapting their work to its environment has redeemed them from pretentiousness – and their sheer longevity has arguably demonstrated the need they claim to be answering, albeit in a seemingly inimitable way.

Welfare State employ 'found' circumstances in a manner which has perhaps taken the concept of 'environmental theatre' to its extreme. More loosely defined as any performance event in which the playing space either by its nature or by refashioning forms an intrinsic part of the action, and usually embracing audience and actors in a shared setting, environmental theatre took (and takes) many forms. At its simplest, an 'environment' might thus amount to a set design exploding outwards from the stage – as, for example, did John Napier's for *Fortune and Men's Eyes*. Spectators at the Open Space were thus required to have their fingerprints taken before groping their way down a bleak iron fire-escape, and entering an auditorium which overlapped into the block of grimly claustro-phobic prison-cells to which the action might just as readily (if less imagin-atively) have been confined – as indeed it eventually was when the production later transferred to a traditional West End theatre, the Comedy.

But other early practitioners employed a more organic, Grotowskian approach in their attempts to link audiences and action through stage settings, whether in the prolific and outgoing work of Lumiere and Son, or in the more austere and often demanding experiences mounted by TOC. Under the direction of Naftali Yavin until his premature death, TOC was 'The Other Company' – so called to distinguish it from Ed Berman and Jim Hiley's very different but associated Dogg Troupe. This attempted an altogether different kind of 'environmental' involve-ment with its audiences – often of deprived London children, perhaps taken by the 'Fun Bus' to derelict land which the ebullient Berman later became more concerned to utilize for inter-active urban agriculture than theatre.

AGITATIONAL THEATRE IN THE SEVENTIES

The spirit of the sixties outlived its decade in the theatre, but not in the nation at large. Thus, a Conservative government had been returned in 1970, and pro-ceeded to rule for four years in chronic conflict with the still-powerful trades unions, until it was finally (and unexpectedly) brought down by an ill-advised attempt of the prime minister, Edward Heath, to make political capital from the miners' strike of 1974. The interim saw the formation (or galvanizing into total opposition) of numerous groups who, following the (at first rather lonely) example of CAST, were more political than aesthetic in orientation.

Most were more or less comfortable with the term 'agit-prop' to describe their work – though the only company actually to adopt the name soon changed it to Red Ladder, which was among the first to take its shows to factory gates, strikers' and union meetings, and working men's clubs and pubs. Others soon followed suit, including Belt and Braces and General Will, for whom David Edgar wrote a number of 'occasional' plays – that is, works rooted in particular issues or events which they were not intended to outlive. One such was *Rent, or Caught in the Act* (1972), through which the company made a lively melodrama out of the unlikeliest of material – a parliamentary bill to restrict subsidies for council housing.

Edgar was hugely prolific during this, the earliest period of his work, theatricalizing subjects as various as the Common Market, a strike in a motorcycle factory, the Festival of Light's crusade against pornography, the Concorde aircraft, and (while most writers – Arden apart – were still uneasily avoiding the subject) the worsening situation in Northern Ireland. He wrote also for his own former university, in Bradford – a city which had become highly active theatrically, its College of Art theatre group having achieved a hefty political impact through pieces created and directed by Albert Hunt. Of these, *John Ford's Cuban Missile Crisis*, which rendered the near-end of the world into hilariously parodied terms of a western movie, was an object-lesson in the making of strong political points through the medium of fast-moving, debunking comedy.

It was during the early days of the Heath government that one of the few 'fringe' figures who had already made a name for himself in the established media, John McGrath, by now disillusioned with the radical potential of television, formed the 'different kind of touring theatre' which was 7:84 – its name taken from the statistic, central to the company's oppositional stance, that 'seven per cent of the population owns 84 per cent of the wealth'. Using plays by McGrath himself – and early on also by Trevor Griffiths, the Ardens, and Adrian Mitchell – the company split into two in 1973, its separate Scottish wing achieving an instant success with its opening production of McGrath's *The Cheviot, the Stag, and the Black, Black Oil*.

This play was about the exploitation of the Highlands, whether by the clearance of crofters in favour of grouse or by the more insidious incursions of the multinational oil companies. And the Scottish 7:84 company outlived its English counterpart in part because similarly identifiable national concerns ensured it the sympathy of a society already in process of being radicalized – the minority of Conservative Members of Parliament in Scotland thus growing steadily smaller even when the party was enjoying a landslide south of the border.

THE GROWTH OF COMMUNITY THEATRE

But while McGrath claimed to recognize in England, too, the residue of an urban working-class culture which he aimed once again to tap, here rural communities tended to be not only more conservative but also more insulated and tightly-knit (not least in their suspicious reception of histrionic incomers). They thus needed the careful nursing of a locally-based company with an intimate knowledge of their special history and problems: and from the recognition of such a need the 'community theatre' movement grew. 'Community', of course, was as much a weasel word in the seventies, used to justify all manner of worthy and unworthy aims and achievements, as 'excellence' has become in the nineties. But when it worked – usually by means of highly portable and often loosely-knit plays, with locally-derived themes which drew upon the life experience of their audiences – community theatre managed to evoke a kind of creative nostalgia while retaining an abrasive edge of social criticism: it was oral history, a century or a few days old, given shape and an imaginative shove in the right direction.

Obviously, the more continuous and close was the involvement of a group with its location, the more successful was its work. And so, whether dealing with cutlery-making in Sheffield, hop-picking in Kent, poaching in the Midlands, rural deprivation in Devon, or urban blight in Covent Garden, the best shows, in which the special knowledge of audiences was sympathetically driven and directed by the actors' own craft skills, offered a mutual learning experience in the humblest village hall or urban social centre. Much of this kind of community theatre was highly politicized, but some – notably Ann Jellicoe's various ambitious attempts to sift a town's local history into a latter-day pageant – remained determinedly neutral. And in Stoke-on Trent Peter Cheeseman continued to plough a straight and striking documentary furrow of his own.

Some workers in the community field came to concentrate upon more distinctive needs which their earlier work had identified – hence the new genre of 'reminiscence theatre', through which companies such as Fair Old Times in the West Country not only took theatre to but made theatre with the very elderly. At once a valuable therapy and a sometimes powerfully 'real' theatrical experience, reminiscence theatre can also create a true sense of empowerment – another weasel word, but for all its easy misuse none the less descriptive of the perceived need to give back to people a sense of control over their lives, or in the case of the elderly an affirmation of the dignity of their own pasts.

From the ferment of regionally-based enthusiasms also emerged those effervescent activity-centres for grown-ups known as 'arts centres' – some clearly created in the laid-back image of the original Arts Lab, others more earnest and didactic in their missions. And while some, again, were attached to or associated with existing theatrical, artistic, or educational institutions, many were stand-alone ventures, surviving on a shoestring and the goodwill of poorly-paid staff. The ambiences they created were thus as various as the impulses from which they sprang: but almost all welcomed the theatrical itinerants of the fringe, within a broader context of culture suffused with camaraderie, coffee, and vegetarian quiche.

Around 150 arts centres were in existence within a decade of 1968, but the number dwindled as the wounds inflicted by double-edged cuts in local authority and arts funding began to be felt. Even more vulnerable to funding cuts were those involved in the theatre-in-education movement (TIE) – not the use of theatre *by* schoolchildren, important at another and closely related level though that also became, but the taking of fit-up companies into schools by actors trained (sometimes simply through experience) in working with children. At one time most regional theatres had an associated TIE group (the first, attached to the Belgrade in Coventry, was formed in 1965, thus predating the 'fringe' by several years), but in a worsening economic climate such attendant 'luxuries' were among the first to feel the pinch – not least when the schools, too, became less able to afford the modest cost of such extra-curricular activities.

Of course, a movement so diverse and amorphous as 'the fringe' (whose members were often setting out precisely to break down barriers) cannot be pinned down definitively by such labels as, for convenience of discussion, I have used – though my categories are similar to those first adopted by the pioneering 'listings' magazines *Time Out*, founded (necessarily, in every sense) in 1968 to keep track of all the proliferating activity, at least in London. Three years later, I helped to create *Theatre Quarterly* with the aim of providing, among other things, a more considered, conspective record – and by the mid-seventies we were finding it necessary to issue little supplementary directories in order to offer simply a factual overview of the complex national picture.

Glancing through these, I am reminded of the many, many companies I have had to ignore: the activity seemed ever-expanding and never-ending, its energy and excitement in the very air we breathed. And soon, of course, this spirit began to communicate itself to the institutional theatre – many of the regional theatres, for example, opening 'studios' in which more experimental or 'alternative' work could be carried out, sometimes by visiting but also by resident companies.

This was a well-intentioned development, but one which also had its dangers: for not only might 'fringe' activity thus become ghettoized, but, in a worsening economic climate, the studios, like the TIE companies, were often the first to feel the effects. And if the parent company had been tempted to farm out new plays to its studio, with the initially benevolent aim of subsidizing such work from a safer bill of fare in the main house, a more balanced repertoire was not always easy to restore.

NEW WRITING MOVES INTO THE MAINSTREAM

Of course, to emphasize, as I have done, the move away from individual towards collective creation is not to suggest that worthwhile new writing was never shaped through this process, still less separately from it. Thus, one of the most avowedly political of writers, Trevor Griffiths, remained relatively uninvolved with 'alternative' theatre, having found his feet early and decisively at both the National and the RSC – and of course on television, whose power to reach the largest 'new audience' of all he was concerned to exploit.

Many of the other playwrights who were still emerging through 'traditional' channels remained very much their own men – only one major figure among them so far being a woman, Caryl Churchill, who first worked in the old reliable training ground of radio. So while Arden and a few other writers – notably

McGrath, who had enjoyed an early legit success at Hampstead – were determinedly moving away from the mainstream towards the fringe, it was not long before movement could be detected in the opposite direction. Of the three major playwrights to emerge from Portable Theatre, Snoo Wilson was thus alone in remaining (true to his idiosyncratic vision of a mad world governed by mad-men) largely an 'alternative' figure – the quirkily surreal demands of his work commercially quite unviable, and seemingly also deterring subsidized support.

Plays by his Portable contemporaries Howard Brenton and David Hare were, on the other hand, receiving productions 'upstairs' at the Royal Court as early as 1970, and in the same year, with *Slag*, Hare even broached that bastion of the liberal bourgeoisie, the Hampstead Theatre Club. Brenton and Hare soon built upon their success in the 'established' theatre, sometimes even in harness – either as longstanding co-writers, from *Brassneck* (1973) to the outstandingly successful play about a monopolist newspaper proprietor, *Pravda*, with Anthony Hopkins (1985), or as an experienced, mutually-compatible author-director team.

Individually, Brenton felt that he now needed the larger-scale facilities he secured from the National in 1976 to render his *Weapons of Happiness* on an adequately epic scale – a similar support system underpinning *The Romans in Britain* four years later. As in the controversy over the (almost incidental but highly graphic) homosexual rape scene in that play, he has remained a rough-edged, uncompromising writer, always prepared to declare his continuing commitment to the left – indulging, for example, in some instant sniping against Thatcherite values in *A Short Sharp Shock!* in 1980.

Hare's strength proved rather to lie in close-up analyses of the angst-ridden soul of the British middle classes – these being more covertly political on their smaller albeit microcosmic scale. His working of this vein has proved duly acceptable to subsidized and, indeed, West End audiences – whom Hare first confronted (with *Knuckle*) as early as 1974 – and also susceptible to prestigious casting in films such as *Plenty*. *Teeth 'n' Smiles* (1975), in which the lead singer of a late sixties rock group (originally played by Helen Mirren) performs before audiences she despises while her manager is torn between the urgings of his ideals and his ambitions, captured the conflicts characteristic of Hare's work in a play which began to extend the barriers of his free-ranging naturalism.

In 1974 Hare joined with Gaskill, Max Stafford-Clark, and David Aukin to form a new company, Joint Stock, which, while no more fully 'alternative' than it was of the establishment, none the less made a notable attempt to reflect in its working methods and internal relationships the priority it gave to playwriting. The company thus employed a technique of 'workshopping' its material which caught up actors and writers for several weeks in a creative process of research on-the-ground, while allowing each his or her own authority – and in the process somewhat muting if not diluting the role of the director. The plays which emerged from this process ranged from Hare's own *Fanshen* (1975), a timely analysis of the

Howard Brenton's *Christie in Love*, first performed in 1969 at one of the leading 'receptive' fringe venues, Oval House in Kennington. The action, which is expressionistic rather than realistic, takes place in a pen of old newspapers and rusty chicken wire, representing the murderer Christie's 'garden'. In this scene, he has been goaded into re-enacting one of his crimes with a life-size doll. *Christie* was Brenton's first play for Portable Theatre, which he joined after finding himself the single member of its audience at an Arts Lab performance. Originally the group was apolitical, but, as Brenton put it, an 'anarchic, antagonistic theatre' became 'increasingly one of political content'. Portable plays were taken out on an embryonic fringe circuit of colleges and institutes, arts centres and community halls. The production of *Christie in Love* was among those which brought fringe companies to the Royal Court for the *Come Together* festival in 1970

effects of the 'cultural revolution' in rural China, and Barrie Keeffe's cartoon-like celebration of the Queen's Silver Jubilee, *A Mad World, My Masters* (1977), to Stephen Lowe's adaptation of Robert Tressell's novel *The Ragged Trousered Philanthropists* (1978), which caught up the company in the nitty-gritty of the building trade, and Caryl Churchill's *Cloud Nine* (1979), on the politics of sexuality.

Stafford-Clark, whose earlier career had been with the Edinburgh Traverse, left Joint Stock in 1979 to begin a long residency as artistic director of the Royal Court, where, despite Gaskill's departure in 1972, support for new writing had remained unswerving. Indeed, the play which many believed to best bode forth the 'spirit of 1968', Heathcote Williams's *AC/DC* (1970) – a psychically-charged, some said Artaudian encounter between two schizophrenics and three hip youths in a bizarre pin-ball saloon – was thus premiered at the Court, while Christopher Hampton, David Storey, Charles Wood, Ted Whitehead, Mustapha Matura, and Nigel Williams were among other dramatists who established themselves largely through its good offices. So also did Howard Barker – the writer who has perhaps most fully developed the fringe's pursuit of new formal possibilities into a distinctive postmodernist vision of his own, richly inter-leaving verbal allusiveness and visual invention.

CHANGES AT THE NATIONAL

The two national institutional theatres tried in different ways to acknowledge changes which often questioned the very notion of institutions: but both also began to suffer from symptoms of what Tyrone Guthrie had called the 'edifice complex' – not so much a preoccupation with buildings over what was happening inside them, as he had diagnosed it, but a need to fill proliferating buildings with work which combined consistent quality and box-office appeal. Thus, Peter Hall's first task at the National, when he took over from a reluctant Olivier as artistic director in 1973, was to prepare the company for a massive increase in its scale of operations, necessitated by the imminent move to the South Bank – where, over the years, the abutting slabs of late-modernist concrete which comprise the new National Theatre building seem to have weathered more sympathetically within than without.

Designed by Denys Lasdun, the three component theatres, which opened one at a time in 1976–77, offer three contrasting forms of staging: downstairs, a traditional end-on audience relationship in the proscenium-arched Lyttelton; upstairs, a more enclosing, fan-shaped auditorium fronting the open-stage Olivier; and, alongside, the flexible open space which is the simple rectangular 'box' of the Cottesloe. Containing and cushioning the theatres is a largely inter-connecting outer shell of foyers, restaurants, bookstalls, and bars – not to mention backstage facilities so advanced that some at first defied operation.

Hall's directorial tenure proved to be dogged by controversy, with his own former company, the RSC, consistently appearing able to produce better work on a far tighter budget. However, he did succeed in breaking-in theatre spaces which had at first seemed forbidding to actors – and somewhat unyielding to audiences, which were now drawn not from a coterie of groupies but from an increasing hotchpotch of genuine enthusiasts, sullen school parties, packaged tourists, and business people dispensing cultural hospitality.

Successes of the time included some spectacular revivals from the neglected Jacobean repertoire and, less predictably, outstanding premieres and revivals of American plays from writers as far apart in age and temperament as Arthur Miller and David Mamet. But Hall also continued the process of wooing new and experimental writers, Brenton and Hare among them – while mounting such blockbusters from older hands as Shaffer's *Amadeus* (1979). And to Alan Ayckbourn – a supremely competent farceur, whose plays usually had their humbler origins at the Scarborough base where his first loyalties lay – Hall gave the freedom of the National's technical resources, in return for a box-office appeal unequalled (thus spake the statistics) since Shakespeare. These and other

commercially viable productions now often transferred to the West End, as Hall tried to strike a delicate balance between imaginative repertory-building and limited finances – of which a lion's share was absorbed by the cost of simply keeping the company's three 'edifices' in good working order.

Among Hall's associate directors from this period, Bill Bryden inaugurated an interesting series of 'promenade' productions at the Cottesloe, while Peter Gill encouraged a wide range of young writers through studio productions. To the larger stages he had assigned their own companies and directors – and, following the defection of Jonathan Miller and later Harold Pinter from the original team, new appointments seemed designed to appease feelings that Hall had been in danger of turning an actors' into a directors' theatre.

Thus, one recruit of the early eighties was Ian McKellen, a rising star of his generation who had devoted much of his early career to touring with Prospect Productions, and who in 1972 had helped to create the Actors' Company, with a policy of restoring to the players some of the creative rights they had lost to the director. (As his performance in *Bent*, illustrated on page 358, bore early witness, he also became a leading champion of gay rights.) Another new arrival was Mike Alfreds, founder in 1974 of Shared Experience, a leading 'poor theatre' company, whose members he had not so much 'directed' as co-ordinated in collectively created popular theatre pieces which ranged from *Bleak House* to science-fiction.

THE ROYAL SHAKESPEARE COMPANY

Unlike the National, the Royal Shakespeare Company had remained a directors' theatre since Trevor Nunn inherited the reins from Hall in 1968. At that time, in spite of Hall's own Aldwych association with the plays of Pinter and Edward Albee, and David Jones's championship of the work of David Mercer, new work presented at the company's London base had not been notably successful – and this was taking its toll at the box-office. One of Nunn's first decisions was therefore to change the three-year contract system to one of two years, actors now playing a single Shakespeare season in Stratford and bringing much of this work to London in the following year.

However, this policy had dangers of its own. For in spite of such occasional main-house successes as Tom Stoppard's *Travesties* in 1974, and valiant failures such as Terry Hands's almost single-handed campaign to win proper recognition for the richly Jonsonian but apparently 'unmarketable' talents of Peter Barnes, the Stratford imports were increasingly being mixed with new Aldwych productions drawn from lesser-known English and continental classics: it thus seemed as though the RSC was cutting itself off from developments in contemporary writing just as these were achieving renewed momentum

This fear led to a search for smaller theatre spaces, in which a programme of new and experimental work could be carried through free from top-heavy financial constraints. In 1971, as a first step, the company therefore took a lease on The Place, in London's Euston Road, where the opening production, *Occupations,* by the then relatively unknown Trevor Griffiths, engaged the emergent acting talents of Ben Kingsley, Estelle Kohler, and Patrick Stewart. The play's director, auspiciously, was the first woman to fill that role for the RSC, the no-less-unknown Buzz Goodbody.

Meanwhile, Nunn was putting his own imprint upon the Shakespearean repertoire. His first two seasons saw a unique sequence of Shakespeare's late plays, for which Christopher Morley – whose collaboration with Nunn was arguably to be as influential as had been John Bury's with Hall – created his famous 'white box' setting. This signalled Nunn's wish to bring a new and uncluttered clarity to design even before Sally Jacobs stripped the stage to the bare essentials of a fit-up circus for Brook's acrobatic *A Midsummer Night's Dream* in 1970 – almost his farewell production for the company.

Nunn was not fully satisfied with his directorial work on *Macbeth* until 1976, when in his third production of the play he teamed McKellen with Judi Dench in the most claustrophobic, scantily furnished, and apparently makeshift of spaces. Another of his memorably minimalist classics was a *Three Sisters* conceived in 1978 for the virtually unstructured conditions of a small-scale tour to 'non-theatrical' venues in the regions (a worthy and continuing annual feature of the company's work). But Nunn was no less at home with the grand imperial theme when he took on all four of Shakespeare's Roman plays for the 'linked' season in

The Royal Shakespeare Company's production of *The Winter's Tale*, part of the Stratford season of Shakespeare's late plays in 1969. Although Trevor Nunn's production was strikingly different from Terry Hands's earlier *Pericles*, they shared a basic 'white box' set designed by Christopher Morley. Nunn added only basic, emblematic props – in the early scene here illustrated, the rocking horse providing a nursery motif. It is being ridden by Leontes (Barrie Ingham) and his son Mamillius (Jeremy Richardson), with Judi Dench as Hermione and Richard Pasco as Polixenes looking on

1972, or with the fluidity of music and movement of his *Comedy of Errors* in 1976. And within the wonderfully ramshackle solidity of the world he and designer John Napier created for the three-part *Nicholas Nickleby* in 1980 he achieved the seemingly impossible – sustaining this truly magical experience for nigh-on nine hours, with David Edgar's adaptation capturing not just the essence but a surprising amount of the detail of Dickens's original. Another major new talent – that of Roger Rees as a gawky, withdrawn, yet life-affirming Nickleby – gave coherence to a rivettingly rambling action.

In 1978 Nunn decided to share the responsibilities of artistic direction with his near-contemporary and long-time colleague Terry Hands. Instinctively a director in the grand manner, with a sure feeling for vivid stage pictures which were often illuminated by Farrah's designs, Hands had at first displayed a somewhat erratic brilliance: but he moulded the RSC's second full sequence of Shakespeare's histories (1975–77) very much in his own image, while his *Coriolanus* of 1977 permitted Alan Howard to take full patrician flight – that actor's reverberant style and charismatic presence bringing him as close to the status of matinee idol as the sensibilities of the seventies allowed.

Nunn and Hands, temperamentally very different, remained respectful of each other's complementary strengths, and happy to share the repertoire with a loyal band of associate directors, old and new – among the veterans, John Barton, whose disciplined enthusiasms and skills in verse-speaking became deeply etched into RSC sensibilities. Barton's rare ability to blend academic authority with an intuitive feeling for the changing times made his *Troilus and Cressida* of 1968 a wryly apposite reflection of the permissive society, while his insight in setting his 1976 *Much Ado* against a background of the Indian Raj provided an apt foretaste for Nunn's *All's Well* five years later – its status as a 'problem' play suddenly clarified in the shadow of the First World War.

Clifford Williams, while more frequently taking his talents further afield, also continued to direct for the RSC. His rediscovery of *Wild Oats* in 1976 was only the first of a veritable treasure-trove of minor masterpieces which now began to enliven the Aldwych repertoire – and, like Williams's earlier revival of Shaw's *Too True to Be Good*, was among a growing number of productions to follow Dion Boucicault's *London Assurance* into the West End (helping to boost the RSC's strained resources in a difficult financial period).

As Nunn himself remarked, with the special exception of Hall himself (other-wise engaged on the South Bank), 'no director nominated as an associate has ever left that group either in practice or in spirit': so if the names of directors recur in the memory more often than actors, this is due to the undoubted sense of continuity they helped to sustain. But the loyalty of numerous actors to 'Stratford Shakespeare' has also been remarkable: and to begin a list – Emrys James, Susan Fleetwood, David Waller, Donald Sinden, Janet Suzman, David Suchet, Geoffrey Hutchings, Susan Engel, Michael Pennington, Juliet Stevenson – is not, invidi-ously, to pick out the most 'important' names, but rather to illustrate the wide range of personalities, attributes, ages, and styles which often gave the RSC of this period the 'feel' (if not, given the financial constraints, the actuality) of being a true ensemble.

By the mid seventies the company at last began also to establish itself as an exciting, even natural home for new writing – just as a 'third generation' of younger directors, mostly with their roots in the alternative theatre, was emerging to meet the needs created by the opening of two smaller, studio theatres. Tragic-ally, Buzz Goodbody, the moving spirit behind these 'other spaces', died before she could witness their expansion – or, as she might have preferred to think of it, the contraction of stylistic excesses which they required. Much of the sinewy strength of her own *Lear* in 1974, for the opening season of that little tin shed 'down the road' in Stratford, The Other Place, as also of Ben Kingsley's *Hamlet* in 1975, thus came from seeing how far Shakespeare could be stripped down to the bare essentials, and achieve an incisive immediacy in close-up conditions.

Opposite: The RSC production of *Nicholas Nickleby*, David Edgar's nine-hour adaptation of Dickens's novel – presented generally on consecutive evenings, but sometimes as a day-long theatre marathon. Roger Rees (left) was a gawky, hyperactive and hyperattentive Nicholas, at once impetuous and slightly sheepish – a persuasive theatrical rendering of a character who often comes across as less than forceful on the page. David Threlfall played his faithful companion Smike – a tour-de-force of almost clinically-observed devotion and dependence, hollow-eyed, limbs lagging behind his own intentions. Contrasting interestingly with the clean-edged austerity of the adaptation of *Bleak House* by Shared Experience, the production by Trevor Nunn and John Caird went for the full richness and rough-edged complication of its original – even the set, by John Napier and Dermot Hayes, spilling over into the Aldwych auditorium. There was also a 'play-within-the-play' – the Crummles company's upbeat version of *Romeo and Juliet*, which became a set-piece finale to the first half. The production won over all the critics – even Bernard Levin, who was incredulous that as political a writer as Edgar could have scripted a show 'so richly joyous, so immoderately rife with pleasure, drama, and entertainment, so life-enhancing, yea-saying and fecund, so . . . Dickensian'

The Monstrous Regiment production of *Shakespeare's Sister* (1980), with Chris Bowler, a founding member of the feminist company

Ron Daniels took over the direction of The Other Place in 1977, and in the same year Howard Davies was appointed to open The Warehouse, a former rehearsal studio in Covent Garden, as its London counterpart. In one or other of these makeshift spaces began the important collaboration between the RSC and David Edgar, with his timely anti-fascist play *Destiny*; a sustained renewal of the company's interest in Brecht, led by Davies; the virtual rebirth of David Rudkin as a major theatre writer, supported by Daniels; and the stylistic challenge presented by new and revived work from Edward Bond.

In addition, new plays came from dramatists ranging from Cecil Taylor to Howard Barker, from Barry Keeffe to Nigel Baldwin, and from Stephen Poliakoff and Peter Flannery to Willy Russell – whose *Educating Rita* at The Warehouse, with Mark Kingston and Julie Walters, continued an RSC tradition of success almost by accident with a long West End run and a subsequent film version. However, another transfer, of Jane Lapotaire in the title-role of *Piaf*, by a woman writer, Pam Gems, served only to highlight – as had Goodbody's singularity as director – how largely male dominated the company remained. Significantly, therefore, it was not through the RSC but from Joint Stock and the Royal Court that Caryl Churchill now emerged from her years in radio to become a leading writer for live theatre.

OPPOSING THE DOMINANT CULTURE

The upsurge in feminist consciousness which had been in part a product of 'the spirit of 1968', and in part a reaction against its more patriarchal aspects, cannot but have helped to shift Churchill's career into this new gear. But a feminist consciousness was only one aspect of this writer's broader social critique, traceable in her work from *Owners*, an exploration of the overlapping ways in which people claim rights over others, staged at the Theatre Upstairs in 1972, to *Serious Money*, which achieved its perversely successful West End transfer from the Court in 1987 thanks not least to the self-absorption of the very class of money-changing Thatcherite yuppies it satirized. But there can be little doubt that, as author of *Cloud Nine* with Joint Stock in 1979 and of *Top Girls*, first seen at the Court in 1982, Churchill also become an *eminence grise* for a rising generation of young women, as probably the most influential and accessible of her generation to weaken significantly (if not to break) the male stranglehold over writing and, indeed, directing for the theatre.

Of course, women had been working influentially as directors well before the seventies, from Joan Littlewood – the first inheritor of whose mantle at Stratford East was another woman, Clare Venables – to the veteran Hazel Vincent-Wallace, ploughing the lonely repertory furrow at Leatherhead. More recently, Jane Howell had been prominent at the Court and Denise Coffey at the Young Vic, while leading women figures in alternative theatre included Nancy Meckler, Beth Porter, Pam Brighton, Verity Bargate, and Glen Walford.

But these remained the exceptions: for directing, as Clare Venables observed as late as 1980, was deemed to require the 'strong leadership' provided by men – who were also supposedly better able to distance themselves in times of crisis, when women might be driven to breakdowns by hurling themselves into a 'nurturing' role. By then, such stereotyping was, of course, being questioned by many besides Venables: indeed, in the following year Micheline Wandor produced, in a slim volume nicely entitled *Understudies*, the first of what was to become a steady flow of books about the role of women, past and present, within the theatre.

For all their differences, the movements for women's rights, for gay liberation, and for the assertion of ethnic identity had all turned to the 'theatre as a weapon' around the mid seventies (relatively late in the 'alternative' movement) from a common belief in its efficacy for questioning and rebutting the received expectations of the dominant culture – which was white, male, and heterosexual. The women's and gay liberation movements had, moreover, both found their way into the theatre through earlier, 'situationist' interventions – 'happenings' with a social purpose, aimed at exposing and ridiculing the worst excesses of that culture.

Thus, in 1970 a protest was mounted by the Women's Street Theatre Group at the Albert Hall amidst all the plasticized, exploitative trappings of the Miss World contest, being hosted for television by Bob Hope. And in the following year the group erected, so to say, giant deodorants and sanitary towels in Trafalgar Square at the culmination of the first National Women's Liberation March – while a group of activists from the Gay Liberation Front disguised themselves as nuns to disrupt the inaugural meeting of the anti-pornography movement, the Festival of Light. In all these cases, the aim of achieving massive press coverage was achieved, whether or not at the expense of sympathy for the cause being promoted.

Many women were also coming into theatre through the theatre-in-education movement, where such notable work with a feminist slant as the Bolton Octagon TIE company's satirical 'bedtime story', *Sweetie Pie*, was contrasting the fairy-tale expectations of women with the real-life likelihoods. Another theatre piece which toured widely and successfully to schools from 1974, *My Mother Says I Never Should*, about the promise and the problems of teenage sexuality, was in fact the first production of the Women's Theatre Group – one of two companies to emerge, in 1973, from the 'Women's Festival', hosted by Ed Berman at the Almost Free (by then domiciled in a small theatre in Rupert Street, off Shaftesbury Avenue).

Although organized by the Punch and Judies, a group who had been pioneering women's street theatre since 1971, this festival is generally agreed not only to have led to the emergence of a fully self-aware feminist theatre, but to the Women's Theatre Group becoming its leading spirits. By 1976, however, Monstrous Regiment, with its roots in the established as well as the alternative theatre and its feminist intentions combined with more identifiably socialist

The Monstrous Regiment production of *Shakespeare's Sister*, with Josefina Cupido. A deconstruction of conventional views of marriage, the show also postulated a writing career for Shakespeare's imagined sister

Martin Sherman's *Bent*, the first play with an overtly homosexual theme to enjoy a major run in the West End. Sherman's earlier play, *Passing By*, was seen during the pioneering lunchtime season of gay plays at the Almost Free Theatre in 1975. *Bent*, which opened at the Royal Court in May 1979 and transferred to the Criterion in July, approached the treatment of homosexuals by the Nazis through contrasting a first act, shown here, of conventional camp bitchery with a bleak yet affirmative second half set in Dachau, its focus a stylized dialogue between Max (Ian McKellen, right) and his lover Horst, in which they achieve a verbal orgasm

beliefs, was beginning to vie for that distinction. 'The Regiment' worked with both Caryl Churchill, whose *Vinegar Tom*, about seventeenth-century witchcraft, was their second production, and David Edgar, who collaborated in 1979 with one of the company's own writers, Susan Todd, on *Teendreams* – a rather despairing ten-year retrospective on the ideals of 1968.

Later the company, which had at first been mixed, became an all-women group – its decision highlighting one of the continuing controversies within the feminist theatre community. Among many other early feminist groups were the Sadista Sisters (early arrivals, and punk before their time), Beryl and the Perils, Hormone Imbalance, Pirate Jenny, Mrs Worthington's Daughters, Cunning Stunts, the Chuffinelles – and even a company, Spare Tyre, dedicated to demonstrating that 'fat is a feminist issue'. Some, too, were concerned specifically to raise consciousness concerning lesbian issues – and so formed part of the parallel development of the gay theatre movement.

Gay theatre was also given its initial impetus by the ever-enterprising Berman, who in 1975 placed an advertisement in *Gay News* (itself a manifestation of the recently raised consciousness of the homosexual community) which resulted in an ad-hoc group of gay theatre workers presenting a season of homosexual plays at the Almost Free. One author represented was Martin Sherman, whose *Bent* was later to become the first overtly gay play to achieve a major West End

success when it transferred from the Court in 1979 – its leading actor, Ian McKellen, also being the first 'star' to 'come out' in the cause of gay pride.

To sustain this work, the Gay Sweatshop company was formed, an Arts Council grant successfully sought – and a further season, at the ICA, mounted in 1976. Lesbians were now invited to join male homosexuals in the company, but eventually decided to work independently while remaining under the Sweatshop umbrella – the women's first play being *Care and Control*, about the parenting rights of lesbians. By 1979 independent lesbian groups such as the Siren company were being formed, and both sectors have continued to develop, despite prejudices renewed or confirmed during the eighties by the emerging threat of the Aids virus – and institutionalized with the passing of a (dangerously vague) law against the encouragement of homosexual behaviour in the young.

THE ARTS COUNCIL IN A CHANGING CLIMATE

Without the more liberal legislation of the 1960s which had at last decriminalized homosexual activity, the development of a gay theatre movement would not have been possible, at least as a public manifestation of 'gay pride'. The Labour government, though more passively responsive than its predecessor of the sixties, offered some encouragement to the broader aims of all these companies – an act requiring equal pay for women, for example, at last reaching the statute book, though often honoured more in the breach than the observance. In parliament, the party had been struggling along on a dwindling and eventually non-existent majority, until the widespread industrial unrest of the so-called 'winter of discontent' in 1978–79 led to a withdrawal of Liberal backing and a lost vote of confidence in the House of Commons. The subsequent election of a Conservative administration led by Margaret Thatcher marks the end of this chapter, and of a great deal else besides.

In retrospect, the unhappiness of many members of the Labour and trades union movement with government policies appears hard to understand: but at the time the failure of Labour ministers to control inflation (in part brought about by the geometric increase in oil prices which followed the Arab-Israeli war of 1973) led not only to curbs on public spending, but to levels of unemployment which – almost desirable though they might now appear – at the time seemed unacceptably high. And so far as the theatre was concerned, the harsh economic climate made it difficult for the Arts Council to dispense its modest largesse without offence to some of the ever-increasing number of clients hoping for its support.

Again in retrospect, however, the much-maligned Council of the time, under the Secretary-Generalship of Roy Shaw, seems to have tackled its problems with more honourable intentions, and a good deal more sympathy, than its then-detractors believed. As early as 1969, it had set up a 'New Activities Committee' in an attempt to respond to needs which transcended traditional boundaries, allocating an initial sum of £15,000 for such 'fringe' ventures – a sum which by 1978–79 had risen one thousandfold, to over £1,500,000. Meanwhile, compared with the dozen or so groups who shared the original meagre sum, some sixty companies were now enabled to work full-time, and many more backed on a part-time basis. Regional Arts Associations were also set up and given their own funding, in an attempt to devolve some of the Council's powers of patronage to more knowledgeable and locally supportive organizations.

Some of the Council's initiatives, however, led conspiracy theorists to believe that it was working if not to undermine at least to exert hegemony (a term coming into favour at the time) over the alternative movement. Thus, in the late seventies the Council tried to set up a 'grid' system of reasonably equipped

Ethnic theatre changes emphasis

Though often in danger of being ghettoized and discriminated against, the ethnic minorities of Britain had, however, usually found ways of celebrating their own cultures within an often unwelcoming host society: now, what rather loosely became known as 'ethnic theatre' emerged, as the theatrical rethinking of the late 'sixties married with a new concern within those communities to aim less at unreciprocated 'integration' than at the assertion – and the theatrical reflection – of their own distinctive identities.

The change of emphasis may be detected even by comparing one of the earliest 'black theatre' companies on the fringe, the Dark and Light Theatre, whose main concern was to provide work for black actors within a repertoire largely drawn from the European tradition, with the more radical programming of the breakaway Black Theatre of Brixton, which wanted to mount work meaningful to the black constituency – the aim also of such later companies as Temba and Talawa, to single out two of the longest surviving. Even longer-surviving, Theatro Technis had been founded in 1957 by the dedicated George Eugeniou for the Greek-Cypriot community based in Camden Town. Soon, Tara Arts began similarly to serve the far larger and more geographically diffuse Asian audience.

Mustapha Matura's *Black Slaves, White Chains*, at the Theatre Upstairs, Royal Court, 1975. Four years later Matura (b. 1939) co-founded the Black Theatre Co-operative, its first production his own *Welcome Home Jacko*. The small company of actors, who achieved a distinctive style blending exuberance and discipline, often used as its base the short-lived black community centre, the Factory. In 1983 BTC created *No Problem* for Channel Four television

venues to ensure that touring companies reached a representative range of locations, and when the number of these proved inadequate, a broader and looser network of smaller venues was set up. However, this came to encourage a division of companies between those touring to the first-class and those confined to the second-class circuit – with funding usually reflecting this division, though artistic 'standards' still tended to be set by the more adequately subsidized groups.

Of course, the Council was subject to pressures not only from its clamour of clients – quick to suspect political censorship in the level (or non-existence) of funding allocated – but from opposing right-wing elements, who questioned whether the state should be offering any support at all to those with an openly proclaimed intention of overthrowing it. And this paradox had to be confronted by the companies themselves – as when, in 1976, CAST at last received an Arts Council grant, enabling the group to convert from part-time to full-time activity.

A play put on in 1976 by Foco Novo, *The Nine Days and Saltley Gates*, intended to celebrate the fiftieth anniversary of the General Strike, caused an exemplary furore. Despite its supposedly historic slant, even the title of the piece alluded to parallels between ancient and modern conflicts in the mining industry: and while it was no doubt understandable that its authors should assert that they were 'telling people what happened, not spreading propaganda', such a claim was clearly disingenuous. Following furious attacks on the play from Tory MPs and the *Daily Telegraph*, a beleaguered Arts Council sent its members along to see it, quietly waited for the fuss to die down – and went on funding Foco Novo. The company, however, mounted few further plays so unequivocally political in spirit.

Trying to maintain such a balancing act ensured that the Arts Council was the target of ill-feeling both from clients claiming 'silent censorship' and from opponents believing that it underwrote subversion. Then, as soon as the new Conservative government was entrenched in office, what was to prove a long and rather haphazard process of changes in personnel and policy was set in motion, with what became known simply as 'the cuts'. *Theatre Quarterly*, which I was still editing, was among the first, in 1980, to be told that its funding had been withdrawn: our subsidy had been modest, but its loss was sufficient to cause the journal to close.

Simultaneously, what proved to be an extended process of reducing funding to the university system (while expecting it to cater to an ever-increasing number of students) had also begun, with departments of drama appearing to be singled out for special punishment in the first round of cutbacks. But the retrenchment thus enforced upon the theatre and theatre studies was, of course, little more than a side-swipe in the triumphalist attack the government now proceeded to mount against the painfully-constructed post-war political consensus.

CHAPTER 22   *Theatre and the Marketplace*

The eighties were driven throughout by the supposedly 'Victorian values', moral and economic, of that small shopkeepers' revision of low Tory dogma which became known as Thatcherism. The decade began and ended in recession: in between, the long, slow process of redistributing wealth from rich to poor went into reverse, when tax reductions for the wealthy failed to produce the promised 'trickle-down' effect; and such resources as remained for the welfare state (electorally popular despite the Thatcherite push for 'self-help') were stretched by the need to dole out subsistence to the swollen ranks of the unemployed. Meanwhile, a programme of 'privatizing' the public sector of the economy steadily liquidated the nation's capital assets – a process which even an ageing former Conservative prime minister, Harold Macmillan, likened to selling the family silver. Effectively, the post-war political consensus was destroyed.

At home, an autocratic prime minister overrode opposition, alike from the more accommodating 'wets' in her own cabinet and from effective political opponents – such as she found in the trades unions, which were duly emasculated, or in the largely Labour-dominated metropolitan councils, which were abolished (leaving London without a representative governing body for the first time in a century). Abroad, Margaret Thatcher found a soul-mate in the ageing movie actor Ronald Reagan, the emollient paternalism of whose eight-year presidency struck a responsive chord in his 'fellow-Americans' just as Thatcher's brusque nannying must have met some deep-seated need in a quiescent English (as distinct from British) public.

The decade of the musical

For the commercial theatre at large this was, beyond doubt, the decade of the musical. Ironically, the previously dominant American style, although reinvigorated (and intermittently represented) by Stephen Sondheim, now found itself out-pizzazzed in London by the native British variety, resuscitated under the influence, as much entrepreneurial as musical, of Andrew Lloyd Webber. Following up his early but perennially revived Joseph and the Amazing Technicolour Dreamcoat (1968) with Jesus Christ Superstar and Evita in the seventies, Lloyd Webber – often with Trevor Nunn as his director – went on to build a show-business fortune of fabulous proportions with a steady succession of blockbusting hits, from Cats (1981) via Starlight Express (1984) to The Phantom of the Opera (1986) and Aspects of Love (1989).

Based on a combination of cleverly-hyped expectations, trendy high-tech staging, and tangy if somewhat predigested lyrics and scores, these purveyed an acceptably pasteurized sense of 'experience' – often handily doubling if not conceived as 'concept albums' for the record industry. Soon, even the national companies were lavishing their resources on musicals, whether robust revivals such as Richard Eyre's Guys and Dolls for the National or company-originated spectacles mounted with an eye to profitable transfers. Some such ventures – the National's Jean Seberg in 1983, Terry Hands's disastrous Carrie in 1989 – properly came to grief: but Nunn's production for the RSC of Les Misérables (1985), illustrated alongside, was an instant popular if not critical success. It quickly and calculatedly transferred from the Barbican to the Palace in Cambridge Circus – a theatre which Lloyd Webber had purchased outright in 1982, and which, until Les Mis took up its long occupation, seemed to have become almost a permanent showcase for his own work.

Redolent as much of the black-and-white morality of melodrama as of the B-movies of his youth, Reagan's simplistic dream of a nation (rather than a world) sheltering from nuclear attack beneath a laser-wrought umbrella was instantly named 'star wars' – after a futuristic film. The financial drain of trying to second-guess the dubious technology of this enterprise, later sensibly abandoned, was one cause of the collapse, at the end of the decade, of the Soviet Union and its satellite states – this 'evil empire', as Reagan had earlier described his necessary enemy. But the hopes consequently placed upon what was described (in the characteristic jargon of the times) as the 'peace dividend' soon gave way before the revived

Scene at the barricades from *Les Misérables*, which opened at the RSC's new, purpose-built London theatre, the Barbican, in 1985. Directed by Trevor Nunn and John Caird, this was one of Nunn's final triumphs as artistic director of the company. The production was mounted in association with a commercial management: soon transferring to the Palace Theatre in the West End, it ran on through the decade and beyond

nationalistic hostilities and disintegrating economies of the former communist nations – now being taught, even by supposedly neutral observers, to equate 'freedom' with the ineluctable workings of the 'free market'.

Communist regimes had at least recognized the honours they vicariously accrued through lavish funding of cultural projects. Most continental democracies, too, had long acknowledged the necessity for reasonable state subsidy – not just to protect cost-intensive national institutions, but to promote the greater accessibility of the arts through what the French called 'decentralization'. In Britain the Arts Council had, on its more modest budget, been hesitantly shadowing such examples: but the Thatcher government was disposed rather to encourage, after the American model, arts funding from private sources. Tax incentives (less generous than the American) were duly offered for business sponsorship, sometimes with matching state funding promised for its lucky recipients. (Without irony, a national lottery was also projected as an appropriate source of support for the arts.)

As arts administrators frittered away disproportionate time upon the tactful, usually unrewarded composition of applications for business sponsorship, they thus found it politic to speak in terms of investments and returns, of markets and invisible exports – but were able to offer as collateral only their own, hard-to-quantify prestige. Of course, prestige for sponsors accrued more surely and safely from association with high-profile national companies than from support for experimental or small-scale work. And there was seldom a guarantee that any kind of backing would last beyond the immediate period or purpose for which it had been secured. Forward planning became a near impossibility.

To win private or public support, even the institutional theatre was expected to demonstrate its 'good housekeeping' – a much-favoured term, especially following the outcome of the Priestley enquiry of 1983 into the running of the Royal Shakespeare Company. Expected to carp, the civil-service investigator in the event could find little to fault, and went enthusiastically native: but the resulting boost in state support for the company proved short-lived, and within a few years had to be supplemented by one of the major sponsorship deals of the decade. Thereafter, the RSC logo rode into the nineties in tandem with that of Royal Insurance.

THE ARTS COUNCIL AND THE INSTITUTIONS

The Arts Council of this period seemed chronically pregnant with reports – one of the earliest of which, *The Glory of the Garden* (aptly a product of 1984, a year long synonymous with doublespeak), anticipated the cultivation of 'excellence' at the expense of experiment. Later, the more fully-researched and wide-ranging Cork report into the condition of the profession went largely unimplemented. The Council now found itself besieged on the one side by clients facing cuts in their funding, and on the other by politicians who questioned the need for its existence, while the 'arm's length' principle which had previously protected it from political pressures also came under threat. For this was a government which believed it always knew best – and in 1985 duly blamed a miserly arts allocation on the vocal opposition to its policies of the likes of Peter Hall.

Although some further devolution of funding to regional bodies was accomplished and arguably overdue, the suspicion could not be avoided that this made it all the easier for an otherwise centralizing administration to divide and rule. But because protests from within the profession were largely limited to bleatings over inadequate funds, and thus demonstrably self-interested, they failed, advisedly or otherwise, to address the philosophy underlying the shortage. Philip Hedley, who gradually rebuilt Theatre Workshop into a thriving neighbourhood playhouse for Stratford East, was one of the very few directors who dared to sustain a full-frontal attack on government policies and survive – while other politically controversial companies, such as Joint Stock, Foco Novo, and the English 7:84 company, fell victim one by one to the Arts Council axe. (The 7:84 company was permitted to survive in Scotland – once it had quietly disposed of its founder, John McGrath.)

The Royal Court, under the continuing direction of Max Stafford-Clark, also found itself regularly threatened – at one time by a bizarre proposal to transfer responsibility for its funding to the Borough of Kensington and Chelsea, whose attitude to this unruly presence in Sloane Square varied from the disinterested to the downright hostile. That the Court managed to survive was thanks rather to a succession of well-calculated West End transfers than to state support, as the theatre fell from being third best-funded in Britain to sixteenth.

In consequence, the number of productions at the Court steadily diminished, and Stafford-Clark found it impossible to maintain a regular acting company – never, confessedly, a top priority at that theatre. Elsewhere, to borrow an apt culinary metaphor, the RSC's approach to company-building (as to repertoire) had always tended towards the *table d'hôte*, whereas at the National actors (and productions) were in these years usually offered *à la carte* (though the generalization at once reminds one of such undervalued exceptions as the stalwart Michael Bryant, on the acting strength of the NT, or of Bob Crowley, a regular designer of astonishing range and virtuosity).

However, for a time in the early eighties Peter Hall found himself trying to keep no fewer than five separate acting companies in mutually-compatible harness at the National – an experiment designed, it seemed, as much to secure the loyalties of the people involved as to woo audiences for their shows. Among the most successful directors of the period, following an *annus mirabilis* in 1983 with *Guys and Dolls*, *The Beggar's Opera*, and *Schweyk in the Second World War*, was Richard Eyre: and in 1988 it was Eyre who succeeded Hall as artistic director, with David Aukin as his administrative right-hand-man.

Generally, Eyre kept a looser and somehow friendlier rein on a company now settling into a middle age made enforcedly 'safer' in its choices by continuing economic constraints. But this did not silence grumbles that the NT remained better endowed relative to its output (and considering its failure to sustain a regular

Antony Sher (b. 1949) was one of the major acting talents to emerge from the Royal Shakespeare Company during the eighties. Despite earlier successes in plays by Mike Leigh and Sam Shepard, it was his performance at Stratford in 1982 as a gangling, red-nosed Fool to Michael Gambon's Lear, in a first production for the RSC by its future artistic director, Adrian Noble, which saw Sher's distinctive, athletic genius come to full maturity. Then, in 1984, he played the Richard III portrayed alongside: a warped hunchback whose self-animated crutches made him both bottled spider and slithering toad – yet also genuinely sexy and suavely complicit with his audiences. Sher's other roles included the revolutionary turned reactionary Martin Glass in David Edgar's *Maydays* (1983), the contrasting title parts in Molière's *Tartuffe* and Bulgakov's *Molière* (1983), and the leader of a band of medieval itinerants in Peter Barnes's brilliant black comedy, *Red Noses* (1985). Back in the West End, he wrought some stunning emotional transitions as the lithe, stiletto-heeled drag queen in Harvey Fierstein's *Torch Song Trilogy* (1985)

touring policy) than the Royal Shakespeare Company – which in 1982 at last transferred its London base to the purpose-built Barbican Centre. Conceived in a period of confident expansion but finally born into an age of austerity, the Barbican was variously regarded as a symbol of RSC empire-building and a white elephant – sometimes both. It boasted an almost impenetrable approach, a pleasant enough sweep of a main-house, and a soulless, claustrophobic subterranean studio, aptly dubbed The Pit.

Like the rebuilt Memorial Theatre back in 1932, the Barbican opened with the two *Henry IV* plays, in new productions by Trevor Nunn. But one of its earliest successes was, of all things, *Peter Pan,* in a production by Nunn and John Caird designed to keep the magic while cutting the whimsy, which ran for three successive Christmas seasons. Also in 1982, Adrian Noble made surely the most propitious directing debut at Stratford since those of Hall and Nunn, with a *King Lear* which paired Michael Gambon with one of the most distinctive of the new generation of RSC players, Antony Sher, in a sort of vaudevillian double-act as king and fool. It was Noble who took over when Terry Hands, who had become sole artistic director in 1988, left the company three years later, while Sher sustained his growing reputation with a spidery but astonishingly athletic Richard III, under the direction of Bill Alexander – who now followed Ron Daniels, Howard Davies, and Barry Kyle from studio work into main-house Shakespeare.

In 1986 the RSC acquired another 'edifice' – or rather resuscitated an old one, converting the reliques of the first Memorial Theatre into the glossy but thoughtfully conceived Swan, intended to house the work of Shakespeare's contemporaries and successors. Honourably, in the first few years of its existence it duly staged rare revivals of plays by Heywood, Tourneur, Shirley, and Brome, as well as by Jonson, Marlowe, and the more marketable Restoration writers. Despite its name, the Stratford Swan was no replica 'Elizabethan' showcase, but unexpectedly 'neutral' in the best sense, comfortable and attractive but allowing the play to command the space rather than the space the play. (Meanwhile, Sam Wanamaker's project to recreate the old Globe on the South Bank, as close as possible to its original structure and near to its original site, was coming slowly closer to fruition.)

COMMERCIAL THEATRE – AND INTERNATIONAL THEATRE

Release from institutional office enabled Hall, Nunn, and Hands to draw more regular commercial dividends from their years at the subsidized workface – in 1988 the Haymarket becoming a first London base for the newly-established Peter Hall Company. This theatre had long settled into a role as home for classy revivals, now cast to attract audiences accultured to television – for whom (never mind the play) such sitcom stalwarts as Penelope Keith were the safest attraction. Hall's repertoire largely of old and new classics was later star-spangled by Dustin Hoffman, tempted back to the stage to play in *The Merchant of Venice* at the Phoenix in 1989.

Although its theatres were custom-built to reflect the social hierarchies now being reinstated, astronomic overheads and break-evens in the West End increasingly limited its output to shows which had not only been pre-packaged but also pre-sold. As on Broadway, nothing less than a smash-hit now made economic sense, 'moderate' runs being allowable only for a leavening of small-cast, modestly set plays – preferably by the likes of Tom Stoppard, Alan Ayckbourn, or Michael Frayn. One-person shows were also allowable – such as those in which Barry Humphries alternated the high-suburban glamour of his 'housewife superstar', Dame Edna Everage, with the slovenly philistinism of his antipodean cultural attaché, Sir Les Patterson. Throughout the decade, too, over-dependence on the tourist trade left the theatre vulnerable to changes in the international political or economic climate,

Kenneth Branagh in the title role of *Henry V*. Like Antony Sher, Branagh emerged as a major talent with the RSC, for whom he played this vulnerable, rather reserved Prince Hal in 1984: but he went on to assert his actorly independence, directing his own *Romeo and Juliet* (1986) and acting in his own play, *Public Enemy* (1987), before helping to create the Renaissance Theatre Company, whose inaugural *Twelfth Night* of 1987 was followed by a sellout Shakespeare season at the Phoenix in the following year

a terrorist threat turning a dozen or so houses 'dark', a boom leaving good 'product' awaiting a home. Proven successes from the National and the RSC were also cost-effectively transferred.

Between recessions, in 1988, the failed businessman, best-selling pulp novelist, and loyal (if accident-prone) Thatcherite Jeffrey Archer took a nibble from his fortune to buy the Playhouse Theatre on the Embankment – but neither this venture nor a brief attempt in the same year to convert the Royalty into a sort of National Theatre for middlebrows survived the ensuing slump. More worthily and success-fully, the Theatre of Comedy – a brainchild of the veteran farceur turned impresario Ray Cooney, dedicated to the discovery and display of contrasting comic styles – colonized several theatres from a first base at the usually ill-starred Shaftesbury.

Two other new companies, though alike classically sustained, proved radically different in most other respects. The English Shakespeare Company, created in 1986 by Michael Bogdanov and Michael Pennington, was director-based, and happily disrespectful of bardic authority in its updating and contemporary allusions: its *Wars of the Roses* sequence of the Shakespearean history cycle was an international success, from Berlin to Tokyo and from the Windy City of Chicago to London's no less windy Waterloo Road. But the Renaissance Theatre Company, formed in 1987 in part as a vehicle for the precocious talents of Kenneth Branagh (whose chutzpah to my taste outshone the charisma which held others in sway) was firmly in the orthodox if largely-displaced tradition of actor-management, and remained rever-ential towards its posthumously resident dramatist.

Branagh's season at the Phoenix in 1988 showed that Shakespeare could still prove good box-office in the West End – at a time when, ironically, its former home, the Old Vic, was struggling to find a new identity. Following the departure of the National, from 1977 to 1981 the theatre had provided a metropolitan base for the touring Prospect Theatre, and was then purchased by the Canadian impresario Ed Mirvish: but despite the subsequent beautification, and a brief and stormy flirtation with the wayward directorial genius of Jonathan Miller, the theatre found itself lacking a distinctive mission – at the very time when, a few hundred yards away, David Thacker was giving a purposive new lease of life to the Young Vic, a rather spartan but clean-cut house too often avoided on account of the school parties which had provided its necessary life-support.

Down river at Hammersmith, too, Peter James was reviving the fortunes of the Lyric – the baroque glories of the old, demolished theatre having been transplanted into an unlikely modernist shell in 1979. Here, and in the studio theatre attached, James was among several directors now beginning to give a less parochial look to the London scene. Also in Hammersmith, the more utilitarian (and more adapt-able) Riverside Studios played host to numerous visitors from abroad, ranging from the depressive Pole, Tadeusz Kantor, to the irrepressible Italian, Dario Fo – whose blend of old-style *commedia* and new-style agitprop made him a seminal influence (and, ironically, also a West End success) early in the decade.

One of Peter Hall's most imaginative later appointments at the National was of Thelma Holt, formerly of the Open Space and the Round House, and now given special responsibility for bringing leading foreign companies to the South Bank – whence an eclectic blend of influences briefly wafted while Holt made a brave stab at resurrecting the World Theatre Seasons of old. In Cardiff, meanwhile, the Chapter Arts Centre had become a year-round receptive venue for foreign practitioners at the cutting-edge of their craft. But most resolute of those who followed in the footsteps of Peter Daubeny were a pair of young, independent entrepreneurs, Rose Fenton and Lucy Neal, who, in 1981, emerged seemingly from nowhere (having travelled seemingly everywhere) to assemble the first London International Festival of Theatre – a feat which, almost single-handedly, they managed to repeat biennially throughout the decade and beyond.

FROM ALTERNATIVE THEATRE TO CHAMBER THEATRE

In its production-intensive occupation of a profusion of both high and humble venues, LIFT was the closest the capital came to emulating the concentrated energy of the Edinburgh Festival – where the appointment of Frank Dunlop as artistic

The Actors Touring Company in their adaptation of the third play, *Ubu in Chains*, of Alfred Jarry's proto-absurdist Ubu cycle (1985). ATC was one of several small-scale touring companies who tended in the eighties to concentrate on rejuvenating the classical repertoire. Notable among the others were the irreverently stylish, visually exciting, and always fast-moving Cheek by Jowl; Shared Experience, with a rougher, more baroque style and concentrated narrative line; the far-flung Footsbarn company; and the vibrantly responsive, self-defining Medieval Players

director led to 'official' offerings now more truly representative of world theatre, playing alongside the more erratic but still-proliferating productions on the fringe. On the London 'fringe', meanwhile, the Old Red Lion in Islington, the Gate at Notting Hill, and the Latchmere in Battersea – where a bustling Arts Centre also flourished – were among the new venues which enlivened a decade when truly 'alternative' excitements were becoming harder to find.

Thus, the trend on the fringe (with not a little assistance from carefully directed funding) was away from political commitment and 'agitprop' towards such glitzier displays of mannered exuberance as those which earned and sustained a glowing reputation for Cheek by Jowl – who would typically take a major or minor classic, rejig it in their own extrovert manner, and let it burst afresh upon their audiences. Cultural conservatism underlying a veneer of stylistic flamboyance could also be detected in the work of such groups as the Actors' Touring Company and Theatre de Complicite (accentless by choice) – often excellent of its kind, but essentially 'chamber theatre' rather than in any meaningful sense 'alternative'. Not unexpectedly, therefore, Declan Donnellan and his designer Nick Ormerod from Cheek by Jowl made career moves to the National which were natural and contented (where Mike Alfreds's earlier transition had been dissonant and fraught).

As the fringe went upwardly mobile, an increasing distance began to be felt between such small but prestigiously-maintained theatres as the Almeida at Highbury or the Donmar Warehouse (as the RSC's old Covent Garden studio was

now renamed) and more makeshift venues in halls or pubs, however imaginatively fitted-up. Among the newcomers were the Finborough Arms in Fulham, the Hen and Chickens on Highbury Corner, and the Man in the Moon in Chelsea. This suggested the need for some new distinction of convenience, analogous to that separating 'off-Broadway' from 'off-off-Broadway' houses in New York.

Ethnic theatre was now able to draw upon a growing stable of writers of Afro-Caribbean or Asian roots – among them, Edgar White, Michael Abbensetts, Caryl Phillips, Tunde Ikoli, Mustapha Matura, Farrukh Dhondy, Barrie Reckord, Hanif Kureishi, and Jacqueline Rudet. Several of these were also working in 'mainstream' theatre – as were many gay playwrights, for whom a prevalent, almost overwhelming concern, both humane and artistic, was the emergent threat of Aids. In its own constituency, gay theatre found itself under threat not only from the new prejudices thus provoked, but legally and financially too, from what became known simply as 'Clause 28' – a section of the Local Government Act of 1988 which (with dangerous vagueness) forbad support for activities promoting homosexual behaviour.

THE RISE OF ALTERNATIVE COMEDY

Some gay groups and performers, from the satirical drag act Bloolips to the high-camp but low-intensity Julian Clary, responded with an outgoing and often outrageous humour to their situation. Indeed, throughout the decade John McGrath's belief in the power of the 'compilation bill' was validated less in the work of theatre companies such as his own than through the emergence of what quickly became known as 'alternative comedy'. This is generally dated from the opening in 1979 of the Comedy Store in Dean Street, Soho – a sort of do-or-die showcase for all who dared brave its well-lubricated audiences and infamous valedictory gong, first wielded by Alexei Sayle.

Early graduates of the Comedy Store included most of the team collectively known as the Comic Strip – besides Sayle himself, Rik Mayall, Adrian Edmondson, Nigel Planer, Peter Richardson, Robbie Coltrane, Ben Elton, Dawn French, and Jennifer Saunders. These variously wrote, directed, and appeared in a sequence of one-off spoofs for television, displaying a wide variety of parodic styles – their common element a sort of laid-back, pre-emptive postmodernism. The first 'Comic Strip' was, significantly, transmitted in November 1982 on the opening night of Channel Four – the closest British television came to offering an 'alternative' channel, and a haven for innovatory talent before the market and the ratings supervened.

However, it was the BBC which elevated Mayall, Edmondson, and Planer into cult figures for an adolescent generation through their engagement, also in 1982, in *The Young Ones*, an anarchic bed-sitcom of high-pitched, chronic mid-youth crisis. By 1985 this had its mildly more mature female equivalent, when Tracy Ullman and Ruby Wax joined French and Saunders as flatmates in the appositely named *Girls on Top*. All these performers went on to develop their acts and stage personae far beyond their alternative origins, while remaining largely faithful to

Opposite: Jennifer Saunders, Adrian Edmondson, Dawn French, and Peter Richardson (plus Timmy the dog) in *Five Go Mad in Dorset* – the first Comic Strip production, transmitted on the opening night of Channel Four on 2 November 1982. This ebullient send-up of Enid Blyton's children's stories shared only its tongue-in-cheek truth to style with successors which otherwise parodied genres as various as sixties films striving to be *nouvelle vague*, self-consciously rough-cut television documentaries, on-the-run road movies, slow-burning westerns, and trendy feminist dystopias. Combining streetwise culture with post-modern pastiche, the series was of uneven quality, its offerings varying from the irrepressibly comic to the self-referentially clever: but all engaged energies and stretched muscles unfamiliar in television comedy. Only Blyton was twice targeted – with another saga of retarded pubescence, *Five Go Mad on Mescalin* (1983)

their spirit – Elton becoming the best-loved and despised of the solo comics, his chirpy stream-of-consciousness eliding satire and scatology into a radical rhetoric of humour.

More typical, of course, were the multiplicity of obscure stand-ups and double-acts who now began to appear in no less obscure pub and club venues up and down the country. Whether or not, as some claimed, comic performance thus came to define the cultural aspirations of late eighties youth as rock'n'roll had for their parents in the sixties, its resurgence as a vehicle for radical social and sexual comment was certainly surprising – for the medium had long been marked by its inherent conservatism and regular resort to sexual and racial stereotyping (explained if not justified by Bergsonian and Freudian theory).

FEMALE AND MALE

One of the minor, madder myths perpetuated by such stereotyping was that women lacked the skills – perhaps, some pontificated, the sense of humour – to command an audience in stand-up comedy. This myth was now shattered by the veritable explosion of female comic talent – not only 'alternative', but, in the work of such artists as Victoria Wood, closer to the tradition of cabaret than of the drinking club. The complacent 'post-feminist' assertion that, in the battle for equality, a ceasefire if not a victory had been achieved may have been (no, *was*) demonstrably false in such realms of male chauvinist piggery as the Houses of Parliament or the City of London: but in the theatre it did seem that the assimilation of women into areas which had before been almost unthinkingly male-dominated was well advanced – without, confessedly, much in the way of 'affirmative action' to speed along the process.

Female directors, for example, now became a felt presence. Any list of notable entrants to this branch of the profession would thus have to set alongside such male newcomers as Declan Donnellan, Nicholas Hytner, Stephen Daldry (who won the Royal Court succession in 1993), and Sam Mendes a rather larger female contingent, including Susan Todd, Sue Dunderdale, Di Trevis, Deborah Warner, Jenny Topper, Katie Mitchell, Phyllida Lloyd, and Garry Hynes – not to mention those women who chose to confine their work to feminist or lesbian rather than mainstream outlets.

So far as acting was concerned, there had for many years been more women than men struggling for security in a craft which was becoming increasingly over-crowded and underemployed (leading to proposals that entrance should be limited to graduates of accredited acting schools). But whereas successful male performers had always included the physically atypical, the eccentric, and even the downright ugly, with only a due proportion of handsome matinee-idols, the attributes of the aspirant actress had normally been expected to include, if not beauty, at least prettiness or 'charm'. This presumption of sexual allure – which posed problems even for the most glamorous actress as she approached middle age – now began to change with what seems, in retrospect, decisive suddenness.

Opposite: Juliet Stevenson as an assertively masculine Rosalind, with Fiona Shaw as a fiery Celia, in Adrian Noble's RSC production of *As You Like It* (1985). Stevenson and Shaw were just two of the numerous actresses (some named on pages 373–4 of the text) who rode happily roughshod over older assumptions about their style and expected range – part of the process through which women began to reclaim a wider role in mainstream theatre. This resulted not only in an influx of new women writers, but a revived interest in the work of previously ignored dramatists from the historical repertoire – ranging from Aphra Behn, whose *The Rover* was staged in 1986 during the opening season of the RSC's new venue for experimental classical work, the Swan, to the American expressionist of the thirties, Sophie Treadwell, whose *Machinal* was to provide a later triumph for Fiona Shaw at the National in 1993

Any roll-call of actors who worked memorably during the eighties would thus expectedly encompass a wide range of styles and physical characteristics. Consider, not quite at random, such names (besides those of Sher, Branagh, and Gambon) as Bob Peck, Simon Callow, Alan Rickman, Gerard Murphy, Michael Pennington, Brian Cox, Rupert Everett, Ian McDiarmid, Mark Rylance, and Simon Russell Beale. But now, thankfully, a similar list of actresses who emerged or fully blossomed during the decade evokes no less broad a spectrum of qualities – including beauty and charm, sure enough, but among many less conventional virtues, and with a fair dash of rough-edged quirkiness thrown in for good measure.

A further not-quite-random sampling to suggest such infinite variety might thus include Juliet Stevenson, Harriet Walter, Julia Mackenzie, Miranda Richardson, Frances de la Tour, Patricia Routledge, Brenda Blethyn, Imelda Staunton, Zoë

Wanamaker, Tilda Swinton, Maggie Steed, Maureen Lipmann, Imogen Stubbs, Kathryn Hunter, Frances Barber, Nicola McAuliffe, Alison Steadman, Josette Simon, Julie Walters, and Fiona Shaw. No less important, the many and diverse styles here represented were beginning to be served by a fairer distribution of female roles, in terms alike of quantity and of their centrality to a play's action.

Although this was in part due to the increased responsiveness of male play-wrights, women writers for the theatre were also becoming more numerous. An instant recall of dramatists of the eighties could thus set such names as Louise Page, Andrea Dunbar, Sarah Daniels, Maureen Duffy, Timberlake Wertenbaker, Winsome Pinnock, Tasha Fairbanks, Ann Devlin, Charlotte Keating, and Helen Edmundson alongside those of Terry Johnson, Doug Lucie, Michael Wilcox, Peter Flannery,

Nicholas Wright, Alan Bleasdale, Anthony Minghella, Robert Holman, Jim Cartwright, Willy Russell, Stephen Poliakoff, Hanif Kureishi, Ron Hutchinson, Nick Dear, and Martin Crimp – suggesting at least a widening breach in the virtual male monopoly of old.

These listings serve well enough their chief purpose – of suggesting the welcome reinforcement of women's numbers in all branches of theatre. But to resort, as I have done, to such representative roll-calls of both sexes is also implicitly (so why not explicitly?) to acknowledge the difficulty of making instant assessments of so many careers still in formative progress, let alone considering their relative significance. In the absence of consensual verdicts, trying to evaluate theatrical experiences so close to one's own recent life experiences can only tempt one into the optimistic

Brian Friel's *Translations*, which transferred from Hampstead Theatre Club to the National Theatre in 1981. Here, a derelict tramp (Sebastian Shaw), saturated in folk knowledge of classical and pagan gods, and the pretty but uneducated Maire (Bernadette Shortt) are among the ill-assorted pupils in one of the Irish 'hedge-schools' of the 1830s, through which the peasantry attempted a measure of self-education in the face of a British government concerned only with the 'translation' into English of the Irish culture and language. The play had already been presented in Ireland by the Field Day company, founded in 1980 by Friel and the actor Stephen Rea. Based in Derry, Field Day worked throughout the decade to create a non-sectarian but committed theatre for the whole of Ireland. Their later productions included Friel's *The Communication Cord*, *The Carthaginians* by Frank McGuinness, Thomas Kilroy's *Double Cross*, and Stewart Parker's *Pentecost*

oxymorons and hopefully illuminating adjectives through which personal taste assumes a cloak of objectivity.

No less, then, will any selection of the major plays of the eighties reflect my own prejudices – in this case, a preference for those few which shared and also shed new light upon my own depressed view of the state of the nation. Among these – some obvious choices, some not – were Louise Page's *Falkland Sound* (1983), Hare and Brenton's *Pravda* (1985), Churchill's *Serious Money* (1987), Alan Ayckbourn's *A Small Family Business* (1987), Doug Lucie's *Fashion* (1987), Peter Flannery's *Singer* (1989), and Hare's *Racing Demon* (1990) and *Murmuring Judges* (1991).

Among plays which worked more allusively, Nick Dear's *The Art of Success* (1986) found its analogies in the times of Fielding and Hogarth, while Wertenbaker's *Our Country's Good* (1988) drew illuminatingly upon Farquhar's *Recruiting Officer* (with which it played in tandem at the Court) to make its points about colonialism and class. Brian Friel's *Translations* (1981) similarly explored elements of the continuing Irish 'troubles' by portraying the rape of the nation's language and cultural heritage during the nineteenth century. *Translations* was the inaugural production of the Field Day company, based in Derry, whose cross-sectarian and cross-cultural approach to its community's problems valiantly spanned the decade following its creation in 1980 by Friel and the actor Stephen Rea.

'HERITAGE', SPECTACLE, AND THE THEATRE OF THE STREETS

In the entertainment industry as in the nation at large, however, the eighties preferred the escapist refuge offered by history to any insights it might offer into present-day problems. Indeed, with manufacturing industries being run down and even service industries deflected into the 'service' of the boom-or-bust philosophy, the 'heritage industry' seemed at times to be the only sector of the economy set for sustained expansion. The new vogue for commodifying the past led, among much else, to 'interactive' encounters with Jack the Ripper in the murky vaults below London Bridge Station, or with bucolic Chaucerian pilgrims in the shadow of Canterbury Cathedral. Even at Madame Tussaud's a homogenized history of London came complete with sounds, smells, and other environmental illusions.

The taste for spectacle reached into the future as well as synthesizing the past, and in the old Trocadero on Piccadilly Circus one could thus experience the full horror of a twenty-minute 'alien invasion'. But just as dioramas appeared primitive in the age of cinemascope, so will even the battery of computerized effects there employed seem unsophisticated before the holographic and silicon-rooted shows of the near future – when miniaturized circuits will also be capable of sensitizing every part, including the most private, to the closeted experience of 'virtual reality'.

Of course, no foreseeable electronic wizardry will be able to supplant that sense of participation and communal celebration which humanity still seems to need – and to derive from live entertainment before a live audience. Whether at the level of 'high' or 'low' art – of Pavarotti in the Park or of Band Aid in Wembley Stadium, to cite two contrasting mass events of the eighties – spectacle on a grand scale thus continued intermittently in fashion. That this was in part a reaction against the domesticating tendencies of television did not, of course, deter the medium from domesticating such events for couch-potato consumption.

A humbler, partial, and more widely remunerative reaction in favour of live performance was the vogue in pubs and clubs for 'karaoke' – a Japanese-originated craze which, through a subtle use of backing tracks, gave amateurs the sense of personally rendering some favoured 'standard' or current hit. Consciously or not, the creators of 'karaoke' thus managed simultaneously and effectively to interweave the three instincts from which most modern participatory performance derives – the folk-rooted need to celebrate shared cultural values; the no less ancient desire of the professional entertainer to turn that need into personal profit; and its more recent manipulation, by those controlling the means of mass communication, to increased dependence upon technology.

More humbly still, as the old fruit and vegetable market left Covent Garden and an artsy-craftsy shopping precinct took its place, street entertainers began to return in force to central London – as to railway stations, subways, pedestrianized town centres, and postmodern shopping malls throughout the land. They enjoyed no subsidy or security – and remained subject to the weather and the whims of passers-by, as itinerant performers have always been. Some followed a 'new age' trail by choice, turning up one week at Glastonbury, the next at the Hat Fair in Winchester, like strolling players of old: but others, the new underclass of 'masterless men', slept haplessly on the streets as well as begging a living there. A return to the roots of theatre? Or the restoration of an ignoble cultural 'heritage', as the nation reneged on its duty, only belatedly recognized, to shield its people from such deprivations?

Not that such support for the arts as remained was always happily deployed. In 1990, for example, one regional theatre chose to suspend its home-based repertoire and to double its ticket prices in order to guarantee a fixed return to the Peter Hall Company for its visiting production of *The Wild Duck*. In the event, derisory audiences left the theatre badly in debt – a debt it chose to expunge by closing down its theatre-in-education team. It would be unfair to name the theatre, for in other respects it had an honourable record in its field: but the tale is only too typical of a decade of distorted values and misplaced priorities.

Also in 1990, and also for lack of funding, the RSC closed down (albeit temporarily) its Barbican stages, leaving London for the first time in thirty years without the invigorating presence of the company from Stratford. At the Aldwych, for so long its makeshift but maybe happier London home, a British star of American TV soaps, Joan Collins, was reimported in September, to lend glamour to a revival of Noël Coward's *Private Lives*. In a nation where – or so Margaret Thatcher had declared – there was no such thing as society, private lives were, presumably, what it was all about. By the time the production closed in January, the prime minister had herself fallen victim to the law of the jungle she espoused.

Epilogue

In epilogues to plays of the Restoration and eighteenth century it was conventional, and so acceptable, for the actor to occupy a multiplicity of roles, speaking simultaneously as a character from the play just concluded, as spokesperson for all 'actors in role' who have ever sought applause from an audience – and as him or herself, a member of a particular company chatting (albeit in verse) with the particular occupants of pit, boxes, and gallery on that particular night.

Sometimes such boundaries are stretched or overstepped within the play itself. When, in *Love's Labour's Lost*, the callow youths are condemned to spend twelve months growing up before their ladies will even consider their protestations of love, Berowne wryly reflects: 'That's too long for a play.' Not that it is, of course: Shakespeare himself casually leapt over sixteen years and a good many more miles to give the later lovers of *The Winter's Tale* time to grow up and opportunity to meet – even personifying Time as a chorus to advise us accordingly.

On the whole, the effect is less distracting than Shakespeare's attempt in his very next play, *The Tempest*, to encapsulate past action in retrospective narrative – as if he were showing that he *could* work, when he chose, within neoclassical confines. Restoration critics were, of course, distressed by his more usual practice of ignoring such edicts – which reminds us that what makes for 'verisimilitude' in one age often seems strained and unnatural in another. Imaginative leaps in time and space are now easier for us to take than the supposition that a play needs to exist in the same dimensions as the audience watching it.

Unity of neither time nor place was insisted upon by Aristotle, and although the old schoolmaster did stipulate unity of action for dramatic poetry, he also pointed out that one of the advantages of the alternative, epic mode was its freedom to develop a many-stranded plot. And epic was in Aristotle's time (and for two millennia afterwards) a performing mode, as was yet a third form in his taxonomy of imitation, the 'lyric' – for us either the most personal kind of verse or, more relevantly here, the words of a song, today most likely performed to the accompaniment of that distant descendant of the lyre, the electric guitar. The *Poetics* even anticipates that distinctive reintegration of rhythm, metre, and performance that we call rap poetry.

How have I found my way back to Ancient Greece at the end of a book about the British theatre? Because Aristotle, so far from being the prescriptive old pedant he is often painted, or the necessary enemy constructed by Bertolt Brecht, was in truth very open to all performing possibilities, and often very modern in his explication of them. Even his argument that action in a play is more important than character (a clear offence against the romantic revival and the individual psychology promulgated in its wake) was less classical in its terms than existential: he suggests, in effect, that, on stage as in life, 'existence precedes essence' – character being shaped not through some 'essential' selfhood but through a succession of actions taken, especially at moments of 'existential choice'.

Shakespeare's plays – as the old argument about 'nature versus nurture' in *The Winter's Tale* reminds us – do not on the whole work like that. His characters seem to pre-exist in ways that made plausible the earnest biographical conjectures of critics such as A. C. Bradley, directors such as Stanislavsky – and in due course psychoanalysts, driven like Ernest Jones to deconstruct Hamlet's Oedipus complex. The actuality of Marlowe's Barabas or Jonson's Volpone or Webster's Flamineo is less readily anticipated: such characters are constructed from what they do, and they bode themselves forth to an audience accordingly.

This is not to say that one sort of character or play is *better* than another. But if there is, as the cultural materialists claim, a 'Shakespeare myth', it has to do not only with the appropriation of our 'national poet' by the social, cultural, or political elite (as his pedestalled presence on the old twenty pound note bore its emblematic witness), but with the danger that a theatre saturated in Shakespeare tends to absorb or transcend other stylistic options. Jonson has been a chief sufferer, for his plays and characters do not so much 'develop' as reveal themselves, his scenes working less as stages in an organic process than as a succession of 'turns', as if on a variety bill. His actors thus need – but are unlikely today to have received – a thorough grounding in the verbal and physical skills of what we would consider (a touch condescendingly) 'stand-up' rather than 'regular' comedy.

Nowadays the British theatre is ill-equipped to conduct such comic business. The Theatres Act of 1843, while often welcomed as ending the monopoly of the patent houses, divided the theatre along class lines instead. This had the effect of hastening the day when 'going to the theatre' became a socially acceptable way of passing an evening of a certain length – an accession of 'respectability' welcomed by many earlier histories, but deplored in mine. In due course came the confinement of West End theatre within a quasi-naturalistic straitjacket, and the loss even of the stylistic flair through which the last generation of great actor-managers redeemed the ordinariness of their repertoire.

Meanwhile the music halls were finding employment for a variety (indeed) of performing skills, which included the physical, vocal, and mimetic as well as the comic. They were also giving a new home and new twists to the 'compilation bill' – now considered inartistic or uneconomic, as 'legit' theatre confined itself to offering a single play in three or five well-regulated acts. A few theatre artists of the present generation have tried to rediscover and make newly relevant a formula that can claim an honourable class and artistic pedigree, but against its virtual takeover and commercialization by the broadcasting media theirs has been an uphill though honourable struggle.

Given the constraints imposed upon most commercial 'product' by assumptions grounded in Shakespeare, Stanislavsky, and the class structure, it can, then, be no accident that many of the theatrical memories I personally cherish have been the work of young or amateur actors less weighed down by that stylistic inheritance – their 'inexperience' here translating as freshness and openness, where experience means only what a despairing John Arden once described with heartfelt irony as the 'rectilinear' need to 'do things properly'.

Thus, in Arden's terms, the curvilinear richness – the sheer rewarding *different-ness* – of Jonson was first revealed to me back in the early sixties not by Tyrone Guthrie's Old Vic *Alchemist* (whose resolute updating was, I later realized, a valiant attempt to overcome differences that should have been confronted), but by a student production of *The Devil Is an Ass* in a cramped Edinburgh hall. Too young to have seen the fabled visit of the Berliner Ensemble to London, I first discovered the new and challenging theatrical language spoken even by minor Brecht in an ill-equipped converted chapel in north London, where Unity Theatre was staging a play I had not heard of then, and for that matter have never seen since, *The Visions of Simone Machard*.

The daring elision of comedy and tragedy with music – and an acknowledged complicity with the audience – in *The Hostage* and *Oh, What a Lovely War!* showed that even West End theatregoers could be tempted into abandoning their normal expectations: yet these and other Theatre Workshop shows were best experienced in Stratford East, where it was no accident that the bar had the feeling of a well-run pub rather than the grudging concession it so often seems on Shaftesbury Avenue – greedy managements compelling cash from a thirsty audience made to queue for most of the interval in a shoebox for a warm, overpriced gin and tonic.

Not, I hasten to add, that it is merely the absence of comfortable bars (sure enough, an inheritance of the Theatres Act) that has led to my rarely feeling thrilled by an evening in a West End theatre. But the Royal Court, the Royal Shakespeare Company (especially at the Aldwych), and the National Theatre have all, at different periods, been almost second homes – places where one seemed assured of a welcome and sustaining repast. No theatre experience has been more joyous, indeed, than one I was initially (from past acquaintance with all-day theatrical junkets) rather dreading: but the nine hours of the RSC's *Nicholas Nickleby* proved a wonderful affirmation of what theatre can be – life-enhancing on stage, and generating among its audience a rare sense of communality.

Although the set of *Nicholas Nickleby* was so luxuriant that it burst the bounds of the stage, the actors were also capable, when appropriate, of creating props from their own bodies – a stage-coach, for example, articulated into motion from the agile amalgamation of intertwined arms and jogging legs. Often, indeed, the very sparsest of sets have been the most rewarding – especially (and unsurprisingly) for Shakespeare, whose *Twelfth Night* I saw most perfectly performed on a Royal Court stage empty but for a few benches, and with the actors clad only in jeans and tee-shirts, in a production (by George Devine) mounted for a single Sunday evening – to cheer everybody up after the poor critical reception of the weekday production, which happened to be *A Midsummer Night's Dream*.

Occasionally an unexpected collision between the theatre and the outside world has added a resonance of its own, as when I spent an afternoon at the Aldwych at the height of the Cuban Missile Crisis, watching the 'sandbox' *Troilus and Cressida*, which spoke its message about the futility of war with almost unbearable irony. Later, though, it was a 'fringe' production which captured with stylistic ingenuity but unswerving and clear-sighted commitment the bizarre quality of that moment when the world stood poised on the edge of extinction – the comically cathartic reworking of the crisis by the Bradford Theatre Group, under Albert Hunt's direction, in terms of a John Ford western movie.

Middle-aged nostalgia has no doubt added its rosy veneer to my memories of some of these productions. And there is no doubt that, measured in terms of sheer quantity, the theatre would appear to be in a flourishing state: the invaluable *Theatre Record* thus listed 311 London productions in its first year of publication, 1981, a figure which had risen to an almost unbelievable 721 by 1993. And a glib dismissal of mere 'quantity' will not do – at least, not in favour of the expected alternative of 'quality', with its presumption of deadly 'excellence', of 'doing things properly'. If the theatre is to survive as a living force in our society, speaking to more than just its aficionados, it needs more often, in Arden's sense, to *do things improperly*.

Certainly, naturalism is not enough, perhaps never was – as witness the accommodating ease with which commercial theatre cushioned its initial shock. Not for much longer will the theatre even be able to claim the superior virtues of its sheer physical proximity and sense of potential danger over the pasteurized versions on film or television screens – for it will soon be possible to programme even accidents into a virtual reality far more comfortably and persuasively digitized than performed. Rather, we need to recognize and reclaim the rich complexity of performance and performing kinds – to agree with Aristotle that the telling of tales and the singing of songs is as much part of the rich tapestry of 'imitation' as the enactment of a comedy or a tragedy; and with the speaker of the epilogue (or the chairman of a music hall) that our response to performance works at many levels of simultaneous perception, and should enhance them all.

As this book goes to press, the British prime minister has just issued a call for the removal of beggars from the streets. It was a previous government's attempt to legislate against such 'masterless men' – many of them, then as now, old soldiers – that created the conditions for the growth of the Elizabethan theatre. Patronage often limited to a livery and a dead man's wardrobe made that theatre both passably respectable and passably loyal – just as the often miserly patronage of today elicits the necessary loyalty (well, the necessary compliance) involved in the constant applications, reports, audits, and all the other insidious manifestations which confirm us as hapless 'customers' in a market economy.

The beggars may be swept from the streets, into whatever equivalent of garbage bins the government devises: all the more does the theatre need its rogues and vagabonds, its masterless men and free women, to say *no* to such meanness of spirit with as fresh and vibrant a voice as it needs also to shout *yes* to the cussedness, complexity, and richness of life.

Reference guide to The Cambridge Illustrated History of British Theatre

Chronology

Glossary

Who's who

Select bibliography

Chronology

75 BC, *c*: Roman theatre at Pompeii

55 BC, Caesar's first invasion of Britain

44 AD, Roman conquest of Britain. Traces of theatres dating from first century at Canterbury and Catterick

155 *c*: Roman theatre built at St Albans. Theatre at Colchester rebuilt

200 *c*: Tertullian, *De Spectaculis*

312 Conversion of Empire to Christianity

395 Division between the Eastern and Western Roman Empires

398 Actors excommunicated by Church

401 *Confessions* of St Augustine of Hippo

410 Beginning of withdrawal of Roman legions from Britain

438 Theodosian Code limits movements and costumes of actors

450 *c*: Anglo-Saxon invasions begin

533 Last recorded theatrical performance in Rome: theatres closed?

568 Fall of Rome

597 St Augustine's conversion of Kent

605 *c*: Construction of theatre at Yeavering

664 Synod of Whitby establishes Romanized Christianity in England

670 *c*: The 'Hymn' of Caedmon

686 Nominal conversion of England to Christianity completed

730 *c*: Original composition of *Beowulf*

791 Alcuin at Court of Charlemagne

800 Charlemagne Holy Roman Emperor

816 Council of Aachen forbids clerics to watch theatrical entertainments

856 Beginning of Viking invasions

871 Reign of Alfred the Great, to 899

920 *c*: Earliest traces of *Quem Quaeritis* trope

960 *c*: Hrotsvitha's Terentian plays

975 *c*: The *Regularis Concordia*

1066 Norman conquest of England

1185 Oxford University established

1209 Franciscan order of friars founded

1215 Magna Carta

1217 First Dominican friars in England

1224 First Franciscan friars in England

1290 Expulsion of Jews from England

1300 *c*: *Interludium de Clerico et Puella*

1311 Feast of Corpus Christi proclaimed

1337 Beginning of Hundred Years War

1348 First visitation of the Black Death

1351 Statute of Labourers. *c*: *Pride of Life*

1362 *c*: First version of *Piers Plowman*

1376 First mention of York Cycle

1378 Great Schism in the Church

1381 Peasants' Revolt

1382 Expulsion of John Wycliffe from Oxford

1385 *c*: Chaucer's *Troilus and Criseyde*

1392 First mention of Coventry Cycle

1415 English victory at Agincourt. *c*: *The Castle of Perseverance*

1422 First mention of Chester Cycle

1450 Jack Cade's rebellion. English expelled from Normandy. *c*: Wakefield and N-Town Cycles flourishing

1455 Beginning of Wars of the Roses

1465 *c*: *Mankind*

1471 First printing of Terence's plays

1476 Caxton's press at Westminster

1484 Plautus's *Aulularia* performed in Rome

1485 Defeat of Richard III. Henry VII establishes House of Tudor

1495 *c*: *Everyman* and Medwall's *Nature*

1498 Plays of Aristophanes printed in Venice. *c*: *The Play of the Sacrament*, *Fulgens and Lucrece*

1509 Accession of Henry VIII

1513 *c*: *Hickscorner*

1515 *c*: Skelton's *Magnificence*

1517 Luther's theses posted at Wittenburg. Rastell's *The Four Elements*

1520 Henry VIII and Francis I at Field of the Cloth of Gold. John Heywood active

1529 Fall of Wolsey. Henry seizes York (later Whitehall) Palace

1531 Henry proclaimed Supreme Head of the Church in England. Redford Master of Paul's Boys

1532 Machiavelli's *The Prince*

1534 Udall headmaster at Eton

1535 Suppression of the monasteries begins. Coverdale's Bible

1538 John Bale active

1539 Publication of the Great Bible. *c*: Redford's *Wit and Science*

1540 Lindsay's *Satire of the Thrie Estaitis*

1545 First Master of the Revels appointed

1547 Accession of Edward VI. Westcott Master of Paul's Boys. Udall's *Ralph Roister Doister*

1553 Accession of Mary I. *Republica*. *Gammer Gurton's Needle*

1558 Loss of Calais to the French. Accession of Elizabeth I

1562 The 'Thirty-Nine Articles' of the Church of England. *Gorboduc*

1566 Gascoigne's *Supposes*

1568 *The Marriage of Wit and Science*

1569 Last performance of York Cycle

1572 Act for punishment of vagabonds

1574 Queen grants patent to Leicester's Men

1575 Leicester's entertainment at Kenilworth

1576 Last performance of Wakefield Cycle. The Theatre and first Blackfriars open

1579 Stephen Gosson's *School of Abuse*

1587 Execution of Mary Queen of Scots. Rose built. Marlowe's *Tamburlaine the Great*. Kyd's *The Spanish Tragedy*

1588 Defeat of the Spanish Armada

1591 *c*: Shakespeare's *Henry VI*

1592 Plague closes theatres for two years

1594 Companies reorganized: emergence of Chamberlain's and Admiral's Men

1596 Building of second Blackfriars

1598 Jonson active. *Isle of Dogs* controversy

1599 First Globe playhouse opened

1601 Essex's rebellion. 'War of the theatres'

1603 Accession of James I. Plague. Royal patronage required for players

1604 Peace with Spain. Alleyn retires?

1605 Beginning of collaboration between Jonson and Jones on court masques. Red Bull built? Guy Fawkes's plot

1606 Beaumont and Fletcher active

1609 Plague. c: King's Men begin winter playing indoors, at the Blackfriars

1611 c: Shakespeare retires

1614 Hope and second Globe opened

1615 c: Cockpit theatre built

1616 Death of Shakespeare. Jonson's *Works*

1622 New Banqueting House in Whitehall opened. Massinger active

1623 'First Folio' of Shakespeare's plays. Fortune theatre rebuilt

1625 Accession of Charles I and marriage to Henrietta Maria. Plague. Death of Fletcher. Shirley active

1627 Death of Middleton

1629 Charles's eleven-year personal rule begins. Salisbury Court opened

1630 Plague. Cockpit-in-Court opened

1632 Death of Dekker. Brome active

1633 Prynne's *Histrio-Mastix*

1634 Chapman and Marston die

1636 Long plague closure

1638 New masquing house in Whitehall

1640 Commencement of 'Long Parliament'. Last court masque, *Salmacida Spolia*

1642 Civil wars begin. Theatres closed

1643 *The Actors' Remonstrance*

1644 Interior of Globe dismantled

1647 Some public acting. Folio of Beaumont and Fletcher's plays published

1649 Trial and execution of Charles I. Commonwealth proclaimed

1650 Prince Charles flees. Many playhouses by now pulled down

1653 Cromwell becomes Lord Protector

1654 Suppression of illicit playing

1655 First Lord Mayor's Show since 1639. Playing at Red Bull

1656 Davenant staging plays at Rutland House. Hope theatre pulled down

1658 Cromwell dies. Davenant at Cockpit

1659 End of protectorate. Playing at Cockpit and Red Bull

1660 Restoration of Charles II. Issue of patents to Davenant and Killigrew. Actresses permitted

1661 Duke's at Lincoln's Inn Fields

1663 King's at new Theatre Royal, Bridges Street (burned down 1672)

1665 The Great Plague: theatres closed

1666 The Great Fire. Dryden active

1668 Betterton and Harris managing Duke's. Etherege active

1671 Dorset Garden theatre opened

1673 First appearance of Mrs Barry

1674 New Drury Lane theatre opened

1678 Popish Plot and exclusionist crisis

1682 Formation of United Company

1685 Accession of James II

1689 William and Mary succeed following the deposition of James II

1690 First appearance of Colley Cibber

1695 Betterton leads breakaway company to Lincoln's Inn Fields. Congreve active

1698 Jeremy Collier's *Short View* published. Wilks joins Drury Lane company

1702 Accession of Queen Anne

1705 Opening of Queen's theatre, Haymarket

1707 Union of England and Scotland. Death of George Farquhar

1708 Companies reunited at Drury Lane

1709 Betterton's company returns to Queen's. Rich expelled from Drury Lane

1710 The triumviral management of Cibber, Doggett, and Wilks. Death of Betterton

1714 Accession of George I, and end of Tory hegemony. Rich takes company to Lincoln's Inn Fields. Steele at Drury Lane (to 1720), with Quin in company

1715 Jacobite Rebellion

1720 South Sea Bubble. Opening of Little Theatre in the Haymarket

1721 Walpole comes to power

1722 Steele's *The Conscious Lovers*

1727 Accession of George II

1728 Phenomenal success of Gay's *The Beggar's Opera* at Lincoln's Inn. Fielding's first play produced

1729 New theatre opened in Goodman's Fields

1731 Giffard manager at Goodman's Fields. George Lillo's *The London Merchant*

1732 Rich opens Covent Garden theatre. Giffard builds new playhouse in Goodman's Fields

1733 Defection of actors under Theophilus Cibber from Drury Lane

1736 Fielding's company at the Little. His *Pasquin* performed

1737 Fielding's *The Historical Register for 1736*. Licensing Act tightens censorship and monopoly of patent houses

1741 Macklin's Shylock at Drury Lane. Garrick's first performance at Goodman's Fields, Giffard having resumed acting there in 1740

1742 Fall of Walpole. Giffard's company moves to Lincoln's Inn Fields

1743 Secession of Garrick and Macklin

1745 Second Jacobite rebellion. Lacy manager at Drury Lane

1747 Beginning of Garrick and Lacy's joint management at Drury Lane. Foote's 'concert formula' at Goodman's Fields

1751 Retirement of James Quin

1752 Local Licensing Act empowers magistrates to authorize local playing

1757 Pitt becomes prime minister. Home's *Douglas*

1760 Accession of George III

1761 Death of John Rich

1763 Garrick's removal of spectators from the stage. Patent theatres damaged during riots over half-price admission

1765 Watt's steam engine. Foote granted patent for the Little Theatre. Lyceum and rebuilt Sadler's Wells opened. Bickerstaff's *The Maid of the Mill*

1769 Garrick's belated Shakespeare jubilee celebrations at Stratford-upon-Avon

1771 De Loutherbourg engaged by Garrick

1775 Sarah Siddons's first, unsuccessful debut: returns to the provinces. Sheridan's *The Rivals*

1776 American Declaration of Independence. Sheridan takes over Drury Lane

1779 De Loutherbourg's designs for *The Wonders of Derbyshire*

1782 Sarah Siddons's triumphant return to Drury Lane. Enlargement of Covent Garden. Opening of Royal Circus (later the Surrey)

1783 Debut of J. P. Kemble as Hamlet

1788 Opening of Astley's Amphitheatre

1789 French Revolution. Macklin's last appearance as Shylock

1792 Further enlargement of Covent Garden. Holcroft's *The Road to Ruin*

1793 War against France begins

1794 Kemble opens enlarged Drury Lane

1797 Mutinies of Spithead and the Nore. 'Monk' Lewis's *The Castle Spectre*

1799 Napoleon becomes First Consul in France. Sheridan's *Pizarro*

1800 Highland clearances. Morton's *Speed the Plough*

1802 Kemble and Siddons move to Covent Garden. Holcroft's *A Tale of Mystery*. Peace of Amiens halts war for one year

1805 Battle of Trafalgar. Master Betty phenomenon. Liston makes first appearance

1806 Astley's Olympic Theatre opened

1808 Covent Garden burns down

1809 Drury Lane burns down. Kemble's attempt to raise prices at new Covent Garden provokes 'Old Price Riots'

1810 c: Prince of Wales's Theatre opened

1811 Regency of Prince of Wales

1812 New Drury Lane opened. Siddons retires. Napoleon's invasion of Russia

1813 Pocock's *The Miller and His Men*

1815 Battle of Waterloo. Treaty of Vienna draws post-war map of Europe

1816 W. C. Macready's debut at Covent Garden

1818 Kemble's retirement. Patent houses install gas lighting. Royal Coburg Theatre opened

1819 Peterloo massacre. Opening of Adelphi Theatre. Madame Vestris's debut

1820 Accession of George IV. c: Opening of Coal Hole song and supper rooms

1821 Moncrieff's *Tom and Jerry*

1824 Repeal of the Combination Acts

1825 Poole's *Paul Pry*

1827 First appearance of Charles Kean

1828 Wellington prime minister (resigned 1830). Jerrold's *Fifteen Years of a Drunkard's Life*. Pavilion, Whitechapel, opened

1829 Catholic emancipation

1830 Accession of William IV. Liverpool to Manchester railway. Vestris's management at the Olympic. Jerrold's *Mutiny at the Nore*. Ducrow at Astley's

1831 Faraday demonstrates electro-magnetic current

1832 Reform Act abolishes 'rotten boroughs' and extends franchise. Grecian Saloon opened in City Road

1833 Death of Kean. Bunn's duopoly at patent houses. Dramatic Copyright Act

1834 Peel becomes prime minister. Poor Law Amendment Act

1835 Debut of Charles Mathews at the Olympic. St James's Theatre opened

1837 Accession of Queen Victoria

1838 Beginnings of Chartist movement

1841 Macready's management at Drury Lane (to 1843). Britannia, Hoxton, opened

1843 Theatres Act ends patent monopoly

1844 Phelps's management at Sadler's Wells (to 1862)

1846 Repeal of the Corn Laws

1847 Vestris and Mathews at Lyceum. Covent Garden reopens as Royal Opera House. Mogul Saloon opens. Charles Morton at Canterbury Arms, Lambeth

1848 Year of revolutions abroad. Royal theatricals move to Windsor

1850 Beginning of Charles Kean's management at Princess's (to 1859)

1851 Great Exhibition at Crystal Palace

1854 Crimean War. Madame Vestris retires

1861 American Civil War (to 1865). First Oxford music hall opened

1863 Taylor's *The Ticket-of-Leave Man*

1865 The Bancrofts' management at Prince of Wales (to 1879)

1867 Robertson's *Caste*

1868 Gaiety Theatre opened

1870 Franco-Prussian War. Vaudeville Theatre and Opera Comique opened

1871 Paris Commune. Irving's first appearance in *The Bells*

1875 Ellen Terry's Portia at the Prince of Wales. H. J. Byron's *Our Boys*

1878 Irving takes over Lyceum

1880 Ibsen's *Pillars of Society* at Gaiety

1881 D'Oyly Carte opens the Savoy Theatre, lit by electricity. Saxe-Meiningen Company appears in London

1885 Pinero's *The Magistrate*. Edwardes joins Hollingshead at the Gaiety

1886 Benson begins management of annual festivals at Stratford-upon-Avon

1887 International Copyright Convention. Tree's management at Haymarket

1889 Ibsen's *A Doll's House*

1890 Alexander at the St James's

1891 Independent Theatre Society formed. Ibsen's *Ghosts* produced, and Shaw's *Quintessence of Ibsenism* published

1892 First Labour MP elected. Wilde's *Lady Windermere's Fan* and Shaw's *Widowers' Houses*

1893 Daly's Theatre opened. Pinero's *The Second Mrs Tanqueray*

1894 Poel's Elizabethan Stage Society formed

1895 Irving knighted. Tree in *Trilby*

1896 Northcliffe's *Daily Mail* launched Lumière brothers' films in London

1897 Forbes-Robertson's Hamlet. Tree at Her Majesty's Theatre. Jones's *The Liars*

1899 Wyndham's Theatre opened

1900 Tree's *A Midsummer Night's Dream*

1901 Accession of Edward VII

1902 Irving leaves Lyceum. Barrie's *The Admirable Crichton*

1903 Women's suffrage movement

1904 Vedrenne-Barker management at the Court. RADA founded

1905 Aldwych theatre opened. Barker's *The Voysey Inheritance*

1906 Reformist Liberal government elected

1907 Queen's Theatre opened. Shaw's *Caesar and Cleopatra*

1908 Mrs Horniman's Manchester Repertory at Gaiety Theatre

1910 Accession of George V. Galsworthy's *Justice*

1911 Parliament Act. Reinhardt in London

1912 Barker's Shakespearean productions at the Savoy

1913 Barry Jackson forms Birmingham Rep

1914 First World War (to 1918). Shaw's *Pygmalion*

1916 Entertainments Tax introduced

1919 Bridges-Adams at Stratford. Maugham's *Home and Away*

1920 Playfair's *Beggar's Opera* at the Lyric, Hammersmith. Shaw's *Heartbreak House*

1923 Formation of Oxford Repertory and Cambridge Festival Theatres. Coward's *The Vortex*

1924 Gielgud's Romeo, Evans's Millamant, Thorndike's St Joan. First minority Labour Government formed

1926 BBC incorporated. General Strike. Travers's *Rookery Nook*

1927 Arts Theatre Club opened

1929 Wall Street Crash. Coward's *Private Lives*, Shaw's *The Apple Cart*

1930 Gielgud's Hamlet

1931 Economic crisis and 'National' government landslide. Sadler's Wells rebuilt. Coward's *Cavalcade*

1932 New Shakespeare Memorial Theatre opened. Priestley's *Dangerous Corner*

1935 Gielgud and Olivier at New. Novello's *Glamorous Night* at Drury Lane. Eliot's *Murder in the Cathedral*

1936 Accession of George VI. Spanish Civil War begins

1937 Olivier and Richardson at Old Vic

1938 Munich crisis. Gielgud directs Evans in *The Importance of Being Earnest*. Dodie Smith's *Dear Octopus*

1939 Second World War (to 1945). CEMA and ENSA formed

1940 Wolfit's Shakespeare seasons

1941 Old Vic bombed: company on tour

1942 Clunes goes to the Arts

1944 Old Vic at New Theatre. Littlewood's Theatre Workshop formed

1945 Labour election landslide. Atomic bomb on Hiroshima. Olivier's Oedipus. Priestley's *An Inspector Calls*

1946 Jackson at Stratford. Old Vic School and Young Vic formed. Arts Council incorporated. First Edinburgh Festival

1949 Quayle at Stratford. Eliot's *The Cocktail Party*

1950 Old Vic rebuilt. Fry's *Venus Observed*

1951 Festival of Britain. Labour loses office

1952 Accession of Elizabeth II

1953 Theatre Workshop to Stratford East

1954 Behan's *The Quare Fellow. Dry Rot*

1955 Commercial television begins. Hall directs Beckett's *Waiting for Godot*

1956 Suez crisis and Hungarian revolution. English Stage Company at Royal Court, and Osborne's *Look Back in Anger*. Visit of Berliner Ensemble

1958 Belgrade Theatre, Coventry, built. New plays from Arden, Wesker, Behan, Delaney, Jellicoe, Mortimer, Pinter, Shaffer

1959 Mermaid Theatre and Nottingham Playhouse opened

1961 Royal Shakespeare Company created, under Hall, in Stratford and at Aldwych. *Beyond the Fringe* at the Fortune

1962 Cuban missile crisis. Olivier at Chichester. Brook-Scofield *Lear*. RSC experimental season at Arts

1963 National Theatre opens at Old Vic. RSC's *Wars of the Roses*. Littlewood's *Oh, What a Lovely War!* Traverse Theatre, Edinburgh, opened

1964 Labour government. Olivier's *Othello*. Brook's 'Theatre of Cruelty' season. First World Theatre Season at Aldwych. Orton's *Entertaining Mr Sloane*

1965 Bond's *Saved*. Pinter's *The Homecoming*

1966 People Show begins performing

1967 Ayckbourn's *Relatively Speaking*. Stoppard's *Rosencrantz and Guildenstern*

1968 Student activism against Vietnam War. Arts Lab, Open Space, and Theatre Upstairs opened. Numerous 'fringe' companies formed. Theatre censorship ended. *Hair*. Grotowski in Edinburgh. Nunn succeeds Hall at RSC

1969 Resurgence of Irish troubles

1970 Brook's *Dream*. Young Vic opened. Conservative government (to 1974). Heathcote Williams's *AC/DC*

1972 Olivier's Tyrone in *Long Day's Journey*. Half Moon and Crucible, Sheffield, open

1973 Women's Festival at Almost Free

1974 Miners' strike. Labour government. Stoppard's *Travesties*. Joint Stock formed. The Other Place opened

1975 Gay theatre season at Almost Free. Ayckbourn's *Norman Conquests*. Gray's *Otherwise Engaged*

1976 Opening of new National Theatre

1977 Hands's histories with Howard at RSC. Warehouse opened. Prospect at Old Vic

1978 Hands joins Nunn directing RSC

1979 Thatcher prime minister. Stafford-Clark at Royal Court. Sherman's *Bent*. Comedy Store opened. Rebuilt Lyric, Hammersmith, and studio opened

1981 Noble's *King Lear* with Gambon and Sher. First LIFT festival. Friel's *Translations. Cats*

1982 Falklands crisis. RSC's Barbican Theatre opened. Channel Four starts transmissions

1983 Eyre's *Guys and Dolls*

1984 Arts Council's *Glory of the Garden*. Sher's Richard III, Branagh's Prince Hal. *Starlight Express*

1985 Hare and Brenton's *Pravda. Les Misérables. Torch Song Trilogy*

1986 RSC's Swan Theatre opened. Bogdanov and Pennington form English Shakespeare Company

1987 Renaissance Theatre Company formed. Ayckbourn's *A Small Family Business*. Churchill's *Serious Money*

1988 Eyre succeeds Hall at National, Noble succeeds Hands at RSC. Peter Hall Company formed

1990 Fall of Margaret Thatcher. Hare's *Racing Demon*

Glossary

agitprop originally an early Soviet theatrical style combining 'agitation' and 'propaganda': hence, theatre in the 1960s aimed at spreading socialist beliefs through similar means

alternative theatre largely synonymous with FRINGE THEATRE, but often used from the late 1960s to suggest a more consciously subversive intention

anti-masque farcical interlude played by professionals within a MASQUE

apron part of the stage projecting beyond the PROSCENIUM arch

archimima leading female performer in a Roman MIME

archimimus leading male performer in a Roman MIME

box one of several enclosed seating areas on the perimeter of an auditorium

breeches part male role played by an actress (in *breeches*, or trousers)

burlesque in British usage, a satirical pastiche of an inflated or otherwise targeted theatrical style

burletta originally, a comic play with music; by the early nineteenth century, any play licensed to be performed at a minor theatre, officially a piece of one act with five or six songs

caesura felt pause or natural breathing space in a line of verse

chamber theatre intimate performance, often in a limited space and with pared-down scenic requirements

comedy dramatic work, often though not invariably funny, but always with a reconciliatory, 'happy' ending. Its characters are conventionally of a lower class than those of TRAGEDY

commedia dell'arte style of Italian comedy from the sixteenth century, improvised from an outline scenario, some of whose stock characters found their way into early English PANTOMIME

compilation bill programme of varied style and content, as found in MUSIC HALL

Cornish rounds circular earth-works with raised perimeter, used as theatres for late medieval Cornish MYSTERY PLAYS

coster comedy low comedy usually of urban life (as among costermongers)

débat formalized style of debate, found in some early Tudor INTERLUDES

discovery in the Elizabethan theatre, actors or a scene already set on stage; critically, the moment of *anagnorisis* (realization or revelation) in a TRAGEDY

droll short comic sketch or extract from a play, popular in the Commonwealth as a means of evading restrictions on more formal playing

dumb-show a role or character performed through gestures, without words

entr'acte 'between the acts': hence specialist 'turns' then performed

euphuistic ornate, high-flown style of language, after Lyly's *Euphues* (1580)

fabliau short verse tale of ordinary life, usually coarsely comic

farce comic play of ordinary people caught up in awkward sexual or social situations, often with an emphasis on physical action and reaction

fringe theatre 'unofficial', usually small-scale productions, originally at the Edinburgh Festival, now any such

gallery an upper, usually cheaper, tier of seats – hence also its occupants

gods the topmost GALLERY of a theatre, closest to the ceiling, and its occupants

Harlequin the lover of Columbine and rival of Clown in English PANTOMIME. Masked, and in spangled or parti-coloured costume, he derived from a stock character of Italian COMMEDIA

heavens the underside of the roof, so painted, protecting the stage of an Elizabethan outdoor ('public') theatre

heroic drama serious (not invariably tragic) and often spectacular play on the themes of love and honour, briefly in vogue following the Restoration

humours, comedy of style so named by Jonson to denote comedies concerned with ridiculing affectations (from the medieval medical belief in bodily fluids which governed human behaviour)

interlude term used to describe several kinds of short play in the later medieval and early Tudor periods. Some were farcical and secular, others (see MORALITY PLAY) of religious import

jig Elizabethan speciality dance or playlet with the clown as protagonist

limelight form of stage lighting, popular in the nineteenth century, producing its strong focus by directing a blowpipe flame against a block of quicklime

locus (plural *loci*) playing place meant to denote a specific location in medieval drama, as distinct from the generalized area or PLATEA

lord's room in the Elizabethan public theatre, a box on the first tier, perhaps facing (perhaps above) the stage, for a patron or some other important visitor

ludius, ludia Latin terms for male and female performers respectively

lycopodium a powder consisting of moss spores, used in the nineteenth century for stage effects

masque in the Jacobean court theatre, a form of spectacular entertainment, with dancing and acting by aristocratic amateur performers, and often an ANTI-MASQUE performed by professionals

melodrama following German and French models, any play with musical accompaniment; by the early nineteenth century a popular English style of sensational (or later domestic) play usually featuring characters from ordinary life and observing POETIC JUSTICE

mima female player in a Roman MIME

mime (1) in Roman theatre, short playlet, probably semi-improvised, mixing farce, satire, burlesque, song, dance, and acrobatics according to the skills of the itinerant performers; (2) a performance in DUMB-SHOW *mimus* (plural *mimi*) male player in a Roman MIME

Minnesinger twelfth- or thirteenth-century German writer and singer, often noble, of love-lyrics

morality play modern critical term for an INTERLUDE of didactic purpose, in which a figure typical of mankind is confronted with characters personifying virtues and sinful temptations

mummers' play a folk drama taken from house to house, usually at Christmas: hence *mumming*, often used more loosely for itinerant folk performance

music hall popular variety entertainment which began in song and supper rooms and pubs in the early nineteenth century, and later flourished in purpose-built halls until after the First World War, when it was eclipsed by revue, cinema, and radio

mystery cycle a sequence of MYSTERY PLAYS performed in the course of a day by different guilds of a particular town, usually at the Feast of Corpus Christi

mystery play a late medieval play from a MYSTERY CYCLE, dramatizing an event from the scriptures; sometimes *miracle play* is used synonymously, but more helpfully this distinguishes a non-scriptural play dramatizing a saint's life

naturalism a literary movement originating in the nineteenth century, which held that human behaviour was scientifically determined by natural laws, and should be so portrayed in art. Not fully synonymous with REALISM, though often so used

ordinary poet resident playwright for an Elizabethan or Jacobean theatre company, thought to have been contracted to write two plays a year

pantomime from the later eighteenth century in England, a theatrical entertainment with stock characters, such as HARLEQUIN, derived from the Italian COMMEDIA DELL'ARTE; during Victorian times, this developed into a Christmas entertainment more often based on a nursery tale, with topical allusions, songs, and star performers in cross-dressing roles

pantomimus masked, solo player of all the roles in a Roman dance-drama, performed in DUMB-SHOW to musical accompaniment

patent an exclusive right to perform legitimate drama, first conferred by the crown at the Restoration, and long confined to two companies, whose monopoly largely survived until 1843

patent house theatre used by a company whose manager held a PATENT

penny gaff in the nineteenth century, roughly fitted-up theatre for the poor, with an admission price of one penny

Pepper's ghost an illusion produced by a sheet of glass reflecting on stage the image of an actor below the stage

performance art a modern form combining elements from the visual arts, such as painting or photography, with acting, dance, and/or music

pit originally, the ground floor of a theatre or its occupants; later, the area remaining behind the encroaching front stalls. The useage survives in *orchestra pit*

place-and-scaffold staging form of staging for the late medieval MYSTERY CYCLES, in which several scaffold stages representing specific localities (LOCI) are grouped around a generalized PLATEA, the action moving between them

platea Latin term for the generalized playing area in medieval theatre, as distinct from the LOCUS representing a specific location

Plautine comedies comedies by or in the style of the Roman comic poet Plautus (*c.* 250–184 BC)

poetic justice critical precept dating from the late eighteenth century, requiring that the fates of characters in plays are morally appropriate to their actions

proscenium strictly, the front part of the stage between the curtain and the orchestra; since it is now bridged by a *proscenium arch*, often used loosely to signify the arch itself, or, in *proscenium staging,* to suggest the invisible 'fourth-wall' through which NATURALISM often has its audience 'overlook' a play

realism originally used in opposition to *idealism*; later, a less deterministic style than NATURALISM (though often confused with it), associated with a depiction of a less 'shaped' but often harsher view of the surface of life

repertoire the range of plays available for performance; more loosely, a *repertory company* often played these consecutively (rather than interchangeably, as *true repertoire* requires)

rondeau a short medieval poem with closely knit rhythms and a distinctive refrain

simultaneous staging elaborate form of PLACE-AND-SCAFFOLD STAGING, in which the full sequence of a medieval MYSTERY CYCLE is played around a town square or other large performing space

station-to-station staging performance of the different parts of a MYSTERY CYCLE at a series of open-air sites to which the plays were moved by means of wagons

tableaux vivants living pictures, in which the action, if any, is in DUMB-SHOW

Terence stage a medieval misconception of how the comedies of Terence (*c.* 190–159 BC) were performed, a narrator in a booth speaking the parts of players who mimed their roles

tire archaic form of *attire:* thus an Elizabethan theatrical dressing room was a *tiring house*, and the person in charge of costumes was the *tire-man*

tragedy a serious play dealing with the fall of a basically good protagonist owing to a flaw in character or misfortune, climactic deaths usually ensuing

tragi-comedy a play in which a tragic tone establishes expectations overturned by a happy ending

trope originally, a verbal or musical embellishment of the mass; by the later middle ages, including the 'dramatization' of biblical events so inserted

troubadour eleventh- to thirteenth-century writer, usually aristocratic, of lyrics of courtly love, in a tradition originating in Provence

trouvère a medieval narrative or epic poet of northern France

Who's who

Select bibliography

General and Reference

The only recent comprehensive history of British theatre is the eight-volume *The Revels History of Drama in English* (London: Methuen, 1975–81). This includes helpful chronologies and bibliographies, but multiple authorship makes for variations of emphasis and authority both within and between the volumes; and although theatre as well as drama is fully considered, the discussions can be off-puttingly discrete. The volumes cover: I, Medieval Drama; II, 1500–1576; III, 1576–1613; IV, 1613–1660; V, 1660–1750; VI, 1750–1880; and VII, from 1880 (the eighth deals with American drama).

Allardyce Nicoll's earlier *A History of English Drama* (Cambridge UP, 1923–46, revised 1952–59), supplemented by his *English Drama 1900–1930* (Cambridge UP, 1973), is still useful, especially for the periods where the massive 'Hand-List of Plays' which concludes each volume has not been superseded. A useful concise summary of available information about plays within an earlier but more limited compass is Alfred Harbage's *Annals of English Drama 975–1700*, revised by S. Schoenbaum (London: Methuen, 1964).

Many of the books considered below contain guides to further reading in their own areas, but two magisterial general bibliographies exist – for works published down to 1900, *English Theatrical Literature, 1559–1900: a Bibliography*, by J. F. Arnott and J. W. Robertson (London: Society for Theatre Research, 1970); and picking up from there, John Cavanagh's *British Theatre: a Bibliography, 1901–1985* (Mottisfont: Motley Press, 1989). Providing fuller detail and annotation, but with a distinct emphasis on drama at the expense of theatre, are a series of bibliographies in the 'Guide to Information Sources' series (Detroit: Gale Research Company, 1976–82): *English Drama to 1660, Excluding Shakespeare,* by Frieda Elaine Penninger; *English Drama 1660–1800*, by Frederick M. Link; *English Drama 1800–1900*, by L. W. Conolly and J. P. Wearing; *English Drama 1900–1950*,

by E. H. Mikhail; and *Modern Drama in America and England 1950–1970*, by Richard H. Harris. Don. B. Wilmeth's *American and English Popular Entertainment: a Guide to Information Sources*, (Detroit: Gale, 1980), complements these in its own field.

Pictorial Documentation

The preparation of this *Illustrated History* has confirmed how poorly the theatre has on the whole preserved its own traces: indeed, the only complete 'iconography' remains Joe Mander and Raymond Mitchenson's *Picture History of the British Theatre* (London: Hulton, 1957). But scholarly accounts for earlier periods do now exist: these are Clifford Davidson's *Illustrations of the Stage and Acting in England to 1580* (Kalamazoo: Medieval Institute Publications, 1991), and R. A. Foakes's abutting *Illustrations of the English Stage, 1580–1642* (London: Scolar Press, 1985). Nothing adequately fills the long gap thereafter, though usefully selective pictorial accounts include Iain Mackintosh's *The Georgian Playhouse* (London: Arts Council, 1975) and Richard Southern's *The Victorian Theatre: a Pictorial Survey* (Newton Abbot: David and Charles, 1970).

Mander and Mitchenson also compiled richly illustrated histories of aspects of the popular theatre, all sub-titled 'A Story in Pictures': *Pantomime* (New York: Taplinger, 1973); *British Music Hall* (London: Studio Vista, 1965); *Musical Comedy* (London: Peter Davis, 1969); and *Revue* (New York: Taplinger, 1971).

Medieval and Early Tudor

The new *Cambridge Companion to Medieval English Theatre*, edited by Richard Beadle (Cambridge UP, 1994) offers a discursive overview, whereas Ian Lancashire's *Dramatic Texts and Records of Britain to 1558: a Chronological Topography* (Cambridge UP, 1984) is concerned with the smaller details – not easy to use, but far more fun than its title may suggest. On the earlier part of the period, Richard

Axton's *European Drama of the Early Middle Ages* (Hutchinson, 1974) remains stimulating, but for an exciting account of the whole range of popular and itinerant performance Allardyce Nicoll's *Masks, Mimes, and Miracles* (1931, reprinted New York: Cooper Square, 1963) has yet to be surpassed. For the later Middle Ages, Glynne Wickham's *The Medieval Theatre* (London: Weidenfeld, 1974) sets the period in a continental context, as does William Tydeman's *The Theatre in the Middle Ages* (Cambridge UP, 1978) – the latter being helpfully complemented by Tydeman's more detailed, production oriented study, *English Medieval Theatre 1400–1500* (London: Routledge, 1986). A.P. Rossiter's *English Drama from Early Times to the Elizabethans* (Hutchinson, 1950) is astute and charming, though now becoming dated: it might be usefully compared with *Medieval Drama*, by Christine Richardson and Jackie Johnston (London: Macmillan, 1991), which is approachable though well grounded in modern theory.

On the liturgical drama, Karl Young's massive *The Drama of the Medieval Church* (Oxford UP, 1933) remains crucial, but must be used alongside O. B. Hardison's *Christian Rite and Christian Ritual in the Middle Ages* (Johns Hopkins UP, 1965). Rosemary Woolf's *The English Mystery Plays* (Routledge, 1972) is the fullest general survey, though rather literary in emphasis. H. C. Gardiner's *Mysteries' End* (Yale UP, 1946) deals with the suppression of the cycles. 'Casebooks' containing critical materials of varying quality include *Medieval English Drama*, edited by Jerome Taylor and Alan H. Nelson (Chicago UP, 1972); *Medieval English Drama: a Casebook*, edited by Peter Happé (London: Macmillan, 1984), and, perhaps the most useful of these, *Medieval Drama*, edited by Neville Denny for the 'Stratford-upon-Avon Studies' series (London: Arnold, 1973).

An expansive analysis, ground breaking in its assessment of pageantry and other forms of dramatic spectacle, will be found in the three volumes of Glynne Wickham's *Early English Stages* (Routledge, 1959–81). For the early Tudor period, the solid historical approach of F. P. Wilson in *The English Drama 1485–1585* (Oxford UP, 1969) contrasts with *From Mankind to Marlowe* (Harvard UP, 1962), by David Bevington – an admirable introduction to the transitional period before the great age of Elizabethan drama, which is no less scholarly for its felt enthusiasm. On the interludes, T. W. Craik's *The Tudor Interlude* (Leicester UP, 1958) refreshingly emphasizes performing conditions, and is worth reading alongside Richard Southern's more quirkily individual *The Staging of Plays before Shakespeare* (Faber, 1973). Robert Potter's *The English Morality Play* (Routledge, 1975) deals with matters of theme, form, and influence.

Late Elizabethan to Caroline

Rather than selecting a few random items from the many shelvesful of Shakespearean studies, I am recommending a bibliographical resource which will serve as a guide to further reading on individual areas of interest. *Shakespeare: a Bibliographical Guide*, edited by Stanley Wells (Cambridge UP, 1990) necessarily reflects the literary-critical emphasis of the Shakespeare industry itself: but it also includes chapters on general Shakespearean studies, on his theatre, and on new critical approaches. For a broad background picture of the age, the documentation assembled by G. Blakemore Evans in *Elizabethan–Jacobean Drama* (London: Black, 1989), makes a good companion to the now-standard (and regularly revised) survey of staging, company histories, and theatre practice, Andrew Gurr's *The Shakespearean Stage 1574–1642* (Cambridge UP, 1981).

Three volumes in the Routledge 'Theatre Production Studies' series – Michael Hattaway's *Elizabethan Popular Theatre* (1982), Peter Thomson's *Shakespeare's Theatre* (1983), and Keith Sturgess's *Jacobean Private Theatre* (1987) – explore plays and companies, assembling evidence of production methods. My own *Shakespearean Concepts* (Methuen, 1989) provides a dictionary-style guide to the ideas and assumptions underlying the drama of the period.

Two works by G. E. Bentley focus attention on theatre practitioners, as their titles suggest: *The Profession of Dramatist in Shakespeare's Time* (Princeton UP, 1971) and *The Profession of Player in Shakespeare's Time* (Princeton UP, 1984). Bertram Joseph's *Elizabethan Acting* (Oxford UP, 1951) was a brave early venture into this uncharted territory: now, David Bevington's *Action is Eloquence: Shakespeare's Language of Gesture* (Harvard UP, 1984) explores technique wearing its scholarly disciplines lightly, as did an earlier classic, M. C. Bradbrook's *The Rise of the Common Player* (London: Chatto, 1962). A wise but provocative study of one distinctive 'line' is David Wiles's *Shakespeare's Clown: Actor and Text in the Elizabethan Playhouse* (Cambridge UP, 1987). On masques and masquing John Orrell's *The Theatres of Inigo Jones and John Webb* (Cambridge UP, 1985) makes an erudite companion to the essays collected by David Lindley into *The Court Masque* (Manchester UP, 1984).

As broad in scope as its title hints is Robert Weimann's *Shakespeare and the Popular Tradition in the Theatre* (Johns Hopkins UP, 1978), while Alan Dessen's *Elizabethan Stage Conventions and Modern Interpreters* (Cambridge UP, 1984) looks beyond the words of the text to what we may deduce from the stage directions. On the theatres themselves, Christopher Edwards has edited a handy little conspective booklet summarizing the available evidence, *The London Theatre Guide 1576–1642* (London: Bear Gardens Museum, 1979). More expansively, Richard Leacroft's *The Development of the English Playhouse* (London: Methuen, 1973), on which I have drawn for the isometric reconstructions used in this volume, comes into its own from this period onwards. Opposed viewpoints on audiences are compared and assessed in Andrew Gurr's *Playgoing in Shakespeare's London* (Cambridge UP, 1987).

The mass of material on the regular drama tends towards literary criticism, but *The Cambridge Companion to English Renaissance Drama*, edited by A. R. Braunmuller and Michael Hattaway (Cambridge UP, 1990) provides a context both in performing conditions and in broader social terms, and includes full guides to further reading on individual authors as well as general topics. Less up-to-date but more detailed and fully annotated guides to study of the dramatists may be found in four volumes under the general editorship of Alfred Harbage from the University of Nebraska Press: *The Predecessors of Shakespeare* (1973), *The Popular School* (1975), *The New Intellectuals* (1977), and *The Later Jacobean and Caroline Dramatists* (1978). Lisa Jardine's *Still Harping on Daughters* (Harvester, 1983) was a seminal work in the development of a feminist critique of this most apparently chauvinist of theatres.

The later Jacobean and Caroline periods have recently been rescued from neglect by some first-rate studies. Margot Heinemann's *Puritanism and Theatre* (Cambridge UP, 1980) began a revaluation continued in Martin Butler's *Theatre and Crisis, 1632–1642* (Cambridge UP, 1984). The elusive theatre of the Commonwealth period remains largely unexplored, with Leslie Hotson's *The Commonwealth and Restoration Stage* (1928, reprinted New York: Russell, 1962) still the standard authority for the earlier part of the period its title delimits.

Restoration and Early Georgian

Here, the definitive reference work is the multiply-authored and no less multiply-volumed *The London Stage* (Carbondale: Southern Illinois UP, 1960–68). The equally massive *Biographical Dictionary of Actors, Actresses, Musicians, Dancers, Managers, and Other Stage Personnel in London, 1660–1800*, edited by Philip H. Highfill et al (Carbondale: Southern Illinois UP, 1973–), is just what its title claims, except that 'dictionary' understates the extent and quality alike of the contributions, which often constitute definitive, albeit encapsulated, accounts of their subjects.

In the first volume of what will become a substantial series, 'Theatre in Europe: a Documentary History', David Thomas and Arnold Hare have tried to assemble all the major contemporary materials pertinent to their period, *Restoration and Georgian England 1660–1788* (Cambridge UP, 1989). For a critical overview, the introductions which originally prefaced the main chronological sub-divisions of *The London Stage* have been published separately in five paperback volumes as *The London Stage: a Critical Introduction* (Southern Illinois UP, 1968). While the emphases vary widely between the various editors, these remain suggestive guides to the period as it develops.

Recent years have seen a small but welcome trickle of books on acting and production styles – Peter Holland's *The Ornament of Action* (Cambridge UP, 1979), Jocelyn Powell's *Restoration Theatre Production* (London: Routledge, 1984), and J. L. Styan's *Restoration Comedy in Performance* (Cambridge UP, 1986). The varying approaches are no less instructive than the individual merits of these works. On the written drama, Robert D. Hume's *The Development of English Drama in the Late Seventeenth Century* (Oxford UP, 1976) is by far the best and fullest modern account, replacing conventional labels with categories which suggest the concerns of the time rather than the tidying-up instincts of later critics. Earlier studies still worth reading include Norman Holland's *The First Modern Comedies* (Harvard UP, 1959) and Kenneth Muir's *The Comedy of Manners* (London, 1970), while John Loftis's *Comedy and Society from Congreve to Fielding* (Stanford UP, 1959) moves us further forward into the eighteenth century.

A collection of essays, *Restoration Drama*, edited by John Loftis (Oxford UP, 1966), includes both L. C. Knights's influential attack on the drama of the time and F. W. Bateson's defence. Fidelis Morgan's *The Female Wits* (London: Virago, 1981) is a lively and accessible account of the women playwrights of the period: this is taken further, both historically and analytically, in Jacqueline Pearson's *The Prostituted Muse* (New York: St Martin's, 1988).

The standard work on the Collier controversy remains *Comedy and Conscience after the Restoration*, by Joseph Wood Krutch (New York: Columbia UP, 1924). On the major individual practitioners, the biography by Mary Edmond, *Rare Sir William Davenant* (Manchester UP, 1987) sets its subject's activities within the theatre he helped to shape, as does Judith Milhous's *Thomas Betterton and the Management of Lincoln's Inn Fields, 1695–1708* (Carbondale: Southern Illinois UP, 1982). An unusually stimulating and wide-ranging miscellany is *The London Theatre World, 1660–1800*, edited by Robert D. Hume (Southern Illinois UP, 1980).

There are few specialist studies of the theatre of the earlier part of the eighteenth century, though two works by John Loftis – *Steele at Drury Lane* (California UP, 1952) and *The Politics of Drama in Augustan England* (Oxford UP, 1963) – are both helpful, and the fascinating decade before the Licensing Act has at last been given focused attention in Robert D. Hume's *Henry Fielding and the London Theatre 1728–1737* (Oxford UP, 1988). Two brief accounts, Cecil Price's *Theatre in the Age of Garrick* (Oxford: Blackwell, 1973) and Allardyce Nicoll's *The Garrick Stage* (Manchester UP, 1980), take the history of the theatre down to the eve of the Siddons era, while Leigh Woods's *Garrick Claims the Stage* (Westport: Greenwood, 1984) considers its subject as emblematic of his times. On the audiences of the period, there is Leo Hughes's *The Drama's Patrons* (Texas UP, 1971).

In more specialist areas, Roger Fiske's *English Theatre Music in the Eighteenth Century* (Oxford UP, 1973) seems set to remain authoritative as long as has Sybil Rosenfeld's *Strolling Players and Drama in the Provinces* (Cambridge UP, 1939). Miss Rosenfeld's *A Short History of Scene Design in Great Britain* (Oxford: Blackwell, 1973) provides an introductory context for her ampler *Georgian Scene Painters and Scene Painting* (Cambridge UP, 1981), which could itself usefully be read alongside Richard Southern's *Changeable Scenery* (London: Faber, 1952).

Late Georgian and Victorian

John Loftis's *Sheridan and the Drama of Georgian England* (Oxford: Blackwell, 1976) is more fully concerned with its primary than its secondary subject, but helpful none the less for the immediate post-Garrick years. Despite its title, George Rowell's *The Victorian Theatre* (Cambridge UP, 1978), takes up the story from 1792, while Joseph W. Donohue's *Theatre in the Age of Kean* (Oxford: Blackwell, 1975) is helpfully concise in its coverage of this more limited span. Ernest Bradlee Watson's pioneering *From Sheridan to Robertson* (Harvard UP, 1926) remains useful among the few general surveys, though its moral judgements are now open to question.

Michael Booth's *Prefaces to English Nineteenth-Century Theatre* (Manchester UP, 1981) provide sound contexts, but Booth's *English Melodrama* (London: Jenkins, 1965), which helped to break the ground in this long despised field, now needs reading alongside Bruce McConachie's *Melodramatic Formations* (Iowa UP, 1992) – which, though American in emphasis, is a model of new historicist theory intelligently and illuminatingly applied. Despite its opaque main title, Martin Meisel's *Realisations: Narrative, Pictorial, and Theatrical Arts in Nineteenth-Century England* (Princeton UP, 1983) makes some vital connections in this and other areas. On late Georgian pantomime, David Mayer's *Harlequin in His Element* (Harvard UP, 1969) is near-definitive, as is A. H. Saxon's *Enter Foot and Horse* (Yale UP, 1968) on the equestrian drama. Sadly, the music hall awaits its definitive historian, but it can boast a splendid bibliography: *British Music Hall, 1840–1923*, compiled by Laurence Senelick, David F. Cheshire, and Ulrich Schneider (Hamden: Archon Books, 1981).

Significantly, there is no general survey of the mid-century theatre. But on the later Victorian period, George Rowell's *Theatre in the Age of Irving* makes a good starting point, and could be usefully read alongside not only his selection of *Victorian Dramatic Criticism* (London: Methuen, 1971), but also Russell Jackson's collection of annotated documents from contemporary sources, *Victorian Theatre* (London: Black, 1989.) Two works on the playhouses themselves are nicely complementary: Victor Glasstone's *Victorian and Edwardian Theatres* (London: Thames and Hudson, 1975), a richly illustrated, architecturally informed overview; and Diana Howard's *London Theatres and Music Halls, 1850–1950* (London: Library Association, 1970), which is replete with facts and references for further study. Mander and Mitchenson's *Lost Theatres of London* (London: New English Library, 1975) also deals largely with this period, while Terence Rees's *Theatre Lighting in the Age of Gas* (London: Society for Theatre Research, 1978) is (aptly) illuminating, and pleasantly non-technical.

Michael Booth's *Victorian Spectacular Theatre* (London: Routledge, 1981) is one of the few studies of production methods, while David Mayer's *Henry Irving and The Bells* (Manchester UP, 1980) restores this absolutely central work to a legitimate life. On acting, the conclusions in Michael Butler's *The Rise of the Victorian Actor* (London: Croom Helm, 1978), have been challenged by and should be considered alongside one of the several recent works of corrective feminist emphasis, Tracy C. Davis's *Actresses as Working Women* (London: Routledge, 1991).

The essays in a collection edited by Joseph Donohue, *The Theatrical Manager in England and America* (Princeton UP, 1970), are complemented by such individual studies of the leading managers as William Appleton's *Madame Vestris and the London Stage* (Columbia UP, 1974), Alan Hughes's *Henry Irving: Shakespearean* (1981), and J. C. Trewin's *Benson and the Bensonians* (London: Barrie and Rockliff, 1960). Moving towards the new century, Hesketh Pearson's *The Last Actor-Managers* (London: Methuen, 1950) remains useful, as does Frances Donaldson's more recent *The Actor Managers* (London: Weidenfeld, 1970).

Early Twentieth Century

The Edwardian theatre as a subject for discrete study has received fuller critical attention than the inter-war period. Among general introductions are J. C. Trewin's *The Edwardian Theatre* (Oxford: Blackwell, 1976); James Woodfield's *English Theatre in Transition 1881–1914* (London: Croom Helm, 1984), and Ian Clarke's *Edwardian Drama* (London: Faber, 1989). On the 'other' theatre of the period, John Stokes's *Resistible Theatres* (London: Elek, 1972) uncovers

elusive areas, while Andrew Davies's *Other Theatre: the Development of Alternative and Experimental Theatre in Britain* (London: Macmillan, 1987) takes its story forward from here.

Two books which deal with the inter-war theatre very much in the spirit of the times are J. C. Trewin's *The Gay Twenties* (London: Macdonald, 1958) and *The Turbulent Thirties* (London: Macdonald, 1960) – as indeed does John Gielgud's idiosyncratic but insightful *Notes from the Gods: Playgoing in the Twenties* (London: Nick Hern Books, 1994). Richard Findlater's *The Player Kings* (London: Weidenfeld, 1971) is largely concerned with Gielgud and others who made their acting reputations in these and the following decades.

Outside the West End, Norman Marshall's *The Other Theatre* (London: John Lehmann, 1947) remains an exemplary insider's account, while George Rowell and Anthony Jackson look in *The Repertory Movement* (Cambridge UP, 1984) at the history of regional theatre in these years and beyond. Both *Theatres of the Left 1880–1935* (London: Routledge, 1985), edited by Raphael Samuels *et al*, and Richard Stourac and Kathleen McCreery's *Theatre as a Weapon* (London: Routledge, 1986) consider the Workers' Theatre Movement, within respectively its transatlantic and continental contexts. Colin Chambers's *The Story of Unity Theatre* (London: Lawrence and Wishart, 1989) also begins here.

Later Twentieth Century

The immediate post-war period has been critically neglected of late, but John Elsom's well-focused *Post-War British Theatre* (London: Routledge, 1979) starts here, as does his collection *Post-War British Theatre Criticism* (London: Routledge, 1981). At the time, Richard Findlater's *The Unholy Trade* (London: Gollancz, 1952) assembled an astonishing amount of information on the workings of the theatre business, while J. C. Trewin's collection, *Theatre Programme* (London: Muller, 1954), looked at all aspects of theatre from both the practitioners' and the critics' viewpoints.

Kenneth Tynan's various collections of theatre reviews – notably *Tynan on Theatre* (Harmondsworth: Penguin,

1964) – are essential and compulsive reading for the decade or so around 1956. Three anthologies of interviews with those most closely involved, plus other performance documentation, provide background to the subsequent decades: *The Encore Reader*, edited by Charles Marowitz *et al* (London: Methuen, 1965), later reprinted as *New Theatre Voices of the Fifties and Sixties*, as a companion volume to my own *New Theatre Voices of the Seventies* (London, Methuen, 1981) – itself a sequel to a volume edited by Charles Marowitz and myself, *Theatre at Work* (London: Methuen, 1967).

Among critical studies, Laurence Kitchin's *Mid-Century Drama* (London: Faber, 1960) remains useful, while John Russell Taylor's *Anger and After* (London: Methuen, revised edition, 1978) is as much of the late fifties as about it – and the same could be said for a comparably involved survey of the years after 1968, Catherine Itzin's *Stages in the Revolution* (London: Methuen, 1980). Michael Billington's *One Night Stands* (London: Nick Hern Books, 1993) is well-selected from over two decades of overnight criticism – and his *The Modern Actor* (London: Hamilton, 1973), while not limited to the contemporary scene, is one of the few insightful studies of this difficult area.

On the most influential companies of the period, there are Howard Goorney's *The Theatre Workshop Story* (London: Methuen, 1981); two contrasting studies of the vintage years at the Royal Court – Irving Wardle's *The Theatres of George Devine* (London: Cape, 1978), and a compilation by Richard Findlater, *At the Royal Court* (Ambergate: Amber Lane Press, 1981); and Sally Beauman's *The Royal Shakespeare Company* (Oxford UP, 1982) – this latter complemented by Colin Chambers's study of the RSC's studio theatres, *Other Spaces* (London: Methuen, 1980). On the alternative theatre movement, a collection of essays edited by Sandy Craig, *Dreams and Deconstructions* (Ambergate: Amber Lane Press, 1980) remains seminal, while John McGrath *A Good Night Out* (London: Methuen, 1981) is a brave attempt to construct theory from the hard school of experience.

Acknowledgements

Every effort has been made to obtain permission to use the copyright material listed below; the publishers apologise for any errors or omissions and would welcome these being brought to their attention.

Title page, 326, 366, Reg Wilson; Half title, 94r, 95l, 115, courtesy of the Henry E. Huntington Library, San Marino, California; 2, Museo Nazionale, Napoli/SCALA; 3, The National Museum of Wales; 5, Aerofilms Ltd.; 7, 29, 35, 43, 70, 77, 82, 83, 94l, 95r, 96, 140, 141, 184, British Library, London; 8, Mary Evans Picture Library; 11, courtesy of the Governing Body of Christ Church, Oxford; 12, Collections/Brian Shuel; 14, from R. Gilder: Enter the Actress, reproduced by permission of the Syndics of Cambridge University Library; 15, Bibliothèque de l'Arsenal/Bibliothèque Nationale; 17, 19, Michael Brooke; 18, Bildarchiv Foto Marburg; 21, 40, 53, 89, 92, 109, 120, 149, from R. Leacroft: Development of the English Playhouse, published by Methuen, reproduced by permission of Reed Consumer Books; 22, Bodleian Library, Ms. Anct F.3.13, fol.3r; 24, Bodleian Library, Ms. F.2.13, fol. 47; 26, Bibliothèque Nationale; 31, Bibliothèque Nationale/Flammarion-Giraudon; 32, by courtesy of the Dean and Chapter of Westminster; 36, courtesy of West Yorkshire Archaeology Service; 38, 42, Sonia Halliday; 39, 78, The Master & Fellows of Corpus Christi College, Cambridge; 45, 121, from H & R Leacroft: Theatre and Playhouse, published by Methuen, reproduced by permission of Reed Consumer Books; 47, by permission of the Folger Shakespeare Library; 50, 130, 134, 235, The Royal Collection ©1994 Her Majesty the Queen; 54, British Library, London/photo by Bridgeman Art Library; 55, Sarah Campbell Blaffer Foundation, Houston, Texas; 59, from Craik: The Tudor Interlude/by permission of the Syndics of Cambridge University Library; 61, Guildhall Library, Corporation of London; 62, Bodleian Library (detail from The Kermess of St George); 63, N. Mason-Smith; 66, ©Crown Copyright. Historic Royal Palaces; 67, La Belle Aurore/Steve Davey & Juliet Coombe; 72, from Greg: Dramatic Documents; 74, 75, 106, by permission of the Governors of Dulwich Picture Gallery; 81, by permission of the Marquess of Bath, Longleat; 79, 93, by permission of the Syndics of Cambridge University Library; 87, by permission of the Trustee of the Will of the Eighth Earl of Berkeley, deceased; 88, Andrew Fulgoni; 98, 110, 111, Devonshire Collection, Chatsworth. Reproduced by permission of the Chatsworth Settlement Trustees; 102, A Private Collection; 103, 119, 123, 127r, 146, 150, 162, 197b, courtesy of the National Portrait Gallery, London; 114, Bodleian Library, Oxford; 118, from Works, by permission of the Syndics of Cambridge University Library; 122, 133, 152, 230, 240, 245t, 251, 262, 268, 290, from the collections of The Theatre Museum, by courtesy of the Board of Trustees of the Victoria & Albert Museum; 128, from The Empress of Morocco, reproduced by permission of the Syndics of Cambridge University Library; 132, from Hamlet, 1709 ed, reproduced by permission of the Syndics of Cambridge University Library; 137, 157, 159, Harvard Theatre Collection; 138, 211, The Garrick Club/E.T. Archive; 143, 151, 165, 167, 182, 189, 193, 194, 195, 202, 203, 210, 215, 216, 218, 219t, 222, 223, 224, 226, 232, 244, 245b, 252, 254, 257, 258, 259, 263, 267, 271, 272, 274, 276, 277, 278, 279, 280, 281, 282, 283, 284, 289, 300, 301, 302, 304, 306, 320, 323, 328, 330, 331, Mander & Mitchenson Theatre Collection; 154, Cincinnati Art Museum, The Edwin and Virginia Irwin Memorial; 160, 192, 214, 239, 249, University of Bristol Theatre Collection; 163, Yale Center for British Art, Paul Mellon Collection; 170, Somerset Maugham Theatre Collection, London/Bridgeman Art Library, London; 173, courtesy of the Board of Trustees of the National Museums & Galleries on Merseyside (Walker Art Gallery, Liverpool); 178, Museum of London; 185, 186, copyright British Museum; 206, from the RSC Collection, with the permission of the Governors of the Royal Shakespeare Theatre; 190, 212, 227, 242, by permission of the Board of Trustees of the Victoria & Albert Museum; 219b, from Planché: Court Favour, reproduced by permission of the Syndics of Cambridge University Library; 237, The Hampden-Booth Theatre Library at The Players; 247, Mary Evans Picture Library; 255, Lewisham Local History Centre; 256, Mansell Collection; 261, British Library, Colindale; 291, 325, Shakespeare Centre Library, Stratford-upon-Avon; 293, BBC Photo Library; 294, Arcaid/Richard Bryant; 296, National Museum of Labour History; 299, 305, Mander & Mitchenson Theatre Collection (photo by Angus McBean); 308, John Vickers; 315, Beata Bergström, Stockholm; 316, 319, Angus McBean; 335, courtesy of the Belgrade Theatre, Coventry; 338, 345, 349, 354, 356, 357, 358, 360, 367, 373, 374, Donald Cooper ©Photostage; 341, Mander & Mitchenson Theatre Collection (photo by John Haynes); 342, 352, Morris Newcombe; 351, Arcaid/Richard Einzig; 363, ©Michael Le Poer Trench/Performing Arts Library; 369, Sarah Ainslie; 370, Channel Four

Index